THE MORALITY OF HAPPINESS

The Morality of Happiness

JULIA ANNAS

New York   Oxford
OXFORD UNIVERSITY PRESS

Oxford University Press

Oxford   New York   Toronto
Delhi   Bombay   Calcutta   Madras   Karachi
Kuala Lumpur   Singapore   Hong Kong Tokyo
Nairobi   Dar es Salaam   Cape Town
Melbourne   Auckland   Madrid

and associated companies in
Berlin   Ibadan

First published in 1993 by Oxford University Press, Inc.
200 Madison Avenue, New York, New York 10016

First issued as an Oxford University Press paperback, 1995

Oxford is a registered trademark of Oxford University Press

Annas, Julia
The morality of happiness / Julia Annas.
p.   cm.   Includes bibliographical references and index.
ISBN 0–19–507999–X; 0-19-509652-5(pbk)
1. Happiness. 2. Ethics, Ancient. I. Title.
BJ171.H35A56   1993   170'.938—dc20   92–37003

2 4 6 8 9 7 5 3 1

Printed in the United States of America
on acid-free paper

Preface and Acknowledgments

During the years it has taken to write this book, many people have helped me in many ways. I am very grateful to them all, and apologize to those who have been inadvertently omitted.

Papers containing material which eventually became part of the book (usually in much altered form) have been given at the University of Dayton Aristotle Conference; the Boston Area Colloquium in Ancient Philosophy; the University of Texas at Austin Ancient Philosophy Workshop; the Spindel Conference on Aristotle at Memphis State University; the political philosophy seminar at Princeton University; a conference on Tradition and Innovation in Epicureanism at Duke University; University of Oklahoma; University of Arizona; Columbia University; Brown University; Johns Hopkins University; the University of California at Riverside; Brigham Young University; the Social Philosophy and Policy conference on the Good Life and the Human Good; a conference on contemporary perspectives on Greek ethics at the University of Nevada at Reno; the ethics colloquium at New York University; Cornell University; the conference in honour of Gregory Vlastos at the University of California at Berkeley; the Chapel Hill colloquium in philosophy. I am truly grateful for the patience and helpfulness of my discussants and audiences on all these occasions.

Many of these papers have been published; they are listed in the Bibliography. As I wrote the book I have frequently made use of these published articles, but in no case does the book present material unchanged from the article. In some cases I have rethought or recast what was presented in the article. In other cases the article is a study of a particular issue, and I have drawn from this only what was needed to make or support a case which is part of the book's overall structure.

The following have read portions of the book, and have made valuable comments, for which I am very grateful: Nancy Sherman, David Gill, David Furley, David Keyt, Gisela Striker, Mark McPherran, Anthony Price, Christopher Laursen, Dan Blickman, Marcia Baron, Brian Leiter, Jeffrie Murphy.

Terry Irwin, Christopher Gill and Nicholas White have read the entire manuscript of a penultimate version of the book, and made extensive and valuable comments. I am very grateful for these, and for the patience and good will of the readers of a long manuscript. The book has greatly improved as a result. It may be that it has not improved enough in substance, and on some occasions I have had to be contented with noting a problem or disagreement in a footnote, rather than arguing out the issue in the text. The book, as I emphasize, is not a comprehensive study of ancient ethics, but a selective study of one aspect of it, and sometimes I have had to note limitations and continue, rather than risk a loss of focus. But on many issues the book has improved immeasurably as the result of this friendly advice and criticism.

I am extremely grateful to the following people for letting me see their work before publication: William Fortenbaugh for his new edition of the fragments of Theophrastus, Voula Tsouna McKirahan for her new edition (with Giovanni Indelli) of the *Ethica Comparetti*, Paul Vander Waerdt and Phillip Mitsis for their essays on natural law for *Aufstieg und Niedergang der Römischen Welt*, Malcolm Schofield for his book on the Stoic idea of the city, David Sedley for part of his commentary on the Anonymous Commentator on the *Theaetetus*, Fred D. Miller for his book on nature, justice and rights in Aristotle's *Politics*. I am particularly grateful to Nicholas White for letting me read an early version of his own book on morality in ancient and modern theories, which complements my own at many points and has been a valuable help.

I have greatly benefitted from the writings of the following on ancient ethics: Fernanda Decleva Caizzi, Giuseppe Cambiano, John Cooper, Christopher Gill, Anna Maria Ioppolo, Terry Irwin, Mark McPherran, Phillip Mitsis, Martha Nussbaum, Gisela Striker, Mario Vegetti, Nicholas White, Bernard Williams. They will probably think that I have not learned enough, but I am grateful for what I have learned. Two works which I found at a late stage of writing the book, and which I have found illuminating and complementary to my own concerns, are Giuseppe Cambiano's *Il ritorno degli antichi* and Nicholas White's book on ancient and modern ethics.

The following have been published too late for the book to benefit: Malcolm Schofield, 'Natural Law' and Antonina Alberti, 'La teoria epicurea della legge e della guistizia', both in the Proceedings of the Sixth Symposium Hellenisticum; Guido Bastianini and A.A. Long, 'Hierocles', 60 in *Corpus dei Papiri Filosofici greci e latini*, Parte I, vol 1**, Firenze 1992; A. Kenny, *Aristotle on the Perfect Life*, Oxford University Press 1992; T. Irwin, 'Aristippus against Happiness,' *The Monist* 74 (1991), 55–82; R.B. Louden, *Morality and Moral Theory*, Oxford University Press, 1992; G. Trianosky, 'What Is Virtue Ethics All About?', *American Philosophical Quarterly* 27 (1990), 335–44; M. Slote, *From Morality to Virtue*, Oxford University Press, 1992; D. Sedley, 'The Argumentative Structure of Epicurean Ethics'.

And I would also like to thank the following for their help: André Laks, Richard Kraut, John Cooper, Paul Vander Waerdt, David Glidden, Jerry Santas, Michael Slote, David Glidden, Pierre Keller, Jerry Schneewind, Tom Christiano, Richard Bett, Ezequiel de Olaso, Howard Wettstein.

The picture on the jacket, Puvis de Chavannes' *Inter artes et naturam*, struck me as containing some interesting themes which are relevant to what I am trying to do in this book. The title means 'Between the arts (or skills) and nature', and sets this theme in a classical background in which contemporary figures take part. Much of this book is concerned with these two themes in ancient ethics. Nature is what is universal and unavoidable in human beings, and it is also what we aim to achieve in ethics as an ideal which goes beyond what is merely conventional and picked up from our own traditions and society. The skills and arts are modes in which we reflect intellectually and thereby become able to transform and improve the merely given material in us. Virtue, which I shall argue is the locus of morality in the ancient theories, is one such skill; it is by virtue of our rationality that we become able to transform, rather than being dominated by, our human nature. Puvis had aesthetic rather than moral achievements in mind, but the point remains—in this respect, ancients and moderns are doing the same thing, and their theories are mutually intelligible. They meet on common ground. The fact that Puvis' contemporary figures seem dated and part of the past to us merely underlines the point that each generation is modern in its own way, and must make its own interpretation of the ancients to find them intelligible. The fact that we tend to find Puvis' classical form of Symbolism somewhat stiff and remote is also interesting. We find it easier to respond to a Symbolist like Gauguin, who rejected his own artistic tradition for a non-Western one—how well he understood it, or succeeded in rejecting his own artistic assumptions, being another matter. (Gauguin, who admired Puvis, said 'He is a Greek whereas I am a savage, a wolf without a lead in the forest.') It is in fact quite hard for us to respond to the classical visual tradition in an artist who is making a serious intellectual engagement with it. But it is worth the effort; and I hope that the same goes for my own intellectual engagement, in this book, with the ancient tradition of moral philosophy.

This is very much my 'Arizona book'; it was conceived, worked on and brought to its penultimate version in the first five years I spent at the University of Arizona, from 1986 to 1991. I am most grateful to my colleagues in the Philosophy Department, and to the Social and Behavioral Sciences Research Institute for generous relief from teaching during that period. I am also grateful for a most friendly and supportive atmosphere. I would like to thank John and Carol Armstrong for extensive help in preparing the indices. The book is dedicated to my husband, David Owen, and to our daughter Laura, who have helped me with love and support during the book's gestation, and at all other times.

Tucson, Arizona   J.A.
March 1993

Contents

THE MORALITY OF HAPPINESS

Introduction

Ancient Ethics

This book is a contribution to the history of ethics. But it is not a 'history of ancient ethics'. It is a book about the form and structure of ancient ethical theory. Hence it is restricted in scope and selective in its interests. This is not the comprehensive account of ancient ethics which we badly need, but I hope that it will clear some preliminary ground and make the production of such a work more feasible.[1]

The primary aim of this book is historical: to study the ancient theories from a systematic and thematic point of view. Historical study of ancient ethics, however, is more elusive and difficult than historical study of ancient physics, or logic; for the perspectives of our own which we inevitably bring to study of ancient accounts of nature and reasoning are not as disputed in their very nature as our ethical perspectives are. Thus when we study ancient ethical theories, we cannot avoid reflecting on our own expectations as to what an ethical theory is. To go directly to the texts without any such reflection might look like a more strictly historical way of proceeding. But in fact, if we do not reflect on our own ethical perspective we shall just carry it with us unnoticed. A great deal of discussion of ancient ethical theory is flawed, in my view, because the authors have carried over to their study of the texts, unquestioned, their own expectations as to what an ethical theory is and should do.[2] But this hinders understanding, and tends to produce an attitude that is either over- or under-critical. Before we rush either to praise or to blame ancient theories for not, for example, providing detailed solutions to hard cases, we should ask ourselves whether the ancients shared the view that this is the kind of thing which an ethical theory ought to be doing. And we can hardly produce an adequate answer to this if we have not reflected on the centrality or otherwise of our own assumption that this is something which an ethical theory ought to provide.

Thus although this is a historical study, it is guided and formed by systematic and thematic concerns which arise from reflection on modern as well as on ancient ethics. I have done this not in order to make the ancient theories seem fashionably interesting. (If they are not interesting in their own right, any such attempt would only falsify them, in any case.) My purpose has been the opposite: to have the best chance of finding out the intellectual structure of ancient ethics, rather than imposing on the subject our own conceptions of what the appropriate structure is.

---

[1] In Michael Frede's terminology, this is a work of doxography; I am concerned to give an account of past theories, from a present viewpoint which is inevitably selective both as to which theories are still philosophically live and as to which terminology will be best understood. See Frede (forthcoming). However, the term 'doxography' is currently understood in such a pejorative sense that I hesitate to use it to label the book.

[2] For interesting discussion of some twentieth-century examples of this, with regard to ancient philosophy more generally, see Cambiano (1988) and N. White's forthcoming book.

Ancient and Modern

Because of these considerations, this book may also be of interest to those who have a serious interest in moral philosophy even apart from its history. In recent years, there has been a growing sense that there is something deeply inadequate about the view that when we systematize theories about our ethical views we are faced with the traditional option, a simple choice between consequentalist and deontological ways of thinking. If this is our option, then we must choose between calculating consequences to discover the right way to act, or rely on moral rules to guide us positively and negatively. But this is to take a modern journey with a mediaeval map—an artificially neat map combining detail in places with large unsatisfactory areas, unexplored and assigned only to monsters. In the last decade much attention has been paid to an option not even marked on previous maps—that of so-called virtue ethics. Philosophers have begun to take seriously the idea that morality might be importantly concerned with the agent's view of her life, with happiness and with virtue.[3] And, since these notions are the controlling ones in ancient ethics, there has been a growth of serious interest in ancient ethical theories, particularly that of Aristotle.[4]

There are many reasons why ancient ethics should appear as a source of fresh insights in areas neglected by most of twentieth-century academic moral philosophy. Ancient ethical theories are concerned with the agent's life as a whole, and with his character. Concern with character and choice, with practical reasoning and the role of the emotions, is central rather than marginal. This has seemed to many to be a useful corrective to modern theories which operate with a narrow and abstract notion of what is relevant to morality, and which are frequently criticized for producing theories which are seriously at odds with our conceptions of what matters in our lives.

Ancient ethics, further, is not based on the idea that morality is essentially punitive or corrective, 'the notion that morality is a life harassed and persecuted everywhere by 'imperatives' and disagreeable duties, and that without these you have not got morality.'[5] Its leading notions are not those of obligation, duty and rule-following; instead of these 'imperative' notions it uses 'attractive' notions like those of goodness and worth.[6] Ancient ethical theories do not assume that morality is essentially demanding, the only interesting question being, how much does it demand; rather, the moral point of view is seen as one that the agent will naturally come to accept in the course of a normal unrepressed development.

---

[3] See Foot (1978), Wallace (1978), Dent (1975) and (1984). There is a survey of recent work in Pence (1984). See also Louden (1984), reprinted in a collection containing other useful papers, Kruschwitz and Roberts (1987); also Baron (1985). Recent collections are French, Uehling and Wettstein (1988); *Philosophia* 20.1–2 (1990), special issue on virtue ethics; Flanagan and Rorty (1990). For a clear and vigorous discussion of common misunderstandings of virtue ethics, see Hursthouse (1991).

[4] See MacIntyre (1981) and (1988); Williams (1981a) and (1985).

[5] Bradley (1876), Essay VI, p. 215. Bradley's own brilliant account of ethics owes much to the leading ideas of ancient ethics; but it has been uninfluential in the mainstream of analytical moral philosophy.

[6] The distinction is drawn in these terms by Sidgwick (1907), p. 106; it governs the way he reads ancient ethics in his history of ethics (1931). It has been influential in the way constrasts have been drawn between ancient and modern ethical theories (not always to the benefit of the former). See Larmore (1990), N. White (forthcoming b).

Stated thus generally, these advantages of ancient ethics are genuine, and it is clearly sensible to look to ancient ethics in the hope of remedying some of the gaps and failures of understanding that are felt in modern ethical theories. Nonetheless, there are reasons to be cautious, rather than enthusiastic about the idea of approaching ancient ethics from the primarily therapeutic viewpoint of remedying what are seen as our own deficiencies.[7]

To be any good, a study of ancient ethics (like this one) has to take its subject matter seriously, whether it aligns with our concerns or not. If we foist onto Aristotle or Epicurus ways of thinking that we find currently fashionable, we shall merely do bad history. And if what we find is not relevant to modern concerns, this is just something we must accept. It is entirely possible that ancient ethics is like ancient physics, which we study without being able to accept the theories as ours.

We might consider this warning needless, since when we read ancient ethics we do not find concepts as remote from ours as form and matter. Ancient ethics centres on the notions of happiness, of virtue and of the agent's deliberations about his life as a whole.[8] These are notions which we recognize from our everyday ethical deliberations without any difficulty. We appeal all the time to the place of certain projects and values in a person's life taken as a whole, to the notion of a life which is satisfactory, and to qualities or dispositions of people which are admirable or deplorable. We probably do not use the *word* 'virtue' often, if at all,[9] but of course it does not follow from this that we do not recognize virtues and vices; few use the *word* 'deontology' either, but that does not mean that we cannot recognize duties and obligations. When we read Aristotle on the virtues, or Epicurus on pleasure, it certainly seems as though we understand what is said unforcedly, that we know how to use, and extend the use of, these very concepts.

Does it follow from this that when we read Aristotle we are rediscovering our own tradition, finding our own roots? Some have thought so, and have concluded that we have been thinking all along in terms of virtue and happiness, and that it is only bad moral philosophy that has obscured this fact from us. If this is so, then the study of ancient ethics will have a very direct and exciting relevance to our own ethical thought: it will *be* the way we think ethically, and although there will be some aspects of ancient thought that we cannot carry over to the modern world, the central insights of the ancients will be our insights.

Here, unfortunately, the unexciting intellectual virtue of caution is required. Ancient ethics is indeed relevant to modern moral philosophy. But if we rush to establish similarities too soon, they will peter out. Only if we take due account of the sources of deep difference between ancient and modern ethics will we also do justice to the deep similarities. There are, I think, three major sources of differences between ancient and modern ethics, all of which we must bear in mind.

[7] A therapeutic viewpoint can be seen even in the title of Taylor's (1988). For a good discussion of this issue see Striker (1988).

[8] Ancient ethical thinkers are all sexist in that the agent they discuss in ethics is always male. Women are sometimes discussed, but always as a special case. I have not followed them in this; I have tried roughly to alternate genders when talking of ethical agents in both modern and ancient ethics. This sometimes produces an odd effect with ancient texts, but the oddity is superficial.

[9] Williams (1985), p. 9: 'The word 'virtue' has for the most part acquired comic or otherwise undesirable associations, and few now use it except philosophers'.

First, modern ethical thinking is the product of several ethical traditions. One is that of the Judaeo-Christian religious framework of ethics: the idea that morality is in some way guaranteed by God. Most prominent, however, are the two types of ideas which when made systematic by theory we call deontology and consequentialism. The former embodies the idea that the basic questions in ethics are those concerning what one ought to do and what one's duties are; the latter embodies the idea that the fundamental ethical questions are rather those as to how one should produce the best consequences.

Thus, even if study of ancient ethics were to redirect us towards concern with virtue and happiness in our own moral thought, this would not provide us with a complete alternative framework; for we have an ethical framework which is concerned not only with bravery and cowardice but also with duty and obligation, and with producing the best outcomes. Rather, studying ancient ethics may help us in a more indirect way. We shall see in this book that surprisingly many of the features characterizing aspects of modern morality—rule-following, the notion of duty, appeal to what is beneficial or useful—do have a place within the ancient theories. But, because they have a place within the ethics of virtue, their role and status are very different from those of their modern analogues. Studying ancient ethics, then, will not lead us to reject, in favour of virtue, notions like rule-following and appeal to benefit; but it may make us rethink the role they play in modern theories, and the ways we relate them to virtue and goodness. And this is a realistic goal, unlike the idea that we could jettison or replace notions which have a settled place in our moral theories.[10]

Second, we find it natural to make a number of demands on a moral theory which ancient theories do not make. It is a common modern assumption that a moral theory should help us to decide what it is right for us to do, and in particular, that it should help us to resolve moral dilemmas and difficult moral cases.[11]

It might be replied to this that no theory can, on its own, settle hard cases for us; all theories, whether deontological, consequentialist, or virtue-based, direct us towards the principles we need to apply to produce right answers, but this does not mean that they give us the answers; *we* apply them to give the answers.[12]

There is a difference here, however, between ancient and modern theories. Ancient theories assume that the moral agent internalizes and applies the moral theory to produce the correct answers to hard cases; but the answers themselves are not part of the theory. Nor are they produced by the theory in the sense that applying the theory to a simple description of a hard case will automatically generate

[10] Some modern writers have been undeniably incautious here. See Scheffler (1987), p. 416: if our ethical concepts are in many ways opposed to those of the ancient Greeks, 'and if this opposition is not only correlated with but also partly responsible for the dramatic differences between ancient Greek society and our own, and if moreover any set of ethical ideas can flourish only in appropriate social and historical circumstances, then it seems hard to see how the ideas of the ancient Greeks could have more to offer those living in our society than do the ideas that flourish in our society itself'.

[11] Cf. Louden (1984), p. 229: '[P]eople have always expected ethical theory to tell them something about what they ought to do, and it seems to me that virtue ethics is structurally unable to say much of anything about this issue. . . .[O]ne consequence of this is that a virtue-based ethics will be particularly weak in the areas of casuistry and applied ethics.' Louden's objections are to an ethic that makes virtue primary; more will be said on this below. See also Solomon (1988).

[12] Solomon (1988) presses this objection.

a correct answer. Thus for ancient theories it is true that there is not much to be said in general about hard cases. Modern theories often see it as a demand that they be able to generate answers to hard cases in a comparatively simple way; and to this extent ancient ethics fails to meet modern demands on casuistry. The source of this difference is easy to locate: it is the demand, explicit since Sidgwick, that we identify, systematize and formalize out of our moral thinking certain 'methods' or procedures for coming to ethical conclusions. This demand in turn rests transparently on the demand that ethics become more like the physical sciences; just as they enable us to make particular predictions as to what will happen,[13] so a 'scientific' ethical theory should enable us to make particular decisions very directly, without the intervention of further deliberation on our part. This often goes with a general attitude that ethics, as it stands, is a mess, and needs to be sanitized by scientific methods.[14]

Ancient ethics accepts no such demands; we shall see that the intellectual model it finds appropriate for ethical understanding is quite different. So, to the extent that this demand is prevalent in modern moral philosophy, ancient ethics will again fail to meet all our demands on an ethical theory. It may well be that the demand itself is a mistaken one, and that the methods of ethics are utterly different from the methods of science; if so, the difference between ancient and modern will be to the credit of the former. The reader will probably have formed a view on this by the end of the book. But, whether mistaken or not, the demand and the consequent need, if one rejects it, to argue against it have become a settled part of modern moral philosophy; they do not depend simply on philosophical argument, and they cannot be wished away.

The Structure of Ethical Theory

There is a third point of contrast, the most important. It is a widespread modern assumption that an ethical theory must have a structure of which two things must be true: it must be *hierarchical* and it must be *complete*. By *hierarchical* I mean that some set of notions is taken as basic, and the other elements in the theory are derived from these basic notions. Consequentialism, for example, takes as basic the notion of a good state of affairs, and then defines the notions of duty, and of the admirable kind of person, in terms of this.

What is meant here by basicness? John Mackie expresses a commonly shared modern assumption here when he says,

> a moral theory is X-based if it forms a system in which some statements about Xs are taken as basic and the other statements in the theory are derived from them, perhaps with the help of non-moral, purely factual, premises. But what would make a theory X-based in the most important sense is that it should be such a

---

[13] At least, some of them do; enthusiasts for the analogy generally ignore sciences like biology, where prediction is not so important.

[14] This attitude, very clear in Sidgwick, is still present in modern ethical works which lay great weight on technical and quantitative methods.

system not merely formally but in its purpose, that the basic statements about Xs should be seen as capturing what gives point to the whole moral theory.[15]

It need not be, of course, that the basicness of the basic elements is obvious to most people (consequentialism is notoriously counter-intuitive in this respect). Rather, they are basic in that when the whole theory is laid out these are the elements which explain and justify the other elements, but not vice versa. In consequentialism it is the production of good states of affairs which explains what the right thing to do is, and not the other way round. This kind of basicness is quite distinct from other kinds—for example, epistemological basicness. (Even full-fledged consequentialists need not think that their understanding of duty and character is based on a prior and better understanding of good states of affairs.)[16]

The ways in which theories are hierarchical can differ. Some theories are *reductionist*, claiming that the derived elements can be reduced to the basic ones. The strongest form of this would be conceptual reductionism, the claim that the derived ethical concepts can be reduced to the basic ones. But weaker versions are obviously possible; the derived elements are in some way to be explained and/or justified in terms of the basic ones.

By *complete* I mean that the theory claims to account for everything in its area in terms of the basic concepts and of other concepts insofar as they are derived from the basic ones. Consequentialism, for example, accounts for judgements we make about someone's being cowardly, or hostile, in terms of good states of affairs, and in terms of character insofar as that is seen as a producer or inhibiter of the production of good states of affairs. Unfavourable judgements that we make about cowardice have no independent standing; if our dislike of a cowardly act is justified, it must be because that act in fact produced worse consequences than the alternative.[17]

Until recently, it has often been claimed that modern virtue ethics is like other modern theories in being hierarchical and complete.[18] As a critic of modern virtue ethics puts it:

> Just as its utilitarian and deontological competitors begin with primitive concepts of the good state of affairs and the intrinsically right action respectively and then derive secondary concepts out of their starting points, so virtue ethics, beginning with a root conception of the morally good person, proceeds to introduce a different set of secondary concepts which are defined in terms of their relationship to the primitive element. Though the ordering of primitive and derivatives differs in each case, the overall strategy remains the same. Viewed from this perspective, virtue ethics is not unique at all. It has adopted the

---

[15] Mackie (1978), p. 358.

[16] For perhaps the whole theory develops together in a coherentist way, none of the elements having epistemological primacy. This is a modern concession; Sidgwick feels the need to claim that the principles of consequentialism are 'self-evident' in a way that principles about duty are not.

[17] See Slote (1988).

[18] Or sometimes simply assumed without argument. Cf. Frankena (1973), p. 63: 'What would an ethics of virtue be like? It would, of course, not take deontic judgements or principles as basic in morality. . . instead, it would take as basic aretaic judgements like 'That was a courageous deed,' 'His action was virtuous,' or 'Courage is a virtue,' and it would insist that deontic judgements are either derivative from such aretaic ones or can be dispensed with entirely.'

traditional mononomic strategy of normative ethics. What sets it apart from other approaches, again, is its strong agent orientation.[19]

If this is so, then virtue ethics will differ from other kinds of theory simply in its choice of virtue and character as basic elements in the theory. It will share with other theories the ambition to explain and justify its derived elements in terms of its basic ones, and to account for everything that an ethical theory should account for in terms only of the basic notions, and of others only insofar as they are derived from the basic notions.

But as a claim about all modern virtue ethics, this is not true. A great deal of recent work which centres on virtue has tended to query the demand for hierarchy and completeness. By now it is accepted that virtue theories may be more or less 'radical', and many have found attractive the idea of a 'moderate' virtue ethics, by which is meant precisely a virtue theory that renounces claims to hierarchy and/or completeness.[20] So far, however, there has been little by way of precise and extended study of the form such a theory would take.

Ancient virtue theories, at any rate, do not aspire to be hierarchical and complete. In them, the notions of the agent's final end, of happiness and of the virtues are what can be called *primary*, as opposed to basic. These are the notions that we start from; they set up the framework of the theory, and we introduce and understand the other notions in terms of them. They are thus primary for understanding; they establish what the theory is a theory of, and define the place to be given to other ethical notions, such as right action. However, they are not basic in the modern sense: other concepts are not derived from them, still less reduced to them. For example, all ancient theories understand a virtue to be, at least, a disposition to do the morally right thing; but the notion of the morally right thing to do is not defined or justified in terms of (still less reduced to) the disposition to do what will produce or sustain the virtue. We need to grasp in its own right what is the morally right thing to do. Indeed, if we do not do this, we will not have understood what makes this disposition a *virtue*, rather than some disposition which does not involve morality. Similarly the good of others is introduced in ways which make it formally part of the agent's own good; but we fail to grasp its place in ancient theories if we think of it as derived from or justified in terms of the agent's own good—for if that were the case, we would be misconceiving what the good of others is.

Ancient ethics has a structure—the notions of happiness and virtue are primary in it—but it is not a hierarchical structure. Lack of hierarchy leads directly to lack of completeness; the non-primary elements are not derived from the primary ones, so *a fortiori* the theory cannot account for everything it aims to account for, in terms only of the primary elements and the others insofar as derived from the primary ones.

It is important not to confuse this with a modern suggestion that the ethics of virtue is autonomous and independent of other areas of morality.[21] The modern

---

[19] Louden (1984), p. 228. (But for second thoughts see Louden [1990].)

[20] See, for example, Baier (1988), Louden (1984) and (1990); also Hudson (1986), esp. chapters 1–5, 10, on non-reductive theories of virtue.

[21] See Trianosky (1986).

suggestion is that judgements about what people should do have no direct connection to judgements about what people should be like, what characters they should have. This certainly avoids the problems that accrue to the assumption that an ethical theory must be hierarchical and complete. If we accept that, then virtue must come in either as a derived element in a theory making duty or good states of affairs basic (which trivializes it) or as a basic element in an ethics of virtue in which duty and other elements are derived from it (which poses numerous problems).[22] But the price of making virtue independent of other elements of morality is a high one. We normally say that both people and actions are brave, just, and so on. If we must separate judgements of character from judgements of acts, large areas of our moral discourse turn out to be systematically ambiguous. Further, to leave judgements about acts and judgements about agents unrelated is surely to give up too soon in terms of systematizing our moral judgements in a theory. Ancient theories do not have the strong structure which we find in many modern theories, especially those which are consciously based on a scientific conception of theory. But they do have *some* structure. They are not like some modern forms of virtue ethics which are consciously a-theoretical, and do not even attempt to bring their basic concepts together in a single structure.[23]

Ancient ethical theories are *theories*: the notions of final good, virtue, nature, happiness and so on are systematically connected. A difficulty in one of these areas is likely to show up in others and to weaken the entire structure. Hence I have felt free to use the word 'theory' throughout to describe what I am talking about. Ancient theories, however, are unlike modern ones in not being hierarchical and complete; and one of the main results of the book will be, I hope, to make this clear, and also to make clear how important this is for our understanding of ancient ethics.

Applications

What then do we get from a study of ancient ethics? First and foremost, we get what we get from any history, if it is honestly done: a sensitivity to the options that we now take increased by understanding those that we now no longer do, and a grasp of our own intellectual situation deepened by seeing what its sources are.

We renew our emphasis first on the notions of happiness, final end and virtue in our own thinking, and put them more firmly in an *ethical* context. For, although we respond to talk of cowardice and generosity, of the good life and happiness, the trend of moral theorizing in the twentieth century has been such that it has been hard to take these thoughts seriously as part of moral thinking. They have remained important in everyday thinking, but most moral theories have not found room for them, and reflection on them has tended to migrate into popular psychology.[24]

---

[22] I do not go into these problems here; see Louden (1984), Solomon (1988). The most prominent one is that an ethics of virtue (so understood) cannot produce an account of right action that is not trivial.

[23] This is recognized in Louden (1990). This issue is further discussed in Part V.

[24] In our society we have to turn to popular self-help manuals to find extensive discussion of questions of the best life, self-fulfillment, the proper role of the emotions, personal friendships and commitments, topics which in the ancient world were always treated in a more intellectual way as part of ethics.

Studying ancient theories in which happiness and virtue are not only respectable but central concepts may encourage us to give these notions more respectful and serious attention when we reflect on our own use of them. Increased attention to ancient ethics could make modern ethics more realistic, readier to take seriously thoughts that have never left the lives of most people but which most ethical theories brusquely banish or downgrade.

Second, studying theories that are not hierarchical and complete may open our minds to the possibility of kinds of theories that are different in form from the ones we are used to. This may encourage a more critical attitude to the theories that we do have, and an awareness of their limitations. In particular this may encourage a more critical attitude to the common assumption that the model for an ethical theory must be that of a scientific one, with basic and derived concepts, and with reduction and theoretical simplicity seen as major aims. We may come to find alternatives other than accepting this picture or rejecting theory altogether as an aim in ethics.

Third, modern virtue theorists may benefit from seeing the formal basis of and limitations on ancient ethical theories, which are theories of virtue. It is the aim of this book to show that ancient theories share a formal framework (which one may miss if one concentrates on just one theory, like Aristotle's) which, despite the deep differences, may be fruitful to consider for modern writers exploring the general structure of a virtue theory.

And finally, modern virtue ethics can benefit not only from the broad patterns of ancient theories but also from their detail. One disadvantage that has been felt by modern writers on virtue is the lack of agreed context for discussions of happiness and the various virtues. When it comes to distinguishing among kinds of virtues, or their connections, or the connection of happiness with the good of others, it sometimes seems as though the debate lacks rules, that the writers are making their way through a medium with too little resistance. Useful insights are often made, but sometimes it is not clear quite what we are to do with them, what is the exact context of debate in which they make a contribution. Ancient theories are well worked-out; often debates developed between different schools, giving a context for the development of important positions. Again, we cannot take over the debates; but studying them may give us a better idea of what is at stake in our own.

The Plan of the Book

The first part of the book examines the notions of a final end and of virtue, the core notions in ancient ethics. I begin by tracing what for ancient ethics is the entry point for ethical reflection: it is the agent's reflection on her life as a whole, and the relative importance of her various ends. This contrasts strongly with modern theories, for which hard cases and ethical conflicts which are often taken to be the spur to ethical thinking. The notion of a final end emerges from considerations about the ways in which the agent's ends and priorities fit together, and from the dissatisfaction which it is assumed that most thoughtful and reflective people feel about their lives and their priorities. Ancient ethics takes its start from what is taken to be the fact that people have, implicitly, a notion of a final end, an overall goal which enables them to unify and clarify their immediate goals. Ethical theory is designed to enable us to reflect on this implicit overall goal and to make it determinate. For, while there is consensus that our final end is happiness (*eudaimonia*), this is trivial, for substantial disagreement remains as to what happiness consists in. (Because of this verbal agreement, ancient theories may conveniently be referred to as eudaimonistic.)

The other major concept in ancient ethics is that of virtue. Because the ancient notion is so different from what we generally understand by virtue, I discuss virtue from several angles: the dispositional aspect of virtue, the way in which developing a virtue affects one's emotional and affective side, the intellectual development which virtue demands, and the demands which an ethics of virtue does and does not make on the structure of ethical reasoning. After some more minor points the part closes by discussing two issues. One is the general assumptions which ancient theories make as to the relationship of virtue to our final end. The other is the extent to which virtue, in ancient theories, is the locus of what we call specifically *moral* value and the moral point of view. I argue, against the modern orthodoxy, that in ancient theories virtue does occupy the conceptual area which we assign to the moral, despite obvious differences. The result of this is that ancient ethics is concerned with what we would characterize as the place of morality in an agent's life. The other three parts explore three aspects of this point.

Part II is concerned with the role in ancient theories of the appeal to nature to ground or justify the theory in some way. I begin by distinguishing ancient concerns here from modern concerns with 'naturalism'. I then look at the role of nature in various ancient theories: Epicurus, the Sceptics, the Stoics, Aristotle and later Aristotelian theories. One result of this is to show that nature figures in these theories in several ways; 'the appeal to nature' does not refer to one monolithic strategy. Nonetheless, analogies can be discerned, and nature figures, roughly, in two roles. One is to give the constraints which all theories must respect; some things are inevitable for human beings, and a theory which is to be livable by human beings must take account of them. Other than the Sceptics, however, all ancient theories hold that within these constraints there is a great deal which humans can do to achieve a better, rather than a worse, life. All appeal to human rationality as what enables us to do this; some are more optimistic than others as to what human reasoning can achieve. Thus nature appears also as a goal which ethical theory can help us to reach. Nature in this sense is not an ethically neutral, 'purely factual' notion. I conclude the Part by discussing the kind of justification for an ethical theory which such a conception of nature can provide, and by contrasting it with what modern theories characteristically demand by way of justification.

Part III examines the role in ancient theories of the interests of others. It is very often assumed that ancient theories must be, at some level, egoistic, just because their starting point is the agent's reflections on his life, and because they demand that the agent have concern for his acquisition of virtue. I begin by discussing those ancient theories that do arguably have a problem with allowing the interests of others a non-instrumental role in the agent's overall goal, namely those theories that hold that our final end is pleasure or tranquillity. Other theories, however, assume that the interests of others will have intrinsic value for the agent. Their differences come in the scope that other-concern has. Aristotelian kinds of theory assume that other-concern will extend only as far as 'friendship' or commitment to particular other people. Stoic kinds of theory, on the other hand, take it that other-concern will extend beyond the range of personal acquaintance and commitment, and eventually result in the virtuous agent having concern, from the moral point of view, for any rational being. In this part I also consider justice, which has been found a problem for eudaimonistic theories. It is often assumed that in such theories justice can figure only as a virtue of character along with the other virtues, and that this leaves ancient theories with nothing to say on the subject which is most prominent in modern discussions of justice, namely the justice of institutions. I show, by considering various theories, that this is mistaken, and also that justice fits into ancient theories better than is often thought.

The final part raises again the question, how eudaimonistic theories can really be theories of happiness. The more we take into the account the point that ancient theories of virtue are theories of what we characterize as morality, the harder it is for us to take them seriously as theories of happiness. I look at two kinds of theory: those, like Epicurus' and the Sceptics', which lay more weight on the idea that the happy life must be a life which the agent enjoys and is positive about, and consequently have problems in giving virtue a non-instrumental role, and also the theories which begin by giving virtue a large role, and consequently have to be extremely revisionary about our conception of happiness and its intuitive suggestions. The major obstacle to our achieving an adequate understanding of ancient ethical theories is the difficulty we are bound to find in giving due weight both to the point that these are theories of happiness, however redefined, and the point that they are theories of morality.

In the conclusion I bring together some of the results of the different parts, and draw some conclusions about the structure of ancient ethical theories.

It is plain, even from this skimpy summary, that the method followed in this book is to let the structure of ancient ethical theory emerge from the material. In each of the parts I bring together various different theories, by comparison, or through the debates between them, in order to let the similarities and differences in their treatments of nature, or the interests of others, emerge. In every case the result is that we can discern different content in the same form, different ways of answering the same questions.

Some readers may find this way of proceeding unsatisfactory. It would certainly be neater and more satisfying if I first laid out clearly what I take the main theses of ancient ethical theory to be, and then presented the material as illustrative of these theses. A book written in this way would first lay out the bare abstract structure of ancient ethical theory, making clear what the alternative possibilities are, and then fill in the details from the various ancient texts. I have consciously rejected this way of proceeding, for two reasons. One is that I am too aware of the difficulties of establishing the form of ancient ethics to feel confident in presenting any such bare structure. Such a project is worthwhile, but will have to build upon more cautious studies, including the present one. Where ancient ethics is concerned, we have all too many confident pronouncements about what is and what is not essential to it- often pronouncements which are backed by knowledge of a very limited number of the ancient theories. A project like the present one, which tries to extract the structure from comparative treatment of several theories, has a better chance of not prejudging important issues at the start, and of letting the wide variety of ancient ethical options register more effectively. The second reason is that such a finished theoretical grid laid over the material from the start would inevitably have a coercive effect on the reader; if the material is presented merely as illustrative of an existing definite plan, it will be read more one-sidedly. My way of proceeding leaves it more open to the reader to agree or disagree in an informed manner with the conclusions I draw. Of course the material is not presented in a wholly neutral way—there can be no such thing; but I hope that for all that, the reader can see whether or not the structure I discern is really there. I have obviously not been able to follow through systematically every significant feature of every theory. Rather, I have tried to lay down the main lines of what is needed to get a grasp of the shape of ancient ethical theory.

Methodological Issues

There are (at least) three kinds of difficulty the reader may feel, which I shall try to isolate and (to some extent) meet. First, presenting the material thematically— discussing virtue in ancient ethics, rather than Aristotle on virtue—necessitates frequent cross-referencing, some repetition and some passages where an important point has to be taken for granted and explored only later on. These expository problems come from the rich and dense nature of ancient ethical theories; explaining what a virtue is, for example, requires following up in detail several kinds of consideration, some of them complex. No simple linear explanation is possible which would go from what is clear and obvious to modern thought to what is less so; rather, several strands in the notion—the emotional side, the intellectual side, the structure of reasoning- have to be introduced separately and brought together at the end. I do not think that this procedure in fact creates major difficulties for a modern reader, and I have kept the cross-referencing as clear as I could. The problems a modern reader has with ancient ethics are less those of grasping abstruse or unfamiliar material than those of coping with an unfamiliar standpoint on familiar things.

Second, confusion may arise over the words 'ethical' and 'moral'. One of the major theses that this book hopes to establish is that ancient ethical thought is a recognizable form of *moral* thought. That is, the ancient theories are theories of what modern moral theories are theories of; they are not a different, lost form of thought that we can study but have no practical interest in. I have emphasized one failing I hope to avoid: that of seeing ancient ethics as too readily available for our use. But I hope also to avoid the opposite failing: that of seeing it as so fundamentally different from modern moral thought in content and method as to form a disjoint alternative. This is a fairly influential view, and I shall examine the arguments for it in detail in the final section of the first Part. I shall thus talk of ancient ethics as a form of morality, even though at several places it is necessary to contrast some aspects of it with aspects of modern morality.[25]

[25] Apart from these sections of the book, I have discussed this issue in Annas (1992c).

Finally, the project of discussing the issues of ancient ethics in a way that brings the different ancient theories together is vulnerable to two kinds of complaints, especially from philosophers whose field this is. One is that it is misleading to compare pieces of ancient theories—says Aristotle on virtue with the Stoics on virtue. We can understand the relevant piece of each theory, it is claimed, only if we make the effort to understand the whole theory: how virtue fits into Stoic ethics, and possibly how Stoic ethics fits into Stoic philosophy as a whole. This objection points to something: parts of a theory lack support if extracted from the whole theory, and are open to misinterpretation. But I do not think this danger serious enough to undermine the project. Sustained discussion and comparison of the different schools' ethical theories will, I claim, show this to be just as legitimate as the comparisons of modern moral theories with which we are more familiar.

A more robust form of this complaint is that ancient ethical theories are not in fact sufficiently independent of the rest of the philosophical theory in question for us to be able legitimately to extract and compare them. It has been claimed, for example,[26] that Aristotle's main ethical claims depend in a substantial way on prior Aristotelian metaphysical principles. And it is sometimes assumed that Stoic and Epicurean ethics depend in a strong way on their physicalism. In this book I do not have the scope to meet these claims directly, by examining all the metaphysical theories in question. I hope that the argument of this book will establish that ancient ethical theories can be legitimately studied in a relatively autonomous way. For the book finds a structure common to philosophers whose metaphysical principles are mutually conflicting; what is thus shared cannot be dependent on the metaphysical principles (though of course I would not go so far as to claim that *nothing* in ancient ethics depends on such principles).

The second kind of complaint takes the form of a claim that there is not enough in common between, say, Aristotle, the Stoics and Epicurus on virtue for a study of virtue in ancient ethics to establish anything except what is too general to be of interest as a position in ethical theory. This kind of complaint can only be met by the book as a whole; what it tries to establish, for a number of issues, is that we can in fact find in substantial outline the forms and limits of ancient ethical theory. Such a case can only be made cumulatively, and the book should be judged as a whole. Any philosophical reader is likely to disagree with my reading of the evidence on some points, on philosophical grounds; indeed one thing I hope the book will do is to stimulate discussion on several problems in ancient ethics which become more salient when different theories are compared. But it is begging the question to assume that ancient ethical theories are so different that we cannot find clear and specific positions which show us the formal and limiting framework of ancient ethics, and display the different theories as taking up different options within it.

The book does not pretend to be a guided tour to the ancient systems of ethics; I have not tried, on each issue, to list what each theory has to say on it, but have discussed only those theories that define the terms of the debate or significantly add to it. Thus the book does not form a comprehensive account of ancient ethics.[27] The

---

[26] Irwin (1988b), chs. 15–21.

[27] At present there is no such account which is extensive enough to deal with the arguments of the different theories in much detail. See, however, Vegetti (1989) and Prior (1991).

selections and omissions are guided by the overall aim of producing a clear account of the intellectual structure of ancient ethics. I have been aware throughout that this is a difficult task, and risks inadequacies on both the historical and the philosophical side. I have persevered because it seems to me one of the most important tasks in studying ancient ethics.

Who Are the Moderns?

Throughout the book, when I refer to modern ethical theories, what I have in mind is one or more of the range of types of ethical theory which enter into live debate and dialectic among moral philosophers at the present day. For these are the theories which actually shape our ongoing understanding of what ethical theory is, and provide the presuppositions we need to be aware of in trying to recover historical understanding of very different kinds of theories. Hence I have had in mind for the most part theories of a consequentialist, deontological and virtue ethics type; I have tried to make it clear when I am referring to a feature of one of these types of theories, and when to assumptions which are more generally shared. I have occasionally referred to theories of a different type,[28] but have tried to be careful in making clear when a theory is one which is not currently regarded as a type of viable ethical theory, one which forms part of the current dialectic.

One major objection to this proceeding is extremely obvious. Is this not a somewhat parochial way of proceeding? Perhaps it is just a matter of temporary fashion that these are the theories which are at the moment the ones which are taken seriously. Would it not be better, especially in a work which takes seriously the task of accurately delineating the options in ancient ethics, to try equally seriously to give a historical account of the major intellectual trends in modern ethics, dealing not just with the options which face us now but with the historical traditions which underlie this situation, and which shape our options for us?

I agree entirely that when one wants to contrast ancient with modern ethical theory, it would be most desirable to have a full historical understanding of the forms of modern as well as ancient ethical theories. But at the moment it does not seem that we have either, and it does not seem sensible to try to work at both ends of the contrast, ancient and modern, at the same time; any such attempt is bound to be thoroughly confusing, and probably confused. In this book I have concentrated on exploring the ancient texts, from the basis of what I admit to be a less than full historical understanding of modern theories. To achieve a proper understanding of the kind of contrast that exists between ancient and modern ethical theories we need, in addition to studies like this one, studies which clarify the modern options in ethics, on the basis of historically informed understanding of them.[29] Only then will we be in the position needed to give a satisfactory answer to questions about the ways in which ancient and modern ethical theories are similar and different. In the meantime, I have stayed aware of my deficiencies in understanding modern ethical

---

[28] For example, Bradley, as a representative of the Hegelian school of ethics.

[29] Work of this kind is presently being done by Schneewind. See his (1990a), (1990b), and (1991) as well as his (1993) and forthcoming paper. The forthcoming book and papers by N. White are also valuable contributions to this project.

theories, and hope that my claims about the ancient theories do not actually rely on a parochial understanding of particular contrasts with modern theories.[30]

Who Are the Ancients?

The book has one important limitation: I start the enquiry with Aristotle, and focus on Aristotle's own writings, the early (and sometimes middle) Stoics, the Sceptics, the Cyrenaics, Epicurus and later writers of Aristotle's school, called Peripatetics. I occasionally refer to later Stoics of the Roman period, and to other later writers, but my main concern is with ethics from Aristotle to Cicero—for Cicero, though not himself an original philosopher, is our source for some major debates.

Why start with Aristotle? Aristotle is the first thinker whose works we possess at any length who writes a work called *Ethics*, dealing systematically with ethical theory. It is Aristotle who first lays out for us the framework of Greek ethics (and hence Aristotle who figures largest in the first part of the book), and subsequent schools walk in his footprints; they share his view that ethics is a distinct subject matter with certain agreed starting points—the importance of the agent's final good, of an account of virtue and the place in it of the emotions, of the role played in the good life by commitments to others- and certain settled areas of contention: all agree that our final good is happiness, but disagree as to how that is to be informatively specified.

Thus this book is not a 'history of Greek ethics' of the kind which starts from texts with recognizably ethical material, such as Homer, and goes through the Sophists, Socrates, Plato and Aristotle. For while all these figures are of interest for ethics, they are not of equal interest when one's concern is with explicit ethical theory. From this point of view it is Aristotle who opens the debate, and the Hellenistic schools who further it; and hence the book concentrates on these.

Still, a few words are in order about the omission of systematic discussion of the Sophists and Plato. The Sophists can indeed reasonably be seen as the real originators of ethical and political theory. They discussed *nomos*, law or convention, and the ways in which it contrasts with nature or *phusis*. They raised and discussed questions like the source of authority of the laws and the nature of society. Why not then begin with them? The reason is simply that the remains we have of their ethical ideas are too fragmentary to come to conclusions firm enough to use in a systematic study of Greek ethical theory. Of the three major figures relevant to ethics, Protagoras,[31] Antiphon[32] and Democritus, the first two still give rise to continuing

---

[30] Where they do, I rely on critics to point this out. It is worth noting, however, that (apart from mentioning the methodology of Rawls' *A Theory of Justice*) I do not engage with modern contractarianism. Although this has some forebears in ancient *political* theory, it is quite alien to ancient *ethical* theory, and so is unhelpful from the interpretative point of view. (I would also claim, though of course it cannot be argued here, that the contractarian model cannot capture morality as that is understood in the eudaimonistic, deontological and utilitarian traditions, and represents a radical departure from the notion of morality which this book aims to understand.)

[31] Protagoras' views come down to us mainly through their very hostile presentation in Plato; see Woodruff (forthcoming). See also Nill (1985); Barnes (1979), vol. 2, ch. 10 (b)-(d).

[32] On Antiphon see Saunders (1977-78); Furley (1981); Barnes (1979) ch. 9 (a); Nill (1985). On the

controversy as to what their ideas were, and fundamentally differing interpretations are current;[33] and the relation of Democritus' ethics to his atomism is still disputed.[34] This situation is especially frustrating in the case of Democritus, as he came to be regarded, in the Hellenistic period, as something of an ethical pioneer, and was regarded as having adumbrated an ethical theory which Hellenistic thinkers took to be primitive, but recognizably like their own in form. Unfortunately we possess no fragments relevant to this highly interesting claim,[35] and scholars disagree as to whether Democritus really did pioneer a eudaimonistic form of ethical thinking, or whether he merely put forward some suggestive claims which later ethical theorists interpreted in an anachronistic way, in line with their own developed theories. The latter option is generally seen as the more plausible.[36] So, although I shall refer to these earlier thinkers for specific arguments where this is relevant, I shall not begin with them, to avoid starting on a speculative and uncertain note.

The exclusion of systematic discussion of Plato may surprise and dismay more people; and of course I am *not* claiming that Plato can be left out of histories of Greek ethics. But in a book which examines explicit ethical theory Plato is problematic, because of his deliberate use of the dialogue form and his consequent rejection of systematic discussion of ethical theory. There is no Platonic dialogue which is 'about ethics' in the way that the *Nicomachean Ethics* is about ethics. Each dialogue has its own theme, or group of themes, which often do not answer neatly to our subject divisions. Even the dialogues which are most obviously relevant to ethics, like the *Republic* or the *Philebus*, are also, and equally, about metaphysical and epistemological issues. And even in the dialogues which are most clearly about ethics, Plato in using the dialogue form deliberately refrains from identifying and laying out his own position. It would be extremely naive simply to identify Plato's position with that which is allotted to Socrates in a given dialogue. And even if we do, we find immensely different positions occupied by Socrates in different dialogues; the structure of Platonic ethical theory is greatly underdetermined by what we find in the dialogues.[37]

Thus if we study 'Platonic ethics' we face a problem of extraction: we have ourselves to select and extract the subject matter of ethics, and this is our imposition of a later framework on a writer who deliberately writes in a very different way. Of course this is a perfectly legitimate procedure. But it points up the large differences

---

papyrus fragment, which has recently been re-read and re-edited, with striking changes, see Decleva Caizzi (1985), (1986a) and (1986b); also Barnes (1987).

[33] For Protagoras, Antiphon and other figures like Gorgias (but unfortunately not Democritus), see Classen (1985).

[34] On Democritus see Vlastos (1945–6); Taylor (1967), 6–27; Nill (1985); Barnes (1979) ch. 9 (d).

[35] For the claims, see Cicero *de Finibus* V 23, 87–88; Arius Didymus ap. Stobaeus, *Eclogae* II 52.13–53.1. The latter passage also contains a long comparison of Democritus with Plato in the *Laws* on reason and pleasure (53.1–20). I discuss the Hellenistic revival of interest in Democritus as an ethical thinker (in striking contrast to Aristotle, who ignores his ethics while paying much attention to his physical theories) in my (1993d).

[36] See Kahn (1985) and Striker (1990). For the view that Democritus was the first to produce a systematic ethical theory see Gosling and Taylor (1982). See Farrar (1988) for a discussion of Democritus which stresses the political significance of his ideas.

[37] This situation is most striking in the case of the hedonism apparently defended by Socrates in the *Protagoras*. There is no consensus as to whether the hedonism is Socrates' or Plato's, and, if Plato's, what its relation is to positions defended by Socrates in other dialogues.

between Plato and a writer like Epicurus. Whatever our problems with Epicurean texts, we are in no doubt that Epicurus wrote about a subject called ethics, and that we are looking for his systematic thoughts about that. Plato, however, chose to write dialogues, not treatises; so to write about 'Platonic ethics' is already to have made certain important decisions about interpreting Plato and to have taken a stand on very contentious matters. In a project designed to let the structure of ancient ethics emerge from the material examined, clearly the less reliance on contentious premises the better.

In the case of Plato there are additional problems. One is the perennial 'Socratic problem'. Within Plato's dialogues can we distinguish a distinctive 'Socratic' position from a later 'Platonic' one? And if so, what relation does the former bear to other accounts of Socrates, such as Xenophon's? This problem is especially pressing in ethics, where we seem to see some clear changes between dialogues. In recent years the old, confident assumption that we can distinguish a 'Socratic' from a 'Platonic' ethics has crumbled somewhat; it has increasingly been seen to rely on naive ways of reading the dialogues, and the whole idea of Platonic 'chronology' has been increasingly questioned. Another problem is the status of Plato's arguments. Are the arguments put forward by Socrates simply Plato's own arguments? Or is Plato more interested in exploring arguments and issues than in building up a system of ethics in the first place? This would certainly explain why he chooses the form of writing that he does. The more seriously we take this possibility, the more problematic it becomes to see particular arguments as simply part of a single system of ideas. This is another area where old views are under fire and old certainties are crumbling.[38]

Aristotle probably develops his ethical position by way of reaction to some Platonic theses as well as by reflecting on common opinion. And some of the Hellenistic schools, while rejecting Plato, take Socrates as an exemplary ethical figure.[39] But, during the period of debate with which this book is mostly concerned, Plato's ethics did not figure as a contender; Plato's own school held no substantive ethical views of its own, but limited itself to criticizing those of others.[40]

It is, of course, perfectly legitimate to try to extract a 'Platonic ethics' from the dialogues. But we should be aware that this involves both strong methodological assumptions and a very large amount of system-building and priority-choosing on our part. And equally, once we have extracted the framework of ancient ethical theory from later writers, it is legitimate to go back and apply it to Plato's works, if we are both cautious and clear about our methodological assumptions. We need, in fact, a work or rather several works on Platonic ethics to help us to understand the following: the distinguishing features of 'Socratic' ethics and how they differ from 'Platonic' ethics; the theory of the 'middle' and 'later' dialogues, and the relation of

---

[38] Some traditional preconceptions as to how to read the 'Socratic dialogues' are attacked in Kahn (1981a). Kahn's position in this and other articles is usefully discussed by McPherran (1990a). Recent collections of articles which explore the methodological problems are Griswold (1988) and Klagge and Smith (1992).

[39] See Long (1988a). Among these are the Cynics, who will not figure much in this book, just because, while they are important in some respects (notably of helping to popularize Socrates as an ethical exemplar in the Hellenistic period) they did not contribute to the development of explicit ethical theory, which is the concern of this book.

[40] See Annas (1992b).

this both to the ethical theories of the Old Academy and to the later position of Middle Platonists such as Plutarch. It is clearly of great interest to examine the extent to which modern readers of the dialogues agree, or disagree, with later writers in the ancient world who read Plato in the light of more developed and explicit expectations about ethical theory. However, I hope it is by now clear why a book with the aim of this one has to start with Aristotle.

Sources

All translations are my own. A 'Cast of Characters' at the end of the book gives brief information, relevant to the concerns of this book, about the major figures discussed.

Aristotle

Aristotle's ethics have come down to us in three versions: the *Nicomachean Ethics* (*NE*), which has the best text and has in the twentieth century been the main focus of study; the *Eudemian Ethics* (*EE*), which shares three books with the *Nicomachean* version and covers roughly the same issues, but which sometimes differs and has a much more problematic text; and the *Magna Moralia* (*MM*), a compendium or textbook of Aristotelian ethics.[41] Since the nineteenth century there has been intense scholarly debate over the chronology and authenticity of these works.[42] While the *Nicomachean Ethics* remains the main text studied, there has been an increasing tendency to use the *Eudemian Ethics* also. Scholarly debate over whether the *Eudemian Ethics* is earlier or later than the *Nicomachean Ethics* has settled down inconclusively, and the most widely shared assumption is that both are by Aristotle, the *Eudemian Ethics* probably earlier. The *Magna Moralia* remains more controversial, and I go along with the majority view that it is a handbook produced in Aristotle's school not long after his death. The view that it is a juvenile production by Aristotle, predating both *Nicomachean Ethics* and *Eudemian Ethics*, has also been argued.[43] For the purposes of this book the point is not of enormous importance, since I am concerned with the general form of Aristotle's views and the

---

[41] For the *NE* I use the Oxford Classical Text (Bywater), and for the *EE* and *MM* the Teubner (Susemihl) as well as the recent Oxford Classical Text of the *EE* by Walzer and Mingay. There are translations with commentaries on all three by F. Dirlmeier: *Eudemische Ethik*, Berlin 1962, *Nikomachische Ethik*, Berlin 1966, *Magna Moralia*, Berlin 1968. There are many commentaries on the *Nicomachean Ethics* in English, notably J. Burnet (London 1900) and H. Joachim (Oxford 1955), and a full and useful one in French—*L'éthique à Nicomaque*, R. A. Gauthier and J. Y. Jolif, Louvain 1970. The best translations in English are W. D. Ross' Oxford translation, revised by J. O. Urmson in the Revised Oxford Translation, ed. J. Barnes (Princeton 1984), and the translation with notes by T. Irwin (Hackett 1985a). The *MM* has not been so well served. For the *EE* see the partial translation with notes by M. Woods (Oxford 1982).

[42] See von Arnim (1924); the works by Dirlmeier cited in the previous note; Kenny (1978). Kenny defends the position that the *EE*, rather than the *NE*, is Aristotle's mature ethical treatise.

[43] Cooper (1973).

ways in which they can be developed; the *Magna Moralia* is good evidence for this even if it is not by Aristotle himself. Also important for Aristotle's ethical theory are the *Politics* and the *Rhetoric*, the latter being a useful source for commonsense views on ethical matters.

The Stoics

No complete work by any early Stoic has come down to us; but for Stoic ethics we have the benefit of three continuous accounts by later writers, which contain material much of which goes back fairly directly to early Stoic writers.

(1) Cicero in *de Finibus* (*On Final Ends*), Book III, presents an account of Stoic ethics put forward by a Stoic spokesman.[44]

(2) A collection of extracts by the fourth-century writer John Stobaeus contains a long extract on ethics, generally attributed to Arius Didymus, court philosopher to the Emperor Augustus.[45] The extract falls into three parts: (a) an introduction, in which Arius draws from two other writers of the first century B.C., Philo of Larissa and Eudorus of Alexandria (this introduction is of great interest for considering the general assumptions and formal framework of ancient ethics); (b) an account of Stoic ethics and (c) an account of Peripatetic ethics. The account of Stoic ethics is a handbook resume. There is at present no English translation available, but I am working on a translation with notes for the Clarendon Library of Later Greek Philosophy.

(3) Diogenes Laertius, a writer of a ten-volume *Lives of the Philosophers*, of uncertain date but probably in the second century A.D., puts into his *Life of Zeno* an account of Stoic philosophy as a whole. The section on ethics clearly derives at many parts from the same sources as the Arius Didymus account (2), and the two usefully complement each other. The only available English translation is that in Volume 2 of Diogenes in the Loeb Classical Library, but I shall use my own translation, which was done together with that of the Arius passage, so that the two are consistent.[46]

The Cyrenaics

The Cyrenaic school, traditionally founded by Socrates' follower Aristippus, seems to depend extensively on Aristippus' grandson, Aristippus the Younger, for its theory and arguments. Our main sources for this are the second book of Diogenes Laertius,

---

[44] I follow Madvig's text of the *de Finibus* (1876; reprinted Hildesheim 1965). Translations are available by H. Rackham in the Loeb Classical Library (Cambridge, MA 1914, repr. 1971), and by Wright (1992).

[45] I follow the text of C. Wachsmuth (1884). The attribution to Arius of the Stoic section is not certain, but it is plausible. On this and other issues see Fortenbaugh, ed. (1983).

[46] I use the Oxford Classical Text, though this is not very satisfactory. A new text by M. Marcovich is forthcoming. The only complete English translation is by R. D. Hicks in the Loeb Classical Library (Cambridge, MA 1925, repr. 1972). On Diogenes' treatment of the Stoic and other schools see Giannantoni, ed. (1986).

and passages in later authors, principally Sextus Empiricus.[47] There were later figures in the Cyrenaic school, some of whom made considerable alterations in its theories. The fragments of all the Cyrenaics can be found in three collections,[48] but English translations are available only of the major sources. Much about the Cyrenaics remains puzzling, but there is an increasing amount of accessible discussion.[49]

Epicurus

Epicurus' own major work on ethics is lost, but we possess a short exhortatory work, the *Letter to Menoeceus* (*Ep Men*). This and a short account of Epicurean ethics are in Diogenes Laertius' *Lives* Book X. Apart from this we have to rely on fragments of or about the ethical works preserved in later writers; on fragments of later Epicurean writers like Philodemus preserved on papyri from Herculaneum; and on passages in the long Epicurean poem *On the Nature of Things* written in Latin by the first century B.C. poet Lucretius. We also have long speeches for and against Epicurean ethics in books I and II of Cicero's *de Finibus*.[50] Reconstruction of the form and much of the content of Epicurean ethics is more hazardous and uncertain than it is with other ancient theories. English translations are available of Epicurus apart from the papyrus fragments, Cicero and Lucretius. For papyrus fragments of Epicurus and other Epicurean writers we are dependent on modern editions, only some of which are in English.

Hybrid Theories

Aristotle's School, the Peripatetics

Aristotle's school developed his ethical ideas in ways that were heavily influenced by later schools, especially the Stoics. Our best source for this later version of Aristotelian ethics, which I shall refer to as Peripatetic to distinguish it from Aristotle's own works, is the account of Peripatetic ethics in Arius Didymus.[51]

[47] For Sextus see below under Sceptics.
[48] Giannantoni (1958); Mannebach (1961); Giannantoni (1990).
[49] For bibliography see the discussion of the Cyrenaics in Part III.
[50] The standard text of Epicurus is *Epicuro: Opere*, ed. G. Arrighetti (Turin 1960). H. Usener, *Epicurea* (Leipzig, 1887, repr. Stuttgart 1966) collects ancient evidence and testimonia on Epicurus. Because Diogenes Laertius transcribes three letters and many sayings of Epicurus in his Life, much of the evidence can be found in Diogenes (see n. 46). Apart from the Loeb Diogenes, an English translation of Epicurus can be found in the edition by C. Bailey (Oxford 1926), which however omits papyrus fragments. We know the work of later Epicureans principally through the Herculaneum papyri; the writer most relevant to this book is Philodemus, and references to those of his works referred to in the book can be found where these are discussed. The standard edition with translation of the Roman Epicurean Lucretius is by C. Bailey (Oxford 1947, repr. 1986). A variety of English translations of Lucretius are available.
[51] On Arius see n. 45. At present no English translation is available, but one is forthcoming in the Clarendon Library of Later Ancient Philosophy, by S. White, in his translation with notes of Cicero *Fin* V (the theory of Antiochus).

Antiochus

Another figure is relevant here: the first-century philosopher Antiochus of Ascalon.[52] Antiochus was a member of the sceptical Platonic Academy who broke away to set up his own school in opposition to prevailing sceptical trends. He turned back to positive or 'dogmatic' teaching. And he thought up the idea that what he called the 'Old Academy' of Plato's successors was the source of a common tradition shared by all the schools of his day except the Epicureans. In ethics he maintained that Plato and his successors, and Aristotle and his school, shared a fundamentally similar ethical framework, and that this was also the position of the Stoics, whose innovations were merely tiresome verbal ones. While nonsense as history, Antiochus' thesis enabled him to build up an ethical theory which is basically Aristotelian, but with heavy Stoic influences. In Book V of *de Finibus* Cicero has a supporter of Antiochus' theory present it at length; and in Book IV he uses Antiochus' arguments against the Stoic theory.[53] Antiochus' ethical theory has not received much serious attention, partly because it is supposedly based on history which is blatantly false, partly because it is an avowed mixture of Aristotelian and Stoic elements, an enterprise which most scholars have seen as doomed. But Antiochus' use of Stoic elements to recast fundamentally Aristotelian ideas is actually of great interest in itself as a contribution to debates between Stoics and Aristotelians on important issues. And Antiochus' project brings him in many ways near to the Peripatetic, Stoic-influenced version of Aristotelian ethics in Arius Didymus.[54] We shall see that there are many important areas of disagreement between Aristotelian and Stoic ethics, and that these hybrid theories have interesting contributions to make to them. Until recently, these theories have tended to receive scholarly abuse or condescension as being 'eclectic'. But familiarity with ethical *debate* enables one to see that 'eclecticism' is not necessarily an unintelligent combination of diverse elements; it may be a sophisticated attempt to avoid problems with theories which are untenable in their unqualified form.[55]

Sceptics

There are two major sceptical schools in the ancient world:

(1) The Academics. In the third century B.C. Plato's Academy turned to scepticism under its head, Arcesilaus. The tradition was carried on, notably by the brilliant Carneades, until the Academy petered out in the first century B.C.[56] Arguing in the tradition of Socrates, the Academics left no writings of their own, but many of

[52] See Glucker (1978) and Barnes (1989).

[53] For the *de Finibus*, see n.44.

[54] Many scholars have thought that this passage is based on, or is actually a version of, Antiochus' ethics. However, the passages are sufficiently different, even if they do have a common source, that it is better to keep them distinct rather than risk confusion by conflating them. They provide quite different solutions to some Stoic difficulties with Aristotle's ethics, for example (see chapter 20).

[55] Cf. the collection of studies in Dillon and Long (1988). I make some remarks on the interest of these hybrid and eclectic theories in my (1990a).

[56] Glucker (1978); also my (1992b).

their arguments have been preserved, along with evidence about their attitude to our final end and the good life.

(2) The Pyrrhonists. This was a breakaway radical movement from the Academy in the first century B.C. They took their inspiration from the legendary figure of Pyrrho, an earlier sceptic who left no writings. Our major source for Pyrrhonism is the extensive work of Sextus Empiricus, a doctor probably of the third century A.D., who wrote a shorter and a longer account of Pyrrhonism with a collection of Pyrrhonist arguments in all areas of philosophy. For ethics the relevant sections are the account of the sceptic's life and aims (which we have only in Book I of the shorter work, *Outlines of Pyrrhonism*) and the sections of ethical argument in both the *Outlines* and the longer work, *Against the Professors*.[57]

General Sources

Some authors serve as sources for more than one school. Plutarch, a second-century Platonist philosopher, wrote many works from which we get useful information about Academics, Stoics and Epicureans, though its value is lessened by Plutarch's hostile and polemical attitude. Alexander of Aphrodisias, a second-third century commentator on Aristotle, is our source for much valuable information about Stoic-Peripatetic debate, and for what Alexander takes Aristotle's own position on the issues to be. Galen, a third-century doctor, who wrote voluminously on many philosophical topics, is our best source for some issues, for example, the Stoic theory of the emotions.

Long and Sedley (1987) is a collection of extracts from Sceptics, Epicureans and Stoics, arranged topically. Volume 1 contains English translations, and volume 2 the original texts. Inwood and Gerson (1988) is a collection of passages from Hellenistic philosophy translated into English, with notes. Gerson and Inwood translate entire passages rather than collecting extracts by topic. Both these collections are valuable; I have not referred to passages in them, since their selections of ethical material differ considerably from mine.

---

[57] Sextus' arguments 'against the ethicists' are found in the last part of book III of the *Outlines of Pyrrhonism* (*PH*) and in book XI of *Against the Professors* (*Adversus Mathematicos* [*M*]). For Sextus I use the Teubner text (Mutschmann, revised Mau). The only complete English translation is that by Bury in the 4-vol. Loeb edition (Cambridge, MA 1933–47, repr. 1967–71). The Sceptical 'Modes' or argument-forms are translated, with commentary and an introduction to ancient scepticism, in Annas and Barnes (1985).

I

The Basic Ideas

1

Making Sense of My Life as a Whole

The Entry Point for Ethical Reflection

In ancient ethics the fundamental question is, How ought I to live?[1] or, What should my life be like? This is not taken to be in origin a philosopher's question; it is a question which an ordinary person will at some point put to herself. Many ordinary people may of course be too unreflective, or too satisfied with convention, or just too busy, to pose the question. But it is assumed that people of average intellect with a modicum of leisure will at some point reflect on their lives and ask whether they are as they should be, or whether they could be improved. And it is widely assumed that, while there are plenty of people around with ready answers, the only answers which will satisfy an intelligent and reflective person will come from ethical philosophy. In the period concerning us, there are many philosophical schools offering competing philosophies of ethics: the question is answered by Aristotle and by later Peripatetic followers, by Epicurus, by the Stoics and by the Sceptics, and their answers are very different. But there is no serious disagreement as to this being the right question to ask, and as to its being philosophy which provides the answer.

To us, the question, What should my life be like? may seem too particular to be a properly ethical question. Shouldn't ethics be about duty, or rights, or the good, rather than about my life? But it may also, oddly, seem too general. Couldn't a wide variety of answers be given, ranging from the life of ruthless egoism to the life of saintly self-denial; and isn't there something unfocussed about a question that allows so wide a range of answers? In either case, how can *philosophy* help here? If the question arises from everyday kinds of thinking about and dissatisfaction with one's life, how can we be furthered in finding the answer by the very abstract kinds of reflection that philosophy gives us? And so we have got out of the way of expecting philosophy to answer the question, What should my life be like? A great deal of modern literature and psychology arises from and revolves around the way people reflect about their lives and whether they are the way they should be, but thought about one's life is no longer seen as central to ethical philosophy, at least to ethical theory. At best the question is seen as marginal, to be answered when the main lines of the theory are already established.

---

[1] Classically posed by Socrates in the first book of *Repub* (352 d): *hontina tropon chrē zēn*. The neutral way I have posed the question is, I think, the most suitable.

27

In the ancient world we find that there is a single kind of concern for one's life being as it should and the kind of person one is, which arises unforcedly in most people, which is the subject of much of literature, and which is the natural starting point for ethical reflection. If we follow through the way in which this concern arises, we shall come to see how ethics can develop from this point, rather than from other points which we find more familiar, such as bizarre problems forced on us by new technology, or a search for justification for familiar rules.[2] In due course we shall see how a question which may seem to us both personal and vague could be seen, in the ancient world, as the only compelling starting point for ethics.

We should recognize that the fact that this is the starting point is not simply a matter of inertia, or lack of moral imagination. The ancients were perfectly aware of the existence of moral disagreement over hard cases. Aristotle, for instance, gives as an example of a typically ethical premise, in the *Topics*, the problem 'whether one should obey one's parents or the laws, when there is a conflict'.[3] And they were also quite aware of the need for principled help in coming to make everyday decisions; Cicero says that noone would dare to call himself a moral philosopher if he had nothing to say about the rules and principles that we need to guide our decisions in most areas of life.[4] But these issues do not determine the structure of ancient ethics; it is never felt that the point of ethical theory is to help us to solve hard moral problems or to determine our rules of everyday duty. These are seen as tasks to be fulfilled once the outline structure of ethics has been got right, not as tasks which form that structure itself.[5]

We all think in retrospect about actions we have done and feelings we have had. For me to think about my life as a whole requires something further—I have to step back to some extent from my immediate present and projects, and think about my past and future. How have I come to have the projects I now have, and the attitudes I now have to those projects, and to many other things and people? To think about my life as a whole is to ask how I have become the person I now am, how past plans, successes and failures have produced the person who now has the present projects and attitudes that I have. And it is also to think about the future. How do I see my present plans continuing? Am I happy to go on living much as I have done, or do I hope, and perhaps intend, to change my commitments and attitudes?

Ancient ethics gets its grip on the individual at this point of reflection: am I satisfied with my life as a whole, with the way it has developed and promises to

---

[2] Of course many people in the ancient world came to take morality more seriously as a result of striking personal experiences or reflections; and from Aristotle onwards there is a tradition of philosophical writing which aims to 'convert', to shock people into rethinking their lives. But what they are to be jolted into is the kind of reflective concern that *can* arise unforcedly in their own life; a *protrepticus* or 'conversion writing' urges the hearer to take what is the natural entry point for ethical reflection.

[3] *Top* 105 b 19–23. Anticipating the later division of philosophy to some extent, Aristotle distinguishes logical, physical and ethical premises and problems. It is not surprising that he thinks of conflicts in this case, since he is considering cases for debate and discussion. I owe the reference to Charlton (1990).

[4] *Off* I 4–5. Cicero emphasizes the importance of *praecepta* (rules, principles), and the ubiquity of *officium* or duty in every area of public and private life. The place of rules and duties in ancient ethics will be discussed at greater length below in chapter 6.

[5] I return to this point in Part V.

continue? For most of us are dissatisfied with both our achievement and our promise, and it is only the dissatisfied who have the urge to live differently, and hence the need to find out what ways of living differently would be improvements. Ancient ethics has nothing to say directly to those who have never reached this point of reflection about their lives or are unimpressed by it: the dull and the complacent, for example. These people can benefit from ethical philosophy only indirectly, through doing what books, or other people, tell them to do. The arguments and conclusions of ethical philosophy will be effective only with those who have come to them through worrying about real problems: recommendations as to how best to live will have force only with those who have wondered for themselves about how their lives are going.

Nor can ancient ethics say much to or do much for those who are not prepared to carry the lessons of ethics into their plans for living. Aristotle is making this point when he says that it is 'futile and useless' for young people to listen to his lectures on ethics, since

> they tend to follow their feelings. But our aim is not knowledge but action. It makes no difference whether they are young in age or immature in character; the deficiency does not depend on time, but on living according to one's feelings and pursuing particular ends. Knowledge is no use to people like this. . . .But knowledge of these matters is extremely useful to people who form their desires and act according to reason.[6]

Aristotle is actually making the point that ethical reflection will not get going until we advance from thinking about and acting on particular ends to thinking about and acting on 'reason', rational reflection. Even those of us who are not dull and complacent will not usually detach ourselves from emotional engagement with present concerns and think about our life as a whole when we are young; those who never do, the immature, form another group of people on whom ethical thinking has no direct hold. As a later writer puts it:

> [I]t is not the person who listens eagerly and takes notes at philosophy lectures who is ready for philosophizing, rather the person whose state is ready for transferring the lessons of philosophy into action, and for living accordingly.[7]

Aristotle in the opening chapters of the *Nicomachean Ethics*[8] traces carefully for us what is implied in this stepping-back from particular concerns to reflection on one's life as a whole, and what we discover when we do it. Aristotle first establishes that 'every skill and every investigation, and similarly every action and choice, seem to aim at some good; which is why the good has been finely characterized as that at which everything aims.'[9] A skill like medicine, he goes on to say, has health as its aim; likewise in an individual agent every 'action and choice' aims at some good. Aristotle takes this point to be simply obvious, one that anyone would accept when thinking about it. We may think that two points are being fused here: the point that

---

[6] *NE* 1095 a 4–11.
[7] Arius 104.17–22.
[8] In contrast to the *Eudemian Ethics*, which begins from thoughts about happiness and goes on to our notion of the final good.
[9] 1094 a 1–3.

each action and choice of an individual are end-directed, and the point that they are directed at the good. We might reject both, or accept the first but not the second.

In fact, the first point is convincing enough if we interpret 'action and choice' sensibly. We may do some things which are pointless or spontaneous, but these are not clear examples of actions or choices. Aristotle himself tends to treat choice as necessary for a proper action, and choice as requiring deliberation, so here he clearly means that everything that we do that is brought about by deliberated choice is end-directed.[10] This has the advantage of sounding as platitudinous as Aristotle takes his claim to be. It leaves it open that much that we do is not action in this sense, but assumes that action is what ethics is mostly concerned with. And this seems reasonable. Ethics is concerned primarily with our considered actions and choices, and with the things we do that reflect our deliberations, not with pointless or spontaneous things we do, like kicking the leaves as we walk along. The claim here is that action and choice have an end-directed structure. And this is a convincing claim, at this level of generality. It is certainly plausible, on reflection, that when I do something or decide to do something, I want there to be a certain outcome, but I want something further as well: I want to *bring about* that outcome, not just to have it happen. My action or decision is seen as a way of bringing about the envisaged outcome, and thus as directed at it as an end or goal.[11]

Must it, however, be aimed at something *good*? Is Aristotle not ignoring the fact that many of our deliberated actions have aims that we recognize to be no good, or positively evil? These cases are easy to deal with, however. I may act to achieve some pleasure, say, which I recognize to be no good—no good relative to my other aims. But in the context of the particular deliberation, the pleasure I aim at is *a* good I hope to get. And in general it is hard to understand the performance of a deliberated action unless the agent saw something good in the outcome he was trying to bring about. Even the case where an agent aims at something she considers positively evil, the action is incomprehensible unless there is some aspect somewhere of the aim which gives the agent a good to try to bring about (if only the pleasure of revenge, etc.). The claim that all action is aimed at some good has in fact an intuitive plausibility (which is all I am trying to establish here), arising from the thoughts we have when we try to understand the actions of others and ourselves. We can understand actions and decisions as given structure by the attempt to achieve some good; and it is hard to see how else we are to understand them. Nothing hinges on the agent's being right, or even consistent.[12]

[10] This need not imply that the agent consciously went through a process of deliberation; in a person of good dispositions deliberation may not have to be explicit. I take it here that we have a rough grasp of what deliberation is; the issue is discussed further in the section on the role of practical reasoning in virtue. The restrictions here on the notion of choice have led some to hold that 'choice' is not a good translation of Aristotle's term *prohairesis*, but allowing for some variations, the core uses of 'choice' in English seem to imply deliberation, spontaneous 'choices' being regarded on reflection as 'picking' rather than 'choosing'.

[11] Of course many complicated issues of action theory open up here, and what I say is rough and crude. But what is at stake here is merely the way in which it is natural for an agent to think about her own actions.

[12] It might be objected that there are very many different ways in which things can be good, and that examining this might undermine one of the assumptions of this argument, namely that all deliberated actions aim at things which are good in a relevantly similar sense. This point did not impress the ancients; very thorough examination was made of the different ways in which things can be good by both the Stoics

Aristotle's second move[13] is to point out that some ends are subordinated to others, and that where this is so we value the subordinated end less than the end it is subordinated to, the one it is sought 'for the sake of'. His examples are from skills and kinds of knowledge, but this is just an analogy; what interests him is the idea that in a given individual his ends might form a hierarchy. People do not make bridles just for the sake of it; their activity is given point by there being an activity of horse-training, of which making bridles is a part. Similarly, my life is not just a series of, so to say, one damned end after another. Some ends are given their raison d'être by forming part of a hierarchy in which they are subordinate to other ends. I do not, for example, try to hit a ball over a net just for its own sake. This action has point by being done 'for the sake of' playing tennis, a wider end which includes this and other things. Playing tennis, in turn, makes sense as something I do by being done for the sake of the wider end of keeping fit. It does not take much thought to see that most of the ends we aim at in our deliberated actions are 'nested' in this kind of hierarchical way.

Aristotle now shows, in a famous passage, that if we put together these obvious thoughts, they imply something which is in a way also obvious, but substantial.

> If, then, there is some end (*telos*) of the things we can do, an end which we wish for because of it itself, while we wish for the other things because of it; and if we do not choose everything because of something else (for it goes on *ad infinitum* that way, so that desire is empty and vain)—then it is clear that this would be the good, and the best [good]. So surely as far as our lives are concerned knowledge of this has great influence, and just like archers with a target we would be more likely to achieve what we ought?[14]

This argument, which has been interpreted as a simple fallacy, or an argument with extreme but hidden complexity,[15] is best taken as just drawing out the intuitive consequences of what we have been given. Take any action of mine: intuitively I understand it as being aimed at the production of some good. But if I ask again why I pursue this good, the answer will typically be that it is nested in a hierarchy of goods. I hit the ball over the net, ultimately, for the sake of keeping fit. I buy the vegetables at the supermarket, ultimately, for the sake of living happily with my family. I take the mid-term exam., ultimately, for the sake of having a satisfying career. The immediate ends or aims of these actions don't provide a full explanation of why the agent did them, what she thought good about doing them. I can say, for example, that I took the mid-term to get a good grade in the course, but this is in turn only intelligible given my having some aim that makes sense of my having *this* goal.

But now the question arises, can we really stop with the higher-level ends we have come up with—keeping fit, having a family, having a career? Each of these looks like one of the ends Aristotle is talking about: surely I want to keep fit for its own sake, even though I want to hit the ball over the net only as a way of

---

(Arius 58.5 and 68.24–74.22; cf. Diogenes VII 94, 96–101) and the Peripatetics (Arius 134.7–137.12, a passage whose heading is, 'In how many ways 'good' is applied'). See Sharples (1983b) and Furley (1983).
[13] 1094 a 9–18.
[14] 1094 a 18–24.
[15] See Kenny (1969); Williams (1962); Kirwan (1967).

contributing to keeping fit? Aristotle wants to give us a dilemma. Either we want one thing for the sake of another, and this just goes on without stopping—and we can see that this infinite regress can be ruled out, since if in this way there were nothing we wanted for its own sake, desire would be empty and vain, whereas we know that desire is not empty and vain. Or, claims Aristotle, there is one final good, one thing we want just for its own sake, while everything else is wanted for the sake of it. That is, our desires are organized around the achievement of a single end, unified by the attempt to reach a single goal. But isn't there a third option? Can't I want to keep fit, have a career and so on, as aims all of which I want for their own sake? Why must there be a single final end, one good at the end of the line?

The argument could be completed by inserting a premise to the effect that, while it might be possible to have several such ends, it would never be *rational* for an agent to do this. For, within the boundaries of one life, two ends, like that of physical fitness and career ambition, are going to be competing for time and energy: there are bound to be occasions when one has to subordinate an action promoting one of them to an action promoting the other. When this happens, how will the agent decide? If he just has these aims, both of which are sought for their own sake, and no established way of giving one of them priority, he will have no rational way of choosing between them when he has to do so: he will be reduced to following whim, or tossing a coin, and this is unsatisfactory when what is at stake is two aims both of which have importance in one's life.[16] Aristotle, however, has not introduced any premises about rationality, so this seems an unsuitably strong way of filling out the argument. The same goes in general for other attempts to show that there is bound to be something unsatisfactory about having more than one aim in one's life that is wanted for its own sake.

Aristotle might be making another kind of assumption which he does not mention: that while we might have more than one aim in life which we want for its own sake, like keeping fit and having a career, still these can also be aimed at for themselves *and also* for the sake of a further or wider aim; but there will only be a single aim in our life which we aim at *solely* for its own sake and not for the sake of any further aim. The trouble with this is that Aristotle introduces this refinement later in his discussion and we have no warrant for reading it back into this passage.

Aristotle's argument has no missing premise, I think, because it is not an argument about what it is rational to do, or a good thing to do, but an explication of what we do do. Aristotle thinks that the third alternative just collapses into the second. I do not in fact stop with several aims that are wanted for their own sakes. I do in fact ask of keeping fit and having a family what the point is of my having these aims; the questions that began with hitting the ball over the net pause when I get to keeping fit, but they do not stop there. And when I do go on to ask why I keep fit,

---

[16] See Cooper (1975), ch. 2, part 1, for a defence of this view. Lear (1988) characterizes the life in which one is drawn by conflicting ends as a neurotic one. Cooper emphasizes the fact that in the *EE* 1214 b 6–14, Aristotle says that one should set up such a goal, since not to have one's life organized round a final end is a sign of great stupidity. But the standard view, in other schools as well as in the *Nicomachean Ethics*, is that it is a fact that we have a final end. The *Eudemian Ethics* passage may merely mean that, while we all do in fact have a final end at some level of articulation, it is a sign of stupidity not to have one's life so organized in an explicit and articulate way.

and so on, I see in the end that there is a single answer: I do all these things, simple and complex, because I see them as contributing to my *telos*, my final end which is my final good. Once I start reflecting at all on the end-directedness of my single actions, there is nowhere to stop short of a single final end.

Is this line of thought compelling? Surely, we may say, it is psychologically possible to live a life in which one has several ends which are not subordinated to a single end, or even mutually co-ordinated. Aristotle at least recognizes this possibility, when he speaks at the end of *Eudemian Ethics* I 1 of people who think that living happily is composed of two or more aims, such as virtue, pleasure and so on.[17] These people, however, are presumably unreflective people who have not yet thought through the implications of reflection on one's life as a whole. Aristotle does not tell us what they are missing, but it seems clear that he takes it that one cannot consistently stop at two or more ends if one is thinking of one's life as a whole. Felt discomfort with the idea of two or more unco-ordinated ends will pressure the agent to continue towards a single final end.[18]

Supposing that this is how we think—why do we do so? Aristotle does not say; again he finds it simply obvious. When I reflect that I pursue A for the sake of B, B for the sake of C and so on, I am standing back from my present plan and widening my vision to take in the past and future ramifications of that and other plans. Asking why I hit a ball, take exercise and so on involves the progressive detachment from individual projects that leads to the view of my life as a whole. I ask not what my three (or whatever) final ends are, but what my single final end is, because a single final end is what is required to make sense of a single life as a whole. Once I start reflecting on my ends, the thought goes, there is nowhere to stop until I reach the end which my life as a whole is aimed at reaching. The entry point for ethical reflection was thought about my life as a whole and where it is going; so I cannot stop until I reach a single end, since only this will enable me to reflect effectively on my life as a whole. Modern thinkers have found the notion of a single final end uncompelling (at least without added assumptions about rationality) because they have not taken thoughts about one's life as a whole to be the starting point for ethical reflection. For the ancients, however, it is unproblematic that the agent thinks of her life as a whole and that, in mature people with the chance to stop and think about their lives, ethical thinking begins from this.

We might object that sometimes at least we can specify no such end. Perhaps the best I can do is to specify a few ends like health, career and so on, but cannot come up with any characterization of a wider end that I pursue all these ends for the sake of. There are two possible answers here. One is that I can in fact come up with such a characterization, though a thin one—happiness; we will return to this claim several times in the course of this book. The other is that it does not matter if I cannot come up with any non-trivial specification of my final end. Why would we expect me to have an informative specification of my final end just from reflecting on my other ends and the way they hang together? For that I need moral philosophy.

---

[17] 1214 b 3–5.

[18] Thus the question is not being begged against pluralism; or rather, ancient theories are compatible with some pluralist claims, for example the claim that the different kinds of value that we pursue are not reducible to a single kind. Ancient theories insist, however, on the importance of the point that the agent's life has a unitary *structure*.

All the schools in our period have their own informative specifications of what my final end is; but that comes after much theoretical thought about ends, virtue, right action and much else, not after the informal reflection we have followed so far.

I have tried to show how, from simple reflections on obvious thoughts, we can get to the key notion of ancient ethics, that of the agent's final good or *telos*. I have expanded on Aristotle's brief argument, perhaps at the risk of tedium, to show that it is not Aristotle's invention, or indeed a specialized philosophical argument at all, but a summary of thoughts easily available to any intelligent person who begins to reflect on the implications of what he is doing. But the result is substantial, even if easily achieved, because, as we have seen, thoughts about my life as a whole lead to thoughts about my final end, about the kinds of aims I have developed and pursue, and the way that these hold together.

It may seem that we have got to this point too easily. Are there strong assumptions doing hidden work? And how does the notion of a final end serve as a basis for further philosophical thought?

The Agent's Final End: Considerations and Formal Constraints

First, some linguistic points. An agent's end is her *telos* (*finis* in Latin), sometimes also translated 'aim' or 'goal'. Aristotle uses as interchangeable the word *skopos*, which literally means a target (in the passage 1094 a 22–24 above he introduces it with the metaphor of archers shooting at a target).[19] But this is unfortunate. A target is a thing you shoot at, and by extension a thing you obtain; whereas an agent's end is not the thing, but rather his getting the thing. *Telos* suggests the agent's activity, her doing or getting something, and the Stoics mark this by distinguishing sharply between the agent's *telos*, his doing or obtaining something, expressed by verbs, and his *skopos*, the thing done or obtained, expressed by nouns. Aristotle's later followers reject this innovation,[20] but it remains true that *telos* suggests an end or goal not in the sense of the thing aimed at but in the sense of the agent's aiming at that end: 'A *skopos* is the target to be hit, like a shield for archers; a *telos* is the hitting of the target.'[21]

Ancient ethics is sometimes labelled 'teleological' because it starts from the point that the agent has a final *telos*. But 'teleology' is used for a variety of ethical

---

[19] This metaphor reappears in Stoicism for the agent's attempt to secure her final end. See Chapter 19, pp. 400–403.

[20] For the Stoics see Arius 77.1–5, and cf. the difference between 'being happy' and 'happiness' in 16–27, and the claim in 26–27 that being happy is the same as getting happiness (not the same as happiness). The Peripatetics pedantically reject this useful distinction in favour of more old-fashioned ways: Arius 130.21- 131.6. Simplicius (*In Phys* 303.30–33) says that 'younger' Peripatetics used the word *skopos* of a nearer goal like health, keeping *telos* for the final good. This is, however, a different distinction, and a more trivial one, than that between object aimed at and aiming at it.

[21] Arius 47.8–10. Unfortunately this passage is clearly either abbreviated or lacunose; it leads on from a discussion of Plato, but Wachsmuth rightly inserts a verb to start a new section. It is unclear whether the point is introduced as a purely Stoic distinction, or as one more widely shared. The passage continues, 'They mean an activity of ours towards our final end [*telos*]'. 'They' may well be Stoics, but the juxtaposition of *telos* as activity and *telos* as goal aimed at is very harsh; presumably abbreviation has removed a transition here.

positions, and care is needed. What we have seen so far is a concept of the agent's final end and final good which emerges from within her deliberations. 'Teleology' is best avoided for the present topic; it has got attached to the issue which will come up in Part II of whether the agent's final good is not merely what makes sense of her life from her point of view, but is also objectively determinable from outside those deliberations.

As we shall see, the agent's final end is generally taken to be happiness. But before we get to that, there are several points of substance about the agent's final end which emerge from reflecting on the way an agent sees his life as unified by the fact that all his projects and attitudes hang together and tend in a certain way (even if he can as yet say little useful about the direction in which they are tending).

The notion of a final end emerges when we think about the way our actions are directed or aimed at the good; and clearly we can aim at the good in many ways, and with a variety of motivations. However, we find that a standard definition of our final end is as 'the ultimate object of desire', *to eschaton tōn orektōn*. This is a definition shared by Stoics, Peripatetics and Sceptics.[22] What is meant here by 'desire'? We must beware here of assumptions deriving from Hume that tend to oppose desire to reason, and to take it for granted that desire is just a kind of wanting which we happen to feel whether there is good reason for it or not, whereas reasons are capable of generating a different kind of motivation. For the ancients, desire, *orexis*, is the most general kind of motivation to do something that we can have. It covers wanting of various kinds, and also covers the motivation generated by reasons, including ethical reasons. So this characterization of the end does not imply that there is any special kind of motivation that we have to our ends; rather, it implies that our motivations, of all kinds, are so structured that there is something 'ultimate' which forms them into an organized whole by being the end towards which they all tend. If our final end is in fact virtue, then virtue is our ultimate object of desire. This does not reduce virtuous motivation to wanting; rather it brings under the umbrella of desire the way we are motivated by reasons of virtue.

A second point that emerges in various ways is that even at an intuitive level my final good is felt to be importantly different in kind from the particular goods I aim at. The author of the *Magna Moralia* asks how we are to consider our final good. It is the best of the goods we aim to have, but that does not make it a good that we can count together with the other goods. Take all the goods we aim at by way of obtaining and keeping health—playing tennis, eating well, etc.; and then take the good all these aim at, being healthy. Which of all these is best? Clearly, being healthy. (If playing tennis were better than being healthy, we would seek health so we could play tennis, but this is to get things backwards.) But if we say that health is the best of all these goods, we would get the absurd conclusion that it was better than itself; and the same goes for our final good.[23] The point is that the final good is good, but not on the same scale of goodness as the goods that we seek for their sake. Aristotle

---

[22] For the Stoics see Arius 76 21–4; for the Sceptics see Sextus, *PH* I 25; for the Peripatetics see Arius 131.4. It is not found in Aristotle himself, but Alexander is happy to characterize happiness this way (*de An* II, 150.20–21, 162.34).

[23] 1184 a 15–24.

makes the same point in a passage[24] where he says that happiness is the final good, since the final good is choiceworthy, and happiness is choiceworthy in the right way—that is, by being the kind of thing that is not counted along with other goods.[25] The final good, then, is not the kind of thing that can be straightforwardly put on a scale of goodness with the other goods that we recognize. This is a point which receives more stress in some theories than in others; it is a point of dispute between the Stoics and the Aristotelian schools how far we should press it.

What is the relation between the final good and the other goods? One suggestion is that the final good just is the collection of all the goods we aim at, taken together. It is not one of the goods, nor is it something separate from them. Rather, we seek a final good just by seeking all our other goods in an organized way. This is the answer of the author of the *Magna Moralia*[26] and also of a later head of Aristotle's school, Critolaus, who characterized our final end as 'the fulfilment of all the goods'.[27] But this kind of answer was regarded as open to the criticism that it represents our final good as something too passive, making it into just another thing that we aim at, whereas what I aim at in my life as a whole is not just goods, not even all the goods I aim at, but something further, namely *my getting* these things. Hence Critolaus was criticized on the grounds that he should have said something like 'activation' rather than 'fulfilment', stressing the fact that our aim is not just the goods, but *making use of* the goods.[28] Our final good, that is, cannot just be goods, whether objects or states of affairs; it is more closely related to our own activity than that.[29] Aristotle seems to be pointing to this kind of suggestion in the notion of our final end when he says that aiming at honour will not do as a final end, for honour seems to reside in the people doing the honouring rather than in the people honoured, whereas we guess[30] that the good is something that belongs to us[31] and is hard to take from us. And he applauds his own account for its result that the end turns out to be actions and activities.[32] People do feel, then, that our final good cannot be something that other people could give us; it must be something we can achieve for ourselves. And so my final end involves my activity: it is not a thing or

---

[24] 1097 b 16–20

[25] See Irwin's translation of the *NE* and notes (1985a) for two alternative renderings; also S. White (1990) and (1992).

[26] 1184 a 25–30.

[27] *to ek pantōn tōn agathōn sumpeplēroumenon*, Arius 46.10–13.

[28] Arius 13–22. The replacement would stress *to chrēstikon tēs aretēs*. Arius adds a criticism of Epicurus on the grounds that in making the aim pleasure and regarding it as a state of equilibrium, he makes our end too passive, not something involving our activity (*dia to pathētikon hupotithesthai to telos, ou praktikon [hēdonē gar]*). Critolaus' definition is also criticized at Arius 126.14–16; see Chapter 20, section 1.

[29] Hence the stress on happiness as involving activity and use of goods in Aristotle and the Peripatetics (see, for example, *Pol* 1328 a 37–8, 1332 a 7–10) and *MM* 1200 a 34–24: one function of virtue is to be able to make right use of goods when we have them. Cf. also the Stoic insistence that our *telos* is being happy, not happiness, i.e., activity, not a state of affairs, which could be merely a *skopos*.

[30] *NE* 1095 b 22–26. The word is *manteuometha*, which literally means to divine or foretell the future. Aristotle seems to mean that we feel this strongly, even though we can give no rational basis for the belief. Perhaps 'feel intuitively' is the right idea.

[31] The word is *oikeion*, something which is one's own, familiar to one.

[32] *NE* 1098 b 18–19; he adds 'for thus it becomes one of the goods of the soul, not an external good'. Aristotle means that it is something that I do, not an object or state of affairs that I could get or that someone could give me.

state of affairs that others could bring about for me. As Arius puts it, reformulating Aristotle's ethics and defending the claim of virtue to be the candidate for the content of our final end:

> Since the superiority of virtue is great both in what it can produce and in being chosen for its own sake by comparison with the bodily and external goods, it accords with reason that our final end (*telos*) is not a fulfilment (*sumplēróma*) of bodily and external goods, nor getting them, but rather living according to virtue among all or most and the most important bodily and external goods.[33]

This idea, that my final end or goal essentially involves my own activity, and is not a good that others could just as well get for me, is important for our understanding of the ancient theories.[34]

It goes some way towards explaining the almost complete absence in ancient ethics of anything resembling consequentialist ideas. The object of my rational overall aim is my acting in one way rather than another, my getting or using goods rather than just the goods themselves. Thus my final good could not be a good thing, but neither could it just be a good state of affairs. These are ruled out right from the start by the fact that they have no essential connection to my activity; somebody else could get and present me with a good thing or state of affairs, but this would be irrelevant to my final good, which it must be up to me to get.[35]

We can see from this why in ancient ethics there is a built-in difficulty in taking seriously a theory which presents as our ethical aim the production of a state of affairs, and subordinated to this the question of what we do to produce that state of affairs. The only ancient candidates for such a theory are forms of hedonism. Of these, we shall see that the main such theory, Epicureanism, is not consequentialist; its conception of the kind of pleasure which is our final end does not make that a state of affairs to the achievement of which the nature of our actions in achieving it is irrelevant. This is because Epicurus takes the eudaimonist framework of ancient ethics seriously.[36] More marginal candidates are the theory discussed in Plato's *Protagoras*, and the Cyrenaics. They are, as we shall see, consequentialist, but just for that reason run into systematic trouble with the basic notions of eudaimonistic ethics.[37]

[33] Arius 126.12–18. In l. 16 I read the MSS *autōn* rather than Usener's conjecture *hapantōn*. Arius denies that our final end is getting goods, not because he rejects the idea that it is getting or doing rather than just being presented with states of affairs, but because he puts stronger conditions on it. The passage continues with a similar statement about happiness; see p. 45. The rejected definition is that of Critolaus; see p. 36, and chapter 20, section 1.

[34] It greatly helps us to understand those theories which make virtue necessary or sufficient for our final end, and which construe virtue as a kind of skill which makes use of, and controls our acquisition of, non-moral goods.

[35] This idea, that the agent's activity matters as much as outcomes for morality, is not prominent in modern moral philosophy of the Anglo-American type, although it has been more prominent in traditions which derive more from Hegel. Bradley's theory of self-realization is the only major statement of this kind of view in the Anglo-American tradition, and within that tradition it has not been nearly as influential as consequentialism. Recent sophisticated forms of consequentialism have tended to try to soften the theory's stress on states of affairs as opposed to the actions which bring those about, but this threatens to lose the main point of the theory.

[36] This will be fully dealt with in Part IV; see also chapter 10, and Annas (1987).

[37] See chapters 10 and 16.

It is also not surprising that ancient ethics, with one marginal exception, never develops anything like the related consequentialist idea of a maximizing model of rationality. If my ethical aim is to produce a good, or the best, state of affairs, then it is only rational to produce as much as possible of it. But ancient ethics does not aim at the production of good states of affairs, and so is not tempted to think that rationality should take the form of maximizing them. Rather, what I aim at is my living in a certain way, my making the best use of goods, and acting in some ways rather than others. None of these things can sensibly be maximized by the agent. Why would I want to maximize my acting courageously, for example? I aim at acting courageously when it is required. I have no need, normally, to produce as many dangerous situations as possible, in order to act bravely in them. Again, the only exceptions are forms of hedonism, but of these the major version, Epicureanism, is not a maximizing theory;[38] it is only the Cyrenaics who maximize (and run into trouble thereby).[39]

A third substantial point is that the intuitive notion of my final good that has emerged clearly implies that I see my life as a whole as some kind of unity, for the final good unifies and organizes all my other aims and goods. So far this unity is only very weak and thin, since we as yet lack a substantial characterization of the final end; but nonetheless it is not trivial. The final end is not unlike the modern notion of a life-plan, the idea that all my activities make sense and are ordered within an overall plan for my entire life. On either view, someone whose life centres on whatever present wants or aims that she has, without regard for the entire life, is stuck at a provisional or immature stage; she has failed to complete the reflections we traced. But should we so regard these people? Some modern theories have defended the idea that it could be rational to care, not for one's life as a whole but merely for one's present aims; that this is not immaturity but an alternative strategy.[40]

We do in fact, not of course in everyday life but only when we reflect in a rational way, think of our lives in terms of a final good or life-plan; those who fail to do so are either missing something, or urging us to uproot the way we think about our lives. One ancient school, the Cyrenaics, did in fact do this. They claimed that our final good was pleasure, which we could best achieve by seeking maximum intensity in pleasurable experiences. But they explicitly admitted that this was not happiness—that is, that they were recommending that we not think in terms of our life as a whole, but abandon our normal ways of thinking about ourselves.[41]

---

[38] See chapter 2, section 4.

[39] See chapter 10.

[40] See Parfit (1984). Compare the less extreme line taken by Slote (1983), who interestingly accepts much of the ancient framework of thinking about one's life in terms of goods one achieves and virtues that one cultivates in oneself, but argues that these should be regarded as relative to a stage of life, not a life as a whole.

[41] Diogenes II 87 (Mannebach [1961] 169, Giannantoni [1958] 172). The end, they claim, differs from happiness, for our end is particular pleasures, while happiness is an organization of pleasures which form its parts, including past and future pleasures. Happiness is clearly the intuitive way of thinking of an overall end, but the point does not depend on happiness and could be recast in terms of our rejecting an overall end in terms of an end that consists only of particular pleasures. Later Cyrenaics held strikingly differing views of happiness, thus conceived; see chapter 11.

We have no evidence to suggest that the Cyrenaics thought through the extent of the changes they were recommending, or seriously examined their possibility. For the claim that we think in terms of a single end or life-plan is supported by a claim about the way human nature develops. All schools in the ancient world agreed that even before we can reason about our lives we have an instinctive tendency to think of our lives as wholes. We have a pre-rational tendency to a 'sub-end' or *hupotelis*. Even a baby is aware of itself as a whole being, and not just a series of experiences. When we as babies seek pleasure, freedom from pain or the things that are naturally good for us, like health, activity and so on, we do so as self-aware wholes, in ways that do not have to be learnt. As we become rational beings we get better and better at articulating our *hupotelis*, the instinctively given end that we seek as whole beings, as a *telos*, an end that can be rationally articulated and defended.[42] And so in thinking of our lives as wholes we are not choosing one alternative rather than another equally available one; we are doing something which is, in the modern phrase, 'hard-wired' into us.[43] Arius, from whom we get the passage about *hupotelis*, says rightly that although the actual word is not in the older philosophers, the thing itself is. This is why we do not typically find arguments to show that it is rational to think of one's life as a whole, to see one's activity as given shape by a single final end. This is taken to be what we do anyway; at least we all do it instinctively, and the more reflective do it in a reflective way. We do not all do it well, of course, and we need philosophy to guide us in doing it better.

The final substantial point about our final end is that there are constraints on it which can be called formal ones. These are important in many arguments, since they serve to rule out some candidates for specifying our final end, not on grounds of their particular content, but on the prior grounds that they are not the right kind of thing to be our final end, since they fail these constraints. Aristotle is the first to spell these out as part of an explicit theory, in a passage where he is arguing that happiness meets these conditions:[44]

> There appear to be several ends (*telē*), but we choose some of them because of something else, e.g. wealth, flutes and tools in general, and it is clear that they are not all complete (*teleia*). But the best good appears to be something complete. So, if there is only one that is complete, that would be what we are searching for;

[42] Arius 47.12–48.5. Alexander of Aphrodisias devotes an essay to the question of what Aristotle thinks the *prōton oikeion* is, i.e. the first thing that we seek as being akin or familiar to us (*de An* II 150–153). This is (though not verbally) the same question as the one that concerns Arius: what do we start from, as an aim that we seek as conscious wholes, in order to end up with the right deliberated and chosen final end?

[43] At least, it is hard-wired into us that we do this instinctively. How much we reflect about what we do, and try to modify or improve it, will depend on the individual. So it is not ruled out that one might try to live a Cyrenaic or Parfittian life; merely emphasized that this would be a life lived in defiance of a very basic instinct, and so unlikely to succeed.

[44] In this passage Aristotle adds what looks like a third condition, that it is most choiceworthy, but not by being a good that is counted together with the other goods. This does not seem to be a single point (and does not survive as a distinct concern in later theories). The point about choiceworthiness seems to be a verbal point; the word *haireton* seems to be most naturally used for what we value for its own sake and not relatively to anything else (hence its distinction from other terms by the Stoics [see p. 167]). The point about not being counted in I have dealt with above as part of the intuitive suggestion that the final good is somehow different in kind from the goods which it organizes and to which it gives direction.

while if there are many, it would be the most complete of them. We say that what is pursued for its own sake is more complete than what is pursued for something else; and that what is never chosen because of something else is more complete than things that are chosen both for themselves and because of something else; and that something is *simply* complete if it is chosen always for its own sake and never because of something else. . . .The same result follows from self-sufficiency (*autarkeia*): for the complete good seems to be self-sufficient. By self-sufficient we do not mean for someone by himself, living a cut-off life, but rather for parents, children and wife, and in general for friends and fellow-citizens, since humans are by nature social (*politikon*). (But we must put a limit to this- if we extend it to parents and descendants and friends' friends it will go on *ad infinitum*; but we must investigate this another time.) We posit as self-sufficient that which when isolated by itself makes life choiceworthy and lacking in nothing.[45]

What is it for our final good to be (1) complete and (2) self-sufficient? Completeness is here explained as an end's putting a stop to desire (desire in the broad sense indicated above, of course). If I desire A because of B, but B just for itself, then B is complete and A is not; B has put a stop to my desire. We could call this *finality*, as suggested by the linguistic link between *telos* and *teleion*. Aristotle indicates here that B might be wanted for its own sake and also because of some further C, and represents this, in a way which is consciously odd, as a matter of degrees of finality, introducing the comparative and superlative forms of *teleios*. But finality is not all that Aristotle has in mind here. Finality is compatible with the relation being purely that of means-end: I want the tools for the sake of doing the job, but if the job could be done without them I would not want them. But the ends we have such as keeping fit and having a career are not in this way means to the end of our final good, means which we would dispense with if we could. What Aristotle has in mind is indicated in the earlier passage where he used the analogy of one skill including in itself the ends of subordinate skills. An individual's ends form a hierarchy, just as the skills and branches of knowledge do. The end of the most authoritative kind of knowledge, he says, 'will include' the ends of all the subordinate kinds of knowledge. One end can, then, be more complete than another by including it (not just by stopping desire at a further point). Let us call this *comprehensiveness*. By completeness, then, Aristotle means to include both aspects: Our final good, the ultimate object of our desires, is complete in that it is not just final but final because comprehensive. Some ends, of course, can be final without being comprehensive, but the good for humans, the good that gives shape to the aims of a human life, could not be like that. It puts a stop to our desires by including and organizing into a whole the ends of smaller-scale desires.

The second condition, *autarkeia*, usually though not completely satisfactorily translated 'self-sufficiency'[46] is more puzzling. Aristotle tells us that 'we posit' a definition of self-sufficiency, suggesting that this is a stipulative definition. Perhaps it

---

[45] NE I 7, 1097 a 25–b 16.

[46] See Cole (1988–9), who studies the occurrence of *autarkeia* in Aristotle in contexts of friendship, *megalopsuchia* and the origin of the state, and concludes that something like self-determination is nearer to the suggestions of the Greek than is self-sufficiency. (I have more doubts about her further conclusion, that something like the modern notion of autonomy is implied.)

is slightly odd to call a final good self-sufficient; Aristotle's discussion certainly suggests that the natural application of the term is to a person's life rather than to a person's final good.[47] A person's life is self-sufficient if it lacks nothing; as Aristotle points out, this is compatible with the agent's having a wide range of dependencies and needs that arise from a life embedded in family and state concerns, and the basic idea is not that of being able to go it alone, like Robinson Crusoe, but of being independent of a certain range of pressures and needs, those that can be regarded as external to the kind of life chosen. Thus my life can be self-sufficient, even if as a parent my well-being is dependent on the well-being of my children, if having and caring about children is one of my chosen aims. Dependencies that arise from my chosen projects are not seen as exposing me to the mercy of external factors in the way that I am so exposed by dependencies inflicted on me by things that are not part of my life as that is formed by my chosen projects.

Since Aristotle introduces his point by the self-sufficiency of lives, we would expect him to say that a final end is self-sufficient if it makes the person's life so. And this is in fact what he says: a self-sufficient end makes the person's life choiceworthy and lacking in nothing. We must understand the final clause from our grasp of the self-sufficiency of lives. That is, for a life to be lacking in nothing does not imply the absurdity that it contains *everything*, or even everything that is, in fact, worth having. Rather, it must contain everything that is required by the deliberated projects that that life contains. The life can still be self-sufficient, even if it contains a dependency on, say, children, if that dependency flows from concerns and projects which are a deliberated part of that life.[48]

This position, that it depends on my chosen aims whether or not my life is self-sufficient, might seem to ascribe to Aristotle an uncharacteristic kind of subjectivism. But on reflection this appearance dissipates. Aristotle is simply making the commonsense point that whether my life is self-sufficient depends on where in it the sources of need are. This in no way implies subjectivism about needs; Aristotle, along with all the other ancient schools, holds that it is a quite objective matter what my needs are, and whether I can in fact so order my life as to make it self-sufficient.

A final end, however, can only be self-sufficient in this sense if it includes all the agent's subordinate aims. If it did not, there would be a source of lack in the agent's life which was not part of her final aim; but then the agent would not be self-sufficient, as far as her aims go. So self-sufficiency also implies comprehensiveness: a final end which is self-sufficient must include all the agent's other ends. Finality does not, but we have seen that for a good to be final for a human being it must in fact be comprehensive.

Subsequent philosophers all diverge from Aristotle in two ways. First, they all drop self-sufficiency as a condition on one's final end. There is no trace of it even in the updated Peripatetic version of Aristotelian ethics produced by his own school.

---

[47] I am grateful for comments from Terry Irwin on this point.

[48] This might seem to run against *NE* 1170 b 17–19, where Aristotle says that the good person must have what is choiceworthy for him, or he will be lacking in that respect. (And thus, since friends are desirable for the good person, he must have these, or be in an important way lacking.) Taken by itself this passage certainly suggests the absurd view that a life is not self-sufficient if it lacks *anything* desirable for the person, not just what is desirable given a certain life-plan, and this is hard to reconcile with 1097 b 8–14. I suspect that the later passage is a careless formulation.

Self-sufficiency itself remains as a concern in ethics, and it is frequently important. The Stoics emphasize self-sufficiency.[49] Epicurus mentions it frequently, and it is a major concern of his ethics.[50] It is arguably a major factor in the Sceptics' conception of their final end.[51] In ethical theory generally it is important for the person living the good life to be self-sufficient; sometimes, as in Epicurus, it constrains the content of the good life.

Completeness, however, appears in all schools as the most important formal constraint on our final end. It is stressed by Peripatetics,[52] Stoics,[53] Epicureans[54] and Sceptics.[55] What is meant by completeness is what Aristotle means: finality and comprehensiveness. It does not occur to anyone to separate these two points explicitly—rather surprisingly, since the alternative account of the final end as the ultimate object of desire (see p. 35) could be taken to concern finality alone. This account, however, seems not to have been taken as definitive of the final end, as revealing what our final end is. In general the crucial definition of the final end is one which brings in completeness, where this is understood as involving both finality and comprehensiveness. A final end can in fact put a stop to desire only by being comprehensive; so, when we are talking about final ends, the two are naturally taken together.

A Picture of My Life as a Whole

The distinctive nature of the starting point for ethical reflection will make a great difference to the shape of different ethical theories. We can perhaps appreciate this from a passage of Seneca:

> Our entire life is made up of parts, with larger circles enclosing smaller ones. There is one which contains and surrounds all the rest; this extends from our day of birth to our final day. Another envelops the years of our youth. One cordons off all of our childhood in its circuit. Then there is a single year, containing in itself all the seasons by whose multiplication life is made up. A month is encircled in a narrower circle. The smallest revolution of all is made up of a day, but even here we go from beginning to end, from sunrise to sunset. . . . Some say that a

[49] See SVF III 272, 275 (definitions of *autarkeia*), and the claim at I 187, III 49, 67, 208, 685 that virtue is *autarkēs* for happiness. The Stoics also develop further the stress Aristotle lays on the virtue of *megalopsuchia* or 'greatness of soul' as a disposition that enables the agent to rise above things. See also Diogenes VII 127.

[50] Many passages praise self-sufficiency as a great good: *Ep Men* 130–131, *VS* 44, 45, 68, 77, U 200, 202, 466, 476. *Ep Men* 122 says that 'we should take care for the things that produce happiness, since when it is present we have everything, and when it is absent we do everything to have it', an informal way of saying that the agent's final end must render him self-sufficient.

[51] Sextus at *PH* III 235–238 and *M* XI 141–167 stresses the way that the Sceptic is less exposed to loss and damage from external factors than other people, because of his commitment to the Sceptical aim. He does not discuss *autarkeia* as such, but this is to be expected, given his avoidance of positive theory in his own person.

[52] Arius 131.2–4. He recommends that we follow the usage of older philosophers and say that the final end is 'that for the sake of which we do everything, while it is not for the sake of anything else'.

[53] Arius 77.16–17.

[54] *Fin* I 42, and cf. I 29.

[55] Sextus, *PH* I 25.

single day is equal to all days in resemblance; for even the longest stretch of time includes nothing that you cannot find in a single day, namely light and darkness, and as we go on to eternity days make these changes more numerous but no different, whether they are longer or more extended. So each day should be ordered as if it were the last in the line, as if it finished off one's life and made it complete.[56]

Seneca does not reject the agent's intuitive picture of his life as something linear, with each successive day added on to what already exists, until we come to the 'last in the line'.[57] But the reflective person will not simply think of his life in this linear way. He will also think of his life as a whole which is available to him in reflection like a circle enclosing his smaller concerns, even the day-to-day ones. Each everyday choice makes sense within a series of larger concerns developed in phases of one's life, especially impressionable periods like childhood. As one develops, the circles get bigger, but the basic point of the metaphor remains: at each level, particular choices take place within, and have to be understood in a context of, larger patterns in one's life. Hence, only by understanding these larger patterns, and in particular having a right conception of one's life as a whole, can one make the right particular choices, and live each day in such a way that it reflects the moral quality of one's life as a whole.

It is easy to see, in an intuitive way, that on this kind of picture it is hard to make sense of some ideas, such as the idea that the present phase of my life might be a 'present self', psychologically connected to but not part of the same whole moral life as a 'future self'. Such ideas were not conceptually unavailable to the ancients, and we shall see that one school, the Cyrenaics, did develop them. But they are felt to put strain on the natural course of ethical reflection. Nor is it easy, given this picture, to see what would motivate a person to live their life around an aim such as maximizing something. For this would at once pull out of shape the idea that the way one lives each day reflects the extent to which one has understood, and thought about, one's life as a whole. In the course of this book we shall see more precisely why such ideas are not at home in ancient ethical theory.[58]

Happiness

Each of us has a final good, it has been so far argued, in that when we stand back a bit from our ongoing projects and ask why we are doing what we are doing, we do not find a satisfactory halt until we get to the final end which makes sense of our life as a whole. We may, however, have no substantial specification of what that final end is. We do, however, always have one to hand, and though it is a thin one, it helps to focus the discussion further. As Aristotle puts it:

Most people are pretty much agreed about the name [of the final good]; for both the many and the refined call it happiness [*eudaimonia*], and suppose that living

[56] *Ep* 12.6–8.
[57] The phrase, *cogere agmen*, is a technical term for bringing up the rear of a military column.
[58] The Stoics also use the image of concentric circles to illustrate the progressive expansion of our self-concern; on this see chapter 12, section 2.

well and doing well are the same as being happy. But as to what happiness is, they
disagree, and the many do not characterize it in the same way as the wise. For the
many characterize it as something evident and clear, like pleasure or wealth or
honour, some saying one and others another—and often even the same person
says something different, saying after falling ill that it is health, and when in
poverty that it is wealth. And when they are aware of their own ignorance they
admire people who say something lofty and beyond them.[59]

It is a platitude, according to Aristotle, that we all seek *eudaimonia* as our final
end.[60] The thesis is, however, not tied to one word, or one notion. Being happy,
Aristotle says, is identified with living well and doing well. In the *Eudemian Ethics*[61]
he says that our concern is directed to what will produce 'living well and finely (if it
is invidious to say blessedly [*makariōs*]'. 'Blessed' (*makarios*) is a loftier and more
pretentious word than 'happy' (*eudaimōn*), but they are interchangeable (other than
stylistically). Arius says firmly that it makes no difference which word you use.[62]
What Aristotle is pointing to is the fact that people have a broad idea of a life's going
well, being happy or satisfactory, and that all regard this as what their final end is.
For ancient ethics the next step comes when ethical philosophers show us that many
intuitive views must be wrong—wealth and honour are not the right kinds of thing
to aim at if one wants a happy life—and suggest more satisfactory alternatives. But
modern interpreters need to spend longer with this notion of happiness, because it is
so different from our own that it is important to avoid misunderstandings.

In ancient ethics, happiness is introduced via a broad notion of a life's going
well, and as a thin specification of our final end. In fact, questions about our final
end are sometimes not carefully distinguished from questions about happiness, since
it is taken for granted that happiness is just what we all think that our final end is.[63]
Thus, happiness clearly inherits many of the points that we have seen are generally
held to be true of our final end. Happiness, says Arius, is the best thing in one's life,
or the greatest of one's goods, or the most important.[64] Happiness is one of our
aims, but in being the final, overarching aim it is thought of as different in kind from

[59] *NE* 1095 a 17–26.

[60] Cf. *Rhet* 1360 b 4–9.

[61] 1215 a 9–12

[62] Arius 48.6–11, esp. 9–11. Unfortunately there is a corruption at the end of the sentence; after 'it
comes to the same thing' (*eis tauto sundrameitai*) there is the meaningless *tois telikois*. Wachsmuth in the
app. crit. suggests either emending to *tois loipois* ('as far as the rest is concerned') or adopting Usener's
more radical emendation which supposes that several words have dropped out and makes the corrupt
words part of the next sentence. In any case, the crucial claim, that it makes no difference whether one
talks of *eudaimonia* or of *makariotēs*, is unaffected by the corruption. Although Arius is a later writer, this
passage tends to support the position that there is no important difference between these terms for
Aristotle. See Irwin's (1985a) translation, p. 338 (Glossary s.v. *blessed*) and Nussbaum (1986a) pp. 330–34,
for defence of the claim that Aristotle uses the terms with no marked difference of sense.

[63] Thus Arius at 131.2–6 gives two definitions of the *telos*, as 'that for the sake of which we do
everything, while we do not do it for the sake of anything else', and 'the ultimate object of desire', and
adds a third, which is an (Aristotelian) definition of happiness: 'living in accordance with virtue in bodily
and external goods, either all of them or most and the most crucial'. And at 130.18–21 he gives
definitions of happiness in terms of activity or use and then remarks that this is also what the *telos* is.
Wavering like this in a technical summary of ethics suggests strongly that happiness had come just to
imply a thin specification of the final end.

[64] Arius 48. 7–9. These are some of the 'simpler' thoughts about it, common to everybody.

our other aims. It can be sometimes thought of as the collection made up of our other ends,[65] but is more commonly thought of as the agent's activity in the pursuit of these ends, as by Aristotle,[66] or as her activity, or making use of other goods, as by later Peripatetics.[67] Happiness is thus thought of as active rather than passive, and as something that involves the agent's activity, and thus as being, commonsensically, up to the agent. This kind of consideration would rule out wealth, for example, right away. Happiness cannot just be a thing, however good, that someone might present you with. At the very least it involves what you *do* with wealth, the kind of *use* you put it to. As Arius says in a reformulation of Aristotle's ethics:

> [Since the final good is not the fulfilment of bodily and external goods, but living according to virtue] therefore happiness is activity (*energeia*) in accordance with virtue in actions that are preferred, as one would wish them. Bodily and external goods are called productive of happiness by contributing towards it when present; but those who think that they fulfil (*sumplēroun*) happiness do not know that happiness is life, and life is the fulfilment of (*sumpeplērōtai*) action. No bodily or external good is in itself an action or in general an activity.[68]

Further, Aristotle reports it as a common thought about happiness that it is 'self-sufficiency of life'[69] and it is assumed to be stable and hard to change.[70] This is no surprise, since happiness is how we specify our final end, which is what includes the ends we have in our life as a whole.

These points are not, of course, true of our notion of happiness. It has often been pointed out that we use 'happy' to describe temporary and even very short-lived states or feelings of a person. Moreover, we apply the word on the basis of the way the agent feels: if he says that he is or feels happy, we tend to say that he is right; there may be more to say about the basis of his claim, but if he says honestly that he is happy, then he is. Happiness can for us be short-lived and subjective.[71] It is sometimes said that by contrast the ancients thought of happiness as longer-term, as applying to a whole life, and as more objective: whether an agent is happy is not

---

[65] As at *MM* 1184 a 26–27: *hē gar eudaimonia estin ek tinōn agathōn sugkeimenē.*

[66] E.g., *NE* 1098 a 16–18: activity of soul in accordance with virtue (and if there are several virtues, in accordance with the best and most complete). Strictly, this is a definition of the human good, not of happiness, but Aristotle has already introduced the idea that we agree that the final good is happiness, and have to find out what constitutes happiness. Compare also *NE* 1169 b 29–30: happiness is a kind of activity, and activity clearly is something that comes into being, and does not just belong to someone like a possession (*hē d'energeia dēlon hoti ginetai kai ou huparchei hōsper ktēma ti*). And cf. also *Pol* 1328 a 37–40, 1332 a 7–10.

[67] Arius 130.18–21. Happiness is the preferred (retaining the MS *proēgoumenēn*) use of complete virtue in a complete life. Or: the activity of a complete life in accordance with virtue. Or: the unimpeded use of virtue in things according to nature. For useful discussion of this passage and other passages in the Peripatetic ethics in Arius where activity and use figure in definitions of happiness see Huby (1983).

[68] Arius 126.18- 127.2. The passage is a continuation of the one on the final good's being activity quoted above, p. 37.

[69] *Rhet* 1360 b 14–15.

[70] *NE* 1100 b 2–3.

[71] Kraut (1979), pp. 167–97, claims, convincingly, that we also have an 'objective' notion of happiness; when we hope that someone will be happy, we are not hoping that they will feel happy even if they are grossly mistaken, but rather hoping that they will have good reason to feel happy. However, Kraut's objective notion of happiness is not to be identified with the ancient notion of happiness, since it is established on different and much stronger grounds.

settled by whether she thinks that she is. But this is misleading. Rather, the ancient concept of happiness was an extremely weak and unspecific one; happiness applies to my life as a whole, and does not depend on my say-so, because happiness is just a thin specification of my final end, and *this* applies to my life as a whole (as has been stressed) and does not depend on my say-so. Happiness is stable, active and objective just because the final good is. In saying that the final good is happiness we are thus adding very little. But that is just what Aristotle says: what we have really done is give the final end a handy name. Thus it is not useful, I think, to compare ancient and modern notions of happiness in general, in advance of closer examination of what the ancient theories are theories of. Happiness in ancient theories is given its sense by the role it plays; and the most important role it plays is that of an obvious, but thin, specification of the final good.

Nonetheless it adds one point which is obvious, but important, to the notion of the final end. Happiness implies a positive view of one's life. If our final good is happiness this does at least rule out conspicuously miserable or frustrated ways of life. Aristotle, for example, regards it as completely absurd to say that a person is happy if they end up on the rack.[72] This is an important intuition about happiness; nevertheless, it is not as decisive as Aristotle thinks, and in the debate about virtue and happiness after Aristotle its role shifted dramatically.[73]

Because happiness does have this suggestion of satisfaction with and positive attitude towards one's life, it tends to be associated, before we have reflected much, with the things that make most people satisfied with their lives—wealth, honour and in general the results of success. We shall see that theories that divorce happiness from this kind of worldly success pay a price. But we have seen already that happiness is vague enough to serve as merely a thin specification of the final good; and we shall find that there are good reasons to develop the ideas that happiness applies to the agent's life as a whole, that it requires activity and that it is different in kind from the other goods that we aim at—even when these developments threaten the positive suggestions that the word happiness tends to have.

The question 'In what does happiness consist'? is the most important and central question in ancient ethics. But although the agent's final good and happiness are the entry point for ethical reflection, the answer to the question 'What ought my life to be like'? is best considered after we have looked at other aspects of ancient ethics.

[72] NE 1095 b 31-1096 a 2. Cf 1153 b 19–21.
[73] See chapters 18–20. I shall return to the question of ancient and modern conceptions of happiness in Part V.

2

The Virtues

1. Having the Virtues

We have seen the importance of the point that I have a final overall goal in doing what I do and in being the kind of person that I am, even if I cannot, from my own resources, give a full or interesting specification of what it is (other than the uninformative description of it as happiness). The crucial questions will then concern my conception of my final end once I make it explicit. Does it turn out to be defective? Is my life perhaps going in quite the wrong direction? How am I to determine which among the competing philosophical alternatives gives me the right guidance in specifying it more closely?

Satisfactory answers to these questions can be given only when we have considered the virtues. We need an understanding of the structure and status of the virtues, since the most important question about my final end is the question What is the place of virtue?

This may seem initially uncompelling to us, given that talk of virtue tends to sound artificial or archaic,[1] and it is important to realize that we share the concern here if not the way of talking about it. The ancient concern for virtue occupies in the most important respects the same place in people's thoughts as is occupied today by concern for morality, and the importance, for the ancients, of determining the place of virtue in one's final end is like the importance, for us, of determining the place of morality in one's life. This has been denied, and the legitimacy of assuming it has to be defended. I do not think that it is a good strategy to begin by trying to show that the ancient notion of virtue matches up with our concept of morality—notably, because there is so much dispute as to what our notion of morality involves; an account satisfying some may seem wrong to others, and thus the conclusions about the ancient theories will be weakened by the disputable nature of the premises about morality. I shall thus proceed indirectly; in this and the following sections I shall simply make the general assumption that ancient theories of virtue are concerned with morality, hoping that the detailed aspects of the theories we shall be considering will support this claim. The general claim will be further defended in the last section, where I shall try to meet objections of principle to the thesis. The result will, of course, fall short of a general positive defence of the claim, but I think that it

[1] Cf. Williams (1985).

is the most one can hope for without entangling one of the main theses of the book in initial dispute.

A concern with virtue, then, is to be taken as a concern with morality; the reason that the first questions as to how to understand our lives and to live them better are questions about virtue, in that intuitively morality is regarded as the central value in a human life.

It can be suggested that we do not, nowadays, regard morality as central in our lives, even if the ancients did. It is not clear, however, that this is true. We can, of course, point to the fact that many, perhaps most people, if asked, might well say that the most important value in their lives is making money, or achieving power; and that if we look at people's lives this kind of aim does seem to be what controls most of what they do. But we have established that what we are concerned with is a *reflective* conception of one's life as a whole; the views of people who have not yet reflected about their lives, or who are incapable of so doing, do not overthrow a theory that is based on what is obtained by reflection. Nor is it clear that we have a contrast here between the ancient and modern worlds; ancient philosophers must have felt much the same about the unreflected deliverances of the majority of their fellow-citizens. The test of the theory as a whole is what reflection delivers and how well that stands up against the demands we make of it. And there is, on reflection, a strong convergence on the thought that morality is, in fact, a central value in human life.[2]

It can also be suggested that, to the extent that we do intuitively think of morality as central in our lives, we are wrong to do so. Perhaps this is a naive view, resting on certain kinds of illusion.[3] So far, however, we are simply trying to understand the ancient theories as they emerge from everyday reflection; this kind of consideration has to be dealt with at a later stage.[4]

The Structure of a Virtue

There are virtues when people are virtuous; a virtue is some kind of state of a person in respect of which she is, for example, brave, generous or just. The modern tradition of virtue ethics tends not to be interested in further differentiation on this score (thus Hume, for example, merely calls a virtue a 'quality' of a person). But in ancient ethical theory considerable attention was paid to three points:

1. Virtues are dispositional.

---

[2] Of course not everyone will come up with this thought. But those who do not will tend to be either those who stick stubbornly to an immoralist view without being able to defend it (and thus without understanding it); or those who have an articulated theoretical alternative. No moral theory can convince the first, and need not try to; and the answers to the second will already be at the plane of reflection.

[3] This kind of suggestion can be found in two of the interlocutors in Plato's dialogues, Thrasymachus and Callicles, and presumably reflects felt problems of the fifth century. It is notable, however, that in the authors on whom this book focusses this radical suggestion is not seen as posing a threatening challenge which it is a primary task of ethical theory to meet. The person who does not see the point of being moral is seen simply as someone with whom it is not profitable to argue about morality.

[4] It is met by the appeal to human nature to ground morality; this is discussed in Part II.

2. Virtues have an *affective* aspect: they involve our feelings, especially our feelings of pleasure and pain, and developing a virtue involves habituating our feelings in certain ways.

3. Virtues have an *intellectual* aspect: they involve reasoning about, and grasp of, the right thing to do, and developed virtue implies good practical reasoning or practical intelligence.

The development of all three points contributes to our understanding of what a virtue is. Aristotle's *Nicomachean Ethics*, which devotes considerable attention to virtue, is our best entry into all three. The discussion will turn up further points which need separate treatment: what form the virtuous person's reasonings take, what the relation is between virtue and right action, whether there is anything in an ethics of virtue corresponding to supererogation. At this point we will be able to return to our initial question, of how virtue relates to our final end, with an improved understanding of how we might go about answering it.

Virtues as Dispositional

Aristotle takes it as obvious that a virtue is some kind of state 'in a person's soul'. In II 5 he argues that there are three kinds of such state: feelings (*pathē*) such as desire, anger, fear, confidence and so on—'in general what is followed by pleasure or pain'; capacities (*dunameis*) 'in respect of which we are said to be capable of having these feelings—being capable of being angry, for example'; and states (*hexeis*) 'in respect of which we are well or badly off towards the feelings—for example, we are badly off towards getting angry, if we do it intensely or laxly, but well off if we do it in an intermediate way'. Aristotle argues that the virtues cannot be feelings, on two kinds of ground. We are, he claims, subject to moral assessment—praised or blamed—for having or lacking virtues, but not for having feelings. This is explained by the second point: feelings are not a matter of deliberate choice; we are said to be affected when we have feelings, whereas virtues are not things that affect us but 'the way we are disposed'. In modern terms, we are not responsible for the way we feel, since it is not entirely under our control; but we are responsible for being virtuous or depraved, and praised or blamed accordingly, so virtue must involve not just our feelings but the way we handle them and choose to deal with them. Obvious as it seems, this is a point of great importance which is not always given its due in modern accounts. A virtue, or a vice, is the way I have *made myself* and chosen to be.[5]

Virtues are not capacities, adds Aristotle, for essentially the same reason. We are not subject to moral assessment for our capacities, because we have them by nature, 'but we do not become good or bad by nature'. I may be naturally endowed with a sunny or a surly temperament, and this is a given about me, a fact that I cannot change. But it is up to me what I do with this temperament, whether I just allow it to flourish or take responsibility for having such a temperament and try to develop it in one way or another.

[5] This emerges as important in considering the question, what the contribution is of our nature to our having the virtues; see Part II, ch. 9.

Virtues cannot be feelings or capacities, then, because we are not adequately responsible for these for them to be virtues. Aristotle concludes by elimination that virtues are states. But what is it about *states* that gives them a defence against this objection? We cannot answer this till we have seen more about the kind of state that virtues and vices are. It is when we have seen what is involved in a *virtue*'s being a state that we can fully see why a virtue has to be a *state*, rather than just the way I feel or the way I can be.

In some ways Aristotle's word *hexis* answers better to our word 'disposition' than to 'state': a virtue like courage is a disposition because it is a condition because of which I am so disposed as to act in brave ways; and this is what a *hexis* is.[6] However, 'state' is the established translation of *hexis*, and Aristotle contrasts it as being more stable with the less stable 'disposition' or *diathesis*.[7] Virtue, then, is a stable state; Aristotle distinguishes exercising a virtue from exercising a skill by the fact that the virtuous person must act 'knowing [that he is acting virtuously], choosing what he does and choosing it for its own sake, and acting from a condition that is firm and unalterable' (1105 a 30–34).

Aristotle's point, that virtue is what we would call a stable disposition, is taken from common conceptions of virtue and regarded as uncontroversial by later schools. We have little explicitly from Epicurus, but the Stoics agree with Aristotle's characterization (though they irritatingly reverse the uses of *hexis* and *diathesis*).[8] It can be regarded as the common property of all the schools. It has caused difficulty to some moderns, even in advance of particular accounts of just what form this stable disposition takes. For if the virtuous person must, to act virtuously, do so from a state which is stable, will not the brave person be acting from habit? And this looks like an unthinking way of acting; the actions I perform from habit are precisely those where I do not have to think about what to do. But how can I rightly be praised or blamed for what is done unthinkingly? This problem is underlined when the state is said to be stable to the point of unchangingness. This makes it look as though the virtuous person acts from a *rigid* disposition to do brave actions, free of any need to worry about whether to be brave, as well as what precisely to do. G. E. Moore brings out the problems with such a conception, claiming rather startlingly that this is how we think of virtue generally:

> There is no doubt that a man's character may be such that he habitually performs certain duties, without the thought ever occurring to him, when he wills them, either that they are duties or that any good will result from them. . . It is because the majority of instances of virtue seem to be of this nature, that we may venture to assert that virtues have, in general, no intrinsic value whatsoever.[9]

---

[6] As I use 'disposition' here, it is simply a condition in virtue of which one is disposed to act; the notion will thus be as complex as is required to give an adequate account of action.

[7] *Cat* 8 b 26–9 a 13, esp. 8 b 27–35: 'A state (*hexis*) differs from a condition (*diathesis*) by being more stable and longer-lasting. Such are kinds of knowledge and the virtues. . . . Justice, temperance and the like seem not to be easily affected or easy to change.' Hutchinson (1986) discusses *hexis* in passages from the *NE*, the *Phys* and *Met*, as well as the *Cat*.

[8] As we shall see (in section 3), the Stoics have a very intellectualist conception of virtue, and tend to cast the point in terms of the stability of knowledge.

[9] Moore (1903), ch. 5, 175–77. Moore never defends the view that this is what we mean in talking of virtue, or his further claim that there is something wrong in meaning more than this when we use the word 'virtue'. He goes on to accuse Aristotle of 'gross absurdity' in claiming that such mindless behaviour

These problems are not much alleviated by the consideration that a fixed character is a product of a period of education and development during which the person was learning to deal with moral complexity. For it still looks as though all the problems arising from moral complexity will be dealt with in *developing* a virtue, while one can change and develop in flexible ways, while the complete virtue itself will just be a rigid source of virtuous actions.

This unattractive picture stems from failure to recognize the internal complexity of a virtue. We should remember that Aristotle *rejects* candidates for the underlying form of a virtue if they are items in respect of which we are passive, things that affect us. Aristotle in fact goes on to define virtue as a state involving choice (*hexis proairētikē*),[10] Thus an honest person's honesty may be 'fixed' in the sense that she is not, and cannot imagine being, seriously tempted to be dishonest. But this does not make her honesty into something like a feeling she cannot help having; rather, she is morally accountable for being honest because this is the way that she has chosen, *and continues to choose*, to be. Thus a virtue is a disposition involving choice in two ways. It is built up from repeated choices and the development of habits of choice. Thus it is unlike mindless habits which are built up merely from repeated experiences that do not involve deliberation and decision. So, although it is indeed developed into a firm tendency to act and decide in one way rather than the other, it does not bring this about by non-rational means, like mere repetition, rote learning, going through the motions. It is simply what happens when one repeatedly decides in the same way—that is, when one's reasoning is consistent and coherent, and one finds that repeated deliberations turn up no reason to reverse one's view. The increasing consistency of behaviour and response that builds up as this happens is thus not a non-rational force threatening the agent's next exercise of rationality. Rather, it should be seen as the increasing effectiveness of the agent's rationality: the dispositions she develops are the result of her deliberations and decisions, *not* of other factors that can be developed in a mindless way.

The second way in which choice enters into a disposition which is a virtue is that not only does it result from choices, but it is on each occasion exercised in making a choice. Thus, if I am thoroughly honest, and decide now not to take something to which I am not entitled, this is itself a choice. My past choices have built up a disposition to be honest, but my present decision is not just a reflex determined by that disposition—it is my endorsement of that disposition. The disposition is not a causal force making me choose; it is the way I have made myself, the way I have chosen to be, and in deciding in accordance with it, I endorse the way I have become.

We can now see why at *Eudemian Ethics* 1220 b 18–21 Aristotle, instancing courage and temperance and their opposites, says that states are what bring it about that our feelings are *reasonable*. The virtues are *rational* states, since virtue is a habit of acting on reasons. However stable, the virtues bring it about that the agent acts rationally, not unthinkingly or mechanically.

---

as virtue is intrinsically good. (Aristotle is also 'highly unsystematic and confused' because he bases ethics on the 'naturalistic fallacy'.)

[10] *NE* 1106 b 36–1107 a 2. *Proairetikē* is just the adjective from the noun *proairesis*, meaning choice. Lacking a corresponding English adjective, translators resort to 'involving' or 'concerning' choice.

Thinking of virtue as a stable disposition brings out something about virtue which is not much stressed in modern ethics. Modern discussions often encourage us to discuss an action in a vacuum without regard to the previous decisions that inclined the agent to do it, or to its effects in terms of the agent's future character. The ancient thought that virtue is a stable disposition, by contrast, reminds us that every action has both a past and a future. It has a past: it resulted from a pattern of reasoning that had developed in the agent as a result of past decisions, and from a pattern of response that had developed in the agent as a result of living with past decisions. And the action has a future: as a result of doing it the agent's disposition will have been reinforced or weakened.

Far from giving a rigid picture of the moral life, this picture emphasizes the way that our moral life is always in a process of development. Everything we do reflects the way we have acted and affects the way we will act. We are all the time faced with new and complex situations; how we deal with them reveals what we have become and affects what we are becoming. Even the stably honest person develops every time she acts honestly; every honest action reflects a determination to continue as she is, a determination that could be undermined by unfamiliar or complicated circumstances. If her honesty is indeed unchangeable, this results not from lack of thought but precisely from continual thought about her honest actions.

Much of the modern misconception of this aspect of virtue ethics may come from Kant, who greatly distrusts the dispositional aspect of virtue. Kant, like many since, thinks that if virtue becomes a stable disposition of the person, then it turns into a rigid mechanical habit in the person, becoming something with respect to which the person is passive, and thus not fully morally accountable. But this is a mistake; virtue is not that kind of state. Kant insists,

> Virtue is always in progress and yet always begins at the beginning. . . . [T]he nature of man. . . .is affected by inclinations. Under the influence of these inclinations virtue, with its maxims adopted once for all, can never settle into a state of rest and inactivity; if it is not rising, it inevitably declines. This is so because moral maxims, unlike technical ones, cannot be based on habit (for basing a maxim on habit belongs to the physical nature of the determination of the will). But even if the *exercise* of moral maxims were to become a habit, the subject would thereby lose the freedom of adopting his maxims. . . .[11]

He is wrong to think this in any way incompatible with virtue's being a stable state; a state which is a rational one involving choice is precisely *not* a mechanical habit.[12]

---

[11] Section XVII of the Introduction to the *Metaphysical Principles of Virtue*, p. 409 of the Akademie edition. I use the translation of J. W. Ellington.

[12] Kantians may retort that Kant is only saying that virtuous activity loses its value if it becomes merely habitual, and is not denying anything that Aristotle would affirm. Kant has, however, a general problem as to how virtue can be dispositional or in any way habitual, if it requires on each occasion the exercise of a strength of will which is independent of the empirical, habit-forming self. There thus seems no room for a developed, rational self in Kant's theory.

2. The Affective Aspect of Virtue

Just by virtue of being humans—'by nature' as the ancients put it—we are susceptible to a wide variety of feelings and tendencies to react. Our development, and especially our moral development, consists in our getting (more or less) control over these feelings and training them in some ways rather than others. This is a process that never ceases, since our lives are not static; we are all the time reacting to different things and experiencing certain feelings and emotions, and the way we do so both reflects how we handled past feelings and affects the way we will handle future ones. It is a process that begins early; children are taught how to train their feelings by a variety of examples and sanctions, and the process becomes ever more conscious and autonomous with age.

Given that virtue is a disposition to do the right thing (problems that we shall postpone till we deal with the intellectual side of virtue), how do feelings come in? A common modern view, deriving from Kant, is that virtues are *correctives* to our feelings, and consist essentially in the strength of will to overcome feelings. For feelings might lead us in the wrong direction as well as the right one; they cannot be guaranteed to lead dependably to the right result. None of the ancient ethical schools share this view. They are all committed, implicitly or explicitly, to several theses that exclude it.

One is that it is important to respect in ethical theory the everyday contrast between someone who does the right thing, but has to battle with his feelings to do so, and thus acts reluctantly and with a sense of pain and loss, and the person who does the right thing and whose feelings endorse the action, and who thus acts gladly and with pleasure. We all do recognize (mostly in our own case) the difference between the merely self-controlled (*enkratēs* in Greek, hence sometimes 'encratic') and the person who does not have to be self-controlled. And we take pleasure or the absence of it in acting to be the chief mark of this distinction. Aristotle draws the distinction in these terms, but it is clearly present in later authors even if they do not use the word, since it is regarded as a matter of common sense:[13]

> People do not consider self-control a complete virtue, but rather less than virtue. For it has not yet become a mean state as a result of harmony of the worse part in relation to the better, nor has the excess of feeling been removed, nor is the desiring part of the soul obedient to and in agreement with the intelligent part; rather it pains and is pained and is repressed by necessity, and lives alongside [the intelligent part] like a hostile enemy element in a civil war.[14]

Another point is that this difference is thought of as a difference in moral development. The person who is self-divided and finds doing the right thing painful is lacking in something desirable which the undivided, non-agonizing person has; self-control is a lower stage than virtue. Modern philosophers often contest this

---

[13] For the Peripatetics, see Arius 128.20–22. The Stoics define *enkrateia* as a subdivision of the virtue of *sōphrosunē* (Arius 60.21, 61.11–12) and so do not explicitly set it up against virtue as a whole. But they recognize, and try to account for, the distinction as a matter of common sense; see Plutarch, *Virt mor* 445 b-d, 446 c.

[14] Plutarch, *Virt mor* 445 c-d. The terminology is influenced by Aristotle, but the whole account is meant to be acceptable to as many different schools as possible.

point on the grounds that we *admire* the conflicted person who beats down his feelings more than we admire the person whose feelings positively encourage generous or just actions. But this misses the point. We can admire someone overcoming a handicap without thinking it preferable to have that handicap. What the ancient theories stress is just the common thought that conflict and stress are signs of something's failing or going wrong, and that a state where these are absent is preferable to a state where they are present. Virtue is not just different from self-control; the harmony in the virtuous between action and feeling makes it preferable to self-control.

A third point is that the ancients think it important to respect in ethical theory the everyday fact that how one's feelings and emotions have developed affects the way one can now achieve a grasp of what the right thing to do is. If virtue were merely control over the feelings, then one could become virtuous whatever one's feelings, perhaps by reading a book and becoming convinced by an argument. For if the feelings are controlled by virtue, then all that matters is to give virtue an intellectual direction; there seems no further role for the feelings to be playing. But in fact this does not happen. Arguments are important in ethics, but on their own they do not make people virtuous; changes in ethical belief have to become rooted in one's emotional life before they become effective. Aristotle stresses the limits of ethical argument until the force of the argument has become effective in the person's life:

> If arguments were self-sufficient for making people decent, they would justly have won many great rewards, as Theognis puts it. . . (1179 b 4–6). Argument and teaching certainly do not have force in all; rather the soul of the hearer must first, like earth that is to nourish the seed, have been cultivated by habits towards taking pleasure in and hating things in a way that is fine. The person who lives by his feelings cannot listen to an argument that directs him away, nor even understand it; how can one persuade someone like this? And in general feelings seem to yield not to argument but to force. So there must be a character there already, somehow akin to (*oikeion*) virtue, loving the fine and repelled by the base.[15]

This does not rule out the possibility that one might have a badly developed character and yet still become virtuous, perhaps by being converted by Aristotle's arguments. What it stresses is that initial intellectual conversion is not enough; if one's character has already so developed that acting in accordance with one's new beliefs is repugnant or difficult, then it takes time and practice—what Aristotle calls 'habituation', the repeated performance of virtuous acts—for one properly to become a virtuous person.

Aristotle himself stresses moral education of the young when considering the development of virtue, and several times emphasizes the importance of a good early upbringing if a person is to become virtuous as a mature adult.[16] He pays less attention to the defective mature adult trying to reform and become virtuous.[17] In

---

[15] 1179 b 23–31. This passage from the end of the *Nicomachean Ethics* is quoted, and stressed, in Burnyeat (1980a); see also Burnyeat (1971), Kosman (1980) and Hursthouse (1988).

[16] E.g., 1095 b 3–13; 1104 b 3–13; 1172 a 19–25.

[17] Though see, for example, 1121 a 20–25; 1152 a 27–33.

the Hellenistic period more attention is paid to the situation of the mature agent who comes to realize the inadequacy of her life hitherto and is 'converted'[18] to a life of virtue;[19] and greater prominence is given to types of writing that aim to jolt and shock people out of bad and vicious habits in order to facilitate such a conversion.[20] However, both Stoics and Epicureans retain the insistence on subsequent practice and habit. On Epicurean virtues we have the rather unhelpful statement of Epicurus (*Letter to Menoeceus* 132) that 'all the other virtues have come by nature from intelligence [*phronēsis*]', which leaves the role of habituation and feeling unclear. However, Epicurus made his followers memorize his sayings, and many Epicurean social practices are best explained as having the aim of the student's internalizing the beliefs required for virtue, so that they become emotionally accepted and part of the agent's attitude and outlook.[21] And the Stoics stress that virtue has to be built up gradually; thinking of it as a skill or craft, they take it to be formed as the different insights that one has over the area come to be 'practiced together'.

All the ancient schools accept these theses, and their implication, that having a virtue is not having the strength of will to correct one's feelings when the latter might lead away from the right action. Rather, having a virtue is having one's character developed in such a way that one not only grasps what the right thing to do is but takes pleasure in doing it; one is repelled by the thought of wrong acting; and one is not seriously tempted by incentives not to do the right action. Virtue is a state of the agent's character and emotions, not merely a disposition to act in certain ways. As Aristotle puts it:

> We must take as an indication of someone's states the pleasure or pain that supervenes on his actions; for the *temperate* person is the one who refrains from bodily pleasures and takes pleasure in this very fact, while the intemperate is the one who is pained by this.[22]

---

[18] The verb is *protrepein*. Aristotle does use it of converting people to a life of virtue: cf. NE 1179 b 7–10, 1180 a 7; and one of his most famous lost works was a *Protrepticus*. But in the Hellenistic period 'conversion writings' became a standard part of moral philosophy. See Arius 40.4–7, 44.12–15, where he is discussing the way different philosophers like Philo and Eudorus present moral philosophy. The Stoics were particularly prolific at producing 'conversion writings': see Diogenes VII 160 (Ariston); VII 36 (Persaeus); VII 174 (Cleanthes); Plutarch, *Sto rep* 1041 e (Chrysippus); D.L. VII 91 (Posidonius). One of their tenets was that only the wise person can convert or be converted to philosophy, since either requires absence of barriers to internalizing the lessons of philosophy. See Arius 104.10–105.4. On this topic, see Nock (1933), especially chs. 1 and 11.

[19] Aristotle's school retains the prominence he gives to habituation (*ethos*); they follow him in focussing on development of the young more than conversion of the mature. The statement of the importance of habituation in Arius' account of Peripatetic ethics (116.21–117.10) is followed by a long account of what is in Stoic terms *oikeiōsis*, the progressive development of our instincts with age into fully reasoned moral commitment.

[20] The most notable example is the Cynic 'diatribe', a kind of sermon. See, e.g., O'Neil (1977) and Dudley (1967). We have some Epicurean examples of this kind of passionate homily in Lucretius' harangue on sex and love in Book IV, and Philodemus' long and passionate presentation of the evil effects of anger in *Anger*.

[21] On memorization see Clay (1983), 74–81, 176–85. On the practices, see Nussbaum (1986b). On Epicurus' intellectualist view of the emotions, see Annas (1989b) (1992a).

[22] 1104 b 3–8. I use 'temperance' as a conventional though not completely satisfactory translation of *sōphrosunē*.

The virtuous person, then, not only does the right thing but has the right feelings and emotions about what she does.

Just this point gives rise to a common modern objection. Having a virtue is supposed to be something I am morally accountable for, since whether I have the virtue is 'up to me', a matter of my choice and something I am responsible for. But it is not up to me whether to have a certain feeling or emotion. At least, however we construe 'up to me', there is a clear intuitive distinction between the way it *is* up to me to do a certain action, and the way it is *not* up to me to have a certain feeling about it. The ancients seem to make an impossible demand: I am generous only if I not merely do the generous thing but have generous feelings; but I cannot choose to have generous feelings in the way I can choose to do a generous action, and so it seems that whether or not I am virtuous is not wholly up to me. As Sidgwick puts it:

> [T]hough Virtue is distinguished by us from other excellences by the characteristic of voluntariness—it must be *to some extent* capable of being realised at will when occasion arises—this voluntariness attaches to it only in a certain degree; and . . ., though a man can always do his Duty if he knows it, he cannot always realise virtue in the highest degree.[23]

Sidgwick concludes from this that virtue presents us with an ideal that we are to aspire to, but that goes beyond what can be demanded of the ethical agent; and this forms one reason for removing it from serious consideration in ethics, since ethics surely cannot be concerned with what is beyond the ethical agent's capacity. This has been an influential conclusion, and still accounts for much of the neglect of virtue in ethics.

This might seem like a problem that ancient ethics should recognize also, if we recollect that virtues are states concerned with choice, states of ourselves that we are responsible for. But in fact no problem is perceived. To see why, we must recall the initial stress on one's life as a whole. When I wonder about where my life is going and whether I can change it, I am asking if my life as a whole might change direction. And when I ask whether I could acquire one of the virtues, I am not asking whether I could become generous *now*. Perhaps I could not bring myself to act generously, given the way my feelings and reactions have developed, or perhaps I could act generously but it would pain me to do so. So I cannot *now* be virtuous. But it is still up to me whether I become virtuous or not; for once I am convinced that it is important to become virtuous, I can take steps to enable myself to act virtuously— by thinking harder before the appropriate occasion and consciously resolving to do so, for example. And by making this into a consistent pattern in my life I can bring it about that acting virtuously is less and less effort on each occasion, and the more I get used to it, the more comfortable I will feel with it, and the more pleasant it will be for me.

A good model is that of breaking a bad habit and establishing a good one. We recognize easily the fact that I may, on the one hand, be unable right now to stop fidgeting, or worrying, while being able to break the habit and get used to a better pattern of living. This is indeed a fairly direct corollary of the point that virtue is a stable disposition: it is up to me to have or lack a virtue in the way that it is up to me

[23](1907) Book III, ch 2, p. 227.

to have or lack a habit; and this is obviously different from the way in which it is up to me to act or not to act right now. Sidgwick contrasts virtue and duty in the way he does because he sees both as ways of characterizing a single occasion of acting. As he sees it (and he has been influential here) either I act out of duty, doing what I should, or I go further and also have the right feelings: but since the latter is not up to me in the way that doing my duty is, it is regarded as a praiseworthy but optional (and therefore not morally required) extra. But this misconceives the way in which having the right feelings is up to me; it is like the way in which it is up to me to have good habits rather than bad ones. I may now, for example, not be able to help worrying, since I have got into the habit of worrying about certain things whether there is good reason or not. But there are clearly ways in which I can stop worrying, if I do two things.

The first is to correct the patterns of acting that are associated with having the wrong feelings. In the worrying case, perhaps I should resolve not to do certain things or to get myself into certain positions. While it may do no good to exhort myself, here and now, not to worry, I can deal with the problem by encouraging some ways of acting and discouraging others in my life. It is by getting used to acting in some ways and not others that I begin to find myself not worrying, or better able to control it if I do.

It may be that I have little idea which are the relevantly better patterns of behaviour and need to appeal to someone else, either for advice or for examples of the better kind of behaviour. I begin by copying what someone else does in order to acquire the right habits of behaviour, and by practicing these habits, I come to see the point of having these habits for myself; I internalize them. If we think of habits, we can see that there is no shortcut. I cannot become generous overnight, however genuine my conversion from meanness to generosity, just as I cannot stop worrying overnight. In each case my feelings change as a result of modifying my behaviour; and to do this I need to be pointed in the right direction to modify it.

Both of these points are stressed in Aristotle's account of the way in which virtue requires habituation. As we read it, we can see that what he is talking about is an everyday fact, familiar every time we try to modify our habits. What is unfamiliar is simply the point that this is what virtue requires.

> The virtues, just like the other skills, we acquire by first activating them. Where we have to learn something to do it, it is by doing it that we learn it; for example it is by building that people become builders and by playing an instrument that they become musicians. In this way it is by doing just actions that we become just, by doing temperate actions that we become temperate and by doing brave actions that we become brave [1103 a 31–b2]. . . . To sum up, states come about as a result of similar activities; hence we must make our activities be of a certain kind, since differences in these are followed by the states. (b 21–3)

There is a second important point, however. Although habit and practice are needed both to stop worrying and to have generous feelings, the process is neither easy nor mechanical. Thought and reflection are needed in two ways. First, I need to reflect before beginning to change my habits. It is clearly no good trying to stop worrying if I have no idea how to do this; and similarly to acquire generous feelings I must have an intelligent appreciation of what kinds of people and behaviour to emulate, what the right general direction is to go in. And second, the process is not a two-stage one of reflecting and then plunging into mindless routine. Rather, I must continue to appreciate how my behaviour is changing, and monitor in an intelligent way the modifications of attitude and feeling as they develop; for letting my behaviour become mechanical will defeat the aim of the process, which is to make the way I am one which I endorse, rather than a mindless pattern of acting. Fully to understand the way in which habituation is directed and informed by intelligent thinking we have to look at what I have called the intellectual side of virtue; but even before doing so it is worth underlining the point that the need for habituation does not render virtue merely 'habitual' or mechanical.

Aristotle's exposition focusses on initial moral development, the formation in the young of good dispositions. He stresses the importance of this[24] to the extent that some have ascribed to him the position that it is impossible for a developed agent to change from vice to virtue. This is surely a mistake, though Aristotle does stress the difficulty of changing one's disposition once it is developed. In any case, the later schools lay more stress on the possibility of converting mature but badly developed people; once convinced that your life is not as it should be, you can change, though because of the need for habituation the process is difficult and requires a process of continual self-monitoring to be successful.

In everything so far the contrast has been an intuitive one: I cannot now, because of my previous faulty habituation, produce to order the feelings required for me to have a particular virtue; but I can change my habits and by thoughtfully monitored practice and habituation change my attitude, and so end up with my feelings in tune with my judgements in the way that virtue requires. This contrast is one that we find exemplified in everyday life (though, as with consideration of our final end, discussion of the way to change our habits tends in our society to be found in popular psychology and self-help books rather than in serious moral philosophy). Philosophers worried about determinism will of course raise the question of whether this contrast is in the end a real one. Changing my habits requires at least that I come to grasp the need for change; and how is this possible if my disposition has developed precisely in the way that needs changing? From the Stoics onwards philosophers had the resources to formulate this problem, so it is not modern anachronism to raise it. Recognition of the possibility of this problem does not, however, serve to erase the intuitive distinction; the crucial claim is that I can change my habits even in cases when it is not true that I can act contrary to habit here and now, and this seems true under many different understandings of how we should analyze the abilities in question.[25]

---

[24] At *NE* 1103 b 23–25 Aristotle says that 'it does not make a small difference whether one has been habituated right from youth one way or another; rather it makes an enormous difference, or rather all the difference'. 1114 a 3–21 suggests a more uncompromising view: Aristotle says that an unjust person cannot stop being unjust because he wishes to, any more than a sick person can get well because he wishes to; they could have helped getting into their state, but once the state has developed it is no longer possible for them not to be like that. He compares a person who can choose to throw a stone or not, but not to retrieve it once thrown. The passage, however, is concerned to stress the point that once you have developed a disposition, you cannot just choose at any point to act contrary to it. It does not exclude the possibility of change by a person convinced of the need for change and with a clear view of how to go about the needed process of rehabituation. Cf. the passage in n. 17.

[25] Cf. Sidgwick (1907), Part I, ch. 5, on the irrelevance of the free-will debate to this kind of question.

Can we say more specifically what state we are in when our feelings are in the correct harmonious relation to our virtuous judgements? Here the different schools seem at least to differ widely, though we shall see that the differences are more apparent than real.

Aristotle famously defines virtue as a state involving choice which is 'in a mean relative to us, a mean defined by reason, i.e., the reason by which the intelligent person would define it.'[26] The 'doctrine of the mean' is a very general formal pattern which Aristotle applies to a variety of material. 'Virtue is a mean' implies that the virtuous person will get it right, where there are two characteristic ways of going wrong, one in the direction of excess and one in the direction of deficiency. Virtue is not opposed to vice, but is rather a way of avoiding vices which are themselves opposed. In the fourth book of the *Politics* Aristotle applies this idea to states: good political institutions, he claims, avoid two opposed ways of going wrong.[27] In his discussion of justice in *Nicomachean Ethics* V, rectificatory justice is defined as a mean between gain and loss,[28] and just acting as a mean between wronging and being wronged.[29] In his discussions of the virtues the doctrine of the mean has a more specific application: the virtuous person aims at the mean in both actions and feelings.[30]

The specific doctrine of the mean involves the claim that the virtues are 'mean states' (*mesotētes*). They are not themselves directly states which embody the mean of anything (kinds of temperament, for example); rather they are mean states because they are the states of someone who has acquired a settled disposition to aim at the mean (*meson*).[31] Such a person might not, of course, actually achieve the mean every time, but would be characterized by having a tendency to achieve it because of regularly aiming at it.[32] What is it, however, to aim at the mean? Aristotle, when he actually spells this out, as he frequently does in his accounts of the particular virtues, does so in terms of what one *should* do or *ought to* do, using the word *dei*, 'one ought';[33] the mean is even associated with *to deon*, what one should do.[34] Thus the 'doctrine of the mean' embodies a platitude, namely that the right disposition to have is one in which one is disposed to act as one should and to do the right thing. But it also involves a claim which is far from a platitude; for it also claims that the right thing to do, involving the right objects, right time, right circumstance and so on, is also a case of the *mean* or intermediate thing to do, where this is located between a way of going wrong which is defective and a way of going wrong which is

[26] *NE* 1106 b 36–1107 a 2.

[27] *Pol* 1295 a 34–b 1. For more discussion of the material referred to in this and the next three footnotes, see chapter 13, section 4.

[28] 1131 b 25–1132 b 20.

[29] 1133 b 29–32.

[30] 1106 b 16–28.

[31] This point, that the virtues are mean states because they aim at the mean, not because they are themselves means or blends of opposing character-tendencies, is clearly defended by Young in his (forthcoming). See also his (1988a) and (1988b).

[32] Cf. 1106 b 27–8: *mesotēs tis ara esti hē aretē, stochastikē ge ousa tou mesou*; cf. 1109 a 20–24.

[33] Cf. 1126 b 4–7: the mean state is one *kath'hēn hois dei orgizometha kai eph'hois dei kai hōs dei kai panta ta toiauta*.

[34] As at 1121 b 12.

excessive. This is a strong claim; it involves, for example, the claim that virtues are not the polar opposites of vices, but rather stand between two vices, while it is the vices which are opposed.[35]

Problems loom at once, however. What is going to count independently as a 'mean amount' of a kind of *action*? Bravery is doing the right thing at the right time, etc. in conditions of danger; how can this correlate with an independently established right number of brave actions to perform? Nor is cowardice well thought of as doing too few brave actions, or rashness as doing too many. For actions the idea of an independent specification of the due or right thing to do as the mean thing to do reaches absurdity right away. Further, Aristotle, despite saying that the mean applies to both actions and feelings (*pathē*), cannot have meant to stress the application to actions; for in introducing the idea that the virtues are mean states in *Nicomachean Ethics* II 6 he brings forward as a useful analogy to virtues the idea that *skills* are also dispositions which aim at the mean.[36] So even if we established a sense in which aiming at the right and due thing amounted to aiming at the mean, we would still not have distinguished virtues from skills.

The substance of the claim that virtues are mean states must therefore lie in the way that they aim at the mean in feelings or *pathē*. The virtuous person aims at the right thing to do, and in so doing aims, indirectly, at having, herself, the right degree of the appropriate kind of feeling. Feelings can be excessive or defective because

> we can get angry and feel bold and have desires and feel anger and pity and in general pleasure and pain both too much and too little, and in both cases not well; but having these feelings at the right time, on the right occasions, towards the right people, with the right aim and in the right way, is the mean and the best thing, which is characteristic of virtue.[37]

Again, there is a *right* way to feel, which we (following the *phronimos* or person of practical wisdom) locate by locating the right time, occasion, etc., and right thing to do. Again, there is the substantial claim that this is also, in fact, the *mean* way to feel, a way intermediate between an excessive and a defective way of feeling. Clearly the idea is no good if it is trivialized, that is, if the mean way to feel is just the right way to feel, or is simply to be identified with the way the agent feels when doing the right thing. But there are also difficulties with any theory which tries to give independent content to the mean amount of feeling involved. What is, for example, the excessive feeling, the mean amount of which is displayed in temperance? The obvious candidate is a raging lust for the pleasures of the flesh, and this would give the right opposition to its opposite, 'insensibility'. But the intemperate person is not always the uncontrolled person clamouring for sex too frequently, or too violently; lack of temperance is shown simply by desiring the *wrong* objects even once, as with Aristotle's person who commits 'adultery' (*moicheia*).[38] Aristotle indeed points out

---

[35] Young (in the articles just cited) claims that this is the main point of the doctrine of the mean.

[36] Cf. 1106 b 4–14. Young stresses the analogy with skills, a point usually under-stressed in accounts of Aristotelian virtue.

[37] 1106 b 18–23.

[38] This point, that what matters is the appropriateness of the objects rather than frequency or intensity, is made by Hursthouse (1980–1), who effectively criticizes the attempt of Urmson (1973) to give independent content to the idea of the mean amount of feeling or emotion.

himself that while virtue is defined as a mean, 'according to what is best and done well, it is an extreme'.[39] The right way to feel might on occasion be extremely angry; this is still 'in a mean' because neither excessive nor defective, but displaying the appropriate amount of anger. (Excess would presumably be feeling extremely angry in wrong circumstances, and defect, feeling only mildly angry in circumstances that should make one extremely angry.) But it is now hard to see how we are not to be forced back to trivializing the idea of the mean amount into that of the due or appropriate amount, whatever that turns out to be.

If we are to give genuinely independent content to the notion of the mean amount of feeling, we would seem to end up with a *moderate* amount of feeling, and the doctrine of the mean would amount to the claim that if the agent has developed the disposition to do the right thing, then she will characteristically feel a moderate amount of feeling or emotion: she will not be either indifferent or highly worked up about what she is doing. Contemporary scholarship rejects any such interpretation as a mistake, and it is indeed hard to square with Aristotle's statement that virtue is an extreme 'according to what is best and done well', but it is interesting that later Peripatetics felt no hesitation at all in describing the theory as that of *metriopatheia*, 'moderation in feeling'. As such it is standardly opposed to the theory of the Stoics, that the agent who has developed the disposition to do the right thing will have *apatheia*, absence of feeling or emotion. We should perhaps have more respect than is usually felt for this interpretation which was, after all, held by people who called themselves Aristotelians.[40] Whatever we think of their view as interpretation, however, it is certainly worth noting that it was stress on feeling, rather than action, and on moderation, that was found lasting in the doctrine of the mean.[41]

Aristotelian ethics was thus generally understood as maintaining that the virtuous agent will act rightly and will have the right amount of the appropriate feeling, where this will be a moderate amount. The Stoics appear to differ completely: they maintain that the virtuous person is *apathēs*, unfeeling,[42] and that virtue requires *apatheia*, absence of feeling or emotion. They stress the importance of the cognitive side of virtue, regarding it in very intellectual ways, and say roundly that there is no degree of feeling that it is appropriate for the virtuous person to have. This thesis is often described as a thesis about the emotions, since the Greek word *pathos* covers both feelings and emotions, and the thrust of the thesis is that

---

[39] 1107 a 6–8.

[40] Terry Irwin has urged on me the view that *metriopatheia* does not involve an adherence to moderation, but just is a name for the view that the emotions and feelings should be regulated, rather than extirpated, where this regulation is ordered by the doctrine of the mean, as expounded above. If so, the later Aristotelians would be better interpreters; but *metriopatheia* would be a very odd word for such a view, since *metrios*, on its own and in other compounds, standardly bears a suggestion of moderation.

[41] See Dillon (1983). Plutarch, *Virt mor*, uses an Aristotelian account of virtue as a mean in order to combat the Stoic theory of the emotions (not actions). Cf. Cicero, *TD* IV 37–50, and Seneca, *Ep* 85, 116 for the view that the Peripatetic view is that feelings should be subject to a limit (*modus*).

[42] At Diogenes VII 117 the wise person is said to be unfeeling (*apathēs*) in a different sense from that in which bad people are unfeeling, meaning harsh and callous. *Apathēs* has to be understood in a special way deriving from that in which the Stoics understand *pathos*.

virtue, far from requiring a settled state of the agent's emotions, demands their elimination.[43]

As often with the Stoics, the startling appearance of the thesis conceals a much milder, and more interesting, core. The Stoics are not saying that the virtuous person should simply *lack* all feeling and emotion. Rather, they define the *pathē* as faulty by definition:

> A feeling, they say, is an impulse which is excessive and disobedient to reason which is choosing; or, an <irrational> movement in the soul contrary to nature. . .; hence every upset is a feeling, <and> again every feeling is an upset. . . . 'Irrational' and 'contrary to nature' are not used in their general sense; 'irrational' is equivalent to 'disobedient to reason'. . . . And 'contrary to nature' is understood in the sketch of feeling as something happening contrary to the reason which is correct and according to nature.[44]

The *pathē*, feelings or emotions that one should not have, are feelings that are already excessive, going contrary to the agent's reason. A feeling or emotion is not a *pathos* unless it is urging the agent to act in a way that goes counter to the reason to act that the agent has resolved on. Hence it is obvious that the virtuous agent will lack *pathē*; to have these is already to be to some degree self-divided and conflicted, and since it is reason that grasps what it is that an agent morally ought to do, the *pathē* that oppose it are obviously undesirable. The virtuous agent will have *some* emotional states, which the Stoics calls *eupatheiai*:

> They say that there are three good feelings: joy, caution, wishing. Joy, they say, is the opposite of pleasure, and is reasonable elation. Caution is the opposite of fear, and is reasonable avoidance; for the wise person will not be afraid at all, but will take care. Wishing, they say, is the opposite of desire, and is reasonable wanting.[45]

Why do the Stoics hold this extraordinary view? One answer lies in their analysis of the emotions, which they take to be beliefs or judgements.[46] The Stoics in fact think that every case of action involves a commitment to a belief about what it is appropriate to do, so the thesis about emotions is just part of a wider account of action. Of course this aspect of the theory is counter-intuitive. Sometimes we *feel* fear, or depression, while lacking any appropriate belief. The Stoic answer is that these are not true examples of emotions, but a distinct phenomenon, *propatheiai* or 'pre-emotions'.[47] Further, even in ordinary cases we think that there is more to an emotion than having a belief. Here the Stoics claim that we are simply wrong: the emotion just is the belief. Suppose, judging some object to be fearful, I feel afraid. If something brings it about that I change this belief, and no longer believe the object

---

[43] Of course emotions are more than feelings; they have an intellectual structure and involve beliefs. I do not think that this extra complexity affects the points I am making here.

[44] Arius, 88.8–89.16.

[45] Diogenes VII 116.

[46] Galen, *PHP*, and Plutarch, *Virt mor,* are our best sources for this aspect of the theory. See Annas (1992a).

[47] See Epictetus fr. 9 (ap. Aulus Gellius, *Attic Nights* 19.1.14–20), Cicero, *TD* III 83, Plutarch, *Virt mor* 449a-b, *Ep* 11, 57.3–5, 71.29, 74.31–2.

to be fearful, then according to the Stoics I am no longer afraid.[48] The thesis that emotions are beliefs helps us to understand why the virtuous person will not have any. For all emotions involve placing value on, and caring about, objects other than virtue. According to the Stoics, virtue has a value and motivational force, quite different from the value and motivational force of other things.[49] And beliefs that attach one to objects other than virtue are all systematically mistaken. Being afraid of something that is not morally evil, or caring about something that is not morally good, presupposes that these things are worth caring about in their own right, whereas for the Stoics this is a misconception, attaching to these things a value which they do not have. There is no scope to discuss this central ethical thesis at this point, but it is clear how acceptance of it leads at once to the initially surprising theses that all emotions are irrational (since, while the beliefs that constitute them provide reasons for acting, they are *ex hypothesi* weak reasons, contrary to correct reason, which aims at virtue) and that we should get rid of them, rather than moderate them (for there is no point in moderating what rests on a complete mistake). We can also see what the *eupatheiai* are. They are affective states which are endorsed by reason. The virtuous person is not affectless; she has, for example, some attitude to danger. But this attitude will be consistent with a rational view of the situation, and so will be 'caution', not fear (fear already implying a wrong view of the situation).[50]

The Stoic theory does at first sight seem extremely perverse.[51] It is tempting to take it simply as a redefinition of what we mean by feeling or emotion, and to dismiss it on the grounds of artificiality. This would be a mistake, however.

One of the most interesting features of the theory is that virtuous action does not require the emotions to motivate it. Indeed, the Stoics are committed to the thesis that emotion is never the right thing to motivate virtuous action, since emotions already involve attachment of the wrong kind to things other than virtue. Whatever we think of other aspects of the Stoic theory of the emotions, it can be seen here as forcing an issue that has remained unclear so far, namely what is the actual *effective* role of the emotions in the virtuous person? So far we have seen that her emotions must be in harmony or agreement with her considered judgements about what she ought to do, rather than being neutral or in opposition and merely controlled or overridden by that judgement. But just what role do these emotions play which are on the side of 'right reason', the agent's correct reasoned judgement as to what she should do? When an agent acts morally, we assume that she acts *because* of her judgement that she should act that way. Suppose I reason that I

[48] Some feeling might persist, of course. It is not clear what the Stoic line on this is. A moderate line might say that there is nothing wrong with having the feeling as long as one does not assent to the belief, and so is not motivated by the feeling. A harsher line would say that having any feeling left over is a sign that you have not fully shed the belief, and so you should aim at ridding yourself of it.

[49] We shall discuss this central thesis of Stoic ethics at more length below. See chapters 5 and 19.

[50] The three sanitized attitudes take the place of desire, fear and pleasure. There is no sanitized attitude to take the place of pain.

[51] The Stoic theory of the emotions has generally been seen as perverse, both in this respect and in their claims that emotions are beliefs. Recent work has done much to show that on the latter point the Stoics are not liable to standard hostile ancient accusations. See the relevant section of Annas (1992a); also ch. 5 of Inwood (1985), Frede (1986), Gosling (1987). Less attention has been paid to the ethical significance of the theory, though see Nussbaum (1987) and Striker, ch. 6 of (1991).

should do a particular generous act. Because I am selfish, this has no weight with me; but by accident (I hear a sentimental song, for example) I have a stray generous impulse and do the act anyway. Clearly I have not acted virtuously; I have done what I should, but not for the right reason. But then what is the effective role of the right emotions which I have if I am a virtuous agent?

If we concentrate on the difference between the virtuous and the merely self-controlled, the answer seems clear: acting because of one's judgement that one should do so is necessary for an act to be a virtuous act, and sufficient for the agent to be merely self-controlled; also having the right emotions that endorse the performance of the act is a further necessary condition for the agent to be a virtuous agent, and hence performing the virtuous act as a virtuous person would.

But if we now concentrate on the virtuous agent, we get a result that can be seen as troubling. For it is not sufficient, on a given occasion, for a virtuous agent to act virtuously that she act because she sees what she should do, and acts because of this. Even the virtuous agent will be acting in a merely self-controlled way unless the relevant emotions are not only present but partly responsible for bringing about the action. Thus a virtuous person who does a generous action will not be acting *generously* unless generous feelings are not only present but partly responsible for the occurrence of the action. Acting because she sees that this is what she should do is not sufficient for her action to be done virtuously. But there are two kinds of consideration that may make us unhappy about this.

One is that the demand seems unrealistic, especially given the emphasis on the role of habituation in rendering a person virtuous. Suppose the agent is reliably and thoroughly generous; the relevant feelings and emotions have all been trained and directed by practice in generous action so that they are quite in tune with it. Does that mean that they play a positive role in every generous action? Surely beyond a certain point it would be truer to experience to think of them as settled, providing no resistance but often simply not called into play in particular generous acts. If a person's generous giving is clearly partly motivated by actual generous feelings, then it seems that the action was not simply the product of a virtuous disposition; some special factor seems in play. There thus seems to be a tension between the thought that virtuous action requires the effective presence of the relevant feelings and emotions, and the demand that virtue be dispositional, the product of habituation.

Apart from this, one might worry about the effective presence of the relevant emotions being a necessary condition for an agent to act virtuously, if one makes certain assumptions about emotions and feelings. For they are under our control only in the indirect way described above; we can alter and direct them only in the way we can alter our habits. On any given occasion, I can see what the right thing is for me to do, and act accordingly just for this reason; but I cannot summon up the right amount of a particular feeling. Still less can I ensure that a particular feeling is partly effective in bringing about the action. It might be thought that this is not true if we stress the dispositional and habitual nature of virtue. If I am virtuous then I am properly disposed in a certain way, say to be generous; on any occasion I will see what is the generous thing to do and have the right attitude towards it. I do not need to summon up feelings specially, because they have *already* been trained in the right direction. This is true, but does not wholly solve the problem. Illness, depression, irritating circumstances can all bring it about that on a given occasion I do not actually have the right feelings, though this does not affect my ability to discern what I should do and to act accordingly. If feelings as well as the judgement are both necessary conditions for the agent to act virtuously, then it seems that the virtuous agent is always in danger of backsliding to being merely self-controlled, given her temperament and circumstances. To escape this we have to make extremely unrealistic assumptions about the strength, stability and force of the virtuous person's feelings.

Thus if we are impressed by the point that even the virtuous person can suffer from deficiencies of temperament and circumstances, and also by the everyday point that often we just do not seem to need the active force of emotions to get us to act virtuously, we may come to think that discerning what the right thing to do is, and doing it for that reason, is in fact sufficient for the agent to act virtuously. The difference between the virtuous and the self-controlled will then not lie in the virtuous having an extra positive source of motivation, namely the right feelings. Rather it will lie in the fact that the self-controlled person is the person with something extra, namely the feelings she has to fight down in order to do the right thing, whereas the virtuous person has no such feelings to overcome. Such a position can stress the need for someone to train and habituate her feelings and emotions in order to become virtuous; and concur that proper training in this respect is what separates the virtuous from the self-controlled. But on this position the result of this training is not a positive, effective role for the emotions in moral action. Rather, it is seen as a removal of actual or possible obstacles to virtuous acting.

Thus for the Stoics, virtue requires getting rid of the emotions because the virtuous person is the person who acts just because of discerning what she ought to do, with nothing to interfere. The self-controlled person is not at this stage yet; she still has to contend with feelings that oppose her doing what she should do. The position rests on a combination of the empirical ground that we do not always need emotion to make us act virtuously, and the theoretical ground that emotions are the wrong kind of thing to produce virtuous action; they can let us down for all sorts of reason, and the fact that the virtuous person does in fact reliably act virtuously shows that she does not rely partly on emotion to do so.[52]

Seneca puts the point forcefully:

> 'What then', [the objector] says, 'will the good man not be angry if he sees his father murdered, his mother raped?' -No, he will not get angry—but he will avenge them, or protect them. In any case, why are you afraid that filial duty even without anger may not be a strong enough motive for him?. . . My father is being murdered—I will defend him; he has been murdered—I will avenge him. But because it is my duty (*quia oportet*), not because I feel bad about it (*non quia dolet*).[53]

An Aristotelian will, of course, be unhappy with this; it seems to allow the emotions too little role in the developed moral life. It is, of course, open to the Aristotelian to modify his position by allowing that in the agent in whom virtue is a developed disposition the emotions are not *effective* forces in the sense of being a

---

[52] For modern discussions of this issue, often in connection with Kantian ethics, see Baron (1984); Herman (1981) and (1983).

[53] *Ira* I 12.

necessary condition on each occasion for the virtuous performance of an action. Rather, their presence might be necessary for the agent to be virtuous, while in the virtuous agent the discernment of what he should do is sufficient to motivate him to do it. The Stoics could reply, however, that they can account for the point that the virtuous person will have certain definite positive and negative attitudes—these are the *eupatheiai*, the attitudes that are sanctioned by a rational view of the situation. However, the Stoics distinguish sharply between this kind of rational attitude and the emotions, and in particular are impressed by the fact that emotions and feelings motivate the agent to action, whereas the *eupatheiai* do not: they are just the attitudes had by an agent in whom rational understanding of the situation is sufficient to motivate her to do the morally appropriate thing. An Aristotelian, on the other hand, owes us an account of why it matters that certain emotions should be present if they are not required to motivate the agent to do the action.[54]

We thus find two very different positions on the role of the emotions in the virtuous person; the debate between Aristotelians and Stoics on this issue formed the major focus of debate.[55] Both these very different positions result from taking seriously the dispositional aspect of virtue and the role of the emotions in distinguishing the self-controlled from the virtuous. That they are so different suggests that this is a deeply difficult issue. It seems at first that the Aristotelians stay closer to common sense, which rejects the thought of getting rid of the emotions. But, once we remove the misleadingly outrageous appearance of the Stoic position, it is arguably as close to common sense, since common sense appears to back the thought that it is sufficient, for the virtuous person to act, that he recognize what virtue requires.[56] Common sense in fact appears to be divided on this issue.[57] We find two theories each of which develops one aspect of common sense to the point that it conflicts with other aspects, as well as with the rival theory. This is a pattern which we shall find again; ancient ethics of virtue, although paying respectful attention to our beliefs and their practical consequences, does not and cannot canonize common sense, since on some points common sense is divided against itself.

3. The Intellectual Aspect of Virtue

The virtuous person has a disposition to make the right judgement as to what he should do. Several issues arise, of which the most fundamental is: on what basis does the virtuous person discern this? Is the right thing to do defined in terms of what the virtuous person discerns? Or is there a standard independent of this that the virtuous person uses? Both alternatives contain problems, and the issue warrants distinct treatment (section 5). I shall also consider separately, in the next section, what the

---

[54] A position might do this which sharply distinguished between judgements about virtues and judgements about actions; but this is not a position any ancient school adopted.

[55] The Epicureans have an interesting theory of the emotions; see Annas (1989b), (1992a). But we lack explicit discussion of the Epicurean position in the present debate. Epicurean emotions are best dealt with alongside the Epicurean theory of natural and non natural desires (chapter 7).

[56] Common sense does not, of course, endorse the thought that it is never right to feel anger, or pity, so it does not support the Stoic theory in its entirety.

[57] Cf. Sidgwick (1907), Part III, chapter 2.

structure of virtuous reasoning is. In this section, I shall look at two issues: 1) the unity of a virtue: how do distinct judgements hang together to form a virtue and what is a virtue's intellectual status? (2) the unity of the virtues: do distinct virtues have distinct intellectual components, or do they in some way share the same intellectual basis?

The Unity of a Virtue

Aristotle compares acquiring a virtue with learning an expertise or skill (*technē*) like house-building or learning to play an instrument.[58] There is something that you learn to do by doing it, and you end up doing it well or badly.[59] He comments that if this were not the case then there would be no need for teachers.

For Aristotle what is important about a skill is that it is the point at which the agent has risen to intellectual grasp of the universal, of what particular cases share. Someone with mere 'experience' can muddle through from case to case, and can even be successful, but the person with skill knows what she is doing and why, and can explain this to others.[60] In the *Nicomachean Ethics* he defines skill as 'a state concerned with making things, which has a true account'.[61] Someone with a skill can give a true account of what he is making—can give, that is, reasons for doing things one way rather than another, for why some products are better than others. Skill crucially involves some level of *understanding* what it is that you are doing in exercising your skill.

This is why skill provides a good model for learning a virtue. The learner, paradigmatically the young learner, begins by picking up what to do in particular cases; he copies his elders or follows their advice.[62] But if he is intelligent he does not remain stuck at the stage of depending on models for each new case or memorizing a list of cases and dealing with each new one by comparing it with past ones. Rather, he develops a sense of the *point* of doing these specific things, and when he grasps this he has a sense of the basis of these previous judgements, which will enable him to go on to fresh cases without mechanically referring back. Like the person who has acquired an expertise in a skill, the learner has acquired understanding of what he is doing,[63] an understanding that can be represented as a unified grasp of the principles that underlie his actions and decisions.

This is, as we shall repeatedly see, the basic point of the skill analogy for virtue. The virtuous person is not just the person who does in fact do the morally right thing, or even does it stably and reliably. She is the person who *understands* the principles on which she acts, and thus can explain and defend her actions. The skill

---

[58] He is not, of course, the first to do so; the analogy with *technē* is extensively developed by the Platonic Socrates, and Aristotle is clearly at times reacting to this. (On this see Annas [1993a].) However, the analogy would not be as important as it is for Aristotle if it were merely a philosopher's position; he clearly regards it as having considerable footing in our intuitions about virtue and the way that these develop on reflection.

[59] *NE* II 1.

[60] See *Met* I 1, especially 981 a 1–b 10.

[61] 1140 a 20–21.

[62] *NE* 1143 b 11–14.

[63] Cf. Sorabji (1980).

analogy requires that the agent reflect and achieve by reflection a unified grasp of the general principles underlying her patterns of action and decision. And thus the analogy marks a strong contrast with modern versions of virtue ethics which regard virtue as a matter of non-generalizable sensitivity; it brings ancient ethics closer to other modern theories which require that the moral agent reflect on, and try to achieve a theoretically unified basis for, her individual moral judgements. The skill analogy, in its various developments, is quite central to the ancient conception of moral theory.

Aristotle insists repeatedly, however, that virtue is not itself a skill, and his grounds for this are interesting. One is that skill is concerned with *making* things (*poiēsis*) whereas virtue is concerned with *doing* or action (*praxis*).[64] This means that they have different aims: 'With making the end [*telos*] is distinct, but not so with acting; for acting well is itself the end.'[65] Weaving produces a rug, pottery-making a pot, whereas bravery 'produces' only a brave action. And, Aristotle insists, the excellence of the rug and the pot 'lie in themselves' and not in the way they were made, hence all that the expert needs is the expert knowledge to produce them; whereas the excellence of the brave action lies not just in it, but in the way it was produced, so that acting bravely requires not just knowledge but a developed virtuous disposition, which motivates the agent in the right way.[66] This contrast, that skill requires only knowledge whereas virtue requires a developed disposition, underlines Aristotle's other contrasts: skill involves a mere capacity (since mere knowledge can be used in different ways, not just the right one);[67] virtue involves more than a mere rational state, since these can be forgotten whereas virtue cannot;[68] in a skill the person who deliberately makes mistakes is to be preferred (to the one who makes mistakes anyway), but the reverse is true for virtue.[69] Moreover, Aristotle insists that virtue is more 'accurate' than skill; the virtuous person has to make precise particular concrete decisions, about matters that do not fall under any expertise.[70]

Aristotle thus stresses the intellectual understanding that the craftsperson has, and hence his independence of models. In calling skill a state, he also recognizes the habituation needed to build up a reliable intellectual grasp underlying the practice of a skill. He chooses to express this position by contrasting skill and virtue.[71] But this is not the only possible response; one could say that virtue, since it shares these features of intellectual grasp and need for habit and practice, is a special kind of skill. Presumably Aristotle insists that virtue is not a skill because skills other than virtue can be practiced in comparative independence of the agent's moral character. But it is a little surprising that Aristotle was more impressed by this point than by the point

---

[64] 1140 a 2–6, 16–17, b 3–4.
[65] *NE* 1140 b 6–7.
[66] 1105 a 26–b 5.
[67] 1129 a 11–16.
[68] 1140 b 21–30.
[69] 1140 b 22–24.
[70] 1106 b 14–17; 1104 a 7–8. Cf. 1122 a 34–5 where someone with a particular virtue is said to be like someone with knowledge in his ability to get right what is appropriate in every single case.
[71] For some modern objections to the idea that virtues could be skills, see Wallace (1978), pp. 44–47, and (1988); for some responses, see Roberts (1984).

that virtue and skill are strikingly similar in their formal structure: both require reflection on what one is doing, and why, an intellectual grasp which is expressed in practice. Possibly Aristotle, who often dislikes his theses to sound counter-intuitive, is impressed by the point that intuitively many skills differ from virtue, for example in having an independently identifiable product, and do not require the level of articulate reflection that virtue requires.[72]

The Stoics, by contrast, are perfectly willing to say that the virtues are skills. They are not missing Aristotle's points; they are just more impressed by the formal similarities.

> [T]hey say that virtue is a disposition of the soul which is in agreement with itself concerning the whole of one's life. . . . All the virtues which are types of knowledge [*epistemai*] and expertises [*technai*] have principles [*theōrēmata*] in common.[73]

We have already seen why they give this intellectualist-sounding account, given their position on the emotions. Nothing much seems to hang on whether a virtue is called an expertise or a branch of knowledge,[74] and we can see why if we look at the Stoic accounts of these. Expertise or skill is 'an organization made up of apprehensions that have been practiced together, aiming at some end that is useful in life'.[75] Thus the Stoics make more prominent than Aristotle does in their account of skill the point that it requires practice and habituation as well as intellectual grasp.

Knowledge is defined as follows:

> Knowledge is apprehension which is sure and unchangeable by argument. In other terms, knowledge is an organization made up of apprehensions such as make up particular [knowledge] and in the excellent person it exists as something rational.[76]

Both definitions point to the way in which 'apprehension' is made firm and in which several 'apprehensions' come to fit together with practice. For the Stoics an apprehension is a grasp of something which is such that the agent could not be wrong about what he grasps. If I grasp something I do not merely have a belief; I am in the state which modern epistemologists would call knowledge of a particular fact.[77] Expertise and knowledge are the results of certain ways in which these apprehensions, or insights as we might call them in the ethical case, become developed into systematic bodies of practical ability. Two points are stressed. Insights must be practiced together to achieve virtue: merely getting a couple of cases

---

[72] We shall return to the latter point shortly; see pp. 71ff.

[73] Arius 60.7–8, 63.6–7.

[74] In Greek *epistēmē*, knowledge, has a plural, *epistejmai*, which we are forced to translate as 'branches' (or 'kinds') of knowledge. *Technē*, skill or expertise, similarly has a plural *technai*; 'expertise' lacks a plural in English just as 'knowledge' does, though we can use 'skill(s)' or 'craft(s)'.

[75] For Zeno as the originator of this definition, see *SVF* I 72, 73, and Sparshott (1978). Sparshott is surely right that what looks like a competing definition of skill as a state which makes a pathway, or which accomplishes things by a pathway, is not a competitor, but a definition of expertise as a human ability, as opposed to *an* expertise, a body of beliefs developed in certain ways. Cf. also Sextus, *PH* III 241, *M* XI 182.

[76] Arius 73.19–24.

[77] Cf. Annas (1990b).

right is not enough—the relevant thoughts have to be brought together in the agent's mind and put into practice in a variety of contexts for the agent to act in the right way constantly and reliably. And a given insight will become firm and reliable only as part of a built-up body of supporting insights. Relevant ethical beliefs come to cohere in a firmer and firmer way as the agent builds up a body of organized and mutually supporting beliefs, and this coherence builds up as the agent's various ethical insights are tested and adjusted in practice. Given this conception of skill and knowledge, the Stoics can, more readily than Aristotle, see virtue as a special kind of skill.

Virtue is not, for the Stoics, just a kind of skill; it is special in that other skills can be said to succeed only when their product is complete—the rug woven, the pot fired—whereas virtue can be said to succeed the whole time it is activated—before the result is achieved and, it will turn out, even if the result is never achieved at all.[78] They also make other claims which derive from further ethical theses, for example the claim that only in the virtuous person can the other skills achieve full consistency and solidity.[79] As we shall see, especially in Part IV, there are points when intuitive analogies from the other skills fall down when applied to virtue. Nonetheless it is absolutely crucial that virtue has the intellectual structure of a skill: it requires reflection and understanding of the basic principles of a practical ability.

The idea that virtue shares its structure with skills, or actually is a kind of skill or expertise, is basic and important in ancient ethical theories. Here we find convergence between ancients and moderns: in ethics it is not enough for the agent just to have some isolated judgements, even if admirable. about right and wrong. A responsible moral agent needs to be critically reflective about these judgements, and to achieve some understanding of their systematic basis. Modern theories do not think of the intellectual structure that is thus achieved as having the structure of a skill in particular; we shall shortly examine some reasons for this. The skill analogy emphasizes not only the point that virtue requires intellectual reflection and understanding, but the point that this understanding is built up through practice, trial and error, experiment and extension of the agent's judgements. Progress in virtue comes not just from critical reflection but also through testing reflective views in real life, from practice in being generous, just or brave.

The prominence of the underlying model of skill brings out some important points in the ancient conception of a virtue. Having a virtue involves having an intellectual grasp which is in an important way unified, and this is so in three ways. First, I must have unified my judgements about bravery, say; I am not yet really brave if I constantly shift my ground as to the proper field for bravery, or the kind of reason which grounds a judgement that someone is brave. Second, although this unified point of view is an intellectual one, it brings with it a unified emotional attitude; for, as we have seen, I cannot become brave just by being argued into it— rather, I have to practice being brave, test and refine my views in actual life, so that growing coherence of my ethical beliefs is directly reflected in growing coherence of my reactions and attitudes. And third, what renders my judgements and reactions

---

[78] This is a point which is of importance for the relation of virtue to happiness, and is discussed in detail in chapter 19.

[79] Arius 73.7–10.

about bravery coherent is my grasp of the unified basis for making them—the point of being brave, by reference to which I can clarify and organize my initial intuitions about bravery. This is seen as the *good* of bravery, the value or worth of being brave. This is not an arbitrary demand; it is a consequence of thinking of the virtues as ways of achieving the agent's (correctly conceived) overall goal in life. The disposition to be brave is unified by a grasp of what being brave, rather than cowardly, contributes to the agent's living well, achieving his final good. (A full grasp of this point must of course await our working through the issues of Part IV.)

Taking skill to be a model for virtue, in that virtue shares the intellectual structure of a skill, thus turns out to have quite strong implications. One is that the virtuous person cannot have become so without being critically reflective. One cannot unify one's judgements and come to see the overall point of bravery without having reflected on the basis of those judgements. The skill analogy brings out the important point that the virtuous person, just as much as the moral agent in most modern moral theories, must be an agent who has reflected on her initial moral judgements and achieved a unified understanding of her basis for making them, on a level which is more general and theoretical than those judgements themselves.[80]

The role of the skill or craft analogy in discussions of virtue is often misunderstood in modern discussions. It is often thought that the model imports what has been called 'the fixed-goal theory of practical reasoning'.[81] If virtue is a craft then our goal in living as humans must be as fixed or definite as the goals of the practical crafts typically are.[82] And this is obviously objectionable; an ethical theory ought not to take for granted at an early stage the highly disputable claim that our ends in life are fixed and determinate. But it is clear from what we have seen so far that this is *not* the role of the human *telos* in ethical reasoning. Given the ways considerations about our overall end enter in, our final end could not be a *fixed* goal means to which we work out. We have seen that thoughts about our final end are produced by considerations which initially give us only a thin and weak specification of it; until we have reflected in depth about the virtues we are in no position to make our final end determinate. We make it determinate in and by developing the virtues; it is not a fixed goal we have in mind as we develop them. Thus to consider our *telos* as a fixed point to guide our thoughts about the virtues is to get matters wrong way round. It is not the object of the skill but the structure and unification of the skilled reasoning that is the crucial point of analogy for ethical reasoning.

To acquire a virtue requires intellectual development. But it is not codifiable; there is no handbook or list of rules to learn from, with the guaranteed result of achieving the intellectual requirement. As with any skill, we can give rules to help the learner, but obviously there is no foolproof recipe or guarantee of success. And so with virtue—success is not mechanical; there are many incalculable failures of temperament or intellect that may thwart the right decision. Grasp of this point helps keep ancient ethics from being tempted by the ideal of a purely mechanical

---

[80] This aspect of the skill analogy is discussed at greater length in Annas (1993a), which also discusses the origins of the skill analogy in Plato's Socratic dialogues.

[81] Wallace (1988), who argues against this conception of the craft analogy and brings out its defects.

[82] This is also the aspect of the craft analogy stressed by Irwin (1976).

decision-making procedure, one which would do the work for us and leave no role to individual deliberation.[83]

There is one large point about the ancient skill analogy which is sociological rather than philosophical, but nevertheless of importance here; it in part explains some difficulties modern versions of virtue ethics get into when they appeal to the analogy. In the ancient world crafts were economically central; references to weaving and pottery were references to jobs people had that were part of the functioning of the ancient economy. Thus, insistence on the common structure of skills and virtue was an insistence that being moral is like *working*; the virtuous person is importantly like the good worker.

This point has to be qualified by the observation that properly living well was thought by all the major schools to require the leisure for reflection, and that some philosophers, notably Plato and Aristotle, insist that working for a living was incompatible with developing the virtues; thus virtue and skill would not naturally be thought as forming aspects of the *same* life. However, their view was not shared by all schools. The Stoics insisted that obstacles to becoming virtuous lay in the agent's character, not his occupation; and while the Epicureans insisted on forming a distinctive philosophical community, this was not because of distaste for productive work. But even Plato and Aristotle, who are most extreme in their contempt for working for a living, have no model but skill for this, and Plato has a surprisingly detailed knowledge of some skills.[84]

In the modern post-industrial world, however, the very word 'craft' suggests craft fairs and other economically marginal activities. Weaving is something done by machines; our model of working is what is done in a factory or an office, neither involving the close relation of producer and product involved in the skill or craft relationship.[85] This is one reason why appeal to the skill analogy in modern virtue ethics may seem unrealistic or nostalgic; crafts just do not play the same role in our lives as they did in the ancient world, nor could they, since we no longer have a craft economy.

We should recognize that for this reason the skill analogy lacks, for us, a certain centrality that it has in the ancient world; this imposes care in our interpretation as well as caution in trying to put the analogy to use in modern virtue ethics. Nonetheless, this does not make it useless for us. We could give less attention to the productive skills proper and focus on skills like teaching or being a doctor, which do not result in a distinct product, as weaving does, and thus play more similar roles in ancient and modern societies. In modern virtue ethics these are indeed often used as examples. Many discussions use sporting and artistic skills as examples. Sport, however, is too trivial a concern, and too linked to aggression, competition and

---

[83] Plato's *Protagoras* contains an interesting attempt to do this by means of the technique of measuring pleasures and pains. See Nussbaum (1986a), ch. 4. (Unlike Nussbaum, I am not convinced that this represents Plato's own position.) What is interesting is how unlike this any serious ancient theory of ethics is. Even Epicurus, who might superficially seem to be putting forward the same kind of theory, is never tempted by a mechanical model of maximizing pleasure. See Annas (1987), and chapter 7.

[84] The detailed description of weaving in the *Statesman*, archaeologically accurate, is the most striking. See Brumbaugh (1976).

[85] Of course even industrialized societies can contain pockets of craft production, such as Navajo weaving; but these are sustained by specialized demand, and are not part of the productive economy proper.

violence, to provide a good model for virtue, and art, though better, is arguably still too limited. More centrally, however, we can take over, without any such adjustment, the point that virtue shares the intellectual structure of a skill; for this answers, as we have seen, to the demand that the moral agent be someone who has engaged in a process of critical reflection about her beliefs, and on this point there seems little dispute between ancients and moderns.

We can thus see why one objection to the skill analogy is without force. Gardeners can and do have expertise without being able explicitly to articulate it and state the principles on which it rests. Does this not imply that skill is an unsuitable model for virtue? But it is clear by now that what matters for ethics in the skill analogy is the point that virtue shares the intellectual structure of a skill, something accessible only to the critically reflective agent. Thus, examples of skills which do not require this are simply examples of skills which are in this respect not like virtue.[86]

The Unity of the Virtues

All ancient ethical theories agree that fully to have the virtues, or even one particular virtue, the agent has to have *phronēsis*. *Phronēsis* is introduced by Aristotle as the 'intellectual virtue' of practical reasoning; it is the state of the developed virtuous person, who not only makes the right judgement and decision on particular occasions, but does so from a developed intelligent disposition, which is the basis for doing so reliably and correctly. As we shall see in the next section, it is a shared assumption that such a disposition is firm in relying on general principles, but must also always be sensitive to the complexities of particular situations. In this section we shall, before considering the structure of *phronēsis* and the basis for the claim that it produces *correct* judgements, look at its role in unifying the virtues.

Phronēsis has commonly been translated 'prudence', and this retains the idea that it is a developed and successful state, but introduces the modern idea, utterly foreign to ancient ethical theories, of a distinct realm of prudence or self-interest, which may be different from that of morality; whatever else *phronēsis* is, it is the disposition to make right moral judgements. A less misleading translation is 'practical wisdom', but this again imports a wrong association, since 'wisdom' in modern English suggests inactive contemplation, and the juxtaposition of this with practice sounds wrongly paradoxical. No translation is completely satisfactory, but the best is probably 'practical intelligence' or just 'intelligence', since the suggestions of inventiveness and problem-solving are more suitable.[87]

Intelligence, then, is the state the agent is in who has learned to reason well about moral matters—not in a particular sphere, but generally. Aristotle makes this point:[88] the intelligent person reasons well about what is good and advantageous for him, not in one area but with regard to living well in general. There are two sides to this development. One is that the agent has mastered the right way of reasoning

---

[86] This point is stressed in Annas (1993a).

[87] In choosing this I have been influenced by Irwin's use of 'intelligence' for *phronēsis* in his translation of Aristotle's *Nicomachean Ethics* (1985a).

[88] *NE* 1140 a 24–6.

about moral matters and can apply it firmly and flexibly. What this involves differs from school to school, some laying more weight on rules, others on means-end reasoning; we shall see this in more detail in the next section. The other side is obvious from what we have seen so far about the emotional side of virtue: the intelligent person will not have to fight his feelings, for in any area his disposition to make certain judgements will have developed along with his disposition to have the appropriate reactions. And since in obvious ways having the appropriate attitude favours the making of the judgements, and vice versa, the person with developed practical intelligence will be a person whose attitudes and emotions are in harmony with his judgements; his judgements are the right ones, and correspondingly his attitudes are the right ones.[89]

In the case of a particular virtue, then, the relation between having the virtue and having intelligence will be extremely close. Aristotle takes up this question;[90] he rejects the idea that there is a merely external connection between having intelligence and being virtuous. Intelligence, he insists, though it is an intellectual state, is not an intellectual state like cleverness, the ability to achieve an aim in an ingenious way, regardless of whether the aim is a good aim or is in harmony with your other aims. People can be clever in achieving all sorts of aims, but intelligence is more than this, though it does involve the problem-solving capacities of cleverness. Intelligence requires virtue; it is the state of the person who makes the right judgements on moral matters, and this is impossible if he is not virtuous. The non-virtuous person's reasonings may fail to start from the right considerations, and may be derailed by temptations. Intelligence, then, requires virtue. This seems clear enough; it is a virtuous disposition that makes the difference between the merely ingenious but possibly unscrupulous person and the person whose decisions and judgements are reliably correct in moral matters. Further, Aristotle insists, virtue requires intelligence. A person may have a fortunate temperament and thus be disposed to act rightly and have the right reactions. But without a developed intellectual disposition to unify and reflect on the reasons for being like this, this is merely 'natural' virtue,[91] lacking a firm intellectual base and hence insecure. Intelligence is called the 'eye of the soul', and someone who has a good disposition but lacks intelligence is compared to a strong but blind person, whose strength serves to harm himself and others as he staggers about. True virtue requires a firm intellectual basis, and thus virtue requires intelligence, the developed disposition to reason correctly in moral matters.

At the level of the individual virtues, it seems obvious that a virtue must have an intellectual as well as an emotional and reactive side: generosity must involve correct judgements and reflection to be *generosity*, rather than a floating sentimental impulse. This much is implicit in the skill analogy. But why should any given virtue require *phronēsis*, the developed disposition to make correct moral judgements in general? Can't I be brave if I make the right decisions about bravery, while possibly going wrong about tact and fairness?

---

[89] We have seen above that Aristotelians and Stoics interpret this role for the emotions in rather different ways, but these differences do not affect what follows.

[90] *NE* VI, especially 1143 b 18–1145 a 7.

[91] See below, chapter 4, for Aristotle's use of 'natural' in this connection.

There are several considerations here. One is that the virtues are structurally similar (at least if we accept the claims made about the structure of the individual virtues). Learning to be generous is not a wholly different kind of thing from learning to be brave. Further, it seems to be empirically the case that as we develop different virtues we not only notice these similarities but also are led to general, non–virtue-specific considerations. We notice, for example, that someone who is generous with what does not properly belong to her is also found telling lies; we not only think about honesty, but may be led to think in more general terms of the place in one's life of honesty and the difference it makes in superficially very dissimilar situations. Considerations like this may begin to start us thinking in terms of the place of each virtue in one's life as a whole.

There is also a push towards unification that comes when the agent articulates why he is virtuous. Ancient theories require that the virtuous agent be able to articulate and defend her reasons for acting as she does and being the way she is, across the board. An individual virtue is not a real intellectual stopping-point; the significant intellectual point is that of the agent who has a correct grasp and the right attitude in every area of life.

The other point can be found in the ancient sources, though not as prominently as we would expect. The agent, as we have seen, acts underivatively from a virtue like bravery when his attitude to and judgements about bravery are unified by his grasp, at some level, of the value of bravery, its contribution to his (correctly conceived) overall good. While there are many questions about this which we cannot satisfactorily answer until Part IV, it is clear even at this stage that this forms a big difference between ancient reasons of virtue and modern moral reasons. It is true of an ancient reason of virtue, as of a modern moral reason, that it gives a non-derivative reason for acting to the agent. The brave agent does a brave action just because it is brave, and not for any ulterior reason; this has the same force as the modern demand that an agent who acts for a moral reason act for that reason and not for any ulterior reason.[92] The point is in each case the same: these are reasons which to motivate in the appropriate way must motivate by themselves; their force cannot be owed to any more basic reasons. Ancient ethics, however, does not give up at this point, leaving it obscure what could be the source of these reasons having this kind of force. Rather, the properly brave person grasps how acting bravely, while done for its own sake, also forms part of her overall good in her life as a whole; indeed understanding this is part of what it is to grasp what bravery is.

Each virtue, then, contributes to my overall good. We can now see a way in which it is natural to think of intelligence, the developed state of correct reasoning in matters of virtue, as unifying the virtues. For virtuous judgement involves correct judgement about what is good in one area of my life. But it will be very seldom that realistic cases of virtuous judgement will involve merely one such area. Bravery involves a correct judgement of the good achieved in one's life by acting bravely, rather than in a cowardly way. But a correct judgement will involve more than knowing that I could either fight or run away, for example. I need to know whether what is at stake is *worth* fighting for. Fighting and refusing to back down over a

---

[92] This is one of the major reasons for regarding the ancient ethics of virtue as being an account of morality. See section 7.

triviality shows not bravery but aggressiveness; someone who fights, perhaps against genuine dangers, for a trivial point of precedence does not understand the proper role in the agent's life of honour. To be brave rather than aggressive, then, the agent must have a correct grasp of the worth of honour and the importance of slights, as well as a correct estimate of what is dangerous. Most concrete examples will expand in this kind of way. To be angry in the correct way, based on a correct judgement and not mere feeling, will involve a right grasp of the importance of what it is one is angry about. So getting it right as to how one should act on a particular occasion will involve a correct judgement not merely as to what good-temperedness requires, but as to what temperance, or fairness, requires. So if having the virtue of good-temperedness requires a grasp of the good achieved in one's life by this virtue, this turns out not to be possible without also having a grasp of the goods achieved by temperance, fairness and so on. For grasping the good of one virtue in the agent's life cannot be done in isolation; the agent needs to see how the various goods in her life are related and adjusted.

This thought, that *phronēsis* underlies all the virtues, since it cannot be employed in one area without involving others, leads, as Aristotle sees, to the point, at first sight surprising, that the virtues are not separable; if you have one you have them all.[93] This thesis of the 'reciprocity of the virtues'[94] is weaker than the thesis of the *unity* of the virtues, as we shall see, but it is still sufficiently startling. Intuitively we think that we can be brave but mean, fair but bad-tempered. According to the reciprocity thesis, this is false. The truly brave person has *phronēsis*, practical intelligence, the disposition always to make correct judgements in the sphere of bravery. But the agent could not have developed this without developing the disposition to make correct judgements in the spheres of all the other virtues also, since the demands of bravery cannot be correctly judged without judging them against the demands of the other virtues.

Thus even to have one virtue fully you have to have practical intelligence; and if you have this, you have all the virtues. Correctly judging the claims of the virtues in any case requires a correct estimate of the place and function of all the virtues in the agent's life as a whole. Hence the *phronēsis* involved in having any virtue unifies the virtues from the agent's point of view. We can now appreciate more fully why Aristotle says that

> the intelligent person seems to be characterized by deliberating finely about what
> is good and advantageous for himself, not in a particular area, e.g., what conduces
> to health or strength, but in what conduces to living well in general.[95]

---

[93] 1144 b 33–1145 a 2.

[94] Alexander of Aphrodisias has an essay on the reciprocity of the virtues (*hoti antakolouthousin hai aretai*) (*De An.* II 153.29–156.27). His arguments feature the points stressed here: one does not have one virtue in full (*holoklērōs*) without having the others; the exercise of justice, for example, involves all the demands (*deomena*, 154.1) of virtue and all sorts of occasions and encounters (*en pasin tois kairois kai pros panta*, 154.16); *phronēsis* unifies the virtues (155.38–156.27). Some of these arguments recur in Alexander's *Ethical Problem* 22 (see Sharples [1990] for translation and notes). See also Irwin (1988a), with the reply by Kraut (1988) and response to this by Irwin (1988a).

[95] *NE* 1140 a 25–28.

Fully to have a virtue involves grasping what it contributes to the good of one's life *as a whole*; and when we think this through we see that all the virtues are unified in the agent's deliberations, so that if you have one you have them all.

This position is the natural outcome of the widely shared thoughts about virtue that we have seen so far: that a virtue is unified in the way a skill is, that its intellectual basis (unlike that of a skill) cannot when developed be limited to one particular area. Nonetheless it may seem objectionable in some ways. It seems, for a start, to give too intellectual a view of the virtues. The thought is that if I really have the virtue of good-temperedness, then I have a correct understanding of the contribution that this virtue makes to my overall good; but I cannot have this without also understanding the contribution that any virtue makes to my good. But should it follow from this that if I have one virtue then I have them all? Could I not have the intellectual basis of the other virtues—the grasp of what they contribute to the agent's good, which enables the agent to make correct judgements in their case—but not have the appropriate emotions and feelings? Intuitively it seems obvious that my judgements and emotions about anger could be in harmony, and my judgements about anger could imply judgements consistent with them about justice, fitting into an overall pattern of judgements about my life—and yet my feelings about justice might be in rebellion against my just decisions.[96]

The answer here must surely be that it is the same with *phronēsis* as it is with the particular virtues: making the right judgements and decisions in an ever more unified and coherent way both presupposes and encourages development of the appropriate feelings and emotions. This is the thought behind Aristotle's insistence that intelligence is not the same as the cleverness that indifferently achieves a variety of aims; intelligence implies virtue, for you are not reasoning *intelligently* unless in your reasoning you are constrained by and sensitive to considerations of virtue.

We might question if this line of thought is as plausible for *phronēsis* as a whole as it is for the intellectual basis of the individual virtues. It might seem threatened by its counter-intuitive consequence of the reciprocity of the virtues, with its corollary that if in any area of an agent's life, for example that of anger, his feelings are not in complete harmony with his decisions, then he lacks any virtue- he is not brave or just, for example. Results like this may make us think that the thesis of the reciprocity of the virtues consists of a truth and a falsity. The truth is that if we think through what is involved in having the intellectual grasp that is an aspect of a single virtue, we will see that it involves having a unified view of one's life as a whole; what matters for bravery is not distinct, in the agent's life, from what matters for justice and even for good-temper. The falsity is that having one virtue fully, that is, having one's feelings completely in harmony with one's judgements in that area, involves having every other virtue fully. It seems obvious that this must be false, because it seems obvious that one's failure to be fully virtuous in one area does not undermine one's being fully virtuous in others.

In theories after Aristotle we find even stronger theses about the relations of the virtues, with no apparent awareness that they are problematic in principle. Several factors may help to explain this: perhaps a more 'practical' view of skill and knowledge than ours, or a greater reluctance to pull apart the intellectual and

---

[96] Kraut's (1988) reply to Irwin and Irwin's (1988a) response to Kraut raise this issue.

emotional aspects of virtue. The most important factor, however, is surely the stress laid in ancient ethics on the agent's view of his life as a whole. We have seen that this is the starting point for ancient ethics, and so it is not surprising that it should emerge as the end point of the agent's reflections about what the right thing to do is. The ancients were quite as aware as we are that intuitively I can be fully just and less than fully brave. But they were readier than we are to accept that this shows that in fact I am *not* fully just after all, because they laid more stress than we do on the agent's viewpoint of the good of her life as a whole. If I am less than fully brave, I am somewhere getting bravery wrong vis-à-vis other values—putting too high a value on security, say. But this imbalance in my values cannot be guaranteed to stay isolated from other values, and it casts doubt on my claim to be fully just, since this imbalance may show up in a context in which justice figures, or may give rise to another one which does. The ancient readiness to accept what seem to us unsuitably strong theses about the unification of the virtues springs from their taking seriously the thought that *one person's* virtues are a unity, since they all reflect *his* considered conception of his overall good.

There is another way in which the non-separability of the virtues seems to lead to implausible consequences: the lines of thought we have just seen imply that there is no conflict among the virtues; all of them find a place in the agent's reflected overall view of his final good, and this could not be the case in a coherent life if different virtues gave rise to conflicting demands. The author of the *Magna Moralia* indeed makes this point quite openly:

> Virtue is not in opposition to virtue; its nature is to yield to reasoning, whatever it commands, so that virtue inclines to whatever reason leads to; for it is reason that chooses what is better. For the other virtues do not come into being without intelligence, and intelligence is not complete without the other virtues—rather they are co-workers with each other[97] in a way as they follow after intelligence.[98]

This thesis does not rule out the existence of moral conflict, but it does rule out moral conflict stemming from conflicting virtues.[99]

Again the thesis offends our intuitions; it seems simply obvious that the claims of one virtue may contend with the claims of another. But the thesis is not that there can be no conflict between the claims of one virtue and those of another, stated at a general level. Rather, the claim is that the virtues as they have developed in an individual will not lead to conflicts in particular cases. And this claim appears to be convincing, as soon as we give due weight to the role of *phronēsis*. If I am really just, then I will, when I am just, apply my understanding of what justice requires; but, as we have seen, this understanding will be incomplete unless I can duly adjust and balance the claims of justice with those of other virtues and their goods. So in a given case, if I make a decision about justice, but this is in conflict with my judgement about what in this case is required by gratitude, this merely shows that I have not got my decision about justice right yet. Because it is the same *phronēsis* that

---

[97] The verb is *sunergousi pōs*, which suggests a later author, since *sunergos* is the regular word for one type of Stoic cause; it facilitates the production of an effect by a cause which can already produce the effect.

[98] *MM* 1200 a 5–11.

[99] A point rightly emphasized by Irwin (1988a), p. 68.

underlies all the virtues, to hold conflicting judgements about different virtues indicates a failure to have achieved a truly global view of one's life and priorities. So the startling-looking claim is merely a further application of the thesis that *phronēsis* underlies and unifies all the virtues in the agent's practical thinking. It in no way denies that the agent might be faced by an insoluble moral dilemma; it merely insists that the source of the dilemma cannot be conflicts within the agent's *phronēsis*.

Ethical theories after Aristotle also accept the importance of intelligence as the intellectual basis of the virtues, and accept it as what unifies the virtues. Indeed they go beyond Aristotle and insist that the virtues are made into some kind of unity by the understanding they share. Epicurus holds this thesis in a somewhat imprecise form. All the virtues, he says,[100] 'have by nature come from intelligence', and he calls intelligence 'the beginning of all [pleasant living] and the greatest good; which is why intelligence is more valuable even than philosophy'. Epicurus seems to regard intelligence as the practical disposition which results from studying and internalizing (Epicurean) philosophy, though sometimes he casts philosophy itself in that role: when Sextus is discussing candidates for being the skill or expertise in living he takes Epicurus' candidate to be, not *phronēsis* but philosophy, which is an activity attaining happiness by arguments and discussions.[101]

We find the Stoics, on the other hand, not only discussing the problem of the unity of virtues in precise terms, but developing an interesting position through debate. *Phronēsis* was for them the 'skill or expertise in living', and they defined it in terms of skill or knowledge of what to do.[102] We have seen that these excessively intellectualist-sounding definitions are a natural outcome of their theory of the emotions.[103] Zeno, the founder of the Stoic school, held 'that there are many virtues'[104] but that they are inseparable; this is Aristotle's view. But he went further than Aristotle in drawing one consequence:

> Zeno admits several differentiated virtues, as Plato does, for example, intelligence, courage, temperance and justice, on the grounds that although inseparable they are distinct and different from one another. But when defining each of them he says that courage is intelligence [in things to be endured, moderation is intelligence in things to be chosen, intelligence in the specific sense is intelligence] in what is to be done, and justice is intelligence in things to be distributed—on the grounds that it is one single virtue which only seems to differ in accordance with the activities by virtue of its relations to things.[105]

Zeno defined the individual virtues as though they were applications of *phronēsis* in different areas. It is easy to see how someone who took seriously the thoughts about virtue and *phronēsis* that we have considered could be led to say this: if the developed intelligence common to all the virtues is required for each, then what will distinguish the virtues beyond the point that intelligence will be differently applied-

---

[100] *Ep Men* 132.

[101] *M* XI 109.

[102] See, for example, Sextus, *PH* III 239–249, *M* XI 170, 184, 197 ff.

[103] On this topic see the excellent review article, Schofield (1984).

[104] Diogenes VII 161.

[105] Plutarch, *Sto rep.* 7, 1034 c-d. I follow the text in Cherniss' edition, *Plutarch's Moralia* xiii.2, Loeb Classical Library, Cambridge, MA, 1976. Note that here *phronēsis* is used in a specific sense as well as the sense of being the general basis of the virtues; this is also apparent in the Galen passage below.

in situations of danger for bravery, of stress for anger, and so on? Plutarch, who is a hostile witness, draws a familiar unwelcome consequence: on this analysis of virtue, are the individual virtues really distinct? Emplasizing the role of *phronēsis* seems to lead not just to the reciprocity of the virtues but to the conclusion that the virtues form a unity: they are all just *phronēsis*, and different contexts of activity do not individuate distinct virtues, but have an external relation to virtue: they are merely its fields of operation.

We do not know Zeno's response, if any, but we do know that one of his followers, Ariston of Chios, who in many respects took an independent line,[106] did hold a strong form of the unity of virtue thesis.

> Ariston of Chios made virtue one in essence [*ousia*] and called it health. And it was by their being somehow in relation to something[107] that he made them different and plural, as if one were to want to call our sight 'white-sight' when it grasps white things, 'black-sight' when it grasps black things, and so on. Virtue when it considers what is to be done and what not to be done is called intelligence; when it orders desire and defines the moderate and timely in our pleasures it is called temperance; and when it takes part in social relations and contracts it is called justice—as a knife is one thing though it cuts now one thing and now another, and fire acts on different materials but by using a single nature.[108]

We have one of Ariston's arguments for this, though it depends on a premise that probably only Stoics would grant,[109] and, more importantly, an attempt to deal with the problem of the counter-intuitive nature of the thesis:

> Ariston thought that there was one capacity of the soul, by which we reason, and held that the virtue of the soul was one also: knowledge of goods and evils. When one has to choose the good and to avoid the bad, he calls this knowledge temperance; when one has to do good things and not do bad, intelligence; courage, when one is confident about some things but avoids others; and when one distributes to each according to his worth, justice. To put it briefly: when the soul recognizes what is good and bad apart from action, that is wisdom and knowledge; but when it comes to the actions of life, it is given several names (those just mentioned), being called intelligence, temperance, justice and courage.[110]

In everyday life we identify and name distinct virtues by distinct areas of action; but our reflective theoretical account identifies what virtue really is, i.e., the intelligence which is differently applied. The needs of practice are different from the needs of

---

[106] See Ioppolo (1980). Ioppolo points out that Zeno's immediate followers often took an independent line, and that 'Stoic orthodoxy' was established only by Chrysippus' successful attempt to meet their points and strengthen a more Zenonian line. Later writers wrongly regard the earlier disciples like Ariston as having been 'unorthodox' or 'heretical' at the time.

[107] One of the Stoic categories; see Annas and Barnes (1985), pp. 134–135.

[108] Plutarch, *Virt mor* 2, 440 e–441 a.

[109] Anon. Commentary on the *Theaetetus* col. 11, 12–40. The Stoics grant that *euphuia*, excellence of natural endowment, is a single state; if this is, then virtue must be also. See Ioppolo (1980), pp. 120–23, 234–36, Schofield (1984), p. 91.

[110] Galen, *PHP* vii 434.31 ff.

theoretical definition and understanding.[111] This passage casts light on the many apparently 'intellectualistic' Stoic definitions of virtue which characterize it merely as knowledge or skill. They are philosophical definitions; they are not meant to undermine or cast doubt on our everyday use in practice of distinct virtue terms.[112]

It seems to have been Chrysippus who established an account of virtue which managed to retain the thesis that there are many virtues, and to treat it as more than a bare concession to practice, while retaining the results of philosophical reflection as to the unifying role of *phronēsis*. What we find as the standard Stoic account is certainly best read this way. The reciprocity of the virtues is explicitly stated and a troubling corollary drawn:

> [The Stoics] say that the virtues are reciprocal [*antakolouthein*, imply one another], not only in that the person who has one has them all but in that the person who does any action in accordance with one of them does it in accordance with all.[113]

We can reconstruct the grounds for this. The person with even one virtue, if she has it fully, has *phronēsis*; but to have this is to have every virtue. But then virtue will consist in *phronēsis*, and what appear intuitively as different kinds of actions (just, self-controlled) will be exercises of the same disposition in different contexts. But then the just person, who acts in accordance with justice, will really be acting in accordance with *phronēsis*. But to do this is to act in accordance with all the virtues.

The Stoics, however, tackle this counter-intuitive consequence. We do not have to conclude, according to Chrysippus, that the good person is always being brave, or the bad person always cowardly or self-indulgent; they are these things only in response to certain definite stimuli.

> All the virtues which are types of knowledge, and expertises, have principles [*theōrēmata*] in common, and their aim, as has been said, is the same, which is why they are inseparable, for the person who has one has them all, and the person who acts according to one of them acts according to all. But they differ from one another in their main points. For with intelligence the main points are, principally, thinking about and acting on what should be done, and secondarily thinking about what one should distribute <and what one should choose and what one should endure> with the aim of doing what should be done unerringly. With temperance the particular main point is rendering one's impulses stable and thinking, principally, about them, and secondarily about what falls under the other virtues, with the aim of behaving unerringly in one's impulses. And similarly courage is principally concerned with everything one should endure, and secondarily with what falls under the other virtues; and justice principally considers what concerns the worth of each person, but secondarily the rest. For all the virtues consider what concerns them all, even those subordinate to one another.[114]

---

[111] I agree here with Schofield (1984), pp. 90–91, against Ioppolo (1980) that Ariston is not himself here indicating a difference between theoretical and practical virtue. Cf. Sextus, *M* XI 184, where it is said that the Stoics explicitly call *phronēsis* an *epistēmē theōrētikē tōn te agathōn kai kakōn kai oudeterōn*, in the context of a discussion of *phronēsis* as the *technē tou biou*.

[112] Ariston's non-orthodoxy on virtue does not affect this point.

[113] Plutarch, *Sto rep* 1046 e; cf. Arius 63.6 ff.

[114] Arius 63.6–26.

How exactly are we to understand 'main points' (*ta kephalaia*)? It is an ordinary imprecise term being used in a technical way. The best way of understanding it is surely via the idea of a perspective.[115] The virtues share their 'principles'.[116] That is, there is no *intellectual* difference between the particular virtues, for the intellectual basis of each of them is simply the global intellectual basis of the virtuous person's life as a whole. But the difference between them cannot reside in emotions. This is directly obvious for the Stoics, since they hold that all emotions are faulty and virtue requires their suppression. However, an Aristotelian could not do much better. For *phronēsis* is a global intellectual basis for the virtuous life as a whole, and its exercise will on any occasion require the appropriate co-operation of many kinds of emotion. What, then, *is* the difference between the virtues? It is an intellectual difference of a kind—but one of priority rather than that of content. To be truly courageous, one must have a global grasp of what courage requires; as we have seen, this will be incomplete until it contains grasp of what justice and the other virtues require, but still there is a viewpoint from which considerations of what courage requires come *first*, and this is courage. Similarly, the viewpoint from which the concerns of justice are taken first is justice, though justice requires a grasp of the concerns of the other virtues also if the proper judging and balancing of different factors is to be successful.

Antiochus takes this conception of the unity of the virtues into his hybrid theory, though without any of the arguments motivating its acceptance, and leaving it somewhat vaguely stated.[117] After sketching the requirements of justice (which he takes, following the Stoics, to requires impartiality) he says that although these are peculiar (*propria*) to justice, they are so in a way which leaves them common to the other virtues, so that justice will both promote and require the other virtues. This in turn is so because, while the virtues are inseparable,[118] still each has its own function (*munus*); courage is shown in toils and dangers, moderation in forgoing pleasures, and so on. Thus the separateness of the virtues is shown in their having distinct areas of application and distinct behavioural expressions. But they are united, Antiochus says interestingly,[119] by each virtue having an other-regarding aspect;[120] this shows itself in different ways, but is most clearly seen in justice. Antiochus thus brings out more explicitly than the other theories do the point that what unites the virtues is not just practical intelligence, but practical intelligence which gives others what is due to them, perhaps at the cost of one's own interests.

On this way of considering it, we can see that what is important about virtue is indeed intelligence, the agent's unified and global grasp of correct priorities in her

---

[115] Long and Sedley (1987, 61 D) actually translate *ta kephalaia* as 'perspectives'.

[116] The word for 'principle', *theōrēma*, means 'theorem' in logical contexts, and expresses the idea that virtuous knowledge is firm and well-established. See chapter 2, section 4, pp. 95ff.

[117] *Fin* V 65–68.

[118] 67: '*haec coniunctio confusioque virtutum*'. . .'*cum ita copulatae connexaeque sint ut omnes omnium participes sint nec ali ab alia possit separari*'. This suggests reciprocity rather than unity, but Antiochus may not care much about the difference between these two; he is mainly concerned to deny that the virtues are independent of one another.

[119] Though without bringing it into any connection with his previous statements about interconnectedness.

[120] 67: '*Quando igitur inest in omni virtute cura quaedam quasi foras spectans aliosque appetens atque complectens*'.

life as a whole. But this does not force us into taking intelligence as monolithic. It takes the form of courage when considerations of how to deal with danger are what come first, and other considerations are brought in mainly to achieve the correct decision in this area. It takes the form of self-control when the first considerations are those of how to deal with bodily pleasures. There is no difference in content; but there is a difference in perspective, the point of view from which you begin. This is the 'prior' or 'first' perspective, not temporally, but in the sense, presumably, that in any situation some aspects will be more salient and others more recessive, and the perspective of bravery, for example, is one from which considerations of bravery are the most salient. We can, then, avoid absurdities such as that the good person is always being brave—avoid them philosophically, and not just by retreat to pragmatic common sense. For the good person's intelligence is always operating, but it is not always operating from the perspective of finding considerations relevant to bravery to be the most salient in the situation.

It is the Stoic account of virtue that best keeps the balance between taking seriously the point that there are many virtues, and also taking seriously the philosophical reflection that establishes what is essential to virtue as being the global grasp of the agent's good unified from the agent's perspective.

A final point: all of these ways in which *phronēsis* unifies the virtues seem to lead to a startling result: nobody is actually virtuous. For if failure to be fully virtuous in any area undermines the claim to be virtuous in any other, then the standard for having any virtue has been set so high (having them all, no less) that it is beyond the capacity of anyone.

Whether this matters depends on the role in the theory played by the notion of virtue. Modern discussions of virtue tend to stay at the level of realistic description; this indeed is one reason why theses like those of the unity or reciprocity of the virtues tend to sound to us odd and unmotivated. In ancient theories, however, although the virtues are introduced as states that we might plausibly have, this is not treated as what defines the notion of a virtue. By the time we have thought through the implications of the affective and especially the intellectual aspects of virtue, we can see that what we see displayed in action may fall short of what is required for possession of a virtue. For what from the outside meets obvious criteria for being a brave action, say, might be performed in a variety of defective ways. The agent may have simply acted in panic or on a stray feeling. Or she may have acted, but without the appropriate feelings, in a merely self-controlled way. Or she might have acted with the proper feelings and as a result of appreciating that the situation called for bravery, but nonetheless may have performed an action that was in some way out of harmony with the balance of values in her life. Once we accept the need to take the structure of a virtue seriously, it points us towards an ideal of the fully virtuous person, which functions as a normative ideal even if never met with in real life. Thus it is not surprising that the fully virtuous person, with complete possession of *phronēsis*, is an ideal, and functions as such.[121]

Something not dissimilar occurs in many modern theories. We begin by looking for the conditions for being a moral agent, understanding this as something which

---

[121] Thus all the theories imply a notion of moral progress, proceeding towards the ideal. For the Stoics this notion of moral progress (*prokopē*) is complicated by their beliefs about virtue; see chapter 19.

actual people sometimes achieve. But as the theory progresses, we find that these conditions are so demanding that no actual people are moral agents. This is not a fault in itself; if we clearly recognize a moral ideal for what it is, we can clearly see its force and appeal. Some modern theories, however, are left with a vast difference of kind between ideal and reality, which they are forced to span with strategies for achieving the ideal indirectly, or for introducing two levels, on one of which the agent accepts the theory while rejecting it on the other. Ancient theories are not driven to these strategies, because the normative ideal of the fully virtuous person is simply the ordinary person who has progressed in becoming virtuous, developing the affective and intellectual aspects until they form a complete harmony.

4. *The Structure of Moral Reasoning: Rules and Insight*

We have seen how important the agent's moral reasoning is. It is because an individual virtue requires correct reasoning that a virtue is not a mechanical habit but the result of practice in giving and acting on reasons. And the demands on this reasoning, when thought through, unify the virtues; for to have even one virtue the agent must be capable of appreciating the values and balancing the priorities involved in exercising any virtue.[122]

What is the structure of this moral reasoning? Different schools give different answers and we find development within schools. We find a refreshing absence of rigid initial assumptions that all moral reasoning must be of the same form or must be reducible to the same form. Modern moral theories often handicap themselves in this way. Thus, consequentialists often assume that all moral reasoning is, or is readily reducible to, reasoning how to maximize some single end (happiness or welfare). This assumption, however, means that kinds of reasoning which are obviously relevant to the attaining of this end, but which are not maximizing (such as following general rules) have to be dealt with in an unsatisfactory way. Either they are excluded as not being moral reasoning, just because they are not of the favoured form; thus following rules gets labelled 'rule-worship' and taken to be a non-moral or even counter-moral thing to do. Or they are given status as moral forms of reasoning by being in some way justified by the maximizing kind; thus following a rule can count as employing a morally respectable form of reasoning if the content of the rule can be justified by maximizing reasoning, or if maximizing reasoning can justify the agent's following the rule, even if it cannot justify the content of the rule, and so on.[123]

In the ancient theories there is no such advance privilege given to a single form of reasoning. What we find is rather an attempt to show how ordinary reasoning can first, in the person who aims to be virtuous, start getting it right, and then develop to the point of full virtue. The fully virtuous person may reason differently from the

---

[122] Though, as we have seen, this need not threaten the distinctness of the virtues, since on any occasion this reasoning will be done from a perspective of a particular virtue, which will consider the most salient particular claims first.

[123] Modern forms of consequentialism have devoted vast amounts of time and ingenuity to this exercise. The kinds of non-maximizing reasoning, and the ways of excluding or incorporating them within maximizing, are more numerous and produce more problems than one example would suggest.

beginner; but the beginner's reasoning is transformed, rather than abandoned or downgraded. Again, skills give us a useful general picture: the expert musician will approach the playing of a piece of music differently from the learner; but this is because she no longer needs to go through the thoughts that the beginner has, not because the beginner is having the wrong kind of thoughts.

Epicurus' is the simplest account of moral reasoning, and the least developed. It can at first sight appear similar to modern consequentialism; for Epicurus holds that our goal in life is to seek pleasure, and the goal of intelligence or *phronēsis* is to achieve this as best we can.[124] A notorious passage in the *Letter to Menoeceus* seems to suggest that the role of practical reasoning is to maximize the agent's pleasure.

> Since this [pleasure] is the primary aim and is innate to us—for that reason we do not choose every pleasure, but sometimes we pass over many pleasures, when greater annoyance follows for us from them, and we judge many pains superior to pleasures, when greater pleasure follows along for us when we endure the pains for a long time. Every pleasure, therefore, because of having a nature which is familiar to us [*oikeian*] is a good, but not every pleasure is to be chosen, just as every pain is a bad thing, but not every pain is always naturally to be avoided. However, one should judge all these matters by measuring together [*summetrēsei*] and looking at the advantages and disadvantages, for we make use of the good on some occasions as a bad thing, and the bad, conversely, as a good.[125]

Many have been tempted to see here a crude anticipation of Bentham's calculus to aid us in maximizing our end, pleasure. But appearances are deceptive; there are two important factors in Epicurean ethics which put such constraints on practical reasoning within it that the model that finally emerges is very different from any modern one.

First, the pleasure which we seek is not a simple feeling, as Bentham assumed. Pleasure is our final end, and as such has to answer to the formal constraints discussed in the previous chapter. At the least, it must be something capable of organizing and focussing all the concerns and aims of my life as a whole; it must encompass everything worthwhile in my life. Pleasure understood as a feeling hardly seems a promising candidate to do this; and Epicurus distinguishes between kinds of pleasure, saying that the pleasure we seek as our final end is static, not kinetic pleasure. Static pleasure is taken to be *ataraxia*, the state of being untroubled, unhindered in one's activities: the condition of normal activity that is not bothered by any interference.[126]

Such an aim, however, is clearly not definite enough to allow of quantification even of a Benthamite kind. Pleasure understood as an untroubled overall state is not

---

[124] Sometimes it is philosophy which has this role, not intelligence; see p. 79. Epicurus thinks that we need practical intelligence to act well, and that we need philosophy to give our practical intelligence the theoretical backing it needs to be securely grounded. He does not greatly care whether we stress the theoretical or the practical aspect of the reasoning required for living well.

[125] *Ep Men* 129–130.

[126] The distinction between static and kinetic pleasures is a difficult one: see Cicero, *Fin* I 37–9, II 9; Diogenes X 136, U 68, *KD* 3. On textual problems in the Diogenes passage see Gosling and Taylor (1982), pp. 388–91. For *ataraxia* as an explication of static pleasure, see U 416, 417 and Diogenes of Oenoanda fr. 2 8–13. Static pleasure is natural in that it results from fulfilling natural desires: cf. *KD* 18, 21, *VS* 21, U 417. On natural desires see chapter 7.

the kind of thing that we can produce units of; nor does it even allow of quantitative comparison of an ordinal kind in any obvious way.[127] Once pleasure is understood as it has to be in an ancient theory where it forms the agent's final end, we see that it is not the kind of thing that the agent can coherently try to maximize.

Second, Epicurus insists that to achieve pleasure the agent must have the virtues. Sometimes his language suggests that the virtues are the best instrumental means for achieving pleasure;[128] but sometimes he suggests that the virtues have intrinsic value for the agent, since virtuous activity makes up and is part of the pleasure (of the right kind, of course) which the agent seeks.[129] On either characterization, however, the agent cannot achieve pleasure by merely calculating the consequences of acts, as in modern theories. Having the virtues involves, as we have seen, having the disposition to do certain acts and also to have achieved a certain kind of affective state. Since having a virtue does not reduce to performing certain acts, the Epicurean will achieve pleasure only by aiming at being a certain kind of person, not by sticking to the limited task of working out the consequences of actions.

So how does Epicurean practical reasoning proceed? At a general level, Epicurus' strategy is just that of all the schools: the agent should aim at being a virtuous person and achieving her final aim, taking care first that this is correctly conceived—which involves learning Epicurean doctrine. He also has a more precise practical strategy, however, in his theory of kinds of desires. All desires are of three kinds, natural, necessary and not necessary. The Epicurean will satisfy only natural and necessary desires, avoiding those which are neither natural nor necessary and whose force derives from faulty beliefs.[130]

Epicurus' account of practical intelligence—good practical reasoning—thus lacks many features defining a modern maximizing model of morality. The end to be achieved is not determinate enough to allow reduction to quantitative calculation. Nor can the end be achieved by working out the consequences of actions alone; for the desired end is the right kind of pleasure, and this comes only to the person who has acquired the virtues to the point of having the desired inner state and not merely producing the right actions. Epicurus' talk of getting less pain and more pleasure has to be spelled out by a strategy of fulfilling only certain kinds of desire, of becoming a certain kind of person, and not merely of doing those actions whose pleasure-producing consequences can be calculated.

Epicurus thus avoids the crudities of modern maximizing models.[131] The cost of this is a certain indeterminacy in Epicurean practical reasoning. Interestingly, we find

---

[127] It might be claimed that there could be degrees of an untroubled overall state, in which case the agent could aim at getting as much as possible of it. Epicurus' view of the completeness of our final end makes this view untenable, however (see chapter 16). The agent could still be thought of as trying to get as near as possible to an ideal which is not itself a matter of degree; but there is no basis for taking this in a quantitative way either.

[128] As, for example, at Diogenes X 138, U 70, 512.

[129] See Diogenes X 138, U 506, *Fin* I 50: virtue alone is inseparable from pleasure; also *KD* 5, *Fin* I 57: virtue and pleasure are mutually entailing; *Ep Men* 132, which repeats this and adds that the virtues have grown to be a part of (*sumpephukasi*) pleasure. See Annas (1987).

[130] *Ep Men* 127, *KD* 29 with scholion, *VS* 21, *KD* 30. There are problems with the division, notably whether all three kinds of desire are really on a level. The topic is discussed in greater detail in chapter 7.

[131] It could be objected that not all maximizing models need be crude; how crude they are depends on how crudely their final ends are conceived. For attempts to get away from the limitations of classic models, see Griffin (1986) and Slote (1989).

in Epicurus the reverse of a line of argument found in Sidgwick and many modern consequentialists. Sidgwick argues that if pleasure is to be a fit end in our lives, it must be understood determinately, as a definite feeling that there can clearly be differing amounts of. Only with such a conception will we avoid vagueness and have something to direct us to definite and unambiguous particular choices.[132] But Epicurus is like Mill in being chiefly struck by the fact the pleasure so understood cannot possibly serve as a *summum bonum*, an overall aim that can plausibly encompass everything valuable in life. Hence he insists on understanding pleasure more broadly, accepting the consequences that pleasure cannot then serve a simple quantity to be maximized, and that trying to achieve pleasure will not give us a simple, effective model of moral reasoning.[133] Clearly Epicurus could not have proceeded in this way if he had thought that his theory required a maximizing model of moral reasoning. This is not so much an insight of Epicurus in particular as simply an implication of taking seriously the eudaimonist structure of moral theory.[134]

Epicurus seems in fact not to have cared very much about the precise form *phronēsis* took. He seems to have relied on a combination of two strategies, one theoretical and one practical, without worrying too much about their precise relation. On the one hand the aspiring pleasure-seeker must study Epicurean philosophy, learn Epicurus' words and internalize doctrines in various ways. This will revise her conception of pleasure and of the virtues, so that her conception of her practical aim, and of the nature of her desires, is now free from pre-Epicurean mistakes. On the other hand, she must scrutinize her desires on each occasion of choice to check that they are now going in the right direction, and monitor them for mistakes: 'To all our desires we should pose this question: What will I get out of it if what I seek through this desire is achieved? And what if it is not?'[135] As long as we combine learning Epicurean theory with practical self-monitoring, Epicurus does not seem to care very much exactly what form our reasonings take. The stress on memorizing Epicurus' saying and doctrines implies that a certain amount of it must take the form of rule-following, though presumably the fully enlightened Epicurean would have internalized these rules so successfully as not to have to keep consciously checking back to them.

Aristotle's account of the form of the virtuous agent's reasoning is much richer than Epicurus'. Virtue is a *hexis proairētikē*, a dispositional state involving choice, *proairesis*. Just because virtue is not a mechanical habit, the virtuous person chooses or decides what to do when acting virtuously. Faced by a temptation to be greedy, I nonetheless act in a just way, say. This decision is not a reflex; it is the product of reasoning into which the claims of both gratification and of virtue have entered. Aristotle calls this reasoning *bouleusis* or deliberation, and discusses it in *Nicomachean Ethics,* Book III, chapter 3. Deliberation is *practical* reasoning: we deliberate about what to do, in a case where we can do something:

[132](1907), Book I ch. 7, Book II esp. chs. 2 and 3.

[133] Sidgwick criticizes Mill for this; his criticisms carry over to Epicurus. See (1907), p. 93 n. 1, pp. 94–5.

[134] How then can Mill be like Epicurus on this score? Mill, in striking contrast to Sidgwick, takes the notion of our *summum bonum* very seriously, and his arguments about pleasure contrast strongly with Sidgwick's because he thinks of pleasure as a candidate for being our overall aim in an entire life.

[135] *VS* 71.

> We deliberate about what comes about through us, but not always in the same
> way, e.g., about medicine and money-making. . . . We deliberate not about
> ends but about ways of achieving ends. A doctor does not deliberate whether he
> shall heal, nor an orator whether he shall persuade, nor a politician whether he
> shall produce law and order, nor does any other such person deliberate about the
> end. Rather they posit the end and enquire how and by what ways it is to come
> about. If it appears that it will come about through several, they consider which
> way will achieve this most easily and finely; if it is produced through one, they
> consider how it is to come about through that, and again how that itself is
> brought about, until they come to the first cause, which is last in the order of
> discovery. For someone deliberating seems to enquire and analyse in the above
> way, as in the case of a diagram. (It appears that, while not all enquiry is
> deliberation—the mathematical kinds, for example—all deliberation is enquiry.)
> The last item in the analysis is the first to come into being.[136]

It has been frequently pointed out that this is not simply means-end reasoning, since
the Greek phrase *ta pros to telos* covers more than the means-end relation. The
contrast is between an end and a way of achieving the end. Sometimes this might be
a means of achieving it; I want to be rich, say, and consider various means of
achieving this. In such cases the means will not be valued for its own sake, but
merely for its contribution to the end; and as a result of this, means will be
interchangeable if they have the same value for achieving the end. But there will also
be cases where what I do to achieve the end bears a more intimate relation to the
end than this. I want a satisfying career, for example: becoming an architect is not a
'mere' means to this, something I value only for its contribution to the end. Rather it
is a way of achieving the end which involves specifying the end in one way rather
than another: discovering the right way of achieving the end involves determining
just what one's end really is.[137] Nonetheless, means-end reasoning does fall under
deliberation, to which it seems essential that there is some working out or problem-
solving. Aristotle indeed illustrates it with an example of mathematical problem-
solving.

The aspect of deliberation which has attracted most modern attention is the
problem of the status of the ends which deliberation achieves. We are, after all,
talking about the virtuous agent. Is virtuous reasoning shown only in puzzling out
how to achieve the agent's ends, and not in deciding what these ends are to be? If so,
Aristotle's picture will be the following unattractive one: the agent by habituation
just comes to have the right ends, while his reasoning abilities are developed only on
how to achieve these ends that he has acquired in a non-rational way.[138]

It is obvious, however, that this is not Aristotle's picture. It is obvious even from
considering the point that deliberation works out ways of achieving the agent's ends
which go beyond being mere means. It is absurd to think that I have, by non-rational
habituation, the end of having a satisfying career, and use reason to work out that I

---

[136] *NE* 1112 b 3–24.

[137] The notion of specification here is taken from Wiggins (1980), which contains some perceptive
corrections of the view put forward by, among others, Allan (1953) and (1955). Nonetheless, I think that
Wiggins runs together two issues, the issue of the status of ends and the issue of the place of rules in
practical reasoning. I deal with them separately below.

[138] There is a surprisingly large secondary literature on this. See Wiggins (1980) and Sorabji (1980) for
references to earlier discussions.

will have this by becoming an architect. As stressed, working out that becoming an architect will be a way of having a satisfying career involves thinking about what my end is, not about a separable means to an already determined end. To reason about how to achieve our ends, we have to reason in some ways about our ends. The orator, as Aristotle says, does not deliberate whether to persuade; but in deliberating about how best to persuade he is bound to reflect on what exactly his end of persuasion is, for how he goes about it will partly determine whether it is, for example, wise policy or demagoguery.

The Book III account, however, does put in the foreground the process of working out, and distinguishes sharply between the end and the way of achieving it. In Book VI Aristotle returns to practical reasoning, this time in the context of the fully virtuous person rather than the person learning to be virtuous. He discusses *phronēsis* or intelligence, and, as we have seen, insists that it involves not only ingenuity and the problem-solving abilities characterizing cleverness, but also virtue; the person with perverted ends will not make intelligent decisions. Aristotle insists, in Book VI, Chapters 2 and 13, that in a virtuous person the ability to reason and having a virtuous state of character are inseparable. There is such a thing as a neutral cleverness, but the virtuous person does not have this *plus* having the right ends; rather he makes the right judgement because his feelings and emotions guide him the right way and make him sensitive to the right factors, and because he is able intelligently to discern what in the situation is the morally salient factor. Intelligence, *phronēsis*, requires that in the agent the affective and the intellectual aspects of virtue have developed together in a mutually reinforcing way.

We have seen from the above sections why this, and nothing less, is the demand made on the virtuous person (by all the schools, not just Aristotle). Here we shall ask what the impact is on our problem-solving picture of virtuous reasoning; and Book VI presents us with a difficulty. In the initial picture the stress was on working out, puzzling through; the analogy was with working out a piece of mathematics. But in the fully developed virtuous agent there is so much stress on the way that thought and feeling work together that there seems no room for working out; in some famous passages Aristotle stresses rather the immediacy of the virtuous person's judgement as to what is right, and the analogue becomes that of perception, of 'just seeing' what the right thing to do is.[139] Some have actually thought that Aristotle is, at least in Book VI, an intuitionist, thinking that the virtuous agent at least does not reason at all about what the right thing is to do, but simply sees what is required. The label 'intuitionist' is dangerous, since in modern moral philosophy it is often used for a position including two theses: that the agent is immediately sensitive to moral factors, rather than reasoning about them; and that this is all that goes on—the agent's judgements have no further backing. Such a position is clearly superficial; but no ancient theory stresses immediacy of sensitivity on its own, without considering its source. The person who is immediately aware of what she should do is the fully virtuous person; her judgements come from a developed virtue, a rational

---

[139] The most striking passage in Book VI is 1142 a 23–30, which says that intelligence is perception of a kind, though not the ordinary kind. See Wiggins (1980); also Woods (1986) and Nussbaum (1985). Note that there are some anticipations before Book VI of the thesis that 'the judgement lies in perception' (1109 b 23, 1126 b 4), but it is only in Book VI that it is worked out in a context which makes clear what the requirements for this are.

as well as emotional state. So the word 'intuitionism' is best avoided; it now suggests too simplistic a position.[140]

There is still the point that Book III suggests that the virtuous agent has to work out what to do before deciding to do it, whereas in Book VI there seems no room for this: the fully virtuous person embodies such harmony of thought and feeling that she does not have to work out what to do: she is immediately sensitive to it. When the mathematical example recurs in Book VI, what is stressed is not the problem-solving but the direct insight into what is needed to solve it:

> Intelligence's object is the final term, of which there is no knowledge but perception—not perception of its special objects but that by which we perceive that the last term in a mathematical case is a triangle, for there is where it stops.[141]

We can see why Aristotle gives us these two pictures. In Book III he is talking about the person acquiring virtue; and the learner does to some degree take his end for granted (since he may still be in part imitating someone or following advice) and does have to put effort into considering, thinking about and working out the various factors relevant to acting (for although he has the right ideas about what to do, they are still not fully internalized; he is still tempted by factors contrary to virtue, since his feelings are still not completely in harmony with his judgements). So the learner will be working out how to achieve his end. But the fully virtuous person will be different, for reasons we have already seen. His virtuous end will be fully internalized; his feelings and emotions will be fully in harmony with his judgements as to what is worth pursuing and what not. Further, as we have seen, these judgements will be strongly unified; as the virtues develop, they do not develop in potential conflict with one another, since they all develop from the unified basis of *phronēsis*. So when such a fully virtuous agent is faced by a decision as to what to do, there does indeed seem no room for, because no need for, working out what to do. Working out would be needed if the agent had to balance conflicting considerations; but, as we have seen, the varying claims on the agent that spring from the sources of the different virtues have already been adjusted. And working out would be needed if the agent had to consider the force of differently appealing factors; but the fully virtuous person will not be tempted by, or take pleasure in, what is contrary to virtue. So to the fully virtuous person it is *obvious* what the right thing to do is. And we find one pattern of practical thinking in the learner, another in the fully virtuous.

Is this problematic? Two considerations soften the apparent harshness of this conclusion. First, even the fully virtuous person may have a hard time making a decision when faced by problems that do not spring from reasons of virtue. On the

---

[140] As Sidgwick, for example, uses the word 'intuitionist', it clearly means only that we grasp something (he thinks, rules or principles) directly and not via working them out from more basic premises. There is no confusion of intuition with a kind of moral sense which picks out qualities 'just by looking'. This confusion was introduced, I suspect, by the work of G. E. Moore, and the debased use of 'intuition' for what we 'just see', as we see that something is yellow, has muddled much twentieth-century discussion. It is still possible, for example, to find discussions which lump together Moore, Ross and Prichard as 'intuitionists', as though they all held a single substantial thesis about intuition, when in fact their theories are strikingly different over what intuition is, as well as over its scope and objects.

[141] *NE* 1142 a 26-29.

one hand, problems are created by bad or inadequate information, uncertainties, difficulties in interpreting empirical aspects of situations. On the other, what creates the need for deliberation and decision may well be those aspects of situations which are due to non-moral factors; money may have to be weighed against ambition, for example. So even the fully virtuous may have a lot of problem-solving and working out to do. Indeed, Aristotle says that it is the *phronimos* who is thought to be best at deliberating.[142] But the virtuous person will have the right framework within which these claims are to be judged.

Second, the fully virtuous person is, as already stressed, a normative ideal to which we aspire. There are certainly no actual people who are immediately and unfailingly sensitive to all the salient moral features of every situation. The point of the ideal is to emphasize the limitations on our forms of reasoning; *we* have to work out what we should do, but that is because of our limitations. The perfectly virtuous person would not work things out the way we do, only in an ever more ingenious way; she would not have to work things out at all.

Thus, the better one's moral reasoning gets, the less one is aware of it in one's life. The better I get at deliberating and working out what to do, the less I will need to deliberate, for the more obvious it will become to me what the morally salient features of the situation in front of me are. We can see that this idea owes something to the model of a skill which is prominent in the ancient conception of virtue, and also something to the stress on development and moral growth that goes with taking virtue and hence character as primary. Ancient theories all share this stress on the difference between being a learner and being morally mature. The ideal agent of modern theories like consequentialism is a perfect reasoner, and the difference between ordinary people and the ideal moral agent is for modern theories often taken to lie merely in the feebleness of everyday ability to reason and the prevalence in our lives of blocking factors, like ignorance, prejudice and laziness. The ideal moral agent, in modern theories, is thus seen as the completely unimpeded reasoner.

Aristotle also has some interesting things to say about practical reasoning in the central books of the *Ethics*; unfortunately these seem not to be thought through and remain suggestive rather than definitive. Further, it is puzzling how they relate to the perceptual, sensitivity model of the virtuous agent.[143] In the central books of the *Nicomachean Ethics* (which are shared with the *Eudemian Ethics*), the *de Anima* and the *de Motu Animalium* Aristotle gives examples to illustrate a thesis about practical reasoning. (It is an interesting point that even in the ethical works, where the context is that of a discussion of the virtuous agent, none of the examples are unambiguously examples of *moral* reasoning.) It would have been significant if Aristotle had pointed out what he took the standard form of an agent's practical reasoning to be, especially if he had indicated whether this is affected by considerations of virtue. One of his examples seems to illustrate just the sort of problem-solving that

---

[142] *NE* 1141 b 8–10.

[143] There is an enormous literature on the so-called practical syllogism. See Cooper (1975); Nussbaum (1978), Essay 4; Charles (1984); Dahl (1984), as well as works which they cite. Here I am more than usually conscious that my own interpretation gives somewhat short shrift to discussions which are scholarly and careful. The interested reader is referred to these works for interpretations some of which do find in Aristotle a coherent and systematic theory.

characterized the beginner in virtue in *Nicomachean Ethics* Book III (except that here the subject-matter does not explicitly involve virtue):

> I need a covering; a cloak is a covering; I need a cloak. What I need, I should make;[144] I need a cloak; I should make a cloak. And the conclusion, the I should make a cloak, is an action. Now he acts from a starting point. If there is to be a cloak, necessarily there must be this first, and if this, *this*; and *this* he does at once.[145]

This everyday piece of reasoning is considered from both the agent's and a spectator's viewpoint; if Aristotle is making a point in moving from 'I' to 'he' that point may be that the considerations that weigh with the agent when reasoning what to do will be the very same considerations as enable someone else to explain what the agent is doing. The problem with this example, however, is that it comes from a passage where Aristotle talks about practical reasoning in a way that does not fit the example. Surprisingly, he talks about *syllogisms* concerned with actions. Aristotle is the inventor of syllogistic logic: he is encouraging us, by his use of terms taken from logic, like 'premise' and 'conclusion', and especially by talk of a conclusion resulting from two premises,[146] to think of something like a syllogism in logic: a sound argument where from two premises of some appropriate form a conclusion is validly drawn. But no piece of *practical* reasoning can be an Aristotelian syllogism;[147] practical reasoning is concerned with particulars, as Aristotle himself stresses, whereas Aristotelian syllogisms contain no singular terms.[148]

Aristotle gives us some examples that do seem meant to be analogous at least to syllogisms in logic. Just before the cloak example he says:

> Here the conclusion from the two premises is the action—for example, whenever someone thinks that all humans should walk, and that he is a human, he walks right away; but if he thinks that no human should now walk, and that he is human, at once he stays still.[149]

But these examples, as is obvious enough, are not remotely the same kind of thing as the cloak example. Where that reproduced a piece of practical reasoning that someone might go through when working out what to do, these examples do not reproduce examples of anyone's practical reasoning. They contain sound reasoning

---

[144] The word here is *poiēton*, a gerundive form, not a first-person form.

[145] *MA* 701 a 17–22.

[146] Aristotle has, just before the cloak example, talked of the 'conclusion' resulting from 'the two premises'. For an extremely thorough and useful survey of Aristotle's use of syllogistic terminology in connection with practical reasoning, see Charles (1984), Appendix 3. The prevalence of these technical terms shows that Aristotle's use of *sullogismos* cannot be explained away as loosely referring to reasoning, rather than to syllogisms.

[147] I am irresistibly reminded of the satiric efforts of a logician, Lewis Carroll, to squeeze pieces of such reasoning into syllogistic form, in his lampoon 'On the New Belfry of Christ Church, Oxford'. Here is a 'Syllogism in *Festino*: (1) To restore the character of Ch. Ch., a tower must be built (2) To build a tower, ten thousand pounds must be raised; *Ergo*, No time must be lost.' An earlier example, 'in *Barbara*', goes: '(1) Wooden buildings in the midst of stone-work are barbarous (2) Plain rectangular forms in the midst of arches and decorations are barbarous, *Ergo*, The whole thing is ridiculous and revolting'.

[148] At least Aristotle makes no provision for propositions containing singular terms, though there are a couple of odd occurrences of singular terms in the *Pr An*; see Patzig (1968) pp. 4–8.

[149] *MA* 701 a 11–15.

about what I should do, if I am a man and all men should walk; but, despite the 'at once', these thoughts could never lead anyone to walk. For we need the reasoning which is to lead to a *particular* action, and *this* certainly does not follow from the two premises. The decision that could lead to a particular action would only follow given certain massive background assumptions which are not in the reasoning itself. The same holds for Aristotle's other examples of such reasoning: we get little pieces of sound (if obvious) reasoning, not cases of working out what particular action I ought to do.

How can Aristotle put such dissimilar things together? There is no really satisfactory account of this. Perhaps the safest conclusion is simply that Aristotle was struck by the fact that more than one pattern of practical reasoning displays an interesting feature: if one accepts the premises, then, unless something goes wrong, one *has* to act on the conclusion. It is irrational to accept, either that one thinks A good and B a reasonable means to it, or that X ought to be done and now is the time to X—and fail to act accordingly. Aristotle was clearly struck by the analogy that this phenomenon bears to the fact that, in the case of the theoretical syllogism, it is irrational to accept the premises and refuse to accept the conclusion. In both cases there is a kind of *necessity* involved. He seems to have been tempted by the analogy with theoretical reasoning to use, in practical contexts, terms from his own logic, such as 'premise', 'conclusion' and 'middle term'. Some have concluded that he was further tempted to try to work out a canonical form of practical reasoning and perhaps establish which were the valid forms of argument. This goes far beyond the evidence, and involves forcing many passages more than they can bear. If Aristotle did think of developing this kind of project, he did not take it very far.

The project of the 'practical syllogism' had wider scope than ethics; but it raises *en passant* a point which does concern ethical reasoning in particular. Some of the 'practical syllogism' examples retain the form of achieving an end which is clear in the less formal examples.[150] But some have a quite different form: they contain deontic words like 'ought' or 'must', and as Aristotle points out in one example, they take the form of bringing a particular case under a universal deontic prescription:

> Since one supposition and statement is universal and the other is particular (for the one says that such and such a person ought to do such and such a thing, and the other that this now is such and such a thing, and that I am such and such a person) then what does the moving is the latter opinion, not the universal one, or else both, though the former is more static and the latter is not.[151]

They look in fact like cases of rule-following; and this is reasonable, since moral reasoning does intuitively involve some rule-following (though how much is controversial). Unfortunately Aristotle has not mentioned rule-following at all, so it is not clear what role this is meant to play in the thinking of the virtuous. One solution is this: the fully virtuous person no longer has to work out means to given ends, for reasons which we have seen; instead his virtuous thinking will take the form of bringing situations under moral rules, so that his reasoning will be 'rule-case'

---

[150] *MA* 701 a 16–17; *NE* 1142 b 20–26; 1144 a 29–36; 1146 b 35–1147 a 10.
[151] *De An* 434 a 16–21. See also *NE* 1147 a 24-b 17.

reasoning.[152] This explains why the fully virtuous person can immediately 'see' what he should do, but is also described as reasoning and using universal deontic rules: the immediacy is just that of seeing that this case falls under that rule. This explanation is plausible as far as it goes; but if this were Aristotle's model of the virtuous person's reasoning, it is hard to see why he would have developed the analogy with perception as he does, with no rules in the context. The virtuous Aristotelian's 'perception' of what she should do emerges naturally from stress on the co-operative development of the affective and intellectual sides of virtue. As many have noted, it sits ill with a stress on rule-following, and Aristotle does not give us adequate indication of whether we should try to reconcile them as just suggested, or perhaps by regarding the rules as rules of thumb, extracted ex post facto from the virtuous person's intuitive judgements rather than leading him to them.[153] Nor is it easy to see how the problem-solving model of practical reasoning is to fit in. Perhaps Aristotle is thinking of highly general rules, which could be reformulated without too much strain in terms of the pursuit of some good; 'everyone should walk', for example, could be reformulated as 'walking is a good for everyone'. But nothing of this kind is to be found in Aristotle's texts, and the use of the rule examples, especially in the discussion of *akrasia* in *Nicomachean Ethics* VII 3, seems very hard to square with the problem-solving passages.

Aristotle has in fact not thought through the place of rules in the virtuous person's thought. He moves from the problem-solving picture of the learner to the immediate sensitivity picture of the fully virtuous without following through the question of what the structure of the fully virtuous person's thinking will now be. From the 'practical syllogism' passages he seems to think of it as either still that of achieving an end or that of following rules, but this remains merely suggestive, and neither model is firmly linked to the stress on direct sensitivity. It was left for the Stoics to develop, via an initial period of debate, a more satisfactory and systematic model of ethical reasoning and its continuities and the place in it of rules.[154]

We might ask why rules are supposed to be so important; some modern discussions of virtue ethics clearly associate rule-following with derivative, mechanical reasoning and do not see why it should have a place in mature moral considerations.[155] But against this it should be pointed out that rules are not a product of bad theory but an inevitable part of everyday moral practice. A great deal of everyday moral thinking, especially that involved in teaching or learning anything, involves following and enforcing rules.[156] Unless a moral theory is to throw

[152] Allan (1953) and (1955); see n. 137.

[153] The latter is the view defended by Nussbaum (1986a), chs. 9 and 10, where she talks of Aristotle insisting on the priority of the concrete particular.

[154] Some may find this an inadequate account of the place of rules in Aristotle's ethics. There are certainly passages where Aristotle seems to be discussing rules, for example, *Nicomachean Ethics* IX 1–2, where he discusses conflicts of obligations, and *NE* V 10 and *Rhet* I 13, where he discusses the relation of *epieikeia* or 'equity' to law. In none of these passages, however, does Aristotle show any explicit awareness of the need to find a formal role in his theory for rules.

[155] See, however, Clowney (1990), pp. 49–68, who argues that virtue ethics needs an account of rules if it is not to be seriously incomplete. Clowney emphasizes rules in the realm of justice; but they are also important in everyday virtuous reasoning.

[156] Sidgwick indeed takes rule-following to be what is most characteristic of commonsense morality (though he ignores or downplays everyday judgements of character).

commonsense morality overboard and try to build *de novo* it must deal somehow with the fact that a great deal of moral practice takes the form of following rules. (This is indeed what makes it most puzzling that Aristotle has so little to say about rules and their status in his theory.) There is nothing suspicious about this: it might turn out, for example, that rules are merely a preliminary stage, or that the person who can grasp the point of the rules is thereby empowered to modify them.

We find an example of what is probably a commonsense view of this in a passage from the first-century B.C. head of the sceptical Academy, Philo, paraphrased in Arius Didymus. Philo produces an extended three-part comparison of the (ethical) philosopher to the doctor.[157] The doctor must first persuade the patient that she needs treatment, and the philosopher must persuade her 'patient' that she needs to 'convert', to snap out of her present way of life and try to live better. Second, the doctor must apply the remedies, and the philosopher must provide the aspirant with the right goals, putting her on the right track.

> [Third], medicine's whole effort is directed at its end, that is health, and philosophy's whole effort at happiness. Following the argument about ends is the argument about lives. With medicine it is not enough to introduce health; there is also a need to provide instructions (*parangelmata*) about health; people who pay attention to these will keep the good condition of their bodies. Similarly with one's life there is a need for some principles (*theōrēmata*),[158] through which one will be able to keep to one's end. The argument concerning lives is twofold, one particular and one general. The particular should investigate individual matters, for example whether the sensible person should take part in politics or just live under the government, or whether the wise person should marry. The general one should investigate what concerns everyone: for example, What is the best form of government? Should public office be open or restricted? This general argument should be called political, and ought to be ranked by itself as a part of the section on lives because of its extent and its general application.
>
> Now, if everyone could be a wise person, there would be no need for further sections. . . . But we should take forethought for ordinary people too, who are in fact helped by words of direction, since they are not able to find the time for lengthy details, through pressure of time or an unavoidable lack of leisure. So we should introduce the instructive argument, through which they will have the instructions for security and correctness in making use of each thing, in shortened versions.[159]

Thus the person who has reflected about his life and is trying to live better will need to guide and monitor his life by reference to certain principles, which, as we have seen, can be tailored to his situation just as the doctor's instructions are. Philo adds that there are a lot of ordinary people who would also benefit from advice, but have no time or leisure to consider details, so that there is also a place for shortened and potted handbooks of advice on how to act in a correct way. There seems, then,

---

[157] Since Philo writes as an Academic sceptic, the set of ideas he reports is presumably not original with him, but is the accepted framework for discussion and argument. We do not know whether Philo produced any arguments for or against it.

[158] This is the same word which is used by the Stoics for the principles grasped by the virtuous person, and also for theorems in a logical context.

[159] The whole passage runs from 40.1 to 41.25 of Arius.

to be a considerable place for instructions and principles both in busy unrecon-
structed lives and in the lives of those who are trying to live better under the
guidance of reflection and theory. To return to the medical analogy, living well
requires not only curing your diseases but putting you on the right regime, getting
you to adjust to a new lifestyle. And even those who are too rushed to change their
lifestyle by giving up high-cholesterol foods, smoking and so on will benefit from
following a few of the rules, such as 'Don't eat too much fried food' and so on. In
the same way, those who are changing their lives for the better need continuing
instruction, not just general advice about the end to pursue. If it is appropriate for
them to have a family life, they need to follow the principles enabling them to do
this well.

The Stoic account of virtue, in its developed orthodox form, allows a place for
rules which fits the presumably commonsensical picture which we find in Philo. In
fact the Stoic theory of virtue is the one which takes rules most seriously, and in
which we find most debate on the place and function of rules in a theory of virtue.

Virtue, for the Stoics, requires principles, *theōrēmata*. Partly this is just because
Stoic virtues are skills, and all Stoic skills require principles; this is what distinguishes
them from mindless habits.[160] *Aretē* in the sense of moral virtue is indeed
distinguished from other, broader senses of *aretē*, in which it can refer to the
excellence of things like statues, by the fact that the possessor of moral *aretē* grasps
principles.

The use of *theōrēmata* does not imply that the Stoics think of skills, or virtues,
as deductive intellectual structures, as we can see from the fact that Philo quite
unselfconsciously uses the word for everyday practical principles. However, it does
bring out the fact that the Stoics stress more than Aristotle does one aspect of the
skill or expertise model. The beginner does not just go from particular cases or
models to unified insight; part of learning is grasping general rules to follow, and the
expert takes care to inculcate the right rules. Further, the expert need not be seen as
abandoning the rules; rather, she has internalized them, and follows them, though
not in the conscious, deliberate way of the beginner. While the Aristotelian account
of skill and virtue seemed to offer the beginner little in the way of help other than
particular good examples, the Stoics stress that right from the start there are
determinate rules to follow if one is to proceed correctly. For them virtue involves
rules, because they stress the systematic side of any skill.

Further, the Stoic theory of 'due actions' suggests the need for a place in the
theory for rules. According to the Stoics, some of our actions are *kathēkonta* or 'due
actions':

> [T]hey say that a due action is one which when performed has a reasonable
> defence, e.g., what is consistent in life, which extends even to plants and animals;
> for due actions are seen even in their case. . . . [A due action] is an activity
> which in the conditions in accordance with nature is proper [*oikeion*]. Of
> activities done in accordance with impulse some are due actions, others contrary
> to what is due <others neither due actions nor contrary to what is due>. Due
> actions, then, are those which reason chooses to perform, as holds of honouring

---

[160] See the passages in *SVF* III 214, where *logos. . .kata ta theōrēmata* is distinguished from
habituation (*ethos*), III 278, 295.

parents, siblings and country, and relationships with friends. Contrary to what is due are those which reason does not choose to perform, as holds of things like neglecting parents, disregarding siblings, not getting on with friends, disdaining one's country and the like. Neither due actions nor contrary to what is due are those actions which reason neither chooses to perform nor forbids, e.g., picking a fruit, taking hold of a pen or scraper, and the like.[161]

Performing a due action is doing something of a kind which there is good reason for you to do. Even plants and animals do this: there is good reason for plants to grow towards the sun, for carnivorous animals to hunt, and so on. Due actions in all these cases are ways of obtaining natural advantages for the kind of thing in question; that is why there is good reason to do them. The Stoics say that only virtue is good, everything else being (in their technical sense) 'indifferent'. Non-virtuous items that are naturally advantageous, like health, soundness of body and mind, etc., are classified as 'preferred' indifferents (and their contraries as 'dispreferred'). A due action can then be also explained as one which, whether in humans or in animals, plants, etc., is an action of a kind such as to obtain a preferred indifferent. In Arius' exposition the topic of due action 'follows appositely' the topic of indifferents. The two ways of explaining due action thus fit together: it is an action of a kind that there is good reason to do, that can reasonably be defended; and it is an action of a kind that achieves what is a natural advantage (technically a preferred indifferent) for the kind of thing in question.[162] In the case of animals, and still more of plants, the good reason is not one which is entertained by the thing itself; it is the observer, not the plant, that can see that there is good reason for the plant to grow towards the sun. But in the case of humans, the agent can not only have a good reason, but can be aware of it and act because of it; and hence it is only with humans that due actions become the subject of ethical appraisal.

Not all our actions are due actions; some are morally indifferent. The Stoic moral beginner learns to be aware of the kinds of reason she has for acting, to avoid actions that are 'contrary to what is due' and to perform due actions. Learning to be good starts with learning right behaviour. We have seen that becoming virtuous is acquiring a special kind of skill: one's right actions cease to be dependent on following others in each case or on working out afresh what would be the right way to act; the agent's grasp of the rightness of his acts becomes unified and internalized as his particular insights are tested and adjusted to become a coherent body. And along with this one's feelings become trained not to run against the demands of moral reasoning. The person who has become virtuous, then, will still do the same kind of action as he did before, but will stand in a different relation to it. The beginner did the due action because there was good reason for him to do it, and he did it because of that reason. But this was compatible with his very much not wanting to do it; failing to realize that there were other moral requirements in that

---

[161] Diogenes VII 107–109. Cf. also Arius 85.12 -18. Long and Sedley (1987) translate *kathēkon* as 'proper function'.

[162] This connection of there being good reason to do an action, and its being an action that secures a natural advantage, may make due actions look prudential. This would be wrong; due actions are those which when performed in the right way are virtuous actions, and so the notion of advantage here is not a prudential one. The connection of virtue with advantage can only be fully understood by way of the issues discussed in Part IV.

situation; failing to grasp similar moral requirements in other situations. The virtuous person will do the same action, but will not have to overcome feelings counter to its performance; will discern and balance all the relevant values in that situation; will reliably discern similar values in all relevantly similar situations. This is just the distinction, familiar by now, between the beginner and the fully virtuous person with *phronēsis*, developed practical intelligence. The Stoics mark this distinction by saying that a due action as performed by a virtuous agent is a *katorthōma* or achievement.[163]

The distinction between a *kathēkon* and a *katorthōma* is comparable to the Aristotelian distinction between a virtuous action and a virtuous action performed as a virtuous agent would perform it—that is, from a reliable disposition so to act, and with no need to control countervailing feelings. A later Stoic (Archedemus) said that achieving our end in life is a matter of making all our due actions perfect or complete, i.e., not just doing the right thing but becoming virtuous in the way we do it;[164] and it is clear from extensive passages in Sextus that the virtuous person is distinguished not by what he does but by his disposition in doing it.[165] But the Stoic distinction lays more emphasis than the Aristotelian one on the point that there are *kinds* of action which are such that there is good reason for the ethical beginner to perform them. And this fits with an increased emphasis on rules, which will mark out for the beginner the kinds of action to do and to avoid in acting in ways which will lead to becoming virtuous.

We know also from a dispute in the early Stoa that the place of rules in virtue was a topic of debate, a debate which led to the establishment of a subtle 'orthodox' view. The source of the debate is Seneca's *Moral Letters* 94 and 95.[166] Seneca distinguishes two kinds of items we are concerned with: *decreta*, which he says translates the Greek *dogmata*,[167] and *praecepta*.[168] Either *decreta* are to be identified with the *theōrēmata* discussed above, and the distinction here represents a filling in of a gap, or the distinction replaces an original theory of *theōrēmata*, which was felt to be too simple. Both *decreta* and *praecepta* could be translated as 'rule'; at one point Seneca says that both of them 'give rules' (*praecipere*) and the only difference is one of generality (we shall see, though, that this gives too simple an account of the difference).[169] However, since the debate hinges on differences between the two, we need different terms.

Praecepta are clearly rules; they enter into contexts of telling us what to do, and of how we ought to act. Sometimes examples are given of actual imperatives—'Walk

---

[163] The word *katorthōma* is found in Aristotle for a successful performance; it becomes a technical term in the Stoics.

[164] Diogenes VII 88; cf. Arius 76.10–11.

[165] Cf. Sextus, *PH* III 244; *M* XI 197–209.

[166] Seneca is not here setting out to give us the history of Stoicism; it is clear that these letters are shaped by his own desire to argue for one view (the uselessness of *decreta* without *praecepta*) in *Ep* 94, and a corresponding view (the uselessness of *praecepta* without *decreta*) in *Ep* 95. Nonetheless, we can, I think, see enough of the views of Ariston and the later orthodox Stoics in these letters for us to be fairly confident of the main lines of the dispute.

[167] 95.10. He also calls them *placita* and *scita*.

[168] This possibly translates *parainein*, the verb prominent in, for example, the Philo passage above.

[169] 94.31. Translation is hindered by the fact that, although 'rules' works as an equivalent for *praecepta*, we have no corresponding verb for *praecipere*; the verb 'rules' means something quite different. I have translated as 'gives rules' or 'directs'.

like this; eat like this'.[170] *Decreta,* on the other hand, are associated with giving the 'why', while *praecepta* give only the 'what';[171] they help us to understand and explain the content of rules. They are thought of as *true*; grasping them is getting things *right*. *Decreta* are further associated with getting things right over your life as a whole, not just on a particular occasion.[172] It fits all these points for *decreta* to be translated 'principles'. Principles help us to understand (and justify) rules; principles are more readily thought of than rules as being true or false; and a principled person is someone who directs their whole life consistently, whereas a rule-follower is someone tied to particular directions in certain areas.[173] It would be nice if Seneca had given us an unambiguous example of a principle; the nearest he gets is the claim that the principles of justice mandate not justifying injustice by good consequences, since fairness and justice are rightly conceived only when conceived as intrinsically valuable.[174]

The early Stoic view seems to have been something like the following: you follow rules which tell you what to do, in the course of becoming virtuous. The virtuous person through reflection grasps the principles which give intellectual structure and content to the virtues. Cleanthes, Zeno's successor, claimed that rules were useful, but that following rules was feeble unless based on grasp of principles and philosophical theory.[175] This is a sensible enough position: rule-following is unavoidable to some extent, but rule-following on its own will not get you very far in moral progress, unless you understand the point of the rules.

Ariston, another follower of Zeno, had a radically different and interesting view. He rejected rule-following as a part of moral progress, developing the only really intuitionistic moral theory in the ancient world.

> Ariston. . .considers this part [rules] trivial and not such as to be internalized [*quae non descendat in pectus usque*], containing old wives' rules. Of more use, he says, are the principles of philosophy themselves, and the formulation of the final good; someone who has well understood and learned that, gives himself his own rules [*sibi ipse praecipit*] for what should be done in each situation.[176]

Why can't rules be internalized? This objection is not filled out; from the impression we get from Seneca of the rest of Ariston's views we can suggest two reasons. One is that a rule just tells you to do, or not to do, one kind of thing; you can't build up separate rules into a coherent grasp of virtue. Another is that a rule doesn't relate in

---

[170] For telling us what to do, see, e.g., 94.1, 23. For imperatives see 94.8. Kidd (1978) claims that Seneca, or the early Stoics, show confusion, since particular imperative directions are different from rules. Certainly Seneca shows no awareness of a difference: 94.8 includes: *Sic incede, sic cena; hoc viro hoc feminae, hoc marito hoc caelibi convenit.* But there need be no confusion; the imperatives just mark particular applications of the rules.

[171] 94.11, 95.40.

[172] 95.44.

[173] Compare Singer (1958), pp. 160–96: 'moral principles are more general, pervasive and fundamental than moral rules, and in some sense their sources or grounds' (p. 160) and 'moral principles are to be distinguished from moral rules by the fact that the former hold in all circumstances and do not admit of exceptions; that principles are invariant and do not vary with changes in circumstances or conditions; and that it is impossible for moral principles to conflict with one another' (p. 192).

[174] 94.11

[175] 94.4.

[176] 94.2.

the right way to the agent's intentions; it can give you an external sanction,[177] but it can't on its own get you to feel an internal sanction.

Ariston also puts forward a recurring argument about rule-following. Rules always have exceptions. He charges at one point[178] that to be useful, rules would have to be absurdly detailed; there would have to be, not just rules for marriage, but different rules for marriage with a virgin, marriage with a widow and so on. He also puts forward a more powerful objection, which unfortunately Seneca gives us only briefly:

> Add here that rules produced from understanding ought to be limited and exact [*finita et certa*]. If in any way there is no limit to them, they are outside the realm of understanding; understanding has knowledge of the boundaries of things.[179]

The virtuous person *knows* what to do; while the Stoics exaggerate this point, it seems a reasonable requirement on virtue that the virtuous person *know* what he is doing. But rules could only be the kind of thing that could be known if they were finite and exact; that is, if it were clear just from the rule itself what were the limits to its application, and if it were clear exactly what did and did not fall under it. This is only an objection to rule-following if Ariston is assuming that moral rules in fact do not have these properties; it seems reasonable to assume that this is what he has in mind, especially as it is something which has worried other moral philosophers.[180] Ordinary moral rules are, to a certain extent, vague; when we apply a rule such as 'Don't lie' we implicitly have in mind a kind of *ceteris paribus* clause: we shouldn't lie unless. . . where what we have in mind is an open-ended list of circumstances which justify or even mandate lying, but which we cannot reduce to a finite, closed list of exceptions. This is just the way we normally proceed to apply moral rules; problems set in only when we demand, with Ariston, that the person who makes a decision and gets it right should be able to say *why* she gets it right. For appeal just to the rule will not provide a complete explanation of the application, since the rule applies only *ceteris paribus*, and there is no closed list of exceptions that could be appealed to in order to show that this application was not one of the exceptions.

Ariston's third objection is the one which Seneca makes the most of. Rules are useless if you're virtuous, he claims, and useless if you're not. If you are virtuous, then you don't need rules, because the virtuous person knows what to do, and (if the second objection holds) you can't do this via rules. But if you're *not* virtuous, then rules are still useless, because, not being virtuous, you can't see the point of them, and only external sanctions, which do not speak to the person, can get people to do things that they can't see the point of.

> Those who want [rules] to seem futile say this: If something has got into your eye and is impeding your sight, you should get it out. As long as it is in the way, someone who gives directions—'this is how you'll walk, you'll stretch out your

---

[177] Cf. 95.40 on threats.

[178] 94.14–15.

[179] 94.16.

[180] Compare especially Sidgwick's extended treatment of commonsense rules, in (1907) Book III. He reiterates that they are not precise; they leave open areas of conflict and uncertainty in their application, which we cannot resolve from the rule itself. Sidgwick concludes that ordinary moral rules cannot, for this reason, serve as 'axioms' in a properly scientific ethics.

hand there'—is wasting his time. Similarly, when something is obscuring the sight of the mind and hindering it from discerning the series of its duties, a person is wasting his time who gives directions—'this is how you'll live with your father, and this with your wife'. For rules are no use as long as error overwhelms the mind; if this is dispelled, what is owed to each by way of duty will be clear. Otherwise, you'll be teaching the person what a healthy person ought to do, not rendering him healthy. You're showing a poor person how to act the rich man. . . . I tell you the same about all the vices; you should get rid of *them*, not give directions to do what can't be done while the vices are still there.[181]

'Treat a friend, a fellow-citizen, a partner this way.' 'Why?' 'Because it's just.' But all *that* is handed on to me by the section on justice. There I discover that fairness is to be pursued for its own sake, and that we are not forced to it by fear or induced by gain; and that a person is not just who approves of anything in this virtue save itself. When I have convinced myself of this and thoroughly absorbed it, what use are your rules, which teach me what I know? Giving rules to one who knows is futile; giving them to one who doesn't is too little, for the person needs to understand not just what he is directed to do, but why.[182]

Ariston's objections are still familiar in moral philosophy, though usually not in the context of virtue. His complaint is that rule-following is worthless as a serious part of moral reasoning and moral development. You can follow a rule without knowing why you are following it; and just following the rule will not itself plausibly lead you to see why you are following it. Hence following moral rules can do nothing, morally, for those who do not see the point—those who are already committed to being unjust, greedy, and so on. And if you do see the point, because you are just, temperate and so on, and so do appreciate the good of justice and the other virtues, rule-following seems to have no place. The first charge seems more powerful than the second. It is easy to see that rule-following on its own will not lead the rule-follower to increased moral understanding. But why are rules useless to the virtuous? Might it not be positively beneficial to have rules of some generality to follow, rather than having to face a succession of particular circumstances in turn without ready general guidance? We can construct Ariston's answer here from his second objection. The virtuous person, who has knowledge, does not use rules because these on their own are 'imprecise and undefined'—they are too general to do justice to the particularities of situations, and would lead us to judge in a crude manner.

What is Ariston's positive picture of the virtuous person? Cicero[183] describes it thus: the virtuous person does whatever comes into his head. This is patently the kind of disingenuous misunderstanding that intuitionists have often had to put up with. Cicero's report seems to be a hostile account of the idea that the virtuous person acts on what he sees to be right, where he does not justify this claim by appeal to a general rule. This is supported by Seneca's account of Ariston's positive view.

Someone who is learning to throw the javelin aims at a target and trains his arm to propel what he throws; when he has acquired this power from training and exercise, he makes use of it in whatever way he wishes—for he has learned not to

---

[181] 94.5–6.
[182] 94.11.
[183] *Fin* IV, 43: '*quodcumque in mentem incideret*' and '*quodcumque tamquam occurreret*'.

hit this or that, but to hit whatever he wishes. Similarly, someone who has organized himself with a view to his entire life has no need of advice in particular cases, since he is expert with regard to the whole, expert not as to how to live with his wife or son, but as to how to live well, in which is included how he should live with his wife and children.[184]

Correct action depends on having a virtuous disposition, and this is not a rule-based disposition. The virtuous person has internalized the most general truths of ethics, but is not guided in particular decision-making by rules. Rather, the correct judgement is a product of the virtuous disposition in a very direct way, just as accurate shooting is the direct product of the javelin-thrower's skill, and is not mediated by rule-following on a particular occasion.

Ariston's is the only explicitly intuitionist theory in ancient ethics (though Aristotle's theory is often treated as though it were). Of course it is part of any theory that the agent needs judgement in order to enable him to apply rules properly; but Ariston goes beyond this to a stronger claim, that ethics is uncodifiable: there are no useful general rules mandating right action, or at least none worthy of being taken more seriously than rules of thumb. Virtue not only can but must do without reliance on rules; it is a matter of non–rule-governed insight flowing directly from the state of virtue itself.[185] This kind of theory is in its modern versions standardly faced by the objection that it leaves the agent nothing informative to say by way of justification for her particular judgements. The generous person 'just sees' what generosity requires, and while this ability is produced by, and rests on, appreciation of truths about generosity and its importance, these truths do not justify the particular judgements in the sense of supporting them against alternative particular judgements; the only justification that they get comes from the agent's overall grasp of virtue in his life as a whole. In the ancient world we do not find exactly this objection, but we do find a related one. Chrysippus, the later head of the Stoic school, argued[186] that Ariston made morality empty and trivial. Virtue, according to Ariston, is simply knowledge of good and evil, and indifference to everything else. But as a Stoic he has to hold that virtue is the only thing that is good; so we seem to have, not just a circle, but a very small and vicious circle. We could break into this, of course, if we had some informative way of spelling out what the knowledge of good and evil comes down to. But if we could do this, we could specify informatively what the virtuous person relies on in coming to particular judgements; yet this is just what Ariston denies; particular judgements come directly from the virtuous person's disposition, and cannot be justified in general ways.[187]

Ariston was original in many ways, and his views were later rejected as 'unorthodox' by mainstream Stoicism, which took its lead from Chrysippus.[188] But

---

[184] 94.3

[185] In some ways Ariston is reminiscent of Prichard, although they are rendered dissimilar by the fact that Prichard's ethical framework is deontological rather than virtue-centred. Both, however, explicitly stress that final particular moral judgements are justified by the agent's disposition rather than by general moral rules.

[186] Plutarch, *Comm not* 1071 f—1072 a.

[187] This objection does not rely directly on the notion of *rules*. For this objection of Chrysippus', see Striker (1991).

[188] See Ioppolo (1980) and the discussion review by N. White (1985a).

later Stoics recognized the need to come up with some kind of defence against Ariston's objections to giving rules a substantial place in virtue. There is no answer exactly to the claim that rules cannot be internalized; presumably this point was meant to be met by the position as a whole. But we do have responses on the issue of the nature of rules.

For one thing, the Stoics refined their position on due actions. As we saw, the view that rules are important in ethics goes with the view that there are certain kinds of action which as such are 'due actions' or not, and that we can specify these. We find what looks like a response to Ariston's complaints that moral rules have exceptions that cannot be finitely listed—a refinement in what we can specify as the content of these rules.

> Some due actions are so without circumstances, others are circumstantial. These are without circumstance: taking care of one's health and sense-organs, and the like. In accordance with circumstance are mutilating oneself and throwing away one's possessions. Analogously with what is contrary to what is due. Further, of due actions some are always due, others not always. Always due is living according to virtue, not always due are questioning, answering, strolling and the like. The same account holds of what is contrary to what is due.[189]

Two points are noticeable. If rules are to be guided by the attempt to pick out due actions, then not all rules will hold universally. The only ones which do, seem to be envisaged as highly general, almost contentless rules, such as 'Live in accordance with virtue'. More specific rules would seem to hold in more restricted contexts. Further, even these do not hold without exception; some hold 'in accordance with circumstance', when there is an exception to some other rule. I follow the rule about taking care of my health, for example; there are reasons of a general and reliable kind for health being naturally preferable to sickness and disability. But if disability would get me out of serving a tyrant and having to do wrong, then I should regard it as a rule to mutilate myself when circumstances demand.[190]

Though this produces a more sensible attitude to rules, none of it completely answers Ariston's point about the uncompletability of *ceteris paribus* clauses in moral rules. The only direct answer to this that we find is an unfortunately brief comment in Seneca:

> 'Rules', [Ariston] says, 'are not limited'. Wrong: for they do not lack limits concerning the greatest and most crucial matters. However, they do contain slight differences required by times, places, people—but there are universal rules [*praecepta generalia*] for these as well.'[191]

This meets Ariston head on: rules are *not* 'unlimited' on the points that matter. There is no serious doubt that a rule about truth-telling implies that you shouldn't *lie, cheat* and so on; there are no problems as to which kinds of actions the rules apply to. Difficulties of application are created by the circumstances of application; we get no examples, but 'times, places, people' suggest familiar cases. If someone at a

---

[189] Diogenes VII 109. See N. White (1978b).
[190] The example comes from Sextus' discussion of Ariston at *M* XI 63–4, though it is sickness rather than mutilation there that gets the agent out of serving the tyrant.
[191] 94.35.

party conventionally hopes that I am having a good time, and I'm not, does saying that I am constitute a *lie*, or does it fall under some other rule? And these problems, Seneca claims, fall under 'universal rules'. Presumably, one brings the troublesome case under a more general rule, such as, 'Put integrity before politeness'.

This, however, makes the resulting problem even more obvious. If the lower-order, more specific rules were problematic because there could always be exceptions to them, how could this fail to apply also to the higher-order, more general rules? Should one, for example, *always* put integrity before politeness? And, even if one should, is a conventional remark at a party a breach of one's *integrity*? All the problems that arose for the original rule about lying instantly recur for the higher-order rule.

Could Seneca, or his Stoic sources, have been unaware of such an obvious point? We do not have to suppose so if we take seriously another passage:

> What difference is there between the principles of philosophy and rules, except that the former are universal rules, and the latter, specific ones? Each of them directs [gives rules, *praecipit*], but the former do so in general, the latter in particular ways.[192]

On its own this is puzzling, since there are many other differences between rules and principles. But it shows that Stoics could be impressed by the fact that, whatever these other differences, both rules and principles have prescriptive force of a kind, and it may be that the answer to Ariston is that problems with rules are solved by appeal to higher-order rules of a kind, namely principles.[193] One attraction of this solution is, of course, that only so is there any answer to Ariston. Formal problems with rules can never be solved by appeal to more rules. But one can see as a possible solution that they might be solved by appeal to principles, which have the same kind of prescriptive force as rules, and so can lead the agent to act in the way that rules can, but which have other features that rules on their own lack. We have seen that principles concern not just types of actions but one's life as a whole; they are true or false, so that grasping them is grasping not just a direction to act but truths about nature of justice, or the like; and they explain rules, giving the 'why' and not just the 'what'. It is unfortunate that we lack an example that might make it clear precisely how appeal to a principle could help a problem with a rule; but perhaps it is no accident that we have no such example, since it is clear from the many roles that principles fill that the notion is a complex one, and perhaps is not adequately to be shown in any one example. We can at any rate see in the abstract that problems of conflict or indeterminateness with rules could be helped by appeal to principles which directed attention to the nature of the problematic concept and located it in one's system of values as a whole. And even this establishes a point against Ariston: problems in applying rules don't mean that you have to appeal to a non–rule-governed insight. You can appeal to principles instead, and this appeal does not result in the virtuous person's making judgements which cannot be informatively justified.

---

[192] 94.31.
[193] On this issue see Mitsis (1993).

Ariston appealed to principles too; how does this solution differ from his view? For Ariston, principles are all we need, or can have; we achieve a general grasp of virtue and the importance of our values in our lives as wholes, and then further appeal to rules is useless. The orthodox view is that appeal to principles, far from rendering rules useless, serves to enable us to see the point of the rules we follow, and locate them in our general moral outlook. If this is feasible, then Ariston's choice between rule-following and non-rule-governed insight is a false dichotomy.

Hence we can already see the outlines of the orthodox answer to Ariston's complaint that rules are useless for the virtuous and useless for the vicious. The response is that we don't *just* follow rules, in isolation; we *also* employ principles, so that the virtuous person's moral outlook is richer, and more unified, than Ariston supposes. We find in several places the claim that rules and principles together form an organic whole, all of which should be considered. Principles are the roots of rules, or the elements of which rules are made up;[194] rules are like leaves, which wither without a parent bough (principles);[195] and the following passage uses two organic metaphors and adds another:

> Let us join [rules and principles]. Branches are useless with no root, and the roots themselves are benefitted by the plant they have produced. Nobody can fail to know how useful hands are, and their help is open; but the heart, because of which the hands are animate, from which they take their impulse, because of which they move, is not visible. I can say the same about rules; they are in the open, while the principles of philosophy are hidden away. With holy rites only the initiated know the more sacred ones; and similarly in philosophy these intimate things are displayed to those who have been admitted and allowed into the shrine, while rules and the like are familiar to lay people as well.[196]

The organic metaphors stress two points. One is that rules and principles should not be isolated in our moral outlook, but are both parts of a larger functioning whole, all of which we need. The other is that principles are more basic; they are the driving factor, since the rules depend on them in a way which is not reciprocal. The religious metaphor adds the point that the understanding which the principles provide is not available to anyone, but only to those who have reflected on their lives with the aid of philosophical theory.

In one passage we get a non-metaphorical account of what this implies:

> An action is not correct unless the intention is correct; for this is what the action comes from. Further, the intention is not correct unless the mind's disposition is correct; for this is what the intention comes from. Again, the mind's disposition will not be in the best state unless it grasps the laws governing all of life and inquires what judgement should be made about each thing, and unless it relates the situation to what is true.[197]

We have already seen that it is common ground among all ancient theories that the virtuous person is the person who not only does the right thing but does it from a

[194] 95.12.
[195] 95.59.
[196] 95.64.
[197] 95.57.

correct *overall* understanding. But the orthodox Stoics insist, against Ariston's brave venture, that this is not a matter of insight not backed up by rules. We need rules to become virtuous, because we need to be guided to do the right kinds of things; and unreflective people may never achieve anything more. Those who make progress towards becoming virtuous reflect on the basis of the rules they follow; the virtuous person has an overall grasp of the inner significance of why she acts as she does. Virtue is structured by principles and rules, and does not depend at any point on non–rule-governed insight.

Modern moral theories have made us familiar with the idea that rules should be tested, once we start to reflect on them, against moral *theory*. It is not enough to follow rules, even if there are in fact good reasons for doing so; the reflective moral agent should be able to say *why* he follows the rules he does, and only theory will suffice to show this. We are not, however, used to finding this thought in the context of virtue ethics. Because in the modern tradition virtue has often been misconstrued as a non-intellectual habit, it has often been assumed that virtue ethics is committed to giving a crucial role to direct insight and intuition, and that it stands in opposition to rule-following. The development of the orthodox Stoic theory shows us that this assumption is based on too narrow a view of what the possibilities are for virtue ethics.

Two outstanding questions remain. When we appeal to principles to understand the significance of the rules, can this lead us to break or modify the rules? How revisionary can this process be? Modern moral theories often stress the ways that moral theory can change or revise our original moral opinions, or moral rules. Are the Stoics revisionary, or conservative?

On this issue there appears to have been a change within the Stoa. Zeno and Chrysippus both wrote works called *The Republic*, in obvious competition with Plato to give an account of the ideal society. We know that later Stoics found the content of these works shocking and embarrassing for the school, and this seems largely to have been because both of them stressed the way in which, in extreme circumstances, the right thing to do might be a kind of action which is normally proscribed, such as eating the dead, or incest. Most plausibly this was in the service of claiming that many socially established norms and rules are backed only by convention, and lack a foundation in nature, which is what the truly virtuous will aim to accord with. It is hard to tell just what Zeno and Chrysippus said, especially since many of our sources are hostile,[198] but it seems that in general the idea was that reflection on the principles of morality, in the light of Stoic theory, could lead to the breaking of ordinary moral rules even in cases where this would be normally accounted shocking. (For reflection on Stoic theory shows us what is truly in accordance with nature, and when we understand this, we will grasp that there is nothing natural about many of our established moral rules, and therefore no serious reason for the virtuous person not to break them in certain circumstances.)[199]

Later Stoics, however, were much more conservative about the role of principles in modifying rules. In Seneca the stress is all on the insight that we gather into the

---

[198] Many of the references come from Sextus, who is gleefully disingenuous in presenting these recommendations as part of Stoic advice on how we should live in general. See *PH* III 200, 207, 245–247; *M* XI 191–4. See Diogenes VII 121, 188 for a less tendentious statement.

[199] These issues are dealt with in greater depth in chapters 5 and 13.

reasons why we follow the rules we do, not on ways that we might improve our rules. Indeed, Roman Stoicism is remarkable for its conformism in this respect; Romans were often attracted to Stoicism just because it promised to give them insight into the significance of following established social rules and norms which were not questioned.[200] Stoicism thus began as a revisionary theory, but later development made it clear that the structure of Stoic moral theory is as such neither radical nor conservative, but compatible either with a desire to adapt existing rules or with confidence that existing moral rules are fine as they are. If the Stoic tries to improve existing moral rules, however, then after Ariston he tries to do so by appeal to principles which are accessible to all who reflect properly; he does not rely on his own capacity for insight. In terms of the skill analogy, he is like the expert who, when circumstances demand it, applies the rule in the light of principles behind the rule, rather than the expert who relies on his own capacity for insight, built up by trial and error.[201]

A long overdue question is, Where do the rules come from in the first place? They can hardly be ideal rules, since they are what the non-virtuous beginner starts from. The Stoics tended to start from generally accepted rules of commonsense morality; where else, indeed, were they to start from? In the so-called 'middle' Stoic Panaetius and the later Stoic Epictetus we find a stress on personal and social *roles* as a source of rules of moral behaviour.[202] This has plausibly been seen as an accommodation to Roman ways of thinking, but its interest is not confined to this.[203] Epictetus argues that we can read off many of our rules of action just from considering what roles we have:

> Consider who you are. . .first a human. . .next remember that you are a son. . .next remember that you are a brother. . .next remember, if you are a councillor of a city, that you are a councillor; that you are young, if you are young; old, if you are old; a father, if you are a father. In every case each of these names, when it comes to be reflected on, suggests the actions that are appropriate.[204]

Intuitively this is plausible; but how deep does it go? Do the rules in question really spring from the roles in question, or do the roles merely serve to locate rules which have force independently of the roles? It does seem, intuitively, that I ought to act in certain ways to my parents, just because they are my parents. But if we do not press any deeper, it can seem something of a mystery that roles like those of being a child, parent, sibling and so on can generate genuine moral rules. We may suspect that the real source of the rules is not the roles themselves but rather moral principles which are of general application but which find an important locus in these particular roles.[205] Panaetius certainly argues that one should perform the duties incumbent on

---

[200] See the classic article by Brunt (1975). Cf. also the final section of Annas (1989a).

[201] I thus side with Mitsis in the (1986) exchange between Inwood and Mitsis.

[202] Seneca's examples of moral rules also tend to lay stress on role-governed kinds of behaviour.

[203] Panaetius' views on this are found in the first book of Cicero's *De Officiis* (though of course it is hard to disentangle Cicero from Panaetius). See C. Gill (1988) and (forthcoming). There are several relevant passages in Epictetus, notably *Discourses* II, 10, 1–12; III, 22, 86–92; IV, 2,10. See Brunt (1975), Appendix.

[204] *Disc* II, 10, 1–12 (selectively).

[205] Griffin (1986), p. 222: 'It is characteristic of role-deontology that it stops too early', and p. 221:

one by virtue of one's personality, status and circumstances, only insofar as this is consistent with the moral point of view;[206] and the thought naturally suggests itself that emphasis on roles is best seen as an indirect way of appealing to further principles. Unfortunately neither Panaetius nor Epictetus, nor any ancient philosopher, discusses the relation of roles to rules and principles. It is generally used, as by Epictetus, in intuitive presentations of Stoic ethics, and assumed not to conflict with the results of applying more general moral principles.

We might think that this approach is bound to lead to conflict, especially in a very rigid society. The above discussion shows why this need not be a fatal difficulty. Even if the specific rules have very conventional content, the morally developed person will grasp the general principles that require the application of all the virtues, and so will be able to qualify the conventional role where necessary. Thus, when it comes to acting like a good father, say, the wise person will not just follow society's rules deriving from the conventional role of father; he will do so in a way informed and qualified by his grasp of higher moral principles and the demands of virtue that they contain. We might still worry that in a society which is (as Greek and Roman society certainly was) very rigid about the role of fathers, this would be almost certain to lead to conflict; if so, then role-generated rules would have at best a preliminary and pedagogic role.

In general, we can see that there is no one favoured paradigm of moral reasoning; for all the schools it is more important to stress the differences between the beginner and the fully virtuous than to specify just what forms their reasoning will take. We can also see that, even though there is no one word answering exactly to our 'rule', rule-following is fairly important in all the major theories. While Epicurus takes no official account of it and Aristotle has some interesting ideas which are not worked up into a satisfactory whole, the Stoics do come to grips with the status of rule-following in the moral life.

Rule-following, however, is only one of the ways in which the virtuous and would-be virtuous person reasons. It is plain that an ethics of virtue puts far fewer constraints on the form of moral reasoning than do consequentialist or deontological theories. What matters is to come to make moral choices underivatively, as an expert rather than as a learner. One probably already applies rules, since nobody starts to be virtuous in a moral or social vacuum; what matters is to do this in an understanding rather than a mechanical way. Moral progress is too complex and involves too much of the agent's personality to be guaranteed merely by adopting one form of reasoning rather than another.

5. *Virtue and Right Action*

In this and the next two sections we shall discuss some questions that have arisen within the attempt to set out the general structure of virtue in ancient ethics. One that is pressing, from a modern perspective, is this: A virtue is a disposition to do the

---

'To make his case, a role-deontologist has to be able to specify roles in a way that makes it clear that the related claims do indeed arise from them and not, say, from non-role-related principles hovering in the background'.

[206] Cicero, *Off* I 110.

right thing, in various areas of life, and to have the right feelings and emotions about it. But how does the agent discern what is the right thing to do? Unless she is *correct* about what to do, she will not have a virtue. If she is wrong about what courage requires, for example, then she will not be courageous, but merely foolhardy: she will do the wrong thing, and will have inappropriate feelings and emotions. So it is crucial to have an answer to the question: what here is the standard of rightness? What does the virtuous agent appeal to in working out what is the right thing to do?

It is obviously no answer to this just to point to the model, familiar by now, of the learner acquiring a skill. The Aristotelian beginner follows the example or takes the advice of a mature and virtuous person; the Stoic beginner follows the rules such a person imparts. But how can the beginner be assured that these are the *right* models and rules? We can appeal to society's consensus on this: the brave person learns what the right thing to do is by noting what is counted in her society as the right thing to do. But this provides no justification. Society's consensus is all we need to determine what the polite thing to do is, but with the virtues there is a further question, is this consensus itself right? In any case, society may not have a consensus where it matters: there may be dispute over what is the right thing to do. Is it braver to fight a duel or to refuse? At some periods this has been a real issue.

It is often thought that virtue ethics faces a dilemma here. When we ask what standard I am to use to determine whether what I propose to do is right, the answer, it seems, will either be *derivative from virtuous agency*—it will take the form, 'What the virtuous (brave, generous, etc.) person would do in these circumstances'—or be *independent of virtuous agency*—it will take one of a number of forms, such as 'It would lead to more disutility than the alternative' or 'That kind of thing is always wrong'. The second option, of independence, trivializes everything said about virtue hitherto. The virtues will simply be praiseworthy ways to be, but the basis for this praise will be quite independent of any praise the agent might get for doing the right thing. It is hard to see why the virtues should matter if this is all that they amount to.[207] Antiochus in particular criticizes the Stoics for making virtue the final good and yet (allegedly) appealing to something else, natural advantages, to give us a criterion for right action.[208] And he brings out explicitly the point that discovering a standard of right action is seen as part of what is provided by a discovery of one's final good.

> When we know what the ends of things are, when we understand what the final good and final evil are, we have discovered the pathway for our life and the formation[209] of all our due actions; we have discovered, therefore, something to which to refer each case, and hence a rational way of living well (which is what everyone seeks) can be discovered and achieved.[210]

---

[207] See the article by Trianosky (1986) for a defence of the independence claim. Note that the independence claim is stronger than the claim that the virtues are states which are valuable in ways that are not reducible to the production of virtuous actions. For an excellent discussion of this kind of objection to virtue ethics, see Hursthouse (1991).

[208] See *Fin* IV 46–48.

[209] *Conformatio*, the reading accepted by Madvig; most of the manuscripts read *confirmatio*, establishment or confirmation.

[210] *Fin* V 15–16.

It could not be clearer that a standard of right action cannot be independent of discovering one's final good and the role played in that by virtue.

But if independence is unsatisfactory, what of the other, derivation, option? The right thing to do will be what the virtuous person would do. But then the problem at once shifts: how do we know which are the virtuous people? Appealing to society's consensus will not do, as we have seen. Perhaps, then, we can appeal to virtuous reasoning itself. The beginner does not have good judgement as to which are the right models; but if he is fortunate enough to have good models pointed out to him, then he will begin by making the right judgements; he will have fixed on the right examples to develop a notion of bravery, rather than foolhardiness, say. As he becomes more virtuous he understands the basis of and reasons for bravery; so he can explain to others why one should do this rather than that. So the criterion for right action is indeed what the virtuous person would do. But this is not trivial. The beginner can appeal to it for guidance; and the virtuous person can not merely come out with a judgement, but explain it.

He can explain it, however, only to other virtuous people, or to beginners who are prepared to accept his judgements as giving them the right examples. For only these people already accept, or are prepared to respect, the reasoning typical of the virtuous person. On this position, the virtuous know that they are doing the right thing because this judgement can be defended by, and explained to, the virtuous, and the aspirants to virtue. But, while the virtuous can encourage and defend one another, it seems that they have little to say to the non-virtuous, the person who rejects their judgements or does not accept their examples as fixing the content of particular virtues. The criterion of right action thus turns out to be defended in a way that looks circular. This action is the right thing to do, we are told, because it is what the virtuous person would do; and the virtuous person is the person with the disposition to do just this kind of thing. So on this position the virtuous seem to have nothing seriously to discuss with the non-virtuous: the virtuous person seems already precluded from accepting the non-virtuous person's challenge on any action. All the difficult questions about what it is right to do seem to be begged by the initial choice of examples to fix the content of the virtue. Further, since the beginner is precisely the person who is not yet in a position to make mature moral choices, it seems to be a matter of luck whether one makes the right initial choice of model or not; one might end up vicious through bad upbringing for which one is not to blame. And once one has developed habits of judgement and feeling, these will all go on mutually reinforcing one another, as we have seen; it becomes a mystery how the non-virtuous person could ever become 'converted' to the life of virtue, which to the person who has developed in a different way would seem to have no appeal.[211]

It is tempting to try to qualify the unattractiveness of this position. First, one might query whether the circularity is really so objectionable. The claim that it is, rests on a view of justification requiring that a moral justification have force even to

---

[211] Even the virtuous person might be thought prone to a version of this problem. When she asks, 'What should I do in this situation?' is she really asking, 'What would a brave person do in this situation?'? It is odd if moral deliberation is always to take the form of asking what some ideal version of you would do in this situation. In this form, however, I think that the problem is not peculiar to virtue ethics; a deontologist will ask herself what a dutiful person would do, a consequentialist, what an efficient maximizer would do. Thus the oddity is superficial.

those who reject the basis of that justification; and this is not clearly reasonable. Why should one be able to show a coward that the right action is the brave one? This point, while it has some force, does not dissolve the present problem, for that is not just that the brave may not be able to convince the cowardly, but that the brave may not be able to convince the mediocre or encratic.[212] Agents may dispute about the right thing to do without being positively vicious; on this view it seems that these people have no recourse but to see each other as having developed dispositions which preclude useful mutual discussion. And a reasonable theory ought to allow more substance than this to ethical disputes.

Another response is to deny that we do have an objectionable circularity here. For a virtuous person is not merely a person so disposed as to do the right thing; we have seen at length that she is also a person whose feelings and emotions have developed in certain ways and not others. Virtue expresses itself in the way she is, not merely in what she does. We break the circle if we give due allowance to the point that the virtuous person is a distinctive sort of person: 'this is the right thing to do because the virtuous person would do it' is justified by the appeal made not just to what the virtuous person would do but to the kind of person that the virtuous person is. Again, a good point is being made: virtue is never merely a disposition to do certain things, but always involves the developed state of the agent's emotional side. But again it does not solve the problem, for the kind of appeal being pointed out is an extremely vague one, the force of which is hard to pin down. The brave person is not just a reliable source of brave actions; she is admirable—but exactly how does this fact help to justify her judgement as to the right thing to do? It is an attractive quality, but its attraction is very difficult to specify; and in any case there are people who do not find it attractive at all, and we are back with the original problem, that the virtuous can, it seems, justify their actions only in terms of their virtue, and so only to the virtuous.[213]

When it comes to determining right actions, then, an ethical theory in which virtue is the basic notion appears at a disadvantage. Either right action is determined in a way derivative from virtuous agency, which leads to circularity, or in an independent way, which trivializes the role of the allegedly basic ethical notion. We can see, however, that the problem in this form comes from the assumptions that an ethical theory must have a structure which is hierarchical and complete. Given these assumptions, if character and virtue are the basic notions, we must be able to account for the standard of right action in terms of virtuous character, and of other notions only insofar as derived from them. The only alternative is seen as the total independence from virtue of the standard of right action, which leaves the theory incapable of explaining it, and so rendered trivial.

Ancient ethical theory is neither hierarchical nor complete, although it is a theory within which virtue is primary. How do we fit right action into this picture?

Even pre-reflectively, we make two kinds of judgement in everyday life, about actions and about agents. We judge that he should not have done this action, for

---

[212] Or, as Nicholas White points out, those raising the question from a neutral philosophical standpoint.
[213] See Sidgwick on the problem of the vagueness of the appeal of virtue as a state of character, over and above its production of virtuous acts; and also on the kind of circularity that virtue ethics, on this conception of ethical theory, is likely to fall into: (1907) Bk III, ch. ii, xiv.

example, and we also judge that she is hostile. On the everyday level neither kind has primacy for our understanding; it takes reflection and theory to get people to see either kind as less fundamental than the other. For in our everyday ethical lives we are preoccupied about the question of actions—what we should do, what advice to give, how to solve hard cases—but we are also, and no less significantly, preoccupied by people—whether someone is right for a job demanding certain relations with people that she finds difficult, whether an official is being craven in the face of pressure, and so on. Once we reflect, we will naturally ask how these different types of judgement are related. One answer is that they are just different, and that neither has priority, but this seems feeble once we notice that both people and actions are brave, generous, just and so on. If we want a hierarchical and complete ethical theory, we will make either actions or agents basic, and run into the problems sketched above. But there is another approach.

Most of us want not merely to do the right thing but to understand what it is about it that makes it the right thing; few are content with mindless performance. Our natural first step is to examine the particular reasons we give for doing one thing rather than another. But it is obvious that these have limited potential for our finding some kind of standard for right action; the particular reasons and intuitions of particular people contain a complex mixture of prejudice and convention which is hard to filter out. The next step, therefore, is to move from particular judgements to find the general procedures we follow in coming to those judgements. Many of these procedures will themselves rest on mere prejudice or custom, as with procedures like doing what one's elders tell one to do, or following the Bible, and if we are sociologists we may stay at that point. But if we are philosophers we will pursue the *rational* procedures that we follow in coming to our particular judgements as to what we ought to do. These are what Sidgwick called the *methods* of ethics.[214] Do we, for example, appeal to certain rules? Are we systematically trying to avoid bad consequences, or produce good ones?

At this point ethical theories divide. Deontologists and consequentialists alike focus on the methods themselves. We are to extract them from their everyday application and test them for consistency and for other intellectual virtues, like simplicity. We are likely to find that the procedures we employ contain exceptions and contradictions, and we are to eliminate these in the interests of producing a rational structure of consistent and ordered principles. This is often just what an ethical theory is taken to be. It is likely that most of the principles that ordinary people use in determining what they ought to do appeal both to kinds of rules and to consequences, and most theories will demand that they be ordered in a hierarchy. We go, that is, directly from the agent's employment of particular rational procedures to a theory that is produced by subjecting those rational procedures to various tests and producing a consistent and ordered structure of them. These are then played off against the agent's particular judgements, and may be used to force these to conform, or may be modified in the light of them.

An ethical theory based on virtue, on the other hand, does not go directly from the agent's employment of various procedures to a point of view that goes right through the agent and asks only about the intellectual structure of the procedures.

---

[214] See Sidgwick's Introduction on this; also Schneewind (1977) on Sidgwick's notion of a method.

Rather, it takes it that we first have to see the significance of these procedures *from the agent's point of view* before we can go on to ask these further questions. If the agent aims to produce good consequences, why is this so from the agent's standpoint? Suppose the agent is following a rule, such as, 'Don't do cowardly things'. Why does the agent accept such a rule—what point does he see in it? For virtue ethics, agents are primary for understanding, because if we want to know what the point is of avoiding cowardly acts, we shall understand this best if we look closely at the agent, and what it would be for him to be brave or cowardly.

This is not to say, of course, that virtue ethics is not interested in the further questions about consistency and structure; but it examines our ethical procedures from the agent's point of view first. Because we hope to find illumination about brave acts from brave agents, virtue is primary for our understanding in the theory. But we are looking at agents to understand the point of doing certain acts, not to derive all relevant claims about acts; so agents are not in this theory basic as they would be in a hierarchical and complete theory. Thus in an ethics of virtue initial interest in what we ought to do moves to an interest in the kind of people we are and hope to be, because the latter is taken to be the best way of understanding the former.

Suppose we are interested in the point of doing a brave act. We will naturally look to the brave person. There are two stages to this. First we have to identify the brave person, and while we are still at the stage of enquiring about actions, we have to pick out the brave person as the person who acts bravely. This constrains us in two ways. There are some actions which nobody who is brave could do. In the ancient world, for example, nobody can be brave who breaks the line of battle and runs away. So some kinds of action form clear constraints on having a virtue. Aristotle remarks that there are some kinds of actions which a virtuous person would never do, and some feelings that they would never have.[215]

We cannot give a finite list of examples for each virtue, for circumstances might convert any kind of action on a particular occasion to one that the virtuous person might do under pressure; we have to be content with *ceteris paribus* clauses. Nonetheless, there clearly are these constraints; there is consensus about them, and they are mostly of a negative kind, things that could not normally be acts of bravery, generosity and so on.

Further, there is also consensus on some positive models for each virtue. The beginner learning to be brave will certainly learn to stand up for himself, not give in to bullying and so on. Agreement here rests at a higher level of generality than with the negative constraints—one should not give in to bullying, but there can be disagreement as to whether a particular action is bullying. Thus there is consensus on, so to speak, the centre and the outer edges of what the brave person does. And these are the points from which we begin to teach the learner who wants to be brave.

So we do appeal to consensus as to which actions are brave ones, to get a grip on the brave person. But this is only reasonable; our accounts of what bravery is

---

[215] *NE* 1107 a 8-27. Compare Plato's insistence (*Repub* 442 d-e) that his own (very revisionary) account of justice is constrained by commonsense limits: there are some things that a just person simply would never do.

must have comprehensible points of contact with our everyday judgements about actions. And we appeal only where there *is* consensus: at the outer limits and the centre. We do not need to worry that there are disputed cases, since we do not start from disputed cases, only from those where there is agreement (which will come at a higher level of generality in the positive than in the negative cases).

But then there is a second stage. As we have seen, virtue is in ancient ethics a kind of skill; developing a virtue is developing an intellectual disposition, increasing your understanding of what you are doing and why.[216] Thus the beginner has to start from the shared views of others; but developing a virtue involves the continual testing and adjusting of those views, and bringing them together in a coherent overall picture. And the agent who has done this will have adopted a more critical attitude to the initial results of consensus than she had when learning; for in the process of comparing and adjusting her initial procedures, she will have come to find various gaps and conflicts. Thus the virtuous person may well, as a result of developing a virtue, revise or reject some of the initial judgements she accepted when learning to be virtuous. So the learner begins from certain givens about what it is right to do, but the reflective developed agent will have a critical attitude towards these and all other judgements about actions; and if and when she parts company with the initial consensus, she can give reasons for so doing. The initial judgement might turn out to be inconsistent with other, more important ones, or might be giving excessive importance to a value that is of minor importance in the agent's life as a whole. Since the virtues are ways of living that the agent develops in order to improve her life as a whole, and since, as we have seen,[217] reflection on the virtues tends to unify them in the agent's overall scheme of life, the pressure to revise initial judgements in the interests of consistency and unification of the agent's life will be strong.

Judgements about what it is right to do, then, are neither derived from an independently developed virtuous agent, nor brought in from an independent standpoint. We can now see that both these alternatives are too simple-minded. The relation between the virtuous person's viewpoint and society's consensus as to what it is right to do is better conceived of as a process like reflective equilibrium. The brave person cannot, of course, improvise what the brave thing to do is; but neither is he bound to an already fixed independent principle. We all have to start from the views of those around us as to brave and cowardly acts. But those of us who develop the virtue can return to correct these initial judgements. We do so not from the viewpoint of a theory developed in the abstract, but from the viewpoint of a brave agent, who has thought out and practiced what matters in bravery.

So we contrast intuitions with reflective judgement, which leads us to understand the intuitions, and perhaps to modify them. Different theories have differing views on how much reflective judgement should modify intuition; we have seen above[218] that early Stoics were more radical on this issue than their successors; and we shall see at greater length in Part IV that on the fundamental issue of virtue and happiness they were prepared to be extremely counter-intuitive. Both ancient

---

[216] We have seen above (section 3) that the skill analogy plays a part in directing agents to shared intuitions rather than to a concentration on disputed or difficult cases at the beginning of the enquiry.

[217] In section 3.

[218] In the final pages of section 4.

and modern ethical theories have the thought that we have to start from commonsense morality, though when we reflect on it we may be led to change it.[219]

A residual modern worry is that such a theory is still intrinsically conservative. This worry takes two forms. One is that if a theory avowedly starts from everyday intuitions, it will never get far beyond them. This is an odd worry, since it is hardly confined to ancient ethics, or even virtue ethics more generally. Even Kant presupposes that the normal moral conscience is basically right. Among all forms of ethical theory only some forms of consequentialism give no status at all to everyday intuitions.[220] In any case it is not true that ancient ethics is conservative. We shall see in Part IV just how far revision of our everyday intuitions is demanded by ancient theories.

The other worry is that even a limited dependence on everyday intuitions is dangerous. Even where we in our society all agree, it is logically possible we might be wrong; and if so, the reflection of the virtuous person will have started from the wrong point and will be systematically warped. The process outlined above can correct for error, but not for massive and systematic error. Ancient theories do not explicitly raise this problem, and sometimes they are castigated for complacency. In fact, they are not naive here. They do not take the possibility of massive and systematic error seriously because they rely on a thesis which is examined elsewhere: that the virtues are natural to us.[221] Thus ancient theories never have to ask if we are massively misguided about the virtues, or whether we should be aiming at cruelty and cowardice instead of their opposites. Our consensus about actions on at least the outer edges and core of the virtues emerges from important facts about the way we normally are, our moral psychology; and for ancient ethics no deeper justification is possible than this, the most general truths about human nature.

6. *Ordinary and Extraordinary Virtue*

An ethics based on the obligation to perform certain actions will produce an account of what may be demanded from the ordinary moral agent, and will then have to give some kind of account of what has got labelled 'supererogation': acts which the agent does which go beyond what he is obliged to do, which are admirable but in some way go beyond moral requirements. It turns out to be surprisingly difficult to specify what it is that is good about supererogatory actions: they are admirable and valuable actions, and we praise the agent for doing them, but if this is so, it then seems a puzzle why they are *not* a matter of obligation. It seems as though actions can be admirable for reasons which do not generate obligations to perform them; but this casts doubt on the adequacy of obligation to be the basic notion in ethics. All the

---

[219] We shall see in Part II that in ancient theories this initial reliance on intuition is connected to the kind of justification of ethics offered in terms of our nature. We could not develop the virtues at all unless we lived in a world where most people will develop, not Hobbesian views but views that reveal at least the 'sparks and seeds' of the virtues: the basis for developing the virtues, though one that falls short of virtue and will be criticized by the virtuous agent.

[220] They thereby, of course, make it completely opaque how we could ever start the process of adopting the theory.

[221] See Part II.

same, we do intuitively recognize a category of actions which are admirable but not required of the agent.[222]

In an ethics of virtue, there is no obvious room for supererogation. There is no 'floor' of minimal moral obligation for the agent to rise above; being a fully virtuous agent is an ideal for everyone. The development of virtue is a process that everyone starts and continues to go along; there are no levels that only moral heroes are supposed to reach. However, there is an analogue of the problem of supererogation: the thought that there is a distinction between the virtue that we may all be expected to achieve, and the virtue which only exceptional people may be expected to achieve.

In both of Aristotle's ethical works we find discussion of a peculiar virtue called *megalopsuchia*, a word that has no good English equivalent ('proud' or 'great-souled' is the usual rendering).[223] What makes this virtue special is that it is not one virtue co-ordinate with the rest; the *Nicomachean Ethics* says that it is the 'crown' or 'ornament' of the other virtues; it makes the other virtues greater, and cannot exist without them, since the agent who has it is one who has greatness in every virtue. It is the virtue of the exceptional agent, who has all the virtues to an exceptional degree and thus has acquired this further virtue of being exceptionally virtuous.[224]

What Aristotle says about this virtue is peculiar. The *megalopsuchos* is certainly concerned with honour:

> If indeed [the *megalopsuchos*] thinks himself worthy of great things, and *is* worthy, and especially of the greatest, he would be especially concerned with one thing [honour]. Worth is said to be concerned with the external goods. . . [and honour is the greatest of these]. And even without argument *megalopsuchoi* people appear to be concerned with honour; for they most think themselves worthy of honour, according to their worth.[225]

He seems to be the person who knows that he is worthy, indeed, since he has all the virtues, morally worthy, and who demands appropriate recognition of this from others. This seems to be the wrong concern for a virtuous person; shouldn't the virtuous person care about being virtuous, rather than being intent on *his* being virtuous and its recognition?

There is another strand to this virtue, however. Sometimes the *megalopsuchos* seems to be above ordinary things, including honour, and indifferent to everything but virtue.

> He is not even so concerned about honour as though it were a very great thing. Powers and money are choiceworthy because of honour (at least those who have them seek to be honoured for them), so to a person for whom honour is a little thing so are the rest.[226]

> He does not face small dangers, nor court dangers, because he honours few

---

[222] See the classic article Urmson (1958); also Baron (1987). For an attack on supererogation, see Kagan (1984) (also [1990]). Kagan discusses Heyd (1982), Nagel (1980) and Scheffler (1982).

[223] See *NE* IV 3; *EE* III 5.

[224] For good discussions, see Sherman (1988), Hardie (1978), Rees (1970), Curzer (1990) and (1991).

[225] *NE* 1123 b 15–24.

[226] *NE* 1124 a 16–20.

things. But he faces great dangers, and when he does he is unsparing of his life, since living in any circumstance is not worthy.[227]

This is not notably more attractive; Aristotle points out that the *megalopsuchos* will not bother to do relatively trivial or boring things, only grand actions,[228] and that he does not get upset over everyday matters because he does not take them seriously.[229] But it seems at any rate to be distinctly different from a self-absorbed concern with honour.

The answer to this puzzling combination of features is surely that offered by Neil Cooper,[230] who points to a passage of the *Posterior Analytics*, where Aristotle is wondering whether '*megalopsuchia*' is ambiguous.

> [We should look for what *megalopsuchoi* people have in common]. E.g., if Alcibiades is *megalopsuchos*, or Achilles or Ajax, what one thing do they all have in common? Not being able to stand insult. . . . Again, consider others, e.g., Lysander or Socrates. If here it is being indifferent to good and bad fortune, I take these two and enquire what they have in common that is the same—that is, being unaffected by fortunes and not enduring being dishonoured. And if there is nothing, then there will be two kinds of *megalopsuchia*.[231]

It seems plain that in the *Nicomachean Ethics* Aristotle has ignored his well-founded doubts as to there being a single quality that combines both of these features, and the peculiarities of the passage are largely explained if we see it as an unsuccessful weave of these two strands.[232] What is interesting here, however, is the point that the notion of a 'super-virtue' can take one of two directions.[233] One is that of the virtuous person as outstanding. It is clear from the examples of Achilles and Ajax that this is a continuation of an earlier Greek idea, that of the hero or outstanding person who lives by standards that apply to him and possibly to other heroes, but not to ordinary people. Achilles when insulted, and Ajax when disgraced, do extreme things which most people would not regard as the appropriate reaction, and would even disapprove of. The heroes in question, however, cannot live with what other people could accept, because they have to live with their own self-conception as heroic, that is, extraordinary, outstanding people. (The example of Alcibiades reminds us that thinking of oneself in this way in a non-heroic, ordinary political society is hard to sustain; Alcibiades' high opinion of himself, and his ability to get others to share it, led to terrible disasters for himself and others.) Aristotle is clearly trying to redefine and refine this earlier idea by attaching it to the *moral* hero; the outstanding person is not the heroic fighter but the person who has all the virtues.

---

[227] *NE* 1124 b 6–9.

[228] 1124 b 23–6.

[229] 1125 a 9–10.

[230] N. Cooper (1989).

[231] *Post An* 97 b 7–25.

[232] For concern with honour, see especially 1123 b 15–24, 1124 a 5–7, 1124 a 20–26; for indifference to fortune see 1123 b 30–1124 a 3, 1124 a 12–20, 1124 b 6–9, 1124 b 23–6, 1125 a 9–10.

[233] At the beginning of Book VII of the *Ethics* Aristotle discusses a kind of 'godlike' or 'heroic' virtue, but he makes it clear that this has no application to ordinary life, just like its opposite, brutishness. The *megalopsuchos*, on the other hand, is clearly an (idealized) phenomenon to be found in (idealized) everyday life.

Nonetheless, Aristotle insists, he is and is perceived to be someone special, someone who stands out, and is recognized to do so by the respect and honour he receives.[234]

This is an interesting attempt; it falls down because Aristotle has not given sufficient thought to the internal perspective involved. For the *megalopsuchos* has to have this thought, that he merits greater honour and respect than others do; and this makes exceptional virtue into something self-centred. (Indeed, the more the thought is refined the more objectionable it becomes. The *megalopsuchos*, it turns out, will not pay attention to honour from any old source, for example, only to honour from good people; to most people he will be frankly contemptuous.) But thoughts which centre on the self in this way are antithetical to the development of virtue, not expressive of it. For virtue involves a concern to do the right thing because it is the right thing, and to be the kind of person who does that—not to do the right thing because one is a person who is outstanding at doing the right thing, and thereby worthy of greater respect than others.

It might be countered that these thoughts are not really antithetical. The super-virtuous person does the virtuous thing just because it is the virtuous thing to do; even if he thereby acts because he is outstanding and worthy of special respect, this latter need not be his motive in acting. Thus we need not conceive of the super-virtuous person as actually having the thought that he will act this way because he is an outstandingly virtuous person. And if he does not have this thought, then, even if he is in fact an outstandingly virtuous person and worthy of exceptional respect, the internal perspective can be consistent with virtue.

However, the problem here does not disappear if the *megalopsuchos* does not hold both types of thoughts together consciously at the same time. For if he does not, we can surely ask why not. What is to prevent his from putting together the thoughts of what virtue requires, and what kind of person he in fact is? Unless there is something to prevent him putting together both these kinds of thoughts, then even if he normally did not, and did not require the thought about himself to motivate him to a particular virtuous action, we must ask what the result is of combining the kinds of thoughts. And the result is surely still objectionable; for he will realize that the reason why he does what virtue requires in such a reliable way is that he is the kind of person who is morally exceptional. And this surely makes him, not a recognizable type of exceptionally virtuous person, but someone whose thoughts about virtue run objectionably through himself.[235]

The other idea in play here is that of being above good or bad fortune. Aristotle refines this from the popular idea of being indifferent to worldly things to the idea of being indifferent to anything but considerations of virtue. On this view, the super-virtuous person cares only about what is relevant to virtue, and precisely does not care about honour and other 'external' goods. This brings this idea into sharp conflict with the first, not successfully overcome by Aristotle's focus on getting honour only from the right kind of people.

It is this idea, that the exceptionally virtuous person not only has the virtues, but does not take anything else seriously, which prevails in ethical philosophy after

---

[234] Chris Gill and Dan Blickman have both emphasized to me the continuity that Aristotle is here claiming with earlier ways of thinking about heroic figures. Aristotle is trying to give moral backing to something which he sees as important in Greek culture.

[235] Compare Williams' notion of a 'self-reflexive deformation' of moral thinking in (1981b).

Aristotle; the self-absorption of the exceptional person who needs to be recognized as such disappears.[236] The Stoics define *megalopsuchia* as 'knowledge which sets us above the things which happen naturally in both excellent and bad people.'[237] Compare the argument that virtue is self-sufficient for happiness:

> 'For if', he says, *megalopsuchia* is self-sufficient for putting us above everything, and if it is part of virtue, then virtue too is self-sufficient for happiness, despising even the things that seem annoying.'[238]

The root idea is the same: this is a virtue of the exceptionally virtuous, who is 'above' everything in the sense of being indifferent to everything but virtue.

Even when disentangled from self-absorption and concern with honour, this virtue can seem disagreeable in many ways. The virtuous person is not, either for Aristotle or for the Stoics, someone who is utterly indifferent (in the non-technical sense) to non-moral objects and values; she is just the person with the right priorities, the person in whom moral values control and dominate the rest. Virtue is what is most important for her, but she is not 'above' everything. The *megalopsuchos*, by contrast, is above everything but virtue. Virtue not only structures her concerns but is *all* she cares about; she is not engaged with the sources of non-moral conduct. We can see how this would result in what Aristotle describes: such an exceptional person is not motivated to do ordinary, boring and unspectacular acts of virtue, since she is not as fully engaged as ordinary people are in the non-moral business of living that gives rise to these ordinary acts. Hence her virtuous acts will be limited to the more spectacular kind.

We can see an analogue here to the problem of supererogation in an ethics of obligation. Our aim is to have the virtues; so surely it must be to have them to the fullest extent we can, to have 'greatness in every virtue'? Some people, the overachievers, do do this: they not only have every virtue, they have it 'in spades'. On the one hand, this is admirable; these people have achieved the condition of the ordinarily virtuous person, only more so, so what could there be to criticize? But on the other hand, the extraordinarily virtuous person is above everything but virtue, and so above what concerns us. Her way of being virtuous must inevitably seem somewhat contemptuous to those of us ordinary people who are not above these everyday commitments and concerns.[239] The extraordinarily virtuous person creates a difficulty for an ethic of virtue not very unlike the problem the saint or hero creates for an ethic of obligation: what makes him admirable would seem to be

---

[236] Aristotle's own school does not seem to have appreciated the interest of his account of *megalopsuchia*; it is defined unilluminatingly simply as a mean between extremes (Arius 146.5–6).

[237] Arius 61, 15–17. *Megalopsuchia* is presented by them as a subdivision of courage (60,22), but the actual definition has no relevance to courage especially; *megalopsuchia* is what puts one above everything not particular to virtue.

[238] Diogenes VII 128.

[239] Sherman (1988) brings out this aspect of *megalopsuchia* very well. I agree with her that there is something objectionable in the self-absorption of the *megalopsuchos*, though I have argued that this affects only one strand of the notion. I take issue with Sherman, however, in that I take as indifference to all but virtue, what she takes as 'the exemption thesis': the idea that doing grand deeds occasionally actually lets you off doing many unspectacular everyday virtuous deeds. I think that Aristotle's text (as well as the later Stoic direction of the concept) suggests that the *megalopsuchos* is so indifferent to petty actions that he does not even see himself as trading them for the major ones.

something we should all aim at, but in fact he turns out to be a bad guide for us, since he turns out to lack just what is relevant for our condition. Our other sources for ancient ethics do not pursue the resulting problem, and it is a pity that they did not find it more interesting.

If we are asked, today, what we take supererogation to be, we are likely first to think of striking examples, such as a person choosing to sacrifice his life to save others, rather than finding a clear theoretical notion. And when we ask what it is that matters about these examples we may find ourselves focussing both on the fact that the *action* was praiseworthy but not morally required, and that the *agent* took it on himself to do something which he would not expect other agents to do. It may be, in short, that our notion of supererogation is a blend of the idea of the praiseworthy but non-obligatory act in an ethics of obligation, and of the idea of the exceptional agent in an ethics of virtue. If there is anything to this suggestion, then supererogation might be illuminated for us by paying more attention than is usual to the contribution to it of ideas of virtue.[240]

7. *Virtue and Morality*

So far I have given no explicit defence of an assumption which requires it, namely that ancient concern about virtue is concern about morality. The sketch so far given of virtue and its place in the agent's thoughts about his life as a whole should have made this plausible, but some objections must first be met before we can finally be satisfied that the assumption is justified.

Attempts to show directly that the ancient conception of virtue lines up with our conception of morality are hindered by the fact that there is great difficulty in defining the latter. This is why I did not begin the book with a systematic account of morality and then claim that the account of virtue given in ancient ethics fits that. The success of such a project would depend entirely on the acceptability of the general account of morality offered. But if one believes, as I do, that our modern notion of morality is indebted to several different sources, it is not surprising that any general account of morality offered will seem acceptable to those who accept the emphasis given to the various sources, and rejected by those who reject that emphasis. The obvious danger of skewing the investigation at the start is intensified when we reflect that ancient ethics contains many of the elements of modern ethics, but with very different status. I have, therefore proceeded more cautiously; I have so far discussed ancient theories of virtue in ways which I hope bring out their similarities to theories of morality on the intuitive level. And I shall now try to meet

---

[240] In fact there are many distinctions to be drawn here. We have spectacular kinds of action. We also have the distinction between merely doing a decent minimum and doing more than this; this can be understood in several ways—as fulfilling imperfect as well as perfect duties, or as doing what a virtuous, rather than a merely dutiful person would do; and this can be taken in either an ancient or a Kantian understanding of virtue. There is also the notion of holding oneself to a higher ideal than one would demand of others; and this may or may not derive from a sense that one is, oneself, an exceptional person. It is unlikely that all these features of supererogation can neatly fall under one kind of account, either in terms of virtue or in terms of obligation. What is important is to recognize them all, and not to give a falsely simple account of a difficult phenomenon.

objections to the claim that ancient ethical theories are theories of morality, looking one by one at what have been claimed to be striking contrasts and urging in each case that the contrast is mistaken. If this is successful, we can feel more confident that ancient and modern theories have the same object.[241]

The most important feature of modern moral theories that seems to be lacking in ancient theories of virtue is the thought that moral reasons form a distinct kind, and that there is a crucial difference between moral and non-moral reasons.[242] Ancient claims about virtue, it is thought, cannot be about morality, just because the virtues do not provide reasons which are different in kind from other kinds of practical considerations which appeal to the agent.

It is certainly true that Greek lacks a word or concept closely corresponding to *moral*.[243] Further, ancient theories of ethics do not find an important distinction between *kinds* of reasons; as we have seen, the important distinction is that between the derivative reasoning of the learner and the reasoning of the expert, and this is not a difference between types of reasons. Moral reasons are in some modern theories taken to be distinguished from non-moral ones by their form (for example, being universalizable), but as we have seen, in ancient theories, formal differences between reasons alone are not ascribed weight.

But if we ask what the point is of distinguishing moral from non-moral reasons, we find something that does have a striking analogue. For the point is to show that moral reasons have a special place in our deliberations. Suppose I consider an action in terms of how much it would cost me, how long it would take, and so on. Then I find out that it is cowardly. This is not just another consideration to be taken into account and weighed against the others. If I understand what cowardice is, this reason simply stops the deliberation; this kind of reason does not outweigh, but overrides or in some theories, 'silences' the other kinds.[244] Of course I may do it anyway; to understand what morality requires is one thing, to do it another. The point is rather that to consider this fact, of cowardice, as though it were merely another reason like the others, possibly to be outweighed by profit-making, is to misconceive what cowardice is. Moral reasons are special just because of this role they have in our deliberations: they override other kinds of reason just because of the kind of reason that they are.[245]

But now we have found similarity rather than difference with ancient virtue ethics. For all ancient theories think exactly the same way about the fact that the action is cowardly: this is a consideration which is not just weighed up against the

---

[241] The issue can be found sharply posed in Williams (1981a) and (1985). However, it has been commonly assumed in many discussions in the last two decades that ancient ethics, centring on virtue, represents a distinct alternative to modern morality, rather than just a type of moral theory.

[242] Williams (1981a), p. 251: '[Greek ethical thought] basically lacks the concept of *morality* altogether, in the sense of a class of reasons or demands which are vitally different from other kinds of reason or demand'.

[243] Actually Latin does better; *honestum* in Cicero's philosophical works often should clearly be translated as 'morality'.

[244] The silencing metaphor comes from McDowell (1980). Kant uses it in a pedagogical context ('The Didactics of Ethics' at the end of *The Metaphysical Principles of Virtue*).

[245] This is meant to capture the intuitive concept of a moral reason; nothing I say is meant to beg the question as between internalist and externalist accounts of what it is that actually gets us to act on moral reasons.

profit and time expended, but which sweeps them aside; and to think otherwise is to misconstrue what cowardice is.

The Stoics make this point in the clearest and most uncompromising way.[246] Only virtue, they say, is good; other things that we desire should be called not good but 'indifferent'. This does not mean that we have no more reason to go for them than not; it simply marks the difference between virtue and everything else. Some things, like health and wealth, are natural advantages, and it is rational for us to seek them; these are 'preferred indifferents', illness and poverty being 'dispreferred' since nothing is bad but vice. Along with this goes a whole set of new vocabulary; thus only virtue is 'chosen', while health, wealth, etc., are 'selected'. The point of all this artificiality is to emphasize the special role that virtue has in our reasoning; because it is the only thing that is good, other kinds of reasons are swept aside, rather than weighed up against it.

> We judge health to be worthy of a kind of value, but we do not judge it a good, and we do not think there to be any value so great as to be preferred to virtue. . . . Compare the way the light of a lamp is obscured and overpowered by the light of the sun, and the way a drop of honey is lost in the extent of the Aegean sea; compare adding a penny to the riches of Croesus and taking one step on the journey from here to India—if the final good is what the Stoics say it is, it is necessary for all the value of bodily things to be obscured and overwhelmed, indeed to be destroyed, by the brilliance and the size of virtue.[247]

The analogies suggest two points. On the one hand, virtue is not straightforwardly incommensurable with other things, in the sense of not being on the same scale at all. A penny has the same kind of value (monetary) as Croesus' riches; one step does get you some of the way to India. On the other hand, there is a difference so marked that seriously to compare these items shows a lack of understanding of what they are. Someone who seriously congratulated herself on the progress she had made towards getting to India after taking one step would be showing lack of understanding of what one step is and what the journey to India is; someone who seriously counted a penny as the first step towards a billion-dollar fortune likewise. Similarly, while we can at the intuitive level talk of virtue, health and so on as considerations all of which have value in an agent's life, seriously to compare the value of money as against that of honesty, say, shows a misconstrual of what money is and what honesty is.

This is less familiar to us than the distinction between moral and non-moral reasons, both because the ancients do not pose the issue in terms of different kinds of reasons and because they do pose it in terms of the ways we can and cannot compare virtue and other kinds of things, rather than in terms of moral and non-moral reasons conflicting, with the moral ones overriding the others. (As we have seen, ancient theories lay less weight than modern ones do on conflict and disagreement in morality.) Nonetheless, the distinctions seem congruent in that their point is the same: they are stressing a feature of our practical deliberations, the fact

---

[246] This point is made here in a preliminary and summarizing way; fuller understanding of the Stoic position here will emerge from the sections on the Stoics in the following three parts, especially chapter 19.

[247] *Fin* III 44–5.

that one kind of consideration, if rightly understood, cannot simply be weighed up against the other kinds, but puts them out of the running. Of course, the reasons that modern theories give as to *why* cowardice is to be avoided will be different from the ancient reasons; modern theories may point to alleged formal features of reasons citing the demands of bravery, whereas ancient theories will point us towards analysis of the nature of the virtue of bravery. But there is agreement on the main point: cowardice is not just another reason to be factored in, it is a consideration which stops the others in their tracks and sends us back to square one.

The Stoics are the only school that insist so uncompromisingly on the difference between the value of virtue and the value of any other kind of things. Aristotle does not insist that virtue is marked off from other kinds of thing that we seek, and later his followers, the Peripatetics, defined their position against that of the Stoics by saying that virtue and other kinds of natural advantages are all good, ridiculing the Stoics for saying that things that we all rationally seek are not good. Aristotle is thus not in as strong a position as the Stoics are to mark off the special deliberative role of virtue. Nonetheless, Aristotle insists in different ways that virtue has special kinds of advantages which other goods do not. The virtuous person will take pleasure in being virtuous, even if it leads to disadvantages, or even to wounds and death; thus he is not losing anything by his virtuous activity that can be balanced against the value of virtue. Thus virtue has a special place in relation to the other goods.[248]

Aristotle also describes virtuous action in ways which bring it close to other modern characterizations of what is done for a moral reason. The virtuous person does the virtuous action for its own sake,[249] and because it is *kalon*, 'fine' or 'noble'.[250] The *kalon* is the aim of virtue.[251] Alexander of Aphrodisias later puts the point more precisely: 'Virtue does everything for the sake of the *kalon qua kalon*, for virtue is such as to do things that are *kala* in the field of action.'[252] The virtuous action is thus done for its own sake, without ulterior motive, as is supposed to be true of an action done for a moral reason.[253] And it is done with the *kalon* as its aim, rather than benefit or pleasure, which are the other characteristic human aims.[254] Thus Aristotle recognizes that the virtuous person does the virtuous act for its own sake, and, further, that when she so acts she is motivated in a distinctive way.

Once again we seem to have agreement with the demands of modern morality rather than conflict, since moral reasons are commonly taken to have just these features: to act for a moral reason is to do the action for its own sake and not for any further motive, and it also involves a distinct kind of motivation. Aristotle and the Stoics thus seem to converge on what is expected by modern moral theories. They do so in different ways, however, and Aristotle's position is the weaker (hence

---

[248] Again, this important point will be greatly amplified in Part IV.

[249] E.g., 1105 a 31–2.

[250] E.g., 1116 a 11.

[251] 1115 b 11–13. For more detail, see chapter 18, especially pp. 370ff.

[252] *De An* II 154.30–32: *hē aretē tou kalou charin hēi kalon panta prattei (praktikē gar hē aretē tōn en tois praktois kalōn).*

[253] Aristotle also holds that virtuous actions are done ultimately for the sake of the agent's final end, happiness. (See chapter 1.) It seems that there is a problem here: how can virtuous actions be done for their own sake *and* for the sake of a further end? See Kraut (1976), Engberg-Pedersen (1981). We will not be able properly to tackle this question until Part IV.

[254] 1104 b 30–1105 a 1.

it is no surprise that his is the theory which is most often invoked in contrasts with modern morality). Aristotle insists that moral motivation is distinct from other kinds, but he does not insist on the special deliberative role of virtue which the Stoics press. His position on this issue is in fact not plain. He insists that the virtuous person, who aims at the fine or *kalon*, will take pleasure in being virtuous, and will not regard losses of money and other advantages as important. But his position is, as we shall see, distinctively different from and weaker than that of the Stoics, who take moral and non-moral considerations to be different in kind.

This difference in strength between the Stoics and Aristotle is linked to the differences between their theories on the relation of virtue and happiness. This will engage us at greater length in Part IV, along with an examination of the later hybrid theories which tried to mediate between the two positions. In all these cases there seems no reason to deny that the role of virtue in our deliberations is essentially that which modern theories take morality to have. Only Epicurus does not mark off the deliberative role of virtue in even the weaker way; but just this point forms a standard ancient *criticism* of him.[255]

Modern moral theories often begin from questions about what we do and our intuitions as to how we ought to act, and proceed to examine these judgements and the kinds of grounds we consider relevant to them. The task of moral theory is often taken as being that of clarifying to ourselves, and making more rigorous, our ways of coming to decisions. Some go further and try to regiment these into mechanical decision procedures, but even theories stopping short of this tend to see their primary aim as being that of improving our ability to make decisions as to what we ought to do, often in hard cases like abortion, euthanasia, etc. This feature is often summed up by calling modern moral theories *act-centred*. As we have seen in the introduction, it is widely regarded as a major task of modern moral theories that they directly improve our ability to work out what to do.

We have already seen that ancient ethics does not proceed in this way or see this as its primary aim. The entry point for ethical reflection is not isolated problems in the abstract, but my life as a whole and how it is going; we investigate this by asking what the place is in my life of the virtues. Ancient ethics is often, for obvious reasons, labelled *agent-centred*. The question is, does this constitute a radical difference between the two? If moral theories are mechanisms to help us work out what to do, isn't concentration on virtue and character beside the mark where morality is concerned?

Claims that there is a radical difference often underplay aspects of modern theories that do not relate directly to actions. Modern theories don't simply seek decision procedures; they also ask what the person will be like who reliably makes the right decisions. They have to do this, especially theories which have very revisionary views as to what the right thing to do is, for they have to face the question, why we should accept their views as to what the right thing to do is? Hence they have to examine what the ordinary moral agent is like, and what the possibilities are of revising her dispositions. Further, we have seen that ancient

---

[255] See the criticisms at *Fin* II 44 ff. Epicurus is often interpreted as giving virtue only instrumental value as a means to producing pleasure. I have argued that Epicurus is driven by various constraints into allowing virtue intrinsic value (see Annas 1987 and chapter 16).

theories don't just discuss the good life, with no reference to action; they assume that discovering the right specification of one's final end will *eo ipso* give one a plan of life and guidance as to one's actual deliberations. It is plain on reflection, in fact, that no sensible theory could consider merely acts or merely agents.

The contrast must lie, then, in the relative importance that ancient and modern theories give to acts and to agents. And it at first seems that we still do have a striking contrast. Modern theories, at least the twentieth-century ones, tend to take questions about what one should do to be the primary ones, in that it is only when these are in hand that we can consider the question of what kind of person to be. Crudely put, the good person is the person so disposed as to make the right decisions, do the right thing; but we determine what *that* is without appealing to our notion of the good person. Virtue will thus be secondary; virtue notions will not aid us to derive standards of right action, and so will not be important. Ancient theories, on the other hand, take virtue notions as primary, as we have seen. They do not derive standards of right conduct from the notion of the virtuous person alone, but the good agent is the focus of the theory because we understand right conduct in terms of having the virtues, not the other way around.

It is widely accepted that there is a contrast of this kind between ancient and modern theories. Sometimes, when ancient theories are misunderstood as being hierarchical and complete, this point is made the basis of a complaint that virtue ethics is trivial, since it can determine right action no more definitely than as what the virtuous person would do. However, as we have seen, this mistakes what ancient theories do. Further, even modern theories often do not simply work out a decision procedure in the void and then define the good agent as the person who applies that procedure. For the development of a realistic decision procedure should have been responsive from the start to considerations about the ways people actually do reason. Otherwise it seems doomed to futility.

Any ethical theory, ancient or modern, has to clarify and criticize our intuitive views both on rightness of action and on goodness of agents. There is indeed a difference of emphasis here. For modern theories often demand that the theory contain within itself correct answers to difficult cases, so that the theory can be applied to simply described situations to produce correct decisions. Ancient theories, by contrast, assume that correct decisions are reached by agents who have accepted and lived by the theory; but methods for producing correct decisions are not part of the theory itself. Hence they stress the understanding of the fully moral agent more than modern theories do, and in a way foreign to modern theories, they see the fully moral agent as analogous to an expert compared to a beginner. Ancient theories thus see no force in the kind of consideration moving Sidgwick, for example, to demand that ethics become 'scientific' and explicitly systematize our ways of coming to decisions. In this sense, and only this, they are 'agent-centred' as opposed to 'act-centred'.

Two considerations mitigate even this contrast, however. One is that while some modern theories *aspire* to produce decision procedures and replace our deliberations by 'powerful' formalized systems, this is so far mere aspiration, and there have been no impressive actual results. The other is that the fully virtuous person in ancient theories is an *ideal*; non-ideal people are best advised to consult the theory explicitly, rather than consulting their own understanding. So for ordinary people there seems to be little difference between the ancient and modern situations: there is, in each case, an ideal of ethical reasoning, but we ourselves would be ill advised to think of ourselves as ideal reasoners.

Another difficulty with ancient virtue ethics has been found in the scope of ancient theories. Aristotle in particular gives lists of virtues which range over the whole of social life and cover areas that we would not at all naturally take to be the domain of morality. He opposes, for example, the virtue of 'temperance' or self-control with bodily pleasures, not only to self-indulgence, the 'excess', but also to *anaisthēsia*, 'unfeelingness', the 'defect', a disposition not to enjoy food, drink and sex as much as one should. He also gives sketches of large-scale social virtues, such as that of paying for public works in a tasteful and appropriate manner. But if he is talking about morality, we seem forced to the absurd conclusion that not enjoying food is a moral vice, or that tasteful expenditure is a moral matter. And there are many similar examples.

This point can be partially deflected by noticing that Aristotle is rather unusual in his list of virtues. The standard approach is to list the canonical four virtues of courage, wisdom, temperance and justice, and to analyze other virtues as sub-kinds of these. Further, many of Aristotle's odder views seem to derive from his insistence on applying his idiosyncratic doctrine of the 'mean'.[256] But even so the problem apparently remains in many cases.

Instead of responding that Aristotle's virtues are not a matter of morality, we could, however, ask whether Aristotle is not prepared to moralize more of everyday life than we are. He seems to regard insensitivity to food and drink, for example, as not just a blank physical given, but as an insensitivity which involves a moral insensitivity in some way; and matters like public spending as inviting moral concern. Whether he is right to do so in the case of all his virtues is another matter, of course, but this clearly seems to be his assumption in general.

Is this absurd? Aristotle is certainly making an assumption which is not absurd, and which is shared by all the ancient schools, namely that ethics is not a distinct compartment in one's life. Taste, style and social behaviour generally are not neutral matters, indifferent between the good and the bad: ethical differences will affect all such aspects of your life. Aristotle is unusual in trying to structure actual virtues for all the various aspects of social life; but there is no disagreement on the basic point that the possession or otherwise of the virtues makes a great difference to how one spends money, enjoys food, makes jokes and so on. Your ethical stage of development is relevant in your life as a whole, in every aspect of your interactions with others.

Is this alien to a proper consideration of morality? Only if morality is in fact compartmentalized in our lives, if our stage of moral development has little or nothing to do with the way we live the rest of our lives. Some hold this to be the case, but it is not obviously true, and compelling arguments can be brought against it. As Bradley puts it,

> It is. . . .an error to suppose that in what is called human life there remains any region which has not been moralized. . . . The character shows itself in every trifling detail of life; we can not go in to amuse ourselves while we leave it outside

[256] See section 2.

the door with our dog; it is ourself, and our moral self, being not mere temper or inborn disposition, but the outcome of a series of acts of will.[257]

We can reject this view, but to do so is counter-intuitive in the extreme. And if we do not think that morality can be compartmentalized, then it may not seem very important whether we regard our lives as coming under a wide range of virtues, or as affected by our development in a narrower range of virtues.

The ethics of virtue, as we have seen, takes shape within the framework of a search for an adequate specification of my final end. In ancient ethics this is the entry point to serious ethical reflection; it is taken to be a deep fact about us that we do have such a final end and that when we start reflecting on our lives we do not rest until we have brought the whole of our lives into reflective focus. Further, it is taken for granted that this final end is happiness, though happiness is understood weakly and in an unspecific way. From this point we find two very common kinds of claim to the effect that ancient ethical theories are not engaging with what we take to be morality.

First, ancient ethical theory begins with the agent's concern for her own life as a whole. Modern moral theories, by contrast, often begin by specifying morality as a concern for others; morality is often introduced as a point of view contrasting with egoism. If a basic and non-derivative concern for others is taken to be definitive of morality, then this contrast may be taken to show that ancient ethics is really a form of egoism; and this is indeed a frequent charge, and one that is often extended to modern versions of virtue ethics.

The straightforward claim that an ethics of virtue is egoistic, since the agent is concerned about developing her virtues as a way of achieving her final end, is straightforwardly mistaken. For what are to be developed are the *virtues*, and these are, for example, justice, courage and the like. Some of them have a direct connection with the good of others, for example justice. All of them involve having at least a disposition to do the right thing, where the right thing to do is established independently of the agent's own interests. An ethics of virtue is therefore at most formally self-centred or egoistic; its *content* can be fully as other-regarding as that of other systems of ethics.

Some find this unsatisfactory, however, and find a danger even in formal self-centredness. The thought here is that if the good of others is introduced as the content of the agent's own final good, then it cannot really be the good of *others*; it must reduce in some way to what matters to the agent. This thought can seem compelling to those accustomed to systems of ethics that begin from an underivative concern for the good of others, but on consideration can be seen to be confused. There is no reason, *prima facie*, why the good of others cannot matter to me independently of my own interests, just because it is introduced as something required by my final good. The thought that is frequently suggested is that the good of others must matter to me just because it is the good of others, not because it forms part of my own good. However, there is no reason why this should be incompatible with its in fact forming part of my own good. For an ethics of virtue, the good of others matters to me because it is the good of others, and it is part of my

[257]Bradley (1876), Essay VI, p. 217.

own final good. It is quite unwarranted to think that the second thought must undermine the first.[258]

A more serious objection is that an ethics of virtue can accommodate the agent's concern for others, but not in the way required for a properly moral point of view. For an ethics which begins from the agent's own good, however vaguely specified, can accommodate only concern for particular other people who can comprehensibly enter into the agent's own concerns and projects; it cannot accommodate impartiality, the thought that I matter, from the moral point of view, merely as one among others, and should give my own interests no more weight than those of anybody else. This is a deep issue, which can only be dealt with satisfactorily in Part III; at this point I shall merely remark that as it stands this objection is mistaken also, since the Stoics both begin their ethics from concern for oneself and one's happiness, and end up claiming that the end of this development will precisely be a position where, as far as the claims of morality go, one is indifferent between one's own interests and those of someone one has no knowledge of in a far-away country, 'the remotest Mysian'. Other theories, notably Aristotle's, do not make this claim; but later versions of Aristotelian ethics, responding to the Stoics, do. Whether or not morality, or justice, requires impartiality is a live issue in ancient ethical debate. If we bear in mind that recently there have been several attacks on the notion that morality requires impartiality, we can see that there is no vast gap here between ancient and modern approaches.

The ethics of virtue is not egoistic in any sense; ancient ethical theories are just as opposed to egoism as is Kantianism. And thus there is no lack of fit on this score with modern concerns with morality.

Another kind of objection is sometimes raised at this point. Other-concern aside, how can it be sensible to see ancient theories as concerned with morality in their concern for virtue? For they aim to show us the correct reflective conception of our final end, which is happiness. But how can any theory hope to show us that being moral is the way to being happy? This is again especially salient with the Stoics, who claim that virtue is actually sufficient for happiness. Bentham's reaction to this claim has been shared by many: 'What benefit, in any shape, could be derived from impregnating the memory with such nonsense? What instruction from a self-contradictory proposition, or any number of such propositions?'[259] Understandably, a common response has been to save the ancients from what looks like a silly endeavour, by claiming that they were indeed concerned with happiness, but not so quixotic as to think morality the best way to it. But a better reaction would be to be more patient than Bentham in trying to understand what is meant. For the problem here lies not with our notion of virtue, but with our notion of happiness. It is easy

---

[258] We shall see in Part III that some ancient theories do have a problem in giving a proper role to other-concern, namely the hedonist theories; but even they (with the exception of the Cyrenaics) see it as a goal of their theory to give it such a role. Thus, whether there is a conflict between aiming at one's own good and aiming at the good of others depends on what content is given to one's own good. For theories which specify this as pleasure there is a problem, since there are obvious ways in which aiming at the good of others comes into conflict with achieving one's own good. But for theories which give virtue a dominant or overriding status in one's own good there is no conflict. See also Annas (1992e).

[259] Bentham (1834), p. 300. This reaction was produced by reading Cicero's *Tusculan Disputations* when an undergraduate at Oxford. I take the reference from the opening of Irwin (1986).

for us to fall into Bentham's mindless assumption that happiness must be a determinate and specific state, especially a state of feeling good about something. And of course it is mysterious why anyone would think morality a good strategy for achieving *that*. But we have seen that there is no reason to think that this is what the ancient notion of happiness is. Happiness has been introduced as a thin and indeterminate specification of our final end. It is a mistake to bend the notion of virtue to fit happiness; in the ancient way of thinking it is happiness which is the weak and flexible notion, which has to be modified when we understand the nature of the demands which virtue makes in our lives.[260] Of course, nothing has so far been said to make this claim convincing; we have concentrated on virtue and found it to be the locus of concern with morality, but we will not examine until Part IV the central issue of the relation of virtue to happiness. When we do, however, we will find no reason to go back on what has been established in this part about virtue and morality.

One final common charge that an ethics of virtue cannot be taken seriously as morality remains to be dealt with. We have been using 'virtue' to translate the Greek *aretē* (and the Latin *virtus*). But is this justified? In Greek *aretē* means 'excellence', and is used wherever things or people are excellent. Horses and houses have *aretē* if they are excellent horses or houses. From this point it is sometimes inferred that even for humans the *aretai* are not the virtues. Virtues are states where we are concerned with particularly moral appraisal, and judge that the person can be praised or blamed and, hence, that they were morally responsible for what they did. But if the *aretai* are just the human excellences, there will be no division of kind between being brave or temperate and excellences like being healthy or handsome, no way of marking off an area of peculiarly moral appraisal, where it is assumed that the agent is morally responsible.[261]

This is a venerable charge, going back at least to Hume's fourth appendix to his *Enquiry Concerning the Principles of Morals*.[262] Hume there claims that 'the ancient moralists, the best models, made no material distinction among the different species of mental endowments and defects, but treated all alike under the appellation of virtues and vices.' This implies, of course, that they were not interested in demarcating those actions for which we are morally responsible from those where this is not the case, a consequence which Hume accepts: 'In general we may observe, that the distinction of voluntary or involuntary was little regarded by the ancients in their moral reasonings.' It was only with the incursion of Christianity into moral philosophy, he claims, that philosophers began to be obsessed by the question of voluntariness and hence with the question of moral responsibility—and hence to mark off a specific kind of moral responsibility and moral virtue.

---

[260] For the same reason it is a mistake to assimilate the relation of virtue and happiness to that of morality and prudence. Our determinate modern notion of prudence has no exact analogue in ancient ethical theories.

[261] The work of A.W.H. Adkins has been influential in this respect; for a recent brief restatement of the essentials of his view, as that relates to the theme of this book, see his (1991). The article concludes with an explicit claim that the recent movement in 'virtue ethics' has nothing to learn from ancient 'aretē-ethics'.

[262] Hume also claims that even in English we do not make a marked distinction between what are usually called the moral virtues and other kinds of non-moral excellence. Sidgwick ([1907] III ii) rebuts this.

Hume's analysis and its accompanying diagnosis, have been influential, so it needs to be stated that it is quite false. Aristotle devotes a prominent part of Book III of the *Nicomachean Ethics* to discussing the conditions for voluntariness, precisely because this is required by a discussion of virtue, since 'praise and blame are bestowed on what is voluntary, pardon and sometimes pity on what is involuntary'.[263]

Further, the fact that *aretē* means 'excellence' , not 'virtue', is quite compatible with its turning out to be the case that the excellences of a human life should be the virtues. And this is what we find. The human *aretai*, from Plato onwards, are quite routinely taken to be courage, temperance, intelligence and justice, with other virtues as subdivisions of these.[264] And as we have seen at length, virtues are concerned with choice, and with doing the right thing, from a well-informed judgement as to what is the right thing to do and a firm disposition to feel and react in the right way about it.

No understanding is gained, then, by translating *aretē* as 'excellence', or by pointing to *aretē* as applied to statues and to healthy bodies. For the wider usage coexists with a narrower usage in which the human excellences just are the moral virtues. During the Hellenistic period the distinctness between these two usages was clearly recognized:

> As for *aretē*, it is in one sense generally anything's reaching completion. So it is with a statue. And there is the unreasoned kind, like health, and the reasoned kind, like intelligence. Hecaton says. . .that the *aretai* that involve knowledge and are reasoned are those whose constitution is formed from principles, like intelligence and justice; unreasoned are those that are observed to be co-extensive with those constituted from principles, like health and strength.[265]

Indeed, the use of *aretē* or *virtus* for the moral virtues of a person came to be seen as the primary use, and the application to statues and horses as secondary, as we can see from this account of Antiochus' ethical theory:

> Thus it will come about that the *virtus* of the mind is preferred to the *virtus* of the body, and the *voluntariae virtutes* of the mind surpass the *virtutes non voluntariae*. The former, indeed, are called *virtutes* in the proper sense, and are much superior, because they come about from rationality, which is the most divine element in people.[266]

This passage is hard to translate, just because we start with the broad sense of *virtus* and go on to the narrower sense in which the moral virtues are picked out. Since the speaker explicitly says that the narrower sense is the proper sense of *virtus*, we

[263] Hume says, 'We need only peruse the titles of chapters in Aristotle's Ethics to be convinced' that Aristotle's virtues are not restricted to what is voluntary; there is little sign that Hume perused the chapters. Indeed, while Hume is at home with ancient history, literature and oratory, his grasp of ancient philosophy is surprisingly weak.

[264] Aristotle's messier and less systematic list is untypical.

[265] Diogenes VII 90 (his account of Stoic ethics). Cf. the parallel passage in Arius Didymus' account of Stoic ethics (62.15–63.5).

[266] *Fin* V 38. Cf. 36, where the same point is made, and it is said that memory and in general endowments and talents belong to the class of 'non-voluntary virtues', while the class of the 'great and true virtues' includes practical intelligence, moderation, courage, justice and others of the same kind.

cannot translate with the two words 'excellence' and 'virtue'; but we have no single word that functions in a like way. Alexander of Aphrodisias goes further in saying that when we use 'virtue' of aptitudes and natural excellences, we are using the word in a different sense from when we use it of the virtues which are unified by *phronēsis*, the practical intelligence of the virtuous person.[267] These passages make it clear why non-moral applications of *aretē* and *virtus* are quite irrelevant to their application to the moral virtues.

Objections can, then, be met, and we have no reason not to accept what has, throughout this part, seemed intuitively true, namely that ancient theories of virtue are theories of morality.

We have seen[268] that no ancient theory of virtue can do for us all the things that we have come to expect a theory of morality to do. Nonetheless, we have seen that for all that, ancient theories of happiness and virtue are theories of morality. We have also seen that the framework of ancient ethics is different from what we expect of modern theories, since it is not hierarchical and complete. In Part II we go on to look at the kind of grounding that ancient theories offer to someone who asks why she should take an interest in happiness and virtue. In Part III we look at the way the good of others is located in a eudaimonist theory. And in Part IV we shall explore the thesis which it is a major goal of this book to understand, that virtue is sufficient for happiness. We can already see that it is not misleading to understand this thesis as being the thesis that in the life which gives the agent all that matters, morality will be, not just one value, but a dominant or overriding value.

---

[267] *De An* II 155 24–8: *plēn homonumōs tas epideiotētas kai tas euphuias eiōthamen aretas legein.* Cf. Cicero, *Leg* I 45.

[268] Introduction, pp. 6–7.

II

Justification and the Appeal to Nature

3

Nature and Naturalism

Ancient ethical theories appeal to nature to ground their ethical claims. The appeal takes different forms, and is more prominent in the Hellenistic theories than in Aristotle; but it is important in all of them.

What is the appeal to nature? It is easy to take it to be some form of what is now called ethical naturalism (and indeed ancient theories are commonly called naturalist). A lot depends here, however, on exactly what naturalism is taken to be. Some modern accounts present it purely as an a thesis in metaethics, having no influence on the content of the theory concerned. And it is defined as a single position[1] by contrast with intuitionism,[2] as follows. Intuitionism is the claim that moral properties are irreducible and cannot be defined in or reduced to non-moral terms. So naturalism by contrast is the position that moral terms *can* be so defined or reduced. (And, since either moral terms are irreducible or they aren't, it can come to seem that the only way of avoiding either position is to move to some form of non-cognitivism about morality—the position, that is, that moral statements are not properly true or false at all.)

There is, however, nothing in ancient ethics that corresponds to the thought that a metaethical position belongs to a different order of enquiry from ethics; theses about the way ethics is grounded form an integral part of ethics proper. More importantly, ancient theories are not reductive; in keeping with the way that they do not try to reduce other ethical concepts to those of virtue, they do not try to reduce ethical concepts in general to those that are not ethical. This comes out strikingly in the Stoics, who define our final end as both the life according to virtue and the life according to nature. These are treated as two ways of coming to the same result, neither having priority or grounding the other. If the Stoics in appealing to nature were naturalists in the modern sense sketched above, their position would be impossible even to state coherently.

The ancient appeal to nature thus turns out not to be naturalism—not, at least, as that is usually taken in modern ethics; and it is clear that the differences lie in the structures of ancient and modern theories.

---

[1] See, for example, the classic account in Frankena (1973).

[2] Though common, this is a bad name, and has led to much confusion (the main source of which seems to be G. E. Moore). There is no connection between the thesis that moral properties are irreducible, and the thesis that they are grasped by some kind of intuition, as opposed to reasoning. See chapter 2, section 4, n. 140.

Ethical naturalism can of course be taken more generously than it is in the above account. If we reject the demand to be reductive, and to appeal to wholly 'non-evaluative' facts, we can still be left with something that can fairly be called ethical naturalism, namely a position which insists on grounding ethical claims in facts about nature that support those ethical claims. This is general enough to form a spectrum of positions, of which reductive versions would merely form one extreme, united by opposition to the thesis that ethical claims are ultimately self-justifying. This weaker position of course leaves it open for the supporting facts about nature to be themselves evaluative or even ethical.[3]

Whether the ancient appeal to nature is in modern terms a form of naturalism or not thus turns out to depend on how generous a concept of naturalism is in play.[4] Narrow, reductive notions of naturalism contrast with the ancient theories; more generous ones may turn out to be comparable. It is perhaps because the narrow notion has been the more prominent one in modern discussion that the ancient appeal to nature has been so widely misconstrued, and indeed that any appeal to nature in ethical contexts has received critically rather short shrift.[5] We can agree at any rate that no ancient theories take the line that ethical claims are self-justifying; we can support ethical claims, and in particular we can support them by appeal to nature.

As we have seen in Part I, the framework for ancient ethics is given by claims about the form my final end should take and the place in it that virtue should have, rather than by claims about actions that are required or permitted or about ways to bring about certain consequences. Thus the facts beyond the ethical claims that we need to appeal to will not be 'mysterious facts' corresponding to the rightness of certain actions or the goodness of certain states of affairs; rather they will be facts about people and the kinds of dispositions that they have. The ancient appeal to nature is an appeal to what *human* nature is.[6] We should make virtue the most important thing in our lives, according to the Stoics, because that is what accords with human nature. We should cultivate the virtues only because they enable us to achieve true pleasure, according to the Epicureans, because *that* is in accordance with human nature. Though they disagree about what it is that human nature requires for its fulfilment, they agree that it is human nature that we should look to, if we are to determine the proper place of virtue in our lives.

---

[3] Unfortunately, 'naturalism' as a slogan term has got largely attached to the stronger, reductive version, and doubtless many modern moral philosophers would find it odd to call a theory naturalistic if it appealed from ethical facts to ethical facts about nature. But this is, I think, a superficial problem; the interesting question is rather what the ethical facts about nature would be, and what kind of support they would offer to the rest of the theory.

[4] In Annas (1988a) I consider only narrow, reductive forms of modern naturalism, and 'reach the mildly surprising conclusion that the ancient theories which ground ethics in human nature are not naturalist' (p. 169). The contrast there drawn, however, arguably rests too much on reductive assumptions which not all modern theories make. Some of the material in this part derives from this article, though greatly expanded. I am grateful for responses to this paper (particularly those of the commentator André Laks, whose comments are published with the paper) which have enabled me to think through some of my theses more clearly.

[5] See R. de Sousa (1984).

[6] Though, as we shall see, there are some complications with the Stoics, who also bring in cosmic or universal nature.

In some ways this can seem the merest common sense. 'Nature' is for the Greeks just 'what there is', the world that the sciences study,[7] and (apart from Plato in some other-worldly moods) no philosopher doubted that we humans are part of that world and are subject to scientific study just like other parts of it. However, the Greeks did not regard human nature, as it functions in ethical argument, as uncontroversially as this might suggest. Human nature enters into ethical argument in different ways, as we shall see, but never in the role of uncontroversial 'scientific' fact.

It is interesting to contrast Mill, who, when discussing nature, defines a thing's nature as 'the ensemble or aggregate of its powers or properties'.[8] Given this notion of nature, and the further assumption, which Mill unquestioningly makes, that a moral theory must provide specific prescriptions for conduct, it is hardly surprising that Mill finds it blankly incomprehensible how the latter could be got from the former. Sidgwick agrees; if 'nature' means just the natural world, then everything we do accords with nature anyway, and we have no principled way of distinguishing natural from unnatural impulses.[9]

What is the role of nature in ancient ethics? Sometimes it serves as the inescapable aspects of ourselves, our nature being those features of our lives which we have to plan around and cannot plan away. (Sometimes, more positively, our nature in this sense is taken to be our potentialities to develop in certain ways.) And we also find nature in a stronger role as the goal or end of human development; the natural life is the life led by humans who have developed in a natural way, this being understood as a way in which the potentialities which for us are given develop without interference from other, external factors. It is obvious that this second use of nature presupposes two things. One is that we can in fact distinguish between the thing's or person's nature and outside influences that count as interferences with that nature. Plainly we cannot do this just by looking at what actually happens; everything a person does is a product of *some* combination of factors. We need to distinguish between what the person naturally does and what is done to him by way of interference. The second assumption is that we can distinguish between what forms an expression of a person's nature and what forms a corruption of it— between a natural and an *un*natural development.

We can see at once that the notion of nature in this second sense is not a neutral, 'brute' fact; it is strongly normative. In defending virtue by showing it to be natural we are not pointing from value to fact, or from evaluative to non-evaluative facts. Thus ancient theories are not open to the objection that they over-simplify or trivialize ethics by treating ethical issues as soluble by a quick examination of 'the facts'. For ancient ethics, the facts in question are neither simple nor obtainable by a quick glance; they are facts which take some finding and the discovery of which involves making evaluative distinctions.

---

[7] Hence nature is commonly contrasted with artefacts, the products of *technē*.

[8] Mill (1874).

[9] (1907), pp. 80–82. 'Those who have occupied themselves with this distinction seem generally to have interpreted the Natural to mean either the *common* as opposed to the rare and exceptional, or the *original* as opposed to what is later in development. . . . But I have never seen any ground for assuming broadly that Nature abhors the exceptional, or prefers the earlier in time to the later. . . .'

However, this last point opens up the ancient appeal to nature to another objection, namely that it is circular. The whole point of appealing to facts beyond ethics to ground ethics, it is often thought, is to appeal to something neutral and independent. If we appeal to nature, only to find that to do so we have to distinguish between natural process and interference, and between natural development and corruption, have we progressed beyond talking about what is good and bad in the person?

The circularity objection looks powerful when stated abstractly; its force dissolves, I claim, when we look at the way ancient theories actually make the appeal to nature (which is what this part is devoted to). We find dispute about virtue; this is supported by appeal to nature; there continue to be disputes about nature, but they are not trivial relocations of the original disputes. For disputes about nature raise the question, What in our behaviour and dispositions is natural, due to us and the way we unimpededly develop? and What is unnatural, due to factors external to ourselves? We shall see that ancient theories give different answers to these questions; and they differ in the degree of adequacy of their treatment of related questions, such as, Why do we need philosophy to tell us what our nature is? How can we go so wrong that most of us lead unnatural lives? and so on. What we do not find is simple repetition of the original ethical dispute. We shall return to this issue; for the moment it suggests that the circularity claim is insufficiently subtle.

Thus the ancient ethical appeal to nature resists assimilation to modern appeals from value to fact. As Christopher Gill puts it,

> [Human nature] function[s] rather as a means of articulating ideals which are already part of an ethical framework; . . .even if they figure (more than other ethical norms) as part of a world-view, the world in question is one that is viewed from an ethical standpoint.[10]

The appeal to nature is part of an ethical theory; it supports the other parts, but is not itself an appeal outside the theory altogether.

Two common misunderstandings about the ancient appeal to nature have to be cleared away before we turn to it in detail; for they often obscure understanding of how the ancient theories actually work, and give a wrong general picture of their scope. These points are forcefully stated by Thomas Nagel.

> The Aristotelian alternative [to modern ethical theory] . . . would ground a universal answer to the question of how we should live in a theory of human nature and human well-being. If there were a universal human nature and if, contemplating it from outside, we could see that there was a single form of individual and social life and a set of emotional and practical dispositions that was best for any being with that nature, this would provide an objective basis for the endorsement (for humans) of that life and those dispositions. It would harmonize the internal and the external view, and derive ethics from a true conception of our place in the universe.

> Williams' objection to this is not that it is unintelligible, but simply that it is no longer plausible to believe that such a controlling teleology of human nature exists. Apart from the biological basics, human good is underdetermined by

---

[10] C. Gill (1990a); see also Nussbaum (forthcoming a).

human nature. Moreover we have learned to expect that the dispositions that define any more particular form of life will lose rather than gain in conviction when looked at from outside. . . From outside it is evident that many incompatible perspectives are compatible with human nature; the ultimate support of an ethical point of view can only lie in the agent's actual dispositions, unsanctified by a universal teleology.[11]

There are two distinct claims here. One is that Nagel claims (as does Williams, and as do many others) that the ancient appeal to nature must be an appeal to teleology. Our having natures that are well realized in some ways and not in others is taken to imply that our lives are thought of as having a point as part of a larger scheme; and that this is something that can be established objectively, perhaps through a 'metaphysical biology'.[12]

First, this is not even what Aristotle holds. His view of nature is teleological in the following way: when we look at the world, we find, in some areas, the large-scale fact of massive adaptness to ends. His focus is on the parts of animals: we cannot understand what an animal's parts, such as a liver or a heart, are until we understand what they are for. But this plainly gives us no reason to think that we can sensibly ask what whole species are for, or what the point of their lives is. We can raise this question of species only insofar as we think that they fit into some larger system of which they can be regarded as the parts: what we call an ecosystem. Once or twice Aristotle is tempted to see such larger patterns, but they are not prominent in his thought, and when he does, he finds *biological*, not ethical patterns. For Aristotle it is just as naive as it is for us to ask what the point is of a human life. This is not a well-defined question; for there is no well-defined larger system that a human being is part of. So Aristotle does not have a 'universal teleology'; and the teleology that he does have is not a theory about human lives.[13]

More important is the point that all the Hellenistic schools appeal to nature in their ethical theories, while having the most diverse views on teleology. Epicurus rejects teleology in nature in any place (even in areas, like the parts of animals, where it is in fact highly plausible). The Stoics, on the other hand, do enthusiastically accept a universal teleology: we and other species, they claim, do form part of a larger system, to which we and everything else is well-adapted.[14] Hence the appeal to nature, being common to philosophers who accept and philosophers who reject teleology, cannot depend on teleology.[15]

---

[11] Nagel (1986).

[12] Sidgwick makes the more extravagant claim that we can accept nature as an ethical aim only if we independently accept 'the more or less definite recognition of Design exhibited in the empirically known world' ([1907], p. 81). This is unnecessarily crude, however.

[13] See J. Cooper (1982), who discusses *PA* 696 b 2 ff. and *Pol* 1256 b 15 ff., where Aristotle does seem to find a pattern in which species are adapted to one another (and also occasional extensions to natural phenomena, as at *Phys* 198 b 36 ff). Sedley's (1991) arguments for finding in Aristotle a universal nature working for the benefit of humans are unconvincing, and over-interpret the *Pol* and *Phys* passages. On this passage see chapter 4, pp. 156–67.

[14] This is not as naive as it sounds; the well-adaptedness is not necessarily perceptible from the individual's point of view—not until the individual has developed his reason enough to be able to appreciate 'the point of view of the universe'. See Part III, ch. 12, on Stoic *oikeiōsis*.

[15] This is not to say, of course, that teleology does not play a role in the notion of nature of those philosophers who do accept it.

More weighty is the claim that to make human nature the basis for ethics is to accept something unacceptably constricting: the imposition of a single form of life and preferred set of dispositions on everyone. Nagel is right that we have reason to reject this picture; from the viewpoint of my own deliberations I know that an ethical theory cannot be right that would impose a single way of life on me and everyone else just on the grounds that we are human.

However, what is this 'singleness' of the ethical way of life grounded in human nature? Nagel and many other modern critics clearly think that it is something which constrains the range of specific activities in a single life and implies that individuals, however diverse, should aim at the same specific goal. If this were the case, criticism would be easy; but it is not how we find the actual ancient appeal to nature functioning. We have already seen that reflecting on our final end does not prescribe one range of specific human activities as against another. The importance of reflecting on my life as a whole lies in the opportunity for clarifying and rethinking my priorities and the ordering of my values. To be told that one way of doing this, as opposed to another, is natural, in accordance with human nature, is to be told two things. One is that there are constraints which my reflection must respect and priorities which are not up to me to settle. If it is true, for example, that human nature is so constituted as always to seek only pleasure, then this rules out certain theories as to how I should live—the Stoic and Aristotelian, for a start. It also directs me as to where to discover mistakes in my life. If it is true that I cannot help seeking pleasure in all I do, and if I do not seem to be very successful in this, then I must be making mistakes as to what pleasure is and how to achieve it; and searching for these mistakes, and rectifying them, is bound to revise my way of life.

But the appeal to nature is also an appeal to an *ideal*, an ethical ideal, articulated by an ethical theory, in terms of which I can locate, criticize and modify those elements in my ethical beliefs which rely merely on convention. For beliefs which I have acquired in an uncritical way from my social environment cannot be relied on to be taking me in the right direction; indeed (depending on how revisionary the theory in question is) they can be taken to be faulty and misleading. Appealing to nature gives me an ethical ideal in terms of which to reject those of my beliefs which turn out to conflict with it, and better to understand those beliefs which are in fact in conformity with it. For what is natural about me is objectively so, whereas many of my beliefs may rest on nothing better than convention. But we plainly do not, just from a conception of human nature (as aiming for pleasure, say) conclude that we should all do the same specific things in life.

Ancient theories, then, do not use the appeal to nature to establish a single specific way of life, or to encourage people to ignore their individual differences. Some theories do contain prescriptions for 'ways of life' and for choosing individual goals; but they come in much later, at a different point in the theory. And thus the argument that the ancient appeal to nature must be unacceptably constricting fails.

There remains another version of the objection, however. Even if we accept the above, ancient ethical theory seems to require singleness from human nature in that the ideal ethical life is always one in which all the agent's aims are harmoniously fulfilled and ethical aims are given primacy. We have seen in Part I the ways in which theories tend towards the unity of the virtues, and thus of the unification of the agent's intellectual and affective tendencies. Further, no ancient ethical theory allows that it could be in accordance with nature to give non-ethical aims primacy over ethical; whatever the precise role given to virtue, it does not allow non-virtuous aims to override it. Bernard Williams has claimed this as a fault in ancient ethics, stressing what he calls 'the Gauguin problem'. Human nature is capable of many kinds of development—moral, artistic, cultural, scientific, spiritual. And a given individual may feel that he has to give a cultural or spiritual aim precedence over a major ethical aim (Gauguin providing a striking example). Ancient ethical theory is in this respect, Williams claims, naive. Our aims are many and complex, and we have no reason to believe that in any one individual life all (or even many) worthwhile human aims can be fulfilled harmoniously. Nor do we have any reason to believe that the excellent development of human nature will always give primacy to the ethical.[16]

The complexity that Williams points to is undeniable; does it show that there is something wrong in principle with the appeal to nature? Clearly not. The ancients recognize the diversity and richness of human nature and its capacities as much as we can; they are not denying anything about the way we are (or about the possibility of a Gauguin). They do make the claim that the ideally virtuous agent would have a life which was internally harmonious and unified by her possession of the virtues; but this is a claim about an ideal, not a denial of the way people actually live. Is it, however, objectionable, and perhaps naive, even as an ideal? Whether this is so cannot be determined before we have seen more about the kind of ideal which ancient theories have, and its relation to happiness.

The ancient appeal to nature does not, then, presuppose teleology, and does not impose a single specific set of activities on any human life. Nor is it an appeal to allegedly simple and uncontroversial facts. Rather, as with happiness, the thought is that we all have some glimmerings of what is natural, but that many of us may be very wrong about its direction and implications, and need the help of philosophy, in the form of ethical theory, to improve and correct our views.

The different schools come to very different conclusions as to what is natural. They also differ in their success in uniting the two major roles of nature: nature as the given facts about ourselves which ethical theory has to respect, and nature as an ethical ideal. I shall look in turn at Aristotle, the Stoics, Antiochus, the Epicureans and the Sceptics. Each of these theories brings out different points of interest about the appeal to nature, and taken together they enable us to see what the strengths (and weaknesses) of the appeal are, and what kind of basis it in fact provides for ethics.

---

[16] These claims are interestingly anticipated in Bradley (1876), chapter 6.

4

Aristotle: Nature and Mere Nature

It has often seemed to students of Greek ethics that emphasis on nature to ground ethics in some way is a product of the post-Aristotelian period. Aristotle himself does not define or even characterize our final end as being the life according to nature, like the Stoics, nor does he have anything like the Epicurean appeal to the difference between natural and empty desires. In fact it seems from some passages in the ethical works[1] that nature plays a different and more minor role in Aristotle's ethics.[2] Hence the appeal to nature as a move in ethical justification is frequently seen as essentially post-Aristotelian, flowing from local and external factors present in the Hellenistic period but not in Aristotle's.[3] If this is the case, then the appeal to nature would seem not to be a part of the structure of Greek ethics as we have so far seen that articulated in Aristotle and shared by his successors; it would instead be a temporary phenomenon. As well as its intrinsic interest, then, it is important for the claim of this part to see whether Aristotle does appeal to nature in a way recognizably like that of the Hellenistic schools.[4] If we can show that he does, as I think we can, this strengthens the idea that while the appeal to nature takes different forms in different theories it forms a common element in ancient eudaimonistic ethical theories.[5]

[1] In what follows I shall concentrate on the *Nicomachean Ethics*, since on this issue much of the relevant material comes from the common books (which have been more studied as part of the *Nicomachean* than *Eudemian* version), and in the books which differ the *Eudemian* version does not introduce any important differences. The *Magna Moralia* likewise contains some interesting differences of detail, but not of principle.

[2] Though it has always been noted, often critically, that Aristotle makes a strong appeal to nature in the first book of the *Politics*. That this has not been more closely connected with the ethics reflects the general tendency to study the ethical works in isolation from the political ones.

[3] Also, Aristotle's appeal to nature, outside the over-studied 'function argument' in *Nicomachean Ethics* I, has not been systematically discussed, perhaps because of the mistaken view that Aristotle's ethical theory is essentially a response to common opinions or *endoxa*. (Aristotle's approach to *akrasia* in *Nicomachean Ethics* VII 1–3, which does start from the *endoxa*, is sometimes wrongly elevated to a general strategy in ethics.) But, while Aristotle respects common opinions, appeal to them is not itself part of his method in ethics. For a clear statement of this, see C. Natali (1900a).

[4] I shall not discuss the interesting passages about nature in the *Protrepticus*, since there is doubt as to how much exact Aristotelian terminology we have. That it is the stronger of the two notions that I distinguish which appears there is suggested by passages B 47–50 in Düring's edition.

[5] See Laks' (1988) reply to my article on naturalism in Greek ethics, esp. p. 179, where Laks talks of 'the *fact* that *phusis* has a philosophically different import in Aristotle and in Hellenistic philosophy'. This 'fact' is often implicitly assumed in discussions of Greek ethics. In this section I argue that on thorough examination we find no such fact.

Aristotle does in the *Ethics* and *Politics* often talk of nature in a way that contrasts it with habituation and thus with the development of virtue. Our development, he says, requires not only nature but also habit and reason; nature on its own can be developed either for the better or for the worse, so that it is up to humans to make use of their reason to control their nature by means of habit.[6] We do not, says Aristotle, blame people for faults if we think them due to nature;[7] for what is 'by nature' or natural is not up to us, and so we are not responsible for it.[8] Indeed, he introduces one kind of 'appeal to nature' of a kind at *Nicomachean Ethics* III 5 precisely as an attempt to *evade* responsibility for one's character. An opponent suggests that what is important is to have the right nature to grasp the ends one should, since nature is responsible for our having the relevant aptitudes. Aristotle rejects this: how we conceive of our final end depends on us, he claims, whether we express this by saying that the end does not appear a certain way to us by nature, or whether we concede that it is natural, but insist that it is still up to us how we develop.[9] Plainly Aristotle allows importance to our nature, but takes it to be essential to deny that nature controls ethical development; something is up to us or at least depends on us, and this is distinguished from our nature.[10]

Indeed it is part of Aristotle's explicit account of virtue in II 1 that the virtues do *not* come about by nature:

> From [the point that the virtues come about through habituation] it is clear that none of the virtues of character come about in us by nature. None of the things that are [what they are] by nature is habituated [to behave] otherwise—for example a stone which moves downwards by nature could not be habituated to move upwards, not even if you habituated it by throwing it upwards ten thousand times, nor fire to move downwards; nothing which is naturally one way can be habituated to be another way. So the virtues come about in us neither by nature nor contrary to nature; we are by nature fit to acquire them, but we are made complete through habituation.[11]

Nature is what we start from, but hardly serves as an ethical guide of any kind. Consistently with this Aristotle distinguishes 'natural' from 'full' or 'proper' (*kuria*) virtue, to the advantage of course of the latter.

> It is like this with virtue. Natural virtue stands to proper virtue as intelligence stands to cleverness; it is not the same thing, but similar. Everyone thinks that they have each of their character-traits by nature to some extent, since we are just, given to temperance, brave and so on right from birth. Still, we search for something else to be what is properly good, and for these traits to be ours in another way. Even children and wild animals have the natural states, but without

---

[6] *Pol* 1332 a 38—b 10.

[7] E.g., *NE* 1148 b 31–4, 1148 b 29–31.

[8] 1179 b 20–23: our nature is due not to us but to some 'divine cause', i.e., something outside us and beyond our control.

[9] 1114 a 31—b 25. Note the large number of times the opponent uses words like *phunai, euphues,* etc.

[10] Note that Aristotle claims that something *depends* on us (*para*) at 1114 b 17, the alternative being that virtuous action is *hekousion*, b 20. Nature is a limiting factor. Commonsensically, virtue and vice are up to the agent (*Rhet* II 6).

[11] 1103 a 18–26.

understanding they appear to be harmful. This much appears to be plain, at any rate: it is like a heavy body moving without sight, which chances to trip heavily because of lacking sight.[12]

Hence, Aristotle adds, it is the intelligent understanding which underlies each proper virtue which unites them into one; insofar as we distinguish the different virtues, we are thinking of their natural bases, not the virtues themselves.

Nature in these passages plainly indicates what, for obvious reasons, I shall call *mere* nature. Mere nature is strongly contrasted with what matters for ethical development; it is what we must improve on, not what guides our improvement. But this is not the only usage of nature that we find in the *Ethics* and *Politics*. Aristotle also makes use of a stronger sense, which I shall refer to just as nature, to distinguish it from mere nature; he nowhere explicitly distinguishes the two senses.

Aristotle's most notorious argument, that in Book I from the 'function' or *ergon* of humans, has always been interpreted as an argument which appeals to the appropriate development of human nature. The conclusion that the good for human beings lies in a certain kind of activity, namely virtuous activity, is produced from claims that humans have a characteristic *ergon* or function, which can be discovered by focussing on what distinguishes them from other kinds of living things. However, we should note that Aristotle himself does not prominently present the argument as involving nature; it turns up once in verbal form,[13] but somewhat casually. We cannot press this argument to show that Aristotle has a stronger notion of nature than mere nature in mind. The same goes for some casual comments which presuppose the notion of full rather than mere nature.[14] What we need to find is Aristotle actually using the stronger notion in ethical argument.

There are two parts of the *Ethics* where we indeed find this. One is the discussion of natural and conventional justice in Book V, chapter 7. Aristotle contrasts two kinds of political (or social) justice, natural and conventional. Natural justice is what has the same force everywhere, regardless of what people think, whereas conventional justice lays down as just what was previously indifferent.[15] The force of nature here must clearly be greater than that of mere nature. Aristotle is not contrasting what is conventional with what is just for people before they start on proper ethical development; what is naturally just is just for people who have properly developed. Aristotle here mentions the objection that no justice can be natural, on the grounds that what is natural is not changeable but the same everywhere it turns up—the stock example being that fire burns in both Greece and Persia, while Greeks and Persians count very different things as being just. Aristotle agrees that actual just arrangements are subject to change, but adds that this is consistent with there being a natural justice which is the best everywhere. He does not make the point very clearly or convincingly, and his later commentator

[12] 1144 b 1–12. Compare *EE* 1234 a 24–34. The forward reference to explanation of how each virtue can be both 'by nature' and 'differently with practical intelligence' is not picked up in the *EE* as we have it. Cf. also 1229 a 20–30.

[13] 1097 b 30.

[14] 1179 b 11, 1143 b 6 ff. Such passages contrast, as more or less natural, traits both of which are developed, rather than contrasting a developed with an undeveloped state.

[15] The whole passage is 1134 b 18- 1135 a 5. On 'natural justice' in Aristotle, see the valuable study by Miller (forthcoming).

Alexander does a much better job.[16] For present purposes what matters is that Aristotle attaches importance to there being a justice which is natural, where this is clearly a desirable kind of justice to aim for.

Highly relevant also is Aristotle's account of pleasure in Book VII of the *Ethics*.[17] Pleasure is there defined as unimpeded activity of the natural state (*anempodistos energeia tēs kata phusin hexeōs*).[18] Indeed, the fact that we seek different pleasures, and seek to vary them, is explained by our having variable and unstable natures (unlike the gods). Again, nature here cannot be confined to mere nature. Aristotle distinguishes kinds and levels of pleasure, pointing out that the best kind of pleasure may even be identical with happiness, since the best kind of pleasure will be the unimpeded activity of the best kind of state, and this is intuitively what happiness is.[19] In fact we cannot understand the Book VII account of pleasure in terms of mere nature; the natural state here is not a minimal starting point to improve on, but itself a desirable goal.

The notion of nature that we have found in these passages is best understood via Aristotle's general discussion of nature in *Physics* II 1. There Aristotle distinguishes things with natures from artefacts; the former have in themselves a principle of changing or not changing. 'Nature is a kind of principle and cause of changing[20] and not changing in the thing whose nature it primarily is, in its own right and not incidentally.'[21] The use to which Aristotle puts this notion of nature in the physical works has been disputed over the centuries,[22] but whether or not it provides the scientist with useful tools, it certainly underlines an intuitively acceptable and important distinction. We recognize the difference between a cat and a table in these terms: among the causal interactions which involve the cat many involve the cat's nature, i.e., the way it acts, not just the action of other things on it; whereas with a table there is no such 'internal' source of change or resistance. The obvious antithesis to nature so understood is *force*; forced movement is brought about by other things impinging on a thing in such a way as to overrule the internal sources of change which operate in the thing itself. Aristotle's *Physics* puts to extensive use this idea of the fundamental contrast between natural and forced behaviour.[23] The

---

[16] Alexander, *de An* II 156.29–159.14, an essay showing 'that the just is by nature', *hoti phusei to dikaion*. Alexander claims that humans are normally social creatures (*koinōnikoi*) and points to many aspects of this which would be impossible if humans did not have normally, and not as a matter of forcible imposition, a very general notion of justice. Those who point to the different forms that conventional justice takes, he points out, are presupposing this fact, that humans are social and thus equipped with the prerequisite for social life, a grasp of justice.

[17] I do not go into the question of the compatibility of this account with that in Book X; I see no problem in regarding them both as variations on a single idea. See Gosling and Taylor (1982), chs. 11–15. Nature is not prominent in the Book X account, however.

[18] 1153 a 12–15. The *MM* at 1205 b 6–7 defines it as a restoration from an unnatural to a natural state (*hē de hēdonē esti katastasis ek tou para phusin eis phusin hekastōi tēn hautou*). *Rhet* I 10 shows that Aristotle regards it as uncontroversial that it is, at least usually, pleasant to get into a natural state.

[19] 1153 b 7–19.

[20] The verb is *kineisthai*, literally to move, but Aristotle intends it to cover all kinds of change; see 192 b 13–15. Similarly the contrast verb, *ēremein*, literally to be at rest, covers all kinds of absence of change, not just of motion.

[21] 192 b 21–23.

[22] On nature in the *Physics*, see Waterlow (1982).

[23] See Waterlow (1982), pp. 33–38, for discussion of some implications of this for Aristotle's

natural state in the Book VII of the *Ethics* is natural in this sense: it is the state that results from our nature, i.e., our internal source of change and resistance to change, when other people, and circumstances, are not impinging to produce a 'forced' behaviour. The suggestion in Book VII is that pleasure is just what happens when we achieve unimpeded natural functioning: pain is what we experience when our natural functioning is frustrated. Whether or not this is an adequate account of pleasure can be left aside for now (it certainly does not seem to be, and whatever the relation of the two accounts, the one in Book X is philosophically an improvement); the point of interest here is that it is a perfectly general account, applying quite explicitly to developed ethical states as well as initial undeveloped states. Moreover, the whole account of pleasure is geared to showing how pleasure is a plausible *goal* for humans; so functioning in an unimpededly natural way must likewise be a plausible goal for humans.

Aristotle shows no signs of awareness that the mere nature of Book VI has turned into the rather stronger nature of Book VII. He does, however, quite explicitly put nature in the stronger sense to considerable ethical work in the first book of the *Politics*. In this book Aristotle argues for three substantial conclusions.

(1) The state is a natural form of association. Families come together to form in turn clans and villages. The *polis* or city-state is the natural product of this growth, but is not in turn a natural part of further growth towards larger social entities.[24]

(2) Slavery is natural. Not all existing slave relationships are natural; some are the result of mere force. But the institution has a natural basis in differences between types of people, some naturally fit only to labour for others while others are capable of providing the intelligence needed to make appropriate use of that labour.

(3) There are natural and unnatural ways of making money. Trade, money-lending and in general ways of acquiring money which aim at profit-making and do not relate directly to the satisfaction of needs, are unnatural.

All of these conclusions are notorious. We shall look in detail at them and the arguments for them later in the chapter. What matters for now is that they all manifestly rest on the idea that the nature of humans is not just a pre-ethical starting point but something which provides ethical goals—goals indeed which Aristotle thinks should control political institutions to a great extent. As he says, 'Nature is an end (*telos*), since what we say the nature of each thing is, is what it is when its coming-into-being is completed.'[25] 'Completed' is the same verb (*teleiousthai*) as was used in the 'mere nature' passages for what habituation had to do, in contrast to nature.

Thus the uses of mere nature, which we have looked at, are only half the story. Aristotle also makes use of a much stronger notion of nature as some kind of ethical goal. The stronger notion does not come from nowhere; it is an application of the

---

scientific method, particularly his lack of interest in experimenting in artificially produced circumstances. As she points out, since for Aristotle the behaviour that is most revealing of a thing's nature is the behaviour it manifests when unimpeded by other things, controlled experimental conditions are for him of little use.

[24] See 1253 a 18–29 for a claim about 'natural priority' of the state to its parts.

[25] 1252 b 32–33.

Physics notion of nature in ethical contexts. But it is clearly not the same as mere nature, and it is a pity that Aristotle does not explicitly mark the difference.[26]

Alexander of Aphrodisias, aiming to produce an account of this issue which is consciously Aristotelian, reproduces exactly this problem. By nature we have not the virtues but merely the aptitudes for acquiring the virtues; full virtue requires a developed rational attitude to what nature has provided. But that we can develop this attitude is itself natural for us: for we are rational beings, and what is natural for rational beings is precisely this, having a rational attitude to natural tendencies, and doing so not automatically but in a way that is up to the individual.

> Those who are healthy as a result of nature without effort and taking thought we do not praise, but congratulate. . . and we would do the same, or even more so, in the case of the virtues, if they were present in some people as a result of nature (as indeed we do in the case of the gods). But this is impossible for us, and we should not demand from nature anything impossible, for nature is the measure for the possible and impossible. Virtue is the completion and summit of each thing's proper nature; it is impossible for anything incomplete to be in its completion, and what comes into being is incomplete when first it comes into being. So it is impossible for a human to be born possessing virtue by nature.
>
> However, nature does not fail to contribute to a person's acquiring it; he has from nature an ability and suitability receptive of it, which none of the other animals has. It is because of this ability that humans differ from the other animals by nature, although they are left behind by many animals when it comes to bodily superiorities. Now if we had this ability receptive of the virtues from nature in such a way that we just got it as we advanced and became completed, as we walk and grow teeth and grow a beard, and other things that happen to us in accordance with nature—if so, the virtues would still not be up to us, just as none of these things are. But this is not the way we get them. If intelligence and virtue were inborn in humans like these things, then all or most of us would have not just the ability receptive of the virtues but the virtues themselves from nature, just like getting the other things natural for us; and then there would be no need for praise or blame or anything like that for virtues and vices, since we would have a more divine reason for, and the substance of, their presence.[27] But it is not like this. We do not see all or even most people possessing the virtues, which is a sign of things that come about by nature. We must be satisfied if we find even one such person who through practice and teaching displays the natural superiority of humans with respect to the other animals by adding, through himself, what is necessarily lacking in our nature. Hence the acquisition of the virtues is up to us, and praise and blame are not useless and pointless, and neither are conversions to the better course, and training in better habits in accordance with the laws.[28]

---

[26] Irwin, in his translation with notes of the *Nicomachean Ethics* (1985a), notices under *nature* in the Glossary that there are two 'important aspects' of nature in the *Nicomachean Ethics*: nature # 1, a thing's original constitution or tendency apart from human intervention, and nature # 2, in which a thing's nature indicates its function and the final cause or end to which it tends. Irwin notes that these are clearly distinct, since 'the nature that is to be developed and realized will include some original tendencies, but not all'. The distinction corresponds by and large to my distinction between mere nature and nature proper.

[27] Following Sharples (1983a); for his note on the text here, see p. 162.

[28] *Fat* XXVII, 197.25–198.26. See Sharples (1983a). My translation owes much to this excellent work.

Alexander faithfully reflects the clumsiness of the Aristotelian position, culminating in the sentence in which he says that the person who does develop virtue supplies what *nature* leaves lacking and thus demonstrates the *natural* superiority of those who can do this to those who cannot.

Thus Aristotle and the Peripatetics both contrast nature with human rationality and its workings, and consider the latter natural. There is no difficulty here, of course, if the two senses of nature, for the undeveloped state and for the developed result, are convincingly related. Aristotle does not do this. Moreover, we find the oddity that it is the sense of nature which is most prominent in his work as a whole, that of nature as the source of a thing's inner development, guiding it, if not frustrated, to its final end, which is the least prominent in the *Ethics*. It is nature in the sense of the raw material for ethical development which dominates the *Ethics*, although the other sense is at work also, and blooms prominently in the *Politics*.

We might expect Aristotle to make moves that would convincingly link his use of nature with that of mere nature. He lays great weight on moral education and development; he has all the materials needed to produce an account such as the Stoics were to produce, in which humans develop from mere nature to the ideal which is natural for them, by a process of development which is itself natural for humans to go through. Had he done so, Aristotle would have rendered his ethical uses of nature less awkward. Surprisingly, he does not do so. We can see here, however, a reason why Aristotle's followers in the Hellenistic period were tempted to rewrite and update Aristotle's ethics in an explicitly developmental form. The account of Peripatetic ethics which we find in Arius Didymus recasts material from Aristotle's ethical works in the form of a developmental story.[29] The author begins by repeating Aristotle's point from the *Nicomachean Ethics*, that character (*ēthos*) derives from habituation (*ethos*); nature gives us only the 'starting points and seeds' for right development, which must be completion by habituation and eventually by rational understanding. Virtue requires for its completion nature, habituation and reason.[30] But the author goes on, in a long passage, to present what he evidently considers to be a restatement of this position in more standard Hellenistic terms, principally the Stoic notion of *oikeiōsis* or familiarization. We are from birth, claims the author, 'familiarized to' what is naturally good for us, and alienated from what is naturally bad. Because of our bodily nature we naturally go for what preserves our physical well-being; because we also have mental and rational capacities we also naturally go for what preserves and completes our nature as rational beings. The author gives the story a characteristically Aristotelian rather than Stoic twist by insisting that we are familiarized to external goods (including other people who are objects of our concern), goods of the body and goods of the soul, of which the highest is virtue; thus we conclude that happiness consists in a life of virtuous activity, but one including bodily and external goods. The fact that the story takes this turn is of great interest, and will be considered at greater length in Part III.[31] What matters for now is that at every stage of the developmental story we do what is natural and go for what is natural to us—not just at the early pre-ethical stage but in

[29] Arius 116.18–152.25.
[30] 116.21–117.7; 118.5–6.
[31] This aspect of the passage is discussed in Annas (1990a). See also chapter 12.

becoming habituated to virtuous action and in reflecting rationally upon this.[32] Such a story, in which what we do at every stage of our development is natural for that stage of development, forms an obvious way of bridging mere nature and full nature, nature as what is displayed in the developed form. In 'normalizing' Aristotle's position on nature in the Hellenistic period, Arius is rendering it stronger and more coherent.[33]

We have seen that Aristotle's major use of nature as a guide to our ethical aims is to be found not in the ethical works themselves but in the *Politics*, particularly in Book I, in which three notorious conclusions, of great import for ethics, are supported by appeal to nature. It is thus here that it is useful to see what use Aristotle makes of the appeal to nature as ethical ideal.

The state (that is, the *polis* or city-state) 'exists by nature', according to Aristotle in *Politics* I 2. It does not owe its existence, that is, to convention, as some claim,[34] and is not the product of a 'social contract'. Aristotle does not think that his claim needs lengthy argument; he simply sketches the process by which a state comes into existence by the uniting of smaller forms of community, and then claims that the state forms the natural terminus to this process, and thus displays their nature; for nature, he says, is an end or *telos*—we say that a thing's nature is what it grows to be, not what it grows from.[35] There is no explicit reference to the *Physics*, but we are reminded of Aristotle's claim when discussing nature there that it is the form of a thing rather than its matter which has the best claim to be its nature, precisely because the form is what the thing grows to be.[36]

The first form of community Aristotle mentions is the family, which he regards in two aspects: male and female come together in families to produce offspring, and master and slave come together to form the most basic economic unit.[37] Families

---

[32] A human is familiarized to himself by nature and to what is natural (118.12–14). Apart from the frequent recurrence of *kata phusin* and *para phusin* in the passage, nature supports our affinity to *philoi* at 120.1, 12–13, 121.16, to bodily goods at 123.9 and to the goods of the soul at 123.24 and 126.2.

[33] The account of Peripatetic ethics has the form of Stoic theory, starting from familiarization to oneself and taking over from the Stoics the idea of our being attracted to what is natural or in accordance with nature for us. The Stoic developmental story, however, initially contrasts what is natural for us to go for (what is merely 'indifferent') with virtue, the object of our developed rational attitude; whereas for the Peripatetic account our entire development from initial impulse up to virtue is part of a single natural development. The same is true of Antiochus' theory in *de Finibus* V; on this see Excursus IV in Madvig (1965). See chapters 5 and 6 of this part, and chapter 12.

[34] Aristotle does not deal extensively with this view. In *Pol* III 9 he mentions Lycophron 'the sophist' as the author of a theory of a minimalist state, serving only as a guarantor to citizens of justice. Our evidence is very scanty, however. For the ancient versions of 'social contract' theory, see Kahn (1981b) and Mulgan (1979). Both Kahn and Mulgan make the point that social contract theories were politically neutral; they did not represent a 'liberal' alternative to theories laying more weight on community and the social nature of humans. It is wrong to see Aristotle as a reactionary in this respect, rejecting liberal advances.

[35] 1252 b 30–34.

[36] *Phys* 193 b 12–18.

[37] He feels the need to argue that these are *different* aspects: women are not naturally the menial labour of the household as well as mothers. Greeks recognize this, he claims, whereas 'barbarians', foreigners, don't (1252 a 34–b 9). (Cf. the later claim that Greeks use to buy brides, but now no longer do (1268 b 38–42).) Aristotle regards it as one of the advances of Greek civilization to have freed women from having the role of household labour as well as that of bearing and bringing up children. This interesting and little stressed aspect of his thinking about women is likely not to impress us much, for two reasons. One is its striking lack of realism as a general statement. Only wealthy Greeks could 'free' their

come together into villages, helped by the formation of kinship links. Villages in turn coalesce into city-states, and this forms the natural end of the process, according to Aristotle. He knows, of course, that larger forms of political association exist, the kingdoms of Egypt and Persia for example, which include city-states as parts; but he does not count these as natural units; presumably he regards them as held together by force.[38] Why is Aristotle so sure that the natural process stops with the *polis*, rather than with the village on the one hand or the larger nation-state on the other? Clearly he is relying on the *Physics* idea of nature as an inner source of change; a natural development is one that comes from the thing in question itself, when not interfered with. And if not interfered with, it will be what usually happens:

> A thing is due to nature if it starts from some principle internal to itself and by a continuous process of change arrives at some end. From each principle there comes about, not the same thing in all cases, nor any chance thing, but always something going towards the same thing, if nothing interferes.[39]

The thesis thus appears as a straightforward one about human nature (and at no point relies on false analogies with the growth of animate beings, as is sometimes claimed).[40] Human nature, the claim goes, is such that people's needs will be met, and their interests catered to, only in the city-state form of community.[41] Forms of community either less or more inclusive than this one will lead to some degree of frustration; people can survive in villages, or under the Persian Empire, but they will fail to develop in ways in which they could have developed if the interference of a confining social environment had not been there. Aristotle identifies the level of development that concerns him by saying that it is only in the context of a city-state that people can achieve 'self-sufficiency' (*autarkeia*). We have seen how important this notion is for Aristotle's ethics; our final end must be not only complete but self-sufficient—that is, must not leave us lacking in anything required for a rationally

---

women from labour that contributed to the household economy. It might fairly be claimed, however, that it represents a widespread *ideal* in Greece (and in many civilizations). But second, such a separation of the role of wife and mother from that of productive contributor to the household economy, while historically a source of pride to men, has been a source of frustration for women.

[38] And, of course, acquiescence on the part of the subjects, because of their nature's having been corrupted by upbringing in bad institutions. Aristotle is very unflattering to 'barbarians' and quotes, without endorsing it but without rejecting it either, a line from Euripides to the effect that it is right for Greeks to rule barbarians because the latter are naturally slavish (1252 b 6–9). But he never comes down in favour of the idea that barbarians are natural slaves, presumably because it is empirically too implausible; at 1327 b 20–38 other peoples are compared with Greeks in a way flattering to Greeks, but hardly making them the others' natural masters. The Asiatics, for example, are said to be 'enslaved' because they lack spirit, not intelligence.

[39] *Phys* 199 b 15–18.

[40] The alleged analogy with living things is stressed in the account of these passages in Barker (1906). For useful distinctions as to ways in which Aristotle's theory is and is not an 'organic' theory of the state, see Mulgan (1977) and Kullman (1991).

[41] The *polis* itself is thus not a natural thing, since it does not itself have a nature, but it is 'by nature' (*phusei*) or natural, since to explain why there are states we need only appeal to the behaviour of natural things, in this case humans. Keyt (1991a) claims that there is a deep contradiction between Aristotle's claim that the *polis* is natural and the opposition of nature to skill (*technē*) in the *Physics* discussion of nature; for the *polis* is a product of human skill and intelligence. But there is no real contradiction if it is natural for humans to employ intelligence in contriving to live together. For criticisms of Keyt's view, see Miller (1989) and (forthcoming).

chosen plan of life.[42] Aristotle is saying here that our lives, insofar as they are lived in a reflective rather than instinctive manner, will be lacking in something important if we are not functioning parts of a city-state.[43] Only in this context can we 'live well' rather than just living; for only this form of community demands of us what we would call *political* abilities. If we do not take part in a political community of equals, and live as active citizens, our lives will not develop as they would naturally have done—that is, they will be in some way stunted.

Aristotle's thesis here is, even if we disagree with it, rather convincing; the idea that people are naturally political and social animals (*politika zōia*) is a highly intuitive one.[44] (Part of its plausibility, of course, lies in its extreme generality; Aristotle has not yet distinguished and judged between particular political systems.) The idea of self-sufficiency in terms of which he puts his points is, as we have seen, important in his ethical works; it is one of the formal constraints on an acceptable account of our final end. Aristotle is appealing to commonsense, rather than to established ethical theory, when he claims that we have achieved our natural, unfrustrated development when we are self-sufficient.

Does he, however, have convincing grounds for the claim that we can achieve this only in the context of city-states—that this is the only context in which people achieve the satisfaction of their needs? Here we can see enormous empirical support for the thesis. Aristotle sees Greek history, with some justice, as a progression from monarchy to forms of government in which a group of equals decide political matters among themselves—to city-states, in fact. Moreover, not only were Greeks self-conscious about this and proud of it, but monarchy in the Greek world was a remote, we might say 'mediaeval' fact; Aristotle knew that city-states had been for many generations the only stable form of political association in the Greek world. It has sometimes been thought remarkable that he should be so impressed by the *polis*, given that his own political status was that of subject to the Macedonian kings, and that he tutored Alexander the Great. But surely it is not surprising that Aristotle should conclude, from the vast amount of research he did into forms of government and their history, that city-states were the form of political association that would viably and stably form in the circumstances of Greek culture. What else would be a reasonable conclusion? As for the larger empires like Persia, Aristotle had the best of empirical grounds for the conclusion that these were imposed, and maintained, by force. Thus Aristotle can maintain that city-states are near-universal. They are so, that is, in the conditions of Greek political culture, and their absence in other parts of the world can be explained by the absence of those conditions. Aristotle in taking Greek political culture to be the norm shows, of course, cultural bias, but an understandable one; it is not mere chauvinism, since he is not himself a native product of that culture.

---

[42] See chapter 1, pp. 40–42. On the importance of *autarkeia* for this argument in the *Politics*, see Everson (1988).

[43] 'We' here, of course, are *de facto* free adult males. But Aristotle's point does not depend on this restriction.

[44] Although in modern political theory it has less initial acceptance than the thesis that we are by nature individual 'atoms', narrowly self-interested and requiring some prospect of future personal gain before we can be induced to take an interest in the welfare of others.

Aristotle has good reason to think that the near-universality of the city-state as a political unit indicates its naturalness. For nature, as he said in the *Physics*, is what always happens unless there is interference: external conditions can intervene to prevent natural development, but what happens normally is natural.[45] In the *Politics* itself we do not find the explicit claim that the natural is the usual, but we do find it in an ethical context, so Aristotle cannot have regarded its application to ethics as inappropriate.[46] That the state is a natural form of community, then, amounts to the claim that it is the form of community in which people's needs are most fully met and their interests best ensured; and that this state of affairs is not produced by force or by other external factors like manipulation. It would be plainly absurd to explain the Greek political map by the thesis that people naturally hanker to be the subjects of large empires, but that participatory forms of government are imposed on them and maintained by force and fraud. This could be true in a few cases, or for a short time, but no one could accept it as the explanation of a widespread and stable form of association. What better Aristotelian proof that it is natural?

The appeal to nature in this case, then, seems to have empirical support of a strong kind. The city-state is natural because nature is not only an inner source of change, but also what happens always or for the most part; and city-states are near-universal, and exist stably by their own momentum, and not by external force.[47]

The succeeding claims about the naturalness of slavery run into more trouble. They do so not only because the conclusion is unacceptable, but because in Aristotle's own terms the appeal to nature is less successful.

Aristotle claims that the relation of subordination that holds between master and slave is one example of a general pattern.[48] We see this pattern, he claims, in the relation of men to women, and in other cases also:

> People between whom [and other people] there is as much distance as between soul and body, and man and beast (their state is such that their function is the use of their body, and this is the best they can do)—these are natural slaves, and it is better for them to be ruled in this fashion, as with the other items. A slave by nature is someone who is capable of being another's (which is why he *is* another's) and who participates in reason only so far as to perceive it, but not to have it. The other animals obey not reason but their passions, and the use [we make of slaves] differs only a little; we get aid from both, slaves and domesticated animals, from their bodies towards our essential needs.[49]

[45] *Phys* 199 b 18, 25–6 (see above); *PA* 641 b 24–6.

[46] *EE* VIII 2, especially 1246 a 31—b 1: 'nature is the cause of what is the same way always or for the most part, and chance of the opposite.' The context is a tangled discussion of good fortune, where Aristotle concludes that if some people *regularly* succeed despite bad reasoning, they must have some kind of natural impulses that urge them in the right direction, even though they are not aware of this. See chapter 18, pp. 373–76. See also *MM* 1194 b 37–39, where, in a discussion of right-handedness and ambidexterity the author commits himself to the principle that something is natural if it occurs always or for 'more time' than the alternative.

[47] Aristotle takes this kind of empirical support seriously, as we can see from *Pol* 1264 a 1–8, where he appeals to the length of time during which people have *not* put communism of a Platonic kind into practice as backing for the thought that it is not, in fact, a good thing.

[48] 1252 a 30—b 1; 1254 a 28—b 16.

[49] 1254 b 16–26. Aristotle adds that there are natural physical differences between the naturally slave and the naturally free; but 'often' (32) we see the opposite: slaves with a 'free' physique and vice versa.

Aristotle's conclusion about slavery does not rest on the force of his analogies, however; he could hardly think that analogy could establish so important a conclusion.[50] Rather, the analogies serve only to make more convincing the general thesis that the kind of subordination that concerns him is widespread. For if nature is to be found in what happens always or for the most part, then if slavery is natural we would expect to find its occurrence to be the norm. Aristotle claims that this is in fact the case; we find slavery at the very first stage of the kinds of community that lead to the formation of the *polis*.[51] Right from the start Aristotle insists that what we have is not the mere imposition of brute force, but a symbiotic relationship of reason and bodily strength. (A relationship dependent on brute force could not, of course, be a natural one, for Aristotle.) The paradigm situation for him is one in which one person has the ability to work out a plan of action, but lacks the strength required to put it into effect, while one or more other people lack the ability to work out such a plan, but have enough ability to appreciate its point and to put their greater strength to use in fulfilling it. The analogies of soul and body, and so on, underline the point that we have this kind of symbiotic relationship rather than mere brute enforcement. And Aristotle claims, infamously, that this kind of relationship is founded in nature; some people have the intelligence to co-ordinate the labour of others towards a productive end, while others are endowed with brute force and have mental capacities sufficient only to follow the orders of the more intelligent directors.

It is understandable that when Aristotle considers what forms productive co-operation can take, he comes to the conclusion that it always takes the form of a master co-ordinating and using the labour power of one or more slaves; for that was the form which he saw in every version of civilized society that he knew of. The reliance of ancient civilization, and Greek civilization in particular, on slavery was so pervasive, and so taken for granted, that it is not surprising that Aristotle does not give serious consideration to other ways in which people can combine their labour; he knows, of course, that some free people sell their labour, and he knows of serf and semi-free labour in some states, but he is right in regarding them as marginal, and slave labour as the basic form of production. So, though distressing to us, it is scarcely surprising that Aristotle regards it as natural: if nature is displayed in what happens always or for the most part, then a near-universal phenomenon like slavery must have a natural basis.

Aristotle's theory is in fact nicely judged to account both for the near-universality of slavery, and for the fact, obvious enough to anyone, that many slaves are not by nature fitted for their role; it is imposed on them by force, and they clearly have abilities which go beyond the role of serving another's will, and could, if free, function as well as the free. Aristotle can explain this fact in terms of his own theory, and thereby, he thinks, disarm the arguments of those who argue from it to the conclusion that all slavery is conventional and imposed by mere force. Since slavery is near-universal, and is so necessary and integrated into all social patterns, it

[50] Fortenbaugh (1975a) ch. 3, esp. section 3, claims that for Aristotle natural slavery rests crucially on the analogy of reason and emotion: natural slaves lack deliberative capacity, but are able to understand and follow the results of others' deliberations. Fortenbaugh's arguments are met convincingly in Smith (1991).

[51] 1252 a 30–34.

must have a natural basis. Hence there are natural slaves, i.e., people who have bodily strength, but only enough brains to follow the orders of others. Such people benefit from being slaves, since they do better overall following the orders of the more intelligent masters; the masters obviously benefit from the increased labour power at their command. However, nature is subject to interference from other factors,[52] and in particular wars and violence bring it about that many actual slaves are naturally free. The system doesn't work perfectly; but that doesn't show that there is no such underlying system; indeed Aristotle turns the tables on his opponents by claiming that complaints about the injustice of particular cases of slavery actually support his contention that there is at bottom a just form of the system which isn't working well. Hence slavery is supported by nature in its role as an inner source of change; such a source can of course be interfered with by external factors.

We have to admire, up to a point, the cleverness and neatness with which Aristotle defends slavery as natural, accounting for it as a near-universal phenomenon while not ignoring the patent injustice of its actual manifestations. But even in his own terms the account fails in two rather striking respects. One is that if Aristotle's theory is right, then nature functioning without tampering should produce a majority of humans who are natural slaves, and comparatively few fit to be free. But surely even a pessimist would hardly conclude that most people are actually natural slaves, though not all are actual slaves. Natural slaves have intelligence adequate only to do heavy manual work; if Aristotle seriously believed that a high proportion of actual free people were natural slaves it is hard to see why he values forms of democracy as much as he does. The obvious response to this would be that in the actual world we see nature working badly; there are not as many natural slaves around as there should be. But if the natural course of things has been tampered with to this extent, we might reasonably wonder whether we can conclude as confidently as Aristotle does that there is a natural basis to the existing order as it is.

Aristotle has also failed to justify the actual situation of slavery in the ancient *polis*.[53] What he has justified is the use of slaves for labour power, manual and heavy work. Perhaps he has in mind the ideal of a peasant with one or two slaves. But a high proportion of ancient slavery took the form of house slavery, with slaves performing organizational and personal tasks which required precisely intelligence rather than brawn. Aristotle must presumably have owned intelligent secretaries and stewards, something quite unnatural in terms of his theory. (And we might also note parenthetically that his theory does not fit female slavery at all, though presumably a large proportion of the slave population would be female.) Again, the retort could be that these are not natural forms for slavery to take (as we can see from the fact that they presuppose or generate a need for slaves who would be useless were they natural slaves). But again: if the actual state of affairs involves tampering with and

---

[52] 1254 b 27–1255 a 1; 1255 b 1–4. It is no accident, as we shall see, that in the account of slavery Aristotle twice notes that nature can fail or be interfered with.

[53] This has been seen by many scholars. Some explain the point by claiming that Aristotle is in this book of the *Politics* concerned to distinguish different types of *rule*, not to do justice to actual institutions like slavery. See Natali (1979–80) and Schofield (1990).

corrupting nature to such an extent, how can we conclude that the actual state of affairs, as it is, must have a natural basis at all?

Clever as Aristotle's theory is intellectually, there is a lack of fit between what it justifies and what it needs to justify. It needs to justify the social existence of slavery as it is. But in doing so it has to allow that a great deal of what happens is due to force and other factors interfering with nature; there are natural slaves, but in fact actual slaves are likely not to be natural slaves.[54] In the abstract the two roles of nature fit together, but to explain slavery as it actually is, giving due weight to the clearly perceived injustice of much actual slavery, so much has to be conceded to the operations of force (wars, piracy and so on) that the thesis that slavery as it is requires a natural basis is undermined. We can understand why Aristotle would not appreciate this; slavery was something that he and most Greeks took utterly for granted. We can see why his general philosophical approach of respecting common views would incline Aristotle to reject the view that the entire system of slavery was based merely on force, and would be unstable without it. Still, Aristotle's own arguments do not in the end succeed in repelling that conclusion.

The appeal to nature here falls down in two related ways. One is that the explanation offered for the system, in terms of the existence of natural slaves, is not adequate to explain what it is supposed to explain, namely the functioning of actual slavery. Empirically we find virtually no natural slaves; and an explanation in terms of non-natural interference in the actual system of slavery proves too much; if it works it shows that the actual system is highly perverted and frustrated by various kinds of force, and thus is as it stands not really natural at all. The other failure is that Aristotle infers far too hastily from the thesis that nature is the norm, what happens always or for the most part, to the naturalness of a near-universal social institution. Some role is doubtless played by cultural bias, leading to a failure of imagination: how could something so widespread and accepted be completely unjust, rest on nothing but force? But a role is also played by Aristotle's underestimation of the differences between what we can infer about plants and animals and what we can infer about human nature. The usual may be the natural with plants and animals, but the complexity of human nature allows the usual to be something that is forcibly repressed, unjust and in every way frustrating to normal human capacities.[55] Aristotle is often accused of thinking of the state too 'biologically'. This is wrong if it implies that he thinks of the state as a kind of quasi-biological entity, forming independently of individuals' intentions;[56] but it has some

---

[54] Bernard Williams in his Sather lectures distinguishes Aristotle's 'argument from above' about slavery from his 'argument from below'. The argument from above establishes that there must be something natural about there being the roles of master and slave. The argument from below shows that there are in fact people that fit these roles. What I have argued amounts to the claim that the results of the argument from below do not fit the argument from above.

[55] The application to Aristotle's views on the position of women is too obvious to need drawing out.

[56] At 1252 a 26–30 he says that the union of male and female for reproduction displays a natural urge which is not *ek proaireseōs* (28). But this does not imply that it comes about in a way that is indifferent to the choices of individuals. That the growth of the state is natural does not imply that individuals' decisions are reduced to the workings of some giant organism. Rather the state is natural because it fulfills needs which people have just because they can make autonomous choices. In general, attempts to show that Aristotle's moral and political theory is over-influenced by his biology tend to neglect Aristotle's specific insistence on the rational and free nature of moral and political choice; see, for example, Lloyd (1968).

force if we consider how, even given the extent of his concessions, Aristotle cannot resist the thought that a near-universal social phenomenon must be basically natural.

The empirical appeal to what is near-universal seemed a strength of the argument for the naturalness of the state; it is clearly a disastrous weakness of the argument about slavery. Must both fall together? No; in the case of the state there is not the same need to make concessions to the interfering role of violence, since the state precisely provides the conditions for free, autonomous action. Rather, Aristotle's fault lies in failure to perceive the crucial difference between the two cases. We find not a flat refutation of the appeal to nature, but rather a reminder of the need to be cautious in its use.

It is interesting that the appeal to nature is often criticized on grounds of vagueness, or of failure to provide a ground independent of ethical considerations. Aristotle's grounding of the state and slavery are not open to these objections; they rest more directly on empirical fact than we find in the Hellenistic philosophers. But it is just in this respect that they are most open to criticism. Appeal to the way things usually are, or nearly always are, provides shaky ground for the thought that they are natural.

Aristotle's conclusion that certain forms of money-making are unnatural is in striking, and usually unmarked, contrast to his preceding two claims about nature, in that it makes no use of the idea that the natural is the usual. Nor could it, since Aristotle's claim is that the only natural way of making money, or more generally of making gain, is that of directly producing what meets one's needs, using exchange only as much as is required to satisfy unmet needs and get rid of unusable surplus.[57] And this was hardly a widespread, let alone near-universal mode of gain in the ancient world. Aristotle condemns as unnatural any way of making money which, like trade, produces profit on the exchange for the middleman who has no personal use for either of the exchanged goods, or, like moneylending, makes a profit on the use of money. And, while there was a certain social prejudice (on which Aristotle may be relying to a certain extent) against trade as opposed to farming as a way of life, it could hardly be said that the norm in the ancient world was a mode of economic production which rejected any notion of profit.

Aristotle in fact adopts a radically different approach in this area, concentrating on a socially *primitive* state to display the natural way of doing things. In the process he brings in a new and somewhat contentious idea, rare in his works,[58] that various species are natural resources for one another, the whole forming a large stable system. Thus plants are 'for the sake of', a natural resource for, animals, and animals similarly for humans. The whole is taken to form a stable system because Aristotle has of course no inkling of the ecological disasters that humans can produce; he thinks of the impact on animal populations made by humans as being relatively small.[59] In this context human means of gain are natural, presumably because they fit into the larger 'eco-system' without disrupting it. The present state of affairs is, of course, very different; all kinds of economic and gainful activities have been

[57] Book I, chs. 8–10. See Natali (1990b).

[58] On this, see J. Cooper (1982).

[59] Later the Epicurean Hermarchus displays a similar attitude; he regards humans as threatened by animals (by direct attack or through over-reproduction) but never seriously considers that humans might pose a threat to animals. See the long passage on the origins of society in Porphyry, *Abst* I 7–12.

introduced which completely break with this pattern. (It is worth asking how much more radical Aristotle's account of slavery would have been had he thought in this way, abstracting from the present institution and asking instead about a more primitive state of affairs taken to be very different.) One can of course fault Aristotle's conception of the economically primitive state of affairs. Real societies which are economically undeveloped characteristically display all sorts of practices which Aristotle would condemn as highly unideal: piling up of wealth in the form of treasure, conspicuous display, even conspicuous destruction, as with potlatch. The idea that a faulty attitude to possessions comes in only with emphasis on profit-making is somewhat naive.

Aristotle's procedure is unrealistic about the actual state of affairs because his main argument about types of gain does not in fact rely directly on nature at all. Rather, he argues for the importance of 'limit' in what one seeks. There is nothing wrong with seeking profit, or gain, or possessions generally, as means to something else: the performance of activities which make up the good life.[60] For one's reasoned conception of the good life will set a limit to the amount of money or gain that one will aim to get. After a certain point money-making will interfere with other, more ethically central activities. However, money-making can take over as an activity centred on making money as an end, rather than a means to other ends; and in this case there is no limit to the money that is sought.[61] The point is clear: seeking money or gain for its own sake unbalances a life and perverts its course, whereas there is nothing wrong with making money as a means to facilitating other, more worthwhile activities.[62]

Aristotle's main argument is thus a moral one, and not an economic one; he is not concerned with the inadequacies of the profit motive from the economic point of view, but rejecting its effects in a human life.[63] He does so although this forms an ideal quite contrary to actual practice. Thus the status of the appeal to nature has greatly changed from the previous two; nature here is quite divorced from the usual. Presumably nature here is still the inner source of change; the fact that we are not as indifferent to profit as we should be is a mark of the unnaturalness of our lives, the fact that our nature is frustrated by external forces. But to see what is natural here we have to point to the *ideal* development of human nature. Aristotle can picture it only in terms of a primitive state of affairs.

It is in his third application in *Politics* I of the notion of nature that Aristotle establishes what is to be one of the most important roles for nature as an ethical ideal in the theories which are to follow. Nature as ethical ideal stands in contrast to what is merely *conventional*; and hence to establish what is a natural way of dealing with some aspect of our lives (in this case the economic aspect), we cannot look at

---

[60] Aristotle presumably means this intuitively, and is not assuming substantial theses from his own ethical theory.

[61] 1257 b 25–1258 a 14.

[62] Though Aristotle has great trouble with the idea that the good life might actually involve *making*, rather than just *using*, money: money provides a prerequisite for living well, and thus ought to be there, like health, and so money-making is not part of the organizing knowledge that orders the good life any more than medicine is (1258 a 27–35). This further thought seems to be due mainly to prejudice, however.

[63] As is rightly seen in the classic article by Finley (1970). See, however, Meikle (1991) for a more sympathetic account of Aristotle's contribution to specifically economic theory than is found in Finley.

what happens usually or for the most part, but must appeal to idealized circumstances. It is noteworthy that Aristotle does not comment on the point that this role for nature as ethical ideal stands in contrast to the earlier two, where nature did figure as the usual or standard thing to happen.

Aristotle, as we have seen, moves without comment between nature and mere nature. Is Aristotle's mere nature simply the idea of nature as constraint, those aspects of us that are unavoidable, which we can modify but cannot avoid altogether? In some passages[64] this seems to be the case; but in others[65] Aristotle stresses the point that we are by nature 'fit to' receive the virtues, and what is suggested is that we have natural 'abilities and suitabilities', as Alexander later puts it, for becoming virtuous. Nature shapes our development from the start, though it is habituation, not nature, which actively guides it. (We will not find out which potentialities we naturally have, of course, just by looking to see what characters people actually develop, for, familiarly, nature can be corrupted; we identify them by asking how people would ideally turn out.) Mere nature in this role is more than just a constraint; on the other hand its positive indications are not very specific and certainly do not aim to impose a single kind of life on everyone. We can also see how mere nature comes to be transformed, in the developmental accounts of later Peripatetics, into the starting point of a development which, if nothing interferes, ends in the full display of the thing's nature.

Aristotle's stronger conception of nature as an inner source of change, something revealed in natural development and guiding it towards its end, is taken over from the *Physics*, where it is developed in the context of the natural sciences. It would be wrong automatically to condemn Aristotle for doing this, or to assume that he must be viewing human nature too scientifically; though it is worth noting that it is this more specific and systematic notion which leads Aristotle to his most contentious conclusions about the naturalness of the state and of slavery. The appeal to nature has sometimes been criticized for being vague and unscientific; we can see from Aristotle's uses of nature that insofar as an ancient appeal to nature lays weight on a concept of nature developed in scientific contexts, this turns out to be a liability rather than an advantage.

Aristotle's use of nature is sufficiently like that of the later Hellenistic schools for them to be seen as exhibiting a common pattern of thought. Nature turns up in two roles: nature as mere nature and also as the goal of ethical development. Aristotle's stronger notion of nature relies on his scientific works rather than just ethical considerations; he does not explicitly relate mere nature to nature by a developmental story; and he does not remark that nature as an ethical ideal opposed to what is merely conventional stands in some tension with his scientific conception of nature as what happens always or for the most part. In all these respects we can see the Hellenistic schools, particularly the Stoa, as taking the appeal to nature further and developing it more coherently as an ethical form of argument. The underlying idea, however, remains the same.

---

[64] Particularly *NE* III 5.
[65] Notably II 1 and VI 12.

5

The Stoics: Human Nature and the Point of View of the Universe

The Stoics discuss nature in many parts of their philosophy; in doing so they are often talking about the nature of the universe, which I shall call cosmic nature. Since cosmic nature comes up in many contexts, they regarded it as a unifying feature of their philosophy, a point brought out by identifying cosmic nature with many other things, notably reason, fate, providence and Zeus.[1] Each of these identifications can be understood only by unpacking a large connected system of ideas. It is clear, however, that nature is a leading idea in questions of freedom and responsibility, in metaphysics and in physics. 'The nature of things' matters for the Stoics because they hold strong theses about the way things are: they are determinists, physicalists, teleologists.[2] It appears from some texts that cosmic nature had a role within Stoic ethical theory. For it is a firm part of Stoic ethics that our final end is living in accordance with nature, and some texts make it appear as though we do this by first finding out about cosmic nature and its requirements, and then conforming ourselves to those requirements. The view this suggests is clearly foundational, since to be virtuous we first have to discover nature, and then follow it. Moreover, what seems to be foundational is not human nature, but cosmic nature, of which human nature is a mere part.

> The primary impulse an animal has, they say, is to preserving itself, since from the start nature familiarizes it to itself, as Chrysippus says in *Aims* book I, where he calls familiar to every animal its own constitution and its consciousness of this. For it was not likely that nature would make an animal alien [to itself], nor that having produced it nature would make it neither alien to nor familiar to itself; for in this way it repulses what is harmful and accepts what is familiar to it.
>
> But as for what some say, that pleasure is what animals' primary impulse is for, this they show to be false. Pleasure, they say, if there actually is any, is something

[1] See Plutarch, *Sto rep* 1050 b. Cf. also Diogenes VII 156 where Zeno is said to have called nature (*phusis*) a 'craftsmanlike fire proceeding methodically to bring things about' (*pur technikon hodōi badizon eis genesin*), a definition blending several Stoic ideas about the universe.
[2] Interestingly, *phusis* (nature) is used also for a particular kind of nature. We find in a classification of things that are unified by *pneuma*, a substance with varying degrees of cohesive 'tension', that there is a hierarchy. Lowest are inanimate things, unified by state (*hexis*); plants are unified by nature (*phusis*), which makes them able to grow and reproduce; animals are unified by soul (*psuchē*) which makes them able to perceive and react; humans are unified by *nous*, which makes them able to reason and think rationally about things. (See Origen, *de Princ.* III 1 2–3 = *SVF* II 988.)

that supervenes when nature itself has sought and found what fits the thing's constitution—like good condition in animals and flourishing in plants. Nature, they say, drew no distinction between plants and animals, since plants organize themselves, though without impulse and perception, and in our own case some things go on in the way they do in plants. Impulse supervenes in animals as an extra, and making use of it they go for what is familiar to them; and for them what accords with nature is running their lives according to impulse. But reason has been given to rational animals for more complete authority, and for them what accords with nature rightly becomes living according to reason; for this supervenes as the craftsman of impulse.

Hence Zeno was the first (in his *Human Nature*) to call our aim 'living in agreement with nature', which is the same as living in accordance with virtue, since nature draws us towards it. Similarly Cleanthes in *Pleasure*, Poseidonius and Hecaton in *Aims*. Living in accordance with virtue, again, is equivalent to living in accordance with experience of what comes about by nature, as Chrysippus says in *Aims* book I. For our natures are parts of the nature of the universe. Hence our aim becomes living consistently with nature, that is, in accordance with one's own nature and that of the universe, being active in no way usually forbidden by the law common to all, which is right reason, which pervades everything and is the same as Zeus, lord of the ordering of all that exists. And this is the same as the virtue of the happy person, and a smooth flow of life, when everything is done in accordance with the agreement of each person's *daimōn* [guardian spirit] with the will of the orderer of the universe.[3]

This passage, important from many points of view, appears to give a priority within ethical theory to cosmic nature. We should live in accordance with our own, that is, human nature, and we do that, it appears, by conforming to the cosmic nature of which our nature is a part. And, since cosmic nature can be studied further by Stoic physics and metaphysics, it appears that cosmic nature gives us a foundation here; by deepening our knowledge of it we can deepen our knowledge of what it is we are to conform to in order for us to achieve our final end.

This kind of view often forms the basis of popular or vulgarized forms of Stoicism, though it has been defended as the correct view of reflective Stoic theory as well. But, apart from the point that it is not the view we get from all our ancient sources,[4] there are many problems with it. One is the oddity that cosmic nature is most stressed in later Stoic writers, like Marcus and Epictetus, who have the least to say about it outside ethics, and in fact essentially ignore non-ethical philosophy.[5] But there are more serious objections. First, it does not seem to be an *ethical* position at all. Virtue, on this view, is simply doing what is needed to conform to nature, where that is taken to be cosmic nature, understood in ways that are independent of human nature. But to define virtue as conformity to some standard which is defined

---

[3] Diogenes VII 85–88.

[4] Sextus in *PH* III and *M* XI, and Arius in his account of Stoic ethics, both important sources, do not even feature cosmic nature. And, as we shall see, there are large differences in the role that texts allot to cosmic nature.

[5] For a different interpretation of this, see N. White (1985b), who argues that later Stoics took the view that a general appreciation of the principles of Stoic metaphysics was regarded as sufficient for ethical purposes, without requiring a knowledge in detail of the crucial theses.

in ways that are external to the basis of virtue itself is to reduce virtue to something else: that is, to fail to do justice to the moral viewpoint.

Standardly this kind of objection is met by the claim that for the Stoics cosmic nature is not neutral and non-ethical. Nature, the way things are, is regarded in a thoroughly teleological way.[6] and on a smaller scale all sorts of phenomena are interpreted teleologically. Even the annoyance of bedbugs turns out to have a point; they wake us up in the morning and thus contribute to purposeful human endeavour.[7] The world as a whole exhibits order and rational planning and is all for the best. That this is not always obvious from the viewpoint of an individual human shows merely that we cannot always overcome our limited sympathies and self-centeredness. Virtue consists in regarding ourselves as parts of a greater whole because it is virtue that enables the individual to transcend the point of view of her own interests and appreciate the part that these interests play in a greater plan. Thus ethics requires conformity to cosmic nature because cosmic nature displays a model of rational order, which we as rational beings can come to appreciate.[8]

This way of looking at things is prominent in later Stoics, especially Marcus Aurelius and Epictetus. But it cannot control our whole interpretation. In the first place, the Stoic arguments to show that cosmic nature is providential are very weak. We find Zeno arguing, for example, that

> What employs reason is better than what does not employ reason.
> But nothing is better than the universe.
> Therefore the universe employs reason.[9]

However, even if these arguments were better, we would still find the unhappy situation that we have a peculiarly unsuitable foundation for *ethics*. For, as we have seen, ancient theories are eudaimonist in form. Ethical theory begins from reflection on the agent's final good and how this is to be made determinate in a way which will enable the agent to make sense of her life and correctly order her priorities. The appeal to cosmic nature, however, does the opposite of what is required; it pulls the agent away from the kind of attachment to her own concerns which is needed for useful reflection on her final end to be possible. Suppose I did come to have a definite conception of cosmic nature and its demands on me; this would still not be relevant to any of the concerns I need ethical theory for, until endorsed by reflection from the relevant point of view. But that point of view is the agent's point of view on his own life as a whole and how best to order his priorities. The cosmic point of view, then, is useless for ethics unless endorsed as part of a theory which is

---

[6] Stress is put on this aspect of nature in Long (1970–71).

[7] Plutarch, *Sto rep* 1044 d (mice also encourage us to be careful not to leave things lying around).

[8] For a recent exposition of Stoic ethics which takes this perspective as fundamental, see Striker (1991). Although I disagree with Striker's methodology, I have learned much from this work. A recent book which fundamentally disagrees with this approach is Engberg-Pedersen (1990). Apart from offering an alternative interpretation, however (one based on objectivity and subjectivity rather than the eudaimonist perspective), Engberg-Pedersen does not offer any arguments against the alternative approach, other than the claim that when the Stoics talk of cosmic nature they are being metaphorical.

[9] Reported by Cicero at *ND* II 20. Cicero also reports the obvious counter-examples: one can show by this argument that the universe is wise, happy, eternal, a god. It is most charitable to take this not to be a serious argument from premises which an opponent might be expected to share, but rather an encapsulation of Stoic doctrine, using premises which are already accepted. See Schofield (1983).

eudaimonist in form. There is an analogue here in Kant's insistence that merely accepting some principle, however excellent its content, does not amount to being moral; we have mere heteronomy until the agent independently endorses the principle through the appropriate kind of reasoning on his own part.

Sometimes[10] it is argued that cosmic nature displays to us a structure or pattern of rationality which, when we appreciate it, moves us to conform our own rationality to it. But this merely leaves us with the question, what is the relevance of any kind of pattern to my life, until endorsed by reflection from the point of view from which I rationally order my life as a whole? Perhaps rationality does exhibit a kind of structure, which I can come to appreciate through studying good and bad reasoning, but this is a fact which, while it may be endorsed by cosmic nature, cannot be derived from it without running into the problem of heteronomy that we have just seen.

Further, not only is there this methodological problem, there are problems with the content of Stoic ethics. If cosmic nature is foundational, then it seems that the Stoic answer to the question, what my happiness consists in, must simply be: conformity to cosmic nature; and this is an unexpectedly thin kind of happiness. What kind of *happiness* could be supposed to consist simply in conforming my life to some external standard?[11]

And finally, Stoic ethics is marked by a number of striking ethical theses. The value of virtue is different in kind from that of other things; it alone is good, while they are merely 'preferred indifferents'. Virtue is a skill, a disposition to do the right thing for the right reason. Virtue is a skill of 'selecting' among the indifferents, although the virtuous person may achieve his aim even if the selection in fact fails to produce those indifferents. These theses form the core of Stoic ethics, and to understand the ethical theory we must understand them. Yet it is completely unclear how we could derive any of them, even in a weak understanding of derivation, from the supposed foundation of Stoic ethics, cosmic nature. We are in rather the same position as a logician required to derive some thesis in Stoic logic, such as that there are five indemonstrable argument-forms, from cosmic nature. However, in ethics the situation is even worse than in logic. For we can come to understand the ethical theses in question only from the eudaimonist perspective, and from problems and debates that arise within that perspective, particularly in opposition to Aristotelian versions of ethics. It is true that in later Stoic writers, such as Marcus Aurelius and Epictetus, we do find ethical strategies which seem to be derived directly from the idea that we are all simply parts of a larger whole. But, as we shall see, in just this respect these writers are distinctively different from the early versions of Stoic ethics, in which these strategies are conspicuously absent.

We do best, then, to concentrate on the early sources for Stoic ethics, those in which the eudaimonist perspective is most marked. Arius Didymus, for example, one

---

[10] See especially the articles by N. White and Striker.

[11] The problem has been set out lucidly and forcefully by Long in (1988b). I owe much to this article, although my disagreement is obvious. Long mentions Irwin (1986) as an example of interpretations of Stoic ethics which see it as primarily eudaimonist. He mentions Forschner (1986) as an example of a more Kantianizing interpretation, which downplays the eudaimonistic side. See also Forschner's (1981). In what follows, I am in broad agreement with Irwin's approach, though my own methodology is more radical here than his.

of our three major sources for Stoic ethics, presents it as a eudaimonist theory along the lines set up by Aristotle:

> One's aim, they say, is being happy, for the sake of which everything is done, while it is not done for the sake of anything further; and this consists in living according to virtue, in living in agreement and further (it is the same thing) in living according to nature. Happiness Zeno defined as follows: happiness is a smooth flow of life. Cleanthes also used this definition in his own writings, and also Chrysippus and all his successors, saying that happiness is not other than the happy life, though they do say that *happiness* is set up as a target, while one's aim is *getting* happiness, which is the same as *being happy*. It is clear from this that the following have the same meaning: 'living according to nature', 'living finely', 'living well', and again 'the fine and good' and 'virtue and what partakes of virtue'; and that every good is fine and similarly every foul thing is evil; hence the Stoic aim means the same as the life according to nature.[12]

It is taken as agreed at the start, in ways familiar from Part I, that each of us has a final end, that this is happiness, and that the task of ethics is to specify this more accurately. The Stoic answer to this is that virtue is sufficient for happiness,[13] a claim supported by their extensive discussions of virtue and other kinds of goods. Nature seems to come in here not as a basis but as a result: the life lived finely, that is, according to virtue, will in fact be natural.

But how are we to reconcile a eudaimonist framework with a role, prominent even if not foundational, for cosmic nature? The answer is to be found by looking at the place of Stoic ethics within Stoic philosophy as a whole.[14] The classic pedagogical order in which Stoic philosophy was taught was logic-ethics-physics, the last culminating in 'theology' or the study of the role of God and providence in the universe as a whole. Thus, ethics was taught first as a branch of philosophy in its own right; and the procedures at this stage do not appear to have been very different from Aristotle's. Chrysippus proceeded by 'articulating' ethical concepts, and by using 'dialectical' reasoning about ethics—reasoning, that is, which begins from what is commonly accepted rather than from theses previously established by philosophical arguments. Chrysippus defended the use of dialectical reasoning specifically within ethics, and collected huge numbers of 'plausible' premises for ethical theses.[15] It is in keeping with this that Chrysippus claimed that Stoic ethical theory was highly consistent with life, and answered to our intuitions.[16] Hostile critics like Plutarch

---

[12] Arius 77.16–78.6.

[13] A claim to be examined in Part IV.

[14] I am immeasurably in debt here to a ground-breaking article by Brunschwig (1991), whose modest title belies its importance. Brunschwig's article is clearly the beginning of any wisdom on this topic and should serve to lessen confusion in the future.

[15] Brunschwig points out the importance of the fact that we find titles on dialectical method within the ethical section of Chrysippus' bibliography in Diogenes VII, and the significance of titles like 'On the articulation (*diarthrōsis*) of ethical preconceptions' and 'Plausible premises for ethical theses (*pithana lēmmata eis ta dogmata*).'

[16] Plutarch, *Sto rep* 1041 e-f: Chrysippus claimed that his theory of goods and evils was most in harmony with life, and most grasped the preconceptions we naturally have (*ton peri agathōn kai kakōn logon, hon autos eisagei kai dokimazei, sumphōnestaton einai phēsi tōi biōi kai malista tōn emphutōn haptesthai prolēpseōn*). Cf. 1047 a–1048 b, where Chrysippus says that people are crazy who care nothing for health, wealth and worldly goods; he clearly thinks that the place assigned to these in Stoic ethical theory answers to what people would think who reflected on the content of their intuitions.

argued that this claim was in tension with the position espoused elsewhere, that Stoic ethical theory was highly ideal, and not exemplified in the world round us; but this is obviously captious. How ideal a theory is, is a question quite distinct from the question of how it is established, by reference to our intuitions or by reference to previously established philosophical theory. Of course individual Stoic theses in isolation were always recognized as highly paradoxical ('only virtue is good', for example), but it is equally obvious that these theses lose their paradoxical nature once they are appreciated in the context of the ethical theory as a whole; revisionary theses can form part of a theory which is nonetheless supported by our intuitions as a whole. Whether the Stoics are successful in bringing off this balancing act can be queried; but methodologically their approach is sound.

Ethics was not just studied as a subject in its own right, however. When the Stoic pupil finished his course with 'theology', it is clear that principles about God and cosmic nature were taken to provide a backing of some kind for what had previously been studied in isolation. Plutarch gives us three quotations from Chrysippus, all to the same effect, which make this clear. One goes:

> Again, Chrysippus says in his *Problems of Physics*, 'For there is no other or more familiar[17] way of approaching the account of goods and evils, or the virtues or happiness, than from common nature and the organization of the universe'.[18]

Plutarch himself claims that this shows that Chrysippus in fact back-tracked, and did teach ethics via theology. But, as Brunschwig stresses, all the quotations come from *physical, not* ethical treatises. So there is no problem; cosmic nature has a role not as a part of ethical theory, but as part of a study *of* ethical theory and its place in the wider scheme of Stoic philosophy.[19]

Thus there are two levels on which one studies ethics: first as a subject in its own right, with the proper kind of methodology, in which our intuitions are subjected to reflection and articulation, and theoretical concepts and distinctions are introduced which explain and make sense of our intuitions; and then later (if one advances that far) as a subject within Stoic philosophy as a whole.[20] What kind of role, however, does cosmic nature play vis-à-vis ethics when introduced at the later stage? Does it provide missing foundations for a subject which is incomplete without them? It is already clear that this would be implausible, since it is quite unclear how cosmic nature *could* provide the foundations for Stoic ethics in particular, or help in

---

[17] The Greek is *oikeioteron*: I have translated 'familiar' to keep contact with the translation of *oikeiōsis* as 'familiarization', but the word can normally mean 'proper' or 'suitable'.

[18] Plutarch, *Sto rep* 1035 c-d (all three quotations).

[19] Plutarch also claims that Chrysippus actually prefixed ethical treatises with phrases about cosmic nature and Zeus (*Sto rep* 1035 b). But this is feeble; as Brunschwig points out, Plutarch himself compares this to prefixes to decrees, which do not form part of the content proper.

[20] Brunschwig himself sees the difference between the two stages more in terms of method: 'the provisional account of Stoic ethics, based on the articulation, *diarthrōsis*, of ethical prenotions and using definitional techniques, has a dialectical status; the definitive account of Stoic ethics, based on theological first principles and using deductive procedures, has an apodictic status.' We need not choose between the two as to which is the correct way to do Stoic ethics. In this chapter I argue for the greater importance of what Brunschwig calls the provisional view; it is the view which we find in our sources, until Epictetus and Marcus Aurelius, and it is the view which we find engaged in debate with other ethical theories, forming part of the rational competition for the allegiance of people concerned about ethics.

any way to produce its distinctive theses. But we can also see, from the way that Cicero makes his Stoic speaker bring in cosmic nature in his account of Stoic ethics in *de Finibus* III, that its actual role was most probably quite different.

Cato gives an extensive account of Stoic ethics, beginning with our natural development, and going on to arguments about virtue and happiness. He concludes with a discussion of justice and of friendship, and finishes up[21] by saying that to the virtues already discussed the Stoics add dialectic and 'physics', treating each as itself a virtue. Dialectic helps us argue well and protects us against taking on errors. 'Physics' does five things for us. It tells us about the world as a whole, which we need to know if we are to live in accordance with nature. It enables us to judge truly about goods and evils by discovering the rationale of the nature and life of the gods,[22] and telling us whether or not human nature is in agreement with the nature of the universe. It enables us to appreciate the force of ancient maxims and proverbs, such as 'Know yourself' and 'Follow God'. It enables us to see the importance of nature for fostering justice and friendship. And finally it enables us to understand our attitude of piety and gratitude towards the gods. Cato then remarks that he is getting carried away by his admiration for the way that Stoic doctrines all fit together, and returns to ethics proper.

Clearly, all these things that physics does for the person who has learned ethics up to this point concern her *understanding* of ethics. Learning about cosmic nature helps us to set our human concerns in a wider picture, and thus get a better view of their significance; it enables us to feel more secure about our basic ethical judgements when we put them in a larger context than ethics; it enables us to bring together isolated and scattered ethical dicta, and see them as contributing to a single set of ideas; and it gives us a more profound understanding of phenomena of our moral lives, such as justice, friendship and our relation to the gods. It is clear why we need to do ethics first, before theology; until we do ethics in its own right we have no idea what it is that we are setting in a wider perspective.

The perspective of cosmic nature does not add any ethical theses, nor does it change or modify those we already know. What we get from the wider perspective is increased understanding of a subject whose content has been established without that wider perspective. If cosmic nature were a first principle within ethics, then here, if anywhere, we would have expected to find direct derivations of particular ethical theses purely from cosmic nature. But this is just what we do not find; by the time we get to appealing to cosmic nature as a first principle for ethics, the content of ethics is already established. We shall see that later Stoics differ in just this respect.

This might be thought to trivialize the perspective of cosmic nature unduly. Suppose one has become convinced of the truth of Stoic ethical theory, but is innocent of Stoic physics; then acquires Stoic physics and theology and sees how they give a perspective within which Stoic ethics can be understood. Surely this does add something, namely the thought that conclusions that have been reached on eudaimonist grounds can also be seen as conforming to the cosmic perspective. This

[21] *Fin* III 72–74.
[22] Or: of nature and of the life of the gods; but I take it that we have a hendiadys which corresponds to universal nature in the next clause.

is true; but we should hesitate to regard it as an addition of content to Stoic ethics. If I am convinced that virtue is sufficient for happiness, then when I acquire the cosmic perspective I acquire the thought that this is not just an ethical thesis, but one underwritten by the nature of the universe. But what actual difference can this make? It cannot alter the content of the thought that virtue suffices for happiness, for I understood that before if I understood the ethical theory. Nor is it easy to see how the cosmic perspective can give me any new *motive* to be virtuous; if I understood and lived by the ethical theory, I already had sufficient motive to be virtuous, and if awareness of the cosmic perspective adds any motivation then I did not already have a properly ethical perspective before. When we think through what is involved in understanding and living by Stoic ethics as that is grasped at the first stage, we can see that nothing can be added by the cosmic perspective except a deepened grasp of the significance of Stoic ethics as part of a wider world-view. As far as content and motivation are concerned, this leaves the ethics where it was. And this thought is supported by the fact that, when we follow through the major ancient ethical debates in which Stoic ethics figure, cosmic nature is nowhere to the point. Clearly the Stoics engaged in ethical discussion, and their opponents tried to meet their ethical claims, in a way independent of cosmic reason; and presumably this is because this is what was appropriate at the level of *ethical* debate.[23]

We are justified, then, in starting from the eudaimonist perspective, and treating Stoic ethics as a theory which, like other ancient ethical theories, begins from reflections on happiness and the agent's final end. It would be wrong to *begin* from cosmic nature to give us the shape of Stoic ethics.

As it is, the theory that we find is hard enough to understand. For the formal account of Stoic theory gives us a set of problematic equivalences between living happily, living according to virtue, living in agreement and living according to nature. The last two are said not to be different; this must be because Zeno originally defined the final end as living in agreement whereas his successor Cleanthes expanded this to living in agreement with nature.[24] We do best to follow the ancient consensus that these two formulae come to the same thing (even if *we* can think of interpretations that would make them differ), which reduces the options. We shall now look at the thought that living happily is living according to virtue, examining the relationship of this to the thought that it is also living according to nature. The discussion will inevitably be selective, leaving much out for examination in Parts III and IV; what matters for now is to see the relation of virtue and nature in Stoic theory.

Living according to virtue, according to the Stoics, is sufficient for happiness, since happiness is what benefits us and virtue is what is truly beneficial. Virtue is in fact the only thing that is truly good, good being defined as what is truly beneficial.[25] These are theses which will receive further examination later in the book. For the present what matters is that the Stoics do not understand the thesis that virtue suffices for happiness in a way which excludes a rational degree of concern for

---

[23] The major examples of these debates are discussed in chapter 12 and in chapters 18–20.

[24] Arius 76.3 ff. But see Diogenes VII 87, where the fuller version is ascribed to Zeno. On the notion of agreement or consistency here see Inwood (1985). See also chapter 19.

[25] See Sextus *PH* III 169 ff., *M* XI 22 ff.; Diogenes VII 103; Arius 69.11–16.

things we normally call goods—health, strength, wealth, power and so on. The Stoics call these indifferents, explaining the odd term as follows:

> [They say that] 'indifferent' is conceived of in two ways. In one way it is what is neither good nor evil and neither to be chosen nor to be rejected. In the other, it is what is not such as to move either impulse or counter-impulse, and in this sense some things are said to be utterly indifferent, e.g. <whether the number of hairs on one's head is odd or even, or> whether to stretch out one's finger this way or that, or to pick up something in one's way, a fruit or a leaf. It is in the former way that we should say that the things between virtue and vice are said by the Stoics to be indifferent, certainly not as regards selection and counter-selection. Hence some have selective value, others counter-selective disvalue, but this is in no way contributory to the happy life.[26]

Virtue has a value which is different in kind from the value of other things like health and wealth. This difference is expressed in several ways, one of which is the way that the Stoics invent a whole new terminology, saying that virtue is chosen whereas the indifferents are only selected, and another of which is the way that these things are said to be indifferent from the viewpoint of virtue, even though we have 'impulses' for some of them and 'counter-impulses' away from others. That is, we go for some things like health, and avoid others, like illness. Why do we do so, especially if, not being virtue, they do not serve to make up the happy life? The answer is that we go for these things because it is *natural* for us to do so.[27] There would be something wrong with a human who consistently shunned good health and sought sickness.[28] Hence some things are 'according to nature' (*kata phusin*), such as health, strength, soundness of the senses and so on; they are natural advantages. Others are 'contrary to nature' (*para phusin*), such as disease, weakness, mutilation and suchlike; they are natural disadvantages. Others are neither according to nor contrary to nature, such as 'the constitution of soul and body, according to which the former is capable of receiving false appearances, and the latter capable of receiving wounds and mutilations and the like'.[29]

Things that are indifferent, then, will be natural advantages, natural disadvantages or neither. Natural advantages have value (*axia*), and natural disadvantages, disvalue, and some have more and some less. Thus, not only are we bound to go for them, since it is our nature to do so, but we can have better reason to go for, that is, to 'select', one than for another, or for more rather than less of the first. They are still indifferents; but indifferents which have greater or lesser 'selective value', the kind of value, that is, which matters when one is selecting among them. Because the Stoics limit 'good' to virtue, they cannot say that some of these are greater goods than others; rather they have to introduce the terminology of calling some 'preferred indifferents' and others 'dispreferred indifferents'. The Stoics' opponents claimed

---

[26] Arius 79.5–17.

[27] Thus, we select, but do not choose (in the strict sense) to go for health, wealth, etc.; although in any particular action we will choose to go for a certain level of health or wealth and a certain way of achieving them. Terry Irwin has stressed the importance of this point.

[28] Although there could of course be circumstances in which this was the rational thing to do; hence one of Ariston's objections to the idea that what nature provides us with are substantive but general moral rules. See Part I, pp. 99ff.

[29] Arius 79.18–80.6.

that they were really comparing goods in awkward terminology, but there is good reason for it; comparison of natural, indifferent things is quite distinct from considering their appeal against that of virtue.[30]

Since we are aiming at kinds of natural state, such as health, the Stoics accept that there are kinds of action which we should perform, namely those that tend to bring about that kind of state. Hence they accept that we have 'due actions' or *kathēkonta*. This is defined as 'what is consistent in life, which when done has a reasonable defence.' There are kinds of thing any living thing ought to do in order to survive and flourish; but only in rational humans does this take the form of recognizing a kind of action as due and acting accordingly—that is, doing what I ought because I recognize that I ought to do it.[31] We have already seen this idea from a different perspective, that of moral rules, in Part I. It is because there are kinds of actions which are due actions for us that we recognize rules prescribing and forbidding kinds of actions. As we have seen, the idea that there could be such general but substantive rules was not uncontroversial in the early Stoa, and it became established only with refinements about 'circumstances'. But the refinements are not relevant from the present point of view; what matters is the line of thought that there are rules prescribing and forbidding certain kinds of action because, among the things that we are naturally attracted to and repelled by, some have greater and some lesser value of a kind. A due action gives rise to a rule because due actions are those that select, among the indifferents that are natural to us, those of greatest value.[32] Chrysippus said, 'Where am I to begin, and what am I to take as the starting points of due action and the material of virtue, if I pass over nature and what is according to nature?'[33]

Living performing due actions is not yet, however, living virtuously. A person is virtuous only when his due actions are 'complete'—when they are not only what he ought to do, and done because he recognizes this, but done from a fully virtuous disposition, one, that is, in which the reasons offered are unified and based on understanding, and the emotional and other responses are fully harmonized with the reasons held. Several Stoic definitions of our final end make it clear that our aim is to live selecting natural things, and thus performing due actions—but doing this in a certain way, which amounts to living virtuously.

> Zeno defined one's aim as follows: 'living in agreement'—that is, living according to a rationale which is single and in agreement, on the grounds that those who live in conflict are unhappy. His successors, articulating this further, produced 'living in agreement with nature', taking what Zeno said to be an incomplete predicate. Cleanthes, his first successor as head of the school, added 'with nature', and he gave the following definition: 'one's aim is living in agreement

---

[30] This is another point which will become clearer when more extensively discussed (in Part IV).

[31] Arius 85.12–18.

[32] In the above I have followed the order in which the topics of indifferents, natural things, value and due action are introduced in Arius' account of Stoic ethics. I take it that there is a point to this ordering and that the above captures something like its motivation. Of course there is an obvious gap between the above and the idea that we have seen in Part I, that we can find what our due actions are by examining ordinary morality and our social roles. Due actions are aimed at what is natural for us; why should conventional morality have captured that? This issue will arise at the end of this section.

[33] Plutarch, *Comm not* 1069 e.

with nature'. Chrysippus, wishing to make this clearer, expanded as follows: 'living in accordance with experience of what comes about by nature'. And Diogenes: 'being reasonable in the selection and counter-selection of the things according to nature'. And Archedemus: 'living making all one's due actions complete'. And Antipater: 'living selecting things according to nature and counter-selecting things contrary to nature invariably'. Often he also added: 'doing everything one can invariably and unalterably towards obtaining the things that are preferable according to nature'.[34]

Our aim is not to get the things which are natural for us, but to do so in a particular way: rationally, firmly, consistently. How does this amount to being virtuous? We have seen[35] that the Stoics regard virtue as a kind of skill (*technē*), and that skill is an intellectual grasp that builds up, becoming ever firmer, through trial and error. As they put it, virtue is the skill concerned with life productive of happiness.[36] Why, however, should the buildup of rational coherence and firmness in the recognition and performance of due actions amount to the particular skill which is virtue?

The Stoics do not at any point produce an argument to prove that a developed rational attitude will in fact come to grasp the moral point of view. Neither does Kant; both theories assume that there is a moral point of view, and that it is only by developing our rational powers (rather than by, for example, calculating empirical consequences) that we will come to grasp it. For both theories the existence of the moral point of view is simply a deep fact about the world, and in the last analysis it explains facts about humans, not the other way round.[37] Kant pays considerably more attention than the Stoics do to the question what exactly we grasp, in formal terms, when we grasp the moral point of view. The Stoics say little that is precise about this, and we are to some extent forced back on reconstruction. They devote attention to a quite un-Kantian concern, the question of how we come to grasp the moral viewpoint, and tell a developmental story that culminates in this.[38] The Stoics have been criticized for offering a developmental story rather than a rational justification, but they have good grounds for doing so. On the one hand, no rational justification of this claim is possible; that there is a moral point of view is a *datum* for the theory to cope with, not a conclusion that it has to establish. On the other hand, the Stoics want to relate our rational grasp of this point of view closely to the development of our empirical nature.[39]

The developmental story starts from the point that it is simply natural for us to go for some things rather than others, since it is natural for us to preserve ourselves and further our existence. This is based on the idea that by nature we find some things 'familiar' and beneficial for us, and go for them, while we find others harmful and naturally avoid them.[40] We start from nature, then, as what we are stuck with,

---

[34] Arius 75.11–76.15.

[35] Chapter 2, section 3.

[36] Alexander, *de An* II 159.34.

[37] This is one point, therefore, where the cosmic perspective studied by theology might well add some understanding for the advanced student. But what matters for morality is already obvious before we do any metaphysics, as indeed it is for Kant.

[38] For Kant this is beside the point, since the genetic story concerns only our empirical nature, and there is a sharp discontinuity between this and our rational nature.

[39] Cf. Inwood (1983), Striker (1983).

[40] The progress of *oikeiōsis*, as the process is called, is dealt with in more detail in chapter II, where a key text, Cicero *Fin* III 20–23, is translated in part.

our needs to eat, drink and so on. As we grow, and become more rational instead of living merely by impulse, we become more aware of what it is about the things that attract and repulse us that matters to us. We thus become able consciously to choose to do things. We move on to choosing to do and avoid kinds of things which benefit or harm us, and to do so following rules; we are now performing 'due actions'.[41] We become virtuous by doing these actions in ever more consistent, thought-through and reliable ways; we develop a virtue, that is a kind of skill in acting rightly.[42]

At this point, the point of becoming virtuous, we do what nowadays is called grasping the moral point of view. From the major passages describing what happens at this point[43] we can describe it in two ways. One is that we now grasp for the first time what is truly good; we appreciate that the value of virtue is quite different from that of other kinds of values. In one metaphor, it is like being introduced by a friend to a third party, whom we then value far more than the original friend.[44] The other is that we now grasp for the first time that what matters is acting on a certain kind of reason, rather than achieving the results of so acting; acting virtuously will normally result in our achieving the correct selection of preferred indifferents, but even if nothing of the kind results we should still act virtuously, because of the kind of reason which virtue provides.[45] What is it about our reasoning which connects it with the point about recognizing the distinctive value of virtue?

Unfortunately the Stoics here do a much less thorough job than Kant of examining the formal features of the reasoning which leads us to grasp the peculiar value of virtue. There is nothing corresponding to Kant's introduction of universalizing one's maxims, of seeking a purely formal object for moral reasoning, and so on. The Stoics merely refer to rational consistency and agreement. Cicero makes his Stoic speaker refer to 'the order and so to speak the harmony of the world' and 'what the Stoics call *homologia* and we can call agreement'. The idea is that we can appreciate rational consistency, which is not just the consistency of reasons for getting what we happen to want, but the consistency of reasons that are reasons that a rational person would have and act on.[46] We come to see that rational consensus makes a claim on us which has nothing to do with, and indeed can override, our own desires and wants, and also override reasons that have reference only to the satisfactions of those desires and wants.

[41] See chapter 2, section 4.

[42] See chapter 2, section 3.

[43] Particularly Cicero, *Fin* III 20–23. See N. White (1978a), for an extended discussion. White is clearly right in insisting that the Stoic theory is not a theory of self-development. When we come to grasp the moral point of view we are not just coming to think of ourselves as rational beings; we are coming to grasp facts about rationality and the good.

[44] The analogue to this in Kant is the grasp that nothing is good without qualification but a good will. Kant takes this to be our initial insight, prior to any insights about actions and duty.

[45] The analogue to this in Kant is the insistence on the importance of moral reasons, and of acting on them even in the absence of the expected results of acting on them, results which may be denied by stepmotherly nature. Note that Kant casts nature as the external world, which can let us down. He is unwilling to do what the Stoics do: think of the agent's reasoning as itself paradigmatically natural.

[46] *Fin* III 21. It would be far-fetched to find here a reference to cosmic nature. The whole idea that there are any such reasons has been attacked by Williams (1981c), who takes the idea of consistency involved to be appropriate only to theoretical, not practical reasoning.

Thus the dispute as to whether the early Stoic definition of the final end was 'living consistently' or 'living consistently with nature' can be seen to be fairly trivial. Living consistently in the relevant sense is living according to the requirements of rationality, which is marked by consistency, rather than according to the conflicting wants of oneself and others. However, this is what it is to live consistently with nature, since human beings *naturally* develop so as to be able to appreciate, and live according to, such rational consistency.[47] The Stoics take it that we can, in the normal course of development of human nature, come to appreciate a rational point of view from which we grasp the force of reasons for action which apply to us, but are distinct in kind from reasons that merely satisfy our own needs; and that this is the viewpoint of virtue, from which we appreciate the distinctive value of virtue. For in any given case, appreciating the special value of virtue will be the same as my having a reason to act on which is distinct from, and overrides, other reasons I have in terms of my own desires and projects.

For the present we can see at least in outline that the notions of living according to virtue and of living according to nature are interdependent. Living according to virtue is a matter of coming to have the right attitude to the things towards which we have natural attraction or repulsion. We start out with natural tendencies; virtue comes when we have developed a rational attitude towards their objects. Nature provides the material of virtue, as Chrysippus puts it. On the other side, living according to nature requires virtue. It is not just a matter of having unavoidable impulses towards natural things like health and away from unnatural things like sickness. For the progression whereby we develop from a concern with these things to a concern for our rational attitude towards them is also natural; it is what is natural for rational creatures, who not only have reasons but can be aware of this, and reflect on their reasons. Thus to understand what living according to nature eventually amounts to, we must understand what it is to live virtuously; for this is what our rational development leads to.

Human nature for the Stoics in fact involves two stages. At first it is a given that we go for what is natural for us, and avoid the unnatural. That is, it is a constraint on us that we must eat and drink, that we prefer comfort and success to pain and frustration, and so on. In Stoic theory, however, this forms the beginning of a developmental story about human nature which concludes with the claim that the developed life according to nature is one in which the original given impulses are controlled and transformed by an overall rational attitude to them. And, although this development is itself natural, there is a distinction of kind between the natural advantages that we feel attraction to, and virtue, the object of our developed rational attitude. Thus, although there is a single process of development from childhood to full rationality, our natural development requires us to grasp, at the crucial point, a difference in kind between what is natural for us hitherto, the pursuit and selection of the preferred indifferents, and what is natural for us as developed rational beings, namely virtuous activity.

The Stoics stress the Kantian idea that morality and the force of its reasons are different in kind from other kinds of goals and the force of their reasons; indeed

---

[47] We shall examine in chapter 11 the way in which Stoic ethics develops both self- and other-concern in rational ways.

they stress the gulf between virtue and our natural objects of attachment. But they also hold that achieving the moral point of view is the culmination of a process of a single story of natural development of rational beings. Virtue is contrasted with what is natural for us, but it is also itself natural as our goal; there is no contrast of our phenomenal and noumenal natures, as there is with Kant, who puts all empirical development and all concern with happiness on the phenomenal side, and contrasts it sharply with the noumenal self, which stands in a highly problematic relationship to anything empirical.

The Stoic view results from taking seriously two points about human nature. One is that it is a *developing* nature; our original given impulses are natural for us, but they are not something we are just stuck with, for it is also natural for us to develop them in some ways and not others, and obviously we can do this better or worse. Nature in the sense of what constrains us—those general aspects of our lives that we cannot alter—is seen as the starting point of a process that develops as we develop. The other point is that human nature is *rational*; this is indeed what gives our development its continuity, since our maturity is a matter of maturing rationality. And since, in Stoic theory, reflection on rationality and its requirements leads to adopting the moral point of view, human nature is such as to develop morally insofar as it develops rationally, that is, in the way which is natural for rational beings.

The two-stage way in which nature is relevant for human beings is clear in a passage of Hierocles:

> Nature is a just teacher, since selection of due actions should be in agreement with her arrangement. At any rate, each living thing lives in a way that follows its own natural arrangement. Indeed, so do all plants, in accordance with what is called living in their case; they don't, however, make use of reasoning and counting and selections from things investigated—plants make use only of bare nature, since they do not share in soul,[48] and animals make use of appearances that draw them to what is familiar to them, and urges that get them going. To us, however, nature gave reason, which will itself in and with, or rather before all matters discern nature, so that, fixed on it as though on some brilliant stable goal it can select what is in agreement with it and organize all of our lives in a due manner.[49]

Insofar as we are not rational, we follow nature the way plants and animals do; but when we have rationally developed, we can follow nature *consciously*, taking it as an aim instead of merely being constrained by it.

A complex theory thus rests on the comparatively simple thought that human nature is what is natural for developing rational beings. The sometimes extreme or paradoxical theses which the Stoics draw from this should not obscure the extent to which their view is intuitive and broadly acceptable. Nature is not just the intractable aspects of ourselves, within which we can manoeuvre; we cannot understand what our nature is without stressing the fact that we are developing and

---

[48] Nature in the sense of *pneuma* of the tension required to unify animate but not perceiving things. See above, n. 2.

[49] 53.2–12 in von Arnim (1906). The passage comes from a work on marriage.

rational beings, so that what is natural for us is precisely to develop in a rational way. When this is separated from the Stoics' own particular claims about rationality, it can be seen to express a view of nature which neatly unites several commonsensical points about what is natural for us.

We can by now appreciate why the Stoics regard living according to virtue and living according to nature as equivalent, although this, like many Stoic claims, is unhelpful or even misleading in isolation. For the virtuous life turns out to be not just a life containing natural impulses, but the life which follows the demands of nature, which lead us by developing our rationality to take a distinctive attitude to those impulses- the life according to nature, in fact. And, as we have seen, no life is lived according to nature unless it is lived virtuously. It is the same life, looked at in two ways each of which stresses one of the elements in it. As Cicero says,

> When the Stoics say that the final good is living in agreement with [*convenienter*] nature, what this means is, I think, the following: always to be in accord with [*congruere*] virtue, and to choose the things which are in accordance with nature, if they are not in conflict with virtue.[50]

Virtue and nature are thus interdependent; each is needed to give an account of the other. We can now see not only that but why there must be something inadequate with the initial suggestion that the agent could first discover the requirements of nature without bringing in virtue, and then become virtuous by conforming to that. Nature is not an independent basis for virtue in that way. Rather, as we might expect given the Stoics' tendency to stress the overall coherence of a theory, virtue and nature both function as parts of a theory which is built up as a whole; neither has priority.

Nature so far is, of course, human nature. There is, however, a complication, and we find a dispute in the early Stoa. Zeno's definition of our final end came from his book *Human Nature*; we then find that

> By nature, consistently with which we ought to live, Chrysippus understands both that which is common and also human nature in particular. But Cleanthes accepts only nature which is common as that with which we should be consistent, not the particular one as well.[51]

How are we to understand the role of 'common' here? When we develop in the way natural for rational beings, this leads us to grasp the distinctive importance of rational consistency and the distinctive value of virtue. The Stoics go on to make further claims about the effect this has on our conception of our relations with others. This other-directed aspect of Stoic ethics will be discussed in more detail in the next part; for now it is important merely to see that for the Stoics the rational point of view is one from which we come to appreciate what is 'common' to all, namely our status as rational beings. The fully virtuous Stoic will ignore, as irrelevant, differences between people that are not sanctioned by the rational point of view; and will thus come to have no more concern for his own interests, from the moral point of view, than for any other rational being.

---

[50] *Off* III 13. Panaetius is mentioned in the preceding paragraph, but there is no good reason to think that the view is not an orthodox one; it fits well with the quotation from Arius (p. 163).

[51] Diogenes VII 89.

So the dispute may have been as follows: Cleanthes held that being virtuous consisted merely (or perhaps principally) in holding the point of view from which one gives one's own interests no more weight than those of any other rational being. This certainly fits with what we have seen to be his uncompromising position on moral rules;[52] for he held that moral rules were no use unless grasped in their dependence on basic principles. Cleanthes in fact seems to have thought that the best way to express the moral point of view was that of removing the agent from her own concerns and making her take an impartial and abstracted view of her situation.[53] And he held that we are 'parts of the *cosmos*'.[54] In these respects Cleanthes is far closer to later Stoics like Marcus than he is to other early Stoics, who do not share these tendencies.[55] It is not surprising that the peculiarities of his view, like those of Ariston's, did not survive in the central Stoic tradition. Indeed we can see that Chrysippus' approach is far more sensible. He recognizes that virtue requires that we grasp that our rationality is common to all other rational beings, but refuses to make this alone definitive of the moral point of view; it is also important that we reflect on the importance of rationality in our own lives, and on the contrast, in a single life, between the value of rationality and the value of other kinds of things.

Virtue, then, requires us to live in accordance with human nature- not just in the sense in which we cannot avoid living the kind of life which humans do, but in the sense that, being rational, we not only have reasons but can reflect on them and consciously try to organize our lives in accordance with them.[56] It emerges, because of the very strong conditions which the Stoics put on rationality, that living in accordance with nature requires us to take the moral point of view, from which we recognize the distinctive value of rationality and virtue; and this, further, compels us to recognize that this rationality is common to all humans as rational beings; thus from the moral point of view we should give our own position no more weight than that of any other rational being. How does all this relate to cosmic nature?

The only passage from which we get any help as to the role of cosmic nature within Stoic ethics is the passage of Diogenes Laertius quoted at the start of this chapter. There we find that living in accordance with nature is introduced as being the same as living in accordance with virtue; an idea we have tried to untangle. Then we are told that living consistently with nature just is living 'in accordance with one's own nature and that of the universe'. The reason we are given for this is that 'our natures are parts of the nature of the universe'. But the further characterizations that

---

[52] Chapter 2, section 4.

[53] Compare his advice on getting rid of the emotions, so clearly unrealistic by comparison with Chrysippus', at Cicero, *TD* III 76.

[54] Stobaeus, *Ecl* 1,17,3; Eusebius, *Praep Ev* XV 15.1 = Arius fr. 29d.

[55] But how can he be, on this account, if he shares with other early Stoics an ethical framework which distances them from the kinds of ethical strategy we find in Marcus and Epictetus (below)? Cleanthes is on any account distanced from the other early Stoics by his intense religiosity; his *Hymn to Zeus* shows that he thinks of virtue as obeying divine commands. He thus has a religious, rather than simply ethical reason for deriving ethical conclusions directly from highly general principles about the nature of the universe: he sees these as embodying the will of Zeus, to which we should conform.

[56] Panaetius introduced the very interesting idea that we should, in our ethical development, pay attention also to our *individual* natures; but this is not taken to licence any development which could come into conflict with what is required of us just as bearers of human nature. See C. Gill (1988). Seneca, in *On the Happy Life*, also develops the theme of individual nature; see Asmis (1990).

we get, of living in accordance with nature, do not add or modify anything that we have already been told. Living in accordance with cosmic nature is 'being active in no way usually forbidden by the law common to all, which is right reason'. That is, we should act in accordance with rationality, which is common to all humans. But we know this already from reflecting on human nature. What is added is the idea that this is a *law* of some kind. Reason is represented as a prescriptive force. So much is of course already implicit in the relatively large role which the Stoics allot to rules and principles in virtuous activity, and again in a way reminiscent of Kant, the Stoics represent the recognition of the force of a moral reason as a kind of respect for law.[57] We are also told that this right reason 'is the same as Zeus, lord of the ordering of all that exists'. This underlines the fact that rationality is found not just in me, but in all humans, and possibly in other parts of the world also. Nothing in all this, however, gives us a new foundation of any kind for the role of reason in humans. Indeed, the passage continues by saying, 'And this is the same as the virtue of the happy person'. We are being shown the kind of way in which an ethical thesis can be further understood within a wider world-view.

Within Stoic ethics, then, working 'dialectically' and from 'plausible' premises which are widely shared, cosmic nature is not a first principle. It is not a foundation needed for specific ethical theses.

If we turn to later Stoics of the imperial period, particularly Marcus Aurelius and Epictetus, we do find cosmic nature used as a first principle within ethics; and the results are rather different. We find both of them insisting that the force of moral demands is underscored by their being put in a cosmic setting (although, as already remarked, it is somewhat odd that they insist on this, since they devote no attention to the physics establishing the cosmic perspective itself). But we also find that they treat cosmic nature as being itself a basic principle for ethics. They stress the thesis that our natures are part of cosmic nature, so that we are parts of a greater whole. And they take this to have direct ethical repercussions. In particular, we commonly find two strategies.

One of these can be called the 'only a part' strategy. I am a part of a greater, cosmic whole; hence I should think of myself as *only* a part of a larger whole. I should distance and detach myself from my own point of view, and see my situation as merely part of a whole in which my point of view is unimportant. 'For every part of nature that is good, which the nature of the whole brings along, and which is such as to sustain that.'[58] The virtuous person will see his task as being primarily that of bringing his own point of view into conformity with that of the larger whole, as part of which he functions.[59] This strategy results in a recurring feeling of transience and impermanence,[60] and also in a feeling of personal insignificance; since one is only part of a larger whole, nothing that one does really matters.

> When you get annoyed at something, you have forgotten this, that everything
> happens according to the nature of the Whole, and that the error is not yours-

---

[57] See chapter 13.

[58] Marcus, *Meditations*, II 3. Cf. II 3,4,9, X 6,7, XII 26. Cf. Epictetus *Disc* I 12, 24–26; II 5, 13, 24–29; IV, 7,7.

[59] For a vivid presentation of this strategy, see Barnes (1991).

[60] Cf. IV 23.

and, further, that everything that comes about has always come about, and will
come about, and is everywhere now coming about. And you have forgotten this,
how great is the kinship of a human for the entire human race; for it is a kinship
not of blood or semen but of rationality. And you have forgotten this also, that
each person's rationality is god and has flowed from yonder; and that nothing is
private property to anyone—one's child, one's body, one's very soul have come
from yonder; and that everything is but supposition; and that it is only the
present moment that each person lives, and this that he loses.[61]

The idea that we are akin to all humans by virtue of our rationality is orthodox
Stoicism; but we do not find in the early Stoics the relentless stress on abstraction
from one's own viewpoint, as being merely part of a larger whole, which leads so
directly to the felt sense that all is 'but supposition' and that we have only the
present moment.

The other strategy can be called the 'alienation' strategy. Thinking of oneself as
only part of a whole leads to a positive alienation from one's own point of view, and
thus to a loss of a sense of the significance of things experienced from one's own
point of view. Marcus tells us that appearances which 'pierce through things' and
enable us to 'see them as they are', appearances that we should aim to have over our
whole lives, are ones like these:

> As when we get the appearance with gourmet food and similar things to eat, that
> this is the corpse of a fish, and that the corpse of a bird, or a pig; or again, that
> the Falernian wine is the pressings of a bunch of grapes; and that the robe with a
> purple border is sheep's wool dyed with shellfish blood; and where sex is
> concerned, that it is the friction of an entrail and the jerky expulsion of
> mucus. . . .[62]

'The way things are' is the way from which they have no significance for us of a
normal human kind. The alienation strategy is arguably in tension with orthodox
Stoicism, which casts no aspersion on our natural attraction to the preferred
indifferents as such, merely insisting that we do not confuse this with the all-
important grasp of the value of virtue.

We are perhaps likely to find these strategies impoverished, compared with early
Stoic theory; but whatever our attitude to them, they are *different*. They come from
taking cosmic nature seriously, within ethical theory, as a first principle. The absence
of thoughts like these from early Stoicism is a strong indication that in early Stoicism
cosmic nature did not play this role. There are certain ironies about the change of
view. We find that the very people who lay such strong and immediate stress on
cosmic nature are the people who apparently pay no independent attention to
physics, the area of study from which cosmic nature should be properly appreciated.

Nature in Stoic theory is not a non-ethical foundation for ethics, a physical and
theological notion from which ethics is derived. Nature as that is relevant to
ethics—the determination of our final end—is human nature, and since human

---

[61] XII 26. For a more sympathetic discussion of Marcus, see Rutherford (1989).

[62] Marcus, VI 13. Arguably the alienation strategy is more characteristic of Marcus than of Epictetus,
and may indicate aspects of his thought which are not properly Stoic. Personal meditations are a very
different thing from lectures, and in any case Marcus is not obliged to monitor himself for Stoic
orthodoxy, as a Stoic teacher might. See Rist (1982).

nature is rational its natural development will be a development of rationality. Human nature is part of cosmic nature, but in doing ethics, as opposed to studying the role of ethics in physics and theology, cosmic nature does not determine ethical theses. And even human nature is not an independent foundation for virtue; virtue and nature are interdependent elements in an overall theory.

If this is so, however, have we not gone too far to the other extreme, and given nature too trivial a role in ethics? If we cannot understand what virtue is without seeing that it is the natural development, in rational beings, of our given attitudes to natural advantages; and if we cannot understand what human nature is, without seeing that its proper development ends in virtue, then nature would not even seem to be the more illuminating concept.

Nature in Stoicism, however, plays recognizably the same two roles that we have already seen emerge in other theories. First, it is what we start from because we have to—the inevitable aspects of ourselves. And second, it is what gives us an ethical ideal; and to produce this the Stoics of course do not make claims about nature just from looking at the way that people actually behave. They hold indeed that virtue is the natural development, in rational humans, of their given attitudes to natural advantages, and that human nature is displayed in virtue. But all actual people are to various degrees unnatural; we cannot help having the right instincts, but we go wrong in our rational development of them. Nature is an ideal concept, or rather it is best displayed in its ideal version. The Stoics hold this openly, indeed blatantly, claiming that the ideal wise person is the only person who really sees and hears properly, knows the truth, can run a household, be a king, be rich, be handsome and so on and so on. As they put it in consciously paradoxical ways, the ideal *is* the norm. We cannot, then, find out about human nature just by observing people. It is a theoretical concept, and we need the right theory to get it right. And similarly with virtue. Virtue is displayed in its proper form only in the completely virtuous person, but since this is an ideal we have no direct empirical access to this. We have two theoretical concepts, and it is unsurprising that we have to work at and with both of them together.

At the same time we are not free to do so *a priori*, merely to produce a neat theory. For the Stoics are empiricists about concepts (as indeed about everything). We acquire them as a result of repeated experiences, and so those who live generally similar lives will acquire similar concepts. Of course with more complex concepts belief and argument play a role; some of our concepts are infected by false beliefs and some depend wholly on them, so that there is an interplay between our reasoning and the given content of our concepts when we try to clarify or revise them. Thus there is room for revision and mutual improvement of the concepts we have of nature and of virtue when we use each to explain the other. Our understanding of nature, for example, becomes progressively fuller as we see that natural development involves not mere given attitudes to natural advantages but the all-important rational attitude to them. Thus Stoic virtue is grounded in nature in that we understand virtue better when we see that it is natural; we start, however, with a dim grasp of nature, and do not fully grasp what it is to be natural until we understand its full development in virtue.

This model of mutual bootstrapping and overall adjustment of theory is a promising one, and charges of circularity miss its point. It is arguably a more suitable

model for ethics than the model of deriving ethical conclusions from independently
established principles. We may fail to notice it if we concentrate only on the striking
and counter-intuitive nature of many of the Stoics' conclusions: virtue is sufficient
for happiness, for example, and the emotions should be removed rather than
moderated. Both of these are said to be established by nature, but they are
established neither by appeal to what people are actually like (this would, of course,
refute them), nor by *a priori* speculation as to what human nature requires. What we
find are attempts to get us to clarify and refine the ethical ideas we have. As a form
of ethical argument the attempt persuasively to redefine a familiar and basic notion
can be quite powerful. In many cases we lack the arguments by which the Stoics did
try to establish their conclusions, but we have enough to see that they did try to
argue from 'common conceptions' or what is intuitive, to reach their counter-
intuitive conclusions, and that ethical arguments about nature can be expected to
take this form.

Far from serving as an independent basis for ethics, nature as an ethical aim has
been considerably redefined in terms of the moral theory and its demands. But Stoics
have a sophisticated enough methodology to meet the objection that this renders the
notion of nature trivial in ethics. With both nature and virtue we start from our
intuitions, but go beyond them in response to particular ethical arguments and the
demands of parts of the ethical theory. There could be no notion of nature, helpful
in ethics, which was independent of any ethical arguments.

One important lack tends to make the Stoic arguments about natural
development less convincing to us; they have no good theory of error to explain why
we all live such unnatural lives. The nearest we find is a remark of Chrysippus that
'in bad[63] people corruptions about good and bad things come about because of the
convincingness of appearances, and because of the way they are instructed'.[64] Most
people go wrong because they do not have the strength of mind to question the way
things appear or what they have been taught by others. But this merely raises the
question, Why are we surrounded by misleading appearances and bad teachings?
How did we get into a state where everyday experience will guide us to live
unnatural, bad lives?

The Stoics can respond that their account of moral development contains an
explanation for this. It is natural for us all to go for natural advantages, the preferred
indifferents. Most of us simply fail to go on to the next stage of development, of
appreciating the distinctive kind of value that virtue has as compared with the kind
of value which preferred indifferents have. Thus grown people who live lives in
which they give too much value to goods like health and wealth are just suffering
from a case of retarded or defective development. They have started on the course
to moral maturity, but have stopped too soon.

To this the objection could be reformulated as the objection that if moral
development is a natural process one would not expect most people's development
to be so easily arrested. How does it happen that not only do most people fail to
develop properly, but they organize society in ways which positively discourage the

---

[63] *Phauloi*, the word used by the Stoics for those who are not ideally good wise people. This way of
talking falls out naturally from making the ideal the norm (see p. 177).

[64] Reported in Galen, *PHP* vii, 320 de Lacy.

proper development of human nature? For this further problem the Stoics have no direct explanation. They take us the way we are now, and assume that we will agree that this is an extremely defective condition to be in. They have nothing general to say as to why we are all living such unnatural lives. We shall return in the conclusion to this part to the question whether or not this matters.

6

Antiochus: The Intuitive View

Antiochus of Ascalon, originally a member of the sceptical Academy, rejected scepticism in favour of a dogmatic synthesis of his own, which he claimed to be the real tradition of the Academy.[1] We have an account of his ethical theory in Cicero's *de Finibus* V, from which it is clear that Antiochus reflected on contemporary disputes, particularly those between Stoics and Peripatetics.[2] It is a hybrid theory, drawing on several sources and responding to a variety of arguments. Antiochus clearly went for maximum agreement and compromise (arguably at the cost of rigour),[3] thinking it more valuable to bring out the consensus between different theories than to argue unprofitably about the differences. The theory is strikingly Aristotelian in content, though Antiochus tries to incorporate important aspects of Stoic moral theory; it is most usefully viewed as an Aristotelian reaction to the Stoic challenge, and can often be fruitfully compared with the account of Aristotelian ethics to be found in Arius Didymus.[4]

Antiochus' theory has not aroused much enthusiasm among historians of ethics, who have tended to prefer the original theories and to dismiss such hybrids as 'eclecticism', by which is often meant unintelligent scissors-and-paste combination of pieces without regard for context.[5] Antiochus has not helped his own reputation by the falsely historic way in which he presented his theory. It was, he claimed, the essential tradition of the 'Old Academy' of Plato and his immediate followers and of

[1] For the fragments of Antiochus, see Mette (1986–7). The major modern work on Antiochus is Glucker (1978), which, however, concentrates on his epistemology and relation to the sceptical Academy. For a survey of his views, see Dillon (1977). Barnes (1989) is both learned and entertaining; unfortunately it contains little on the ethics. On the ethics, see Hunt (1954a) and (1954b).

[2] And, despite his rejection of the scepticism of the Academy, he made use of Academic arguments, especially some by Carneades.

[3] This is certainly the way it is presented in *Fin* V. Piso, the spokesman for Antiochus' ethics, is charged with introducing inconsistency into a theory which is consistent in its Stoic version. (See Part IV, pp. 419–23.) Piso deals with the charge most unsatisfactorily, and it is clear that Cicero thinks that the theory is basically weak (cf. 95).

[4] See the Introduction, pp. 22–23. It too uses a Stoic framework, beginning from *oikeiōsis*, but adapts it in order to come to Aristotelian conclusions; this it achieves mainly by denying the kind of difference the Stoics demand between virtue and other kinds of value, treating virtue and the 'natural goods' as merely different sorts of good. Further, the Arius passage also extends the role of nature greatly from what we find in Aristotle. However, Antiochus lays much more explicit weight on nature and the possibility of resting ethical conclusions on nature, so in the present context his seems the more useful theory to concentrate on.

[5] For a revaluation of 'eclecticism', see Dillon and Long (1988).

Aristotle; and also of the Stoics, who had misleadingly changed a great deal of the terminology.[6] This claim will obviously not stand up as history. We need not, however, charge Antiochus with dishonesty, since he was plainly not concerned with history in the way we might be; rather he thought that what he was doing could rightly be seen to be in a tradition forming the core of Platonic, Aristotelian and Stoic ethics, and thus presented himself as the heir of all these traditions. We do not share his viewpoint and thus tend to think of an attempt to unite these traditions as misguided. But whether traditions can rightly be seen as similar rather than different obviously depends on the kind and level of the question you are asking, and we can see why Antiochus, preoccupied with questions which had been debated by Stoics and Peripatetics for generations, and finding current repetition of the divergences leading nowhere, would find it a worthwhile task to distinguish a common core to these traditions.[7]

From the standpoint of a study of ancient ethics like the present one, which tries to find the common intellectual structure underlying different ethical theories, a hybrid theory like Antiochus' can be of particular use; for it displays clearly both the kind of consensus that could be claimed between different theories and the kinds of tensions felt between them on various issues. Antiochus will be of particular help in considering the place of virtue in happiness, since his ethics is designed to mediate between Stoics and Peripatetics on this score. But he is also of interest with regard to the appeal to nature. He adopts elements of both Stoic and Aristotelian theory in developing his own account of nature; and this gives us a chance to see the use of nature in these theories in a way which is detached from the theories and employed to come to different conclusions from the original ones.

Antiochus makes nature very prominent in his theory. A resume of the theory begins like this:

> The first part [of philosophy], dealing with living well, they sought from nature and said that we must obey it, and that nowhere else but in nature was to be sought that final good to which everything is referred. And they established that to have achieved everything from nature in mind and body and in life is the ultimate choiceworthy thing and the final good.[8]

---

[6] Cf. 74: just as other thieves change the marks on stolen property, so the Stoics changed the terminology of the theory they took over. This move enables Antiochus to use a great deal of Stoic material for his purposes (it has also encouraged some modern scholars to find in Theophrastus or other Peripatetics early versions of characteristically Stoic items like *oikeiōsis*).

[7] Barnes (1989) gives a sympathetic account of Antiochus' syncretism over his whole philosophy; see esp. p. 81: '[I]n the early part of the first century B.C. Antiochus' syncretism will have seemed both true and illuminating. In logic, the struggle of his time was between scepticism and science; in physics, the tussle concerned a mechanistic atomism on the one side and teleology and a material continuum on the other; in ethics, there was a duel between virtue and pleasure. In each of these great battles the Old Academics and the Peripatetics stood shoulder to shoulder with the Stoics: Plato, Aristotle and Zeno formed a philosophical triumvirate defending the republic of knowledge and virtue against the barbarian attacks of sceptics and voluptuaries.'

[8] Cicero, *Varro* 19. The speaker is summarizing the theories of the 'Old Academy', i.e., Antiochus' hybrid theory.

Antiochus begins conventionally enough by stressing the importance of having a correct conception of our final good (para. 15),[9] and asks what this must consist in. Briefly, it is that it must consist in virtue and also in possession of 'natural goods' of which health, strength and beauty are examples (para. 18). Antiochus reaches this conclusion somewhat circuitously and in a way that raises various questions. He claims to be taking over 'Carneades' division', a framework produced by Carneades the Academic sceptic to classify all possible ethical theories. There is a lack of fit between this division and the use Antiochus makes of it,[10] and it is not clear why Antiochus feels the need of it. The theory he is going to develop is an intuitive one, and he would have been much better off basing it on our intuitions about what our final end must contain. I shall here pass over the complexities of the 'Carneadean division' and merely extract what Antiochus does for his own purposes.

There are, he claims, three kinds of candidates for being the first things to which we feel natural attraction: pleasure, freedom from pain and 'primary natural goods'. He dismisses the first two without argument (para. 21) on the grounds that 'we are born for greater things'. We may well find this too swift; many, including some utilitarians, have in fact claimed that pleasure is the sole object of all our desires. The appeal here is essentially to intuition: we cannot reasonably conceive of ourselves with pleasure as our final end. The appeal is presumably to the thought that pleasure could not be complete and self-sufficient, as a final end must be.[11] The same is assumed to hold of freedom from pain. Thus we are left with primary natural goods as the object of our natural impulses.

As already indicated, this is a curious procedure, since one would suppose it obvious that we have natural impulses for health, strength and so on. All Antiochus is adding here is that we really do want these things and not the pleasure or freedom from pain that we get out of having them, a point that seems intuitively acceptable. These things are the first or primary objects of our natural impulse; they are the things we cannot but want, nature marking out the limits of what is possible for us. This is why they are specified so broadly:

> What they call the primary natural goods include integrity and security of all

---

[9] All references of this form in this section are to the paragraph numbers in Cicero, *Fin* V.

[10] The division makes extensive use of Stoic ideas, comprehensible in an Academic argument against the Stoics, but more awkward for Antiochus, who in this passage is stressing the *Aristotelian* nature of his theory. It begins by characterizing practical intelligence, the intellectual basis of virtue, in Stoic fashion as 'the art (*technē*)' of living, making the point that every skill must have a subject matter distinct from itself. This must be something 'adapted to our nature'; the claims of pleasure and freedom from pain are dismissed and the only candidate left is 'primary natural goods' (*prima secundum naturam*). Practical intelligence, we are told, develops an account of morality (*honestum*) which takes the form of aiming all our actions at pleasure, freedom from pain or natural goods, even though these are not actually obtained; it is the '*consilium ita faciendi*' which is sought for its own sake, not for its results. Unsurprisingly, only the third version is taken seriously. Thus virtue is introduced in a way which fits only the Stoic theory. Further, when virtue is introduced later in his own theory, it does not figure in this role at all, but rather as a kind of good which we go for. On these problems, see Striker (1986a) n. 16.

[11] So it does not take seriously the moves Epicurus can make to show that pleasure of a certain kind can in fact be complete and self-sufficient. See chapter 20. Antiochus seems to stay on the level of intuition, on which it is true that pleasure is inadequate as a final end. He repeats at (para. 30) that we cannot even understand the claim that we love ourselves for the sake of something we get out of it, such as pleasure. Rather it is the other way round; we get pleasure precisely because we love ourselves. This is just an appeal to common sense.

one's parts, health, sound senses, freedom from pain, strength, beauty and the like. There are similar primary goods in the mind, like sparks and seeds of the virtues.[12]

As we have seen, nature forms the general and overall constraints on us: these are the kinds of things we inescapably want.

These impulses alone, however, cannot serve to direct us to our final good; that must also include virtue (hence our final good will be 'composite'). Why? Again Antiochus is relying on intuition in insisting on this right at the start. It is plausible that most people would agree that their final end had to include morality; few people would on reflection think that a complete and self-sufficient good could be completely amoral. Antiochus is not aiming to prove that virtue must be overriding in our lives, only that it must have an important place, along with other values; and for this he is right in thinking that he has more intuitive support than more rigorous theories.

To put the notion of nature to use Antiochus specifies it in two ways. First, he points out that each kind of living thing has its own nature, so that living in accordance with nature will imply very different consequences for plants, animals and humans, since they have different natures. Thus, starting like the Stoics from the general claim that all living things love themselves and seek to preserve themselves (para. 24ff.), Antiochus goes on to spell out the very different consequences this has for humans and other living things. For humans, because they are rational, can become aware of and reflect on their own reasoning. In a remarkable passage (paras. 39–40) Antiochus describes a vine, which has a life and a natural development, and is naturally helped or harmed by certain things. Suppose it acquired the animal faculties of perception and action; in that case it would be able to do for itself all the things which are now done by the external force of the vine-dresser; but although it would protect its vine-nature it would no longer be a vine, but a vine-animal, since it would be aware of and protect its animal faculties as well. Similarly if it acquired a human mind, it would become a vine-human; while it would use its mind to protect its plant and animal aspects, it would also use it in the ways humans use their minds, and would be in fact an oddly shaped human, rather than a thinking plant. Thus, Antiochus concludes (para. 41), what is crucial is to know one's own nature clearly and to find out what matters for one. Children aren't aware of having a mind that can be used rationally, but as they develop they take more and more pleasure in using their minds and eventually realize that excellences of the mind matter more than excellences of the body.

The second stage, therefore, is to reach a clear understanding of what human nature is. For Antiochus it is only human nature which is at stake, with no direct backing from cosmic nature. Uncontroversially, he says that human nature involves both body and soul (para. 34), so that we discover what proper human development is by examining both physical and mental excellences. He takes it to be uncontested

---

[12] Para. 18. Later as the theory develops we can see why our potential for being virtuous develops out of rationality. But in this passage it is awkward, because we are still officially within the terms of the Carneadean division, in which virtue is not one of the natural goods sought, but a developed rational skill in dealing with the natural goods. See n. 10. The 'seeds' of virtue that we find here probably derive from Aristotle, *Hist An* 588 a-33, where Aristotle talks of *ichnē kai spermata* of future states.

that bodily excellences are health, strength and so on, and that excellences of the mind are of two kinds, the non-moral, such as memory and talents in general, and the moral ones- the virtues, such as courage, moderation and so on. (He is not crudely begging questions here, since he is establishing only that the virtues are taken to be excellences of the mind; this does not show either that we do develop them or that we give them a special status.)

Antiochus needs to show, and does try to show, that we value these kinds of excellences for their own sake (para. 46ff;), since it is not enough just to show that we recognize them as part of standard human development. We attach intrinsic importance to healthy and sound bodily states, he claims, arguing that we try to produce the appearance of this even at the cost of the reality. We value intellectual activity for its own sake also; here Antiochus appeals, very plausibly, to children's natural curiosity to discover things, with no thought of what they get out of it. As for valuing the virtues for their own sake, he admits that we have the potentiality for this rather than the actuality (paras. 59–60). But that we do have this is shown by our consensus on certain clear cases of morality (paras. 63–65).

Hence the life according to nature will be one in which the goods of body and soul are valued, and also morality; the latter will be important, but not at the cost of all the rest, since our development has led us to value all of them and given us no reason for sacrificing any. Antiochus notably takes a Stoic rather than an Aristotelian view of what morality entails, in demanding that when I am virtuous I will be, when virtue requires it, impartial between my own interests and those of any other rational being. I achieve this, supposedly, by extending my sympathy from myself out towards others I am attached to and thence ultimately to everyone (para. 64). Antiochus locates this, rightly, within justice, but adds that since all the virtues are unified by having the same intellectual basis,[13] they all involve other-directedness and impartial moral thinking (paras. 67–68). Plainly Antiochus thought this the account of morality that was conventionally required.[14]

The culmination of our natural development, then, is to value all natural goods, bodily, mental and moral, for their own sake, and to value them in the right way— that is, with the later and 'higher' goods taking precedence over what they follow. The person who develops naturally finds virtue to be so important that it suffices for the happy life (*vita beata*), but the other natural goods are also needed for the completely happy life (*vita beatissima*)—a problematic thesis which will occupy us in Part IV.

As with the Stoics, Antiochus' story makes double use of nature. We appeal to human nature first to give us a general and overall idea of what about us is inescapable. But we also appeal to nature to find what we can do about these aspects. For the good life involves taking up a rational attitude to these inevitable aspects of our lives, and reason is what naturally characterizes humans like ourselves: a normal human life is one in which reason develops until maturity. So a natural human development is one that goes from perforce accepting our given drives to

---

[13] On Antiochus' version of this thesis, see chapter 2, p. 82.

[14] We may find it remarkable that he presents it as part of a basically Aristotelian ethical system, since Aristotle's ethics contains no such demand of impartiality. Presumably Antiochus thought that any ethical theory, even an Aristotelian one, must accommodate what was in his day seen as a requirement of morality. The issue is discussed in detail in chapter 12.

self-consciously reflecting on them and developing a rational attitude to them; and both the starting point and the end point of this are natural. Antiochus, however, does not combine this, as the Stoics do, with an insistence that rational development culminates, when it reaches a grasp of morality, in grasping that moral value is different in kind from all the other kinds of values that the person has been attracted to so far.[15] He rejects, as being pedantic and basically silly, the Stoic insistence that virtue alone be called good, with new terms worked out for all other kinds of values. Health, strength and virtue are all goods, he insists; virtue may have a privileged role, but it is for all that the same kind of attractive thing, a good, as other values, and the process of development from primitive urge to rational self-consciousness is an uninterrupted one.

Antiochus has been much berated for misunderstanding Stoic theory, and it is true that, especially in his arguments against it,[16] he shows little effort to appreciate what motivates the sharp Stoic cutoff between virtue and other kinds of valuable things. From his own point of view, however, we can see why he had little patience with it. He starts from and stresses natural development, from given and unarguable beginning to rational and self-conscious end, and in this the Stoic gulf between kinds of values is awkward, and his alternative, which lessens the distance between moral and non-moral value, both smoother and more intuitive. Antiochus is quite right to see this as the crucial point if you stress nature as a basis for ethics, and his theory can be seen as a protest against both treating moral development as a continuously natural process and insisting on a sharp separation of moral from other value. He certainly puts his finger on a difficult point in Stoic ethics, and at the very least shows that this puts some strain on the use of nature. Humans are supposed to have potentialities not only to recognize moral and non-moral values but also to grasp that the former are different in kind, and that moral value not only trumps non-moral value but is value of a kind which cannot even be straightforwardly put on the same scale as non-moral value. Is a position as strong as this simply the normal achievement of uncorrupted human nature? Kant, and the Stoics, certainly thought so; but Antiochus has not been alone in finding this counter-intuitive. We shall find, in Part IV, that this dispute as to the results of normal human rational development mirrors a dispute about the status of virtue in our final end; and on this issue also Antiochus appears as the champion of our intuitions against those whose theory develops our intuitions to lengths that are themselves counter-intuitive.

Antiochus' form of naturalism is not, of course, simply an appeal to the way people actually are, and, although he sees his theory as converging on Aristotelian results, he makes no use of the Aristotelian idea that nature can be seen in what happens always or for the most part. For Antiochus claims that our natural development culminates in valuing virtue for its own sake and in a way that gives it a special role[17] in our life with regard to other values; and an empirical survey of most people's opinions would almost certainly reveal that for most people virtue is not consistently seen as more important than other values, nor valued intrinsically rather than as a means to other ends, for example, honour and reputation. Nor do we have

---

[15] For, according to Antiochus, the culmination of ethical development is not a grasp of a notion of good which goes beyond what is originally good for human nature. See N. White (1978a).

[16] In *Fin* IV.

[17] Exactly how special, we shall examine in Part IV; it is only touched on in this section.

to suppose that Antiochus thought otherwise. All that he takes to be established by experience is that people are capable of valuing virtue for its own sake. Nature, he says, gave us merely the seeds or the beginnings of virtue (paras. 59–60); nobody can say that people are not capable of virtue, but it is up to us individually to develop actual virtue. What, however, makes us think that we are even capable of this? Antiochus points to consensus here (paras. 61–63), but qualified in two ways. One is that people agree in moral judgements on a very general level: who is so unlike a human being, he says, as not to be repelled by wickedness and to approve what is moral? Further, he says, there is agreement on certain cases, picking very easy and uncontroversial cases. Everyone hates the traitor ready to sell his country for personal gain; everyone approves of friends ready to sacrifice their lives for each other. These judgements, he insists, are shared by the ignorant many and not just the refined few.[18] Nonetheless, such agreement in intuitions can establish only that people sometimes and to some extent value virtue for its own sake. They cannot establish that they do so consistently, or when their own interests are at stake; above all they can't establish that people even sometimes give virtue the right place in their scheme of values.

Antiochus' reliance on intuition can be seen as a weakness rather than a strength. What in the theory drives us to give virtue even a large importance as compared with other kinds of goods? The Stoics can justify their claim that virtue must be overriding by appeal to the considerations which Antiochus finds so silly, which distinguish moral value as totally different in kind from other kinds of values. But once morality is seen as merely another kind of good, what justifies saying not only that people can and sometimes do value it, but something as strong as this:

> Thus I will venture to call the other natural things 'goods'; I will not cheat them of their old name rather than think up a new one;[19] but I will place the great bulk of virtue in the other scale of the balance. That scale will weigh down both earth and sea, believe me.[20]

It is at this point that the Stoics can retaliate and claim that Antiochus, having rejected a special status for virtue, cannot on the basis of appealing to nature alone give virtue the status he wants for it in the agent's life. The claim that it is natural for us to give so much weight to virtue certainly does not emerge from our intuitions about traitors and loyal friends, and Antiochus is in the position of building on and going beyond our intuitions, but without any convincing grounds elsewhere in his theory for going as far as he does or stopping when he does.[21]

Nature in Antiochus' theory is simply human nature, and at no point is there any appeal to cosmic nature. When (para. 44) he says that to understand our nature we must study nature in general, it is still human nature that he means; he appeals to Apollo's command to know ourselves rather than to physics. Antiochus takes over a

---

[18] Para. 67. Perhaps this point has been inserted by Cicero himself, of course, who is putting the theory into the mouth of a Roman aristocrat.

[19] The text is corrupt in this clause (see Madvig *ad loc*), but the corruption does not affect the sense of what follows.

[20] Paras. 91–92.

[21] This is another point which is mirrored in the dispute as to the status of virtue in our final end; see chapter 20.

great deal of Stoic ethics: their developmental type of theory, their appeal to nature, their stress on rationality as what characterizes humans, and their insistence that the development of a rational attitude will lead the agent to be impartial between himself and others from the moral point of view. However, he makes no room in his theory for cosmic nature. He does not have a second stage, as the Stoics do, in which the ethical theory which was studied dialectically is then seen in a wider context and grasped in the light of principles about cosmic nature. And, consistently with this, he does not even bring cosmic nature into the ethical theory proper; for him it plays no role at all. The successful way in which he takes over so much of Stoic theory without it gives further support to the suggestion that it does not play a structural role in Stoic ethics either.

7

The Epicureans: Rethinking What Is Natural

According to Epicurus, our final end in life is pleasure. This may seem surprising, given the antecedent formal conditions on what a final end must be. It might seem hopeless to think that pleasure could be complete, since there are many ends we have, such as virtue, which are not means to or parts of pleasure. Further, how could it be self-sufficient, since we seem to have needs that are not satisfied just by pleasure—needs to enquire, for example? And it is implausible to think of pleasure as somehow constituted by our own activity, as something that is not passively given to us but carried out in what we do.

Epicurus, like Mill, is aware of these problems, and like Mill tries to solve them by distinguishing kinds of pleasures, one more worth pursuing than the other. Unlike Mill, however, he does not flagrantly introduce a non-hedonic standard into his characterization of them, by saying that one kind is 'higher' than the other, but tries to show how there can be two different kinds of pleasure, one fit to be our final end while the other is not. One kind of pleasure is kinetic, the other 'katastematic' or static.[1] The examples used in discussing the distinction in *Fin* II 9 make it fairly clear: the pleasure of drinking is kinetic, that of having drunk, static. Kinetic pleasure is the pleasure you feel as lack or need is being removed. Static pleasure is what you get when pain has been removed; it can be varied, though not increased.[2] Epicurus identifies our final end with what he calls tranquillity or *ataraxia*, which is static pleasure.[3] Thus the pleasures that come from fulfilling needs do not form our final end; what is complete and self-sufficient is static pleasure or *ataraxia*. Though we need kinetic pleasures, they are not enough to amount to our final end in life.

In Part IV we shall examine the problems Epicurus has in giving virtue a place in this final end. What is relevant for this part is that static pleasure is *natural*, the pleasure of being in the *natural* state. This is only said in so many words in two late

---

[1] See *Fin* 1 37–9, II 9, Diogenes X 136, U 68, *KD* 3. There are much-discussed textual problems in the Diogenes passage; see Gosling and Taylor (1982). None of our sources are very full or explicit. See Annas (1987).

[2] Presumably the variation comes from variation of the activity pursued when one is in a state of static pleasure.

[3] *Ataraxia* and *aponia* are static pleasures (Diogenes X 136). The end of the blessed life is bodily health and *ataraxia* (*Ep Men* 128); a few lines later it is said that the beginning and end of the blessed life is pleasure, so unless we have a sudden switch of final ends, *ataraxia* is just a specification of the kind of pleasure that can be our final end. This is what we find at 131, where Epicurus says that when we call pleasure the end we mean not profligate pleasures but absence of bodily pain and mental *tarachai* or troubles: that is, the kind of pleasure which is elsewhere said to be static rather than kinetic.

188

sources,[4] but we find in Epicurus an interesting set of claims which illuminate the naturalness of the Epicurean final end. We find a certain amount of intuitive appeal to the idea that pleasure is right for us, is what we go for unless other considerations force us otherwise. Thus Epicurus says[5] that all pleasure is good because its nature is familiar to us (*dia to phusin echein oikeian*). And he is described by later writers as saying that pleasure is the first thing we find familiar.[6] This notion is not proprietary to Epicurus; all the Hellenistic schools claimed that their favoured end is what is really *oikeion* for us.[7] Epicurus also claims that we need no argument that pleasure is to be sought or pain avoided; these things are obvious. And he appeals to the nature of newborn children and of animals, who seek pleasure without being directed to do so.[8]

None of this goes very far, however. The passage from the *Letter to Menoeceus* continues with the point that, while all pleasure may be good because it is all 'familiar' to us, still it is not all to be chosen, for choosing a pleasure may lead to greater pains. To be theoretically interesting, an account of the naturalness of pleasure ought to give us more of a guide than this as to how to achieve it; for a clear conception of our final end is supposed to provide a guide as to how to act. This is what we find in the theory of natural desires that is prominent in Epicurus and, I shall argue, developed in a later Epicurean, Philodemus.[9] Our final aim is pleasure—the kind of pleasure that is natural, in accordance with human nature. This will we achieve if we fulfil our natural desires; and the widespread failure to achieve it (and thus to be happy) results from people fulfilling, or trying to fulfil, desires that are not natural. Hence Epicurus insists, 'To all our desires we should pose this question: What will I get out of it if what I seek through this desire is achieved? And what if it is not?'[10] Although we do not find, in the passages of Epicurean ethical theory that we have, much that explicitly gives us the structure of the theory, it is clear that Epicurus makes an appeal to nature to support his idea that pleasure is our final end. For the kind of pleasure that is our final end is natural, and we achieve this by following natural desires; and the latter is conceived of as a concrete practical strategy.

It is often thought that Epicurus had a crude proto-Benthamite calculus to guide us in achieving pleasure. This is because in a famous passage of the *Letter to Menoeceus* (129–130) he tells us that we use 'measuring' to determine when to forgo pleasures because of greater future pains, and to accept pains because of greater future pleasures. But it is a mistake to think that this gives us a quantitative measure

---

[4] U 416 (Olympiodorus on the *Philebus*, 294 Stallbaum; U 417 (Plutarch *Non posse* 1099 c). At *Fin* I 23 nature is said to set up pleasure and pain as our final ends for choice and avoidance, and similar thoughts are common; but I have stuck to passages which distinguish the two kinds of pleasure, only one of which can form our final end.

[5] *Ep Men* 129.

[6] Our *prōton oikeion* (U 398, 509).

[7] PHerc 346, an Epicurean treatise on ethics edited by M. Capasso, defends the Epicurean notion of the *oikeion* against that of most people who think that ambition and aggression are 'familiar' to us.

[8] *Fin* I 29–30.

[9] Gisela Striker has suggested to me that the theory may have its origin in passages in Plato's *Repub*, especially 558 d–559 c and 571 a—572 b; and that possibly the generic/specific distinction developed below may go back to the passage about correlatives at 438 a ff.

[10] *VS* 71.

of pleasure of the kind that the early Utilitarians produced. As often, Epicurus uses misleadingly crude language for a position which is in fact not crude; the language of measurement of pleasures has to be understood in terms of the theory of natural desires, not the other way round.[11]

We have a few statements by Epicurus on his classification of desires:

> We should reflect that of desires some are natural, some empty. Of the natural, some are only natural and some are necessary. Of the necessary, some are necessary for happiness, some for comfort of the body, and some for life itself.[12]

> Of our desires, some are natural and necessary, some are natural but not necessary and some are neither natural nor necessary, but come about dependent on empty belief.[13] An ancient scholion to this adds: By natural and necessary Epicurus means those that bring relief from pain, e.g., drink when we are thirsty; by natural but not necessary he means those that merely vary the pleasure, without removing the pain, e.g., expensive food; and by neither natural nor necessary garlands of honour and the setting up of statues.

> We should not force our nature, but persuade it; and we shall persuade it in satisfying the necessary desires, and the natural ones if they do not harm, and by harshly refuting the harmful ones.[14]

Epicurus is using two distinctions here: natural versus empty and necessary versus non-necessary, putting them together to produce a threefold classification. He nowhere explains exactly how this is done, and it is best to examine them separately.[15]

Natural desires are opposed to empty desires, which are desires which depend for their existence on an empty belief. What then are empty beliefs? They are at least false, but the notion of *empty* implies more than this. There is an established idiom in Greek in which 'empty' is used for what is futile or pointless,[16] and so an empty belief is not a simple factual error but a mistake which renders your efforts pointless, sidetracking your life away from the right way to happiness. Empty beliefs then are errors which are harmful and dysfunctional for the agent.

Since empty beliefs are all false, we would expect that natural desires would be desires which depend only on true beliefs; but this seems far too weak. And in fact we find that natural desires are understood not solely by contrast with empty desires, but as being desires that come from human nature; thus we have to ask what general account Epicurus has of nature and the natural.

We do not possess in any of our extant passages a substantial Epicurean account of what it is for a thing to have a nature. Nor does this seem due merely to the state of our sources: Epicurus' philosophy of science contains nothing like Aristotle's careful discussion of scientific concepts like those of nature and change. (There is in fact little or nothing between very high-level principles of atomism and low-level

---

[11] See chapter 2 section 4, for a rebuttal of the idea that Epicurus has a maximizing theory which conceives pleasure quantitatively. On Epicurus' crudity of expression, see the end of Annas (1987).

[12] *Ep Men* 127.

[13] *KD* 29.

[14] *VS* 21.

[15] What follows, on Epicurean desires and Philodemus on anger, draws heavily from Annas (1989b).

[16] As at Sophocles, *Electra* 330–331: *theleis thumōi mataiōi charizesthai kena.*

scientific explanations.) However, we can glean from the texts we do have various notions of nature which Epicurus employs. Thus he uses it for what is objectively there,[17] and for a thing and the way it is, as opposed to its qualities and relations.[18] He also uses 'the nature of X' or 'the X nature' in a way that verges on periphrasis for 'X';[19] thus a thing's nature is what it is (what it really is, we might say) as opposed to what merely happens to be true of it, or is true of it only by virtue of its relation to something else.

This might seem rather meagre, less helpful than Aristotle's idea of nature as an internal source of changing or being changed. We might also wonder why Epicurus feels entitled to it, since nothing in the principles of atomism demands it, and indeed Epicurus is hostile to teleological ideas which go along with that of nature in Aristotle (and the Stoics). However, we can see why Epicurus might regard it simply as an intuitive point, everyone readily accepting, in everyday life, that there is a distinction between the way a thing really or naturally is, and what merely happens to be true of it, or is true of it only in relation to other things.[20]

This is probably all that Epicurus is in fact relying on. Epicureanism is concerned to answer to widespread intuitions; we have these as a result of developing *prolēpseis* or concepts from our experience, so that if they are widespread they must answer to something that is there.[21] We can see, however, that the initial notion of nature that Epicurus is appealing to is not very substantial. All that it implies is the formal point that there is such a thing as the way humans really are. This is not trivial, of course; even the formal claim supports the idea that there are general truths about our desires and the ways we should handle them, which rest on our shared humanity. And the contrast of natural with empty desires suggests that what is natural is contrasted with what is both mistaken and harmful. But none of this rests on a substantive antecedently established notion of what human nature is, and still less implies any antecedent ability to pick out what is natural and what is not. We cannot rely on Epicurus' theory of human nature to understand what he says about natural desires; it is the other way round.

What of the other distinction, that between necessary and non-necessary desires? A desire is necessary if we cannot be happy, or healthy, or even alive, if we do not have the object of that desire.[22] The desire is called necessary, then, because it

---

[17] *KD* 7: if people who are in fact wrong were right, they would have achieved *to tēs phuseōs agathon*; cf. *KD* 25, U 471; U 423; *KD* 31: *to tēs phuseōs dikaion*; *Ep Men* 133; *VS* 25; Arrighetti [37] [35]: if the *metron* is not *em phusei* then we should not even consider time to exist.

[18] Cf. Arrighetti [24] [48] 7,17; [24] [49] 4,8,27: the *eidōla* are 'natures' which are 'full of void'; *Ep Her* 71: we should not deny the existence of qualities on the ground that they lack 'the nature of the whole'; *sumptōmata* do not have the rank (*tagma*) of nature *kath'heauta*; ibid. 68: we cannot conceive of *sumbebēkota* like natures *kath'heautas*; the *kath'holas phuseis* are contrasted with both *sumptōmata* and *sumbebēkota*, ibid. 40 and 48.

[19] Plutarch comments on this usage (U 76). Cf. Arrighetti [29] [5], where 'air's nature' = 'air'; [34] [21] 4,11,16: the nature of the atoms has not contributed to the bad dispositions of some; Usener 84: 'immortal natures' for the gods; *Ep Pyth* 97,113: 'the divine nature' for the gods.

[20] Compare statements such as that atoms constitute the nature of the soul (*Letter to Herodotus* 65; nature is weak towards evil, but not towards good, for it is sustained by pleasures but broken up by pains).

[21] Though it is possible that we have infected our concepts of things with bad theory and false beliefs. On *prolēpseis*, see Long (1971), and Glidden (1983) and (1985).

[22] *Ep Men* 127.

is necessary for us to have its object: that is, its object is something that we *need*, rather than just want. It is tempting to link this to the ancient scholion on *KD* 29, which says that these are the desires which bring *pain* if not satisfied. Non-necessary desires will just be desires whose objects we do not need, and which do not bring pain if not satisfied. Plainly, both necessary and non-necessary desires can be natural.

Epicurus puts together the two distinctions by specifying three kinds of desire: natural and necessary, natural and non-necessary and neither natural nor necessary, identified with empty desires. But there seems to be a problem with this classification,[23] as we can see by considering *KD* 30:

> When there is an intense effort in those natural desires which lead to no pain if not gratified, these come about in a way that depends on empty belief, and they fail to be dispelled, not because of their own nature, but because of the person's empty opinionating [*kenodoxia*].

From this it is clear that one and the same desire can be either natural and non-necessary, or empty, depending on what the agent's attitude and other beliefs are. We could say, for example, that desire for lobster is a natural but non-necessary desire.[24] But if the agent turns out to *care* very much for lobster, making efforts to get it and sulking if it is not on the menu, then the desire becomes an empty one, for it now depends on the belief that getting lobster, as opposed to something else to satisfy one's hunger, is worth caring about. And this is an empty belief- it is false and it gets in the way of the agent's happiness, for she is involved in the nuisance and expense required for frequent lobster consumption. Thus the same desire (desire for lobster) can be either natural but non-necessary, or not natural at all, depending on the agent's attitude and other beliefs. But how can the agent's other beliefs have so powerful an effect?

We are tempted to turn to other characterizations of natural desires, to see if they can help to fill out the notion of what is natural in a helpful way. Natural desires are, for example, supposed to be *easy* to fulfil: 'Thanks to [our] blessed nature, which has made what is necessary easy to provide, and what is hard to provide not necessary.'[25] One could retort, however, that it is easy to fulfil the desire for lobster—*if* you have plenty of money; likewise easy to fulfil the desire for political office—*if* you have power and means, and so on. Natural desires are also said to be limited[26] and to vary the pleasure produced, rather than increasing it.[27] But these seem likewise unconvincing and open to obvious counter-examples.

The key to understanding the theory is, I suggest, an assumption which is nowhere made explicit in the texts, one which will give us the right way of marking off the natural desires of humans in such a way that they contrast in the right way with empty desires, and divide in the right way into necessary and non-necessary.

---

[23] Cicero (*Fin* II 26–7) faults the division, complaining that since *natural* is the genus of which *necessary* and *non-necessary* are the species, the three classes are not co-ordinate, as Epicurus wants them to be. This is a fairly superficial point, but Cicero is right in finding the division problematic.

[24] The example is suggested by the scholion on *KD* 29: 'by natural but not necessary [Epicurus] means those that merely vary the pleasure, without removing the pain, e.g., expensive food'.

[25] U 469. Cf. also *KD* 15.

[26] *KD* 15.

[27] Scholion on *KD* 29.

The assumption is that desires which for humans are natural and necessary are *generic*. That is, they are desires *for food, for shelter* and so on, without specification of *what kind of* food, shelter and so on. My desire for food springs from my nature as a self-maintaining organic being which needs to replenish itself every now and then; and it is necessary that I fulfil this desire if I am to continue as such a being at all, and *a fortiori* as a healthy and happy such being. Hence if I do not fulfil it I will be in pain, and fulfilling it removes this pain. Thus we explain the various characterizations of natural desires. And if natural and necessary desires are generic, for food rather than for any particular kinds of food, then they contrast in the right way with empty desires, for they do not rest on any false beliefs. Since I *need* food, drink, etc., my desires for them do not involve me in any mistakes. They will also contrast in the right way with natural and non-necessary desires if these are taken to be *specific*, specifications of the desire *for food*. The desire *for lobster* will be a specification of the desire *for food*. It is not necessary, because as a human being I do not have a *need* for lobster. I have a need for food, but not for *that* kind of food, as opposed to food in general. However, consuming lobster is plausibly taken as varying the pleasure of fulfilling the desire for food (even if according to Epicurus' theory it never increases it).[28]

If the difference among the natural desires between necessary and non-necessary is that between generic and specific, we can see why Epicurus would end up with a threefold classification, even though two of the classes are species of one genus. For, while it is true that all natural desires contrast with empty ones in involving no false belief, there is an important difference between the necessary and non-necessary ones. The generic desire for food cannot involve false belief; desiring food is something I have to do, given my nature, and does not rest on any belief. But the specific desire for lobster, while it need not, can involve false belief—for, as Epicurus points out, I can come to have the wrong attitude to lobster, and instead of merely regarding it as a kind of food, a way of stilling my hunger, I can come to care about having *it*. If I do, then I have the empty belief that there is something about lobster worth caring about in its own right, and not just as a means to nourishment. Hence it is important to stress not only the difference between natural and empty desires, but also the difference between the necessary (generic) and not necessary (specific) ones. We can further see why a given desire could well fall into either the natural and non-necessary or into the empty category; for it is only when what we desire is a specification of what we have a need for that false beliefs can give it undue importance; so only on the specific level can false beliefs corrupt the non-necessary desires, converting them into empty ones.[29]

---

[28] Cf. the scholion on *KD* 29.

[29] This suggestion seems to me to make the best sense of the texts that we have. It should be admitted that it differs from the only ancient source which interprets the classification of desires in terms of degrees of specificity—the scholion on Aristotle's *Nicomachean Ethics* quoted in U 456. This gives desire for food and clothing as examples of natural and necessary desires; desire for sex as an example of a natural but non-necessary desire; and 'the desire for such-and-such (*toionde*) food or such-and-such (*toiasde*) clothing or such-and-such (*toionde*) sex' as examples of desires which are neither. We have no reason to give this scholion authority, however, and it faces difficulties. (1) It cannot accommodate *KD* 30, which plainly implies that a desire can be either natural and non-necessary, or empty. (2) It makes the necessary/non-necessary distinction artificial; surely we have as much a need for sex as for clothing? One can (as Martha Nussbaum does) defend the view that all natural desires are unspecific, on the grounds

Epicurus' position, then, is, very generally, that we achieve our final end, happiness, by achieving the kind of pleasure (static pleasure, *ataraxia*) which fulfills the required formal conditions[30] and which is natural to us. We do this by trying to fulfil only two kinds of desires: (a) natural and necessary desires, desires which we cannot avoid having because they come from the needs we have by virtue of being human, and (b) natural and non-necessary desires, particular specifications of those desires which depend on our beliefs, and which can go wrong and become empty if our beliefs are mistaken.

The difference between necessary and non-necessary among the natural may have seemed a somewhat scholastic one. But we can see its importance if we try to further fill out the content of what, for Epicurus, is natural. It is tempting to focus on the characterizations of natural desires as those that it pains us not to fulfil, and those that are easy to fulfil, and to think that what Epicurus has in mind are simple bodily desires, for food, drink and so on. This is encouraged by some of his sayings which seem to make bodily satisfactions crucial for happiness.[31] But this cannot be the whole story, as we can see from the way the later Epicurean Philodemus says that the emotion of anger 'is unavoidable, and is called natural for that reason'.[32] Anger is an emotion which requires belief and reasoning. If it is part of our nature because it is unavoidable, then our nature requires more than food, drink, etc.; but where do we know how to draw the line?

The answer is given by the fact that necessary and non-necessary desires do not mark out different ranges of objects; rather, the non-necessary desires specify the former. Thus when Philodemus says that anger is inevitable for humans, he does not mean that all cases of anger are inevitable. Rather, the associated desire—the desire for retaliation—is inevitable for humans, like the desire for food. But it is not inevitable how we express that desire, any more than in the food case. We have seen that with food it is unavoidable that I shall desire to eat; but it is up to me how I fulfil this desire given what is in front of me. If I get too attached to particular things to eat, my desires become empty; they stay natural only if, while enjoying particular edibles, I do not get too focussed and stuck on them—if I remain as satisfied with alternative fare that is as nourishing. With anger, according to Philodemus, there is an analogous phenomenon. It is inevitable that, being human, we feel a desire for retaliation when harmed or insulted; hence it is inevitable that we feel a kind of 'natural anger'. Natural anger involves feelings that are painful or 'biting' in themselves,[33] but need not involve further pain. For there is a right and a wrong way to express anger. Anger which comes from a settled disposition and 'results from seeing how the nature of things is, and from having no false beliefs in comparative

---

that what renders a belief empty is the agent's coming to regard one particular thing as not only needed but irreplaceable, the good Epicurean view being that all objects of natural desire are replaceable, and attachment to any particular objects irrational and dysfunctional. The problem with this view is that it requires KD 30 to say that intense attachment *replaces* one kind of desire by another, an interpretation surely less plausible than the one sketched above.

[30] Whether it does in fact do so will be examined in Part IV.

[31] Cf. U 409, the notorious statement that 'the beginning and root of every good is the pleasure of the stomach; even what is wise and extraordinary has reference to this'.

[32] XXXIX 29–31 of *Anger*. For this interesting but difficult work, see the edition by G. Indelli (Bibliopolis, Naples 1988).

[33] See *Anger* XXXVII 24–XXXVIII 8.

measurements of losses, and in punishments of those who do harm'[34] is natural and produces no 'disturbance' (*tarachē*) in the agent. But the agent may have false beliefs, in particular the belief that retaliation is good and enjoyable in itself. This tends to lead to other false beliefs, particularly overestimation of one's own losses and the other person's gains, and thus to further resentment:

> Desiring to punish, as though it were something enjoyable, a desire which is coupled with great anger, is silly, and is characteristic of people who think that this is the greatest good and turn to it as though to something choiceworthy in itself, and think that otherwise they could not punish people, and it is entwined with a harsh disposition, as we have shown and will display again as we proceed. . . .[35]

This is an empty desire, being based on a false and harmful belief, and the anger it grounds is called empty anger. Philodemus not only contrasts natural with empty anger, but also, as the end of the quotation suggests, gives us extensive descriptions of people in the throes of empty anger, showing us how unlovely this is and enabling us to see that harsh, intense anger depends on the belief that retaliation is a good thing.

In the case of both anger and the desire to eat there is something which we cannot avoid, and which is natural and necessary. We cannot help wanting to eat something, or wanting to retaliate to harm in some way; these are human needs. But there is something which is not necessary: how we deal with these desires and allow ourselves to express them. We always in fact eat A rather than B, get angry in a reasonable or in a violent way; and there is a right and a wrong way of doing it. The right way is still natural; only the wrong way, which involves false, 'empty' beliefs, is not natural. In the case of desires, the wrong way involves fixating on a particular object for its own sake rather than just as a means to satisfying the desire. In the case of anger, the wrong way involves taking retaliation to be, not just something required, but something good and appealing in itself; hence the wrong way sanctions violent and intense anger. But despite the differences, the structural similarity is plain: we go against our nature only by following empty beliefs.

Epicurus' notion of nature is thus considerably more subtle than is often thought. He does not think that we can mark off a distinct class of activities, such as eating and drinking, as being natural. Rather, all of our activities are natural in one way, and in another any of our activities can be natural or not, and which it is, depends on us. Nature constrains us all in the sense that humans cannot but need food, drink, and so on; but this is a weak and basically commonsensical point. On a particular occasion, when I eat bread because lobster is not available (or eat lobster and enjoy it, but would not mind if it were not available), I am not *constrained* by my nature, but what I am doing is natural: it is in accordance with my nature because it is fulfilling a need in a way that does not create a trouble or problem for my life. If I put everyone out to have lobster, or eat bread ungraciously because lobster is unavailable, I am not acting naturally; I am fulfilling a need, but doing so in a way which will leave me in a more problematic state afterwards. And this in turn is because the belief I am acting on is false. Thus in any given activity, of whatever

---

[34] *Anger* XXXVII 33–39.
[35] *Anger* XLII 21–34.

kind, there is an aspect which is natural and one which need not be. Even the faulty and wicked cannot avoid acting naturally in that they have to fulfil their basic needs; but the particular way they do this can involve empty beliefs, and hence empty, unnatural desires.

Obviously there are implications for the way we are to find out which desires are natural, as we must if we are to examine every particular desire to monitor our Epicurean progress. We have to work from two directions. On the one hand, we are given very general direction by reflection on what human needs in general are. Some of this (eating, drinking, sleeping) is uncontroversial; but not all is. We have seen Philodemus claim that we have a need for some form of retaliation to harm; Epicurus also thinks that we have social needs, in particular for friends and for life in a stable society. For he is not just concerned with what we need barely to stay alive; of necessary desires 'some are necessary for happiness, some for comfort of the body and some for life itself'.[36] But of course what we need for happiness is more controversial than what we need for staying alive. It might seem that Epicurus is condemned to hopeless circularity here: happiness is natural, but what is natural is what we need for happiness. However, we should remember that there is a distinction between happiness as a general formal notion and a specific candidate for happiness. Epicurus need not, and does not, depend on his own substantial account of what happiness is, to establish what our general needs are. He is, rather, relying on intuitive agreement that once we have satisfied our bodily needs we have further needs to achieve a satisfactory life, however that is construed. Everybody agrees that to be happy we need *some* kind of personal attachments, *some* kind of social context and so on. From this direction, then, we establish only very general tendencies of human nature, nothing definite enough to distinguish between different ways of achieving happiness.[37]

From the other direction, we distinguish natural (non-necessary) from empty desires by finding empty beliefs and showing how some desires rest on them. Here what we appeal to is definitely controversial, for an empty belief, as we have seen, is not just a false one, it is false and harmful. In fact the whole notion of 'empty' is clearly a technical one, dependent on Epicurean theory to give it its sense. While we nowhere get a definition, we can put together some Epicurean points about it. Empty beliefs are false, and ground the empty desires and emotions that are contrasted with the natural ones; they are also sometimes identified with harmful beliefs; and the suggestions of 'empty' are such that empty beliefs are those that lead the agent to do what is in fact pointless and futile, even if it matters from the agent's point of view. (This indeed seems to be why they are harmful.) Plainly, then, we shall not make headway in identifying empty beliefs until we have taken on quite a lot of Epicurean theory.

Such dependence on theory need not be a fault, or lead to circularity. But it does in the event lead to a strikingly *revisionary* Epicurean theory of what is natural. Epicurus' ethical theory makes claims to be empiricist and commonsensical; we start

---

[36] *Ep Men* 127.

[37] Interestingly, Philodemus talks of 'natural wealth' at 14.19 of 'On Household Management' (book IX of *Vices*); and this recalls *KD* 15, where 'the wealth of nature' is contrasted with the wealth of empty beliefs. What is meant, however, seems to be simply a degree of wealth compatible with living according to natural desires; wealth is hardly natural in the sense of being unavoidable, as anger is.

from feelings of pleasure and pain which need no argument to establish them as the foundation for ethics.[38] But the theory ends up rather far from common sense; and ancient Epicureans were famous for establishing, in Epicurus' Garden and other similiar communities, a way of life radically different from that pursued by ordinary people. This is not surprising if one considers the theoretical assumptions that lie behind the identification of empty beliefs.

One of these is the elevation of self-sufficiency as an important value. We have seen[39] that a formal condition on my final good is that it be self-sufficient; Epicurus, who talks of the self-sufficiency of people rather than ends, interprets it stringently: we must not fix our desires on particular objects, for if so we make our happiness contingent on obtaining those objects; and this threatens our happiness, for the objects may not be available. This is why we should satisfy our natural and necessary desire for food with what is available, being happy with bread and water, appreciating cheese if it is available but adjusting happily if it is not.[40] The classic statement of this aim is at *Ep Men* 130–131:

> Self-sufficiency we consider a great good, not so as to make use of few things at all times, but so as to make use of few if we lack many, genuinely persuaded that the pleasantest enjoyment of luxury is had by those that least need it, and that everything natural is easy to obtain, while it is what is empty that is difficult. . . . So growing accustomed to simple and inexpensive means of living is productive of health and makes a person unhesitating when faced with the necessary employments of life; it disposes us better when at intervals we do come on luxuries, and it makes us unafraid of chance.

We can see how this fits into the pattern we have seen above: we should not be ascetic and try to repress or minimize needs that we have; rather we should ensure that the ways we satisfy those needs involve no belief that any particular way of satisfying them is indispensable. For if it were, then achieving a satisfactory life would be outside our control to the extent that it is not under our control to ensure that these particular objects are available.

If beliefs about the importance to us of particular things and people in the satisfaction of our needs are empty beliefs, then two large assumptions are being made about our nature. One is that human nature does not require the making of particular commitments for a satisfactory life. This is an assumption that emerges in Epicurus' ambivalence towards family life and the general Epicurean preference for larger and more diffused forms of community, for weaker dependence on a number of friends rather than stronger dependence on a small family unit.[41] It is a controversial assumption, which we shall examine later, in Part III. The other assumption is that it is natural to be risk-aversive. Epicurus urges us to acquire an attitude to our desires which makes us maximally flexible in fulfilling them, since

---

[38] See *Fin* I 29–31.

[39] Part I, pp. 40–42.

[40] See U 181 for the bread and water, 182 for the cheese. Cf. *KD* 15, 21, 26, *VS* 59, U 202.

[41] Cf. O'Connor (1988). Nussbaum, in (1989), discusses Epicurean objections to romantic love, with its fixation on one object, and the lack of realism and of true caring that this can lead to. P. Mitsis (1988) ch. 3, 'Friendship and Altruism', discusses the various tensions in Epicurus' account of friendship, concluding that it raises severe problems for his account of his final end in terms of pleasure. The subject is discussed in chapter 11.

otherwise we risk disappointment. But it is not clear that we do always, nor that we should, rank security of fulfilment above other factors in this way, and Epicurus has no arguments to show why it should be more natural to do so.

If we look again at what Philodemus says about anger we can see another important assumption: the importance of avoiding *tarachai* or 'troubles'. Troubles are what interfere with the unimpeded running of one's life; static pleasure or *ataraxia* is a state where there are no interferences in one's pleasant activity. Put thus abstractly, it sounds clearly desirable; but specific applications are less convincing. Philodemus, we recall, claims that the good Epicurean will not feel violent, 'empty' anger once he loses the empty belief about the desirableness of retaliation. He will regard it as something 'most necessary', something he has to do, but as unpleasant, like drinking foul-tasting medicine and undergoing surgery.[42] What effect will this actually have?

> But someone will say: But if it is because of being harmed in intentional fashion that he gets angry, and he is harmed by someone to the highest degree, how will he not experience great anger? how will he not have a strong desire to pursue the person? To this person we will say that he will be alienated in the extreme from the person who inflicts such harms on him, or is obviously going to inflict them, and he will hate him—that just follows- but that he does not experience great trouble. Nothing external is worth much, since he is not even susceptible to great troubles in the presence of great pains, and much more is this so with anger. Terrible sufferings are the natural result of stupidity.[43]

This is disturbing in two ways. One is the way in which the insistence that the fulfilment of natural desires not involve the agent in 'troubles' shifts the emphasis from what is happening to make the agent angry, onto the agent's own state. This emerges in Philodemus' frank 'interiorizing' of the agent's good: it is wrong to get angry about things to the point of disturbing yourself, since these are 'external'.[44] He even says rather complacently that it is stupid to suffer a great deal from things that make you angry; if getting angry about something *bothers* you, then the belief that makes it bother you must be an empty belief; and since your aim is tranquillity, you should try to shed it. This kind of example encourages the thought that Epicurean happiness is bought at the price of adjusting the agent too thoroughly to the world, that it is too passive a conception of human life.

Second, the notion of anger that we are left with is a very redefined one. Feeling natural anger will merely involve seeing that one ought to retaliate, that it is something required or 'necessary'; it will not involve the kind of feelings that anger normally does. We can see this clearly in Philodemus' own comparison with gratitude. Since to the good Epicurean external things do not matter whether good or evil, he will not be very grateful for benefits, just as he will not be very angry at wrongs; he will see a grateful response as something that has to be done, but will not feel positive about it (for that would imply the [empty] belief that it mattered).

[42] *Anger* XLIV 9–22

[43] XLI 32–XLII 14.

[44] This is marked in Philodemus, but not in Epicurus. In this form it may represent Stoic influence. For other examples, see *Anger* XLVII 39–42, XLVIII 18–24; *Rhet* II fr. XX 5–10; *Grat* II 5–6. Cf. also Diogenes of Oenoanda fr. 41 Chilton 1–3.

Natural anger and natural gratitude look nothing like our emotions; it seems that the emotions that it is natural for us to have are more like the emotionless states of an agent whose priority is not to be disturbed by the impact on her of others and the world generally.

In fact Philodemus himself embraces an even more extreme position: the naturally angry person is called the 'unangered' (*aorgētos*) person, and we seem to get the conclusion that to be naturally angry is not to be angry at all (as we understand that) but merely to *pretend* to be:

> In general, we should know that the person who is purely unangered will give the appearance of an angry person, but not for long, and if he gives it for longer is not deeply [angry], but just not such as he seems to be. Thus those who have the completely opposite disposition [from the angry person] give the appearance to such an extent that even a wise person such as *Epicurus* gave some people the appearance of being like that.[45]

Epicurus means his appeal to nature to be empirical and to appeal to what we can agree on; but here we find an extreme redefinition of what is natural. Even if we are not very clear about anger, we intuitively think that the angry person is acting on strong feelings, and that these may well cloud judgement and lead to violent and intense response. Now we find that the *natural* way to be angry is to have no such feelings, but rather merely to be aware that one must respond in certain ways: angry behaviour is a show put on for the benefit of others, while the good Epicurean feels nothing herself but distaste for what she does.[46]

We seem here to find a tension between the appeal to nature as to something *inevitable* and the desire to find out what is natural by removing false beliefs; for the latter leads us to extensive revisions in our notions of the natural. The tension should not be exaggerated, and there are two factors modifying it. One is that what is inevitable is what is natural *and necessary*, the very general directions that our needs take; and this leaves room for revision as to the specific ways in which we fulfil our needs. And this suggests another point: the appeal to nature is not meant to be an appeal to obvious facts, or to be read off from the specific ways that people actually do fulfil their needs, just for the above reason: unless they are pathologically disturbed, people cannot go wrong on the general kind of need they can fulfil, but there is plenty of room for them to go wrong on the specific ways in which they actually fulfil them. Hence the appeal to nature cannot avoid involving theory, and surely must involve revision to some extent of our everyday notions of the natural. (And we should remember that Epicurus is impressed by the point that most people are extremely unhappy, and clearly mistake their own needs at some level.) The problem is not that the appeal gets us to rethink how we fulfil our needs, nor that it appeals to theory to do so. The problem is rather that the theory contains such strong assumptions that our notion of the natural is revised to a degree that can well seem unacceptable. Indeed, what we find in Philodemus could be thought to undermine the advantages of distinguishing the necessary from the non-necessary

---

[45] *Anger* XXXIV 31–XXXV 5.

[46] The Stoics also hold that the natural way of being angry is not to be angry at all, but merely to pretend if necessary (cf. Seneca, *Ira* II 13–14). But they have a much more developed theory to mitigate the counter-intuitiveness of the position.

within the natural: when we find that feeling natural anger seems equivalent to feeling no anger at all, we may think that the revision in the ways we are to fulfil our basic needs has ended by denying those needs. Perhaps we should indeed not feel any anger; but if so, in what sense is natural anger inevitable for us, as Philodemus says it is?

Of course this problem about revision need not be a problem across the board; Epicurean views on the emotions may possibly be more extreme than in other areas of life.[47] But there does seem to remain tension between the appeal to nature as what in our lives is inevitable, and the particular revisionary form that the theory takes in its Epicurean form.

Given his very revisionary account of what is natural for us, does Epicurus have any theory of error to explain why most people live so unnaturally, and why they need philosophy to show them what is natural for them? He can appeal, of course, to the fact that most people fear death, and fear the wrath of the gods, and to his own diagnosis of unhappiness as allegedly springing from these fears.[48] But these again depend heavily on specifically Epicurean arguments; they do not seem to provide independent support for the account of what is natural. Once again, it need not be a fault in a theory that part of it in isolation does not convince someone who does not accept the theory. But it does seem to be a weakness in an ethical theory that an important ethical conclusion seems extremely counter-intuitive unless one accepts not only the ethical theory, but other large Epicurean theoretical claims.

In Epicurus we see very clearly something which is in general true of all ancient ethical theories. The appeal to nature is meant to ground some of the ethical claims; it is not taken to be a trivial reformulation of those claims. But the appeal to nature is not a claim from ethics to something quite outside ethics. The nature that is appealed to is an ideal nature, an ethical ideal. It can nonetheless be appealed to as support for some ethical claims just because it is a highly general ideal; we are all likely to agree that it is natural for us to seek some form of food, shelter, community, hostile response to aggression and so on. However, as we have seen, the specific way in which this ideal is developed depends largely on strong Epicurean theses which the non-Epicurean is not likely to accept. Epicurus' extreme beliefs about self-sufficiency and the like force us to see in his case what is true generally: the appeal to nature is not an appeal outside ethical theory to neutral fact; it is an appeal to an ethical ideal, and therefore may ground some of the claims of an ethical theory, but not in a way that avoids dependence on the theory. Epicurus illustrates one danger of this; the more a theory revises the specific content of the natural, the less it can use the appeal to nature to ground other parts of the theory.[49]

---

[47] And possibly more influenced by Stoic views that emotions should be removed; Philodemus' *Anger* certainly shows trace of Stoic influence in some parts. See Annas (1989b).

[48] See Lucretius III 830–1094 for an analysis of the effects of fearing death. In the *Ep Men*, a popular introduction to philosophy, Epicurus focusses on beliefs about death and the gods, rather on than theoretical questions such as the nature of a final end.

[49] Hence the Stoics, who have an explicitly holistic theory, are in a better position to use the appeal than is Epicurus, who, because of his empiricism, does have a foundational approach.

8

The Sceptics: Accepting What Is Natural

Ancient sceptics, diverse though they are, are alike in their fundamental difference from all other ancient philosophical schools (and from modern forms of scepticism): they are a school without a set of doctrines. They distinguish themselves from other schools not in their beliefs but in having no beliefs, and in not even being committed to a distinctive methodology.[1] To be a sceptic is indeed to have a certain intellectual position, but it is unlike all other philosophical positions in having no positive content. As our main ancient source, Sextus Empiricus, puts it,

> What scepticism is, is an ability of opposing apparent things and things thought of in whatever way, an ability by which we come, through the equipollence [*isostheneia*] in opposed objects and statements, first to suspension of judgement [*epochē*].[2]

Why would anyone go in for this? The sceptic (allegedly) begins like everyone else, searching for the truth, especially in those matters with which philosophy is concerned. But whereas most people think that after some investigation and argument they are entitled to believe in some substantial theses (or to believe that these theses are not true) the sceptic is not satisfied. He not only investigates but identifies himself as a continual investigator and enquirer.[3] He tests any thesis proposed for his acceptance in the most effective way, by trying to argue for the opposite. The sceptic is, as Sextus indicates, the person who is best at 'opposing' claim to claim, arguing not-*p* for any thesis *p* put forward as being true.

The sceptic thus pits herself against the 'dogmatist', the person who does accept certain theses as being true. What the sceptic rejects for herself, and attacks in other people, is thus not mistaken belief as such, but commitment to *any* belief, something they call 'rash (or precipitate) assent'. Modern sceptics accept beliefs in one area and on the basis of this attack beliefs held in others; ancient sceptics, more radically, are committed to no beliefs at all.[4] They are committed only to the process of enquiry

---

[1] For a general introduction to ancient scepticism, see Annas and Barnes (1985).

[2] *PH* I 8. Sextus goes on to add that a second result is untroubledness (*ataraxia*); I shall deal with this below as one of the things dividing Pyrrhonists from other sceptics (chapter 11).

[3] The term 'sceptic' comes from the Greek *skeptesthai*, to enquire. But ancient sceptics were not tied to this way of describing themselves: see *PH* I 7.

[4] Modern scepticism about value, in particular, tends to take this form; philosophers are usually sceptical about values on the basis of unsceptical acceptance of other beliefs, usually about science. See Annas (1986). For an argument that modern moral scepticism need not be thus local in nature, see Bett (1988).

itself. Sextus claims that enquiry honestly pressed will lead to *isostheneia* or equipollence: one will find that, after the issue has been thoroughly argued and thought through, there is in fact as much to be said for not-*p* as for *p*; one has no rational basis for choosing between them. When this turns out to be the case, the sceptics claim, the result is suspension of judgement (*epochē*); one can, as a matter of fact, no longer come down on one or the other side of the question. When you see that the arguments for and against *p* come out equally, you will no longer be able to commit yourself to *p* as to a rationally defensible thesis. You may be left with your original inclination to accept *p*, rather than not-*p*, since this may have sources that are not dependent on rational argument; but that is another matter.

But how can the sceptic argue if she is not committed to any set of beliefs, or any preferred method of arguing? Sceptical argument is always *ad hominem* (in a non-pejorative sense); the sceptic is always arguing against what the opponent accepts, showing the opponent what is wrong with accepting his beliefs. For this purpose she can adopt whatever is required to attack those beliefs and display equipollence on the subject. But the beliefs thus used have no preferred status; the sceptic examines them in turn and finds out what is 'opposed' to them. Nor is the sceptic tied to any canons of method or argument. She will accept those that are current in the philosophical tradition of the day. For those are the ones that will effectively convince people; opponents will be indifferent to attacks in a mode they do not accept (as we can see from the case of analytic philosophers who are indifferent to deconstructionist attacks, and deconstructionists who are unmoved by analytical criticisms). But this does not canonize the tradition for her; she will use the modes of argument the opponent accepts to attack the beliefs the opponents accept. For if your goal is to get rid of rash assent, *ad hominem* reasoning is the most effective way to do it: your argument against the opponent does not rest on a substantial position of yours, so it cannot be attacked by attacking that position. The sceptic can attack without having to defend.

All forms of ancient scepticism are marked by the features sketched above: absence of doctrinal position; commitment only to the practice of enquiry; enquiry understood as *ad hominem* attack on opponents' positions by establishing the opposite as strongly as the thesis attacked; suspension of judgement taken to be the result of this.[5] But the three main movements of ancient scepticism differed on the further matter which will concern us, namely the extent to which scepticism involves the reflective having of a final end, and the role of nature as grounding the sceptical end. Thus it is best to deal separately with Pyrrho, the sceptical Academy and later Pyrrhonism.[6]

---

[5] I do not here go into important questions which are not strictly germane to my discussion of nature, such as: What is the scope of ancient scepticism?—*All* beliefs, or merely theoretical beliefs established by argument?—nor the contrast between ancient scepticism and modern kinds which focus merely on knowledge claims. See Burnyeat (1983), Frede (1987a), and (1987b), Barnes (1982).

[6] These accounts are selective and focussed on the issue of nature. The works referred to in each section give a fuller picture in each case.

1. Pyrrho

Pyrrho of Elis (c. 360–c. 270 B.C.) is a problematic figure for us; he is the founding father of ancient scepticism, but since he was like Socrates in writing nothing and in attracting widely opposed types of attention his actual position has become overlaid with myths.[7] Our best account of his intellectual position comes from his pupil Timon:

> Pyrrho's pupil, Timon, says that anyone who is going to lead a happy life must take account of the following three things: first, what objects are like by nature; secondly, what our attitude to them should be: finally, what will result for those who take this attitude. Now he says that Pyrrho shows that objects are equally indifferent and unfathomable and undeterminable because[8] neither our senses nor our judgements are true or false; so for that reason we should not trust in them but should be without judgement and without inclination and unmoved, saying about each thing that it no more is than is not or both is and is not or neither is not is not. And Timon says that for those who take this attitude the result will be first non-assertion, then tranquillity (*ataraxia*).[9]

Two things are notable from our point of view: that Pyrrho sees scepticism as in some way a means to a happy life, by way of producing tranquillity; and that he sees it as a thesis about the nature of things. The latter point especially has been taken to imply that his was a naive, dogmatic scepticism. In the above passage he plainly says that we cannot determine whether our judgements about things are true or false, and should therefore suspend judgement about them.[10] Some have interpreted him as grounding this claim on a metaphysical claim about the nature of things; but this is implausible.[11] Pyrrho does make claims about nature,[12] but these should be taken

---

[7] His biography in Diogenes Laertius contains stories that illustrate the thesis that scepticism produces practical paralysis: thus we are told that Pyrrho was indifferent to dogs and precipices, but that fortunately his friends went round making sure that he stayed safe. Some stories illustrate the claim that scepticism leaves a person with no basis for rational choice between alternatives: so we are told that Pyrrho was so indifferent that he would wash pigs and even clean the house. And we also find stories that illustrate the thesis that the sceptic's inner detachment is consistent with living a full and active life: so we are told that he was a respectable citizen and high priest, honoured by exemption from taxes.

[8] Following Zeller's conjecture *dia to* for *dia touto*. The latter gives the sense 'hence', which is followed by many scholars. That reading must be rejected, however, for several reasons. First, the Greek as it stands is unsatisfactory; there is no particle, and the grammar of *mēte. . .mēte* is unexplained. But there are also philosophical reasons. (1) It makes Pyrrho a naive dogmatist, claiming that very strong and unintuitive conditions hold for all objects, and dogmatically drawing an epistemological conclusion from this. But Pyrrho could hardly have failed to notice the conflict between making this claim and urging the loss of beliefs. (2) Further, Pyrrho later served as a prototype for the life without beliefs, something incomprehensible on the dogmatic reading. (3) On the dogmatic reading Pyrrho gives no argument for his claim that things cannot be grasped, known, etc.; on the preferred reading we get a reason for this in our inability to establish firm beliefs. This matters, since classical scepticism crucially sees suspension of judgement as arising from the practice of enquiry; it cannot be called into being by a dogmatic claim. (4) On the dogmatic reading 'equally' makes no sense. On the preferred reading it has a clear role, in the appeal to conflicting appearances and equipollence.

[9] Aristocles in Eusebius, *Praep Ev* XIV 18 2–4. The translation is that in Annas and Barnes (1985), p. 11. The passage is 53 in Decleva Caizzi (1981).

[10] Though he does not use the word that was to become standard for this, *epochē*. P. Couissin argued convincingly that this concept is a product of the sceptical Academy's debate with the Stoics: see (1929b).

[11] Without some move his position is obviously self-undermining, something too naive to ascribe to

together with the rest of the evidence we have about him, in which it is prominent that he takes the sceptic to end up in what was later called suspension of judgement, and in which he stresses the role of the 'appearances', the way things appear to someone who is not prepared to commit himself dogmatically to its being true that things are that way.[13] To make sense of the fragmentary evidence about Pyrrho, we have to construct an overall position not unlike that of later sceptics (who must have thought as much, since some of them appealed to Pyrrho as a forebear). Because of intellectual difficulties we are led to suspend judgement on all matters of belief, following the way things appear to us to be, but not committing ourselves to their actually being that way. But we are not as reduced as we might appear at first to be. First, we can use concepts like that of nature to organize our experience at the level of appearance; we can talk about the natures of things, and indeed must if we are to make sense of our experience as a whole, but the content of this is accepted as appearance, not as dogmatic commitment. Thus the notion of appearance is a sophisticated one; we can not only accept particular experiences but make sense of them in terms of concepts like nature, without falling into dogmatism.

This is important when we consider the role played by happiness. It seems that Pyrrho recommends scepticism as a successful way of trying to be happy. But how is this possible without a prior dogmatic commitment to the existence and importance of happiness as a human goal? Some have seen the answer in an interpretation which makes Pyrrho naively inconsistent: he recommends scepticism without noticing that this rests on a prior commitment to substantial belief. But it is a more reasonable approach to the evidence overall to take Pyrrho's claims about happiness to be part of his claims about nature: a way of making sense of our experience without dogmatic commitment. The thought then is that while we cannot with honesty, because of intellectual difficulties, rationally commit ourselves to definite views about human goals and what is natural for us, we cannot help making sense of ourselves in certain ways, prominent among which are the points that humans do have happiness as their major goal and that scepticism does in fact produce this. We cannot help doing this because that is how things appear to us. Thus claims about happiness, taken to be part of claims about the natures of things, present themselves as what we cannot avoid, what we are stuck with whatever our rational endeavours. (Pyrrho can of course only claim this for his own case, and the same goes for all of

---

an influential figure in a sophisticated intellectual environment. Many interpreters therefore, without evidence, take Pyrrho to have exempted his claim about things' natures from the scope of suspension of judgement- see, for instance, the discussion in Long and Sedley (1987), and Decleva Caizzi's (1981) notes. For a convincing rebuttal of the dogmatic interpretation, see Stopper (1983).

[12] Apart from Decleva Caizzi 53, the most important text is Decleva Caizzi 62, another passage from Timon. In it Pyrrho is represented as making a claim about 'the nature of the godlike and the good'. See Decleva Caizzi's notes for a defence of the traditional reading, which makes it a dogmatic claim not merely about nature but about everlasting nature. For a more convincing interpretation, see Burnyeat (1980b), and for radical doubts about this difficult text, see Stopper (1983).

[13] For testimonia linking Pyrrho with reliance on appearances, see Decleva Caizzi 55, 62, 63 A-C, and Diogenes IX 104–5. It forms a prominent part of our evidence. Long and Sedley (1987) oddly take Pyrrho's views on values to be reports of appearances, in the manner of later scepticism, while ascribing to him dogmatism about the nature of things. But values are (for the ancients) a considerable part of the nature of things; it is strange to be dogmatic about the determinability of something while suspending judgement as to whether it is good.

us.)[14] As it does for Epicurus, nature appears as what is inevitable. But our attitude to it is, for the sceptics, more passive, because claims about the natures of things, including our own nature and tendency to seek happiness, are precisely what we cannot rationally commit ourselves to; they are the views we find ourselves holding after rational enquiry has left us suspending judgement.[15]

2. The Sceptical Academy

In the middle of the third century Plato's Academy was turned by its head Arcesilaus to scepticism; under him and later Carneades it became famous as an anti-dogmatic school until it petered out in the first century B.C.[16] They adopted the practice of *ad hominem* argument, representing it as a revival of Socrates' methods. They also held that argument and enquiry, when pressed, resulted in *epochē*, suspension of judgement- a rather unSocratic feature, which seems to be taken over from Pyrrho. What distinguishes them from other ancient sceptics is that they never present enquiry and argument, and the suspension of judgement that they allegedly lead to, as means to happiness or tranquillity. The sceptic searches for truth because we all do; and we all do because that is the way humans are. This is not subordinate to a further aim.[17]

Thus the Academic Sceptics do not have to ask whether we enquire *in order to* be happy. But they do have to face the question how an intellectual practice that leads to suspension of judgement relates to everyday life. If one suspends judgement about some matter, how will one ever act on it? For Arcesilaus we have two interesting pieces of evidence. One passage[18] says that Arcesilaus did have a 'criterion for action', since he had to enquire about how to live one's life, and this requires a criterion since happiness, the aim of one's life, depends on having one. We then find an elaborate (though puzzling) argument to the effect that the person suspending judgement will guide her actions by the criterion of 'the reasonable' (*to eulogon*). But how can Arcesilaus hold this without committing himself to a dogmatic position, inconsistent with his practice? One influential response has been to read the argument itself as *ad hominem*, directed entirely against the Stoics; but there are

---

[14] Although the sceptic could certainly say that it seems to him that there are other sceptics, if his practicing of sceptical method seems to him to have achieved results. It is not clear whether Pyrrho's methods are sophisticated enough to allow this. For later Pyrrhonism, which engages with this issue in a more thorough way, see below, end of this chapter, and chapter 11, section 3.

[15] Pyrrho says nothing (that we have record of) as to what our rational enquiries are, or why we should think that they always leave us in suspension of judgement, or why tranquillity, of all things, should ensue on oue ceasing to make rational commitments; the later Pyrrhonists have more to say on these matters.

[16] On the sceptical Academy and its interpretation of Plato as a sceptic, see Annas (1992b) and (1988b). On the history of the Academy, see Glucker (1978).

[17] See Striker (1981a). Sextus at *PH* I 232 says that Arcesilaus made *epochē* a *telos* or final end. If he did, he would face similar problems to the Pyrrhonists: how can enquiry be genuine if you are doing it in order to get certain results? See Ioppolo (1986) ch. 6. But in this passage Sextus is foisting tranquillity as an end on to the sceptical Academy, as well as suspension; we have good reason to think that Sextus is unreliable and disingenuous when distinguishing his own kind of scepticism from others, and this testimony is best dismissed.

[18] Sextus, *M* VII 158.

difficulties with this.[19] The position seems to be Arcesilaus' own; so we need some account of how it does not undermine the rest of his position.

Another important passage[20] shows Arcesilaus meeting the objection that the sceptic cannot act. Suspension of judgement, Arcesilaus claims, removes assent to beliefs; the sceptic cannot be committed to the truth of a claim that he has subjected to thorough enquiry and argument. However, action does not require this: it requires only 'appearance and impulse': the world strikes the agent as being a certain way, and the agent responds; his impulse 'leads him naturally to what appears to be good'. Once again it is difficult to explain this away as *ad hominem*, but how can it fail to be dogmatism?

The reference to 'naturally' gives us the key, along with another passage[21] where it is said that 'in arguing he would somehow naturally use, 'I say that. . .' and 'So-and-so (naming him) won't assent to that.'', something in which he was followed by his pupils. Arcesilaus regarded his responses, including his intellectual responses, as grounded by what is natural. In other words, we suspend judgement in the face of intellectual difficulties; but are not thereby paralyzed practically, since nature leads us to act even without rationally grounded assent.

This appeal to nature is clearly not an appeal to our simpler, non-rational side. It is supposed to be natural to us to argue, and to demand rational grounds, as well as to respond in their absence; for we are rational creatures. Arcesilaus is thus relying on the whole of our nature, intellectual and non-intellectual. Enquiring comes naturally to us; so we are naturally led to feel the force of the intellectual difficulties, and to end up in equipollence, and thus in suspension of judgement.[22] This is a demand of part of our nature, the intellectual part. But we aren't just intellects; the whole of our nature demands that we respond even when our intellects are not satisfied. Thus, we find an intellectual problem as to how we can act while suspending judgement; and there is no intellectual solution to this. But this does not matter; for it is a *fact* about our nature both that we cannot find a solution and that we act anyway.

As a solution, this is reminiscent of Hume's.[23] The appeal to nature makes both what causes the intellectual problem and what circumvents it part of our nature. Thus the appeal to the whole of our nature avoids introducing any dogmatic element into scepticism: nature is just the way things are bound to appear to us, what is inevitable for us intellectually and otherwise. On the other hand, by the same token what is natural for us cannot afford the basis for any criticism of what we intellectually accept; we turn out to be passive with respect not just to our needs but our reasoning. It has been suggested that Arcesilaus was influenced by the teaching

---

[19] The purely *ad hominem* reading of the sceptical Academy goes back to a seminal article by Couissin (1929a). For this passage, see Ioppolo (1986), Annas (1988b), and Maconi (1988).

[20] Plutarch, *Ad Col* 1122b-d. On this argument, see Striker (1980).

[21] Diogenes IV 36.

[22] Why? Why can't we sometimes come to firm conclusions? The Academic sceptics took it to be a *fact*, not a demand of reason, that honest enquiry finds reasons to be equally balanced, at least in philosophical matters. Later under Philo the Academy came round to the view that some intellectual positions are in fact more persuasive to us than others, when all the arguments are in; but with this they encountered difficulty in maintaining their position as sceptics.

[23] I make the comparison briefly in Annas (1988b). I also explore the contrast between Hume and the Pyrrhonists in (1993b). See also McPherran (1990b).

of older Academy leaders, particularly Polemon, who stressed the importance of nature as grounding our ethical aims.[24] But in the Academics the appeal to nature changes its role. That it is natural cannot be a reason for doing one thing rather than another, since I will do what appears to me to be best, and whatever that turns out to be is natural. Nor can it be a reason for thinking one thing rather than another, since it is equally natural for me to reason out the cons as well as the pros on any issue. Nature is no longer that subset of facts about me which are inevitable; everything that I do or say is equally inevitable, and thus equally natural. If our nature is thus our whole nature, so understood that whatever effect one part of it has on the other parts, the result is equally natural, then the natural gives us a criterion of action in a rather strange sense: nothing that we do could count as not following it.

The role of nature in the Academics is thus quite consistent, and does not threaten their scepticism.[25] But something seems to have gone wrong; nothing that we do now counts as failing to follow nature, thus disappointing our expectations that nature would be selective in directing us to one way of living rather than another. Even if we take the point that nature does not direct us to one specific way of life only, it seems too far to the other extreme to appeal to nature and get an automatic rubber-stamp for whatever way one is living. We are told that Arcesilaus' own behaviour was ethically impeccable,[26] but this cannot have been because he was trying to follow nature. Thus in one way a consistent scepticism does not change anything, since it provides no basis for internal criticism of what we do. But in another way it does, since pre-reflectively we expected the notion of nature to be a normative guide, and if the sceptics are right it is no such thing.

3. *Later Pyrrhonists: Sextus*

As a reaction against the increasingly modified scepticism of the Academy in the first century B.C. one of its members, Aenesidemus, founded a newly radical form of scepticism, taking its name and inspiration from the radical figure of Pyrrho. This is the scepticism represented for us by Sextus Empiricus. In a more sophisticated form, it restates the position, and inherits the problems, of Pyrrho.

Like Pyrrho, Sextus rejects any dogmatic appeal to nature, but puts great reliance on nature as what we are inevitably bound to accept by way of 'appearance'. The Pyrrhonists in fact frequently see their intellectual task as one of rejecting enquiry into the nature of things in favour of resting with the appearances.[27] Sextus

---

[24] See Ioppolo (1986), pp. 146–56.

[25] I have not dealt with Carneades, whose *pithanon* or 'what is convincing' (or 'persuasive') as a criterion of action raises several issues which would take us beyond the scope of this section. See Bett (1989) and (1990).

[26] Diogenes IV 37–8, VII 171.

[27] The entry under *phusis* in Janáček's Index makes this clear. (Appearances are also contrasted with things 'in themselves' or 'absolutely'.) The sceptics also renounce enquiry into things that are 'naturally unclear (*phusei adēla*)'.

pours scorn on the notion of nature, on the grounds that there is so much undecidable dispute about it among the dogmatists.[28]

However, Sextus also appeals to nature in his account of 'how the sceptic can live'—how suspension of judgement does not lead to practical paralysis. The sceptic suspends judgement as to how things really (or 'in their nature') are, but can live by the appearances—things inevitably impress themselves on him as being one way rather than another. The way this leads to everyday action is divided into four:

> Thus, attending to what is apparent, we live in accordance with everyday observances, without holding opinions—for we are not able to be utterly inactive. These everyday observances seem to be fourfold, and to consist in guidance by nature, necessitation by feelings, handing down of laws and customs, and teaching of kinds of expertise. By nature's guidance we are naturally capable of perceiving and thinking. By the necessitation of feelings, hunger conducts us to food and thirst to drink. By the handing down of customs and laws, we accept, from an everyday point of view, that piety is good and impiety bad. By teaching of kinds of expertise we are not inactive in those of them which we accept. And we say all this without holding any opinions.[29]

It is puzzling that nature is given as only one of the four aspects of everyday observances (*biōtikē terēsis*); and this seems illogical. Why is nature responsible for our perceiving and thinking, but not for handing down customs and teaching skills? It is also odd for nature to be contrasted with the 'necessitation' of feelings, since nature is standardly what we cannot avoid rather than what we can. Moreover, when Sextus talks, in *PH* III and *M* XI, of the sceptic's life, he seems to be employing a wider notion of nature. In both passages he contrasts two aspects of life- what depends on belief and what is necessitated.[30] Evils that depend on belief, such as thinking pain a bad thing, can be eliminated; for the sceptic will come to lose this belief, suspending judgement on the matter. But we cannot get rid of what is necessitated, such as the pain; change in belief leaves that stubbornly there. This is the basis of Sextus' conclusion that the sceptic will achieve 'moderate feeling' (*metriopatheia*) in matters that are unavoidable, and untroubledness (*ataraxia*) in matters of belief. We cannot avoid the nuisances of pain, hunger, etc., but we will, allegedly, mind them much less if we have shed beliefs, particularly the beliefs that pain, hunger, etc., are bad things.[31] The contrast is between aspects of our lives that we cannot avoid and aspects that we can have an effect on. We have seen that this is the Epicurean conception of what nature is; and at one point we find Sextus identifying what is necessitated with what is natural.[32] This is an easily understandable contrast; but it fits awkwardly with Sextus' account of everyday observances. The problem seems to lie, however, in Sextus' consistently sceptical practice. The sceptic does not in his own person accept substantial theses, or the legitimacy of

---

[28] In the Third Mode (*PH I* 98). The claim is somewhat puzzling, since Sextus' lengthy demolitions of dogmatic claims in the study of nature do not include that of nature itself. See Annas and Barnes (1985).

[29] *PH* I 23–24.

[30] For a particularly clear example of the contrast, see *M* XI 142–3.

[31] Because of this recognition of negative factors in our lives which we cannot eliminate, the Pyrrhonist conception of happiness is markedly less optimistic than those of other schools. See chapter 17.

[32] *M* XI 156. He does so by way of introducing a poetic quotation.

substantial concepts like that of nature; he uses them to dislodge other substantial theses or concepts, but is always ready to attack them in turn. Hence there is no internal sceptical drive to consistency in their use. Even when rejecting dogmatic commitment to nature, Sextus is happy to use it in several different contrasts: nature versus convention, nature versus appearance and so on. But Sextus' overall position is reasonably clear. The sceptic relies on nature to guide her in the absence of commitment to beliefs, precisely because what is natural is just those aspects of us which are unaffected by our beliefs.

The Pyrrhonists systematically oppose having beliefs to being affected by appearances; thus when we suspend judgement and lack beliefs, we are not thrown back on nature in an undifferentiated way, but are rather left with the content of our beliefs intact, but accepting that content as something forcing itself on us rather than as something we rationally accept. Thus losing beliefs, for a Pyrrhonist, is not a matter of shedding information, but rather of retaining the information but losing one's original attitude to it: one cannot help being impressed by the thought that grass is green, virtue good and so on, even though one cannot rationally accept either because of appreciating the equal force of considerations on the other side. Thus when losing commitment to beliefs throws us back on nature, as being what is necessitated about us, we are left not with a cognitively impoverished set of attitudes, but rather with a different, detached state of mind towards the attitudes that we had before. Thus the Pyrrhonist seems well-equipped to meet the standard complaint that in appealing to his final end, which he takes to be natural, he is covertly introducing committed, dogmatic claims; he can admit to accepting the content of those dogmatic claims, but not as a dogmatist would.[33]

Sextus in fact presents the sceptics with a full-scale account of our final aim and of scepticism as an optimal way to reach it, quite on a par with those of other schools:

> Now a final end [*telos*] is that for the sake of which everything is done or considered, while it is not itself done or considered for the sake of anything else. Or: a final end is the final object of desire. Up to now we say that the final end of the Sceptic is untroubledness [*ataraxia*] in matters of opinion and having moderate feelings [*metropatheia*] in matters forced on us. For Sceptics began to do philosophy in order to decide between appearances and to apprehend which are true and which false, so as to become untroubled; but they came upon equipollent dispute, and being unable to decide this they suspended judgement. And when they suspended judgement, untroubledness in matters of opinion followed fortuitously. . . . A story told of the painter Apelles applies to the Sceptics. They say that he was painting a horse and wanted to represent in his picture the lather on the horse's mouth; but he was so unsuccessful that he gave up, took the sponge on which he had been wiping off the colours from his brush, and flung it at the picture. And when it hit the picture, it produced a representation of the horse's lather. Now the Sceptics were hoping to acquire untroubledness by deciding the anomalies in what appears and is thought of, and being unable to do this they suspended judgement. But when they suspended

---

[33] It is of course difficult to give an independent definition of 'accepting the content'; intuitively we can understand it as the cognitive state, whatever that is, which the detached sceptic shares with the dogmatist.

judgement, untroubledness followed as it were fortuitously, as a shadow follows a body.[34]

Pyrrhonism is here clearly put forward in the way any ethical theory is: it is taken that we will agree that we have a final end, and the sceptic tells us how we shall achieve it if we follow his recommendations rather than those of his rivals. But this introduces a problem which we find neither in the Academics (who do not present scepticism as a way of achieving our final end) nor with Pyrrho (who does not stress the importance of enquiry). Is the sceptic not dogmatically putting forward scepticism as a recommended way of life?

The immediate answer is by now obvious: Sextus is not in the above passage competing with the dogmatists in rationally recommending scepticism; rather he is in good sceptical fashion recording what appears to him to be the case—the way things cannot but strike him—but without commitment to believing it. Thus Sextus in talking about the sceptic's end is not going beyond what it is inevitable, and natural, for him to do.[35] But this response has troubles of its own.

That the sceptic has a final aim, and that this is untroubledness, is something *internal* to her reasonings; she does not have, so to speak, one appearance after another, but organizes them by the notion of a final end, which is an appearance organizing other appearances. Now it seems plausible that, in an ancient setting, the notion of a final end should be an appearance that persists in all or most people after ethical debate. But the claim that this is untroubledness is much more controversial. We have seen[36] that conceptions of the agent's final end which fill it out as something passive are controversial; the idea that one's final end should in some way consist of one's own activity is a fairly central idea. This does not mean, of course, that argument cannot dislodge it; but it does mean that as part of Sextus' appearances it is more idiosyncratic than he seems aware of. We can grant to Sextus the point that, *if* untroubledness is our aim, then scepticism as described seems the best way of achieving it. But the problem comes when we ask why we should accept that untroubledness is our aim. As presented, of course, it is just part of what Sextus finds it natural to accept; but most people will not find it thus natural to accept, unless they have been through the same intellectual course as Sextus, which will have influenced them to accept it.

Is this a problem for the sceptic? It certainly raises the question sharply, what the status is of Sextus' account of the sceptical end. If he is not putting it forward dogmatically, but just recording what he finds it natural to accept, then if his readers do not find it thus natural there will be nothing further to say or do. But this seems to conflict with the picture Sextus presents of himself as concerned to convert others to the sceptical end, in particular the therapeutic picture he presents of himself as curing others of false belief, and of himself as doing this because he is a 'lover of humankind'.[37] Is Sextus not committed at least to furthering his own

---

[34] *PH* I 25-6, 28-9.

[35] For more on the status of the sceptical final end, see chapter 17.

[36] In chapter 1.

[37] The classic statement of this is at *PH* III 280: 'the sceptic, because of his love of humanity, tries as far as he can to cure the belief and rashness of the dogmatists'—*ho skeptikos dia to philanthrōpos einai tēn tōn dogmatikōn oiēsin te kai propeteian kata dunamin iasthai logoi bouletai*. On the therapeutic

appearances, so to speak—to getting others to share them? And if so, he appears to think that untroubledness is a good thing, that it is preferable for people to be sceptics, and so on—In short, he appears to have a committed and positive attitude to the contents of his appearances, something which makes them no longer just a matter of nature and necessity imposing itself upon us.[38]

The obvious answer from the sceptical side is that having a positive attitude to one's own appearances—untroubledness as our aim, scepticism as the desirable means—is not to be analyzed as having appearances *plus* having a positive commitment to them, something which would plainly be unsceptical. The problem comes from having too limited a view of what our nature is. What is natural, and unavoidable for us, is not passivity towards our appearances—that would not be a human response—but an active, critical use of them. Sextus' philanthropic concern to make others sceptics (because that would be so much better) is itself part of his appearances, what is natural for him. He is detached from what he puts forward in the sense that he is not committed to believing it to be true, as the dogmatists do; but that does not condemn his acceptance of it to be wooden and blankly passive. The natural human response is to *live* by appearances; and in the case of intellectual appearances, this means actively holding to them and living by them.

If this is the case, however, then living by the appearances seems to come to just what most people mean by having beliefs, and scepticism seems to have eliminated itself. The pursuer of the sceptical final aim will indeed be just like any other person with an ethical aim. She will have gone through sceptical arguments which left her detached from her beliefs; but this very detachment will be something which makes no difference when it comes to acting on what she accepts.

It will be said at this point that scepticism produces detachment from one's beliefs by removing commitment to them; and *that* cannot leave everything where it is. The sceptic who has lost commitment will no longer identify with his beliefs; it will be as though he observed them going on inside him, but without identifying with them, or with their outcome.[39] The sceptic can respond that it is not clear that this is what detachment has to be. If we are so to understand what is necessary and inevitable for us that it is natural for our response to our appearances to be an active and critical one, then detachment will not have the alleged effects. We may well then ask what there is left for detachment to be; and though it is possible to sketch a conception of detachment which would not preclude immersion in the practical,[40] it is then far from clear how this could be a plausible candidate for human happiness. What is clear is that detachment has to be understood in a very special way if it is to be something that makes no difference to the sceptic's ability to live like others.

---

dimension of Pyrrhonism, and its potential conflict with the sceptic's lack of commitment to belief, see chapter 11.

[38] See McPherran (1988).

[39] For this charge, see Burnyeat (1983). In Annas (1986) I endorse the view that sceptical suspension of judgement and detachment will lead to a passive and uncritical attitude to the content of ethical beliefs, and thus to a radical difference between the sceptic and others. I now think that the sceptic can respond to this, along the lines suggested here, though the response is ultimately unsuccessful, since it pays the price of extending the scope of what is natural so far that the point of its original introduction is lost.

[40] See the end of McPherran (1988) for interesting suggestions about this and parallels from Buddhism.

Sceptics can accept this, and it is clear that Sextus sometimes does, namely when he claims that scepticism does not attack ordinary life.[41] To the objection that scepticism then seems a waste of time, since it has got one no further than when one started, the answer is that scepticism only seems a waste of time to someone who no longer needs the sceptical process of enquiry—that is, the *successful* sceptic. By the time it seems superfluous, it has already done its job. Scepticism will only be a perceptible presence in the life of someone who has not yet got what he needs scepticism to achieve—namely untroubledness, by intellectual or other factors.

Thus the sceptic can avoid dogmatic commitment at any level. But this is done by expanding the notion of what is natural and necessary to us, to the point where it covers the whole of the original area which was to be divided between the natural and the alterable realm of belief. Nature has again been stretched to the point where everything the sceptic does is natural. And so once again, while there is a clear sense in which scepticism leaves everything the way it was before, there is also a sense in which it never can; for we pre-sceptically took nature to be a selective normative ideal, and if scepticism is to work, this must be a mistake.

Scepticism and Epicureanism share a surprising number of features,[42] and it is clear that their approaches to nature are shared up to a point. Nature is those aspects of us and our lives that are inescapable, unalterable by our beliefs. Nonetheless, our beliefs can be effective, since they determine the specific way we deal with those inescapable parts of our lives. Sceptics and Epicureans agree that it is inevitable not only that we will feel pain and hunger, but that we will have some kind of negative attitude to these things. What is up to us is to manage and alter the beliefs that bring it about that our attitude takes one particular, harmful or helpful form. The theories, however, diverge very radically as to what we can do about our nature. The Epicureans, as we have seen, have a highly revisionary and theoretically loaded idea of what is natural when false beliefs are removed. But although the sceptics are equally sanguine as to the feasibility of removing our beliefs, they are in the end left with a view of nature so unrevisionary as to be totally unselective.

The sceptics in accepting nature avoid the problems accruing to the Epicurean revision of what is natural, and do more justice to our view that nature is those aspects of ourselves that are inevitable; indeed this is the aspect which they stress, to the point of losing any ability to use nature selectively to point us in the right direction towards ethical progress. But this in effect nullifies the appeal to nature; it has lost its force as a normative ideal.

There are two possible retorts to this conclusion about the sceptics' use of nature. One is to deny that we do in fact have an expectation that nature will give us a selective ethical ideal. This does not just imply, of course that we do not have an explicit *belief* on the matter; scepticism can hardly rely on beliefs. Rather, it must be the case that even after reaching suspension of judgement on all the relevant matters, we still do not have any expectation, of a non-rational kind, that nature will guide us in a normative way. How plausible is this claim? Even in the twentieth century, when rational appeals to nature are out of fashion, it is still possible to affect people

---

[41] For a discussion of Sextus' various claims about scepticism and everyday life (*bios*), see Barnes (1982). This issue will recur again in chapters 11 and 17.

[42] See Gigante (1981), and the discussion review by Fowler (1984).

adversely against a practice by calling it unnatural. In the ancient world this was even more deep-rooted, and the idea that the sceptics would find themselves with appearances that were completely indifferent and neutral as to the normative force of nature must have seemed highly implausible.

Another retort is to deny that scepticism does leave everything where it is. Perhaps losing our beliefs does not leave us with all the same appearances; maybe losing some beliefs will in fact have an effect on some of our appearances. Losing my belief that wealth matters, for example, will in fact leave me more indifferent to wealth than before; the original appearance need not be affected by the loss of commitment to the corresponding belief, but as a matter of fact will tend to weaken.[43] So the sceptic will end up living a different life from others, and this will be because of his attachment to nature.

Even if this is right, however, nature does not seem to be functioning as a *normative* ideal in the ordinary sense. The sceptic can say, 'If you achieve suspension of belief you will in fact come to live a more natural life—look at me', but in so doing he is not giving me a reason for seeking it. *That* would be merely re-infecting me with dogmatism, since I would be seeking the natural life as though it were valuable. The only way to achieve the natural life is indirectly, by not seeking the natural life but by doing what will in fact achieve it (this being constant enquiring which will lead to suspension of judgement).[44] And this hardly leaves nature a role as a normative ideal in terms of which we are to select and reform our priorities. Does this matter? Yes, for it is part of the pre-theoretical view of the world that nature is such a selective normative ideal, and a theory which nullifies this is taking something away from us. The sceptic can of course admit this, and say that the gain is well worth the cost, but this returns us to the problem that he can give us no reason for thinking this; he can merely point to the sceptical way of life and hope that we find it attractive.

---

[43] This position is argued for powerfully by McPherran (1986) and (1990b).

[44] And by this point, as Nicholas White has emphasized, it cannot *matter* to the sceptic that it is the natural life that is being aimed at.

9

Uses of Nature

This survey has shown that the conventional picture of the role of nature in ancient ethics is seriously amiss. Instead of the remorseless imposition of a single way of life on everyone, suitable or not, we have found nature figuring at the most general level of our lives. Instead of metaphysical biology we have found appeal to humans' social and political instincts. Instead of appeal to a Great Pattern in the world to which we have to conform, we have found that the real appeal, even in the Stoics, is to human nature. Two kinds of roles emerge as the central ones for nature in ethical theory.

One is a limiting role: nature is those aspects of ourselves that we cannot change but must work with. This can be seen negatively or positively. Negatively, nature in this sense is inevitable and thus constrains what we do. We have seen that, because nature is conceived of as our most general and overall features, the inevitability of nature does not imply that there is nothing we can do to live better or worse; it is up to us to specify our lives in ways such that things that we have to do—eating, getting angry, seeking company—are done in the right way rather than the wrong. We can do a great deal, by way of reforming our beliefs, to enable us to live more naturally; living according to nature does not have to be a passive acquiescence. And it is not achieved by switching from one, corrupt set of activities to another, natural set; rather, what is needed is a change of your attitude to the activities you have. (This may, of course, result in a change of your way of life; but this is dictated by your change of attitude, not the other way round.)

Nature as our given material can be viewed more positively as our given potential for certain kinds of development. This is one role which it has in Aristotle: the natural virtues are not proper virtues, but states, natural because unchosen and merely a matter of temperament, which have the potential to become real virtues when the agent reflects on her reasons for acting and develops the intellectual basis of real virtue. Alexander develops this Aristotelian idea more explicitly.

But nature is not just the given aspects of ourselves; nature can function as an ethical ideal, as the correct way of developing the given aspects of ourselves. In ways that differ between the different theories, we find different ideals of the natural life. Moreover, the schools do not just differ doctrinally; they differ in the way that their ideals are intuitive or counter-intuitive, given ordinary moral beliefs. Thus we can assess the success or failure of the appeal to nature in the different schools in many different ways. Is the account of what is natural too counter-intuitive, and in particular too far from the first notion of nature, the inevitable, intractable aspects of ourselves? How much weight is put on it within the theory? and so on. In all cases, however, the notion of the natural is frankly dependent on ethical notions. We have seen that the one account which has a more empirical basis, Aristotle's in the *Politics*, runs into serious problems from its empirical commitments.

The Stoics are the first to produce an ethics that appeals to nature and is prominently a *developmental* one; this enables them to take as primary the points that human nature is developing and rational. Thus we get a more sophisticated use of nature which combines the idea of nature as the inevitable aspects of ourselves with nature as indicating a goal of development, one that can be corrupted. We begin, for the Stoics, with given impulses to 'natural things' like health and strength; but because we are rational beings the natural development for us is one in which we develop our rationality and come self-consciously to adopt a rational attitude to these things and to our pursuit of them. This approach, once introduced, proved very powerful; we find both later Peripatetics and Antiochus using it, and adapting it to reach conclusions about morality that are less counter-intuitive than the Stoics' and more like Aristotle's. The great attraction of developmental theories was presumably the way in which in them nature gives us the starting points for ethics, and also indicates our ethical goal, in that natural development for humans is towards rationality, and it is rational thinking that develops into moral thinking.

There are thus some grounds for seeing the developmental type of theory pioneered by the Stoics as the most successful ancient form of the appeal to nature; certainly while Aristotelian ideas remained popular they were recast in this form, which integrates the two roles of nature better than Aristotle or his later commentators like Alexander do.

The theories are thus naturalistic in two ways. First, they are concerned to produce a theory which is realistic, which respects the limits of human nature. All the theories, especially the developmental ones, start from very general facts about humans which we cannot ignore; ethical theory works within these limits, rather than taking off from a starting point unrelated to human nature and trying to accommodate it later in the day. To start from this point, rather than from some other, makes a considerable difference; in particular, ancient theories do not face the problem that some modern moral theories, particularly consequentialist ones, do, namely that of producing highly counter-intuitive conclusions which no one could live by, and then being driven to 'two-level' solutions in order to enable agents to act on them. Ancient theories often do come up with ideals which are far from real life, but they can (especially the developmental ones) make it clear how one gets to the end point by a reasonable progress from the starting point. For the starting point, human nature as what is inevitable in us, precisely guarantees that the theory is to be a livable one.

Second, ethical development, which is not a given but is precisely what is up to us to achieve, is itself natural; this is again a point most successfully captured by the Stoics, once more because of the developmental form of their theories. This is the part of ancient ethics which modern readers are apt to find most unsympathetic. Partly this is because the claim is manifestly a normative one, whereas we expect the appeal to nature to be to non-normative 'fact'. Partly it is because the ancient claims are so plainly revisionary, whereas we expect nature to be an empirically specifiable notion. These points will be dealt with shortly.

Even apart from this, however, the idea that nature indicates ethical goals in any way can seem hopelessly vague. General facts about human beings can put realistic bounds on an ethical theory, but how can they give us any but the most uselessly vague positive direction? Stoic and Stoic-influenced theories answer this by stressing the development of rationality. What is distinctive about the natures of humans is just that they can come to understand their own relation to their nature, reflect on and modify their given impulses. While this answer is, I think, true, it is also true that ancient theories remain satisfied with merely suggestive versions of it. Ancient theories are content to find the connection between developed rationality and morality just obvious, instead of analyzing it more closely. Further, they are content to find its connection with nature obvious also. The developmental theories tell us over and over again that it is natural for humans to develop their reason in just the same way as it is natural for plants and animals to develop their own characteristic powers. But this ignores the fact that reason is not clearly a single power but a cluster of powers, exhibited in many different ways, intellectual and practical. Is it equally natural for us to appreciate good reasons for acting as to prove theorems, for example? This question is raised by Aristotle, whose *Nicomachean Ethics* contains in Book X an extended claim that our final good resides in intellectual contemplation, whereas the rest of the book has understood our final end to be achieved by practical reason; and the merits of the 'active' and 'theoretical' lives were debated in the Hellenistic period.[1] But in ancient theories the concept of rationality is under-discussed and too much taken for granted. Modern discussions have perhaps over-compensated for this; but certainly we are justified in finding too little said about the naturalness of the development of rationality, and about the move from rationality to morality.

It is abundantly clear that the ancient appeal to nature is not naturalism if that is understood as an appeal from value to fact, or from controversial to uncontroversial fact. It is true that all theories insofar as they think of nature in the role of constraining general facts about ourselves have to be realistic to be convincing, and to appeal to what would generally be agreed. And even developmental accounts try to be empirical about the first stages of human development, 'going to the cradle' as they put it[2] to observe the ways in which children develop. Still, it is clear that nature is more than this: the life according to nature is the virtuous life, and this alone shows that we do not find what is natural just by looking at children or, indeed, normal adults. As often stressed, nature in ancient ethics is a theoretical term, for we are being given an ethical ideal. This is not circular: we do not try to back up ethical

---

[1] I have not in this book touched on the endlessly discussed question of whether Aristotle's 'intellectualism' in Book X is consistent with the rest of the work. My own view is that the problem is a spurious one, since the *Nicomachean Ethics* as we have it is not a work which Aristotle wrote, which 'Book X' and the other books are parts of. Both our *Ethics*, like the *Physics*, *Politics*, etc., are collections of lecture notes, probably put together by Andronicus, when he prepared his edition, because these were the papyrus rolls he found on the same topic. (Andronicus' own catalogue does not even seem to contain our *Nicomachean Ethics*; there is considerable doubt about its origin as a distinct work. See Kenny (1978). There is no reason to expect these collections to be unified like a modern book (there are several ways, not just this one, in which they are not) and thus no reason to try to harmonize texts as different as the ones we call 'Book I' and 'Book X'.

[2] Cicero, *Fin* V 55.

claims by appeals to nature which turn out to rely on just those ethical claims. Nor is the appeal to nature empty merely because it does not get us out of the scope of ethical argument. We have seen that, in the different schools, it does plenty of substantial, often controversial and certainly rationally discussable work. In particular, it is an important element in the revisionary aspect of ancient ethical theories; what is natural is opposed to what is merely conventional. When we begin to reflect on our lives and search for the true ethical theory to help us to live better, we start to ask which goals and principles we accept merely because of the influence of institutions and other people's unreflected views—what in our unreflected views, in other words, is respected for merely conventional reasons. The appeal to nature is an appeal to an ethical ideal that gives us the means to locate and correct the merely conventional element in our moral thinking.

What kind of *justification* can it then provide? None, on certain views of justification. If to justify a theory we have to reduce it to some other kind, or define its terms of some other theory which is independent of it and in some requisite way better grounded, then ancient theories provide no justification through nature. On the other hand, they clearly do *something* when they, for example, distinguish natural from empty desires, or describe our natural development in ways that begin with the behaviour of infants. Whether we call it justification or not depends on our preconceptions about what that is; ancient theories seek at least to increase our understanding of them by pointing us to human nature as a reference point. The best model for this kind of increased understanding is a holistic one: we appeal from ethics to nature, but to understand nature properly we have to bring some ethical understanding to bear, so that we clarify the two concepts together. Hence the Stoics, who have an explicitly holistic model for their theories as a whole, express the place of nature in ethics most successfully.

We are here reminded forcefully that ancient ethical theories do not have a rigid and 'scientific' structure. They are not hierarchical and complete as far as concerns their internal structure. Nor, when it comes to basing ethical claims, do they regard appealing to nature on the model of appealing to, still less reducing to, a more secure independent domain. We have some intuitive independent grasp of human nature; but the bigger the role nature plays in an ethical theory, the more it is shaped by ethical considerations from the theory itself. The explanation is provided by overall holistic adjustment and interplay between theory and intuitions; it is more like reflective equilibrium than scientific reduction.

This may strike us as far too weak to be interesting. At this point we should always ask ourselves whether we find the ancient theories weak only because we are demanding something which is inappropriately strong. It may be that we are over-influenced by a scientific model, and will not accept anything as increasing our understanding in ethics unless it explains the ethical in a scientific way. If so, it may be salutary to look at the ancient theories, whose intellectual model is practical skill, not science.[3]

We might fairly ask, however, whether the notion of nature is strong enough to serve to adjudicate between the different theories. This is harder to determine than

---

[3] This will certainly reinforce any doubts one may have as to why science is supposed to be relevant as a model for ethics in the first place.

at first appears, as ancient writers sometimes claim that it can; in particular, we often find Epicurus rejected on the grounds that 'we are born' for something higher than pleasure. But it is hard to see how in fact the theories can use nature neutrally to criticize one another. Facts about the behaviour of the newborn, for example, would seem to be a good candidate; but in fact they only reveal that the same behaviour can be interpreted in different ways. The Epicureans take newborn behaviour to show that the infant's basic aim is for pleasure; the Stoics take it to show that the infant is aiming at self-preservation. Further, once we move on from the newborns, each theory develops its own constraints on nature, so that a Stoic, claiming that the natural life requires an appreciation of the difference in kind between virtue and other kinds of value, will be met by a Peripatetic claiming that the natural life requires us to appreciate moral and non-moral goods as simply different kinds of good, with no such sharp divide. It is not that each theory has its own concept of nature; rather they share the general notion of nature, but since each specifies it in accordance with its own demands they will naturally end up with conceptions of nature which cannot help to judge between the theories but rather stand or fall together with each theory. Here again we find that the ancient notion of nature is unspecific and essentially weak. Schools can of course differ in the degree to which they actually redefine the natural in terms of their theory; we have seen that the Epicureans seem open to criticism on this score, since if the natural is so far redefined as to call into question the very distinctions we started from, we seem, to have lost the advantage of appealing to nature in the first place, and Epicurus' ethical theory is indeed at certain points highly unrealistic.

Is it, however, a weakness in the ancient theories that they do not appeal to a notion of nature which is neutral between the theories? It would surely be more realistic to regard this as a *strength* of the ancient appeal to nature. For it is not clear that there *is* any such thing as a neutral, theory-independent conception of human nature; and philosophical discussion has emphasized many difficulties in establishing any such thing.[4] Even among those who claim that there is such a thing, there is intense and radical disagreement as to just what human nature, established independently of ethical argument, is, and as to the kind of influence on ethics that is produced by insisting that there is a substantial human nature which ethics has to take into account.[5]

The aspects of human nature that we can agree on without appeal to any theory are highly general: we all need food, shelter, community and so on. But these are just the kinds of facts which for the ancient theories establish nature in the sense of what is inescapable about us. As soon as we proceed further, and try to show that more specific human needs are natural, we run into the problem that what one theory

---

[4] Feminist philosophers have done a great deal of recent work on this. See, for example, Jaggar (1983).

[5] See, for example, the articles in the collection edited by Paul, Miller and Paul (1991). Many of the authors believe that biology or sociobiology can establish important truths about human nature in an ethically neutral way, but they disagree radically as to whether this establishes constraints which ethics must respect (particularly with respect to the claims of altruism and gender differences) or whether human nature is so plastic that modern technology can transform it, and that ethical judgements will change to match. For a modest attempt to explore the potentialities of the concept of human nature with respect to gender justice, see Annas (1992d).

asserts another denies, and that the very terms of the debate are disputed. But this is just what we find in ancient ethics; the Epicureans differ from the Aristotelians, say, on the natural way of being angry, because they start from very different conceptions of our final end. So before we take it as a criticism of the ancient theories that they fail in fact to establish a strong theory-neutral notion of human nature, we should ask ourselves seriously whether we think that any such thing can be done.

We all, of course, start from living conventional and unsatisfactory lives; nobody comes to ethics a blank sheet of paper. Ancient ethics tells us to live more natural lives. But this is never conceived as a simple task, nor as a simple switching of our activities. The Cynics, street preachers and 'philosophers' with little time for argument, took the crude view that returning to the natural life involved dropping out of your present life and adopting a different set of activities. Serious philosophers, however, always saw that matters are not so simple as this.[6] We want a life that answers to more of our needs, and also gives us a truer view of our needs. This requires more than just switching activities; for if we have not reflected on our unfulfilled needs they are likely to stay with us in the new activities. What it requires is reflecting about ourselves and about our needs and interests are, plainly a complex task. To live naturally, in fact, involves an inner change, without which outer changes are useless; we must start to reflect on what kinds of being we are, what our needs are and so on. Clearly we cannot do this in a way which keeps ethics right out of it. The appeal to nature gives shape to a demand to come to terms with ourselves from the ethical point of view. It is not a repetition of the demand to be virtuous; but, properly done, it will bring illumination about virtue. We will be clearer about what we are trying to do with our lives once we see that our ethical ideals are realistic, that they help us not to be limited and frustrated by inevitable facts about ourselves but to use and adapt them in ways that improve and transform our lives.

One aspect of ancient theories that has seemed objectionable is their seeming feebleness in the face of explaining error. Why do we always start from an unnatural life? Why are things standardly so wrong that we have to struggle to achieve natural activity? No ancient theory gives extensive attention to answering these questions; they do not seem to think it a task for ethics to try to answer the question at the root of them, namely, Why do we go wrong about what is natural for us?

It may well be that they did not consider this a well-formed question. There are lots of particular pressures that explain why we make particular mistakes about what is natural; but perhaps there is no one factor which explains all the mistakes we make about this. So perhaps the question of error was regarded rather like a question about what explains *everything*; there is no one answer, just lots of little ones. This on its own will not suffice, however; for the general question is not self-evidently ill-conceived.

---

[6] In this book I do not discuss the Cynics except marginally; this is because, with their contempt for academic theory generally, they do not contribute to the ongoing discussion of ethical theory which we find in the other schools, and so do not fall within the scope of this book. Of course I am not denying that they would be noted in a comprehensive history of Greek ethics. But with regard to the concerns of this part, their contribution is too unsophisticated to warrant treatment alongside the theories that I have discussed.

What is important here seems to be the fact from which we started; the entry point for ancient ethical reflection is that of reflecting on your life as a whole. From this point of view the agent will be asking how *she* has gone wrong, how she has come to be so out of touch with her real needs, so mistaken in her attitude to her emotions and so on. Clearly, if these are the questions, then the needed answers will be analogous to the ones Chrysippus suggests: the problem lies in taking too seriously what current opinion values, and in being too impressed by 'appearances', the way things strike me, the priorities and values I find myself with. The remedy will just as clearly lie in thinking for myself, in making myself, by ethical reflection, independent of current impressions for my basic values and priorities. But from such a point of view, a general explanation of how everyone in my society has wrong values will not seem very helpful. This shows that everyone is in the same boat that I am in; but I may well have suspected that already, and anyway it scarcely helps me to progress with my reflections.

What this brings out is that there is a certain individualism in the way ancient ethical reflection gets started. I have to start from asking about my life, since no other starting point will do for me. (This does not mean, as we can see by now, that the *content* of my reflections need be particularly individualistic; indeed in ancient theories it hardly ever is.)[7] Further, ethical improvement is seen in terms of my increased rational ability to come to terms with and modify the given aspects of my life. From this point of view, general explanations of error about what is natural, which apply no more to me than to anyone else, will not be much use. They are just more of the input that I have to reflect on, but they cannot in themselves enlighten me, or show me what I need to know. It seems to be concentration on the individual point of entry into ethical reflection which explains the lack of interest we find in tracing general patterns that show our systematic error about what is natural for us.

---

[7] This is the subject of Part III. Claims that the Hellenistic ethical theories, for example, are peculiarly 'individualistic' are (incorrect) claims that the content of these theories is more centred on the individual than previous theories are.

III

The Good Life and the Good Lives of Others

10

The Good of Others

As has been stressed in more than one context, the entry point to ancient ethical reflection is an assessment of one's own life and the way it is going, and ethical thought is thought about how to reorder one's life in a reflective way. It has (far too) often been thought that because of this shaping fact ancient ethics is egoistic. For if I am concerned to achieve my own final end, improve my own life, am I not simply seeking my own self-interest?

The answer to this is clearly no. For what I have to develop, in order successfully to achieve my final good, are the *virtues*, and we have seen that these are the moral virtues- justice, courage and so on. Some have a direct connection with the good of others, most prominently justice, which may involve my surrendering goods I want to others because they have a just claim on them; but all the virtues are dispositions to do the right thing, where this is established in ways that are independent of my own interests. Thus the fact that I aim at my own final end makes ancient ethics formally agent-centred or self-centred, but does not make it self-centred in content; as the ancient theories plainly are not.

Thus if we go on to ask what the place is in ancient ethics of the good and the interest of others, the answer is, on a general level, already obvious. Achieving my final good, happiness, whatever that turns out to be, will involve respecting and perhaps furthering the good of others. For, first, I have no reason, just because of seeking my own good, to treat others in ways that are instrumental to my own good. Second, a virtuous person is committed just by being virtuous to respecting and sometimes furthering the good of others. And third, it is a fact of experience that we do care about the good of other people in a non-instrumental way, even when this is not a direct requirement of virtue; we love our family and friends, for example.

And thus we find that ancient ethical theories treat directly of the good of others in two areas in particular. One is that of *philia*. This is usually translated 'friendship', though it covers more than we usually intend by friendship. Our paradigm of friendship is a chosen relationship implying a fair degree of intimacy; but *philia* covers, on the one hand, unchosen relations of affection such as family relationships and, on the other hand, relationships that involve acquaintanceship but no intimacy, such as those of patron and client, political associations and so on. *Philia* is best thought of as commitment to particular people. 'Commitment' is fairly neutral as between chosen and unchosen relationships: you are committed to both your lover and your sister. It can also be used both of familiar relations (your children) and relations of a more formal and contractual kind (your colleagues). The basic idea is that, among the people that surround you, there is a subset of people to whom you have a prior commitment of energy and concern. Your *philoi* have first claim on you, both in good times when you have benefits to give and in bad times when you have to set priorities for giving help.

The other area is that of justice. For although justice is merely one among the virtues, and indeed, if we stress the unity of the virtues, merely one area in which practical intelligence (*phronēsis*) is displayed, it is often (though not universally) felt that justice is special in character, and needs separate treatment, because it involves the good of others so directly.

The charge of egoism sometimes recurs even at this point. Critics sometimes say that, even though ancient theories do assume that the agent will care about the good of others, indirectly through (non-just) virtuous action and more directly through justice and *philia*, this assumption is not really justified, precisely because the good of others will matter to the agent as part of *her* good. But what does this charge amount to? The good of others ought to matter to me *because* it is the good of others, not because it is part of my own good. But it is no part of the theories we have seen so far that its forming part of my good is the reason why I should care about the good of others. There only appears to be a problem if we are covertly assuming that a theory whose perspective is that of my good must be reducing the good of others to my good.

But although at a very general level there is plainly no problem with a eudaimonistic ethics containing several forms of genuine concern for others, nonetheless at a more specific level difficulties emerge over other-concern. These can be collected into two groups: those arising over other-concern in general and those arising over justice. I shall introduce them in that order.

First, while there is no problem in principle with a eudaimonistic ethics containing concern for others, one might wonder whether there is not a problem in cases where the final end does in fact seem limited to the agent's self-interest. If my final end makes virtue prominent, then the interests of others have to come in; but if my final end is pleasure, why would I care about other people except instrumentally, as means to my own pleasure? This is an obvious problem for all hedonistic theories, at least those that present pleasure as forming the agent's final end.[1] We shall look at two ancient hedonistic theories, that of the Cyrenaics and that of Epicurus, and see how they cope with finding a place for other-concern within this final end. The Cyrenaics shift on the matter; Epicurus avoids some of their problems because he claims that pleasure in the role of final good is a kind of tranquillity, and we shall see what difference this makes. We shall also examine the Sceptics, for their final end is also tranquillity.

Second, given that other-concern is not derived from self-concern, what status does it have? Some other-concern obviously comes from virtue, but what about our concern for other people as such? Is this just something we happen to feel? If so, how deep do these feelings go? Is other-concern just one thing in our lives we happen to care about, or is the source of other-concern as basic in us as the source of self-concern?

---

[1] Thus all ancient hedonist theories face it, and so does Mill, who in *Utilitarianism* presents his theory as eudaimonist in structure. Sidgwick does not, and in this has been followed by the modern tradition of utilitarianism.

Third, how far does other-concern extend? All normal people care about their family and some friends; but should our concern extend further? Should we, for example, care about all our fellow-citizens (in an ancient city-state)? Should we perhaps care about *all* human beings, given that we are human beings? In short, is there a defensible limit to the extension of other-concern, and if so, where does it come?

The answers given in ancient theories to both these groups of questions emerge together from considering the contrasts, and the mutual influence, of Aristotelian and Stoic theories of friendship and of extension of sympathies; we shall consider these in some detail.

The above questions all arise over *philia,* but there are also problems specific to justice and its role. Justice as we have seen it so far in all ancient theories is a virtue of character among others. This at first seems to mark a sharp contrast with modern theories of justice, in which justice is primarily a virtue of *institutions* and procedures, and only derivatively of people. Indeed for this reason it has sometimes been thought that ancient theories have nothing to say about the justice of institutions, or nothing interesting. However, this is to draw the contrast too sharply and to ignore much of the evidence. Some ancient theories do have ideas about the justice of institutions and procedures which are not merely obvious derivatives from what they say about the justice of individuals' characters. In particular, Aristotle and Epicurus have much of interest to say on this score. The question then arises, which we shall try to answer, how this relates to what is said about justice as a virtue of character, and what the implications are for the status of justice in the ethical theory as a whole.

Finally, a note about terminology. I shall not here use the terms 'egoistic' and 'altruistic' (I have used 'egoistic' only in reports of modern criticisms of ancient theories). This is not to deny their usefulness; but they can be distracting in discussions of ancient theories, simply because they have been defined in terms of modern debates which do not apply in ancient ethics. 'Egoism' is standardly used of theories whose content is self-centred or self-interested, as well as being formally agent-centred. Since all ancient theories are formally agent-centred, and the question is, whether some of them are also in fact self-centred in their content, the use of a term standardly implying both can be confusing.

'Altruism' has two distinct modern uses, neither well-adapted to ancient ethics. In one use, it implies merely that one gives the interests of others some weight for their own sake and not instrumentally. In ancient ethics, it is taken for granted that we do do this, the only question being, whether the theory can properly account for it. Altruism in this sense is not perceived, in ancient ethics, as posing any particular problem, or as giving rise to a special debate about egoism and altruism. In another use, 'altruism' is used for the disposition to put the interests of others *before* one's own, to be self-sacrificing. In ancient ethics this is likewise not an issue. This is not because the ancients were more self-assertive and selfish than we are. Rather, it is assumed that virtue will require the agent sometimes to put the interests of others before her own, and that sometimes affection for other people will lead the agent to put their interests before her own. But there is no *distinct* virtue of self-sacrificingness, nor is it thought to be desirable for an agent to be so disposed as regularly to put the interests of others before her own.

Thus to characterize ancient debates in terms of egoism and altruism is to risk confusion and anachronism. I have preferred to use the terms 'self-concern' and 'other-concern'. I hope these have the advantages of sounding comparatively untheoretical, as they are intended to do. All ancient theories assume, as a matter of common sense, that all agents have both sorts of concern. The disputes and problems arise over their relative status and importance.

11

Finding Room for Other-Concern

We have seen that there is no reason in principle why an ethical theory which starts from the perspective of the agent's final end should not allow that the interests of others matter to the agent for their own sake. There is nothing egoistic about the assumption that ethical reflection starts from the agent's coming to reassess his life as a whole. Nor does egoism enter in even when the agent's final end is characterized as happiness—for that is a thin rather than a substantial concept, one which adjusts to other discoveries made by the agent's ethical reflection, rather than *vice versa*. However, some of the ancient theories do have conceptions of one's final end which seem to raise problems as to how, given their content, the agent could in fact have concern for others that did not reduce to concern for their impact on the agent's life. These are the hedonistic theories, those of the Cyrenaics and Epicurus, and the view (perhaps one should not call it a theory) of the Sceptics, who describe their end as Epicurus does, as tranquillity (*ataraxia*). We shall look at these theories to see whether they do in fact face real problems in allowing for other-concern, and, if they do, how this is related to their conception of the final end.

1. The Cyrenaics

The Cyrenaics, so-called from Cyrene, the home town of their originator, Aristippus, are the most radical ancient moral philosophers, since they are the only school explicitly to reject the importance of achieving an overall final end. Aristippus was an associate of Socrates, and figures as a character in Xenophon's *Memorabilia*. In a conversation with Socrates[1] he says that he rejects deferral of any gratification and wishes only to live as easily and pleasantly as he can. He rejects Socrates' objection that this will lead to a life enslaved by other, stronger people who are willing to postpone enjoyment for the sake of further ends, and says that he will retain his 'freedom' by rejecting social ties and travelling in many countries, with commitments to none. A large biographical tradition gathered round Aristippus, as we would expect of someone who so openly flouted Greek expectations about the superior nobility of deferring gratification and pursuing virtue.[2] We can gather from this

---

[1] II 1. Aristippus appears also in III 8, but we learn little from this about his own views.

[2] In Xenophon's exchange, Socrates urges Aristippus to ponder Prodicus' Choice of Heracles, in which the hero chooses between the sensuous appeal of Vice and the austere bidding of Virtue. Xenophon's Socrates here represents the conventional view on the matter, as often.

227

tradition that Aristippus held certain views, chief among them that 'he enjoyed pleasure from what was present, and did not laboriously chase after the enjoyment of what was not present.'[3] Consistently emerging from the tradition is the image of a person who pursues what is presently attractive, quite explicitly at the price of commitment to ideals which require self-control and deferral of gratification. There is a paradoxical quality to this which comes out in the divergent kinds of stories told of Aristippus. On the one hand, Aristippus presents himself as living the 'free' life, the life that is under the agent's control. It is this aspect of his life which makes him a follower of Socrates, who became a model of many different kinds of self-driven lives, independent of conventionally held values.[4] Thus an often-repeated story has him saying, of his association with the courtesan Lais, that he possessed her—she did not possess him; and that what mattered was not to avoid pleasures but to be in control of them rather than controlled by them.[5] Aristippus may have taken Socrates as his model because of the attractions of the autonomous life, regardless of its content. Or he may have thought that taking pleasure as one's end was a reasonable interpretation of what Socrates thought about seeking one's final good. Here we have the ambivalent evidence of Plato's *Protagoras*, where Socrates is represented as building up a theory which takes the rational pursuit of one's end to be a pursuit of pleasure, but where he is also shown distancing himself in elusive ways from this theory. Scholars still divide as to whether Plato presents Socrates as espousing the theory seriously, or merely as arguing *ad hominem*, drawing out implications of what his hearers would accept. Without taking a definite line on the *Protagoras*, we can accept that a kind of hedonism could be seen as an interpretation of what Socrates held. Further, we possess an interesting papyrus fragment of a Socratic dialogue in which Socrates espouses hedonism.[6] So we can see that hedonism could be seen as one legitimate interpretation of Socratic ethics (whether or not we take it to be a reasonable interpretation). It may be, then, that the Cyrenaics saw Aristippus as a Socratic figure not merely because of his stress on the autonomy of his life, but also because they saw hedonism as a genuinely Socratic theory.

On the other hand, Aristippus' own form of pleasure pursuit, focussed clearly on pursuing the present pleasure rather than caring for past and future, has little to do with Socrates' stress in the *Protagoras* on hedonism as a rational overall strategy to ensure maximum pleasure over one's life. The *Protagoras* theory in fact points in quite the other direction, since it stresses the irrationality of going for the present pleasure just because it is present, a viewpoint that leads to misjudging the pleasantness of what is far away in time just because it is far away from the present.[7] Aristippus breaks with all theories that stress one's life as a whole, rather than isolated episodes—and this would include the *Protagoras* theory.

---

[3] Diogenes II 66, fr. 51 in Aristippus (IV A) in Giannantoni (1990), *Socratis et Socraticorum Reliquiae* (Bibliopolis, Naples 1990), vol. 2.

[4] See Long (1988a).

[5] Diogenes Laertius II 75. See Giannantoni frs. 86–100 for variations on this theme.

[6] In the papyrus Socrates and a companion discuss his reasons for not defending himself at his trial; Socrates argues that death is no less pleasant than life, to a sensible person, and his companion replies that this is convincing to those who, like themselves, 'consider pleasure to be the best end of life'. The papyrus dates from the third century B.C., but the language suggests a fourth-century date for the text. There is a short discussion by Jonathan Barnes on pp. 365–66 of *Phronesis* XXXII (1987).

[7] See *Protag* 356a-357a, esp. 356c.

Moreover, although Aristippus stresses his freedom and autonomy, the project of pursuing the present pleasure in fact leads to the need for a maximally flexible lifestyle, one which requires adjusting to circumstances to such an extent as to make the claim of autonomy look rather hollow. Thus the Diogenes Laertius Life introduces him as 'capable of adjusting to place and time and person, and of playing a part fittingly in every circumstance', and this is the burden of the stories that follow. Some of them show him adapting bravely to adverse circumstances, or throwing away money when it became too heavy, and so on. But the stories that were found most memorable were those in which he figures as a toad-eater and lickspittle, usually at the court of Dionysius I of Syracuse. In the most famous, Plato refuses, and Aristippus agrees, to amuse the tyrant by wearing women's clothing at a banquet. Sometimes Aristippus is given a tag from Euripides' *Bacchae* to the effect that even in these circumstances he can retain independence of mind; but the tenor of the story is clearly that Aristippus would do anything, however degrading, to obtain pleasure—that a hedonist is bound to adjust to the demands of circumstances so thoroughly as to leave himself no basis for self-respect.[8] The tradition about Aristippus is clearly marked less by admiration of the autonomous life than it is by the thought, common in some modern anti-utilitarian writings, that if one's own pleasure is the aim then one cannot take ordinary morality seriously, and so will not be ashamed to do any kind of action, if only it produces pleasure. Such flexibility clearly struck most Greeks as shameful rather than admirable.

The tradition about Aristippus also shows him as quite strikingly uncaring about others. He coarsely refuses responsibility for fathering a courtesan's child, and when reproached for exposing his infant son 'as though it had not been produced by him' replies, with stunning brutality, that phlegm and vermin are also produced by us, but we throw them away as far as we can, since they are useless.[9] These stories are no more likely to be literally true than the others, and we know that in fact he had a daughter, Arētē, whom he probably taught because she figures as a philosopher in her own right. Nonetheless, the stories, like others in the tradition, show us how Aristippus' hedonism was generally perceived, and answer to something in it.

Modern scholars are divided on the issue of whether Aristippus, besides leading a colourfully hedonistic life, also founded the Cyrenaic school in the more substantial sense of working out philosophical doctrines which formed the basis of the school's later position. The general consensus is that he did not, and that Aristocles is right in saying that it was Aristippus the Younger, his grandson, who first clearly defined the end as living pleasantly, something merely implicit in the life and writings of the elder Aristippus. While dating within the school is problematic, we can fairly safely regard the younger Aristippus as belonging to the generation

---

[8] See Giannantoni frs. 25–43 for anecdotes about Aristippus and Dionysius. In the banquet story, the clothing that Aristippus and Plato are asked to put on seems originally not to be women's clothing, but just clothing of a rich material, probably used mainly for women's garments. In some versions, e.g., Sextus (*PH* I 155, III 204) it has become a woman's garment. The exchange from the *Bacchae* has Aristippus reciting a line that casts him as a woman: *kai gar en bakcheumasin ous'hē ge sōphrōn ou diaphtharēsetai.* (The version in the Suda has the more dignified *ho nous ho sōphrōn*, which avoids this.) Given the very strong and rigid Greek views on masculinity and its appearance, this anecdote clearly served as a hostile *reductio* of Aristippus' ideas: 'there was *no length* that he would not go to.'

[9] Both stories at Diogenes II 81 (the first is 88 in Giannantoni, the second 135).

before Epicurus, and the three later unorthodox Cyrenaics, Anniceris, Hegesias and Theodorus, as being Epicurus' contemporaries.[10]

The explicit Cyrenaic theses about pleasure certainly fit the image put forward by Aristippus.[11] Our final end, they claim, is pleasure, defined in a very precise way; pleasure and pain are both movements (*kinēseis*), not settled states. Later Cyrenaics distinguished this view from Epicurus': pleasure is not just absence of pain and trouble, but something more positive—an actual movement.[12] Further, one pleasure does not differ from another, and no pleasure is more pleasant than another. Pleasure is conceived of as a single feeling, experienced in different circumstances but itself always the same. This is a notion of pleasure that we associate with crude empiricists like Bentham, and in the Cyrenaics it is explicitly linked with a crude empiricist epistemology; they held that we could have no experience, and hence no knowledge, of physical objects, only of our *pathē* or experiences of them.[13] If pleasure is a feeling that we have access to only by direct experience of it, we can see why there is stress on *present* pleasure. Past pleasures have vanished and future pleasures are not yet around; so why should I care about them in comparison with present pleasure, which I *can* experience?[14] Hence the most radical Cyrenaic thesis:

> They think that our end differs from happiness [*eudaimonia*]. Our end is particular pleasure, while happiness is the organization [*sustēma*] of particular pleasures, in which are included both past and future pleasures. Particular pleasure is choiceworthy for its own sake, but happiness not for its own sake, but for the sake of particular pleasures. That pleasure is our end is given credibility by the fact that from our childhood we are familiarized to it[15] and when we get it we seek no further, and avoid nothing as much as pain, its opposite.[16]

The Cyrenaics alone among ancient schools rejected the importance of one's life as a whole for one'e ethical perspective. What matters is the pleasure one can experience, and this is one's end. The Cyrenaics seem to have made no serious attempt to argue that this kind of *telos* could meet the conditions of being complete and self-sufficient, and it is hard to see how they could have done so. From the doxography it

---

[10] The Aristocles passage is ap. Eusebius *Praeparatio Evangelica* XIV, 18.31. It is IV A 173 and IV B 5 in Giannantoni. The view that the elder Aristippus did not found the school's philosophical doctrines is defended in Giannantoni (1958) and in Classen (1958). It is accepted by A. A. Long in his (1992) and (forthcoming) articles. Mannebach (1961) modifies the thesis somewhat, as does Döring (1988). Mannebach and Döring tend to see the later Cyrenaics as responding to Epicureanism, and to find chronologically distinct layers stratified in the doxographical tradition. A. Laks (1993) argues for a more unitary view of the doxography.

[11] For the orthodox Cyrenaic view, see Diogenes II 86–93 (Giannantoni IV A 172).

[12] Some trouble has been caused by the fact that the Diogenes passage says that there are only two *pathē*, pleasure and pain, whereas the Aristocles passage (above) distinguishes three states (*katastaseis*), painful, pleasant and neither. Rather than find changes in the theory, it is surely best to distinguish the states of being in pain, pleasure or neither from the experiences of pain and pleasure themselves.

[13] On this theory see Glidden (1975) and McKirahan (1992).

[14] See Athenaeus XII 544 A-B (Giannantoni IV A 174).

[15] The verb is *oikeiousthai*. This indicates that the passage derives from a later author using the originally Stoic term to describe earlier theories. Ascribing an elaborate theory of two sources of instinctive motivation (see chapter 12, section 2) is inconsistent with other aspects of the Cyrenaic theory, particularly their lack of place for other-concern. The Cyrenaics seem to have meant only that we have a natural attraction to pleasure, something noted already by Aristotle and Eudoxus.

[16] Diogenes II 87–88.

seems that the best they could have done would have been a crude move like Bentham's, basing ethical on psychological hedonism; if pleasure is the only end that we can go for, then it must be the only thing we can find worthwhile in itself.[17]

From this point of view, one's life as a whole has no particular significance, and so happiness is defined in terms of the end, as a collection of pleasures. Happiness retains its sense of something extended over one's life, but is thought of as made up of memories of past pleasures and anticipations of future pleasures, as well as of experiences of present pleasures. It does not motivate the agent in any way independent of her motivation to pursue particular pleasures. This still leaves it with an instrumental role. Memories of past pleasures, for example, do not form part of one's aim, but they could help one to achieve it. However, the Cyrenaics are unenthusiastic even about this limited instrumental role of happiness, considering it a bore and a nuisance to collect together the pleasures which make up happiness.[18]

This explicit rejection of overall concern for one's life is the source of three striking Cyrenaic tenets. First, while they recognize the reality of purely mental pleasures which do not depend on the body, they hold that bodily pleasures are superior, and more to be aimed at; this seems clearly to be because they are more vividly experienced, and the Cyrenaics discount the advantage that mental pleasures have, one stressed by Epicurus, namely that they help to give us a view of our life as a whole more than bodily pleasures do.[19] Second, since pleasure is our ethical end, and the obtaining of pleasant experiences obviously has little congruence with following established ethical norms, they can allow no independent ethical weight to the latter.

> They think that nothing is just or fine or base by nature, but only by convention [*nomos*] and custom. However, the good person will do nothing outrageous, because of the penalties imposed, and because of people's opinions.[20]

Finally, and most germane for our purposes, they allow no genuine concern for others. 'A friend is for the sake of usefulness,[21] for a part of one's body is also cherished, as long as it is there.'[22] Friendship and justice, the two main forms of other-concern, are thus judged to have no intrinsic value. Justice is merely conventional, and should be observed merely as a strategy to obtain pleasure, or because the alternative would be greater pain from penalties. And friendship has merely instrumental value; a friend is like a part of oneself that one cares about while it is there, doing its job, but which one gives no thought to when it is no longer there. An absent friend is thus like an amputated toe; it does nothing for you, and it would be silly to care about it. Further, while the toe is still attached it would be silly

---

[17] This *may* be unfair. The doxography contains interesting suggestions of the theory that pleasure alone is a *natural* end; thus people fail to pursue it if they are *perverted* (Diogenes II 89), and the wise person will not feel envy, love or superstition because these depend on empty belief, while he will feel pain and fear because these are natural (Diogenes II 91; both passages in Giannantoni IV A 172). The problem is that 'empty belief' is a characteristically Epicurean term (see chapter 7), suggesting that the doxography has been contaminated by Epicureanism on this issue.

[18] Diogenes II 90 (Giannantoni IV A 172); the word is *duskolōtatos*.

[19] Diogenes II 89–90 (Giannantoni IV A 172). Contrast Epicurus' view at *de Fin* I 55–57.

[20] Diogenes II 93 (Giannantoni IV A 172; Diogenes II 93).

[21] The word, *chreia*, may be particularly Cyrenaic; Aristippus judged lice, unwanted babies and phlegm to be *achreia*, useless.

[22] Diogenes II 91.

to have a detached concern for its interests, apart from concern for it as a functioning part of your body. When we reflect that in Greek 'friend' (*philos*) covers one's family as well as chosen acquaintances, we can see why Aristippus is represented as killing off an unwanted baby son on the grounds that it was useless. What reason could he have had to care about it, if it did nothing for him?

The example, however, shows us how counter-intuitive the Cyrenaic view is on this point. All our concern for and attachment to others is irrational and wrong, unless it furthers our own pursuit of pleasures. One might try to mitigate the harshness of this, as utilitarians have tried to do with some versions of utilitarianism, by pointing out that usually a family and friends will in fact be 'useful' to the agent; they increase the chances of obtaining pleasure by providing a secure background for his activities. Obtaining pleasure on one's own is thus considerably less efficient than obtaining it in a context where one has family and friends. This reply can never be adequate, however, for it would give one no reason to care about those people who are not useful to one: old and dependent parents, for example, unwanted babies, friends when they need you more than you need them. Moreover, the extent to which the Cyrenaics could use this defence is limited to begin with, since they stress the burdensomeness of pursuing particular pleasures via seeking happiness, an organized and planned way of getting pleasures. If one is really more likely to obtain particular pleasures by adapting to circumstances in a maximally flexible way, like the Aristippus of tradition, then friends will be of only limited value even instrumentally.

The Cyrenaics are the only ancient school who openly ascribe to other-concern only an instrumental value (and limited at that) and thus definitely subordinate it to self-concern. And this flows directly from their setting up as our final end a kind of pleasant feeling which is important to the agent only as her own experience. Devaluation of other-concern goes with a de-emphasis of one's life as a whole, as opposed to one's experiences.

The three later branches of the Cyrenaic school, known by the names of their leaders Hegesias, Anniceris and Theodorus, develop interesting variants on the orthodox theme. They all have distinctive views about the importance of the agent's life as a whole and about the role of other-concern. With them the school fragments and finally peters out; to the extent that they were responding to Epicurus they were deemed unsuccessful, and henceforth it was Epicurus' version which was the standard form of hedonism.

Hegesias of Cyrene maintained the orthodox view that our *telos* is pleasure (and the avoidance of pain), but combined this with a far more pessimistic view of our chances of achieving this. This emerges in some striking theses.[23] First, he declared that all the major circumstances of life, riches, poverty, even freedom and slavery, were indifferent as regards 'the measure of pleasure.' None of them as such produces pleasure any more than pain. Even life is not always desirable. If people think any of these kinds of things desirable in themselves, it is because they are misled by their comparative rarity or frequency in their own lives.[24] Further, this is coupled with

---

[23] For Hegesias, see Diogenes II 93–96 (Giannantoni IV F 1).

[24] Long (forthcoming) aptly compares the Ninth Mode of Aenesidemus; similar arguments are appropriate here to show that no kind of thing has positive or negative value in itself. We would,

another depressing fact, the prevalence of chance and suffering; because of the vulnerability of both body and soul, happiness is 'completely impossible'. Only fools think life is worth it; the wise realize that it is indifferent as regards what matters, namely pleasure. These gloomy thoughts earned Hegesias the nickname of the 'Death-persuader' and led to a story that King Ptolemy forbade him to lecture because of the number of his students who committed suicide.[25] It is strikingly paradoxical for this philosophy to be *hedonism*. Hegesias simply thought that hedonism was the least irrational strategy for dealing with life, giving the wise advantage in avoiding evils, if not achieving positive goods; it seems to have no other recommendation.

Hegesias did cling to the orthodox insistence that our end is particular pleasures, not overall happiness, and in conformity with this he carried over and even strengthened the orthodox view on other-concern:

> There is no such thing as gratitude or friendship or benefaction, because we do not choose these things for their own sakes, but because of their *uses* - if they are absent the former do not even exist. . . .
>
> The wise person will do everything for his own sake; there is no other person whom he regards as equally valuable with himself. Even if he thought that he would reap the greatest advantages from someone, they would not be equal in value to what he himself produces.[26]

Hegesias underlines the selfish aspect of the doctrine, to the point of agreeing that strictly on this view there is no such thing as friendship; an instrumental concern does not amount to friendship as we conceive of that. On this view, of course, there is nothing very glorious about the self-centred life; it is the best we can achieve in a bad situation, and does not amount to anything but minimizing evil. The strengthened insistence on absence of other-concern, we should note, goes with a strengthened insistence on the pointlessness of trying to organize and reflect on one's life as a whole.

Anniceris of Cyrene is said in one source to have 'restored' the Cyrenaic school and replaced it with the Annicerian.[27] Perhaps this represented a re-formation in view of the increased pessimism of Hegesias; it also seems to represent an answer to some Epicurean ideas. He stoutly restated the Cyrenaic claim that our end is pleasant experience, against Epicurus' claim that it is a state of untroubledness, calling the latter the state of a corpse. And he reiterated that we have no fixed end for our life as a whole; rather, each action has its own fixed end, in the form of the pleasure that the action produces. But he modified the total view very considerably:

> The school of Anniceris . . . allowed friendship in life, as well as gratitude,

---

however, also expect something like the arguments of the Tenth Mode; but their absence may just be due to our sources.

[25] Before we dismiss this as ludicrous invention, we should remember the number of people who have committed suicide as a result of reading *The Sorrows of Young Werther* and the poems of Sylvia Plath.

[26] Diogenes II 93, 95 (Giannantoni IV F 1). Cf. also Epiphanius *adv. haer.* III 2,9 (Giannantoni IV F 2), who stresses the point.

[27] Strabo XVII 3,22 (Giannantoni IV G 1).

honouring one's parents and acting on behalf of one's country. Hence, on account of these, even if the wise person receives annoyances, he will none the less be happy [*eudaimonēsei*], even if he gets only a few pleasures. The happiness of a friend is not choiceworthy for its own sake; for it is not something that one's neighbour can experience. Reason is not self-sufficient for making us confident, and above the opinions of the many; we must become habituated, because of the bad disposition which has grown up in us for a long time. A friend is accepted not only because of his uses—if those failed we should no longer keep company with him—but also on account of the goodwill that comes about, for the sake of which we endure hardships. Indeed, one who posits pleasure as the end and is annoyed when deprived of it nonetheless willingly endures this on account of his love towards his friend.[28]

This is a striking attempt to modify the orthodox view in the direction of common sense. Like a tender-minded utilitarian, Anniceris denies that his theory really does conflict with common sense, as it clearly seems to do. Thus he boldly claims that the successful Cyrenaic will be happy, even though he has no fixed end for his life as a whole. And, although the theory cannot allow him to value a friend other than instrumentally, nonetheless the phenomenon of real friendship can be saved—we will sometimes rightly subordinate our own interests to those of our friends.

At first sight the attempt seems simply hopeless. Happiness (*eudaimonia*) just is an overall aim; if we have no overall fixed end, then whatever our state it cannot be happiness. Similarly, if we regard a friend instrumentally, it cannot be rational to sacrifice pleasure because of our feeling for our friend. Anniceris' position seems more salvageable if we make an assumption about his reasons for modifying the traditional view. He may have maintained that our only *telos* is experiencable pleasure, but disagreed with other Cyrenaics that it was hard to attain, doing so by allowing that what is commonly regarded as other-concern and moral behaviour in fact do produce pleasure. Thus he disagrees empirically with Hegesias; rather than denying that other-concern produces pleasure, and so concluding that a Cyrenaic abolishes other-concern, he claims that other-concern produces pleasure, so that a Cyrenaic can expand his strategy of obtaining pleasure by bringing in other-concern. The same holds for happiness; there is something to be said, he thinks, for the commonsense policy of seeking one's final end via reflection on one's life as a whole; this, then, is something which the good Cyrenaic should make use of.

We are likely to agree with Anniceris rather than Hegesias as to the pleasure potential of commonsense modes of thinking. But in incorporating them into Cyrenaic thinking Anniceris took on a problem afflicting some modern indirect versions of utilitarianism: a systematic double-mindedness about commonsense modes of thinking. Cyrenaic theory can ascribe no intrinsic value to concern for one's life as a whole, or to other-concern. Instead of rejecting them, Anniceris urges us to exploit them for their usefulness in producing the theory's goal, particular pleasures. But we can only do so effectively if we go along with the commonsense view of these, namely that they have intrinsic value. I will only sacrifice my own pleasure for a friend if I am concerned for the friend's interests for their own sake; I will only be happy with few pleasures if I attach intrinsic value to being happy, i.e.

[28] Diogenes II 96–97 (Giannantoni IV G 3).

having an overall view of my life, as opposed to achieving particular pleasures. But if I am a Cyrenaic these beliefs are mistakes; I *can* only value my own pleasure, not that of someone else, which I cannot experience, and I *cannot* attach positive value to an overall state which is short on particular pleasures. So the strategy of getting particular pleasures by co-opting commonsense beliefs works only if one can accept the commonsense beliefs to put them to work, while discounting them from the viewpoint of the theory. There is no sign that Anniceris was aware of this fundamental problem, one awaiting many philosophers who have tried to domesticate a radical moral theory by claiming that we can accept both it and common sense.[29]

In Theodorus of Cyrene we find a considerable shift away from the main planks of the Cyrenaic view. He was mainly famous for his atheism, about which we know little. Although he did not reject the view that our end is particular pleasures, he took the remarkable step of elevating mental pleasures, as against the orthodox view that bodily pleasures are what matter, since we experience them. Theodorus held that our aim should be *chara* or mental pleasure, this being the goal of *phronēsis*. Because this is what matters, *phronēsis* is a good, and bodily pleasure only intermediate between good and evil. Our goal is thus to be intelligent rather than to seek pleasant experiences, and Theodorus is a hedonist only in name; a main feature of the original idea was that we seek pleasant experiences because pleasure is a feeling which is always the same whatever its source. Theodorus, like Mill, abandons this idea and thereby the motivation for the original theory.

Theodorus rejects other-concern, though for different reasons from the other Cyrenaics. Friendship does not exist between fools; for when the usefulness is removed, so is the friendship. Thus he accepts the orthodox hard line; the theory effectively abolishes other-concern. But for the wise it is different; there is no friendship there because 'they are self-sufficient and do not need friends'.[30] Self-sufficiency is one of the marks of a final end; it contains everything worth having for one who has made a rational choice of that end. Theodorus is moving towards the more mainstream thought that someone who has successfully achieved her final end has a *life* which includes everything worth having. This is a thought that orthodox Cyrenaics have resolutely resisted: our final good is particular pleasures, not a satisfactory life. Thus Theodorus weakened on the central point of Cyrenaic hedonism, the rejection of the ethical framework of eudaimonism. The Cyrenaic school petered out in fragmentation and different kinds of compromise.

The Cyrenaics are interesting from the viewpoint of this book because they are the exception that proves the rule. They reject the standard assumption that ethics starts from reasoned reflection on one's life as a whole. And they reject the standard assumption that the agent who does so has reason to incorporate in her life some measure of genuine other-concern. In the school's vicissitudes we can see a pattern:

---

[29] It is psychologically possible, no doubt, to be double-minded in real life by training oneself in selective attention, selfishness, and so on. But this is different from the claim that one could be double-minded when what is in question is a theory that one has reached by reflection. For reflective awareness will tend to make the agent aware of the roles of selective attention and other such factors.

[30] For Theodorus, see Diogenes II 98–103 (Giannantoni IV H 13).

these two assumptions tend to be upheld together or modified together. The connection seems to be direct. They reject eudaimonism because their final end is getting pleasant experiences. And this end seems to be a necessarily self-centred one. The Cyrenaic epistemology underlines this point; I cannot value someone else's experiences equally with mine, for I cannot experience them. If what I value can only be what *I* experience, I cannot value others, or their interests, in any but an instrumental way.

It thus seems to be the narrow conception of their final end which leads the Cyrenaics to their distinctive theses. In the process they show something of great interest about ancient ethical theory. The generally accepted assumptions about ethical theory—that it starts from reflection on one's life as a whole, that it demands some measure of other-concern—put great strain on a hedonistic theory. For hedonism, as critics like Bradley have stressed, is insensitive to the natural contours of a human life. And hedonism, if pleasure is construed as pleasant feeling, cannot account for other-concern; pursuing my own pleasure is the only rational thing to do. Modern forms of utilitarianism, from Sidgwick onwards, which have tried to avoid this consequence, have done so only by drawing on very strong independent assumptions about the demands of rationality, which allegedly force us to pursue the pleasure of others equally with our own. The Cyrenaics, unwilling to make these strong assumptions, are left with the only ancient ethical theory that, except for Anniceris, denies the reality of other-concern.

It is clear that this was not found very plausible; the Cyrenaics were a minority school, remembered mainly for views later regarded as absurdities to be avoided. The tradition about their originator, Aristippus, presents him in ludicrous and unedifying ways. When Epicurus was formulating what was to be the only influential hedonist theory in the ancient world, it is clear that he was motivated to avoid ending up in the Cyrenaic position, and that he did so by designing a form of hedonism which would not fall foul of our assumptions about other-concern and our life as a whole.

2. *Epicurus*

Epicurus is also a hedonist; our final end is pleasure, he affirms. Further, he is an empiricist, and insists that the pleasure we seek must be conceived of as experienced bodily pleasure or as derived from experienced bodily pleasure. He has no idea how to conceive of the end, he says, if he removes pleasures such as those of taste and hearing, the pleasures of sex and of seeing beautiful objects.[31]

Nonetheless, instead of rejecting other-concern, or bringing it in merely via commonsense beliefs, Epicurus both insists on the reality of other-concern and presents it enthusiastically as promoted by his theory. His account of justice is complex and will get separate treatment; here what is relevant are his famous effusions about friendship:

---

[31] U 67, 413. Cf. the comment at U 409 that the pleasure of the stomach is the beginning and root of all good.

> Friendship dances round the world, proclaiming to us all to wake up and congratulate one another.[32]

and

> The noble person is mainly concerned with wisdom and friendship, of which the former is a mortal good, the latter an immortal one.[33]

and many more.

There is an obvious problem in this combination of views, which emerges in a famous saying:

> All friendship is choiceworthy[34] for its own sake; but it takes its origin from benefit.[35]

A theory that starts from the thesis that my final good is pleasure, where this is construed as my own pleasure, experienced bodily pleasure or deriving from this, nonetheless insists that I can and do feel genuine other-concern, and that the relationships deriving from this are a most valuable part of my life. How can this come about?[36]

The answer lies in the fact that Epicurus takes seriously, as the Cyrenaics do not, the eudaimonistic framework that he shares with other ancient ethical theorists. In particular he takes seriously the thought that an agent's final end must be complete, as we can see from this passage where an Epicurean is speaking:

> Thus we are enquiring what the final and ultimate good is, which, in the opinion of all philosophers ought to be such that everything must be referred to it, but it itself referred no further. Epicurus locates this in pleasure.[37]

Thus Epicurus places himself in the tradition which the Cyrenaics reject.[38] He further stresses self-sufficiency: the person who achieves the end, pleasure, will have a self-sufficient life.[39] So Epicurus is committed to giving us an account of pleasure which can show how it is possible for pleasure to be our final end, meeting these conditions. He is, in fact, in exactly Mill's position; Mill realizes that it is easy enough to show that happiness (by which he explicitly means pleasure and the absence of pain) is desirable as an end, but far from easy to show that it is the *only* thing desirable as an end.[40] How could pleasure be the kind of end which encompasses all our other ends?

---

[32] *VS* 52.

[33] *VS* 78.

[34] *Hairetē*, Usener's emendation. The text reads *aretē*, 'virtue'. The main problems with the text are that friendship is in Epicurean texts repeatedly compared with virtue, but nowhere else said actually to be a virtue; and that the received text is very harsh Greek. Long (1986), pp. 305 and 319, defends the MS reading on the assumption that a verb such as *nenomistai* has dropped out.

[35] *VS* 23.

[36] For a sympathetic discussion, see Long (1986) and Mitsis (1988) ch. 3.

[37] Cicero, *Fin* I 29. Cf. I 42.

[38] Epicurus' ethics have rightly been seen in a eudaimonistic framework by Striker (1981b) and Hossenfelder (1986) and (1985), pp. 23–39 and 102–124. The discussion here draws on material in Annas (1987).

[39] See *Ep Men* 130–131, *KD* 15, 21, 26, *VS* 59, U 202.

[40] Chapter 4 of *Utilitarianism*.

Despite his insistence on the importance of bodily experience in our conception of pleasure, Epicurus argues that not every kind of pleasure is fit to be our final end, and the kind that is, turns out to be very far from simple experience. There are, he claims, two kinds of pleasure, kinetic and static (katastematic).[41] Unfortunately we lack an extensive theoretical discussion of the difference, but the examples in *Fin* II 9 are fairly clear. The pleasure of drinking is kinetic, that of having drunk, static. Kinetic pleasure is pleasure felt as a need or lack is removed; static pleasure is pleasure resulting when pain has been removed.

There is more to be said about the difference between these two kinds of pleasure, and we will return to this in Part IV, but for present purposes what matters is simply that our final end is static, not kinetic pleasure, and is often referred to as *ataraxia*, the state of not having *tarachai* or troubles. It is often translated as 'tranquillity', but the suggestions of the English word are perhaps too negative.[42]

> When, therefore, we say that pleasure is the end, we do not mean the pleasures of
> the dissolute and those that lie in enjoyment, as some suppose who are ignorant
> and disagree with us or take it in a bad sense, but rather not being pained in body
> and not being troubled [*mē tarattesthai*] in soul.[43]

Ataraxia is negatively defined; it is the state in which you are not frustrated or hindered in what you are doing. You are functioning normally and nothing painful or unpleasant is interfering. Static pleasure is thus not the pleasure of absence of activity, but the pleasure of being in a state where you are functioning with no interference. It is easy to see from this why this kind of pleasure is *natural*,[44] and why many have seen a parallel here between Epicurus and Aristotle's account of pleasure in *NE* VII, where it is defined as the unimpeded functioning of the natural state. Aristotle in that passage wonders whether pleasure so conceived could be our final end;[45] the pleasure of normal unimpeded functioning, unlike a bodily sensation, is something which could comprehensibly be our final goal, an end adequate to include everything we aim at for its own sake.

Having shown that he has an account of pleasure that could serve, in the abstract, as a final end, since it meets the formal conditions (whether successfully or not we shall consider in Part IV) Epicurus then claims that obstacles to this can be met: the most obvious candidates for being ends which we do not seek for the sake of pleasure are in fact sought for its sake. These are the virtues, and friendship. The virtues are dealt with at greater length in Part IV; for the moment we just need to note that Epicurus claims that we will not in fact achieve the kind of pleasure which forms our final end unless we live virtuously.

> It is impossible to live pleasantly without living intelligently and finely and justly,
> <or intelligently and finely and justly> without living pleasantly; for the virtues

---

[41] *Fin* I 37–9, II 9, Diogenes X 136, U 68, *KD* 3. There are severe textual problems with the Diogenes passage; see pp. 388–91 of Gosling and Taylor (1982).

[42] On 'tranquillity' as a translation for *ataraxia*, see Striker (1990).

[43] *Ep Men* 131.

[44] See chapter 7 for the Epicurean strategy of following natural desires to achieve our end.

[45] 1153 b 9–31.

have grown to be a part of[46] living pleasantly, and living pleasantly is inseparable from them.[47]

Epicurus is expanding the notion of pleasure (at least *ataraxia*, the pleasure which is our final end) so that living virtuously is part of what living pleasantly is. We shall return in Part IV to the success of this strategy; it is at any rate clear that this is what the strategy is. It is also clear that it does not derive from any obvious thoughts about pleasure. Rather, the pressure comes from the formal conditions on what our final end must be. If our final end must be complete and self-sufficient, and if pleasure is our final end, then pleasure must be complete and self-sufficient. So pleasure, at least the kind that forms our final end, must be the kind of thing which can include everything that we seek for its own sake. And so it must include, in some way, living virtuously, since this is something we seek for its own sake.

It must also include friendship. For having a friend is like living virtuously—it is something we do for its own sake. To do it for an ulterior motive would be to reject the notion of virtue, or other-concern. So Epicurus, rather than taking the reductive Cyrenaic attitude to friendship, accepts it and shows that a life aimed at pleasure can include it, just as it can include the practice of the virtues.

> [The Epicureans] claim that friendship cannot be separated from pleasure, just like the virtues, which have been discussed. Isolation and a life without friends are full of hidden traps and fears, so that reason itself advises us to secure friendships; when these are obtained our spirits are strengthened and cannot be parted from the hope of getting pleasures. Just as hate, jealousy and contempt stand in the way of pleasures, so friendships are not merely the most loyal aids to pleasures but also their producers, both for one's friends and for oneself. One enjoys them in the present, and is also inspired with hope for the following and future time. So, since we cannot in any way keep a firm and continuing pleasantness in life without friendship, and since we cannot have friendship itself unless we love our friends equally with ourselves—this is in fact brought about in friendship, and friendship is linked with pleasure. For we are equally glad along with our friends' gladness, and suffer equally in their troubles. And so the wise person will feel the same towards his friend as he does to himself, and will, on account of his friend's pleasure, undertake the same efforts that he would on account of his own. The same things should be said about friendship that were said about the virtues, how they are always connected to pleasures. Epicurus said it wonderfully in almost these words: 'The same belief that strengthened our spirits not to fear either eternal or lengthy evil, has discerned that in this space of our life it is the protection of friendship which is the most secure.'[48]

This passage can seem initially perplexing. On the one hand, the benefits of friendship to the agent are stressed; friends produce security and thus freedom from pain and frustration, and, more positively, they enable and help to produce the positive pleasures of joint activity. This all seems to suggest a basically self-centred view: I need friends because they are useful to me. Yet alongside this we find quite unambiguous declarations that we love our friends as much as ourselves and have

---

[46] *Sumpephukasi.* My translation is influenced by Mill's expression for his solution in *Utilitarianism* ch. 4.

[47] KD5. Cf. *Ep Men* 132.

[48] *Fin* I 66–68.

equal concern for their pleasures as for our own. This makes up a coherent view if we bear in mind the point stressed above, that the pleasure we seek as our final end has to be complete—it gives our concerns and activities point in a way that they do not give it point. One prominent concern we have is friendship. Further, Epicurus recognizes that friendship implies real other-concern; to allow into one's life a concern for others for their pleasure-productive usefulness would not be to allow in *friendship*. He even says that we have *equal* concern for our friends' interests with our own and love them equally with ourselves, something clearly not true of all friendships; he seems to be showing that he can account even for what seems the most difficult case for him. Given these two points, we must seek, as our final end, the kind of pleasure which is produced by allowing genuine friendships into our lives. If we did not allow that pleasure was our ultimate reason for seeking friendships, then pleasure would not be complete, and thus not our final end. If we treated friendship purely instrumentally, we would be allowing not *friendship* into our lives, but something else.

So if, as Epicurus holds, pleasure is our complete final end, and we also need real friendships, then we are forced to his conclusion. We need, in our lives, real friendships, which may sometimes involve caring about others as much as about ourselves. What gives this its point in our lives is ultimately pleasure. But this does not lead to selfishness, or to viewing friendship instrumentally; for pleasure as our final end has been expanded to include the pleasure from genuine other-concern. The argument is, as the Epicureans saw, exactly the same as with the virtues; the pleasure we seek is expanded so that we achieve it precisely by having non-instrumental concern for virtuous action and the interests of others.

Epicurus' position is an interesting one. It is certainly not met by the objections brought against it in *Fin* II 82 ff., which are probably typical of ancient anti-Epicurean arguments. The objector claims that if friendship is sought for the sake of pleasure, then it can only have an instrumental value; if you love your friend because friends make you feel secure, then you are precisely not loving your friend for his own sake. And if friendship does have only an instrumental value, then its status is shaky; money is usually better at producing security than friends are. This objection simply refuses to take seriously the Epicurean claim that we can and do value friends intrinsically, even though our overall aim is pleasure.

Perhaps there is some excuse for this in the fact that the Epicurean position is not set out very clearly. What Epicurus needs, though he does not produce it, is a two-level view of the kind worked out by modern utilitarian theories. In making and keeping friends, we do not refer every act of friendship to increasing our overall pleasure; rather, we accept as our aim that of having genuine other-concern for our friends. But the aim of this whole policy, of having friends rather than coping with life in some other way, is guided by the aim of increasing our pleasure. Thus pleasure is our aim when we are thinking of the policy as a whole; but it is not our aim in individual acts of friendship, which are aimed at the friend's good for its own sake.

Unfortunately, we cannot wholeheartedly ascribe such a view to Epicurus even implicitly, to make sense of his different claims about friendship (and virtue). For, to the extent that he seems aware of two-level views, he rejects them. One of his prominent sayings is,

> If you do not on every suitable occasion refer each of your actions to the end

given by nature, but stop short[49] and make your avoidance or choice with reference to something else, your actions will not be consistent with your theories.[50]

This saying is isolated, but nonetheless significant, and we possess no contrasting discussion which would weaken its force. Taken as it stands, it rules out the kind of two-level view needed to make all Epicurus' claims about friendship and pleasure consistent. It seems to imply that in every act of friendship I should be asking myself, not about the welfare of my friend, but directly about my own final end, pleasure. And if we take this seriously, it is hard to find Epicurus' position a stable one. I am to help my friend at my own expense, say, and yet at the same time do this with a view to my own final end, pleasure. Epicurus claims that this does not commit me to a narrow, instrumentalist view of my friend's interests, because the pleasure I am aiming at is not a narrow, selfish pleasure, but a kind of pleasure which I can get precisely from doing things like helping friends. But here the problem is obvious. How can I get pleasure from genuine concern for my friend, unless I can regard my friend's good as an intrinsic good, regardless of any pleasure that I get out of it? But if this is possible, then when helping my friend I don't, after all, need to keep one eye on my own pleasure.

Epicurus' position is thus not a stable one; to be so, it would need a clear distinction of levels of concern which is nowhere apparent, and which on the face of it would contradict one of Epicurus' explicit sayings. Further, even if Epicurus did have a clear two-level view, this would bring problems of its own, for it would involve a kind of schizophrenia. While helping my friend I would bear in mind only my friend's needs, while with another part of my mind remaining aware that the point of all this activity in the first place was simply to obtain pleasure for me. Yet I would carefully avoid bringing these thoughts together, for if I did, there would be a risk that the thought about pleasure would interfere with my helping my friend.

On a two-level view, normal human moral activity depends on the agent's having two kinds of thought, but always keeping them carefully compartmentalized in his mind. This creates a problem if, as with Epicurus' theory, the two kinds of thought are pretty certain to conflict when brought together. When faced by a friend in need, I cannot both react as a friend would react and also at the same time allot my concern in proportion to the outcome in terms of pleasure for myself. Yet what could justify keeping the two kinds of thought apart? It is clear that without special effort the two kinds of thought are bound to come into collision on occasion. But if they are kept apart deliberately, this would seem to be itself the result of a meta-deliberation about the agent's priorities; but if this involves a concern to avoid conflict, it seems that the meta-deliberation must itself have considered together the very two kinds of thought that it is concerned to keep apart; it segregates them because it already knows that they are going to conflict.

A theory which hopes to avoid this systematic self-deception needs to distinguish levels of the self, one more enlightened than the other and capable of

---

[49] *Prokatastrepseis*, a puzzling word. Bailey translates 'turn to'; Hicks, 'swerve aside'; Arrighetti has 'ti volgerai ad altro'; Bollack (1975) 'tu t'éloignes'; LSJ suggests 'stop short' for this passage. There seems at any rate to be a clear contrast with straightforwardly applying the principles.

[50] KD 25.

fooling or manipulating the less enlightened level.[51] But this is an unfortunate picture of ordinary moral deliberation going on in one person; even if we are not repelled by the idea of inner manipulation, we need further moves to show us how these different levels could be unified into one functioning agent. Epicurus is thus perhaps wise to reject the option of a two-level view. But then he remains stuck on the ground floor with the problem of giving the interests of friends intrinsic value within a hedonistic theory.

Given the unsatisfactoriness of Epicurus' ways of dealing with his obvious desire to allow other-concern intrinsic value in the agent's pleasant life, we can see why hostile critics attacked the view on the assumption that it allowed friendship only instrumental value. Further, we find some Epicureans producing defences of friendship which presuppose only that it has instrumental value for the agent.[52] Cicero's Epicurean spokesman in *Fin* I adds, after the account which seems to go back to Epicurus, two more, which are rather different. The first relies on association: we begin by loving friends merely for their usefulness, but just as familiarity produces affection for buildings and places, so the progress of friendship leads to a 'blossoming' of affection for the friend's own sake. The second presents friendship as the result of an agreement (*foedus*, literally treaty) between wise people to love each other as much as themselves.[53]

The first of these is clearly feeble. It can give no account of friendships that arise quickly. Moreover, what guarantee have we that association will produce results which are morally desirable? Perhaps attachment to places leads to mere sentimentality; why should it be different with people? And in any case, for association to work in a way producing the desired results, the agent would already have to have an idea of disinterested affection. Familiarity with a place need not lead to disinterested concern for its welfare; nor need it do so with a person, unless the agent already has an idea of what it would be to love someone for her own sake—but in this case association is not doing the relevant work.[54] The second argument might initially seem more promising; but again, while the notion of a contract might provide a mechanism, it could never produce what the agents are represented as already having: the aim of valuing one another for their own sakes. (We have no warrant for reading into Epicurus any of various modern theories which try to derive other-concern from compromises between different agents' self-concern.)

Even apart from the unclear status of genuine self-concern in overall Epicurean theory, there are objections that can be raised to the account of friendship. If the point of having friends, as a policy, is to enhance the agent's overall pleasure, we can see how this would lead to having friendships which would make one feel secure, and also to forming relationships which would increase one's opportunities for pleasure. But this would still seem to indicate the appropriateness of caution about committing oneself in certain respects. Genuine friendship implies a willingness to pledge oneself to activities which are unrewarding for oneself, for one's friend's

[51] R. M. Hare's later moral philosophy develops this strategy.

[52] There is an analogue in the case of virtue. Some of Epicurus' own statements about it seem to give it the status of a mere means to pleasure. See further Part IV, pp. 339ff.

[53] *Fin* I 69–70. Mitsis (1988) ch. 3, esp. pp. 104ff., gives forceful arguments against these options.

[54] Indeed, one might regard this 'argument' as being, not a distinct argument, but an attempt to produce a mechanism for reaching genuine other-concern in the first place.

sake. This is especially clear in close family kinds of friendship (which we tend to call 'personal relations' and the like rather than friendship). Parents, for example, will sacrifice years of their life to bring up a retarded child; grown children will care for aged tiresome parents; people will often forgo things of importance to themselves for a sibling or a spouse. Even in chosen friendships one partner may sometimes have to accept fairly long-term stretches with nothing in it for him, when his friend is depressed or in trouble. It is not clear that Epicurus can allow for this kind of case. Would an Epicurean not be committed to breaking off the relation (or putting the child or parent in an institution) when the relationship could clearly contribute neither to her security nor her enjoyment? Epicurus can generate other-concern, but not *enough* other-concern for the agent to be prepared to accept great losses for the sake of other people.

Besides, some friendships at least imply a deep *personal* commitment. Epicurus' spokesman in *de Fin* I 65 mentions legendary examples of such friendships, such as those of Theseus and Peirithoos, Orestes and Pylades, and claims that Epicurus' Garden produced far more examples of friendship as notable. But it does not seem that Epicurus' theory can really allow for close personal attachments such as these. These are relationships where it is crucial that the partners do not regard each other as in any way replaceable. Each is attached to just that person, for good or ill for their own life. On Epicurus' theory such relationships would seem to be irrational; attachment to the person has come quite detached from concern about the agent's own pleasure.

Furthermore, we can see from Epicurean practice that they rejected some socially established forms of relationship. They regarded it as best to live in small communities like Epicurus' own Garden, and while this did not exclude arrangements like marriage, it is clear that an individual's affection was spread further than was normal Greek practice. Instead of the usual partition of a small area of private, family life in which affection was expressed, and a public life in which political alliances were made (by men, at least), the Epicureans rejected public life and enlarged the private area of affection. Thus what we think of as the private emotions were extended further than a small family circle. And a natural result of this would be a downplaying of the importance of intense and exclusive relationships. In a famous passage Lucretius attacks romantic love and the intensity it evokes;[55] but even apart from this, Epicureans were committed to taking as their paradigm of personal attachment one that put less weight on the individual, irreplaceable nature of its object than our notion of friendship or personal attachment does.[56] Thus, if accused of giving too limited an account of friendship, Epicurus could reply that he has given an account of the only kind of friendship which it is reasonable for an Epicurean to have. Other kinds—intense romantic love, for example, do not aid, or even detract from, the Epicurean final end, and an Epicurean account of friendship will reasonably exclude them.

There remains a certain tension, however, given that Epicureans invoked famous romantic friendships in the first place, and especially given Epicurus' claim that the wise person will love his friend 'equally with himself'. This, and Epicurus' great

[55] IV, the final section. On this see Nussbaum (1989).
[56] This is further argued in O'Connor (1989).

enthusiasm for friendship, indicate that at least sometimes he was inclined to think that his theory could account for all the forms of friendship that we intuitively recognize. How these are to be related to the thinner and more psychologically hygienic extended forms of attachment in Epicurean Gardens is hard to say.

3. *The Sceptics*

The Sceptics, as we have seen,[57] are a school with no theory and no beliefs; they are merely committed to the practice of enquiry. However, one Sceptical school, the Pyrrhonists, also claim that they have a final end, and specify it as *ataraxia*, freedom from being troubled—the same as Epicurus'.[58]

There are many problems attaching themselves to this claim, some of which we shall revisit in Part IV. First, it seems initially odd for sceptics to be putting forward views at all, never mind substantial views about our final end. Sextus tells us what the sceptic's final end is:

> Now a final end [*telos*] is that for the sake of which everything is done or considered, while it is not itself done or considered for the sake of anything else. Or: a final end is the final object of desire. Up to now we say that the final end of the Sceptic is untroubledness [*ataraxia*] in matters of opinion and having moderate feelings [*metriopatheia*] in matters forced on us.[59]

The sceptic achieves untroubledness by investigating all matters of belief until he comes to see that on every disputed question the considerations on each side are equal; suspension of belief is the result, and this produces untroubledness. Some things are 'forced on him' like pain and hunger, and he will be bothered by these, but 'moderately' because he lacks the beliefs which most people have about these, and which are the real sources of people's unhappiness about them.

Sextus must, if he is consistently sceptical, be merely reporting on his own appearances, the way things continue to strike him even after he has examined all relevant beliefs, found them to be in hopeless and equally-balanced conflict, and suspended judgement on them. This procedure already raises questions about the reality of others. Sextus does not say, 'It seems to *me* that untroubledness is the end'; rather, he tells us what 'the sceptic's' end is. Why is he confident that what he says so much as has application to other people? Why is he entitled to think that there are other people at all? As always, Sextus' reply is that he is not *entitled* to think this, or to hold any other belief on the subject; but at the end of all the arguments *pro* and *con*, he is left with things appearing to him to be that way. So for the sceptic, not only the content of what he says about the final end, but also the assumption that other people are even listening, and the prediction that what has happened to him will happen to them, are part of his own appearances. Things seem to him to be that way; but none of it makes up a belief that he is committed to.

---

[57] Chapter 8.

[58] The Academic sceptics never make such a claim about *ataraxia*, or indeed about having a final end.

[59] *PH* I 25; cf. 25–30.

Thus, while Sextus is perfectly entitled to give us the content of his appearance that the sceptic's end is untroubledness, questions do arise as to why he should expect other people to finish up with this appearance. Is it in fact part of most people's appearances that we think of ourselves as having a final end? and in particular untroubledness as a final end? The second assumption arguably weakens Sextus' position; what if, at the end of the argumentative day, most of his interlocutors ended up with the appearance that *ataraxia* was too passive to be a final end, and that our final end, whatever it turns out to be, must involve an element of striving? Sextus, of course, cannot *argue* against such a position; he can merely report that this is how it seems to be to him—and, of course, he can find problems with the opposing view. Sextus in fact represents all truth-seekers as motivated by the desire to be free of troubles,[60] an even bolder claim, and one even less likely, one would think, to commend itself to most people after all the arguments.

Sextus' appearances thus contain quite substantial assumptions as to how most people will react to arguments and see matters. If he expects to interact intellectually with others, rather than be left to report his own appearances in isolation, it must be true that most of his interlocutors assume that our final end is untroubledness, the only interesting question being whether Dogmatism or Scepticism is the better way of attaining this. Sextus can, of course, try to get his interlocutors to share the view that untroubledness is the natural state, the state we are left in when we have got rid of all the beliefs we had that were causing us trouble or worry. But, again, he cannot *argue* this; he has to hope that this is the appearance that they will end up with after his arguments.

When Sextus turns to ethics, the part of philosophy most relevant to our final end, we find another assumption that invites question: the thought that it is commitment to ethical beliefs that brings anxiety and trouble, and suspension of ethical belief that brings relief and composure.[61] Again, one would suppose intuitively that this was not the response that most people would have to initial reflection on ethical argument.

But, even if we are completely satisfied as to the content of Sextus' own appearances, and the assumptions these involve as to what most people accept and what they expect from ethical argument, one problem remains. Why should the sceptic even want to argue with others? Why should she care if they are troubled and unhappy? If the sceptic has achieved her own end, and is free of troubles, what could possibly motivate her to argue with others, write books of sceptical arguments, give an intellectual shape to sceptical philosophy?

The answer is that

> The Sceptic, because of being benevolent [*philanthrōpos*], wishes to cure by argument [*logos*] the opinion and rashness of the Dogmatists, as best he can. So, just as the doctors for bodily cases have remedies which differ in amount, and apply the strong ones to those who are suffering greatly, and the milder ones to those suffering more mildly—so the Sceptic puts forward arguments which differ in strength; he uses heavyweight ones, which can powerfully set right the

[60] See *PH* I 12, 29.
[61] On this see Annas (1986).

Dogmatists' case of opinion, on people gravely afflicted by rashness, and uses the milder ones on people who have a superficial and easily cured case of opinion, people who can be set right by milder types of plausibility.[62]

The sceptic has a *therapeutic* aim. Most people are suffering from the disease of dogmatism, and the sceptic is their doctor. Philo of Larisa, the last head of the sceptical Academy, developed at length the analogy between the doctor and the philosopher in a passage we have already seen.[63] The idea that philosophers (of all kinds) are like doctors, and can cure diseases of the soul, is a Hellenistic commonplace;[64] even the sceptics, who hold no beliefs, see their task in this way. The therapeutic model explains a great deal about Sextus' practice: his use of *ad hominem* premises, for example, and his interest in the persuasive power of arguments rather than their validity. But it merely raises again, with greater force, the question of how the sceptic can aim at helping others. How is this consistent with seeking his own end of untroubledness?

There is one very direct answer. Even when the sceptic has done the best job he can on his own beliefs, and achieved a stable state after suspending beliefs on all the matters that had troubled him, he can still be disturbed by other people's problems; they form, for him, a nuisance or *tarachē*, trouble. The successful sceptic is no longer made anxious by their arguments, having been through them, but it just does, as a matter of human nature, bother him that other people hold beliefs, and so are unhappy and troubled. Perhaps the sceptic's *philanthrōpia* lies in this, that he can never achieve full *ataraxia* while there are other dogmatic, and therefore unhappy, people around.

This is a perfectly sceptical answer, not committing the sceptic to any beliefs. Again, it makes us wonder about the confidence with which Sextus generalizes about 'the sceptic': wouldn't it be more plausible for most sceptics, having coped with their own beliefs and suspended judgement, to be indifferent to the concerns of others? It is, after all, one's own beliefs, not those of others, that were supposed to make one so unhappy in the first place. Would the residual unhappiness the sceptic feels at the dogmatism of others not be rather trivial compared to the large amount of happiness he feels having suspended judgement about his own beliefs?

Suppose, however, that human nature just is, as a matter of fact, very social and sensitive to others, so that sceptics always find that, even when they have got rid of the worries attaching to all their own beliefs, they are still left with concern for others, and a desire to cure them of their troubles. Still, the sceptic is left in an odd position over this concern. For the sceptic will not be exercised about others' mundane problems like toothache, poverty or unrequited love. These could only bother him if he believed that these were bad things, which of course he does not- he does not believe that anything is good or bad after working through the sceptical arguments about ethics. What can really bother him, it appears, is only the intellectual problems of other people—their dogmatism or holding of beliefs. It is

---

[62] *PH* III 280–81. This passage is notorious for its further claim that the Sceptic will sometimes use arguments he knows to be weak, if they are all that is required for conviction. An instrumental attitude to reason and argument flows directly from the therapeutic model.

[63] See chapter 2, section 4.

[64] See Nussbaum's (forthcoming b), for an extended study of this aspect of Hellenistic philosophy, especially with regard to the emotions.

this, rather than physical or emotional problems, which the sceptic proposes to cure, for he cures by means of *logos*, argument or speech, and what he cures is simply the 'rashness' of the confident holder of beliefs. And the sceptic is presumably bothered only by those things which he proposes to cure.

The sceptic's other-concern can, then, be genuine—but it would not be very comforting to the sceptic's unsceptical friends. If I hold beliefs, especially value beliefs, I will know that my sceptic friend will be extremely bothered by this, and will exert himself to cure me of them. He will argue with me to bring me to the point of equipollence, and thus to suspension of belief, which will in turn cause me to become untroubled, and thus no longer a source of trouble to him. He will not be at all bothered, on the other hand, by my financial ruin, divorce, or cancer, for he does not believe these to be bad things, and they are things which he does not have to feel bad about, since they are things which he does not experience. As an example of other-concern, this seems highly selective and eccentric. One would hardly rely on one's friendship with a sceptic.

The sceptic can produce a reply to this, which is that, though it may sound brutal to say so, financial ruin, divorce and cancer are indeed trivial problems compared with the holding of beliefs. For it is only my beliefs that these are bad things which makes me so upset about them; and if I suspended judgement about them and no longer had these beliefs, I would cease to mind about them (until the cancer became painful, of course). The source of what bothers me about these things is my beliefs; and thus the sceptic is indeed a true friend, since he cares about what matters. Sympathy over these things would merely encourage me to care about them, and so make things worse; it would be like a doctor's prescription which removed immediate pain but encouraged the underlying condition. The sceptic will help only where what he does will indeed help rather than hinder; thus he is a true friend.

Even if we accept this, it still leaves the sceptic with one of the less attractive features of the doctor; he knows better than you do what is wrong with you. The sceptic, of course, will not, like the doctor, claim to *know* what you really need; it is simply that he will only be bothered by what ails you, your beliefs, not by the other matters which bother you only because of your beliefs. His benevolence extends only where it is needed. There remains a great asymmetry between the sceptic and his friend. The overall state of the successful sceptic is sensitive only to irritation by the holding of beliefs. Thus he will be moved to be philanthropic only to suffering Dogmatists, and to those not necessarily in ways that they would appreciate. And towards another successful sceptic he would not seem to be moved to be philanthropic at all. The sceptic's other-concern would appear to be purely reactive.

It is easy to imagine a response to all this. Why should the sceptic's benevolence be construed so narrowly? Perhaps the result of suspending all beliefs will be to leave one *actively* benevolent to others, not just irritated into curing their beliefs. There is nothing to rule this out, but if it turned out to be the case it would surely force some revision of the sceptics' characterization of their end as *ataraxia*, freedom from trouble. For it is an essential feature of active benevolence and other-concern that it opens you up to troubles of all kinds. If you care actively about your friends, you will be bothered by their cancers and divorces. But this is a clear threat to your own *ataraxia*. Thus in a different way the sceptics face Epicurus' problem with other-concern. If your aim is to achieve your own *ataraxia*, then this would seem to disable you from caring about others, at least in ways that do not reduce to protecting your own untroubled state. And thus the therapeutic strain in Pyrrhonism sharpens the problem a Pyrrhonist has with accepting active other-concern into his life at all.

One thing that has clearly emerged from this chapter is that there is indeed a problem, in ancient ethics, for theories whose final end is given a narrow content, one which focusses our aims on achieving experiences of certain kinds. This is obvious for hedonistic theories like the Cyrenaics', which claim that we aim at producing present pleasant experiences. But it is also a problem, of a more subtle kind, for the Sceptics, who do not dogmatically claim that we do or should aim at anything, but who nonetheless are confident enough about the appearances that argument will leave us with to give us a whole ethical framework, in which our final end is an experienced state depending on the way things appear to us. Such theories face the problem that their final end does not plausibly appear to be complete, to be an end such that it gives point to everything else that we do, while not being given point by any of them. And one large aspect of this is that such theories seem unable to give any place in their achievement of the final end to genuine other-concern, even in the limited form of friendship or commitment to particular other people.

The fact that the Cyrenaics, other than Anniceris, produce such wildly counter-intuitive accounts of friendship underscores the fact that it was an intuitive demand in ancient ethics for the ethical agent's life to contain, unproblematically, some measure of genuine other-concern. As we shall see, problems arise over the scope of this concern, but it seems to have been a basic intuition that some friendship, some concern for others for their own sake, is a part of every life that can be a candidate for the reflected ethical life. Here Epicurus contrasts interestingly with the Cyrenaics. He rejects the narrowness of their final end, partly in order to be able to claim that his theory does allow for genuine friendship. Indeed, he turns this to advantage, proclaiming friendship as a special feature of Epicureanism. While we cannot be sure of the chronology, it is very likely that the maverick Cyrenaic Anniceris was responding to this move on Epicurus' part by trying to modify the harshness of the original Cyrenaic theory. But the early failure of the Cyrenaic school, in contrast with the durability of Epicureanism, suggests that for a Cyrenaic it was too little too late.

From this discussion it emerges that in ancient ethical theory two theses exert a considerable pull: theories that flout them are seen as counter-intuitive, so that to be acceptable a theory must at least try to do justice to them. These are that our final good must be complete, and that the ethical life must contain at least a measure of genuine other-concern.

None of the discussion in this section has focussed on more than a measure of other-concern, namely concern for particular other people and special commit-ments—the concerns that go under the name of friendship or *philia*. We might well think that an ethical theory should require other-concern of greater scope than this; and indeed we find a debate, to which we turn, on just this point between Aristotelian and Stoic theories. Even Epicureanism has so far established merely that it tries not to reduce other-concern to self-concern, not that it has established the ethically appropriate range of other-concern.

12

Self-Concern and the Sources and Limits
of Other-Concern

1. Aristotle on Friendship and Self-Love

Aristotle devotes two books of the *Nicomachean Ethics* (and a correspondingly large section of the *Eudemian Ethics*) to *philia*, which is best translated 'friendship' despite the reservations noted above. He is not concerned to demonstrate that concern for others for their own sake is possible, either for ordinary people or for the virtuous; that he simply takes for granted. In fact, he usefully shows us that this is part of our intuitions in a passage in the *Rhetoric*, where he is setting out various views, not as part of a theory of his own, but as what we all accept:

> Let loving [*philein*], then, be defined as wishing for someone what one thinks to be goods, for their own sake and not one's own, and being such as to do such things, as far as one can. A friend [*philos*] is someone who loves [*philōn*] and is loved in return, and those who think that this is how they relate to each other think that they are friends. Granted this, it is necessary that someone is a friend if he shares someone else's pleasure in good things and pain in distressing things, for that person's sake and not for any other reason.[1]

This point is taken up and developed in the extensive treatment of friendship in the *Nicomachean Ethics*.[2] 'They say that one should wish good things to a friend for his sake' (1155 b 31); and Aristotle accepts this widely shared intuition and builds on it. His own major contribution is to distinguish three different kinds of friendship, depending on the reasons one has for having a friend. One can, in a friendship, seek either what is 'expedient' or useful, or what is pleasant, or what is good. Friendships based on usefulness or pleasure are inferior to the other kind, and people who have them are friends to a lesser degree;[3] the best or perfect kind of friendship is one in

---

[1] *Rhet* 1380 b 36–1381 a 5. This passage, and the whole of the chapter (II 4) is rightly stressed in Cooper (1980).

[2] *NE* VIII and IX. Cf. the corresponding treatments in *Eudemian Ethics* VII and MM II 11–17.

[3] Aristotle seems to vary between the *Eudemian Ethics* and the *Nicomachean Ethics* as to how the relation of the different forms of friendship is to be characterized, and the *Nicomachean Ethics* version is certainly understated. See Fortenbaugh (1975b) and Walker (1979) for the technical aspects of the problem. Cooper (1980) defends the view that all three forms of friendship are really friendship in the substantial sense that all involve disinterested concern for the friend's good; so does Nussbaum in her treatment of friendship in Aristotle in (1986a), chapter 12, part II. Price, in ch. 5 of (1989), gives the matter a thorough discussion, concluding that the inferior forms do not really fulfil this condition and

which each person is friends with the other because of that person's goodness, specifically his good character—indeed this kind of friendship is often called friendship of character.[4] All the kinds of friendship suppose the truth of the basic intuition about friendship, namely that to be a friend is to wish well to the other person for his own sake, not instrumentally, as a way to your own good. Usefulness and pleasure friendships, however, are based on features of the person which are relatively superficial and transitory, and so these friendships themselves inherit these features. But friendship based on good character is based on something which is essential to the person: indeed, the good character can be said to be the person in that the person will, as we put it, identify with her settled good character-traits more than with other, more superficial possessions such as the ability to be useful or pleasant. This kind of friendship is one in which one is friends with the person fully for their own sake, for in valuing the person's character one values the person.[5]

Many features of Aristotle's theory of friendship have been sources of continued controversy and discussion. Is Aristotle right in connecting so intimately the ideas of valuing a person and of valuing the person's character? Must concern for character be so closely tied to concern for goodness of character? And is Aristotle right in thinking that there is any one phenomenon which answers to the basic idea of wishing well to someone for her own sake, and yet takes such diverse forms as valuing her for her good character, her capacity to amuse, her useful connections? These questions are tangential to the present concern, however, which is how Aristotle deals with the limits and the source of other-concern.

It is at once evident that Aristotle assumes a large restriction on other-concern by giving an important place in the good life to *philia*, rather than to concern for the interests of others however close or distant one's commitment to them. This does not, of course, mean that he thinks that there is no such thing as the latter, but he does not discuss it under the heading of ethically required other-concern. *Philia* is other-concern restricted to those people to whom one has a certain kind of commitment. The commitment can be deep, as with friendships based on good character, or shallow, as in utility friendships; it can be continuing or transitory. It can be based on mature choice, as with adults developing an acquaintance, or can arise from an unchosen relationship, as with family relationships, which Aristotle includes, indeed illustrating *philia* by a mother's love for her child,[6] despite the fact that such relationships do not really fit into any of his types of friendship. But *philia* involves some kind of personal commitment. For Aristotle, the pursuit of our final end does not directly imply any concern for 'the furthest Mysian',[7] someone living in a far-off foreign country, with whom we have no personal ties at all.

---

that Aristotle is thus using *philia* in a broad way to cover some relationships which fail this condition, even though his main interest is in relationships which meet it.

[4] Such friendship is referred to as friendship 'of the good' (e.g., 1156 b 7–9) or 'because of the good' (e.g., 1157 a 19–20); it is referred to also as 'friendship of character' (e.g., 1164 a 12–13) or friendship 'because of character' (e.g., 1165 b 8–9).

[5] This has aroused strong opposition; cf. Vlastos (1981a). For a subtle and sympathetic attempt to defend Aristotle here, see 'Perfect Friendship in Aristotle', ch. 4 of Price (1989).

[6] 1159 a 27–1159 b 1.

[7] At *Theaet* 209 b Socrates complains that the conditions introduced so far for distinguishing something in one's thought will not in fact distinguish Socrates' thought of Theaetetus from one of Theodorus or of 'the furthest Mysian'. The phrase apparently suggests proverbial remoteness, together

We can easily think of sociological reasons why Aristotle should assume that other-concern should be thus limited. He thinks of the moral agent not as an isolated individual relating morally to each other isolated individual, but rather as the product of moral education in particular contexts—the family, the peer-group, the city. He thinks of moral character as being displayed within the same contexts which develop it. And if our final end involves moral activity, and moral activity is the exercise of moral character which has been developed in a specific social context, how can our final end demand moral activity outside that context? If we have not developed morally in any context which includes the furthest Mysian, how can the furthest Mysian make a moral demand on us? What could it be? Such considerations cannot, however, succeed in the end even on the sociological level. For the Stoics also make the same assumptions as Aristotle does about the limited group contexts in which moral development takes place; but they do not hesitate to conclude that morality, when developed, recognizes the force of unrestricted other-concern; the furthest Mysian does have a moral claim on us, even if we grew up in Athens.[8]

Does Aristotle have any arguments to show that achieving our final end requires friendship, rather than some different kind of other-concern? There seem to be two. One is that friendship assists self-knowledge; for we can discern and evaluate the characters of others better than our own, and in the best kind of friendship, based on goodness of character, we appreciate that our friend's character is sufficiently like our own for friendship to give us the opportunity for self-discovery. Friends are required because (a) only in other people can we find a 'reflection' of ourselves that will give us an objective assessment of ourselves and (b) only friends among other people provide us with the degree of intimacy we need for us to find out anything deep and lasting about ourselves.[9] The other is that sharing activities with friends enables us to carry on these activities in a more continuous, pleasant and effective way than we could if we were limited to individual efforts. The good, flourishing

---

with a certain contempt; John MacDowell in his translation (Oxford 1973) translates, 'the remotest peasant in Asia'. The Anonymous Commentator on the *Theaetetus*, in his note on *Theaetetus* 143 d, introduces the furthest Mysian in the moral context of the requirement of justice, according to the Stoics, that one be impartial to everyone, even if you have no personal ties with them. Perhaps the commentator uses the example because he has the later *Theaetetus* passage in mind; in any case it is a suitable example to make the point about impartiality in moral theory.

[8] Very general claims are sometimes made at this point, to the effect that in the Hellenistic age people became more 'individualistic'; they identified less with *polis*-life and became more isolated and anomic. But there are, of course, many things that 'individualistic' might mean; of course there were *some* general cultural changes, and *some* ways in which people became more interested in what we might call their individual differences, but it is difficult to make out a general claim about Hellenistic 'individualism' which is both supported by Hellenistic culture and history and is also strong enough to be interesting. Thus differences between Aristotle and the Stoics cannot be explained just by the claim that Hellenistic people were more 'individualistic' and less *polis*-minded.

[9] Cooper clearly brings out the importance of the question, why the good life requires *friends* in particular. I follow Cooper in thinking that the present argument is most clearly formulated in the *MM*, 1213 a 10–26 (which of course renders it a later restatement for those who do not accept the authenticity of the *MM*), though it is also adumbrated at *NE* 1169 b 28- 1170 a 4. Nussbaum stresses this argument, emphasising the requirement of mutual intimacy if the knowledge obtained is to be practical knowledge— that is, not a bare cognitive grasp but knowledge which already embodies the right affective disposition.

human life is made up of activities, and a context of shared and joint activities enables people to achieve a level of activity, particularly ethical activity, which would otherwise be beyond their reach. Political activity is doubtless the prime example of this point. Again, we can see why friendship, rather than unrestricted other-concern, is required for this; what is needed is a context of familiarity and intimacy before many activities can be sensibly shared.[10]

These arguments undoubtedly show that in achieving the good life we are greatly helped by having friends. If we have a supportive context of friends, we are more likely better to understand ourselves and better to achieve our moral goals. Do they, however, show more than that friends make this easier for us? Are friends actually required? Our answers to this will depend on how needy and insufficient we think we are as individuals for the achievement of the good life.[11] If we are pessimistic, we will think that an individual has no hope of achieving her final end with any degree of success without support from friends.[12] If we are more optimistic, we might think that friends are not necessary for an agent to achieve a good life, though they make things a great deal easier and allow the agent to achieve more than he otherwise would have done. Either way, we can see that friends, rather than a random bunch of other people, play a helping and enabling role for the agent trying to live a good and thoughtful life. That friends are useful to us in this role does not, however, imply that our concern with friends must at bottom be instrumental, that we might dispense with friends if we got a really good self-knowledge manual or a really good secretary. For, while friends help us cope with our weaknesses, and thus render us more self-sufficient, our dependence on friends, if they are really friends, opens us up to weakness and gaps in self-sufficiency of a different kind. Friends may let us down, and even if they are the best kind of character-friend and thus reliable in what matters, they may die, or leave town, leaving us exposed. An instrumental argument for friendship must therefore show less than is required.[13] Friendship is thus intrinsically good; even when we do not actually need what friends can give us, they are worth having for their own sake. They enhance our life by the knowledge and activities that they further, even if we could in fact get by without them.

These arguments have some force; they show that, even if a good life contains different kinds of other-concern as well, friendship would still add something, be worth having. But they do not, of course, show that or why we should be concerned with friendship as opposed to those other kinds of other-concern. Given Aristotle's very broad conception of friendship, it covers relationships which do not involve

---

[10] Cooper isolates this argument also, focussing on *NE* 1170 a 4–11. He discusses the strengths and weaknesses of both arguments.

[11] J. Cooper points out that these arguments 'in a certain way . . . both emphasize human vulnerability and weakness' ([1980] p. 331).

[12] A lot depends on what we take 'friend' to imply here. It seems too pessimistic to think that the agent is doomed without strong personal friendships; many worthy lives have been led without this. If we take 'friend' to cover wider and more superficial relationships, it seems more plausible; but in this sense the agent would be very unusual in lacking all friends. Here we are hindered by the problems over whether Aristotle does think that all his forms of friendship in fact share a common core of disinterested goodwill (see n. 3).

[13] Nussbaum stresses the extent to which regarding friendship as a constitutive part of the good life opens up the agent to the problems of contingency, and stresses the limitation this puts on instrumental defences of friendship.

intimacy, and thus many kinds of other-concern which we would not naturally range under friendship. But no kind of Aristotelian friendship will extend to the furthest Mysian; concern for other people to whom we have no particular commitment at all does not come into the theory.[14] It is true that at the very beginning of the *Nicomachean Ethics* discussion of friendship, when gathering together beliefs that show why friendship is ethically important, Aristotle gives as some of these beliefs:

> There seems to be a natural friendship of parent for offspring and offspring for parent, not only among humans but among birds and most animals, and among members of the same species for one another,[15] and especially among humans, whence we praise lovers of humanity. One might see in one's travels how every human is familiar to[16] and a friend to another human.[17]

However, Aristotle's own theoretical account of friendship could hardly be said to do justice to either of these two kinds of relationship; indeed, they can scarcely be said to turn out to be cases of real friendship in the end, given that account. Particularly puzzling is the praise 'we' give to lovers of humanity; if this is seriously meant as praise of those who feel commitment to other humans just as such, and regardless of any shared context, then not only does it find no echo elsewhere in Aristotle's ethics, it seems incompatible with the importance given elsewhere to the contexts of family and polis.[18] No theory of a complex ethical phenomenon can do justice to every pre-theoretical intuition; Aristotle's reflective theory emphasizes the importance and ethical potential of particular commitments, taking no serious account of unrestricted other-concern. However valuable his account of *philia*, it leaves a felt gap in the theory; we shall see that all later theories take seriously the ethical demands of the furthest Mysian.

Friendship is, as we have seen, a genuine concern for the other's good; so any attempt to reduce this to self-concern, or any other distinct motivation, must fail, for it would give an account not of friendship but of something else. Nonetheless, one might try, non-reductively, to explain friendship as a form or development of something else, and this is what Aristotle interestingly does. In *Nicomachean Ethics* IX 4 and 8 he relates friendship to self-love, making the first move in a debate which his later followers were to develop more ambitiously, and with a greater sense of its importance than Aristotle seems to feel.[19]

---

[14] Cf. Benson (1990).

[15] This is sometimes translated 'members of the same race', as by Irwin. I take the neuter *allēla*, however, to indicate that Aristotle is not thinking of different races of humans, but of different species more generally; he has just been talking about animals, and goes on to stress the case of humans.

[16] The word is *oikeion*, which also means 'akin to'. In the books on friendship, particularly when talking about family and kin relationships, which fit badly into his account of friendship, Aristotle frequently uses *oikei-* words and their compounds. See n. 26.

[17] 1155 a 16–22.

[18] And compare *Pol* 1252 b 5–9, where Aristotle endorses the view that Greeks are superior to 'slavish' barbarians; presumably a 'lover of humanity' might miss this point.

[19] The following passage draws on material in two of my articles, Annas (1977) and (1988c). I have been helped by the comments of Richard Kraut, who was my commentator at the conference from which the second article comes, and whose comments were particularly helpful.

In *Nicomachean Ethics* IX 4 Aristotle gives us five marks by which people define friendship, marks which he himself accepts.[20] A friend is one who (1) wishes and does good (or apparently good) things to (or for) a friend, for the friend's sake, (2) wishes the friend to exist and live, for his own sake, (3) spends time with his friend, (4) makes the same choices as his friend and (5) finds the same things pleasant and painful as his friend. But, Aristotle goes on, all these marks are paradigmatically found in the good person's relation to himself. 'Each of these seems to belong to the good person by virtue of his relation to himself, and he relates to his friend as he does to himself, for the friend is another self.'[21] Friendship is thus explained as the extension to others of a relationship that one has to oneself. One can be guaranteed to hold it to oneself, and can extend it to others because 'a friend is another self'.

Aristotle is aware that intuitively this sounds rather peculiar.[22] He is unconcerned about this, however, because the analysis permits him to account for and clarify the subjectmatter he is concerned with. In particular he can do justice to two points. One is that self-love is what I shall call psychologically primary. For 'each person wishes goods for himself most of all'.[23] My own self and concerns are inescapably nearer and more pressing than the selves and concerns of others are. This strikes Aristotle as an important psychological fact. It does not, of course, imply that I can care for others only in a way that makes them instrumental to my own concerns. Nor, on the other hand, does it imply that I *should* put my own concerns first, or even that it is morally permissible to do this. The other point is that, as is familiar by now, friendship is a concern for the other person's good for their own sake, not an instrumental concern. The thesis that a friend is another self does justice to both these points. Aristotle is claiming that we can in fact extend self-love in certain respects, can come to relate to a friend in some of the ways we relate to ourselves.[24] We start, as a matter of psychological fact, with self-concern; but we can, also as a matter of psychological fact, come to extend to others the relevant aspects of that concern, and so come to care about their good for their own sakes.

This is plainly not an *argument* to show how, granted only self-concern, we can get to other-concern. If it were, it would be without force, since the premise that a friend is another self would simply beg the question. Rather, Aristotle is here explaining friendship in terms of relationships which are clearest in the case of self-love. The ability we have to extend concern to others is treated as just as much a fact as our ability to have self-concern; neither is reduced to the other or treated as more explanatory. The procedure thus rests on common sense; we think self-love to be

---

[20] He refers to this passage at 1168 b 3–6 in a way making clear that he does endorse them, even though they are introduced only as what people think.

[21] 1166 a 29–32.

[22] At 1166 a 34-b 2 he says that one can have friendship to oneself only insofar as one is two or more; and he argues at length in V 11 that a person cannot properly be just or unjust to himself. Of course this does not contradict his analysis: there may be a basic relation one has to oneself and then extends to others, and *this* relation one can have to oneself 'only insofar as one is two or more'. But the points Aristotle notices certainly underline the unintuitive nature of his analysis.

[23] 1159 a 11–12.

[24] Not in all or most of the ways; to have for a friend exactly the type of concern I have for myself is an *excess* of other-concern, which is not admirable (1166 b 1–2). The five marks of friendship list the ways that are relevant.

psychologically primary, but this does not *eo ipso* undermine our confidence that we have genuine other-concern.[25]

Aristotle says little about our ability to extend concern to others, and seems on the whole to take it for granted. In *Nicomachean Ethics* IX 4 he is talking about mature forms of friendship between ethically developed adults, and does not ask about the original or instinctive form of this concern. When he is talking about family and kin relationships, he says some suggestive things which later followers were to develop,[26] but Aristotle himself does not do this—partly of course because such relationships do not fit well into his own analysis of friendship.[27] *Nicomachean Ethics* IX 4, then, is close to common sense in its treatment of self- and other-concern. Aristotle does not question that we achieve concern for others for their own sake; that we do this by extension from self-love simply accepts both this and another fact, the fact that self-love is what, psychologically, we start from.

In another passage, however, self-love appears in an analysis which is anything but commonsensical, an analysis whose counter-intuitive nature Aristotle seems positively to stress.[28] The passage begins with Aristotle appearing to do what he often does, namely opposing a set of reputable views or *endoxa* to another set, or to a theory, showing that they conflict; and then developing an answer which does justice to what is true in both sides and showing that when this is rightly developed the conflict turns out to be merely apparent.[29] But there are unusual aspects to this passage. Aristotle says that, on the one hand, we have beliefs like the following: self-love is blamed, and people think that it is bad people who do everything for their own sake, while a good person acts morally, because of the fine (*kalon*), doing this the more the better he is, and also acts for the sake of a friend, letting his own interests go.[30] These are not just casual beliefs—they are, if anything is, ground-floor, basic beliefs in ethics; the entire *Ethics* tries to do justice to the facts that good people act morally and have concern for others. Then, surprisingly, we are told that these accounts are 'reasonably' in conflict with 'facts'.[31] What are these 'facts'?

---

[25] For different interpretations, which treat the commonsense level of explanation as more superficial, see Kahn (1981c) and Alberti (1990a).

[26] The word *oikeion* and cognates such as *sunoikeiousthai* occur not only in the sense of being proper or appropriate, but in the sense of being akin or related to. In some passages, e.g., 1161 b 18 ff., they are used in the sense of feeling akin to or feeling affinity with; at 1162 a 1 ff this is contrasted with the sense of literally being akin. At 1161 b 16–24 Aristotle, saying that parental love is the basis of all family friendship, adds that parents love their children 'as being something of themselves', since one's offspring is regarded as a detached part of oneself, just as one's hair or teeth are detachable parts of oneself. This idea of extended self-concern suggests the later Stoic theory of *oikeiōsis* (see section 2), and some scholars have seen in these passages the adumbrations of an earlier Peripatetic theory of *oikeiōsis* (see section 3).

[27] I discuss in the 'Self-Love' paper, but not here, two other aspects of the *Nicomachean Ethics* IX 4 passage: Aristotle is concerned with perfect friendship, not the lesser kinds, and he identifies the self with the agent's practical reasoning. Neither affects the issues discussed here.

[28] It is perhaps significant that while *EE* VII 6 and 12 and *MM* II 11.47–50 and 15 contain material analogous to that in *NE* IX 4, nothing in the *EE* corresponds to the more striking *NE* IX 8. *MM* II 11 13–14 corresponds to it closely, however, though with one striking discrepancy (see p. 262).

[29] Aristotle claims that this is what he is doing at 1168 b 12–13.

[30] 1168 a 29–35.

[31] *Tois logois de toutois ta erga diaphōnei, ouk alogōs* (1168 a 35-b 1). The customary suggestion of the *logos*/*ergon* contrast is that *logos* is what is in some way merely a matter of expression, while *erga* are

People say that one should most love (*philein*) that which is most *philos*, most of a friend. But this is the person who most wishes goods to someone for that person's sake, even if nobody knows. And each person stands most in this relationship to himself, since he stands most to himself in the five ways of which friendship was defined as the extension to others. Various proverbs suggest this too.[32] Aristotle is appealing to the psychological primacy of self-love established in IX 4, but has converted that into a claim that one *should* most love oneself. What is the status of that claim here, since it was no part of IX 4 itself? Perhaps Aristotle thinks that many people are inclined to think it reasonable to put one's own interests first, just because self-love is psychologically primary; whether he thinks this reasonable or a muddle, he certainly endorses the thought here as a *prima facie* problem.

Whatever the oddity of the conflict which Aristotle has established, there is no doubt about his solution to it, and clearly he commits himself to this, regardless of the status of the conflict he presents it as solving. The answer to this lies, he says, in distinguishing how those on each side understand self-love, being *philautos*. Those who think it bad are identifying the self with the lower, irrational part of the soul, which is gratified when the person is eager to get the most money, honours and pleasure for himself. It is a very different matter, however, to love oneself in the sense of awarding oneself what is truly best, and of gratifying the 'controlling' part of oneself, one's practical reasoning.[33] Those who say that self-love is bad are therefore talking about something different, not *true* self-love.

Aristotle recognizes that his own view sounds paradoxical:

> If someone were constantly eager to be the best of all in doing just actions, or temperate ones, or anything else concerned with the virtues, and in general always acquired the fine [*to kalon*] for himself, nobody would call *him* self-loving, or blame him. But this person *would* seem to be a self-lover even more [than the other kind].[34]

It is noteworthy that Aristotle is defending a thesis which in ordinary life everyone would reject; he generally takes this to show that something has gone wrong with the argument.[35] Here, however, he consciously defends a paradoxical position, and does so by showing that the thesis in question, that the good person should be self-loving, is compatible with the beliefs it seems to conflict with. Instead of rejecting the thesis on the basis of the beliefs, he introduces a special sense of 'self-love' in terms of which to reconcile the beliefs. Both our belief that the good person acts morally, and then our belief that he acts for the sake of others, are reconciled with the thesis that the good person is and ought to be self-loving.[36]

---

solid facts or deeds. This contrast is the opposite of what we would expect here; we would expect the counter-intuitive theory to be the merely verbal item, the shared and solid intuitions to be the facts.

[32] 1168 b 1–10.

[33] In IX 4 Aristotle actually identified the self with the practical reasoning; but we do not need that thesis here, only the idea, easy enough to understand, that the agent can identify with either higher or lower aspects of her self.

[34] 1168 b 25–29.

[35] In the *Rhetoric* he records without comment the endoxic view that old people live with a view to advantage, rather than the fine, 'more than they should' because they are self-loving (*philautoi*) (II, 13).

[36] In the (1988c) paper I argue at length at this point against the alternative interpretation of these

First, Aristotle claims that self-love is compatible with moral action. Since the self-lover aims to get for himself most of what he seeks to get, self-love in the moral field commits him, as he sees, to a strange kind of 'moral competition' between virtuous people.[37]

> Everyone welcomes and praises people who are especially eager to do fine actions. And when everyone competes for the fine and strains to do the finest things everything will be as it should in common and each will individually get the greatest of goods, since virtue is like that. So the good person should be a self-lover, for in doing fine actions he will aid himself and also benefit the others, but the wicked person should not, for in following base feelings he will harm both himself and his neighbours.[38]

If everyone is self-loving, then people will compete, for each will be concerned to put her own interests first. But if the self-love is of the right kind, that is, love of the person's practical reasoning, then the resulting competition will be benign, for people will be competing to be virtuous, and this does not have the same results as competitions for what is normally 'fought over' (1168 b 19).[39]

Aristotle is, under the pressure of accommodating to the thesis that the good person should be self-loving, reinterpreting the notion of competition. He has distinguished an ordinary sense of self-love in which the person loves bodily or external goods, and a new, special sense in which the 'real' self-lover loves and identifies with her practical reasoning. This is certainly highly redefined from the sense that most people would give to self-love, and it is not very surprising that the competition between true self-lovers is also redefined, and turns out to be wholly different from the common understanding of competition. Normally, competition is for a limited good, and hence is at others' expense; if I get more you will get less. But when people 'compete to be virtuous' what they do is not at the others' expense, for Aristotle insists that *each* person gets the greatest good, since 'virtue is that kind of thing'. Virtue is an inexhaustible good; if I have more this does not leave less for you. As Shelley said of true love, to divide it is not to take away.[40] Hence competition to be virtuous is not a contest for a limited good, and so does not take away anything from others, or conflict with what is in their interests. This is a competition in which there are no winners and no losers, and things work out for the best for everyone; more like what we think of as *co-operation* than competition.

It is unusual for Aristotle to reinterpret familiar notions in paradoxical ways, and the significance of his doing it here has been underestimated. That this is what he is doing, however, seems clear from another passage in which he introduces the

---

passages put forward by Richard Kraut in his (1989) book, ch. 2. Kraut in his reply to my paper takes the discussion further.

[37] The term is Richard Kraut's (see n. 36). Kraut dissolves this problem by arguing that (1) moral competition spurs everyone on to do better than they would have done without it and (2) Aristotle elsewhere commits himself to strong theses that limit the scope of moral competition and prevent it involving obnoxious results, such as unfairness to others.

[38] 1169 a 6–15.

[39] Cicero at *Am* 32 talks about a kind of moral competition between friends which is reminiscent of this passage.

[40] 'True love in this differs from gold and clay/That to divide is not to take away'. *Epipsychidion* 160–161.

same idea of moral competition (though not there interpreting it in terms of self-love):

> Those who are friends because of virtue are keen to do good to one another . . .
> and when they compete in this there are no complaints or fights. For no one is
> annoyed with someone who loves and benefits him; if he is gracious, he will
> retaliate by doing good. And the winner, getting what he aims at, will not
> complain about his friend; for each is aiming at the good.[41]

The language of competition has been completely reinterpreted; the 'competitive'
urge is to do good to others; one 'retaliates' with benefits. And if 'true' self-love is
love of one's practical reasoning, which will lead one to do virtuous actions, this is
what competition between true self-lovers will turn out to be.

Aristotle also claims, in a passage that has been found notoriously difficult, that
his thesis that one should be self-loving (in the right way) does not conflict with the
other fundamental belief that seemed to make trouble for it, namely that the good
person will sacrifice his own interests for another.

> It *is* true, concerning the good person, that for the sake of his friends and his
> country he will do much, and die for them if necessary; he will sacrifice money
> and honours, and in general goods that are fought over, obtaining for himself the
> fine. He will choose a short period of intense pleasure rather than a long period
> of mild pleasure, and choose to live finely for a year rather than for many years in
> an ordinary way, and choose one action which is fine and great rather than many
> small ones. This is certainly[42] true of those who die for others; they choose for
> themselves what is great and fine. They will sacrifice money in circumstances
> where their friends will get more; for the friend gets money, while he gets what is
> fine, so he does assign himself the greater good. It is the same with honours and
> offices—he will sacrifice all these to his friend; for this is for him fine and
> praiseworthy. It is then reasonable that he seems to be good, in choosing the fine
> in exchange for everything. It is possible to sacrifice actions to one's friend, and
> for it to be finer to be responsible for a friend's action than to act oneself. In all
> praiseworthy matters, then, the good person appears as assigning himself more of
> what is fine. This is the way, then, that one should be a lover of self, as we said,
> but we should not be in the way the many are.[43]

Aristotle has often been thought to fail in this attempt to reconcile self-love with
other-concern. Concern for others, even to the extent of self-sacrifice, turns out to
be formally self-serving after all; even the ultimate sacrifice, dying for another, turns
out to be assigning to yourself more of what matters more. And in the way he
presents the choice to act for others as a choice of the heroic over the humdrum,
Aristotle seems to be assimilating it to a familiar Greek tradition of heroism that is
distinctly self-centred in the desire to shine and excel for a brief and glorious
moment.[44] Aristotle seems to have resolved the apparent conflict of self-love and

---

[41] 1162 b 6–13.

[42] *Isōs* here is usually translated 'perhaps', but seems to have here the meaning of 'certainly', which
later becomes standard for it.

[43] 1169 a 18–1169 b 2.

[44] This is familiar from the *Iliad*, especially in the portrayal of Achilles. Cf. also the words of Glaucus
at VI 206 ff., esp. 208: *aeien aristeuein kai hupeirochon emmenai allōn.*

other-concern by reinterpreting other-concern in a fashion that interprets it away, and leaves him with a theory about self-love which is in fact self-centred. Other-concern here seems to be merely apparent, and self-love more basic.[45] We could lessen the problem by taking this passage in close connection with the previous one, about 'moral competition'. Thus assigning myself the fine is not like assigning myself money or honours; virtue is the kind of inexhaustible good which allows me to have all I need without lessening any opportunities for you. Thus assigning myself the fine does not worsen anyone's position—indeed, since all benefit by the performance of virtuous actions, it improves it. This move appears merely to postpone the problem, however. The more we stress the point that Aristotle has redefined the content of self-loving behaviour, the more striking it remains that self-sacrifice is explained as being, formally, self-love.[46]

A plausible move is to argue that Aristotle is claiming that self-love of the right kind is *consistent* with our intuitions about self-sacrifice; he is not trying to explain self-sacrifice away, but represents the self-sacrificing agent as *also* getting for herself what matters. Her motives will thus be mixed. She sacrifices her money, say,[47] so that her friends can get more money. She does this for her friends' sake, because this is a fine thing to do (and not for any ulterior motive, such as showing off or feeling virtuous). But she also 'assigns the greater good to herself', for in doing a virtuous action she is doing what matters more to her than gaining money, and so gaining what she regards as her good.[48]

Is this position viable? It seems perfectly all right as long as we describe it from outside, in the third person. It becomes more problematic when we ask what form the agent's thought will take from the agent's point of view. Is the agent supposed to be thinking, 'I'll sacrifice this money, so that my friends can gain more, for that is a generous action, and so fine; *and* I'm sacrificing mere money and gaining the fine, so I'm assigning myself the greater good and come off best after all'? There seems to be something wrong with this; the second half undermines the first, at least if they are both being taken to be the agent's characterization of her goals.

It may be retorted that there is really no problem, as long as the agent is thinking of herself as acting out of concern for her friends for their own sakes, and out of concern for herself as pursuing the fine. For pursuing the fine just is doing things like acting for the sake of other people out of concern for them. This indicates, I think,

---

[45] Kraut claims that the problem here dissolves once we recognize that virtuous people are implicitly recognizing bounds on their assignment to themselves of the fine; they recognize a constraint of fairness on maximizing their own virtuous activity. This claim involves interpreting this passage in the light of what is said elsewhere in Aristotle, especially the *Politics*, about fair access to opportunities for political office. I am more reluctant to use other sources to interpret a passage which has very unusual methodological features.

[46] Recall that, faced by a conflict between intuitions about self-sacrifice and a thesis about self-love, Aristotle reacts by making self-love basic (in a refined sense) and explaining away the conflict with the intuitions.

[47] Using Aristotle's example at 1169 a 26–9.

[48] Cf. Irwin's comment on 1169 a 35–b 1, in his translation with notes of the *Nicomachean Ethics* (1985a): 'Clearly the virtuous person's attitude to his friends' good is not entirely selfless and self-forgetful. But Aristotle takes it to be consistent with concern for the friend's good for his own sake. It is because this sort of concern is fine that the virtuous person thinks it is part of his good. Hence the virtuous friend never 'sacrifices himself' if that implies sacrifice of his own interests to another's; but he is no less concerned for the friend's good for the friend's own sake than a 'self-sacrificing' person would be.'

the right lines on which to interpret Aristotle. The agent acts out of self-concern, but where this is concern for oneself as a rational agent aiming at the fine, this will take the form of other-directed and moral action. Thus we remove the conflict, by understanding self-concern not to be the agent's immediate aim. Rather, she aims at helping others for their own sake; doing this is also a case of acting out of self-concern in that her life as a whole expresses concern for herself as a rational agent aiming at the fine.

Thus this passage is far from explaining other-concern away and saying that the agent really acts to gets something for herself when she acts for others. Rather, the aim of helping others for their own sakes is accepted as real and not explained away. The agent, however, also acts from self-love in that what she does shows that her life and actions as a whole display concern for herself—concern for herself, of course, as a rational and moral being. Self-love is not the agent's particular aim; rather, when the agent acts self-sacrificingly, her act is an expression of her love for the life of actively virtuous practical reasoning, which is what she most deeply feels herself to be and to be identified with.[49]

Such an interpretation makes good sense of the curious procedure of IX 8; Aristotle is concerned to save a paradoxical-sounding thesis about self-love, and this is more understandable if he is defending, not the thesis that the agent is always motivated by self-love, but the thesis that the agent's actions express what he values and loves most in his life overall. Further, we can see that the presentation of self-love as heroic is less objectionable than it superficially seems. The virtuous person is not thought of as consciously rejecting the merely humdrum, as though it were beneath her; rather, she does what is heroic, but what motivates her is the thought that this is what virtue requires, not the thought that she will be a hero.[50]

Aristotle does not tell us whether to interpret the claims about self-love in this passage as claims about the agent's particular aims, or rather as claims about what is shown in the agent's life and activity as a whole. It is best to take it as the latter claim, both because it makes better sense of the passage itself and because it makes sense of Aristotle's relation to later Peripatetic developments on this theme. But it remains true that Aristotle throws the idea out rather mysteriously, and it is a pity that he did not explicitly develop it further. Nor does he tell us how the conclusions of IX 8 are to be related to the rest of his ethical writings. The conclusion that acting for another's sake, even extreme self-sacrifice, is really a kind of self-love, is one that cannot be restricted to the discussion of friendship. The virtuous person will often have to act for the sake of others, and put her own interests behind those of others; if this is really a case of self-love, then self-love would seem to be a fundamental concept in explaining what virtue is, since developing the virtues will be an expression of self-love, for it will be an expression of the rational moral agency

---

[49] Thus we have a 'two-level' view of a kind, but not one that leads to the 'schizophrenia' problem, since the two kinds of thought when put together do not lead to conflict. They do so lead, of course, on the common understanding of what it is to be self-loving, but Aristotle makes it clear that that notion here is extremely redefined, in a way precisely defined to avoid conflict.

[50] This does not answer the question why virtue should be thought to be heroic in the first place. Chapter 2, section 6, may help us understand this odd thesis to some extent.

which a true self-lover identifies with. We can only speculate how Aristotle ultimately intended IX 8 to be related to the rest of what is in the ethical works.[51]

However, the discussion of other-concern and self-love in IX 8 is of great interest in itself and as the beginning of a complex development of ideas about other-concern. Aristotle has not defended the claim that self-love even partially motivates the moral or self-sacrificing agent; what is being referred to is just the story of the development of virtuous dispositions and practical reasoning in the agent. It is when we think of the agent's motivation and concern over his whole life that we can see what he does as an expression of self-concern. Wicked or faulty agents show their self-love in greedy or unjust actions; the virtuous agent will show his self-love in acting virtuously, since the self he loves is his developed capacity for practical reasoning, and virtuous activity is the expression of correctly developed practical reasoning. Self-love can thus help explain the development of the virtues; the agent in developing the virtues comes more and more to love the self which is expressed in virtuous action, rather than the self which is expressed in desire for things such as money or power.[52]

As we have seen, self-concern is for Aristotle psychologically primary; we all start there. In IX 8 he makes the interesting claim that the end of our progress in virtue, to the point of doing virtuous actions for the sake of the fine and acting in the interests of others for their own sake—that this is also a kind of self-love. It is, of course, a greatly expanded notion compared with the beginning kind of self-love, for the relevant notion of self has changed; from the intuitive notion of self as what is gratified by obvious advantages to the very special notion of self as what identifies with rational and moral activity.

There are two aspects to this thesis. One is that ultimately self- and other-concern have a common source (not, of course, one that either is reduced to). The other is that this common source is self-love. We begin with self-love of the familiar narrow kind, and out of this we develop other-concern, taken to be self-love of a different, more elevated kind. As we shall see, Aristotle's followers accepted the first of these points but not the second. They accepted that self-concern and other-concern have and develop from a common source; they are not primitively distinct, with distinct sources in us. But they refused to consider this common source to be self-love. Aristotle is the only thinker who begins from ordinary self-love and uses the term self-love also for the end of the developed process, where we have other-

---

[51] Since what we read as the *Nicomachean Ethics* was put together, presumably by Andronicus, from Aristotle's ethical writings (though it is apparently absent from Andronicus' list, and its origin is problematic), there is no presumption that it is unified as a modern book would be; indeed it already contains, in the sections we call 'Book I' and 'Book X', incompatible accounts of the content of *eudaimonia*, and there are also apparently irreconcilable divergencies between the two accounts of pleasure. There are also passages in the *Eudemian Ethics*, notably the concluding passage of chapter 3 of book VIII, which defend, in isolation, bold ideas which have broad implications for the ethical works as a whole which are never explicitly drawn.

[52] See Homiak (1981). Homiak does not discuss the IX 8 arguments, but she argues rightly that, 'self-love is best seen as the cause of virtuous behaviour and not the end for which virtuous actions are done. Because self-love is a higher-order attitude towards planning, it is not a part of one's life-plan and hence not something one strives for *qua* part of one's plan. In this sense, Aristotle's self-love does not constitute someone's purpose or reason for acting: it is not a goal a person strives to achieve. But. . .someone with the appropriate feelings of self-love will act virtuously, as a natural causal consequence of his psychological state' (p. 640).

concern and morality. Later thinkers just find this point too paradoxical. The author of the *Magna Moralia* has a passage which corresponds to *Nicomachean Ethics* IX 8 quite closely, but refuses to call the virtuous person 'self-loving' (*philautos*), reserving the word for common or garden selfish regard, and insisting that the virtuous person should be called 'good-loving' (*philagathos*) instead.[53] The author of the account of Peripatetic ethics which we find in Arius Didymus insists that, though virtue develops from initial self-concern, it 'is not self-loving (*philautos*) on this theory',[54] and treats self-lovingness (*philautia*) as a vice of deficiency in friendly feeling towards others.[55] The ordinary resonance of 'self-loving' was clearly that of *selfish* or *self-centred*,[56] and other authors find this more of a problem than Aristotle does. Antiochus' avowedly Aristotelian theory stresses self-love heavily as the starting point of ethical development, but does not place a form of it at the end point. Aristotle's later followers clearly separated what they regarded as the important Aristotelian point about the common source of self- and other-concern from what they regarded as the unnecessary paradox of regarding the whole process, end as well as beginning, as self-love. They did so in reaction to the next step in the debate, taken by the Stoics.

2. The Stoics on Other-Concern and Impartiality

The place to understand the role of other-concern in Stoic ethics is in their theory (partly discussed already in chapter 5) of *oikeiōsis*. This can seem more mysterious than it really is, because there is no good single English equivalent. I shall use 'familiarization';[57] others have used 'appropriation' or 'making akin to'. The root idea is that of making one person or thing *oikeion* to another. *Oikeion* in turn comes from *oikos*, the house or household. People are *oikeioi* if they are related to you, or in some other way attached to your household; so *oikeion* comes to mean both 'akin to' and 'what belongs to you or is on your side', as opposed to what is *allotrion*, alien, not belonging. *Allotrion* generates *allotriōsis*, for which we do have a single term, 'alienation'; *oikeiōsis* is opposed to this, and although there is no adequate single English word, perhaps 'familiarization' will suggest both the notion of family and that of being close to and coming to belong.[58]

Oikeiōsis itself is the noun from the verb *oikeiō*, to familiarize. This is a three-term relation: X makes Y *oikeion*, familiar, to Z. The relation that concerns the Stoics is that where the subject is nature, and their theory consists of the two following claims: (a) nature familiarizes a human with him/herself; and (b) nature familiarizes a human with other humans. (Hence humans are said to 'be familiarized

[53] *MM* II 13–14.

[54] 125.21–126.2. Even Aristotle recognizes that common sense treats *philautia* as hindering people from living 'with a view to the fine' (*Rhet* II 13); and at *Pol* 1263 b 2–5 he distinguishes *philauton einai* from *to philein heauton*; selfishness, he says, is loving oneself *more than one should*.

[55] 143.1–16.

[56] Cicero uses '*communis philautia*' for the customary vanity and self-centredness of authors (*Att* 13.13.1).

[57] Following a suggestion by Jonathan Barnes. John Cooper suggested that it be followed by 'with' rather than 'to'. It doubtless still sounds odd in many contexts; but so, probably, did the Stoic term.

[58] For a history of the notion and of related ones, see Kerferd (1972) and Pembroke (1971).

with' themselves, or others, 'by nature' being understood.) It will emerge how important it is that these are distinct claims.

The idea behind (a) is found is passages like the following:

> The primary impulse an animal has, they say, is to preserving itself, since from the start nature familiarizes it with itself, as Chrysippus says in *Aims* Book 1, where he calls familiar to every animal its own constitution and its consciousness of this. For it was not likely that nature would make an animal alien [to itself], nor that having produced it nature would make it neither alien to nor familiar with itself; for in this way it repulses what is harmful and accepts what is familiar to it. But as for what some say, that pleasure is what animals' primary impulse is for, this they show to be false. Pleasure, they say, if there actually is any, is something that supervenes when nature itself has sought and found what fits the thing's constitution—like good condition in animals and flourishing in plants.[59]

For nature to familiarize me with myself is for it to be natural for me to find myself familiar, not to be alienated from myself. As Chrysippus argues, it is not likely that we are by nature alienated from or indifferent to ourselves; if this were the case, we would hardly have survived. So we can conclude that we have a natural impulse to preserve and to care about ourselves.[60]

Thus it is natural for us, right from the start, to have a concern with ourselves. We begin with a tendency to self-love,[61] but *oikeiōsis* is not self-love; rather it is the tendency we have both towards developing self-concern and towards developing other-concern. Since we do not ordinarily group these two together under a single concept, it is not surprising that there is no everyday word for *oikeiōsis* and the Stoics need to invent a technical term instead.

The Stoics tell a developmental story, the first part of which we have already discussed in chapter 6. As babies we start out concerned for ourselves in a primitive way, guided by instinct to the basic things that our nature needs—food, warmth, security. We learn the kinds of things to do to get what is natural for us—health, activity, engagement in finding out about the world. From there we move to the ability that rational beings have to follow rules and to perform 'due actions', and thence to the build-up of a virtuous disposition to do these firmly and reliably. Finally, we come to a point when, if our reason develops properly, we appreciate that the value of our getting things rationally is crucially different from the value of our rational activity itself; it is the reasons we act on that matter, not the consequences of acting on those reasons. To realize this is to realize the distinct value of virtue, and its difference from other kinds of value expressed in the thesis that only virtue is good. For realizing the value of virtue is to realize that one has a reason to act which is different in kind from a reason that merely promotes one's own desires and projects. As I have argued above, this claim is very Kantian, except that the Stoics say little as to what it is about rationality that enables it to play this important role, or what the formal links are between valuing one's rationality and

---

[59] Diogenes VII 85–6.

[60] I will not here go into the interesting psychological detail of the process. Later writers particularly emphasize the role of perception and consciousness in their accounts of how familiarization comes about. See the long account by Hierocles in von Arnim (1906). For a discussion of the issue, see Inwood (1984).

[61] Cf. passages in the account of Stoic ethics in *Fin* III 16 ('*sensum haberent sui eoque se diligerent*' and '*a se diligendo*') and 59 ('*se omnes natura diligent*').

recognizing the difference between moral and other value. They merely stress the importance of objective rational consistency.

The essentials of the process are sketched in the following passage from Cicero:

[The Stoics think that] as soon as a living thing is born (for this is the place to start) it feels a concern for itself and is introduced to preserving itself, and to its constitution, and to loving those things that preserve its constitution; and it is alienated from destruction and from those things that appear to bring destruction. They prove it in this way: even before pleasure or pain has touched them infants seek for what conduces to their safety and reject the opposite, and this would not happen unless they loved their own constitution and feared destruction. But it could not come about that they sought anything unless they had a sense of self and for that reason loved themselves. From this we should understand that our first principle of action is drawn from loving one-self. . . . Let us return to the first principles of nature, with which what follows must cohere. What follows is this first distinction: They call 'valuable'. . .what is itself in accordance with nature or such as to produce it; it is worthy of being 'selected' because it has some amount of value (which they call *axia*). They call 'non-valuable' what is the opposite of the above. Thus, the principle being established that things that are in accordance with nature are to be taken for their own sake and their opposites not taken, the first due action (this is how I translate *kathēkon*) is to preserve oneself in one's natural constitution; then to hold on to the things that are in accordance with nature and repel those that are the opposite. When this principle of choice and avoidance has been discovered, there next follows choice together with due action. Then this becomes constant. Then it becomes utterly reliable and in accordance with nature; and it is at this point that what it is that is truly good first comes to be, and to be understood. For a human's first concern is with the things that are according to nature; but as soon as he has acquired understanding, or rather the concept, which they call *ennoia*, and has seen the order of things and so to speak their harmony, he values this far more than all the things he had loved before. Thus by knowledge and reason he works out the position that it is here that the ultimate human good is located, the good which is praised and sought for its own sake. And since this is placed in what the Stoics called *homologia* and we can call agreement—since that good to which all else is referred is placed here, then fine actions and the fine itself, which alone counts as a good, are late to develop, but still the only thing to be sought for its own power and status; none of the primary natural things is to be sought for its own sake.[62]

We have seen before the ideas that there are two fundamentally different kinds of value and that virtue develops via the performance of *kathēkonta* or due actions. Here they are placed in the context of developing familiarization of the person to himself, where this is taken as a progress towards caring about one's reasons for acting more than for the actual achievement of what one reasons in order to get. As we have already seen, this developmental account is not in itself an argument for the conclusion that virtue is valuable in a different way from the results it helps us to achieve; but it supports that thesis by showing how this could be the culmination of a natural development.

[62] *Fin* III 16, 20–21.

What of thesis (b), that nature familiarizes us with other humans? We are told by Plutarch that Chrysippus hammered this point home:

> How is it then that [Chrysippus] keeps on irritating us by writing in all his books—books on physics, for heaven's sake, as well as on ethics—that we are familiarized with ourselves as soon as we are born, and to our parts and to our own offspring?[63]

The passage has often been found puzzling or ludicrous because we plainly don't have offspring at birth. But there is no problem if we take the point to be that at birth we have primitive forms of the instincts both for self-concern and for other-concern. Thus at birth we have the instinct to care for our offspring; of course this will not come into play until we have offspring, but when it does, it is a form of a primitive instinct, not something learned.

It is clear that Chrysippus regards the two forms of familiarization as distinct, and the theory seems from the start to have involved both, though not all passages mention both.[64] Several passages give us the main lines of this kind of *oikeiōsis*: we start from a primitive attachment to our offspring, and from there extend our sympathies outwards to concern for others. Once we have started to do this, we find that there is no rational stopping place until we have concern for every human just insofar as he or she is human. And this attitude, of impartial concern for the interests of all others, is the basis of justice and of communal life.[65] This kind of *oikeiōsis* is often called 'social', and the first kind 'personal'.

This is a very striking claim: our concern for others proceeds from concern for our offspring, who, since we have concern for our 'parts', may be initially thought of as detached parts of ourselves, and ends up with concern for any human being just as such. 'It should be that one human does not find another human alien, precisely because of being human.'[66] One important result of this is that there is no distinctive ethical role here for *philia*, commitment to particular other people. According to the Stoics we have a natural instinct for attachment to other people, which even makes it easy for us to make friends.[67] But this is only an early stage on our development towards a fully impartial view of others and ourselves. We have no ethical reason to stop at, or to be particularly concerned with, attachments to particular other people.

The Stoics are the first ethical theorists clearly to commit themselves to the thesis that morality requires impartiality to all others from the moral point of view,[68] and though this does not imply that *philia* is ethically indefensible, it is bound to lessen its importance. They hold indeed that friendship really holds only among the virtuous, and that relationships with a view to mutual benefit are not really

---

[63] *Sto rep* 1038 b.

[64] Some scholars have suggested that *oikeiōsis* to others or social *oikeiōsis* is a later graft onto a theory which originally contained only the other kind. But this is highly implausible, especially in view of an early co-option of the term for our relations to others by the Epicureans. See Vander Waerdt (1988).

[65] See, for example, Cicero, *Fin* III 62–63.

[66] *Fin* III 63.

[67] Diogenes VII, Hierocles 11, 14–18.

[68] Plato's ethical theory in the central books of the *Republic* can be interpreted to make some such demand, but Plato puts it forward in the context of the metaphysics and epistemology of Forms, and he does not separate the two in any of his later work.

friendship.[69] Friendship thus lacks intrinsic ethical significance. The virtuous are those who will never let particular attachments modify or constrain their fundamental commitment to virtue as an overriding value; and while this is consistent with their retaining some particular attachment, it is clear that morality sets the rules for friendship so firmly that friendship cannot for the Stoics play the kind of positive helpful role in the virtuous life that it does for Aristotle.

The Stoic 'wise person' is someone who has completed the development of *oikeiōsis* in both personal and social forms. Thus he will give rationality its proper place in his life. On the one hand, he will recognize the crucial difference between moral and other value, and will be prepared to act on reasons that reflect this, reasons which do not further his own desires and projects. He will act virtuously. The Stoics hold that virtue is beneficial, indeed, because of its special role, the only thing which is truly beneficial,[70] and they hold that the virtuous person who has achieved both forms of *oikeiōsis* will benefit all equally, as well as himself, in acting virtuously. This thesis sounds peculiar in isolation, and opponents made it sound ridiculous: 'Zeus and Dion, granted that they are wise people, are equally benefitted by each other, whenever either encounters a movement of the other.'[71] But the thesis can be better understood if we take it to apply to virtuous people who have achieved both forms of *oikeiōsis*, for they realize that what matters from the moral point of view is not whether one has any commitment to the people involved, or even knows them, but the fact that all are capable of appreciating the situation from the moral, that is, the rational point of view. Kant thinks of moral action as relating people, not in their actual empirical relations, but as members of a kingdom of ends. The Stoics put the point in terms of virtue and the benefit that virtue brings: the good produced by virtuous action is not the kind of good which could belong to particular people, but belongs to and benefits all who are virtuous, that is, appreciate the kind of good that it is.

> Goods are all common among the excellent, and evils among the bad. Hence the person who benefits someone is himself benefitted, and the person who harms someone harms himself. All excellent people benefit one another, even when they are not totally friends to one another, nor even well-disposed nor in good repute nor accepted as such, on account of not being apprehended as such and not living in the same place. However, they are so disposed as to feel goodwill, friendship, approval and receptiveness to one another.[72]

Thus the mutual benefitting which the virtuous produce is what unites them in a relationship from the moral point of view. We are bound to find this a strange and perhaps unsuitable way of expressing the relationship; we are more used to Kantian ways of expressing this, and benefit may seem out of place. We should remember, however, that 'benefit' here has just the same special sense that 'good' has, since we are talking about virtue. It is the Stoics' way of expressing what is special about a

---

[69] Diogenes VII 124, Arius 108.15–25, Cicero, *Fin* III 70. See Lesses (forthcoming).

[70] For more on this, see chapter 19.

[71] Plutarch, *Comm not* 1076 a. Cf. 1068 f: if one Stoic wise person stretches out his finger intelligently (*phronimōs*), all wise people in the inhabited world are benefitted.

[72] Arius 101.21–102.2. Cf. also 93.19–94.6, and 95.3–9; Cicero, *Fin* III 69.

moral, as opposed to an ordinary, relationship. It is interesting that they contrast it specifically with the limited commitment which is characteristic of friendship.

It seems reasonable to describe the conclusion of the process of social *oikeiōsis* as impartiality, even though there is no distinct word for this in Greek or Latin. For impartiality as that is commonly understood in modern moral theories imposes the requirement that, from the moral point of view, the agent (a) not weight his own interests merely because they are his own and (b) not weight his own particular attachments and commitments merely because they are his own. I am not morally entitled to favour either myself or my mother, just because, outside the moral point of view, I am naturally more attached to my own interests and those of my mother than I am to those of other people.[73] And this is just what the Stoic theory demands of the agent, at the end of the process of social *oikeiōsis*.

Impartiality has seemed to many to be too high a demand for a reasonable morality to make, too much of an alienation from our natural attachments to be a requirement that moral agents can reasonably be expected to respect. The Stoics seem to meet this objection somewhat by their claim that impartiality is the natural outcome of the process of social *oikeiōsis*, a natural development of our instinctive other-concern just as recognizing the moral point of view in the first place is a natural development of our instinctive self-concern. But this is a mere claim. An opponent could object that it lacks psychological plausibility. We possess a long fragment of a later Stoic, Hierocles, which seems to be giving us a psychological mechanism for getting from limited other-concern to impartial moral concern for all; if this is successful, it would meet this type of objection.

> In general each of us is as it were circumscribed by many circles, some smaller, others larger, some enclosing and others enclosed, depending on their differing and unequal relations to one another. The first and nearest circle is the one which a person has drawn around his own mind as around a centre; in this circle is included the body and things got for the body's sake. This circle is the smallest and all but touches its centre. Second, further from the centre and enclosing the first one, is the one in which are placed parents, siblings, wife and children. Third is the one in which are uncles and aunts, grandfathers and grandmothers, siblings' children and also cousins. Next the circle including other relatives. And next the one including fellow-demesmen; then the one of fellow-tribesmen; then the one of fellow-citizens and then in the same way the circle of people from towns nearby and the circle of people of the same ethnic group. The furthest and largest, which includes all the circles, is that of the whole human race.
>
> When this has been considered, it is for the person striving for the proper use of each thing to draw the circles somehow towards the centre and to make efforts to move people from the including circles into the included ones. It is for someone with familial love to [treat] parents and siblings, [wife and children, like oneself; grandfathers, grandmothers, uncles and aunts like parents, siblings' children like one's own, cousins like siblings] and so by the same analogy treat older relatives, male and female, like grandfathers or uncles and aunts; those of one's own age like cousins; and the younger ones like cousins' children.
>
> I have thus briefly given clear instructions as to how to behave to one's

---

[73] Note that the Stoic theory actually stresses the naturalness of this kind of attachment to oneself and one's commitments, as well as the naturalness of being led to take the moral point of view.

relatives, once we have learnt how to treat oneself, parents and siblings, and also wife and children. But there remains the point that we should treat people from the third circle similarly to those in the second, and our [further] relatives similarly to those from the third circle. For the distance in blood, which is rather great, removes some of one's goodwill, but nonetheless we must make efforts towards equating them. We would hit a reasonable mark, if through our own initiative we reduce the distance of this relationship to each person. The basic practical point has been stated; but we should add more, in the ways we address people, calling cousins siblings and uncles and aunts fathers and mothers, and among our further relatives calling some uncles, others nephews and others cousins, extending the use of the name to fit the age they happen to be. For this mode of address would be no mean sign of the efforts we make in each case, and at the same time would stimulate and intensify the drawing-in of the circles we have suggested.

However, now we have got so far, it occurs to me to remember something which is not irrelevant to the division of parents that has been given. We said about that, when we were at the place where we were comparing a mother with a father, that we should allot more affection to one's mother and more respect to one's father. Consistently with this we should now establish that it is fitting to give relatives on one's mother's side greater affection, and those on the father's side greater respect.[74]

Hierocles is admirably clear and specific as to how we are to go about extending our given instinctual sympathies until we care equally for all. But his account is open to obvious criticisms, and if it was the standard Stoic account then it is strikingly weak. We are supposed to call our aunts, for example, 'mother'. This is supposed to make us care more for our aunts than we now do. But first, calling someone your mother does not produce the feelings you have for your mother. As Aristotle points out in his criticisms, in *Politics* II, of Plato's proposals in the *Republic* to abolish the family, if you try to spread family feeling more widely, you don't produce a larger family, you just water down the sentiment. Calling all your aunts 'mother' will then just devalue what you attach to calling someone your mother. However, even if it worked, this might help Plato but would not help the Stoics. For we would still have a version of family feeling. Thinking of my aunts as my mothers brings them closer to me; it does not tend to make me impartial where considering their interests is at stake—rather the opposite. Hierocles' talk of drawing in the circles depicts a situation where I cease to be indifferent to people and regard them more in the way in which I regard people to whom I have particular commitments. But the process is supposed to end up with my having the same attitude to all humans; and plainly what is required is not that I think of all humans as though they were my mothers and fathers. For, obviously, the aim is to think of all humans impartially, giving them all equal concern; whereas my relation to my mother and father is a paradigm of a

[74] Ap. Stobaeus, *Flor* 84.23. This is printed in von Arnim's edition of the Hierocles papyrus as pp. 61.10–62.20. The papyrus also contains some material interesting in this respect. In what is left of col. 9 Hierocles distinguishes kinds of *oikeiōsis* to oneself (*eunoētikē*), to one's kind (*sterktikē*) and to external things (*hairetikē*). In the remains of col. 11 he says that we are a kind of animal which is given to gathering (*sunagelastikon*) and needing others (*deomenon heterou*). This is why we live in cities. We also make friendships easily, by dining with someone or sitting next to them in the theatre. The fragment 52.28 ff (from Stobaeus) adds that we are urged by nature to marry and to form unions.

partial relation, where, because of my commitment to particular people, I favour and cherish them more than others in my relationship with them. Increased partiality to others can never end up with impartiality; Hierocles is producing the opposite of what is required.

It is possible, of course, that Hierocles is assuming that as you draw people from an outer into an inner circle, that circle changes its nature; when lots of women are your mothers, your affection for your mother becomes diluted and spread further. This is suggested by the bizarre proposal at the end that you should love your mother's family (male and female) because you love your mother, and respect your father's family (male and female) because you respect your father. One kind of partiality is being transformed into a different and wider kind. However, this produces a tension in the theory. We pull people from the outer circles into the inner, but at the same time dilute the significance of the inner. But then what was the point of pulling the people in, in the first place? If I start calling my aunts 'mother' but feel for them considerably less than is conventionally appropriate for a mother, then I would seem to be treating them like aunts, and the process has been pointless. It would not be so pointless, of course, if I now treated *my mother* in just the same way; then I would have erased a difference. But note that I would have done it in the opposite way to the way Hierocles recommends: treating a near relative in a less partial way rather than treating a further relative in a more partial way.

It seems that extending one's partial sympathies to more and more people is not the way to reach impartiality. Apart from the implausibility of Hierocles' story, stretched or diluted partiality will never amount to impartiality. Having other-concern for all other humans is different in kind from stretching the particular concerns and commitments I have to particular other people. Thus if Hierocles gives a standard account, the Stoics recognize the importance of impartiality in ethics, but give the wrong mechanism for reaching it. On this point Sidgwick, talking of impartiality as that is required in utilitarianism, seems to be exactly right:

> There are very few persons, however strongly and widely sympathetic, who are so constituted as to feel for the pleasures and pains of mankind generally a degree of sympathy at all commensurate with their concern for wife or children, or lover, or intimate friend: and if any training of the affections is at present possible which would materially alter this proportion in the general distribution of our sympathy, it scarcely seems that such a training is to be recommended as on the whole felicific.[75]

Sidgwick adds that extension of sympathy is actually prone to run *against* the demands of impartiality (which, for him, is of course the demand to increase happiness no matter whose it is—yours, your family's, or the furthest Mysian's).

> [A] man may find that he can best promote the general happiness by working in comparative solitude for ends that he never hopes to see realised, or by working chiefly among and for persons for whom he cannot feel much affection, or by doing what must alienate or grieve those whom he loves best, or must make it necessary for him to dispense with the intimate of human ties. In short, there

[75](1907), p. 502.

seem to be numberless ways in which the dictates of that Rational Benevolence, which as a Utilitarian he is bound absolutely to obey, may conflict with that indulgence of kind affections. . . .[76]

In Stoic theory the rational and impartial demand of morality is not to maximize pleasure; but Sidgwick's point is still relevant. A demand of reason, that one treat all alike, is not the conclusion of a process of extending personal affections: that can result only in weak partiality, not in impartiality. Thus the Stoics (or at least Hierocles) seem to have made a mistake as to the kind of mechanism that their theory requires.

It may be the case, however, that Hierocles is not aspiring to produce a psychological mechanism of a general kind for getting from primitive other-concern to impartiality, but rather taking it for granted that we can do so, and giving us a way of getting us in the right frame of mind to start doing so. Perhaps the picture of drawing in the circles is not meant to be more than a metaphor, to give us the general idea, without giving us an actual mechanism.[77] In that case the Stoics will not be landed with an unsuitable psychological mechanism for getting to impartiality; but neither will they have any defence against the objection that what they claim about social *oikeiōsis* is psychologically implausible.

We do have a very interesting passage from an ancient critic of the Stoics, who charges that their thesis about social *oikeiōsis* leads to implausible and indeed ridiculous results. Like some modern critics of moral theories which require impartiality, he claims that the Stoic theory founders because on this point it is counter-intuitive. He is an anonymous Commentator on Plato's *Theaetetus*, probably from the first century B.C.[78]

> [Socrates] cares for the Cyreneans also [as well as the Athenians] and by the same principle for all humans whatsoever, for we have been familiarized with members of the same species. However, he has been more familiarized with his own fellow-citizens, for familiarization is more or less intense. So if those [the Stoics] who derive justice[79] from familiarization are saying that someone has it equally with himself and with the remotest Mysian, then given this assumption justice is preserved—but it is not agreed that it *is* equal. For this goes against what is evident and our self-awareness.
>
> For familiarization with oneself is natural and non-rational, while familiarization with one's neighbours, while itself natural also, does not happen without reason.
>
> Thus if we condemn the wickedness of some other people, we not only blame them but are also alienated from them; but when people go wrong themselves, they do not accept the opposing claims [?] but cannot come to hate themselves. Thus the familiarization is *not* equal with oneself and with anyone else.
>
> Indeed, even with the parts of ourselves we are not equally familiarized. We do

---

[76] (1907), p. 503.

[77] We could compare the metaphorical pictures of Sun, Line and Cave in the central books of the *Republic*.

[78] Diels and Schubart (1905). See Tarrant (1983) for arguments that the commentator belongs to the first century B.C., and may be Eudorus of Alexandria.

[79] Justice forms a unity with the other virtues, so that the special requirements of justice form part of the moral point of view. The Stoics say very little about what makes justice a special case; see, however, chapter 13, section 3.

not stand in the same relation to an eye and to a finger, not to mention nails and hair, since as regards their loss we are not alienated in the same way, but more or less.

But if they say themselves that the familiarization can be intensified, then there will indeed be benevolence [*philanthrōpia*] but they will be refuted by circumstances [. . .] where it is necessary that only one of them be saved; and even if these circumstances do not arise, they are nonetheless in a position to be refuted.[80]

The author begins by saying that we are not impartial towards all humans; we favour our own fellow-citizens more. (This takes off from Socrates' comment in the dialogue that he cares more for Athenians than for people at Cyrene.) So the initial complaint is that we are in fact partial to some groups of other people, not impartial towards all. The complaint, like all Anonymous' complaints in this passage, rests on 'what is evident', commonsensically obvious.[81] The Stoic response would obviously be that even if we are not *in fact* impartial between our own interests and those of others, we ought to be when this is morally required. This is an adequate response; the theory is only affected if this claim is itself supposed to rest directly on 'what is evident', since it certainly does seem more 'evident' from daily life that people are partial to their own friends and fellow-citizens than that they ought to overcome this when morality is in question. But the Stoics do not think this; they claim that their theory *as a whole* answers to common sense, but this is quite consistent with individual theses in isolation being counter-intuitive.

Anonymous indicates three ways that my concern for myself is ineliminably different from my concern with others. First, personal *oikeiōsis* is 'irrational' while social *oikeiōsis* is not. That is, I do not come to feel concern for myself on the basis of reasons; I just do feel concern for myself- whereas I do not feel concern for others until I have worked out rationally that I should do so. This seems captious, however; the Stoic view is plainly, as the quotation from Plutarch shows, that we have from birth both forms of instinctual concern: concern for myself and my parts and concern for my offspring. We must reason to develop both; it is illegitimate to contrast primitive instinctual self-concern with rationally developed impartial concern for others.

Anonymous may be implying a stronger point, however: that there is something *more* natural and basic about self-concern than about other-concern. I will have self-concern, the thought goes, regardless of what reasons I do or don't have for acting, whereas other-concern rests entirely on recognizing the force of certain reasons; and what doesn't rest on reasons is more basic and powerful as a form of motivation than what does. The Stoics have an obvious reply to this also. Why be so pessimistic about the force of reasoning? In a mature rational adult, do instincts in fact have greater motivational force than reasons, or attitudes based on reasons? Further, even suppose that in a particular agent they do; are they therefore regarded as having more justificatory weight? Faced by a sudden danger to herself and another, an agent may well give in to instinct and preserve herself, while knowing that she should have

---

[80] Col. 5.14–6.29.
[81] Cf. the arguments against impartiality in moral theory in Williams (1976).

rather risked her life to save the other (imagine the example so set up that this is true). But this alone does not justify her action, either to others or to herself.

The second way is this: our attitude to others is different from the attitude we have to ourselves, as is shown by our reaction to wrongdoing. We feel alienated by the wrongdoing of others, but do not similarly hate ourselves for our own wrongdoing. There is surely a correct point here: we know, each in our own case, that we do not in fact regard ourselves as just one among others. It is basic common sense that there is a self-other asymmetry; each of us cannot escape her own particular point of view, and thus each of us has a special perspective on her own actions.

Does this, however, show that my own point of view is always a self-*favouring* point of view? The Stoics can reply that we do not in fact always *excuse* ourselves for wrongdoing in ways that we do not excuse others. And even if we did, would we regard this as a justified reaction? Surely we feel, even before accepting any Stoic theory, that my own point of view as such does not excuse or justify me in what I do. Indeed, we may rather feel that I ought not to favour myself from my own point of view, even if I can. On these first two points Anonymous seems clearly to get the worst of the debate, because he appeals to common sense, but common sense seems not to support him.[82]

Third, Anonymous points out that nature has made familiarization to our own body a matter of degree: hair and nails matter less to me than eyes and fingers do. But if our self-concern naturally turns out to be a matter of degree, then surely our other-concern will be; he is arguing from analogy. Thus familiarization will not serve to produce in the agent *equal* concern for all including herself. The argument is strengthened if we suppose there to be a hidden premise: in the case of self-concern it is clearly *rational* to care less about your hair than about your eyes, so there are at least some cases where it is rational for familiarization to be a matter of degree, and so it seems that it can be rational to care less about human beings as such than about your own family and country. Common sense then supports the claim that it is a rational requirement on a moral theory that you have *some* concern for others, proportionately to your degree of attachment to them, but not that you have *equal* concern for all.

How could the Stoics meet this point? It is stronger than the other two, since common sense seems not to demand *equal* concern for all as a rational requirement on moral choice and action. On the other hand, it does not support favouring of oneself against others either. Does this mean that it favours Anonymous' compromise view? This is a very difficult point to settle. Intuitively, it seems that common sense does not have a definite view on this point; it rejects both extremes without committing itself to a definite alternative. If so, common sense is radically incomplete in this area, and to have a definite view we must turn to one theory or another. Thus the Stoics could claim that, while their theory is not supported by common sense on this point, neither is either of Anonymous' claims: that we favour ourselves, and that we favour others proportionately to our degree of personal attachment to them. So Anonymous can show at most that the Stoic demand for

---

[82] It does not follow, of course, that common sense favours the Stoic theses that Anonymous attacks; but the Stoics do not need this; they only need common sense to support their theory as a whole.

impartiality is not directly supported by common sense, not that it is counter-intuitive and ridiculous.

Finally, Anonymous concedes for the sake of the argument that *oikeiōsis* could be 'intensified'—that is, that we could feel benevolence, a concern broader than that for particular other people. Still, self-concern will win out, he claims, using an example destined to have a long history. In a shipwreck two people struggle for life, but only one can survive. The papyrus gives out here, but we know from another source that the situation is as follows: there are two passengers and only one plank on which to float to safety. Which should have it? The Stoic solution is that the morally worthier one should; and if they are equal in this respect, then they should use a fair random procedure.

> 'If there is only one plank and two shipwrecked men, both of them [Stoic] wise men, would each try to seize it for himself, or would one cede it to the other?' 'One would cede it, and it would go to the one whose life is more of value to himself or his country.' 'What if there is nothing to choose between them on this point?' 'There will be no struggle; one will cede to the other as though the loser by lot or in a game of chance.'[83]

It seems clear that Anonymous' objection was going to be that this is absurd, since in fact anyone in such a position would fight for the plank himself. It would be more interesting, and more in keeping with the stress here on *philanthrōpia*, benevolence, if we had an example of someone wishing to save, not himself but some other particular person to whom he is attached. In a similar modern discussion Bernard Williams has a man saving his wife in a shipwreck.[84] And failure to be impartial is displayed just as much in favouring one's spouse or friends as in favouring oneself. But unfortunately we seem to have the same situation as before: concern for myself versus concern for others. And the Stoics could make the same reply, familiar by now: it is not obvious that we do always favour ourselves in situations like these, and even if we do, we do not regard such partiality as morally justified.

Anonymous may be thought to have more of a point if we remember that *oikeiōsis* is supposed to be a *natural* development. How can something be natural if people do not in fact develop that way? But this objection too can be seen to be without force if we recollect that the Stoics do not think that we find what is natural just by looking to see what people, even most people, do. Nature is a theoretical term in Stoic ethics: the natural life is the life we would ideally live, and the fact that we do not live that way merely shows that we have been corrupted. Anonymous could then retreat to saying that all the same nature must have some empirical footing in Stoic theory; we must originally have acquired the concept empirically and thus there must be some cases where we experience what is natural. However, the Stoics could retort that perhaps our initial experience of what is natural is correct enough to give us the idea, but requires very extensive revision; and since humans tend to be selfish it is our attitude to others that one might expect to be the part of ethics where people most tend to go wrong.

The Stoic theory, then, when properly understood, is not ridiculous or counter-intuitive. Common sense does not favour Anonymous, though it does not demand

---

[83] Cicero, *Off* III 90, from a collection of such problems discussed by the Stoic Hecaton.
[84] In the (1976) article.

the Stoic requirement of impartiality either. The nature of the broader Stoic response to these arguments is fairly clear: they would say that Anonymous is not taking seriously enough the demands of *rationality* in ethics. A rational agent will understand the difference between the requirements of rationality, on the one hand, and on the other, what she wants, or what her own commitments are. So a rational person will see that, though he is bound to love his family more than other people, and care more about himself, this doesn't in itself form a justification for favouring his family or himself.[85]

It is worth noting that Anonymous' objections are very like those that have been brought against Kantianism and utilitarianism; the question is simply whether morality requires impartiality, and the special features of virtue ethics do not come into play. At no point does Anonymous suggest that the Stoics are flouting some formal feature of an ethical theory based on virtue and the agent's final end; he just says that what the Stoics require is too demanding. One might, all the same, reasonably ask how this demand for impartiality can fit into an ethical framework of this kind. The answer lies in the kind of stress the Stoics put on rationality. We are naturally rational beings, and so we will not be satisfied with achieving a final end which is not suitable for rational beings, namely one which involves the requirements of rationality, which will include impartiality. This may sound absurd if it is presented in isolation as a thesis about happiness; but we should remember that happiness in ancient ethics is a vague notion, and we shall see in Part IV the extent to which it can accommodate revisions of our everyday priorities. Further, the Stoic demand is essentially no different from the demand made by some modern versions of utilitarianism. I start from seeking my own pleasure (happiness, welfare). Once I realize that I should do so rationally, I am led to maximize it; and once I take this step I am led by recognizing the requirements of rationality to see that I should maximize pleasure (happiness, welfare) whether it is mine or not. Following up the requirements of rationality leads me to see that my own viewpoint has no rational claim on me just because it is mine.[86]

Thus the Stoic demand, whether ultimately a plausible one or not, is not outrageous; other moral theories make the same demand. It is not an obviously disastrous move in a eudaimonistic ethics; at least other kinds of theories based on the agent's pleasure (happiness, welfare) make the same demand. It does not rest on special features of Stoicism: it rests on strong demands on rationality which are also evident in other kinds of theory. In particular it does not rest on the Stoic view that the universe is an ordered whole of which we are parts; since, as we have seen, this is not a principle from which ethical theses are derived. Further, once the Stoic position about impartiality had been introduced, it was seen as compelling. We find

---

[85] Given that the Stoics, like all the other ancient schools, think that being a moral person is achieving one's own good, we can see why Epictetus says that '[Zeus] has set up a rational creature's nature in such a way that it cannot achieve any of its own goods without contributing to the common benefit. Thus doing everything for one's own sake becomes no longer anti-social'. (*Disc* II 19, 13–14. Cf. III 24, 11.) Achieving the good of all as one does if one acts impartially, just is achieving your own good properly understood.

[86] This line of thought is clear in the work of Peter Singer. There are further problems with utilitarianism, pointed out by Bradley and by Bernard Williams: pursuing pleasure cannot possibly give shape to a life or allow the proper place in an agent's life to his commitments.

later version of Aristotelian ethics, such as those of Arius and Antiochus, taking it over, although with some discomfort, because it was seen as something which a moral theory now had to accommodate.[87]

Another respect in which the Stoics differ strikingly from Aristotle is in having a theory in which self-concern and other-concern are two distinct sources of human behaviour, neither developing from the other. *Oikeiōsis* is a disjunctive notion: it covers the rational development of both self- and other-concern. What these have in common is simply that they are both cases of rational development of the agent's initially narrow, instinctive attitude to a wider and rationally based concern.[88]

Sometimes the Stoic theory is presented as though this were not really the case. Personal *oikeiōsis* is a process in which I develop as a rational being. This can be presented as a development in my view of myself; I start by thinking of myself as a being with desires, attachments and so on, and as I progress in ability to reason I come to think of myself as, or to identify myself as, a rational being. But to do this is just to adopt the impartial standpoint, from which my personal concerns matter no more than anyone else's. So personal *oikeiōsis* will get me to the impartial viewpoint, and social *oikeiōsis* will just be a matter of applying this to others. This is a venerable interpretation; we can find it at the basis of Antiochus' criticisms of the Stoics in Cicero's *de Finibus* 4, and several modern interpreters have adopted it.[89] Nonetheless it is wrong.[90] Our sources do not characterize personal *oikeiōsis* in this way; it is described as a development in which one moves from valuing one kind of thing (natural advantages, which are indifferent) to valuing a distinctively different kind of thing (virtue) and to acting on reasons in a way according with this. Further, this view of the relation of personal to social *oikeiōsis* gives the latter hardly anything to do; all the work would be done by the former, and it would seem a mystery why the Stoics had a two-source rather than a one-source view. In fact, its two-source form is what is distinctive about Stoic *oikeiōsis*.

It could be objected that this creates a problem for the Stoics given that they put such heavy stress on the developmental nature of their account, particularly their appeal to the behaviour of newborn humans and animals.[91] For clearly the behaviour of newborns reveals self-concern; other-concern appears later in the animal's development—much later in the case of humans. Thus if we lay weight on what is revealed at the start of the development, we would be inclined to conclude that self-love is primary, not just chronologically but in some deeper sense. The Stoics, however, seem committed both to emphasising 'the cradle argument',[92] the argument that the behaviour of newborns and the young is important for discovering what is

---

[87] These issues are also discussed in Annas (1992e).

[88] I do not think that the passage at Epictetus I19, 11–15 contradicts this (see n. 85). What the passage says, is that self-concern properly understood is compatible with other-concern, not that other-concern is just an expanded form of self-concern.

[89] See Kerferd (1972), Engberg-Pedersen (1986) and (1991). It is also the interpretation of Long and Sedley in (1987). See also Whitlock Blundell (1990).

[90] See the articles by N. White, especially (1978a).

[91] This objection has been forcefully urged by Inwood. See also Whitlock Blundell (1990).

[92] See Brunschwig (1986).

natural, and to the claim that what appears only late in the development, namely other-concern, is as fundamental as what appears at the beginning.

This need not be a serious problem, however. The Stoics are committed to the thesis that we have two distinct *instinctual* sources of behaviour, which develop and change as we learn to reason but are not themselves created by reason. One of these is apparent at birth, the other not until later; but the question is not just when it appears, but what its nature is when it does appear. If it is, when it appears, not learned and dependent on reason, but instinctual, then it must have been present at birth. Of course there is some awkwardness in saying, as the Stoics do, that at birth we have affection for our offspring; but Stoic theses are often superficially awkward and even paradoxical. There is nothing deeply problematic about the thought that the instinctual basis of our behaviour, which is developed by reason and results in a broadening of the initially narrow sympathy, takes two fundamentally different forms. Other-concern does not appear till later than self-concern, and so its development is complicated right from the beginning by the fact that self-concern has already developed in rational ways. Since properly developed self-concern will lead to virtuous action and then virtuous dispositions, concern for others must come in as part of personal *oikeiōsis*. This is, however, based on reasons, and is quite consistent with its being true that we feel the purest instinctual form of other-concern for our offspring when we have them. Personal and social *oikeiōsis* can be presented as theoretically different developments without its being true that they could develop separately at different times in the same individual.

Stoic theory about other-concern thus differs radically from Aristotelian in two ways. It does so in its view of the scope of other-concern, its insistence on progression to completely impartial concern for all humans just as such, instead of stopping with a form of *philia* or commitment to particular other people. And it does so also in its view of other-concern, its insistence that its source is distinct from the source of self-concern right from the start and not just when it becomes apparent.[93]

3. *The Aristotelian Response*

From the Hellenistic period we have two extensive ethical texts of great interest, hybrid theories in which Aristotelian and Stoic elements are combined. As already stated, I think that it is most fruitful to see these hybrids not as unintelligent pastings-together of diverse ideas but rather as the deliberate complication of theories in order to defend them against problems raised for them by other theories. In the case of both these theories we can see a restatement, in terms of an adapted version of Stoic *oikeiōsis*, of the Aristotelian idea that other-concern can be seen as developing from self-concern. Examining this adaptation, its advantages and some of

---

[93] This does not conflict with Stoic eudaimonism. When I reflect on my final end, and revise it in accordance with Stoic priorities, what I have to work on is the ways in which I have rationally developed my initial endowment of these two kinds of instinct. If I am, for example, very selfish, this is a fault in my rational development, not in my initial endowment. The disjunctive nature of *oikeiōsis* does not threaten the unity of my final end.

the strains it produces, can help us understand the Stoic-Aristotelian debate about other-concern from which these hybrid theories emerge.

One of these theories is Antiochus' system of ethics in Cicero's *De Finibus* V.[94] The other is the long account of 'the ethics of Aristotle and the other Peripatetics' in Stobaeus' *Ecl* II, 116–152, plausibly attributed to Arius Didymus, the Emperor Augustus' court philosopher.[95] There is a large difference between Antiochus and Arius. Antiochus is professedly giving us his own theory, creatively synthesizing Stoic and Aristotelian material to produce something distinctive. Of course, he presents it as the tradition of the 'Old Academy' and claims that it is the original form of the theory that we find fragmented in Aristotle, the Stoics and others.[96] But this historical claim is not really in tension with the idea that the theory is his own; Antiochus' claim is that he has produced a theory which does justice to the best aspects of various theories, while avoiding their faults, and that precisely in doing this he has rediscovered the original tradition from which all the schools represent a falling away. Arius, on the other hand, is not reconstructing a tradition common to Aristotle and the Stoics, but claiming to tell us what Aristotelian ethics are- in a very 'updated' and stoicised framework.

Antiochus is the easier case, since he is claiming to rediscover a tradition common to Aristotle and the Stoics. Thus although his ethical theory is Aristotelian in spirit, his account is not a serious attempt to interpret Aristotle alone.

Antiochus begins his account of ethical development[97] with a resoundingly uncompromising statement:

> Every living thing loves itself, and as soon as it is born acts so as to preserve itself, since this is the first impulse given to it by nature for maintaining all of its life: to preserve itself and to be so affected as to be best affected in accordance with nature.[98]

Human development, including ethical development, is not a progression from self-love to some other motive, but rather a progression within self-love to more and more reflective and conscious views of the self. A human being comes to have an ever better conception of what it is to be a human being—which Antiochus interprets as a conception of himself as a rational being.

---

[94] On this, and on Antiochus, see chapter 6, with the notes.

[95] While I shall refer to the author as 'Arius', it is of course possible that Arius is retailing or paraphrasing another author. On the likelihood of a Peripatetic source for Arius, see Moraux (1973), pp. 273–74, 349–50 and Hahm (1990). But Arius' own attitude is not irrelevant. As Moraux stresses, he was surely aware of Andronicus' new edition of Aristotle, and was a friend of Andronicus' pupil Xenarchus, whose approach to Aristotle's texts was quite different and much more 'modern'. See Alexander of Aphrodisias, *de An* II 150–153, esp. 151.3–18 for Xenarchus and Boethus appealing to *NE* IX 8 when explaining Aristotle's views in terms of *oikeiōsis* and the *protōn oikeion*. This sort of scholarly, text-based activity is not very different from modern journal articles on Aristotle; it is very different from Arius, whose approach remains pre-Andronicus. (On the other hand, it is post-Critolaus: a definition rejected at 126.14–16 is that of Critolaus [cf. 46.10–13].)

[96] Cf. *Fin* V 72–4. Different schools like those of Aristotle, Theophrastus, Erillus, Ariston and others, he claims, have taken and privileged parts of the system; the Stoics indeed have taken it over wholesale, but have changed the terminology.

[97] This is preceded by an argument to eliminate most candidates for being our final end. The argument, based on Carneades, does not fit the rest of Antiochus' procedure; see chapter 6, p. 182 and n. 10.

[98] *Fin* V 24.

It is interesting that Antiochus feels the need to defend this starting point; although it is obvious and undeniable, he says, that every living creature loves itself, nevertheless this should also be demonstrated.[99] He does this by claiming that it is unintelligible to claim that living creatures can hate themselves. Self-hatred would be a state of avoiding everything good for one and seeking out what is bad and destructive; and this cannot be coherently carried out. What we call self-hatred is really only a case of someone unbalanced by a particular motive, and even this would not be coherent unless the person loved himself enough to care about the success or failure of the particular project. Further, Antiochus claims, it is equally unintelligible to claim that someone could be indifferent to their own state. And it is also absurd to think that we love ourselves for the sake of some property or state of ourselves; we can imagine loving virtue, or a friend, for some ulterior reason, but it is unintelligible to imagine myself loving myself for some ulterior reason. It is clear from all these arguments from unintelligibility that by self-love Antiochus means, not self-concern as that contrasts with other-concern, but simply a concern that we cannot but show in staying alive, doing actions and so on. And indeed he goes on to illustrate self-love by our fear of death and non-existence.

Since self-love is understood so broadly, it is not surprising that Antiochus has little difficulty in showing that it develops into love of and concern for whatever we find our nature to be. Thus we mature, on his account, from concern for physical well-being to concern for mental and ultimately for ethical well-being (though, since the theory is Aristotelian in spirit, we retain a concern for physical well-being and other kinds of good as well). The bulk of Antiochus' account of ethical development is devoted to showing how natural human development leads us to value virtue (though not only virtue) for its own sake. In this he is adopting the Stoic developmental story. He does not, however, take over their distinction of personal from social *oikeiōsis*. He concentrates on the agent's development of virtue, and then, when he gets to the virtue of justice, points out that this will require extension of our sympathies to all humans so as to be impartial between their interests and ours.[100] At this point he rapidly goes through the claim that parents' affection for the children gives us the starting point from which we extend our sympathies to family, friends, fellow-citizens and ultimately to all humans. He at once adds that, although this is required by justice in particular, it underlies all the virtues, since they are reciprocal and all involve other-concerned motivation. Thus social *oikeiōsis* comes in rather abruptly when the agent has reached the point of valuing virtue for itself. Antiochus seems to think of personal *oikeiōsis* as a process of coming to think of oneself as a rational being, and social *oikeiōsis* as merely an application of this viewpoint to the case of considering others.[101]

Antiochus has little trouble showing that the ethical agent will be other-concerned, since he has begun with such a broad and capacious notion of self-concern. If self-concern is shown in living a human life (just as a plant shows self-concern for living a plant life) then, given that it is uncontroversial that normal human life shows *some* other-concern, Antiochus will have no trouble accounting

---

[99] *Fin* V 27 ff.

[100] *Fin* V 65 ff.

[101] This is what I argued to be a misinterpretation of the Stoic theory; see above, second section.

for this. The awkward questions come rather when we ask *how much* other-concern Antiochus feels entitled to on the basis of his broad notion of self-concern. Why should Antiochus' agent have sufficient other-concern, for example, to override concern for his own money? or still more his own life? (It is clear that these questions are related to questions we have already seen arise about the place of virtue in Antiochean happiness.) Why in particular should self-love, however broadly understood, lead the agent to the *impartiality* that justice, and perhaps all the virtues, require? Antiochus never argues for this crucial point. Yet this is an important gap, given that he is so insistent that it is self-love that we start from, not a combination of self- and other-concern.

Antiochus' theory is Aristotelian in wanting to start from self-love, and to produce a theory which is formally self-concerned throughout. He is, however, like Aristotle, not concerned to reduce other-concern to self-concern; the agent is formally self-concerned, but the developed moral agent will not be motivated by self-concern—rather, he will be motivated by virtue. However, by offering a developmental account Antiochus forces us to ask a question to which he has no answer, namely, how he can show that self-love will develop into *enough* other-concern to produce an agent who is genuinely virtuous. Appealing to natural sympathies will not suffice; this shows us what we have to start with, but does not on its own show how to get to what is sufficient for morality. Moreover, Antiochus actually makes it harder for himself than it is for Aristotle to do this, since he takes over the Stoic demand that justice requires the agent to be impartial between her own interests and those of any others- probably because by now this was regarded as something a moral theory ought to do. But it is a tall order to get this much out of the natural development of self-concern. We have seen that Antiochus' picture of natural human development from the self-centred to the ethical is an intuitively acceptable one. But when we consider that he accepts extreme Stoic demands on the ethical, we can see that extreme other-concern can only be seen as developed from self-concern at a price—a vague and unrigorous notion of self-concern at the start. The main reason why Antiochus finds his own notion of self-love so obvious, and its alternatives so unintelligible, is that his starting point of self-love contains whatever is needed for ethical development, even when that turns out to require impartial other-concern for all.

Antiochus makes his view on this point uninteresting by making things too easy for himself. Nonetheless, his theory is interesting in other ways, not least the way in which he sees an Aristotelian kind of theory as demanding a single-source developmental account, rejecting the Stoic picture of self- and other-concern as equally basic and co-ordinate.

Arius is more problematic; we find what claims to be a distinctively Aristotelian ethical theory, which nonetheless uses a great deal of distinctively Stoic framework. In particular, the notions of our final end and happiness, which Aristotle in the *Nicomachean Ethics* introduces by a discussion of human 'function' and a careful examination of various common beliefs about the matter, are in Arius introduced by a long passage which develops the notion of *oikeiōsis*. Scholars have tended to react to this point by regarding the passage as a synthesis of the two different theories, one that is muddled or mechanical because the two theories are on the face of it so different; Arius has been seen as a scissors-and-paste compiler with a confused and unoriginal mind.[102] Two monographs[103] introduced the exciting idea that the Stoic-looking material, particularly *oikeiōsis*, was not originally Stoic at all, but was developed by Theophrastus. Arius would then be giving us not a later conflation but a development of originally Aristotelian ideas, from which the Stoics had borrowed. The exciting thesis was, however, definitively exploded,[104] and it is now generally accepted that *oikeiōsis*, and several other concepts prominent in the passage, are Stoic in origin; what we have is a recasting of Aristotelian ideas in a Stoic mould.[105]

This *might*, of course, merely be a matter of intellectual fashion. By the first century B.C., the most plausible date for this passage, the Stoics seem to have dominated ethical discussion, and it may be that even an author professing to give a straightforward account of another theory would find it congenial to do so in terms of *oikeiōsis*.[106] It would, however, be preferable to find a philosophical reason for this procedure, and we can do this if we read the passage as an Aristotelian response to the Stoics on both the sources and the limits of other-concern. The Stoics, as we have seen, rejected Aristotle's stopping at *philia*, insisting rather that rational development of other-concern will not stop until the agent can, from the rational point of view, be impartial between herself and any other rational human being whatsoever. And they reject the idea that other-concern is a special developed sort of self-concern; rather self- and other-concern are distinct instinctual sources of human behaviour.[107]

When in the Arius passage we find a restatement of Aristotelian views in a Stoic framework, it is plausible to see this as an Aristotelian response to Stoic theory. In an obvious way this shows that Aristotelians have given up some things found in Aristotle himself; they have, for example, given up talking of moral psychology in terms of Aristotle's *orexis* (desire) and gone over to the Stoic psychology in terms of *hormē* (impulse).[108] They have given up talking as Aristotle does of the difference

[102] See Diels (1958), pp. 71–72; and cf. Zeller (1961), Teil III Abteilung 1, pp. 635–39.

[103] Von Arnim (1926), Dirlmeier (1937).

[104] By Pohlenz (1940). Pohlenz has been followed on this by Brink (1956) and Moraux (1973), pp. 316–444, and to some extent by Giusta (1964–7). Surveys of the scholarly discussion can be found in Giusta, pp. 74–84, Moraux, pp. 333–50, Görgemanns (1983), pp. 166–68.

[105] See Magnaldi (1991), however, for a defence of the position that there was an original Peripatetic *oikeiōsis*-theory which developed alongside the Stoic version. In her view it is a mistake to find Stoic influence in the Arius passage or *Fin* V; but she does not carefully distinguish mechanical transference of Stoic views from intellectual response to Stoic arguments.

[106] This may seem surprising to us. But Hermarchus, an early Epicurean, uses *oikeiōsis* for a natural affinity between humans in Epicurean social theory (see Porphyry, *Abst* I 7–12, esp. 7); on this see Vander Waerdt (1988). Arius in his introduction to ethics introduces the notion of a *hupotelis* or 'pre-end', an idea which he says older philosophers had, though they lacked the word (see chapter 1, p. 39), and explains this allegedly universal ethical notion by an *oikeiōsis*-story (47.12–48.5). The Anonymous Commentator on the *Theaetetus* calls *oikeiōsis* commonplace and regards Socrates and the Sophists as its originators (col. 7, 20–25).

[107] It is likely that the Stoics were responding to Aristotle's ethical works, though of course we do not know the exact form they found them in; our *Nicomachean Ethics* and the other ethical works are a later production probably of Andronicus' editorial work. For a very exaggerated claim that Aristotle's works were not well known to or a major concern of the Stoics, see Sandbach (1985). By Arius' time it is clear that in ethical philosophy both positions were well known and regarded as alternatives.

[108] The author of the *MM* tends to talk in terms of *hormē* rather than of *orexis*, so possibly there is

between a just act and a just act performed as a just person would do it, and started talking instead of the Stoic distinction between *kathēkon* and *katorthōma*.[109] Similarly, the Arius passage begins with the Aristotelian point that *ēthos* (character) derives from *ethos* (habituation), because we need to complete and perfect what nature gives us as a starting point, but develops this in Stoic fashion, telling a developmental story which uses the Stoic notion of *oikeiōsis*. However, adopting your opponents' terminology need not be a sign that you have adopted their conclusions. Indeed, an effective way to meet an opponent is precisely to neutralize the point that formed an objection to you by taking it over yourself, showing that you can make the alleged objection part of your own position. Rather than repeating your own position in the original terms, you go on to show that you can absorb the apparently troublesome part of your opponents' position without being forced to their conclusions. Thus you come out one step ahead of the opposition rather than one step behind. And, in an intellectual atmosphere where debate tends to start from your opponents' premises, this is an intelligent way to proceed, critical rather than merely defensive.[110] The hybrid nature of the Arius passage can thus be seen as an expression of critical engagement and synthesis, a deliberate attempt to co-opt the (probably dominant) Stoic model in the interests of a non-Stoic conclusion.

The passage opens with the claim, probably supposed to be familiar from Aristotle, that character comes from habituation (*ēthos* from *ethos*), since it is habits and correct upbringing which bring to completion the starting points and 'seeds' which we have from nature.[111] Only humans can do this, since it is a development produced by reason, unlike the 'necessity' which can habituate other animals; human souls have a rational as well as an irrational aspect. The distinction is Aristotelian, though developed in some non-Aristotelian terminology,[112] and with a certain amount of confusion.[113] It is through our reason that we share in what is immortal

---

not much in this change. However, it made clearer the differences between Aristotelian and Stoic views on the emotions, for example.

[109] See chapter 2, pp. 96ff.

[110] There are obvious parallels in the way that modern ethical debate develops, in a similar intellectual atmosphere, where everyone is very conscious that there are several alternative going theories. For example, utilitarianism has moved from a crude rejection of the notion of rights, on the grounds that there is no obvious utilitarian basis for them, to a more sophisticated position which includes the recognition of rights, together with a utilitarian analysis of them which salvages as much of the notion of rights as is compatible with a utilitarian analysis. This strengthens the utilitarian position; for now the rights theorist cannot merely object that the utilitarian ignores rights, but must find a new and more subtle argument, to show that utilitarians cannot *really* account for rights, though they think they can. There are many other obvious parallels in the development of ethical debates. I have developed this aspect of the Arius passage, as an Aristotelian reply to Stoic theory, in Annas (1990a). See also S. White (forthcoming).

[111] 116.21–117.2. Cf. *NE* 1103 a 17–25, *EE* 1220 a 39–b 2, *MM* 1186 a 1. The claim about 'seeds' recalls Aristotle's *Hist An* 588 a 31–33, and Antiochus' similar claims; see chapter 6 n. 12.

[112] 117.2–118.6. Cf. *NE* 1102 a 26–32, 1139 a 3–15, 1103 a 3–7; *EE* 1221 b 27–31; *MM* 1185 b 3–13, 1196 b 15–17. The irrational part of the soul is called *hormētikon*, a Stoic term; and it is further divided in a Platonic-sounding way into the *epithumētikon* and the *thumikon*.

[113] Arius distinguishes a theoretical and a deliberative aspect of our rational side; but then a distinction between the excellences of the rational and irrational parts is apparently lined up with the distinction between theory (and knowledge) and action (the sentence, 117.18–118.4, is admittedly incomplete and may be corrupt).

and divine, though it is by reason that we strive for the perfection or completion not only of our reason but also of what is mortal and bodily in us.[114]

A human first of all 'strives to exist, since he is familiarized with himself'; and hence he is duly pleased by things that accord with his nature, and displeased by those that are contrary to it. Hence he goes for health, pleasure[115] and living, since these are natural, hence choiceworthy and good; and shuns illness, pain and destruction, since these are unnatural, hence to be avoided, and bad. For both our bodies and souls are 'dear' or 'friendly' (*philon*; we have no analogous idiom in English) to us, and so are their potentialities and activities. Hence the origins of impulse (*hormē*), due action (*kathēkon*) and of virtue are to be found in our striving to preserve ourselves. Both the ideas and the terminology here are Stoic, and their development is described in a familiar Stoic way: we start by going for natural advantages, and work out how to do this rationally, i.e., by following reasons. So the beginnings of right action come from concern to obtain natural advantages, and so do the beginnings of virtue, which is explained as being a correct and systematic understanding resulting in correct choice of natural advantages; these are the sphere and the object of virtuous and vicious actions. We have here recognizably the start of an account of Stoic personal *oikeiōsis*.[116]

Arius then insists that, as he will shortly demonstrate, nearly the whole of the Aristotelian system comes from 'these things'; so we expect a continuous account, and are somewhat surprised to find that now what appears to be social *oikeiōsis* breaks in, and we get an account[117] which is very similar to the standard Stoic account of *social oikeiōsis*. We love our own offspring, Arius says, and love them not, or not just, because of the advantages they bring, but for their own sake. (This is indicated by the fact, for example, that we make provision for our children when we die, caring about their welfare even when it will be of no concern to us.)

> But if children are thus loved in accordance with what is choiceworthy for its own sake[118] then necessarily parents also will meet with friendship [*philia*] for their own sakes, and brothers, and the woman who shares one's bed, and relations and other relatives [*oikeioi*] and fellow-citizens; for we have from nature some forms of familiarization towards them also, since human beings are friendly and social creatures. It is not relevant whether some of the friendships chance to be remote and others close at hand to us; each is choiceworthy[119] for its own sake and not just for its usefulness. But if friendship towards one's fellow-citizens is

[114] 118. 6–11. Aristotle's notorious claims about 'immortalizing ourselves' by our employment of reason in *NE* X, 1177 b 31–34, have here been firmly brought down to earth; the employment of reason is not something distinct from our normal activities that involve the body. Cf. Diogenes VII 130: the Stoic view is that of the three lives which are *theorētikon, praktikon* and *logikon*, one should prefer the third, since reason makes us suitable for both theory and action.

[115] Pleasure is a non-Stoic insertion; the Stoics did not consider pleasure to be a natural advantage, but a mere supervention, if that (cf. Diogenes VII 86); but Aristotle's theory gives it a more positive role (though the Arius passage does not contain anything corresponding to either passage on pleasure in the *Nicomachean Ethics*).

[116] 118.11–119.21.

[117] From 119.22–122.7

[118] This is actually a conjecture of Wachsmuth's: *to di'hauth'haireton* for the nonsensical *to authaireton*. There is a parallel at 126.13.

[119] Heeren's conjecture, *hairetēn* for *aretēn*.

choiceworthy for its own sake, necessarily it must be so with friendship towards the fellow-members of one's ethnic group and tribe, and hence with friendship towards all human beings. And indeed all those who save another person are so disposed towards their neighbours, so that they act for the most part not in response to their merit,[120] but in accordance with what is choiceworthy for its own sake. For who, seeing a human being being overcome by a wild beast, would not rescue him, if they could? Who would not show the way to someone who has lost the way? Who would not supply someone perishing from want? Who, finding a spring in a waterless desert, would not point it out by signs to those travelling the same road? Who does not set great store by a good reputation after their death? Who is not repelled by utterances like these, as being contrary to human nature: 'When I am dead, may the earth be mingled with fire' and 'I don't care; I'm all right'. It is obvious, therefore, that we have a natural goodwill and friendship towards everyone, which clearly indicates that it is choiceworthy for its own sake, and also in accordance with reason. For 'there is one race of men and one of gods, and both have their breath from a single mother nature' [Pindar, *Nemean* VI 1, 2.]. But although we have a common love of mankind, what is choiceworthy for its own sake is much more obvious in the relation towards friends that we see regularly.[121]

Here is the standard Stoic model: starting from limited other-concern we move outwards to concern for all humans just as such. Indeed, the way in which this is claimed arguably goes beyond what the Stoics say, and comes close to some Kantian formulations.

The Stoics say only that the agent is ultimately familiarized to the furthest Mysian; the passage here describes our relations to those we do not personally care for, in terms of what is 'choiceworthy for its own sake'. What does this mean? In the use of the notion of choice here, the emphasis is not on the agent's picking and choosing, but on the idea that choice is a response to a certain kind of *value*: something choiceworthy for its own sake is valuable for its own sake and not for some other reason. So, the passage claims, we can love our children, spouse and so on, but we can also come to value them for themselves, that is, come to have an impartial or disinterested concern for them. And we can go on to have this disinterested concern for others whom we didn't love personally to begin with— strangers on a journey, for example. Twice Arius stresses that we come to have this disinterested concern for all humans.

Most interesting is the sentence about saving others, since there we find the claim that in our relations with others we act in recognition of a value which is not only not dependent on whether we have a personal attachment to them, but is also not dependent on their worth or merit. Here we come closest to the view which we find in its definitive form in Kant, namely that people are 'ends in themselves', have a value which is distinctively different from other kinds of values, and which we recognize in acting morally. We get close; but we are, admittedly, not quite there. When Arius says that we do not act in response to these people's merit, he means that we do not respond to these people's social standing, or usefulness to us, but not that we respond to a value that people embody regardless of their stage of moral

---

[120] Accepting *pros axian*, with Usener and Wachsmuth, for the manuscript's corrupt *tas praxeis*.
[121] 120. 8-121.25.

achievement. We don't find Kant's insistence on the value of the agent purely as autonomous rational moral agent, whether in fact morally good or bad. Further, Arius' language does not quite imply, though it borders on it, that it is the people themselves who embody the relevant value; mostly he talks of acting towards people in accordance with what is choiceworthy in itself.[122] Nonetheless, we have a different and striking formulation of the impartiality requirement. If I am familiarized equally to all humans, then from this point of view, the moral point of view, I must regard all humans as embodying a distinct kind of value which I respond to when I act morally towards them. This demand, that moral action be seen as a response to a certain kind of value, something's being 'choiceworthy in itself', is natural if action is seen as always being a response to something perceived as good in some way. It is interesting that this teleological account of moral action results in the most Kantian—sounding passage in ancient ethics. And it is still more interesting, of course, that it occurs in a restatement of *Aristotelian* ethics.

We now return to personal *oikeiōsis*, via a bridging passage which explains what has been done. We have shown, Arius says, that friends are choiceworthy for their own sake; now friends are the greatest of external goods, so we have shown that external goods are choiceworthy for their own sake. But if this is so, with how much more force will this apply to the other kinds of goods—goods of the body and goods of the soul. We find the goods of the body choiceworthy for their own sake—goods such as health, strength and beauty; if so, *a fortiori* we find the goods of the soul choiceworthy for their own sake, without an eye to advantage. And thus, by way of the division of goods into external, those of the body and those of the soul, which was a standard Peripatetic distinction, we return to the Stoic story of personal *oikeiōsis*, though the final part, where the agent comes to care for virtue, as a disposition of rational choice, more than for the results of rational choosing, is expressed somewhat awkwardly. The author points out in several ways that, just from the fact that goods of the soul are more choiceworthy than goods of the body (and these more choiceworthy than external goods) one could conclude that the virtues, which are the goods of the soul, are more worth having than other goods.[123] But there is also a more Stoic-influenced account of how the agent comes to give priority to virtue:

> Virtue makes its entrance, as we have demonstrated, from bodily and external goods; but it turns towards itself and contemplates that it itself is much more something in accordance with nature than the bodily virtues, and is familiarized with itself as with something choiceworthy for itself, and is even more familiarized with itself than with the bodily virtues. So the virtues of the soul are far more valuable.[124]

---

[122] The opening sentences of the passage are the ones that come closest to saying that acting towards someone in accordance with what is choiceworthy for its own sake implies acting towards them as though they were choiceworthy for their own sake.

[123] 124.1–125.13. The author begins this section awkwardly by saying, 'However, one could work this out also from what we said earlier.' There are also some very strained analogies between the different kinds of good; for suspicions that this section is an interpolation, see Moraux (1973), pp. 325–27, Görgemanns (1983), pp. 179–81.

[124] 123.21–27.

Personal *oikeiōsis* ends with the agent identifying with the viewpoint of morality, a stage made vivid here by the personification of virtue as a kind of agent being familiarized with itself.

The conclusion[125] stresses that, although the process has culminated in the agent's concern for herself as a rational, virtuous being, virtue and the exercise of rationality are not the agent's only aims. Rather, we have the Aristotelian conclusion that the agent will also regard bodily excellences and external goods like friends as choiceworthy for their own sake. Arius leans heavily on the Peripatetic distinction of three kinds of good to make clear that the conclusion is not the Stoic one, that virtue is sufficient for happiness, but rather the Aristotelian one, that virtue is necessary but not sufficient, requiring other goods as well. Virtue is greatly superior to these goods;[126] happiness is not a combination of these goods, but rather an active life of virtue which uses or acts on these goods.[127] Happiness is not just good things, but a life of actions, so that the other kinds of goods do not make for happiness on their own, but only as put to service by virtue. But despite the superiority of virtue the other goods are genuine goods, choiceworthy for their own sake, and required for happiness. They are not, as the Stoics would have it, merely preferred indifferents, not straightforwardly comparable with virtue.

We can see that Stoic *oikeiōsis* has been considerably recast. For the Stoics, personal and social *oikeiōsis* are distinct and co-ordinate; neither develops as part of the other. But here we find that social *oikeiōsis* has been inserted into the process of personal *oikeiōsis*. Development of concern for oneself results in concern for oneself as a rational being, but this includes concern for one's friends and other external goods.

One reason for this is obvious enough. This passage has been recast in order to fit the Peripatetic distinction of three kinds of good (external, of the body, of the soul), and this in turn has clearly been done in order that the result will be an Aristotelian, rather than a Stoic, account of the place of virtue in happiness. An Aristotelian account of happiness must make room for all three kinds of good as needed for the agent's happiness, diverging sharply from the Stoics on this score. However, on its own this would provide a merely mechanical kind of reason for the way in which the two kinds of Stoic *oikeiōsis* are combined in this passage; for the desired result could be produced in other and probably more elegant ways. We can get a better insight into what has happened if we remember to see the passage in the context of the contrast we have seen between Aristotle's *Nicomachean Ethics* account of other-concern as a special kind of developed self-concern, and the Stoic account of self- and other-concern as having two distinct bases.

The Arius passage is best interpreted as a sustained attempt to develop Aristotle's ethics from a starting point of self-love, as indicated in *Nicomachean Ethics* IX 8. We have already seen that Antiochus thinks it appropriate to bring in self-love as the starting point of the development which ends in virtuous and other-concerned behaviour, in an Aristotelian spirit; but he is not offering an interpreta-

---

[125] 125.14–128.9.
[126] 126.12–14.
[127] 126.12–127.2.

tion of Aristotelian ethics in particular, but rather 'discovering the tradition' behind several theories. The Arius passage presents itself as an account of Aristotelian ethics, and this may make it appear strange that it does not explicitly start from self-love. We should remember, however, how strained Aristotle's claim was found that other-concern is really a developed form of self-concern.[128] Even Antiochus, who starts his developmental account from self-concern, took that in a broad and arguably contentless way so as to be able to end up with extreme other-concern. And in the Arius passage we find that Aristotle's own terms have been replaced by a developmental account which is taken from the Stoic account of *oikeiōsis*, but adapted so that social *oikeiōsis*, developing concern for others, is made a part of personal *oikeiōsis*, developing self-concern. The transition is ingenious, but despite what looks to us like its complexity, it is made very simply, by interpreting other-concern as concern for one of the kinds of good that self-concern focusses on.

There are three striking external indications that this recast developmental story is explicitly meant to replace Aristotle's *Nicomachean Ethics* IX 8 story about developing self-love. First, when we find the summary of Aristotelian ideas on *philia* in the second half of the Arius passage, we find a small shrivelled remnant[129] of the books on friendship in the *Ethics*. Six types of friendship are listed, namely those appropriate to foreigners, relations and so on; their different bases are listed, together with the claim, from the *Ethics*, that all friendship is for one of the three ends of the fine, the pleasant or the advantageous. However, in place of any consideration of the basis of friendship in one's relation to oneself, we find the following: 'The first friendship, as we said, is that towards oneself, the second towards one's parents,[130] then in turn towards others, relatives and strangers.' This is clearly a reference to the initial *oikeiōsis* passage, and referring to it as to an account of self-love indicates that the account of self-love has been transferred from the account of friendship to become, in expanded form, the introduction to the ethics as a whole, in the form of an adapted developmental account. It is especially notable that the later passage refers to the earlier one as an account of self-love (which it was not explicitly called there). It even uses this to create a highly artificial application of the doctrine of the mean, namely that we should avoid the extreme in friendship towards ourselves, for this carries the reproach of self-lovingness (*philautia*), and the deficiency in friendship towards others, for this carries the reproach of stinginess (*pheidōlia*).[131] This, the one clear reference back in the passage to the first part from the much more doxographical second part, indicates clearly that self-love has been

---

[128] See pp. 261–62.

[129] 143.1–16.

[130] Not one's children, as we would expect. Inwood (1983), pp. 196–97, points out that this links the passage with Antiochus' way of explaining extension of sympathies, rather than the Stoic one, which begins from instinctual affection for one's offspring. There is no real conflict, however; the Stoics focus on the instinctual basis of our other-directed sympathies, Antiochus focusses on the order in which we begin to extend them.

[131] Friendship is not in Aristotle a virtue to which the mean applies. This artificial application clearly post-dates the recasting of Aristotle's ideas in Stoic ways, so that self-love has become the starting point of a continuum which ends with impartial regard for all, a continuum which is amenable to the application of the idea of the mean.

transplanted from its context in the account of friendship to bloom luxuriantly in the updated introduction to Aristotelian ethics.[132]

Second, the initial passage itself, while otherwise parallel in terminology with Stoic accounts of *oikeiōsis*, contains many striking occurrences of *philos*, *philia* and related words.[133] While the terminology of friendship and self-love is not altogether absent from the Stoic accounts, it is not prominent in anything like this way.[134]

And third, the conclusion of the passage seems consciously to reject Aristotle's actual conclusion about a special sense of self-love. 'Virtue is on this theory not self-loving (*philautos*) but social and political; and since we said that virtue is most familiarized with itself, clearly it is naturally familiarized necessarily with knowledge of the truth.'[135] As we have seen,[136] the idea that other-concern is a special form of self-love was found paradoxical. In the Arius passage we find Aristotle's idea separated from its paradoxical expression and developed in different terminology. Stoic *oikeiōsis* has provided an accessible way of making self-concern the starting point of a development culminating in Aristotelian ethical development. To make it suitable, however, the Stoic story has been altered, so that other-concern develops as a stage of self-concern; the whole process, though not called self-love, is formally self-centred at the end as at the beginning. And this is what centrally distinguished the Aristotelian from the Stoic account.

This Peripatetic adaptation of Stoic *oikeiōsis* turns out to be, not a muddle or unintelligent patchwork, but an interesting attempt to provide Aristotle with a restated account of his ethics. This is an account which starts from agreement with the Stoics on a number of points. An ethical theory should be developmental in form, presenting progress to the moral point of view as a development natural to humans. It should show that the moral point of view implies impartiality towards all humans. And it should show how the moral point of view requires us to develop from an instinctive to a rationally aware form of both self-concern and other-concern. But on one crucial point the revised Aristotelian theory rejects a Stoic starting point. It is a one-source rather than a two-source theory; the development of other-concern is seen not as separate from and co-ordinate to the development of self-concern, but as being merely one stage of the latter. Arius makes this point better than Antiochus does; he works to restate Stoic theory into Aristotelian form rather than just starting from a vague and question-begging starting point.

Why does it matter to have a one-source rather than a two-source theory? And can an Aristotelian theory really take impartiality on board? We shall turn to these questions in the next section.

---

[132] This reference back has much exercised scholars. Some, e.g., von Arnim (1926) 81 ff., have used it as evidence for an original Peripatetic *oikeiōsis*-based theory; others, e.g., Pohlenz (1940) 6–40, have treated it as an artificial join between two dissimilar parts.

[133] Very strikingly as 118.20–119.2. Compare also 120.12, 15, 18; 121.17, 23–4; 127.4–9.

[134] Cf. Cicero, *Fin* III 16: '*sensum haberent sui eoque se deligerent*' and '*a se diligendo*', and III 59: '*se omnes natura diligant*'. But in Greek accounts *philia* and *philos* are not prominent.

[135] 125.21–126.2.

[136] Section 1, pp. 261–62.

4. The Debate

Two distinct questions have emerged from the extended comparison of Aristotelian and Stoic theories on the place in the virtuous life of the good of others. One is, What is at stake in the debate between single-source and two-source theories? Why did it matter to an Aristotelian to collapse the two forms of Stoic *oikeiōsis* into one?

As we have seen, Aristotle sees morality as developing from self-love, and also argues that the end result is self-love—a highly special and refined form of self-love, of course. The latter point is universally rejected after Aristotle, as being unnecessarily paradoxical. But a point of contest remains; later Aristotelians insist that morality develops from *one* instinctive source of human motivation, and call that self-love. When they are willing to take over the Stoic developmental framework and terminology to do this, why reject the two Stoic forms of *oikeiōsis*?

One possible Aristotelian objection is that Stoic *oikeiōsis* is a messy and clumsy kind of theory. It explains our moral development in terms of two sources which are simply juxtaposed, and this is less convincing than an account that does it in terms of one. Aristotelian *oikeiōsis* would thus have familiar theoretical advantages of economy and simplicity. Thus an Aristotelian will not disagree with a Stoic as to the reality and importance of other-concern in the agent's life. But she will say that her theory is far simpler and more convincing from the explanatory point of view, for the only original source of human behaviour it needs to posit is self-concern, other-concern coming in as a developed form of this.[137]

The Stoic could respond that explanatory simplicity is not necessarily achieved by having just one source of ethical development. For that source has to contain sufficient internal complexity to be capable of accounting, non-reductively, for actual other-concern in the agent's life. And so we get a dilemma. Either the Aristotelian account is really reductive, and other-concern is reduced to merely a form of self-concern, without independent status; in which case we have failed to account for the data. Or self-concern must be so understood that what develops from it is genuine, unreduced other-concern; in which case we have merely given one name, 'self-concern', to what is in fact a disjunct, consisting of what the Stoics call self-concern and other-concern. Moreover, by so understanding self-concern that what develops from it is both self- and other-concern, the Aristotelians are adopting a position not much less paradoxical than the original *Nicomachean Ethics* IX 8 version; even if self-concern is not reduced to other-concern, we have a highly unintuitive way of regarding it.

The difference here between the schools is a real one, but not a difference about the existence and the importance in the agent's life of other-concern. It is rather a difference about the theoretically adequate understanding of this, and so more like a difference about the basis of ethics.

Another Aristotelian objection could be that the Stoics are wrong in thinking that other-concern does go as deep in instinctual human nature as self-concern does.

---

[137] The continuing appeal of this kind of theoretical simplicity can be seen in Hume's strategy (developed from Butler) in the second Appendix to his *Enquiry into the Principles of Morals* (though he is talking of reductive theories). He locates the appeal of the idea that all action is self-interested in its simplicity, and argues against it by showing that it does not in fact provide us with the simplest explanation.

The Aristotelian could agree with the Anonymous Commentator on the *Theaetetus* that self-concern is instinctive and 'irrational', whereas we only learn to feel other-concern as a result of learning to appreciate and act on reasons. This could be supported by appeal to what we see of human development; babies are totally self-concerned, and we have to be taught to be concerned for others.[138]

It is clear by now, however, what the Stoic response to this would be. We cannot read off the proper course of moral development merely by looking at the chronological development of humans. Young humans do have to learn to care for others, and purely instinctive other-concern does not appear until late in life, when we have offspring. But when it does appear, it does not have to be learned; it is part of our instinctive nature. Thus the Stoics could reverse the argument and claim that the Aristotelians fail to account for the instinctive love of parents for their children; they have to account for it as a learned development, which it is not.[138]

The Stoics seem to have the better of the argument here. The Aristotelians are committed to finding that other-concern is a development of self-concern, and to doing so in a way which does not reduce the former to the latter, but produces more than a trivial redescription of other-concern. The hybrid Aristotelian theories that we have seen cannot be said to have been strikingly successful in doing this.

Another difference between Aristotelians and Stoics does directly concern the making of different concrete ethical conclusions in the sphere of other-concern. We have seen that Aristotle himself sees no ethical pressure to extend other-concern to the point of impartiality, concern for all humans just as rational humans; whereas the Stoics do insist on this. Both the Aristotelian responses we have seen accept the Stoic point on this; Antiochus and Arius both agree that the moral agent will eventually become impartial. But how can such a position be made consistent with an Aristotelian theory, which talks about ethics in a more limited context of one's friends, or one's fellow-citizens? The problem is underlined for the Arius passage by the fact that it ends with summaries from the *Politics* which repeat Aristotle's position that the ethical life is best lived in the limited social context of the Greek city-state. Being a citizen is essential to the ethical life, not a stage on the way to becoming a citizen of the world.[139]

We are familiar from modern ethical theories with ways in which these positions can be reconciled. It might be, for example, that we should ideally have impartial concern for all, but that for most people this is too demanding, so that ethical theory has to put limits on the requirements of morality. On this view, we take ourselves to have duties to our fellow-citizens, but not to the furthest Mysian, because, although we should do the latter if we were ideally virtuous, it would in fact be impossibly demanding for us. An Aristotelian kind of theory would on this account be a compromise between the demands of morality and the reality of human nature. Another tack is to present a more limited morality as actually being the best way, for us limited humans, to get nearer to the demands of moral theory. Since we have some trouble acting on the demands that the furthest Mysian puts on us, we do

---

[138] It is interesting that Aristotle's own account of friendship includes, but has difficulty accounting for, the love of a parent for a child; see n. 6.

[139] The *Pol* passages stand in the way of attempts to read the entire passage as expressing a Theophrastean or early Peripatetic theory of *oikeiōsis* in which our sympathies are extended over a wider area than the city-state. See von Arnim (1926), pp. 142ff., Moraux (1973) p. 341 and n. 83, Annas (1994).

better, on this view, to limit the demands of morality to those we can fulfil. This is not ideal, but actually gets us nearer the ideal than would a system in which we all tried to recognize our duties to the furthest Mysian; if we tried to do *that* we should all fail, whereas as things are we actually achieve our goals some of the time.

These are modern moves; we find no signs in any of our sources of such answers to the problem. Nor do we find any signs of more sophisticated answers to the problem, defences of Aristotle's ethics which would have repelled the attempts of Aristotelians to take on board the Stoic demand for impartiality in ethics.[140] Since the rejection of impartiality as an ethical demand is nowadays often part of an ethical position that harks back to Aristotle, it is a pity that the development of Aristotelian views in his own school, against rivals who did accept this demand, does not reflect any of these arguments. Later Aristotelians simply caved in to the Stoics on this point and accepted the impartiality requirement without even integrating it to the rest of the theory very satisfactorily.

Only in the Arius passage do we find any attempt to do this, and it is of the feeblest. 'But although we have a common love of mankind, what is choiceworthy for its own sake is much more obvious in the relation towards friends that we see regularly.'[141] But this is strikingly false. It is easier to have a disinterested concern for a stranger, towards whom one has no personal attachment, than to have it towards one's child. Perhaps, however, we should emphasize the 'see regularly'; the thought may be that when I see a friend regularly I appreciate what is valuable about her as a person, not just as someone I like. But, while this may be true, it still does not seem that this is 'more obvious' than coming to have disinterested concern for a stranger on a journey (Arius' own example) whom I meet only once.

Further, even if this claim were true, it would not establish what is needed. If other-concern has no logical stopping place short of concern for all people, including the furthest Mysian, and concludes by finding something equally 'choiceworthy in itself' in every case, then the obviousness or not of this in friends as opposed to strangers has no clear relevance. It seems to have no ethical force. In fact, once one accepts the impartiality requirement, it is hard to see how friendship, and the life of a citizen, can have an important ethical role unless some move is made which justifies their importance in terms of the impartial point of view itself; the claim we find in Arius falls far short of that.

On this point also, then, the Stoics seem to have the more defensible theory. This is not, of course, to adjudicate between theories that require impartiality and those that do not; the debate is complex and goes far beyond its ancient beginnings, bringing in issues like relativism which the ancient debate does not deal with. Still, this debate, one of the most central in ethics, clearly has ancient antecedents in this aspect of the continuing debate between Stoics and Aristotelians.

---

[140] Cf. recent work by MacIntyre (1981) (1988) (1990), and Williams (1985). The best and most sophisticated version of these arguments still seems to me to be the one given in Bradley (1876).

[141] 121.22–24.

13

Justice

1. *A Virtue of Character and a Virtue of Institutions*

Justice is generally seen as the most demanding virtue, for it requires the agent sometimes to give up what is in her own interests because of the rights of others.[1] For this reason, justice is the virtue which most strikingly raises the question of the relation of the agent's good to the good of her society. Justice can be exercised among family and friends, but its proper field is that of the wider society in which the agent lives. And thus it can come to seem the virtue which provides problems for a eudaimonistic ethics, one in which ethics is structured around the question of what will best promote *the agent's* happiness.

Plato, in the *Republic*, famously undertakes to meet the challenge of people who claim that justice does not really contribute towards the agent's happiness, because its requirements are in the interests of others. He tries to show that justice really is, in fact, in the agent's interests, and does so by arguing that state and individual are isomorphic and that justice is the virtue which ensures the proper relationship among the parts of either. It is clear by now, however, that we do not need a theory as ambitious as Plato's to answer the problem that justice is a virtue, and so part of what should achieve the agent's happiness, while making demands that do not appear to be in the agent's interests. For happiness is a weak, unspecific notion which it is the business of ethical theory correctly to specify; and we have seen that such specification, in some theories at least, already makes very high demands on the agent's willingness to consider himself as being merely one among other rational beings. Any theory must make some attempt to show that justice is a virtue which the agent needs in his attempt to achieve overall happiness. But, since eudaimonism is not an ethical theory either recommending or requiring self-interest, justice is not a problem merely because it is the virtue which most obviously carries the requirements of the interests of others.

---

[1] In this book I do not have the scope to discuss fully the question of whether ancient theories have anything like our notion of rights. Briefly, however, while it is true that Greek has no word corresponding to our 'right', Latin has *ius*. Further, theses about rights can be understood, even without the word 'right', as theses about various kinds of claims and permissions, and both Greek and Latin have ample vocabulary for these. (See Miller [forthcoming] for an extended discussion of rights terminology in Aristotle.) While ancient theories have no one concept bringing together just what our 'right' does, we have no warrant for concluding that they could not recognize what we call rights.

In fact, the major problem raised by justice, in a eudaimonistic ethics, is the claim not of others as such but of society. So far we have had no difficulty with the conception of the virtues as dispositions of the agent's character. But is not justice also a virtue of institutions? We praise societies, methods of distribution and laws as being just. How are these two applications of justice connected? This issue is especially salient in our attempts to understand ancient theories, because in modern social and political thought it is usually taken for granted that it is the justice of institutions which is primary; people are just in a merely derivative way, namely as being so disposed as to respect the principles or whatever which render the institutions just.[2] The idea that justice could be reasonably taken to be a virtue of character, in any but this secondary way, seems odd, and even arbitrary, in modern theories, and attempts to revive the idea have not had much success.[3] As a consequence of this perspective, ancient theories of justice are often taken to be fundamentally misguided, since they take justice to be basically a virtue of character. It is often assumed that they are then left with an unsatisfactory position, for it is not plausible to hold that a good account of the justice of institutions can be derived from the notion of justice as an individual virtue.

It is true that in ancient theories we find nothing like the ingenuity of detail and expanse of technical expertise that we find in modern theories of justice, especially those of a contractual kind. Nonetheless, I think it is wrong to write off the ancient theories in this area, and to regard them as essentially theories of individual morality only, with no, or no helpful, position on the relation of the individual to the common good, or to the justice of institutions. As often, the picture is more complex than may appear at first sight.

In this chapter I shall first deal with Epicurus' theory of justice, since it brings out with especial clarity the issue which is at stake when justice is taken to be both one virtue of character among others, and also to be what particularly characterizes social institutions. Whatever one thinks of the merits of Epicurus' own solution, it is plain that the problem is clearly recognized. I shall then move on to the Stoics. We have already seen that social *oikeiōsis* is taken to account for justice, and there is a question whether the Stoics have really left room in their theory for a distinct political application of justice. I shall argue that in fact they have not, and that their answer to the present problem is in effect radically to depoliticize the institutional application of justice. There are complications, however; early works by Zeno and Chrysippus seem to address political issues, and some later Stoics made attempts to reintroduce these issues in different form. Moreover, there is the issue of the Stoic conception of 'natural law' and its application in the political sphere.

Aristotle, of course, has, in the *Politics*, an extensive treatment of justice in society; but this has not often been brought into connection with the account in the ethical works of justice as a virtue of individual character. Of all the theories relevant to this book, Aristotle's is the one which most firmly locates the justice of

---

[2] This is very clear in, for example, Rawls (1971). Despite subsequent modifications of the theory, one point which remains constant is that the 'sense of justice' which characterizes people is derivative from the justice of Rawls' principles of justice, and consists in having acquired a disposition to respect, think in accordance with, etc., those principles.

[3] For some well-known criticisms, see Williams (1980). For an attempt to rehabilitate the idea of justice as a virtue of character, see O'Connor (1988).

institutions in the workings of the city-state or *polis*; he does not have a robust conception of justice as demanding duties to those who fall outside the city-state relationships. Here there is a striking contrast with the Stoics. In the later Aristotelian theories that are produced in answer to the Stoics, namely Antiochus and Arius, we find differing responses; Antiochus follows the Stoic tendency to depoliticize the social aspect of justice, while in Arius we find an attempt to retain an Aristotelian concern with political justice within a Stoic framework of other-concern. We thus find a variety of responses to the problem that justice has a social and political aspect, which has to be brought into some kind of relation to justice as a virtue of the individual's character.

2. *Epicurus on Justice*

Epicurus is a particularly interesting philosopher from the present point of view, because in his case we find two quite distinct bodies of evidence. In one, justice is treated as a virtue of the agent's character along with the other virtues; in the other, justice is presented as the result of a contract between people making up a society. The motivation seems quite diverse in these two cases, and it is only recently that philosophical work has been done on the relation between them.[4]

On the one hand, we find that virtue is not only regarded as one among the other virtues of character, but that Epicurus stresses the strong connection that there is between them.

> We are left with justice—to say something about every virtue—but almost the same can be said [as about the other virtues]. I have shown that wisdom, temperance and courage are so linked with pleasure that they cannot be parted or torn away from it in any way; this is what we should judge to be the case with justice, which not only causes no harm to anyone, but on the contrary always adds (?) something[5] both by its own force and nature in making minds tranquil, and also by its hope that there will be no lack of those things which nature desires—if it is not corrupted, that is. Further, just as rashness, lust and cowardice always torture the mind and continually irritate it and are troublesome, so when injustice[6] becomes established in someone's mind, it causes troubles just by the fact that it is there. If it has actually brought something about, however secretly it has done it, it can never feel sure that it will always remain concealed. . . .
>
> There is no reason at all for going astray, for the desires which proceed from nature are easily fulfilled without any injustice, while those that are empty should not be yielded to, for they yearn for nothing that is desirable. And there is more loss in injustice itself than gain in the things that are provided by means of injustice. Thus, to speak correctly one would not even say that justice itself is to be sought for its own sake, but because it produces a high degree of pleasure. For it is pleasant to be loved, and dear to people, because it renders one's life more

---

[4] For excellent work on a topic until recently almost entirely neglected, see Denyer (1983), Mitsis (1988) ch. 2, Vander Waerdt (1987) and (1988), Long (1986), D. Gill (forthcoming).

[5] Madvig (1965) marks a lacuna; some verb such as 'adds' or 'provides' must be understood.

[6] Accepting Madvig's insertion of *improbitas si*.

secure and more full of pleasures. Thus we think that the disadvantages which result for the wicked are not the only reason for rejecting injustice, but far more the fact that it prevents the person in whose mind it stays from ever breathing freely or having peace of mind.[7]

Justice, like the other virtues and for the same reasons, is desirable not in itself but for the contribution it makes towards the agent's achieving *ataraxia* or tranquillity. We will consider later[8] Epicurus' claim that our final end is tranquillity, and the important question whether this commits him, or not, to giving all the virtues merely instrumental status. What matters here, however, is that it is clear that it is the agent's *own* tranquillity that is at issue; possession of the virtues matters just because it contributes to the agent's achievement of his own final end. Thus, the agent's motivation to become just will be, ultimately, hope of achieving pleasure, of the right, tranquil kind, over his life as a whole. The way that this is connected with justice is as follows: injustice springs from the agent's having, and acting on, faulty desires—desires which lead him to act aggressively and greedily. But the person who truly understands how to achieve *ataraxia* will know that and how to satisfy only natural desires—following the strategy we have discussed above.[9] And if he does so he will lack the motives which impel most people to injustice. Hence claims such as the following: 'The greatest fruit of justice is tranquillity [*ataraxia*].'[10] 'The just person is most tranquil, while the unjust is full of the greatest trouble [*tarachē*].'[11]

Problems that we might find with this conception of justice are no different from problems with Epicurus' conception of the virtues generally.[12] But it is initially surprising to find this confronted by extensive passages (mainly a linked section of the *KD*) in which justice appears to be the outcome of a contract between persons aiming at mutual safety from harm. From these passages several points emerge. The agent values justice not, or not mainly, for its direct benefits in terms of her own tranquillity, but in a way that is contingent on others' reciprocating; the motivation to be just depends not on any direct link with one's final end but on the security from fear of punishment that commitment to justice brings; what produces such security may vary, and therefore there is no fixed content to justice, which can vary from society to society.

> Natural justice is a pledge of advantage, towards not harming or being harmed by one another.[13]

> There is no such thing as justice in itself; in people's relations with one another in any place and at any time it is a contract (*sunthēkē*) about not harming or being harmed.[14]

---

[7] *Fin* I 50, 52–3. See also Mitsis' discussion of this passage (1988) pp. 70–79.
[8] In chapter 16.
[9] Chapter 7.
[10] U 519 (Clement of Alexandria, *Strom* VI 2, 266.39).
[11] *KD* 17.
[12] On which see chapter 16.
[13] *KD* 31.
[14] *KD* 33.

Injustice is not a bad thing in itself, but because of the fear that comes with the suspicion that one will not evade those established as punishers of such things.[15]

It is impossible for the person who secretly does one of the things about which people have contracted with one another about not harming or being harmed to be confident that he will evade detection, even if he evades it thousands of times for the present. For right up to death it is not clear that he will evade it.[16]

From a general point of view justice is the same for all, for it is a kind of advantage in people's community with one another. But from the particular point of view of the place and of any other causes, it does not follow for all that the same thing is just.[17]

Of the things deemed to be just by law, what is confirmed as advantageous in the needs of people's community with one another should have the status of being just, whether it is the same for all or not the same.[18] But if someone only sets up a law, but there is no result that accords with advantage in community with one another, then this no longer contains the nature of the just. And even if the advantage according to the just changes, but for a while fits the preconception,[19] it is none the less just for that time—to those who do not trouble themselves with empty sounds, but look to the facts.[20]

Moreover, a long passage from the early Epicurean Hermarchus supplements this picture in two ways. One is that justice is the result of a contract, and that there is therefore no justice between humans and animals, or indeed between humans and other humans who are incapable of understanding or keeping to contracts.[21] Hermarchus follows the point up with unpleasing vigour: with animals that lack reason and so cannot understand laws, our only option, he says, with a bad faith that has been echoed down the centuries, is that of killing them.[22] In any case they do not form part of a social community with humans; and humans in forming social communities 'expel' animals from those communities—not literally, of course, but by classifying them as an 'underclass' in the society that lacks the rights which members of that society have.[23]

Second, the contract aims at achieving what is 'useful', and so far-sighted people could manage with the contract alone; it is only because the mass of mankind is short-sighted and fails to discern what is in their interest that we need sanctions.[24] A far-sighted enough grasp of what is useful and in everyone's interests would suffice for intelligent people; presumably they would be able to make the adjustments

[15] *KD* 34.

[16] *KD* 35.

[17] *KD* 36.

[18] Following Arrighetti's text, *tou dikaiou chōran dei*.

[19] *Prolēpsis*, the general concept. For Epicurus our preconceptions, which are empirically acquired, form a test that theories have to meet.

[20] *KD* 37. Cf. KD 38.

[21] Cf. *KD* 32.

[22] 12.5–6 in Porphyry, *Abst* Book I (the whole passage is fragment 34 in *Ermarco, Frammenti*, ed. F. Longo Auricchio, Naples, 1987).

[23] *Ibid.*, 10.1–3.

[24] *Ibid.*, 7.1–4.

required in the law when conditions change so as to ensure continued usefulness of the system.[25]

We seem to have a contractual account of justice alongside an account of it as a virtue of individual character. Plato, in the *Republic*, tried to replace a contractual account of justice by an account in which it is basically a virtue of the agent's character. Epicurus seems to have revived the contractual theory, but kept the emphasis on justice as a state of the agent.[26] How are we to reconcile these two points?

Until recently the predominant tendency was to ignore the passages in which justice appears as a virtue of character, or to interpret them in the light of the contractual passages; and to interpret these, in turn, as claiming that the only motive for the Epicurean to be just is fear of consequences if detected. This is certainly the view of Cicero,[27] and of Plutarch, who tells us that Epicurus answered the question, 'Will the virtuous person do what the law forbids if he knows that he will not be found out?' by saying that a simple answer to this will not do, and who interprets Epicurus as meaning, 'I'll do it, but I don't want to admit that I will.'[28] On this view, justice is for the Epicurean never more than a second-best, a disagreeable necessity forced on one by the fact that one lives in society and must therefore do the best one can by way of obtaining security from being wronged by entering into a contract to avoid mutual wrongdoing. It is the fear of detection and punishment alone which motivates the Epicurean to be just; and thus, when that fear is rendered groundless, there is a real question whether he has any further motive to remain just. While Plutarch puts the point crudely, it may indeed seem likely that if the consequences of detection are in fact removed, the Epicurean will have no further motive not to engage in pleasure-producing injustice.

This interpretation, however, is hard put to it to explain the evidence that justice is a virtue of the agent's character, and one, moreover, which secures tranquillity. For the strategy just outlined would seem to be a predictably terrible one for achieving tranquillity, of all things. There are at least two reasons why this should be so.[29] One is that if fear of detection is, at least in some circumstances, the only deterrent from injustice for the Epicurean, then he has desires for what can only be obtained by injustice which are, to that extent, unfulfilled, and thus is frustrated and 'troubled' or suffering from *tarachai*; so he will to this extent fail to achieve *ataraxia*. Moreover, it is only the contingent chance of circumstances which determines whether or not the agent is in this position. Ordinarily there will be quite a lot of the time when the contract works in his favour; and so whether or not he becomes frustrated in this way depends not on him but on factors outside himself. But one can hardly have achieved tranquillity if one's state of mind can be at any moment

---

[25] Hermarchus also interestingly allows a role for *oikeiōsis* or natural affinity between people, but limits it to the relevant group, that is, those capable of grasping their long-term advantage. See Vander Waerdt (1988) on this.

[26] However, the contractual theory of justice which Plato has Glaucon and Adeimantus expound at the beginning of *Republic* Book II is not the same as the one Epicurus defends; on this see Denyer (1982).

[27] *Fin* II 71, where Cicero claims that fear as a motive is incompatible with genuine, as opposed to sham, justice.

[28] *Ad Col* 1127 D.

[29] These are essentially D. Gill's (forthcoming) objections.

altered by external factors. Further, this same point undermines the idea that Epicurean justice could be a virtue; for a virtue is, as we have seen at length, a developed disposition to decide and act in certain ways rather than others, with one's emotional side developing appropriately. But it looks as though the contractual view of justice is inconsistent with this. On this view, the Epicurean behaves justly because he calculates that allowing certain desires to be frustrated is rendered worthwhile by the increased expectation of security that comes from all committing themselves to the contract not to harm one another. But this calculation will obviously not be stable, for circumstances will bring about differences in the degree of frustration, the chance of detection and so on; we get the difficult situation mentioned by Plutarch, for example. Thus the Epicurean's commitment to justice cannot be stable, for it rests on calculations which may shift and change in a way that depends on circumstances rather than the agent. Such a shifting basis cannot form the core of a virtue, as that is understood in ancient theories. And yet we find, in the *de Fin* passage, a clear commitment to the idea that not only is justice a virtue, but it forms some kind of unity with the other virtues, since the practical reasoning it involves is shared with them.[30]

There is a clear problem, then, raised by the two kinds of accounts of justice that we find in Epicurus.[31] Since Epicurus can hardly have left such a situation with no solution, but we have no explicit evidence as to what his own solution was, we should try to find a way of reconciling the accounts which is in keeping with what else we can securely conjecture as to the structure of Epicurean ethics. We should, that is, see the ethics as eudaimonist in form, but as also giving an account of justice as a feature of societies. The problem lies in the fact that the individual and social accounts of justice appear to give us divergent motivations for the agent's being just: on the one hand, fear of detection and punishment, a fear shifting with every change in circumstances, and on the other, a settled and motivationally secured disposition to achieve tranquillity by adopting a strategy of following only appropriate desires.

What Epicurus needs, one might think, is something akin to Hume's distinction between natural and artificial virtues; for Hume faces a similar difficulty, since his ethics is formally eudaimonist but also attempts to account for the pursuit of what is perceived to be in the general social interest. However, Hume's distinction makes sense within his own theory, in which virtue is treated in a perfunctory and unstructured way. But within the framework of ancient theory, it appears arbitrary

---

[30] This problem has affinities with the kind of problem that afflicts consequentialist theories which try to include virtues in their theory. If the question of what it is right for the agent to do is determined by reasoning about outcomes which depend largely on factors external to the agent, then this is incompatible with the agent also acting out of virtue, precisely because virtue requires a settled and motivationally stable disposition on the agent's part, one which will not adjust without further ado to differences in external outcome. See Slote (1988), Railton (1988).

[31] Vander Waerdt (1987) argues that for Epicurus an adequate account of justice is given by the idea that following only natural desires will remove the motivation to be unjust. For objections to this, see D. Gill (forthcoming), who argues that this cannot account for (1) Epicurus' repeated insistence on the impossibility of achieving complete security (cf. especially *KD* 34 and *VS* 7) nor for (2) the fact that Epicurus insists that the content of justice may vary with circumstances, so that the motivation to be just must be capable of explaining such differential behaviour, whereas the mere lack of inappropriate desires would seem to explain the same behaviour everywhere. Such an account, Gill argues, threatens to make the contractual account of justice applicable only to non-Epicureans, while good Epicureans will not need it; but this is difficult to reconcile with the totality of the evidence.

and unmotivated. If a virtue is understood in the complex way demanded by ancient ethics, the insistence that justice is an 'artificial' virtue is unhelpful. All the virtues are equally natural, in ways that we have seen, ways which are of course compatible with social conventions playing a role in establishing the detailed content of what are regarded in particular societies as virtues. The notion of an 'artificial' virtue adds nothing until spelled out in terms of some relation between justice as a means of achieving social good and justice as a virtue that the agent has reason to acquire. But this is exactly the problem we need to solve.

The most promising solution to the problem is to assume that justice as a social phenomenon need not require the same motivation as justice as a virtue of the individual's character.[32] Justice as something which facilitates social co-operation rests on the need to provide security, and thus, ultimately, on the fear of detection and punishment in the commission of injustice. But this need not function by producing in each individual a tendency to judge and act, in each case, on the basis of calculations about detection and frustration. Rather, the thought is that it best operates precisely by producing in each individual a tendency to judge and act in ways which reflect the agent's belief that justice is something which conduces to the best life on the part of the individual agent. (Given the rest of Epicurean theory, of course, the best life will be the life of tranquillity, and thus will involve the strategy of living according to natural desires.) If so, then Epicurus will be entitled to think of justice as a genuine virtue, for two reasons. One is that such a tendency can be stable; the agent can acquire a settled disposition to judge and act in ways which relate stably to the (Epicurean) *telos* in the ways required of virtue, without fluctuating along with every calculation about change of outcome. The other is that on this view we can see why justice would be thought to be closely connected with the other virtues; all share their characteristic practical reasoning, which will be largely concerned with the strategy of following only natural desires. One way of posing the problem about justice is as the problem of combining the contractual account with a statement like 'It is not possible to live pleasantly without living intelligently and finely and justly, nor to live intelligently and finely and justly without living pleasantly.'[33] But if justice as a virtue of character can develop in a way which is not directly dependent on the fluctuations of fear of punishment and frustration, we can see how the contractual theory is quite consistent with the above claim. More, we can see how it might actually support it; for the passage continues, 'If a person lacks the conditions for living intelligently and finely and justly, it is impossible for them to live pleasantly.' In the case of justice, there is a complication not present with the other virtues; the conditions for individuals to develop justice as a virtue of character are precisely those that the contractual theory explicates. For justice is a virtue of social groups; and such groups can only come into being under conditions which can be presented as those in which people make a contract to avoid mutual harm.

Thus the contract theory tells us what the conditions are in which people can form societies on a just basis; when these conditions are fulfilled, individuals can develop justice and the other virtues that people need in order rightly to direct their

---

[32] This is the solution developed in D. Gill (forthcoming), to whom I owe a great deal on this topic.
[33] *KD* 5. (Cf. *Ep. Men.* 132.)

lives towards achieving *ataraxia*. Where the conditions of justice are not fulfilled, people are motivated to just behaviour solely by fear of punishment; but where they are fulfilled, people are motivated to be just solely by the desire to achieve tranquillity. Justice can be the virtue that Epicurus wants it to be only in a society where the conditions of the contract hold; but this is not what the Epicurean bears in mind when she is just.

There are three quite important connected points. First, we obviously have a two-stage theory of a kind. The individual just person does not calculate outcomes before deciding to do the just thing, although at another level it is the possibility of such calculations which renders justice an option for her. However, the two stages are not totally independent, for the contract theory presupposes a particular theory of human motivation, and not all such theories are compatible with the Epicurean account of justice as inseparable from a pleasant life. On a very negative or Hobbesian view of human nature, the only motive for committing oneself to a contract could be the fear that one will suffer from the aggressions of others more than one will oneself gain from one's own aggressions; contract theories are associated with theories to the effect that this is the most one can expect from human nature. However, Epicurus, as we have seen, finds human nature to be considerably more plastic than this, and so though, for Epicurus, contracts may well have come about to check mutual aggression, this is not the utmost that they can do; contracts can serve also to educate human nature as to the benefits of co-operation.[34] Thus Epicurus need not regard people as being stuck at the primitive Hobbesian level; contracts serve to co-ordinate co-operation as well as to prevent mutual aggression. And this means that there is no implausibly wide gulf between the two accounts. It is often assumed that a contract theory must rest on a pessimistic view of human nature, and if this were true there would indeed be an implausible leap from the contract providing the conditions of justice to the development of justice in the individual. But Epicurus has an optimistic view of the plasticity and potential of human nature; seeking security from mutual aggression is not the best that human nature can achieve. And so even the contractual theory itself is compatible with natural co-operation rather than continued attempted aggression; it is not in tension with justice as an individual Epicurean virtue, as a primitive Hobbesian account would be.

Second, there is a *prima facie* tension between what we find in Epicurus and the complicated picture of human prehistory that we find in Lucretius V. Lucretius gives us a picture of primitive humans becoming more civilized as they develop social structures; but he also shows these structures being employed badly, and the development of technology, which made civilization possible, making possible also increased destruction and aggression. Lucretius' picture does not show us a uniform development towards justice and increased civilization.[35] Moreover, Epicurus' own

---

[34] Hence, perhaps, the rather gnomic fragment 530 U (Stobaeus, *Flor* 43.139): 'The laws exist for the sake of the wise, not so that they won't commit injustice but so that they won't have injustice committed against them'. The wise or virtuous, at least, are not trapped in a Hobbesian state of nature, even if others around them are aggressive.

[35] See Lucretius V 925–1457, especially 925–1160. On this see Blickman (1989). Blickman also discusses the interesting new fragment 21 of Diogenes of Oenoanda, which apparently discusses a kind of future golden age.

attitude to the actual social structures of his day was deeply ambivalent. On the one hand, he was notorious for telling his followers to abandon the conventional ancient concern with active political engagement, and to 'live unknown' in Epicurean communities like the Garden, the assumption being that political life is impossible without developing unnatural desires—for example, for money and power—which will render the achievement of *ataraxia* impossible. On the other hand, he also allowed that some people simply could not achieve happiness of any kind without such political engagement, and declared it best for them to do so;[36] and his follower Colotes expounded on the benefits of government and civilized society, as opposed to the brutish life that humans would live without such institutions.[37]

There is no real difficulty here, if we bear in mind that Epicurus' account of justice is a *philosophical* account, and as such cannot be expected to match up to any period in history in a simple way. Epicurus' attitude to the political situation of the present seems to be that, while it is in some ways a great improvement on the past, it is still radically defective from the point of view of justice; hence the past gives us some positive, but also some negative indications as to the present. This is just the sensible attitude that many people have always had to their past, the attitude of all who refuse either to romanticize or to demonize it.[38] Hence Epicurus' contractual account of justice is neither helped nor hindered by his account of prehistory or his degree of commitment to the actual political institutions among which he lived. It gives, as such, no support either to the idea that he favoured an apolitical life or to the idea that he supported present political institutions.

The third point is the most important. For the two accounts of justice can be reconciled only by giving Epicurus a two-level theory; and we have seen the problems that this raises in the case of friendship.[39] For it is crucial to the reconciliation of the two accounts of justice that they do not require the same motivation; what motivates the adoption of the contract is not what the individually just Epicurean bears in mind. But we seem to have the same problem as before: how can the two types of motivation be separated? Surely the individual just person will have to bear in mind, at some level, the point of having just institutions in the first place; or what will make the virtue which she is developing *justice*, rather than some other virtue? But if she does bear it in mind, all the former problems seem to arise; it seems that the motivation which is indicated is not that which the individual just Epicurean ought to be bearing in mind.

And we have the same passage from Epicurus which appears to stand in the way of two-level views which separate distinct kinds of motivation in the agent:

> If you do not on every suitable occasion refer each of your actions to the end

---

[36] Plutarch, *de tranq an* 465 F–466 A.

[37] Plutarch, *Ad Col* 1124 D. Long (1986) stresses the positive side of Epicurus' attitude to actual governments, and rightly rejects the idea that he was a 'primitivist' who thought that all government was unnatural and would ideally 'wither away'.

[38] It remains true that in Lucretius, as many commentators have noticed, there is a distinctly pessimistic tendency about his own day, and that correspondingly he shows a greater tendency than we have reason to suspect in Epicurus to fantasize about the past.

[39] And we will see the same problems arise with even greater force in the case of the other virtues, in chapter 16.

given by nature, but stop short and make your avoidance or choice with reference to something else, your actions will not be consistent with your theories.[40]

But it may be that the problem is not as bad in this case as it is in the case of friendship and the other virtues. For in those cases the individual is supposed to have a systematically double-minded attitude to a moral phenomenon in his own life, and problems come from the fact that in performing one and the same action he has to have two incompatible goals in mind. But here the two levels correspond to two different things: the agent's attitude to justice as a way of achieving his own *ataraxia*, and his attitude to justice as a phenomenon which enables him to co-operate with other people. So it is not obvious that the different motivations here must conflict in the way they do in the other cases. For example, the agent might perform an act out of justice, in order to achieve *ataraxia*. Reflecting on why *justice* was required in this case, she might reflect that this is because of the need that human beings, including herself, feel to be secure and free from fear of various kinds. But, because these are different facts about herself, reflection on the second does not interfere with the first, as is the case where the reflection produces two distinct goals for the same action. For the fact that one forms part of society and therefore needs to hold to contracts which ensure the general good does not generate an individual aim in the way that one's aiming at tranquillity does.

We may hold, then, that the demand for consistency between actions and principles is not violated in the case of justice.[41] A particular act of justice is motivated, in the case of an Epicurean, by a desire to be just in order to achieve *ataraxia* (via the theory of natural desires, of course). It is also explained by the contractual theory of justice, and this fact is available to the agent, but the action need not itself also be motivated in the way appropriate to that theory. (If it were, of course, then the problems we have already seen in the case of friendship would arise.) And this is simply because the contractual theory of justice explains why people collectively, in societies, are just; and this need not exhaust (though it ought to be consistent with) their motivation to be and remain just as individuals.

Epicurus' is an example of a theory of justice which faces, and arguably succeeds in resolving, the point that, in a eudaimonistic theory, justice has to be a virtue of the agent's character like the other virtues, and yet some account has to be given of the way in which justice functions as a virtue of societies. Epicurus' account has until recently been misunderstood, both because the contract theory was often taken to exhaust his thoughts on justice and because that theory was misunderstood as implying a pessimistic account of human nature. But it is because he has a contract theory without the expected negative view of the potential of human beings for co-operation that Epicurus is able to give us a theory which conjoins an account of justice as institution-relative and changing in content, with an account of justice as a state which the good Epicurean will invariably pursue.

More could of course usefully be said about the nature of Epicurus' theory itself. It clearly has affinities with contract theories from the time of the sophists,[42]

---

[40] *KD* 25. See the note on this passage in chapter II for textual problems.

[41] This is D. Gill's conclusion (forthcoming), though his attitude to the two-level problem differs from mine.

[42] For some of these links, see Denyer (1983).

and just as clearly represents a rejection of the kind of account of justice in society defended by Plato and Aristotle. In the course of the present enquiry, however, what matters most is to establish the relation of justice as a feature of society with justice as something which the agent aims for as part of her overall achievement of her final end.

3. *The Stoics: Natural Law and the Depoliticized Outlook*

We have seen that the Stoic account of *oikeiōsis* has the consequence that we extend our other-concern in a steadily more rational way until we come to have the same degree of rational other-concern for all other rational beings. Neither *philia* nor the bonds of the *polis* or city-state seem to be ethically defensible boundaries setting limits to the demands of other-concern. With friendship this has the result that particular commitments to others have, as such, a limited and not very important ethical role.[43] What of distinctively political attitudes, developed in the context of the city-state; and in particular what of justice as that relates to political institutions? What is the specific role left for these in Stoic thought? Here our evidence is unfortunately scanty, and the interpretation of it much disputed. The Stoics are the originators of one of the most influential concepts in political philosophy, that of natural law;[44] but matters are complicated by the fact that they do not seem to have meant by natural law what later became its standard form in the tradition. Still, even with these difficulties we can produce a coherent account which is consistent with the rest of Stoic ethics.

We complete the process of *oikeiōsis*, in its two versions, when we have extended our intuitive sympathies in a way which is wholly rational; when we act on, and are aware of the nature of, certain kinds of reason. This is reason as employed by the *sophos* or wise person; it is the normative ideal of reason. The Stoics sometimes characterize this reason as taking the form of *law* and thus as prescribing and forbidding actions. It is also called natural, for reasons which we have seen at length already.[45] The best account that we have from the early Stoa goes back to Chrysippus:

> Chrysippus began his book *On Law* as follows: Law is the king of all things, human and divine; it must preside over what is noble and what is base, and be their ruler and leader; and in accordance with this it must be the standard of what is just and what unjust, and for creatures that are by nature social it must be prescriptive of what one should do and prohibitive of what one should not do.[46]

---

[43] 'As such', because they will also, of course, form the context for much important development of the virtues.

[44] Striker (1986b) correctly points out that the Stoics are the first to have a conception of natural *law*, as opposed to natural justice. Plato and Aristotle think that justice has a natural backing, but they do not think of it as lawlike or prescriptive in form.

[45] Part 2, chapter 3.

[46] Marcianus, *Institutes* book I. Cf. Arius (ref. 98. 10–12): 'The law, they say, is correct reason prescriptive of what one should do, and prohibitive of what one should not do.'

All moral people, insofar as they are moral, will agree in their reasoning, so the content of natural law is perfectly objective; it is the reasoning anyone would come up with insofar as they reasoned morally. However, the *sophos* will be reasoning about particular situations and the rightness or wrongness of particular actions. Insofar as this reasoning is thought of as prescriptive, in a positive or negative way, it is thought of as taking the form of law—but not law of the kind with which we are familiar.[47] For the Stoics, natural law is simply correct moral reasoning, thought of as being prescriptive.[48]

The early Stoics also call natural law divine, and this is not surprising, since they take reason to be what is supremely important, and natural law is simply the prescriptive aspect of correct moral reasoning.[49] Cleanthes, in his *Hymn to Zeus*, identifies it with the will of Zeus, and stresses that it is the 'common' law which applies to all rational creatures.[50] But, although the prescriptive and authoritative aspects of the idea of law are stressed, natural law does not seem to be law in the sense of a body of highly general rules, but simply correct moral reasoning, regarded as making authoritative positive and negative commands.

This point brings out a paradox in the Stoic conception of natural law. Law is what unites a political community, giving a structure to political society and forming the basis for political interaction. It is something essentially public and general. In all these respects it contrasts with moral reasoning, which is what individuals employ in private and particular as well as public contexts, which is characteristically not general in form and which need not take a prescriptive or imperative form. Moral reasoning may employ general rules, but its negative or positive results concern particular actions and options. Yet for the Stoics it appears that natural law is to be identified with the correct moral reasoning to be found in the virtuous individual. And yet this leads to a strange result. Virtuous individuals relate to other virtuous individuals by way of sharing their reasoning and coming to the same conclusions. But they do not in any obvious sense form a political community. Indeed, those who reason morally may often find themselves in conflict with their actual political communities. Is it not perverse to use the image of law for what is shared by people who share a moral, but not a political community?

It is not perverse, for the Stoics are, as often, embracing a superficially paradoxical view quite deliberately; what makes the above consistent is their

---

[47] We can see from passages such as the opening of the *Hippias Major*, the whole of the pseudo-Platonic dialogue *Minos*, and Aristotle's *Rhet* I 13, that it was not very difficult to push someone into holding that the proper application of 'law' (*nomos*) was not to actual, positive law, but to a normative ideal not embodied in positive law, an ideal easily thought of as 'natural law'. See C.C.W. Taylor (1990). However, the Stoic view goes considerably further than this in taking natural law to be something which arguably does not have the form of actual laws at all.

[48] Hence what it prescribes will be *katorthōmata*, right actions done from a virtuous disposition, and performable only by the wise and virtuous. For a detailed defence of this view, see Vander Waerdt (forthcoming a). Vander Waerdt stresses Plutarch, *Sto rep* 1037 c-d, Arius 96.10–97.14, 102.4–10 and Cicero, *Leg* I 18–19. See also Inwood (1986b) and Watson (1971); and see Mitsis (forthcoming) for criticisms of the claim that there is a development in the Stoa on this issue.

[49] Zeno, according to Cicero *ND* I 36, *naturalem legem divinam esse censet eamque vim obtinere recta imperantem prohibentemque contraria*.

[50] Cleanthes, *Hymn to Zeus* line 2: *Zeu, phuseōs archēge, nomou meta panta kubernōn*. In line 20 evil people are said to disregard *theou koinon nomon*. Cf. Diogenes VII 88: *ho nomos ho koinos, hosper estin ho orthos logos*.

acceptance of the claim that moral people form the only (real) political community. Just as the virtuous person is the only (really) healthy, rich, sane person, and so on, so the way in which virtuous people relate to one another in the only relationship which is a (really) political relationship, and their directives the only ones which have the force of (real) law, paradoxical and counter-intuitive though this sounds.

> The Stoics say that the universe is a city in the proper sense, while those here on earth are not really. They are called cities, but they are not. For a city and a people are morally good [*spoudaion*], a kind of refined[51] organization and body of people governed by law.[52]

Some accounts add the point that the 'true' cosmic city is a city of gods and men:

> In the way that a city is described in two ways, as the habitable structure and also as the organization of the inhabitants together with the citizens, so also the universe is like a city consisting of gods and humans, with the gods having the leadership and the humans subordinate. There is community between them because of partaking in reason, which is natural law.[53]

The gods are not, obviously, the gods of Greek religion (though the Stoics made some effort to link them to that by allegory). They are rational beings, superior to humans by virtue of the role that rationality has for them, somewhat reminiscent of the Kantian notion of a holy will. The point is that the reasoning common to rational beings (humans and any others) is represented as a kind of law, because it has prescriptive force;[54] but obviously it is not law as we ordinarily use the term, but law as it would be in an ideal community. The ideal community, consisting of virtuous people reasoning morally, is the locus of law in an ideal sense.

What is meant by such an ideal moral community? As often with the Stoics, we are reminded of a Kantian idea, this time the kingdom (*Reich*) of ends.[55] Moral actions and attitudes are taken to link one to those who share them, in a way like that in which shared political interests link members of a city, but superior in that moral attitudes reflect a correct system of priorities in a way that actual political interests do not.[56] Thus it is at once tempting to think that we have two communities, the actual one we are born into and whose laws we follow, and the 'real' community, that of moral agents, who live under the 'real' law, natural law, which is just the prescriptive content of moral reasoning.

---

[51] *Asteion*, 'refined' or 'civilized'. On the use of this term see Appendix E to chapter 3 of Schofield (1991).

[52] Clement, *Stromateis* IV 26.

[53] Arius ap Eusebius, *Praep Ev* XV 15.4 Cf. Cicero, *Leg* I 22–23, Marcus IV 4.

[54] That this is the order of argument is clear from the passages in Cicero and Marcus: humans are linked by the bond of rationality with one another and with the gods; *therefore* they are linked by law.

[55] There are other aspects of Stoic theory which suggest this also, notably the idea that the virtuous person achieves benefit, of a special kind which equally benefits all virtuous people. See chapter 19.

[56] Schofield (1991) usefully develops the idea of an intellectual community; insofar as one, by virtue of having certain intellectual interests, takes part in certain activities, this links one in a community with others who share those interests, who may well not form part of one's own political community. And to someone with stronger intellectual than political interests, the intellectual community might quite well be more central and important than the actual political one. In this case, of course, we are not tempted to redescribe the intellectual community as being itself an ideal political one.

Let us conceive of two states [*res publicae*], one great and truly common [*publica*], in which are included both gods and men, in which we do not look to one or another corner, but measure the boundaries of our state by the sun, and another one in which we have been enrolled by the accident of our birth. This will be the city of Athens, or Carthage, or some other city, which relates not to all humans but some particular ones. Some people give their efforts to both states at the same time, the greater and the smaller, some only to the smaller, some only to the greater.[57]

Each of us has, contingently, a place in a particular political context; 'but there's another country. . . .'.

Apart from its Kantian resonances, the Stoic representation of moral consensus in reasoning as an ideal political community under ideal law is of tremendous interest in the history of political philosophy. From the present point of view, two points are relevant.

The first is that the idea fits well in Stoic ethical thought, once we appreciate its deliberately paradoxical nature, but that it is awkward to think of law whose content is so unlike that of any actual laws. And there seems to have been a development: in later Stoicism, especially in the Roman period, natural law seems to have been thought of as an idealized version of actual law—that is, as a set of general rules, but one whose content, unlike that of actual laws, is universally applicable. And this is the idea which, under the name of 'natural law', has gone through various influential formulations in political thought.[58] In Cicero, for example, we find natural law described in a way that makes it look simply like an idealization of actual law:

True law is right reason in harmony with nature, extending to all, unchanging, everlasting. It summons us to right action by its command, and deters us from wrongdoing by its prohibition. It is not in vain that it commands or prohibits good people, even though it has no effect on the wicked when it commands or forbids. To obstruct this law is a sin [*nec. . .fas est*]; no modification may be made to it; nor can it be completely abolished. We cannot be freed from this law by either Senate or People. We do not have to look for anyone other than ourselves to explain or interpret it. There will, then, not be one law at Rome and a different one at Athens, or one law now and a different one in the future—rather one law, everlasting and unchangeable, will bind all peoples at all times. And there will be one common master and ruler of all, that is, God, who is the author, arbitrator and mover of this law. Whoever will not obey it will be in flight from himself, and in despising human nature he will thereby suffer the severest penalties, even if he escapes what are considered to be punishments.[59]

---

[57] Seneca, *Ot* 4.

[58] See Vander Waerdt (forthcoming a). If natural law is thought of as having general rules as its content, then it will prescribe *kathēkonta* rather than *katorthōmata*, a large change from the point of view of Stoic theory. See Mitsis (forthcoming b) for criticisms of this; he claims that in the passages which appear to support this, *kathēkonta* should be so understood that they cover, rather than exclude, *katorthōmata*, which are 'perfect' *kathēkonta*.

[59] Cicero, *Rep* III 33. On the relation of Roman law to Stoic views about natural law see Vander Waerdt (forthcoming b). Vander Waerdt shows with much learning that there is no clear Stoic influence on the Roman legal thinkers.

And this is certainly the notion of natural law which we find from Aquinas through Grotius and Pufendorf to Hobbes and Locke, though of course there are variations on the need for God to guarantee the law, and on the rules which form its content. This tradition, however, is not relevant to the early Stoic view on natural law, which makes it simply the prescriptive content of correct moral reasoning.

Second, we must ask what the relevance of natural law is to our initial question: in what sense does it help to form a specifically *political* solution to anything? The answer is clear: the idealized political community, being a simply moral one, is not a political notion at all, and the very fact that the Stoics say that actual cities are not really cities suggests that they reject specifically political discussion in favour of a redefinition of political terms which uses them in a context where political issues do not arise. This suggestion is, I think, correct, and explains why there is so little that we can call Stoic political philosophy. We find various suggestions which we can call political, but there is no one political direction that Stoic ethical theories have to take.

The most notorious contribution of the Stoics to political discussion was Zeno's *Republic*, together with another work of that name by Chrysippus. Zeno's work became so notorious that we are told that later Stoics tried to bowdlerize it, and the references we have to it are often disingenuous, picking out its discussion of various shocking practices and suggesting that it recommended them.[60] It seems clear that Zeno and Chrysippus claimed that there was nothing but convention to support various strongly held taboos concerning sex, disposal of the dead and so on, so that in certain circumstances it would be permissible for the virtuous person to eat dead bodies, commit incest and so on. But the most serious part of the work seems to have been a conscious reply to Plato's *Republic*, Zeno's own projected ideal city. Like Plato, Zeno rejected the force of accepted family ties and relied on a sublimated form of affection to bind together the citizens of the ideal city. Zeno went further than Plato in rejecting standard institutional features of actual cities, such as temples, gymnasia and any coinage. But the most striking feature of Zeno's work, as far as we can tell, was the one in which it most resembles Plato's *Republic*, namely that only the virtuous are citizens of the ideal state. Zeno's answer to the problem of how to improve actual cities is so idealized that it removes those factors that lead to specifically political problems. Like Plato, Zeno abolishes conflict, and does so by abolishing the obvious sources of conflict, namely attachment to goods other than virtue. In a city in which money and status do not matter, and normal family life is replaced by wider affective ties and an instrumental attitude to sex, personal conflicts are likewise obviated. This gives us an idealized model for a political association; but like Plato it gives us no political programme for achieving this. In fact we can best see Zeno's work as an earlier version of the thesis which

---

[60] See Diogenes VII 32–4, 129–131, 187–9. Schofield (1991) chapter 1 argues that the material in the first and third of these passages has already been recast by a sceptical source. Sextus Empiricus makes obviously dishonest use of the shocking material in *PH* III 205–208, 245–49, *M* XI 190–96. Philodemus, *Sto*, especially columns 17–20, gives us the piously shocked Epicurean view of the 'dreadful practices sanctioned by the Stoics'. The earlier parts of the work give us an entertaining view of the lengths to which some later Stoics were prepared to go to avoid responsibility for the ideas in it. See the Introduction in Dorandi (1982).

came to be expressed as the idea that the community of rational virtuous people is the only real city.[61]

Thus we can see that there is a price to be paid for the radical way in which the Stoics answer the question, how the just person relates to actual political institutions, and what she demands of them by way of institutional justice. Like Plato's just agent in the *Republic*, she will take part in the politics of no society but the ideal society, which exists nowhere on earth.[62] This does not mean that she will be inactive politically in her own city, whichever that may be. But her political activity as a Stoic will consist simply in trying, by whatever means are in the circumstances appropriate and morally permitted, to bring the actual state of affairs closer to the ideal. And since what this demands is making everybody moral, no one political programme is indicated.

We do not know whether Zeno and Chrysippus made any concrete suggestions as to how to bring about the ideal state, nor their answers to the related question, how we are to rank actual states for excellence.[63] Early Stoic definitions of justice treat it simply as a virtue of character,[64] and are unhelpful on its political dimension. We know that Ariston stressed the conventional nature of one's ties to one's own state:

> By nature there is no native country [*patris*], just as there is no house or field or smithy or doctor's clinic; each of these comes into being, or rather gets named and called what it is, with reference to whoever is living there and using it.[65]

This underlines the attitude, found in less extreme form in other early Stoics, that political and social institutions are in themselves just indifferents, things with only an indirect relation to moral value.

A Stoic is not of course committed to the view that political institutions are merely instrumentally valuable material on which he is to practice his virtuous development. Preferred indifferents, after all, have genuine value; it is rational to go for them, and they are in accordance with our nature. So a Stoic has reasons independent of virtue for preferring the absence of poverty, coercion and so on. Further, a person who has developed towards virtue and extended the circles of social *oikeiōsis* will realize that from the moral viewpoint she has reason to prefer these things impartially, that is, at the least without arbitrary limitations to particular people. And this might seem to legitimate some sort of political stance. We find the

---

[61] Schofield (1991) argues that the work is 'Janus-faced', and that it was written with a more positive political programme in mind than I have allowed, 'as a contribution to the dialectic of classical Greek philosophy about the proper constitution of the *polis*'. However, 'it opened the way for doing political philosophy in a quite different style, no longer tied to preoccupation with the *polis*, but focused instead on the moral potentialities of man considered as man, not as citizen' (Chapter 4). See however Vander Waerdt (forthcoming a).

[62] *Repub* 592 a-b.

[63] Erskine (1990) argues that the early Stoa was committed to democracy and economic redistribution in a way that the later Stoa rejected. For a critical discussion of this, see Vander Waerdt (1991).

[64] At *SVF* I 197 it is said to arise from *oikeiōsis* (we have seen this from the passage from the Anonymous Commentator on the *Theaetetus*, chapter 12 section 2). At *SVF* I 374 justice is defined as allotting to each their deserts (*to kat'axian hekastōi nemein*).

[65] *SVF* I 371.

Stoics holding that the wise person will take part in politics, especially in states which appear to be making progress towards becoming complete (or perfect), and will legislate, educate people and write useful books.[66] But this is still pretty vague. It would seem to favour negative efforts to remove poverty, injustice, and so on rather than positive efforts to promote a favoured interpretation of justice, say. And it is confined to a level where the Stoic has no reason, just as a Stoic, to favour capitalism rather than socialism, proportional representation rather than first-past-the-post voting systems, democracy rather than a one-party system. For we have no political, as opposed to moral, criteria for picking out which are the states that are progressing, rather than degenerating.

We find an isolated and unmotivated claim that the Stoics held that the best state was a 'mixture' of democracy, kingship and aristocracy,[67] but this gives us little help in the absence of arguments as to what is good or bad about these forms when 'unmixed'. And we have already seen that later Stoicism, particularly in the Roman period, tended to take for granted the importance of social roles and their attached duties, and to start from them in following moral rules, rather than stressing any need to criticize the content of existing duties.[68] Such discussions as we find of the nature of the *polis* are formal and unhelpful,[69] and in discussions of 'ways of life' we sometimes find it assumed that it is morally permissible to 'live off' kingship either by being king oneself or by living off a king's property. Being a king's dependent is obviously one among many ways that a philosopher might make a living; it is not so clear why it is morally permissible to be a king oneself. We certainly do not find a critical attitude to forms of government; they are just some among the indifferents, and there does not seem to be a politically guided way of selecting among them.[70]

The early Stoa did have some things to say which we can call political about actual institutions.[71] Two statements are ascribed to Chrysippus which look very like defences of actual political institutions. In one passage he is said to hold the position that life is like a race, and that one should compete with other people. Tripping up the opponents and other foul play is ruled out, but there is nothing wrong with trying to win.[72] In another passage Chrysippus is said to claim that, just as in a theatre, the space is public, but I am correctly said to have a right to the seat that I have paid for, so in the world the fact that everything is originally common to all is compatible with people having a right to property.[73] The theatre analogy, repeated later by Epictetus,[74] is an extremely interesting one, not least because its force shifted over time. While the Greek theatre was like a modern one as far as seating arrangements went, the Roman theatre was organized strictly on class lines; you could sit only in the part of the theatre assigned to people of your social standing. It

[66] Arius 94.8–20.

[67] Diogenes VII 131. Cicero in *Rep* produces a theory of the 'mixed' constitution in the context of mythical Roman history, and at I 34 there is a reference to Panaetius.

[68] Chapter 2, section 4.

[69] See Arius 103.9–24 for an example, together with the discussion in Schofield (1991) chapter 3 and appendices E and F.

[70] Arius 109.10–110.4.

[71] This issue is discussed in greater detail in Annas (1989a).

[72] *Off* III 42.

[73] *Fin* III 67.

[74] *Disc* II 4.

thus comes to serve as an analogy for more restrictive implications of property-owning than it originally did.[75] Unfortunately, we do not know what reasons were offered by Chrysippus for these claims. We know that his own *Republic* was regarded as being just as extreme as Zeno's, and for the same reasons, so he seems to have held that in the ideal state there would be no property (since caring about property is a barrier to reasoning in a moral way) while in the actual world property is defensible.

Clearly Chrysippus held some version of a two-level view, but it is unclear what form it took. He may have held the weaker view that in the actual world the existence of private property, and the degree of competition with others which this brings with it, is compatible with the possibility of moral progress, so that private property can be justified as a necessary concession to human weakness without giving up on the possibility of progress to an ideal state in which there would be no private property with its associated competition. However, Chrysippus may have held the stronger view (more properly called a two-level view) that private property can be justified as being in fact a helpful means to moral development. Aristotle had justified private property as providing the right context for the development of the virtues,[76] and Chrysippus too may have thought that, given human nature, a system of private property provides a better context than common ownership for moral development.

It is disappointing that we do not have enough evidence to choose between these interpretations. However, the associated scraps of information that we have about further Stoic contributions to the issue continue to leave us in this position, namely of being unsure, when some existing institution is defended, whether this is being done on the basis of the weaker or of the stronger view. And this strongly suggests that the Stoics had no explicitly political 'line' on the matter. What matters is to achieve the right moral ideal. How this is best to be achieved politically is a matter of how best to organize things that are indifferent, and this is something which may vary given the circumstances. It is noteworthy, though, that in general Stoic discussions on this level seem to be basically conservative.

In one very interesting passage Cicero opposes the views of two heads of the Stoa, Diogenes of Babylon and Antipater of Tarsus, on cases where people are buying and selling, and one of the two parties can exploit the other's ignorance, without actually breaking any laws or denying the other party anything he has a right to know. Someone selling a house, for example, may conceal the fact that the house has serious defects.[77] Any comments that Antipater made regarding these cases simply repeat orthodox Stoic views: it is natural to us to have other-concern which can be extended to all other people, so that we care about their interests even if we have no personal connection to them, and so can clearly see that we should not harm their interests even if we could personally gain by so doing. What is more interesting is that Diogenes is represented as making comments which give some kind of defence of the person who restricts himself to respecting his legal obligations

---

[75] This salient point is made by Erskine (1990), pp. 105–110, who notes the more restrictive use of the analogy made by Roman writers.

[76] *Pol* 1262 b 37–1263 b 14.

[77] *Off* III 50–57, 91–92. The whole of both passages is translated, with more detailed comment, in Annas (1989a).

and not violating the legal rights of others. The person who knowingly sells the defective house to an innocent buyer has, he points out, not violated the buyer's rights, since he has not kept back anything that the buyer has a right to know.

Cicero claims that Diogenes is in conflict with the orthodox position repeated by Antipater, but this seems wrong. We have no reason to think that Diogenes recommended the minimalist view that all that is morally required of an agent is that he fulfil his legal obligations.[78] His position is not in conflict with the orthodox Stoic view put forward by Antipater. But Diogenes did clearly stress, in a way that was found striking, the importance of legal obligations and legal rights. Once again, we are left uncertain, because of the nature of our sources, whether he held the weaker or the stronger view—that is, whether he held that fidelity to legal obligations is compatible with achieving Stoic moral progress, or rather that such fidelity is actually the best way, given the way the world is, to achieve Stoic moral progress. (This would be on the following grounds: if we try directly to respect the interests of all others, we shall destroy institutions like buying and selling, which presuppose precisely that we do not directly try to do this; it is by respecting such institutions that we have a better chance of progressing in virtue.) Although we cannot decide between these two options, we can at least say that Diogenes was trying to make some kind of space, in Stoic moral theory, for the claims of institutions like that of buying and selling.

Later we find another prominent Stoic, Hecaton, putting forward what does look like the stronger view. In his book on *kathēkonta* he claimed that

> A wise person should look after his family property, doing nothing contrary to customs, laws and institutions. For we do not wish to be rich just for ourselves, but for our children, relatives and friends, and especially for our country. For the means and resources of individuals are the riches of the state.[79]

And he also claimed[80] that one should, at least *prima facie*, put duty to a treasonable parent above duty to the state, on the grounds that this filial attitude is conducive to there being an excellent state.[81] In both of these cases we seem to find the stronger view: a certain attitude, for instance towards private property, is justified on the grounds that the having of the attitude conduces to a further and morally more universal goal. However, we have no explicit theoretical defence on Hecaton's part, and so no reason to ascribe to him a general theory defending existing institutions on the grounds that they indirectly encourage moral progress.

The absence of a general theory is even more marked where we find discussion of justice. In Cicero's *De Officiis* I we find a discussion, which presumably derives from the Stoic Panaetius, of the ways in which people are justly entitled to property which they own. The question is raised, what the origin is of property rights.

> Things are not private by nature, but become so either by long occupation—e.g.,

---

[78] Hence Cicero's presentation of the alleged disagreement between him and Antipater is in many ways misleading.

[79] Reported by Cicero at *Off* III 63.

[80] *Off* III 90.

[81] He adds, however, that although it is permissible to avoid a choice for as long as one can, if one is forced to choose one should, in the end, choose the state.

people who have at some point entered vacant territory, or by conquest—e.g., people who have acquired them by war, or by law, pact, agreement, lot.[82]

Here the point is being made that it is just for people to keep what they are entitled to, but it is striking that the methods by which people originally acquired their entitlements are a mixed bag, and some of them (conquest and war) are flagrantly unjust. The standing of the discussion of the justice of keeping entitlements is somewhat undermined by the total absence of any discussion of what it is that makes entitlements just entitlements. There seems to be no theory of justice to draw on.[83]

Thus over time we find a repeated pattern: various Stoics defend, or indicate justifications for, a particular political or social institution, while Stoic moral theory continues to insist that the proper application for political terms like 'law' and 'community' is to the situation of ideal moral consensus. What does not emerge is any principled way of linking the two. Indeed, one wonders whether the Stoics ever did have a principled way of linking their moral theory to their discussions of existing political and social institutions. On the other hand, it would be odd if the only grounds for defending private property, legal obligations and so forth, were the fact that they were part of the established social reality that we have to live with. For the Stoics are notably uncompromising about everyday intuitions and common beliefs. It would be odd if our commonsense views about happiness were in need of a great deal of modification, but not our views about private property or laws about sale.

The gaps we find when we look for Stoic political philosophy are not due solely to the state of our sources. For the Stoic answers to political problems, such as problems about justice, are moral rather than specifically political answers. And although we do find fragments of 'applied' philosophy such as the discussions of private property, these are not integrated in any systematic way into the general moral theory.

So the Stoics have no systematic answer to the question, how justice as a virtue of the individual agent relates to justice as a virtue of institutions. As we would expect from the fact that other-concern finds no ethically significant stopping place in the *polis*, they do not regard the justice of insitutions as a centrally important ethical matter. Ironically, in virtue of the fact that they bequeathed to the tradition of political thought the important concept of natural law, their own outlook is a radically unpolitical, even depoliticized one.[84]

---

[82] *Off* I 21.

[83] I do not here discuss the long passage on justice as a virtue in the first book of the *De Officiis*. There is much doubt as to whether its main original features are due to Panaetius or to Roman influences due to Cicero himself. Atkins (1990) and Atkins and Griffin (1991) stresses the Roman aspects of the long and curiously disjunctive account of justice. Even if we put more stress on Cicero's Stoic source Panaetius, we should bear in mind that the account has no parallel in early Stoic texts, and has to be understood as a distinctively Panaetian development, probably in response to Roman intellectual influences.

[84] Although I have not discussed Roman Stoicism, I think that my conclusion is in agreement with that of the classic article by Brunt (1975).

4. *Aristotelian Theories*

Aristotle

Aristotle, in the *Nicomachean Ethics*, treats justice like a virtue of character along with the other virtues. It, like them, is analyzed in terms of the 'mean', and treated as a virtue that is acquired by progressive habituation and increasing rational understanding. In this Aristotle goes along with the standard ancient assumption that justice is a virtue of the individual agent, sufficiently like the other virtues for it to be unified with them by the agent's *phronēsis* or practical intelligence. This way of proceeding has opened Aristotle to modern criticisms that he ignores the distinctive nature of justice.[85]

There are several elements to this attack, which are better treated separately. First is the claim that justice does not fit the special Aristotelian theory of the 'mean'; treating justice as though it did, is simply wrong on Aristotle's part. Second is the claim that Aristotle ignores the institutional aspect of justice, or at best treats it in a marginal way. Third is the claim that Aristotle is fundamentally wrong to treat justice as a virtue of character at all, since it is basically a virtue of institutions, and agents are just in a derivative way, namely in that they are the kind of people who respect and live by the principles establishing the justice of institutions.

As we have seen,[86] the doctrine of the mean, in its application to the virtues, embodies the specific claim that a virtue is 'in a mean' in that it is a state in which the agent aims at a mean in both actions and feelings. As such, the theory applies far more plausibly to feelings and emotions than to actions. The virtuous person, in aiming at being the kind of person who does the right thing, is aiming at having the right degree of the appropriate kind of feeling, the degree which amounts neither to excess nor to defect. The present claim is that this is an inappropriate model for justice, for here there is no application for the idea of feeling the right amount. This would have application only if there were a characteristic range of feelings or emotions such that they standardly produced just actions, whereas excess or defect produced unjust actions. Aristotle on one occasion seems to claim that justice is marked by such a range, namely, one where the excess is *pleonexia*, greed or the desire to have more.[87] But this is very artificial, as he recognizes elsewhere when he says that the vice of excess is committing injustice, whereas the vice of defect is that of *suffering* injustice.[88] Obviously, there is no one range of feeling which could be expressed excessively by taking more than one is entitled to, be expressed 'in the mean' by taking only the due amount, and be expressed defectively by letting others take what one is oneself entitled to. Hence, it appears, the theory of the mean simply breaks down when applied to justice.

Aristotle, however, explicitly says that the theory of the mean does not apply to justice in exactly the way it does to the other virtues. 'Justice is a sort of mean [*mesotēs tis*], not in the same way as the other virtues, but because it is related to a

---

[85] This attack is put most trenchantly by Williams (1980).
[86] In chapter 2, section 2.
[87] 1129 b 1–10, 1130 a 14–b 5, 1136 b 35–1137 a 4.
[88] 1133 b 29–1134 a 16.

mean <lit. is of a mean>, while injustice is related to the extremes.'[89] And what he has in mind is clearly just the point often urged against him: there is no one independently identifiable motivating range of feelings and emotions which produce wrong action at both extremes and right action at the mean point. Hence, justice does not fit the theory of the mean in the specific way in which the other virtues do. But the reasonable conclusion is that what Aristotle has in mind is a more general application of the theory of the mean, under which justice does fall. And this is supported by a passage in the *Politics*:

> If it was well said in the *Ethics* that the happy life is the life according to virtue which is unhindered, and that virtue is a mean, then necessarily the best life is the mean [middle, *meson*] life, namely, achieving the mean which is available to each kind of person. These same definitions necessarily hold of the virtue and badness of the state and constitution; for a constitution is a sort of life of the state.[90]

Aristotle here clearly envisages a general schema of the mean, which applies both to the virtues of character discussed in the *Ethics* and the types of constitution discussed in the *Politics*. What is in mind is a schema in which the right way of proceeding corresponds to a mean between two related extremes, of excess and defect, which correspond to characteristically wrong ways of proceeding. Such a general schema covers the specific account of the virtues, and also Aristotle's schema for discussing constitutions, according to which democracy represents one extreme and oligarchy the other, while the mean between them is represented by Aristotle's preferred form of constitution, *politeia* or 'polity'.[91] Again, distributive and rectificatory justice are both described in the fifth book of the *Nicomachean Ethics* as fitting the model of hitting a mean between extremes.[92] But of course the specific application to ranges of feeling is found only in the virtues, and there need be nothing corresponding in the types of constitution. The 'mean' (*mesos*) constitution is indeed marked by the preponderance of *hoi mesoi*, the people in the middle, neither very rich nor very poor.[93] Of course there is nothing analogous to this in the case of the virtues. What matters is rather that Aristotle is insisting, probably against common sense, that the right way of doing things lies between two corresponding, and opposed, wrong ways of doing them; right and wrong are not a binary opposition. The theory of the mean is thus a general schema in Aristotle, as indeed in other fourth-century writers,[94] and there is no reason to expect justice to fit the pattern of the other virtues in every detail, especially given that Aristotle says explicitly that it is a special case.

More serious is the charge that Aristotle, by treating it primarily as a virtue of individual character,[95] misdescribes justice. It is certainly not true, however, that he

[89] 1133 b 33–1134 a 1.

[90] 1295 a 35–b 1. Aristotle goes on to distinguish three 'parts' of the city, the rich, 'middle' and poor, and declares the mean or middle constitution to be the one in which the 'middle' people dominate.

[91] Aristotle's schematism here is quite marked. For a discussion of ways in which it distorts his views of democracy and oligarchy, see Mulgan (1991). This point is independent of the difficult question of the relation of the 'mean' constitution to the previously discussed 'mixed' constitution.

[92] The former at 1131 a 10–15; the latter at 1132 a 6–b 20.

[93] Creed (1989).

[94] See Hutchinson (1988).

[95] For an article which accepts that this is what Aristotle is doing, but defends it, see O'Connor (1988).

neglects the institutional application of justice. In Book V of the *Ethics*, in which he does discuss justice as a virtue of individual character, he also discusses at length various kinds of institutional justice. In chapter 3 he analyses distributive justice, and in chapter 4, rectificatory justice. These are kinds of justice which can only be understood as concerned primarily with institutions.

Moreover, Aristotle, unlike the Stoics, has much that is substantial to say about institutions like private property, and means of acquiring goods. He explicitly defends private property against the arguments of Plato in the *Republic*,[96] and distinguishes, as we have seen, right from wrong kinds of acquisition of goods and money.[97] There is thus no such gap in Aristotle's theory as there is in the Stoic theory when we ask about the justice of various practices such as acquisition and possession of various goods.

Further, a large part of Aristotle's discussion in the *Politics* concerns political justice.[98] In fact, for Aristotle it is political justice which is central. He does, in a few passages in the ethical and political works, raise questions of justice which arise between people who are not members of the same political unit,[99] and also says that there are forms of justice in the household, which are like political justice, but different from it.[100] But Aristotle focusses on political justice:

> This holds among people who share a life aiming at self-sufficiency, and who are free and equal either proportionately or arithmetically, so that people who do not meet this condition do not have political justice towards one another, only a kind of justice which has a similarity to it. For there is justice among people who have law in their relations to one another.[101]

A great deal of the *Politics* is devoted to issues of political justice, for Aristotle spends much time and energy in classifying various types of 'constitutions' or political arrangements holding between free people, and discussing the question of which type of constitution best achieves political justice. One approach to the problem is to examine which kinds of constitutions aim at the common good:

> It is clear, then, that such constitutions as aim at the common good are correct according to what is just absolutely, but that those which aim only at the rulers' own good are all mistaken, and deviances from the correct constitutions; for they are like the rule of a master, while the city is an association of the free.[102]

Another approach is to examine the notion of equality, since a widespread intuition about justice is that it requires ensuring equality, but not, Aristotle insists, simple numerical equality, but an equality that is proportionate to *axia* or worth. Thus

---

[96] See his criticisms of Plato in *Pol* II, especially chapter 5. On this topic, see Miller (forthcoming) ch. 9, and (1990); also Irwin (1991).

[97] See chapter 4, pp. 156–57.

[98] Modern discussions that stress this aspect of the *Politics* are Nussbaum (1988a), Charles (1988), Miller (forthcoming) and Keyt (1991b).

[99] *Pol* 1324 a 35–b 36; *Nicomachean Ethics* 1161 a 32–b 8; *Eudemian Ethics* 1242 a 19–28. On these passages see Miller (forthcoming). However, as Miller stresses, Aristotle is not committed to there being a kind of pre-political justice which is the source of political justice.

[100] *NE* V 6, 1134 a 24–b 18.

[101] 1134 a 26–30.

[102] 1279 a 17–21.

Aristotle examines extensively the ways in which justice brings about distributions in which individuals have shares of some good, such as political office, in a way whose proportion reflects the proportion in the relation of the individuals' worth or value. In Book III especially he discusses the different interpretations of this idea which lie behind democratic and oligarchic conceptions of justice.[103]

Here there is obviously no scope to go into the detailed argument of the *Politics*, nor to discuss the difficult issue of which is Aristotle's own candidate for being the best political arrangement. What is of importance here is simply to stress two points. One is that Aristotle can hardly be accused of neglecting justice as a virtue of institutions. Large tracts of the ethical and political works are devoted to precisely this issue. The other is that Aristotle's institutional framework for justice is that of the city-state; there is a kind of justice in familial and non-political relationships, but the central kind of justice is that which relates members of a well-defined political unit, the *polis*. With justice, as with *philia*, Aristotle draws a firm boundary to other-concern. Justice, for Aristotle, does not naturally extend into a relationship which links rational humans just as such; while he does not explicitly say that we do not owe duties of justice to people outside our own *polis*, his own account of justice is tailored to the political institutions of the city-state.

There remains, of course, the question of how justice as a virtue of institutions is related to justice as a virtue of character. There are some passages which suggest a Platonic kind of answer—the kind of justice involved is importantly the same.

> There is no fine deed of a person or a city apart from virtue and intelligence; and a city's courage, justice, intelligence <and temperance> have the same force and form [*morphē*] as those in which each person shares [*metechein*] when he is said to be <courageous>, just, intelligent and temperate.[104]

We need not, however, understand this in the strong kind of way that we find in the *Republic*. Aristotle might mean no more than that just people and just institutions are 'the same' at some fairly high level of generality; he certainly is not committed to the idea that people and cities are isomorphic in their internal structure. The obvious candidate for the respect in which Aristotle might think that people and cities are just in the same way is that, as with all the virtues, justice displays the structure of the 'mean'. We have seen that the mean is a very general schema which does not have to be applied to people and to institutions in specifically the same way, so this suggestion is plausible. Aristotle thinks that the just person, who makes just distributions, displays the pattern of the mean; and that distributive justice is itself a case of the mean. Moreover, Aristotle's favoured *politeia*, in which distributions are just, itself exemplifies the mean. People and institutions, then, can be said to be just in the 'same' way, at some admittedly unhelpful level of generality. However, Aristotle never explicitly says that the justice of a city is itself a case of the mean. The *Politics* passage, then, is probably best regarded as an overstatement, which Aristotle is not consistently committed to. His considered view seems to be the more moderate one that just people exemplify the mean, and so do patterns of just distribution, and a type of just constitution. These are all just in the ways

---

[103] It is not obvious what the correct relation is between justice as what achieves the common good and justice as distributing in accordance with desert. I am indebted here to discussions with David Gill.

[104] *Pol* 1323 b 32–36.

appropriate to the kinds of items that they are. Aristotle lacks the urge to reduce any of these types of justice to one basic type.

Aristotle's thus differs from modern theories of justice which regard justice in the individual as being derivative, a disposition to abide by and respect principles of justice which define justice for institutions. However, as is obvious enough, the view that this is the correct relationship is a typically modern one, and we have no reason to expect Aristotle to share the view that justice is primarily, or basically, a virtue of institutions and only secondarily of people. What is more interesting is that Aristotle does not, as is sometimes supposed, reverse the priority, taking people to be the primary locus of justice and downgrading or neglecting its institutional application. Rather, Aristotle has much to say about both, and, in his usual fashion, has no drive to reduce one to the other or to force them under a specific common account.

Although a work like this, which is primarily concerned with Aristotle's ethical framework, cannot provide an adequate account of his study of political justice, nonetheless one point is patent enough: Aristotle's stress on the *polis* as the primary locus of justice. It is in political association that people primarily stand in relations of justice to one another. Aristotle does not deny outright that we owe duties of justice to the furthest Mysian, but he gives us no way of finding out what these might be. He considers justice in the context of the city-state, and of just distributions which produce a political common good.

Later Aristotelian Theories

Later theories of an Aristotelian cast are responding, as we have already seen, to Stoicism, and to the consequent need to restate Aristotle's theories in a form which takes account of Stoicism, whether by opposing or by absorbing Stoic influences in the relevant respect. We find strikingly different responses in Antiochus and in Arius Didymus on the issue of justice and the role of the *polis*.

Antiochus. Antiochus, who after all is not pretending to put forward Aristotle's own ideas in detail, but to be presenting the 'original tradition' behind Aristotelian, Platonic and Stoic ethics, takes the bolder line. He simply takes over the Stoic view of social *oikeiōsis*, in which one proceeds from self-concern outwards to concern for any human, and in which the *polis* does not form a consequential stopping place. Like the Stoics he leaves no room for an interesting political theory; attachment to the *polis* becomes just another attachment to external goods, and the moral outlook becomes a depoliticized one. We do not have much material explicitly from Antiochus on this issue, but one passage in the exposition of his ethical theory in Cicero's *de Finibus* V makes the point clearly enough. The speaker gives an account of justice which is clearly Stoic in structure.

> In the whole of morality [*honestum*] which we are talking about, there is nothing more brilliant, nor of greater extent [*nec quod latius pateat*] than the association of people with other people, a kind of community and sharing of advantages and a real affection for the human race. It is born with us from conception, since children are loved by their parents, and the whole household is held together by marriage and offspring, and gradually spreads abroad, first through kin relationships, then marriage connections, then friendships, then relations of proximity,

then to fellow-citizens and those who are allies and friends politically, and finally embraces the entire human race. This attitude of the mind, which allots to each their own, and maintains this community of human association I am talking about in a dutiful and fair way, is called justice.[105]

This is followed by a claim that justice and the other virtues reciprocally imply one another, the first half of which is rather unclear in its argumentative force, but incidentally brings out a very interesting point:

> For since human nature is so formed as to have something innate which is, so to speak, civic and concerned with one's people (which the Greeks call *politikon*) whatever each virtue does will not be incompatible with human fellowship and with that community and affection I have described.[106]

The speaker is clearly referring to the Stoic type of account just given, and soon to be repeated.[107] He takes it as uncontroversial that this can be referred to by the word *politikon* and the corresponding words in Latin. He has not noticed, or does not care, that this assumes that, in the middle of a supposedly Aristotelian account, *politikon* has lost its connection with *polis* (and correspondingly the Latin *civile* has lost its connection with *civis*). For clearly the *polis* is of no particular importance in this account of justice. Antiochus seems to be aware of Aristotle's more strictly 'political' works, which focus on the *polis*, but he finds it equally natural to use the word *politikon* in a wider sense which is more like 'social', and can figure without remark in Stoic theory.[108] It can of course be argued that the more general meaning is often present in Aristotle also, but nonetheless Aristotle's political works grant a real centrality to the *polis* and to the relationships of justice that arise within it, and show only sparse interest in wider relationships. Antiochus sides with the Stoics, but apparently refuses to see a problem.

Arius Didymus. Arius, as we have already seen, takes the opposite tack on this issue from Antiochus. Although his account of Aristotelian ethics bases it on a form of *oikeiōsis*, and develops other-concern, as the Stoics do, to the point of requiring what we can call impartiality, he nonetheless compromises: 'But although we have a common love of mankind, what is choiceworthy for its own sake is much more obvious in the relation towards friends that we see regularly.'[109] We have seen[110] that this compromise produces problems; for nothing is done to reconcile the results of

---

[105] *Fin* V 65.

[106] *Fin* V 66.

[107] In *Fin* V 67.

[108] At *Fin* IV 5, the speaker, giving a rundown of 'Antiochus' Old Academy', commends the Peripatetics and Academics for their full treatment of the issue which is *civile* in Latin, *politikon* in Greek. Here it does seem, despite the vagueness of the passage, that what is being referred to is 'politics' in the restrictive sense of issues that centre on the *polis*. Unless Antiochus (or Cicero) is being careless, the Antiochean view did not find it important to distinguish between *politikon* as 'of the *polis*' and as 'social'.

[109] 121.22–24.

[110] Chapter 12, section 4.

the Stoic view with the insistence that nonetheless moral demands are 'more obvious' in our close relationships. The problem is compounded when we find that at the end of the long account of ethics Arius adds a section on 'household management and politics'.[111] This section is obviously a compendium of points taken from the *Politics*; various claims are strung together with no such radical reworking as the ethical works have been subject to. This is not to say that there are no changes from the *Politics*; for example, Arius discusses the household as a 'small *polis*' and therefore regards the family as itself the 'first *polis*'.[112] This is in sharp contrast to Aristotle's consistent attitude that household relationships are different from political ones; for example, they do not exemplify political justice, but merely something like it. It seems, then, that Arius is operating with a sense of 'political' that is somewhat weakened from Aristotle's; he even uses Aristotle's famous formula that a human is a political animal (*politikon zōion*) to explain why he will talk about the city-state *and family*. It is tempting to think that he has weakened the distinction between the political and the social.[113]

However, Arius' actual account draws on different sections of the *Politics* so mechanically that it is clear that there has been no radical rethinking of Aristotle's basic ideas. Arius draws on the first book of our *Politics* for a discussion of the household as the origin of the state, and the locus of the relationships which will develop into political ones. There are references to the theory of natural slavery[114] and to the thesis that there are natural, approved ways of acquiring goods.[115] There are references to Book III's account of citizenship, and classification of the different kinds of constitution;[116] and to Book V account of *stasis* or internal conflict in states, and ways in which states can be stabilized or destabilized.[117] More surprisingly, perhaps, there are many echoes of Book VII, where Aristotle sketches his own idea of the ideal state; Arius gives us strings of bits of detail, from the ideal size of the state to the division between the productive classes of people and the citizens proper, to regulations about temples and age for marriage.[118] It cannot be said that this adds up to a particularly coherent picture of what Arius takes to be important about the state, but we can glean a few important points from it nonetheless.[119]

One is that in the Hellenistic period there seems to have been no development of Aristotle's political thought. Whereas his ethical thought was fairly thoroughly revamped, with Stoic terminology taken over in a way reflecting argumentative

---

[111] 147.26–152.25.

[112] 148.8–9, 148.5. He does go on to say that the household contains the 'seeds' of the *polis*, and contains 'sketches' of various political relationships. But one cannot imagine Aristotle, in the *Politics*, endorsing the earlier claims at all.

[113] As has Antiochus (see p. 317).

[114] 148.21–149.4. The sentence may suggest an interesting doubt as to whether slavery is in fact natural. But it may mean only that there are, in fact, slaves by convention as well as natural slaves.

[115] 149.15–24. Again, there is a change of tone, at least; Arius sounds more enthusiastic about money-making and its importance to the household than Aristotle does.

[116] 150.4–5, 150.17–151.8.

[117] 151.9–15.

[118] 150.6–10, 151.23–152.25.

[119] For more on this passage in Arius and its significance for Hellenistic political philosophy, see Annas (1994).

encounter with Stoic theory, Aristotle's political thought found no strong rivals; as we have seen, the Stoics had no real political theory, and the Epicureans were uninterested in this kind of philosophical debate. Thus Arius gives us excerpts and paraphrases from what is clearly our version of Aristotle's *Politics*, without apparently feeling the need to make fresh sense of it in a greatly changed philosophical climate.[120] There is no attempt to harmonize Arius' weakened understanding of the political with his unproblematic excerpting of passages of Aristotle which use the original, stronger sense. Indeed, one wonders at times how much political theory was understood or taken seriously by the writer who excerpted bits of Book VII without remark alongside Book III, for example.

As a result of this, we can see that Arius retains Aristotle's idea that moral development, and the exercise of justice in particular, requires the *polis* as its locus of development and exercise, but that this idea is retained as part of a system of ideas within which it no longer really makes sense. Once one has accepted the Stoic notion of *oikeiōsis* and its result, that one reaches the impartial point of view at the end of the process of moral development, there is a real question, What role is played by the *polis* as a theatre for moral development? As we have seen,[121] there are arguments whereby we can reconcile the importance of the impartial point of view with a special commitment to particular other people; and versions of those arguments can readily be extended to special concern for one's particular political unit. It may be that, while ideally we should have concern for the furthest Mysian, the unknown traveller in the desert, and so on, in fact all that can reasonably be required of us is that we have concern for our own fellow-citizens. Or it might be that it is unrealistic to expect people to develop directly in ways that will lead to impartial other-concern, so that it is best for people's moral development to take place within the locus of the city-state, this being the best way in which people will develop the moral basis that can be led on to impartiality. However, neither of these arguments is present, even in embryonic form, in Arius. What we find is rather a mechanical, and perhaps rather nostalgic combination of thoughts: the Stoics are basically right, and moral development, particularly the development of justice, leads us from self-concern ultimately to concern for all others, whether we are particularly committed to them or not. However, there is also room for insisting that the *polis* is a particularly important area of moral development, since humans are 'political animals'.

This combination of thoughts is nostalgic, because in the absence of arguments like the above, there really is no reason to think that the *polis* is a morally important unit. And we can see signs that Arius does not really think that it is, given his weakening of the notion of 'political' that we saw above, until it includes family relationships, which for Aristotle are in strong contrast with political relationships. Arius, while he does give the *polis* a role in Aristotle's political thought, perhaps shows us the reason why Antiochus simply leaves it out: once you take Stoic *oikeiōsis* seriously, there is, in the absence of further arguments, simply no real role for a specifically political context of moral development, and no reason other than

---

[120] It is of some incidental interest that what Arius is referring to amounts to the content of much of our *Politics*. He does not feel any need to distinguish 'ideal' from 'empirical' parts of the work, treating it as all part of the same project.

[121] Part 3, chapter 3, section 4.

piety to Aristotle to go on repeating points about the ideal *polis* which are no longer doing any work.

5. *Conclusion*

In this book, which is a study of ancient ethical theory, I have clearly not been able to give an adequate account of ancient theories of justice. I have, in this part of the book, merely tried to point up two things.

One is that it is not true that in ancient theories justice is assumed to be primarily a virtue of individual character, with justice as a virtue of institutions neglected, or taken to be trivially derivable from the virtue of individual character. So much is in fact clear just from the existence of Aristotle's *Politics*, where political justice is extensively discussed. But frequently this is not brought into any relation with justice as a virtue of individual character; and the contributions of Epicurus, the Stoics and the later Aristotelians are often neglected. I hope that this section, sketchy as it is, will indicate at least that eudaimonist theories are not simply lacking, or hopelessly naive, on this issue. The Stoics alone do not really have a political theory; but this is because of their particular ethical commitments, not because they have failed to notice the existence of political problems.

Not only do the ancient theories recognize that justice applies to institutions, but they try to relate the justice of institutions to the justice which is a state of just people. Here the Stoics are radical, and in effect depoliticize their moral outlook. But Epicurus and Aristotle grapple with the problem of the political context of the just person's justice. Aristotle assumes that moral life will be developed within the context of the city-state, and that just institutions are crucial to producing the best form of government, within which people will be able to develop the virtues, including of course justice as an individual virtue. Epicurus has a much lower view than Aristotle of the importance of the city-state and political life to the development of virtue; but all the same he develops a view of justice as the result of a social contract, and a plausible view of how the individual just person might go along with the results of that contract.

We thus find a variety of views about the justice of institutions and its relation to the justice of the individual. We do not, of course, find the characteristically modern view that justice is primarily a virtue of institutions, and only derivatively of individuals. The ancient view is more complex. There is also an irony here. It is sometimes claimed that ancient moral theories were dominated by the fact of *polis*-life, and that morality was seen as arising and developing essentially within the ancient community, with the result that ancient morality is less geared than modern to the situation of the individual, and addresses itself more to the agent as a member of a community. What we have seen so far in this book lends no support to this idea; and the contrasts between ancient and modern theories of justice as a virtue of institutions suggest that in some respects this idea is quite misleading. For it is modern theories of justice[122] which regard justice in the individual as merely a matter of adopting and following principles which have been independently established for

---

[122] Rawls (1971) provides a good example.

institutions, often in ways which consciously abstract from the characters of individuals. Ancient theories, even where they find analogies between individual and institutional justice, never attempt to define the former in terms of the latter, or to narrow their accounts of individual justice to mere conformity to what institutions require.

14

Self-Interest and Morality

We can now see, from a survey of the material in this part, why charges of egoism made against ancient ethical theories because of their eudaimonistic form miss the mark completely. The thoughtful person who enters on the path of ethical reflection in the manner of the ancient theories is moving away from self-concern. Insofar as the theories give virtue a non-instrumental role in achieving happiness, they are making morality necessary for happiness; and moral demands will lessen the role in the agent's life as a whole of her own self-centred projects, for their status will be determined by moral considerations, not *vice versa*. Further, all ancient theories recognize that we do, in fact, value others and their interests for their own sake, and not just for our own. And the ancient theories are aware that justice is an important virtue of the individual, and that it is linked to justice as a virtue of social institutions.

The theories differ, as we have seen, in the stringency of the demands that they make as regards the interests of others (just as they differ, as we shall see in Part IV, as to the stringency of the demands which they take morality to make). There is a spectrum; at one end are the Cyrenaics (apart from Anniceris), who hold that one should care for the interests of others merely insofar as these contribute to one's own experienced pleasure, and at the other end are the Stoics, who hold that the virtuous person will give the interests of herself and her friends no more weight from the moral point of view than those of 'the furthest Mysian', some utterly unknown person who is nevertheless entitled to equal concern as a rational human being. Thus, eudaimonism as a type of theory is compatible with an entire range of requirements about the interests of others, varying wildly in their demandingness from those that permit extreme selfishness to those that demand impartiality from the moral point of view. And so it is clear that eudaimonism as such makes no uniform demand or permission where the interests of others are at stake; thus it is radically mistaken to charge eudaimonistic theories with egoism.[1]

Such a wide spectrum of views as to the degree of demandingness made on my happiness by the interests of others points up an important fact about the ancient theories: the notion of happiness involved is a very weak and flexible one, capable of

---

[1] The only theory we have seen which is quite clearly egoistic in the modern sense, that of the Cyrenaics (other than Anniceris) is not really a eudaimonistic theory at all, since the Cyrenaics reject happiness as an overall end. However, we still have a wide range of positions, since Epicurus and the Sceptics patently have difficulties in not making the interests of others purely instrumental to those of the agent, and thus contrast with the Aristotelian, as well as the Stoic, position.

accommodating widely divergent claims from morality and from the interests of others. This is a point which has been frequently stressed in this book, but the results of this part make it particularly salient. As a result, a question is extremely pressing, namely, what sort of happiness is it which is compatible with some of the extreme demands made, in the Stoic theory for example, by the interests of others? This is the question which will be taken up in Part IV. But what has been established so far is that there are no structural barriers in a eudaimonist theory against the acceptance even of a demand for impartiality.

The results of this part make clear one large and interesting difference between ancient and modern theories. The ancient theories, by allotting the interests of others space in the framework of the agent's happiness, do not allow a structural gap to open up within the theory between morality and self-interest. Questions about the importance of the interests of others are posed right from the start in terms of the amount and degree of importance that the interests of others will have within my own conception of my happiness. It is impossible, in a theory of this structure, for me to work out in determinate detail what my own happiness is to consist of, and then, separately, ask whether I have any reason to care about others, and, if so, how much. It is clear by now that working out what my happiness properly consists in *already* requires working out how much the interests of others are to count (how much, in fact, they count depending on the theory in question). Modern moral theories, however, even where they differ greatly in form, often share the assumption that my own happiness, and the happiness and interests of others, can be worked out in quite distinct spheres of my practical reasoning. (Since we tend to associate morality with the interests of others rather than our own interests, this is an obvious source of the common misunderstanding of ancient theories as egoistic.) Indeed, many modern moral theories take it to be a major problem, how I am to reconcile and balance my own interests with those of others. Further, not only is it assumed that these are quite distinct in the agent's practical reasoning, it is sometimes further assumed that practical reasoning actually takes two distinct forms, namely prudential where only my own interests are concerned, and moral, when I, separately, bring the interests of others into my reasoning. Once this is assumed, lengthy discussion often ensues as to whether moral reasoning can or cannot be reduced to a complex form of prudential reasoning.

Eudaimonistic theories do not permit this kind of split to develop. Reasoning about my own interests differs neither in kind nor in its sphere from reasoning about the interests of others. This is, furthermore, the result of a commitment to one kind of theory rather than another. We have no reason to think that ancient Greeks and Romans did not, on an everyday level, distinguish as sharply as we do between their own interests and those of others. No doubt on an intuitive level the distinction of self-interest and the claims of others seemed as prominent to an ancient agent as to a modern. We can appreciate this just from the non-philosophical ancient literature; people in ancient drama, history and oratory pose practical questions in terms of self-interest as opposed to the demands of virtue and the interests of others.[2] Aristotle in the *Rhetoric* makes it plain that most people tended to see the fine, the characteristic aim of the virtuous person, as being associated with acting in the

[2] Nicholas White has stressed the importance of this point to me.

interests of others, as opposed to your own.[3] It is sometimes claimed that the prominence in modern moral philosophy of a perceived conflict between one's own and others' interests is historically rooted, and dates from the breakdown of social consensus (a breakdown which is dated very differently, depending on which social consensus it is which is taken to have broken down). But a glance at the ancient non-philosophical literature shows this to be a superficial analysis. The idea that individuals are in a state of conflict, and that when I think of my interests I am likely to oppose them, in my reasoning, to yours, was just as prominent in the ancient world as in the modern, as a matter of everyday intuition and prejudice.

We learn a great deal about the character of philosophical reflection, then, from the fact that ancient philosophical theories reject this intuitive way of dividing up the sphere of practical reasoning. All eudaimonistic theories are committed to rejecting, as simply mistaken, this very common way of regarding one's reasoning. Indeed, they establish a stronger position as they develop. One very striking mark of this is the prominence of the thesis that virtue is a skill or way of using the non-moral goods in one's life. The idea that virtue is a skill underlines the point that the moral agent is someone who has reflected on her values and has a firm intellectual basis for them; and the fact that virtue is represented as a skill in using non-moral goods underlines the point that moral reasoning is not opposed to prudential reasoning, but carries out what is generally taken to be the major function of prudential reasoning, yet without in the least erasing the important contrast between moral and non-moral value. This is another, frequently unmarked way in which ancient theories, while they answer to everyday beliefs as wholes, are committed to revising some of them. For, however much they otherwise differ, Aristotle, Epicurus, the Stoics and others are committed to the thought that the fact that my interests are, in everyday ways, opposed to yours does not mark a structurally important point in moral theory. The fact, on which Thucydides and other ancient non-philosophical writers harp so incessantly, that individuals see themselves in opposition when it comes to money, power and the like is not a deep fact as far as ethics is concerned. The interesting question is, rather, what amount of weight I should give to your interests and those of others in a correct conception of what my own interests are, what my happiness consists in.

This point has emerged in ancient debate. We have seen that the criticisms of the Stoic demand for impartiality retailed by the Anonymous Commentator on the *Theaetetus* are feeble insofar as they merely point to the fact that people think in self-interested ways. For this is one of the respects in which the theory demands that we improve, and so does not, as it stands, constitute an objection to it. An appeal to selfish intuitions here has no force against a theory which does not allow isolated intuitions probative weight, something no ancient theory does.[4]

---

[3] This point is developed in more detail in chapter 18, pp. 371–72.

[4] The same holds of the arguments 'against justice' which Carneades was famous for making, and of which we have fragments in the third book of Cicero's *Rep* and works deriving from it. (One of the examples, the two drowning men with one plank, turns up also in the Anonymous Commentator; good examples acquire a life of their own in ancient as in modern debate.) Merely pointing out that different peoples disagree about justice, and that established systems of power (like the Roman empire) are unjust, forms no argument at all against the normative and ideal claims of a theory of justice. I have not discussed Carneades' arguments in detail in this book, because they seem, from the state of the evidence, to have been directed against a variety of theories which we cannot clearly sort out; since ancient sceptical

Thus ancient theories, which in this respect are not operating from a different intuitive basis from modern theories, nonetheless are committed to finding a major modern assumption to be a philosophical mistake; the ancient theories find the opposition of my own interests to those of others to be philosophically superficial, something to be accounted for in a moral theory but not something that should give that theory its characteristic form. This is one of the main ways in which theories of a eudaimonistic form distinguish themselves from other moral theories. And plainly we cannot fully assess this difference and its significance until we look more closely at the role played in the ancient theories by happiness, for not until then will we really understand the kind of compromise that the agent is making, in ancient theories, in so conceiving of her own happiness that the interests of others will make strong demands that must be respected before happiness is achieved.

---

arguments were always *ad hominem*, this means that we do not fully understand the arguments themselves. For a view which takes them to be directed against the Stoics, see Striker (1991) section 5. For arguments against this reading see Annas (1989a), especially section 4.

IV

Revising Your Priorities

15

Happiness, Success and What Matters

We have now to return to the question, how any of what we have seen can be a theory of *happiness*. As we saw in Part I, the entry point for ancient ethical reflection is consideration of one's life as a whole, and reflection leads one to the notion of one's final end. Happiness enters as a thin specification of this final end. As Aristotle says,[1] there is consensus that our final good is happiness, but this point is trivial and settles nothing, for there is intense disagreement as to what happiness consists in. Thus there is agreement as to what one could broadly call the form of happiness, though little as to the content.[2] Happiness is the best thing in life, the greatest of our goods. It is different from the other goods we aim at; it is not just another end, but the way we actively pursue those other ends, and so can be referred to as the use we make of those ends. Since happiness is our own activity it is something we do, and so is, commonsensically, 'up to us'.

In the course of the book so far, we have seen that, whatever else is true of the specification of our final end, further conditions must hold. Our final end is natural, in ways which we have seen developed differently in the different schools. That is, it should at a general level respect the fundamental facts about our human nature; and it goes beyond mere tradition and convention to give us an ethical ideal for living. And it must accommodate two crucial points. One is virtue; we achieve our final end by developing the virtues, and we have seen that there is no chance of understanding these non-morally, as merely dispositions to live a successful life where that is understood in neutral terms. Rather, the virtues are dispositions to do the morally right thing, dispositions developed by training our feelings and emotions in morally right ways. The other fact to be accommodated is other-concern. As we have seen, some theories demand (apart from justice) only limited other-concern, restricted to particular other people, while other theories demand that from the moral point of view the agent have equal concern for all humans just as such. Concern for others, for their own sake and not the agent's, must form part of the content of the agent's reflective final end.

As is by now clear, the Cyrenaics are the only exceptions; every other school accepts these conditions as conditions on our final end. Only the Cyrenaics, who consider our end to be the maximizing of intense present pleasure, reject these conditions, and this is because they reject the initial move, that our final end must be

---

[1] *NE* 1095 a 17–26, quoted in chapter 1, pp. 43–44.
[2] On these points, see chapter 1, pp. 44–46.

what we seek in our life as a whole, rather than in experiences within that life. Hence they reject the idea that our final end is *eudaimonia* or happiness, since that already brings in the notion they reject, that our final end should be sought in our life as a whole.[3]

None of this would be problematic if we could take *eudaimonia* to be something other than happiness. For what we have seen so far is the progressive development and filling out of what I have called an ethical perspective. I begin to reflect on my life as a whole; I find, most likely, that the various ends I pursue are not harmonized and tend to conflict and leave me dissatisfied. I reflect on the requirements of morality and (whichever be the philosophical theory I come to adopt) develop my habits of action and deliberation so that I acquire the virtues; in doing so I will both change, adjust and harmonize my ends and will end up with a more coherent set of values. I will do this in accordance with what I find to be natural; again, whichever ethical theory I adopt I will come to see that many of my initial values are recommended solely by artificial conventions, and I will come to try to live a more natural life, by developing the given aspects of my life as a human in accordance with a correct philosophical theory, rather than by merely relying unthinkingly on social conventions. And in doing all this I will come to give the interests of others their proper weight within my own projects; what this weight is will depend on the theory I adopt, and so will my view of the relation of concern for others to concern for myself, but all theories (again, excluding the Cyrenaics) make it clear that the interests of others must have some underivative weight in the agent's reflective final end.

If *eudaimonia* could be taken as something like the moral life, none of the above would raise deep difficulties. We would have an ethical perspective which is distinctive in certain ways, diverging from consequentialism and Kantian theories in its starting point and emphases. We begin from the agent's life as a whole, and the theory's emphasis is on character and disposition. This differs strikingly from theories which begin as attempts to produce a mechanism for solving problems. Nonetheless, such an agent-centred theory, appealing to nature, would look recognizably like a moral theory. But *eudaimonia* is happiness. To non-philosophers the *eudaimōn* life is the successful life, in which the agent has and enjoys the rewards of success, whether those are conceived as money, pleasure or honour.[4] The more we develop the ancient ethical perspective, the more problematic it becomes to see what we have as being an account of happiness.

Modern interpreters are constantly tempted to get rid of this problem. One way to do this is to deny that *eudaimonia* is anything like happiness. But this simply does not answer to the ancient non-philosophical evidence; *eudaimonia* at the very least connotes a satisfactory life about which the agent has positive feelings. Another is to claim that the virtues are not the *moral* virtues; rather they are dispositions whose possession might more plausibly make the agent happy. But we have seen that this cannot be sustained either. Rather, ancient ethical theories are theories about happiness—theories that claim that a reflective account of happiness will conclude that it requires having the virtues and giving proper weight to the interests of others.

---

[3] For the Cyrenaics, see the first section of chapter 11.
[4] See Dover (1974), pp. 174–5, and the introductory chapters of Decleva Caizzi (1988).

We should face an obvious, but frequently ignored, consequence of this: ancient theories are all more or less revisionary, and some of them are highly counter-intuitive. They give an account of happiness which, if baldly presented to a non-philosopher without any of the supporting arguments, sounds wrong, even absurd. This consequence is frequently evaded because it is assumed that ancient ethical theories are morally conservative, concerned to respect and justify ancient ethical intuitions without criticizing or trying to improve them.[5] But this assumption is false, as we have amply seen already. Moreover, this problem over the understanding of happiness is a problem for the ancients and not just for us trying to interpret them. As we shall see in this section, all the ancient theories greatly expand and modify the ordinary non-philosophical understanding of happiness, opening themselves to criticism from non-philosophers on this score.

It is in fact common ground to the ancient theories[6] that, on the one hand, we are all right to assume that our final end is happiness of some kind, and to try to achieve happiness in reflecting systematically on our final end; but that, on the other hand, we are very far astray in our initial assumptions about what happiness is. The situation is the same as with nature; we are all right to want to lead a natural, rather than artificial, life, but we are apt to be misguided about what is natural, and we need ethical theory to clarify this for us. Similarly with happiness; only ethical theory will make it clear to us what happiness really consists in. The two points are connected, of course, since we become happy by doing what is natural.

The point has already been made[7] that when we ask about the relation of virtue to happiness we are not trying to make two equally determinate notions fit together. Rather, happiness is the vague notion that has to bend to that of virtue, not the other way round. We now have a fuller understanding of this point, having seen the depth and extent of the commitment to morality and the interests of others involved in the ancient ethical perspective. So we should not be surprised that ancient theories have counter-intuitive consequences about happiness. Given what we have seen so far, they could not fail to. The conception of happiness that we start with could not possibly be unaltered at the end of the process of reflection and conscious adoption of an ethical theory.

A modern response at this point might well be that, given this situation, ancient theories should just have abandoned the idea of giving an account of happiness. What they say about virtue, nature and the interests of others is compelling; they only spoil things by casting their theories in terms of happiness, condemning themselves to failure by persisting in an unsuitable framework. They should have realized that commitment to virtue leads not to true happiness but to the sacrifice of one's happiness. This point is most often made about the Stoics, but could equally well be made about all ancient theories.

---

[5] This has been especially common with Aristotle, whose method has often been misunderstood as a canonization of common sense. Sidgwick comments on Aristotle's account of the virtues that 'he gives throughout the pure result of analytical observation of the common moral consciousness of his age. . . .This adhesion to common sense, though it involves some sacrifice of both depth and completeness. . .gives it . . . a historical interest. . .' (Ch. 2 section 9, of [1931]). See Part V, pp. 445–46.

[6] Except, of course, the Cyrenaics.

[7] In chapter 2 section 7.

Whether this charge is just, can only be properly judged in the light of the detail of this part. But before embarking on this we should consider what can be said in general in favour of a kind of theory that shows that happiness is really to be found in living a moral life in which you care for others.

Happiness comes in, in the first place, as something that we obviously all go for. Once we see the need for a final end, an end we pursue in some way in every action, there is no better specification than happiness that we can come up with for it. (At least this is true of *eudaimonia* in Greek, and of some uses, at least, of happiness in English, though not all.) For, while we can be said to want other things for the sake of being happy, we cannot be said to want to be happy for the sake of any further end. Before we start to reflect, happiness is our only end which is complete and self-sufficient. And hence it is not so surprising that happiness should be our best initial way in to specifying what our final end is. Before starting to do philosophy, we have no other such way in.

At the end of the day we find that our philosophical reflections have taken us some way from the intuitive suggestions of happiness. For the Stoics, for example, the truly happy person, the person who has achieved his final end, is the virtuous person, even if he suffers poverty, disease and torture. But this does not in itself show that we chose the wrong starting point. For we knew once we started to reflect that reflection would make us change and adjust our ends and thus the things we valued. Ethical reflection is bound to make us change our values and priorities. In fact the whole drive of ancient ethical theory is exactly this: to get us to revise our priorities. This is just as true of Epicurus, who has a more 'intuitive' conception of happiness, as it is of the Stoics. We would not, after all, have *needed* ethical reflection if things had been fine the way they were. We start on the process, characteristically, because on reflection we find that we are dissatisfied with our lives and the way they are going. An ethical theory that left all our intuitions about happiness in place could hardly do justice to the drive that started us reflecting to begin with.[8]

So it can be seen as a success, rather than as a failure, when an ancient theory starts from the intuitive position that we seek happiness, and ends up giving an account of happiness far removed from the content of the original intuitions. (Whether it *is* a success or not depends of course on the success of the theory.) For we start from the only intuitive conception suitable for our purposes, but we revise that in accordance with the revision of our priorities that the theory demands. All ethical theories, after all, start from what we intuitively accept in morality and, in the course of explaining this, subject it to criticism and revision. If we find this especially peculiar in the case of happiness, this may just be because we find it unfamiliar. And there remains the point that 'happiness' for us covers some areas that are not covered by *eudaimonia*. We should not find the project so peculiar if we remember that happy feelings and moods are not relevant, and that happiness applies to a whole life, or to an agent in respect of her whole life, and that it implies that she has a positive attitude to her whole life.

---

[8] The Sceptics illustrate the connectedness of these two points. They do leave all our intuitions in place; at least, any changes to them do not come from reflection and theory (for that would be dogmatism). And they do, arguably, fail to do justice to the initial drive to reflect, which demands a normative theory which does not leave everything the way it was before.

This general point, of course, leaves room for what we find: a spectrum of positions from theories which try hard to do justice to our initial intuitions about happiness, to theories which are more revisionary. We shall see that the development of the debate about virtue and happiness from Aristotle through the Stoics to Antiochus rests on this point of method: how much of the content of our initial intuitions about happiness is it important to retain? All the figures in this debate have answers to this, sometimes quite developed and subtle. (Any initial expectation that the more intuitive the theory about happiness the better, is quickly seen to be too simple.) In this part we shall see what theories share and what divides them on this, the major issue of ancient ethics. What they share is the methodological assumption that they are developing a theory of happiness in developing their ethical theories. What divides them are two connected points. One is their choice of candidate for giving us the content of happiness—pleasure, tranquillity, virtue and so on. The other is their degree of willingness to reject or modify our initial expectations that the happy life is one of satisfaction and success, measured in ways that we pre-philosophically accept.

16

Epicurus: Virtue, Pleasure and Time

Epicurus' theory, although it is a form of hedonism, is (as is clear by now) quite unlike most[1] modern forms, just because he takes seriously the eudaimonist ethical framework. Aspects of this have been brought out already;[2] these must now be brought together as we examine how Epicurus proposes to persuade us that our final end, happiness, is in fact pleasure.

Epicurus is unlike modern consequentialists in that he does not take the pleasure we aim at in all we do to be pleasant states of affairs in the production of which our actions are mere interchangeable means. This consequentialist conception is indeed not to be found in any ancient theory. It might seem that Epicurus comes nearer to it than other ancient theories do, because his theory has sometimes been taken to be one in which rationality takes the form of maximizing—and if what we should do is to maximize pleasure, what other form could this take than maximizing pleasant states of affairs? The only passage that could appear to suggest this is one from the *Letter to Menoeceus* (129–130) which has achieved undeserved fame, since it is from a popular work which does not claim to lay out the structure of Epicurus' theory:

> Since this [pleasure] is the primary aim and is innate to us—for that reason we do not choose every pleasure, but sometimes we pass over many pleasures, when greater annoyance follows for us from them, and we judge many pains superior to pleasures, when greater pleasure follows along for us when we endure the pains for a long time. Every pleasure, therefore, because of having a nature which is familiar to us [*oikeian*] is a good, but not every pleasure is to be chosen, just as every pain is a bad thing, but not every pain is always naturally to be avoided. However, one should judge all these matters by measuring together [*summetrēsei*] and looking at the advantages and disadvantages, for we make use of the good on some occasions as a bad thing, and the bad, conversely, as a good.

Here the language of measurement has seduced many into seeing an anticipation of quantitative hedonism. It seems as though, when we decide on each action, we reduce all the factors involved to pleasure and pain, and do what will produce the most pleasure or least pain. Hence we sometimes 'make use of the good as a bad thing' and vice versa; we pass over a pleasure-producing course of action if it will

---

[1] Mill provides the most striking exception, since he takes seriously considerations of one's life as a whole. I take Bentham and especially Sidgwick to be definitive for the modern tradition of hedonism.
[2] Chapter 1; chapter 2, sections 4 and 7; chapters 7 and 11.

produce more pain in the long run. A role has also tacitly been played in favouring this kind of interpretation by the modern expectation that an ethical theory will provide us with a definite decision procedure; measuring quantities of pleasure certainly offers the most obvious way of providing this for a hedonist.

But the language of measurement appears nowhere else,[3] and is incompatible with the important point that the pleasure which we seek as our final end is not kinetic pleasure, but katastematic or static pleasure, something not amenable to quantitative measurement. Static pleasure is not something which can be measured in a definite way; thus the prospect of getting more of it rather than less cannot be formalized into anything like a determinate decision procedure. Epicurus thinks that we should monitor our moral progress, but we do this not by checking on particular actions, but by scrutinizing each *desire* to see whether it is the approved kind or not.[4] Thus, while Epicurus recommends the commonsensical strategy of trying for more pleasure rather than less, there is no maximizing in the theory; the pleasure that we aim at is just not the right kind of thing to be maximized.

Modern hedonist theories are typically consequentialist in structure, employ a maximizing notion of reason and pride themselves on providing a definite decision procedure for action. Epicurus' theory does none of these things. This is not because he consciously rejects any of these ideas, but because his conception of pleasure as our final end is not such as to provide any of these things. This conception is in many ways odd and unintuitive; we can understand it only when we see how it is produced to meet the formal conditions on our final end, namely being complete and self-sufficient. Epicurus' conception of pleasure is, in other words, tailored to meet the demands on any theory of happiness—that is, of our final end. Thus we need first to examine this conception of pleasure and see how it does fulfil the formal conditions, and then see whether Epicurus can succeed in showing how it can accommodate the further demands on its content, namely that on reflection happiness is seen to require concern for others and the development of virtue.[5]

Unfortunately, we lack any extended Epicurean discussion of kinetic and katastematic pleasure, and much of our evidence for Epicurus' theory of pleasure comes from hostile sources,[6] but we can start from examples which have a good chance of going back to an Epicurean source:

'You must necessarily concede,' [says the anti-Epicurean], 'unless you are firmly obstinate, that the force of pleasure is quite different from the force of having no pain.' 'Well, you will find me obstinate on this point,' [replies the Epicurean], 'since nothing truer [than the claim that they are the same] could be said.' 'Is there, then,' I said, 'pleasure in drinking for a thirsty person?' 'Who could deny that?' he said. 'Is it the same pleasure as the pleasure when thirst has been quenched?' 'No; it is of a quite other kind. Thirst when quenched has a static state of pleasure [*stabilitas voluptatis*], while the other pleasure, of the actual

---

[3] The language of more and less does, but this does not imply the possibility of quantitative measurement.

[4] *VS* 71.

[5] For interpretations of Epicurus as a eudaimonist see Striker (1981b); Hossenfelder (1986) and (1985), pp. 23–39 and 102–24; Annas (1987).

[6] For extended discussion of the distinction, see Gosling and Taylor (1982) chapters 18 and 19, and Mitsis (1988), pp. 45–51.

quenching, is in movement.' 'Why, then,' I said, 'do you call such different things by the same name?'[7]

Here we find the Latin equivalents for static (katastematic) pleasure and kinetic pleasure, and the contrast seems to be that kinetic pleasure is the pleasure you have as a pain or want is being removed, whereas static pleasure is the pleasure you have when there is no pain or want to be removed. Kinetic pleasure is the pleasure of getting to this latter state, static pleasure, the pleasure of being in it. Static pleasure thus seems to be simply the state of having no pain, and Epicurus denied that there was an intermediate neutral state between pleasure and pain: absence of pain just is (static) pleasure. Static pleasure, however, can be varied, though not increased.[8] An important passage, unfortunately corrupt, tells us that 'Epicurus in *On Choices* says this, 'For *ataraxia* and *aponia* are static pleasures" by contrast with kinetic ones.[9] *Aponia* is the absence of pain, and *ataraxia* the absence of *tarachē*, trouble, worry or irritation. And there are many passages where Epicurus tells us that our final end is *ataraxia*, for example,

> When, therefore, we say that pleasure is the end, we do not mean the pleasures of
> the dissolute and those that lie in enjoyment, as some suppose who are ignorant
> and disagree with us or take it in a bad sense, but rather not being pained in body
> and not being troubled [*mē tarattesthai*] in soul.[10]

Clearly, the kind of pleasure which forms our final end is *ataraxia* (sometimes absence of bodily pain is explicitly added, sometimes assumed to be included), and this is pleasure of a static rather than a kinetic kind.

Some ancient critics, for example Cicero, assume that kinetic pleasures are bodily pleasures, leaving nothing but mental pleasures to be our final end. This criticism is connected to the ways that Epicurus contrasts bodily with mental pleasures, to the credit of the latter. If this were so, there would be force to Cicero's claim that Epicurus is equivocating on 'pleasure', or that his empiricism is inconsistent. For bodily pleasures are those that we are aware of in experience, hence, given Epicurus' empiricism about meaning, those that give sense to our uses of the word 'pleasure'. And, since these are the uses that figure in Epicurean claims about the goodness of pleasure, Epicurus would simply be cheating in claiming that our final end is not actually this at all, but something quite different, which seems to have none of the positive features of the first kind of pleasure.

However, even in the absence of specific Epicurean discussions, we can see that this must be wrong. For we have seen[11] that the pleasure which is our Epicurean final end is natural. Epicurus thinks of pleasure not as a uniform sensation that one could get more or less of from different activities, but rather as what results from fulfilling a desire. In seeking pleasure, what matters is that we fulfil those desires which are natural, and the Epicurean strategy for living the best life is directed at finding and

---

[7] Cicero, *Fin* II 9.

[8] Cicero, *Fin* I 37–38.

[9] Diogenes X 136. Unfortunately the clause that should give us examples of kinetic pleasures seems to give us the wrong examples. The claim of the first clause is unaffected, however. For discussion of differing interpretations of this passage see Gosling and Taylor (1982), pp. 388–91.

[10] *Ep Men* 131.

[11] Chapter 11.

following natural desires. Natural desires, however, do not produce mental rather than bodily pleasures; rather the natural/not natural distinction cuts right across that of mental and bodily. Natural desires are those we cannot help having, so that in fulfilling them we are following, rather than forcing, our nature. We have seen that these include desires for food and drink, but also desires like those for retaliation—as we would expect, given that our nature has needs that are both bodily and mental. The important point is to fulfil natural desires in ways that do not rely on empty (that is, false and harmful) beliefs. If we do this, we will remove the pains and lacks that we cannot help but have, and do so in ways that give rise to no further pains or lacks. Whereas if we fulfil empty desires, that is, desires which we have only because we have empty beliefs, we will remove some pains and lacks, but in ways which renew them or bring other, even worse ones; which is why most people, who do not limit themselves to natural desires, lead lives of chronic dissatisfaction and unhappiness.

The picture that this suggests is the following. In living our lives, we should aim at being in a state in which we are not bothered or frustrated by bodily or mental troubles. We can avoid mental troubles by avoiding empty beliefs—and the best way to do that, according to Epicurus, is to internalize and live by the principles of Epicureanism, in particular losing the fear of death, which he believes to be at the bottom of many of our worries. Being human, however, we are bound, just by our nature, to have certain recurring needs and lacks, and, hence, to have certain pains as we become aware of these. The most obvious of these will be needs for food and drink, but we also have certain mental needs, for example, those underlying anger. When we satisfy these needs, we feel kinetic pleasure as the need is satisfied. If we satisfy these needs in the wrong way, relying on empty beliefs, this will result in a state which will be one of dissatisfaction and 'trouble'. But if we satisfy them in the right way, fulfilling only natural desires, the resulting state will be one of complete absence of both bodily needs and mental 'troubles'. This is the condition of static or katastematic pleasure. Our final end, then, is not a state made up of bodily pleasures; nor is it a state in which bodily pleasures are replaced by mental ones. Rather, we aim at being in a condition in which bodily and mental pleasures of satisfying our needs result in a state of satisfaction which is not disturbed by the incursions of further needs and pains.

We can see why static pleasure can be varied but not increased. A condition of freedom from pain and interference is not the kind of thing which can be increased, or vary in intensity. (This is why the Epicurean final end cannot produce a decision procedure for taking action to produce it.) It can be varied, however, in two other ways. One is that the kinetic pleasures produced by satisfying various lacks can be of different kinds. We satisfy our need for food by eating, but as we have seen, there are many ways in which this necessary desire can be specified—many kinds of things we can eat—without falling into reliance on empty beliefs. What we should eat to relieve our hunger depends on circumstances, relative availability of foodstuffs, and so on. The condition in which we are no longer troubled by the need can therefore be produced in a number of varied ways. Further, the condition of *ataraxia* itself allows for variation even when all the needs are met. For *ataraxia* is a state in which nothing, bodily or mental, is interfering with your natural state; but the natural state for humans is not one of inertness, but of varied activity. We achieve our final end, not by doing some particular things rather than others, but rather by doing whatever we are doing in a way which is not hindered or made miserable by pains and 'troubles'. Of course it may well be that some forms of activity are more likely to lead to this desirable result than others; and Epicurus himself lived a specific kind of life in the 'Garden', which obviously stood as an Epicurean ideal form of life. But some Epicureans lived perfectly ordinary lives, and we even find Epicurus on occasion allowing that Epicureans could live a life of political and military activity, if that formed for them the best way of achieving a condition where they were not made unhappy by nagging 'troubles'.[12] *Ataraxia*, then, is a state where you are functioning normally, in ways that do not constrain or flout your nature, and you are not hindered or upset by mental or bodily troubles.[13]

Many have felt some sympathy for Cicero's complaint that this does not look much like *pleasure*, and to follow him when he accuses Epicurus of equivocating: of introducing the notion of pleasure via cases which we recognize from experience, and then of arguing that pleasure is our final end—but pleasure in a quite distinct sense. But if *ataraxia* is not a special, refined mental state, but simply the condition of normal functioning unimpeded by pains or worries, the problem is greatly reduced. For this is a notion of pleasure which we can grasp from our experience quite as readily as the notion of a pleasant experience as a lack or pain is removed. The Epicurean in *de Finibus* II 9 seems quite justified in claiming both that it's pleasant to quench one's thirst, and also pleasant not to need to quench any thirst; and that these are different, but both pleasant. It is true that we do not find any explicit defence in Epicurus of using the same term in his theory for both of these; but they are certainly both natural and intuitive ways of using the term *pleasure*. The sense of pleasure in which pleasure is our final end is indeed markedly akin to that discussed by Aristotle in *Nicomachean Ethics* VII, where he says that pleasure is unimpeded activity of the natural state, and wonders whether this might be what our final end is. Aristotle is indeed more counter-intuitive in this passage than Epicurus is, for, although he recognizes both the pleasures of being in the natural state and the pleasures of being restored to the natural state after interference by illness or pain, he inclines to think that the latter are not really pleasures at all. Epicurus does justice to more of our intuitions here.[14]

However, it remains surprising for a hedonist to come up with a conception of pleasure as our final end which is like Epicurus'. We have only to look at the Cyrenaic theories to see that the thought was obviously available, that we should aim at having as much as we can of the kind of pleasure with which we are familiar in experience when we have a pleasant sensation. Epicurus' notion of *ataraxia* is one which we can see as based in our experience, but it is still notable that he makes this, rather than the kinetic kind of pleasure, our final end. His procedure is somewhat

---

[12] Plutarch, *De tranq an* 465F (U 555).

[13] Bodily pains are awkward here, since it is hard to ensure that you are not troubled by them. In this case Epicurus' move is highly implausible: if pain is unbearable, he says, it won't last long, and if it is chronic, it is bearable (*KD* 4).

[14] On Aristotle and Epicurus, see Rist (1974) and (1972) ch. 6; Merlan (1960). Alexander of Aphrodisias, in *Ethical Problems* 23 (and 26) discusses the ways in which Aristotle can avoid the conclusion that happiness will be pleasure, if pleasure is unimpeded activity of the natural state. For translation and discussion, see Sharples (1990).

puzzling if we think of it as driven solely by the desire to do justice to the nature of pleasure. But it makes immediate sense if we see that he is working in a eudaimonist framework; he wants his final end to be complete and self-sufficient.

That Epicurus accepts that our final end must be complete is clear from the following passage:

> Thus we are inquiring what the final and ultimate good is, which, in the opinion of all philosophers ought to be such that everything must be referred to it, but it itself referred no further. Epicurus locates this in pleasure.[15]

He also regards self-sufficiency as important:

> We should take care for the things that produce happiness, since when it is present we have everything, and when it is absent we do everything to have it.[16]

In many passages it is stressed that the best life is one in which the agent is self-sufficient; indeed this is a theme which is pushed to some lengths in Epicurean ethics, to the point of risk-aversiveness.[17] Accepting these conditions, however, forces Epicurus to develop a conception of pleasure like that of his static pleasure. For intuitively nothing can be more obvious than that the kinetic kind of pleasure is not complete and does not render one's life self-sufficient. Pleasure understood as pleasant experience is manifestly not what gives point to all our activities and renders our lives lacking in nothing. As we have seen with the Cyrenaics, a theory which clearheadedly makes pleasant experience our final end has to reject the idea that our final good is complete and self-sufficient. Further, even outside the framework of eudaimonism this worry is important. Mill, for example, fully realizes that in claiming that pleasure is the agent's *summum bonum* he runs into the problem of completeness. He regards it as comparatively simple to show that happiness (by which he explicitly means pleasure and the absence of pain) is desirable as an end; but he has to show something far harder, namely that happiness thus conceived is the *only* thing desirable as an end. In particular, he recognizes that he has to square this with the recognition that we seek the virtues for their own sake. His solution is to expand the notion of happiness in such a way that seeking the virtues for their own sake counts as seeking happiness, since doing the former counts as part of being happy: 'the means have become a part of the end, and a more important part of it than any of the things which they are means to. What was once desired as an instrument for the attainment of happiness has come to be desired for its own sake. In being desired for its own sake it is, however, desired as *part* of happiness.'[18]

Epicurus' own solution is, I shall argue, not very dissimilar from this. It may seem at first glance as though it is totally different, since we find some very downright passages which appear to give virtue no independent value at all:

> It is because of pleasure that we choose even the virtues, not for their own sake, just as we choose medicine for the sake of health.[19]

---

[15] Cicero, *Fin* I 29. Cf. I 42.
[16] *Ep Men* 122.
[17] *Ep Men* 130–1; *VS* 44, 45, 68, 77; U 200, 202, 466, 476.
[18] *Utilitarianism* chapter 4.
[19] Diogenes X 138.

and

> One should honour the fine and the virtues and that kind of stuff, if they produce pleasure; but if they don't produce it one should leave them alone.[20]

and, quite repellently,

> I spit on the fine and those who emptily admire it, when it doesn't make any pleasure.[21]

And Epicurus' followers continued in this debunking vein; Diogenes of Oenoanda rails against the stupidity of people who would make virtue our final end, rather than something productive of it.[22]

However, we should draw a distinction here. Despite the violently iconoclastic language, Epicurus is actually taking a conservative rather than a radically hedonistic view of virtue. A radical hedonist will revise the content of the virtues in order to remove conflict with her final end; for if our final end is correctly conceived, the virtues can only be dispositions to achieve that, and to the extent that they tend to lead us astray from this they are in need of correction. Thus a radical hedonist will regard courage, say, as a virtue only to the extent that the disposition to do courageous actions tends to help the agent to achieve pleasure; a courageous action done for its own sake and resulting in considerable pleasure-frustration will be considered to be not really a virtuous action. This approach to the problem has commended itself to some modern utilitarians.[23] But Epicurus is not tempted in this direction. Rather, he assumes that the virtues must be conceived of in the commonsensical way, as dispositions to do the morally right thing, whether or not this produces pleasure. Only so would he find there to be a *problem* for the hedonist about being committed to virtue.

It seems from the debunking passages that Epicurus gives the virtues, so conceived, merely instrumental status. But there are also other passages which cast doubt on this straightforward conclusion. We find three interesting characterizations of the relation of virtue and pleasure. First, virtue alone is inseparable from pleasure, while other things, for example food, are separable.[24] It is not clear quite what is meant here. The thought may be that I may get pleasure from food or fail to do so, but I cannot fail to get pleasure from virtue. Or it may be that food is only one among alternative ways to get pleasure, while virtue is inescapable as a way of getting pleasure.

Second, pleasure and the virtues are mutually entailing.

> It is not possible to live pleasantly without living intelligently and finely and justly, nor to live intelligently and finely and justly without living pleasantly. If a person lacks the conditions for living intelligently and finely and justly, it is impossible for them to live pleasantly.[25]

---

[20] Athenaeus XII 546f (U 70).

[21] Athenaeus XII 547a (U 512). This, like the last passage, is supposed to be a citation from Epicurus' *Peri Telous* (*On One's Final End*).

[22] Fr. 26 Chilton.

[23] See Slote (1988) and Railton (1988).

[24] Diogenes X 138 (U 506).

[25] *KD* 5; cf. *Ep Men* 132, *Fin* I 57.

This suggests that both interpretations of inseparability are in Epicurus' mind. I cannot fail to live pleasantly if I have the virtues (as I could just if I had food) because having the virtues entails getting pleasure from them. Further, having the virtues is inescapable as part of living pleasantly, not just one among alternative means to it, because living pleasantly entails having the virtues.

In one passage both these characterizations are brought together and a third is added: the virtues have 'grown to be a part of' happiness.[26] This passage certainly appears to give the virtues a non-instrumental role in the pleasant life. If having the virtues is actually part of the pleasant life, and if the virtues are not to be redefined, but are taken in the commonsense way, then part of the pleasant life is formed by acting and living according to the virtues, i.e., in accordance with dispositions to do the moral thing for its own sake, rather than for any ulterior motive.

There is an obvious analogue with Epicurus' attitude to *philia* or concern for others; and similar problems arise in both cases. Epicurus accepts that the pleasant life must include concern for others; in some places he says or implies that this has no intrinsic value; but his own account demands that the pleasant life include real concern for others, not merely concern for them only to the point that this promotes the agent's happiness. With virtue we have a similar problem in reconciling the debunking passages about virtue with the passages which say that virtue is part of and inseparable from the pleasant life. To some extent the problem here is a matter of our sources and of Epicurus' style. The iconoclastic passages are ripped out of context, and hostile sources may have made them appear worse than they are; perhaps they did not even present Epicurus' own view in the original context. Even if they did, Epicurus may simply have been succumbing, as he often does, to an immature tendency to shock people out of conventional attitudes; thus initial shocking claims might give way to a more nuanced conclusion. And finally, the claim that we choose virtue for the sake of pleasure just as we choose medicine for the sake of health (i.e., instrumentally) may, in the original context, have been designed merely to make the point that virtue is not our final good, without being supposed to give a full account of the relationship of virtue to pleasure.

Still, a problem remains apart from style, one which is well brought out by the ancient objections to Epicurus we find in the second book of *de Finibus*. Epicureans, claims the objector, do not mean the same as ordinary people when they talk about the virtues; a virtuous person does not, as he would have to on an Epicurean account, have pleasure as a final good.[27] Second, in cases where exercising the virtues conflicts with seeking pleasure, the Epicurean cannot be relied on to be virtuous, when external constraints and side-effects are removed; if these are absent he has no motivation not to seek pleasure rather than be virtuous.[28] Third, Epicureanism is not a moral theory that can be openly avowed. For an Epicurean

---

[26] *Ep Men* 132. In translating *sumpephukasi* as 'grown to be a part of' I am obviously influenced by Mill's solution to his analogous problem in *Utilitarianism* chapter 4.

[27] *Fin* II 45–54, 60–73.

[28] II 54–9. Cicero himself does not distinguish this objection sharply from the previous one, but they are quite distinct. The earlier one concerned the adequacy of Epicureanism to account for the way we think of virtue in cases where both sides would act in the same way. But these arguments concern cases where Epicureanism and ordinary morality would *diverge* in the absence of external constraints (like modern 'desert-island' cases).

cannot have the ordinary person's non-instrumental attitude to the virtues; but if he were to admit this, others would naturally distrust him, so he has to conceal the fact.[29]

All these objections are aimed at a theory which *says* that it gives the virtues intrinsic value, but in fact finds it problematic to do so, given that its final end is pleasure. The objections are in fact excellent objections, for they all home in on what is the theory's biggest weakness: its systematic double-mindedness about the status of the virtues. For the Epicurean does not regard the content of the virtues as given by what is required to achieve pleasure; rather, she expects to achieve pleasure by developing *the virtues*, courage, justice and so on. But then what does happen on occasions when practicing a given virtue will lead to clear loss of pleasure? The objections assume that the Epicurean will cling to her final end—pleasure, and thus will stick to the hard line: that is, will break a desert-island promise to a dying person if keeping it will frustrate pleasure, and there are no side-effects; and so on. Further, the Epicurean will have good reason not to admit that this is what she has done; for doing this will, in normal circumstances, lead to great loss of pleasure. Epicurus clearly does not want these results, any more than he wants to accept an instrumental view of friendship; but it is not clear how he is entitled to avoid them.

As with friendship, Epicurus could avoid the problem by explicitly making his theory a two-level one, one in which we aim at being virtuous, on each occasion, for its own sake and without keeping an eye out for pleasure; but also one in which, when we reflect on our life as a whole, we realize that we seek the virtues for the sake of the pleasure that we get from living a life in which we have the virtues. But, while this would give a unified account of all the texts, we seem to find Epicurus explicitly rejecting it:

> If you do not on every suitable occasion refer each of your actions to the end given by nature, but stop short and make your avoidance or choice with reference to something else, your actions will not be consistent with your theories.[30]

And, as we have seen in the case of friendship, Epicurus has good reason to avoid two-level theories, which merely introduce another kind of double-mindedness. At one level we are supposed to be committed to being virtuous for its own sake, while at another we are supposed to be aiming at achieving as much pleasure as we can. But these two levels are supposed not to interfere with each other; something which evidently presupposes a meta-level where the relationships of the two levels are settled—but where all the original problems break out again.

We are left, then, with the conclusion that Epicurus' conception of our final end, namely static pleasure or *ataraxia*, is meant to be complete—to be the end for which we do everything, while it is not done for a further end. And Epicurus makes efforts to show that in this way he can accommodate what he needs in order to make the theory a plausible one—that is, accommodate the development of virtue and concern for others for their own sake in his account of our final end. He recognizes that his view of what we should all be aiming at in life needs to allow in

---

[29] II 74–7. Note that this objection holds only if Epicureans, as a matter of fact, do have an instrumental attitude to the virtues.

[30] *KD* 25. For the puzzling notion of 'stopping short', see the note on this passage in chapter 11, p. 241.

commitments to others, and commitments to morality, or it will not be acceptable as an answer to the question, How ought I to revise my priorities to live a better life? But his answer is not really satisfactory; here we can join Cicero in thinking that Epicurus' ethical intentions are better than his theoretical working out of the answers.

In fact, by this point it may well seem that Epicurus' answers to the basic ethical question of what our lives should be aiming at, are, at least in intention, extremely bland, rather than hedonistically shocking. Again, this may not seem to be the case at first sight, since there are, as usual, some debunking comments taken out of context, where we find Epicurus saying that the beginning and root of all good is the pleasure of the stomach, and that he cannot conceive of the good if he removes the pleasures of taste, sex, hearing and sight.[31] But in the light of the above discussion and the texts considered there, it is clear that it is important to Epicurus to show that his claim that our final good is pleasure can be made consistent with our everyday beliefs that developing the virtues and caring for the interests of (some) others are part of our final end. Epicurus accepts that ethical reflection starts from the agent's life as a whole, and that it develops by accepting, and thinking through the implications of, some claim as to the specific content that our final end ought to have. This acceptance is indeed what distinguishes Epicurus from the Cyrenaics, and in making it he was able to present hedonism as a serious contender to be an ethical theory. Yet it is hard not to see him as having boxed himself into a corner shared by some consequentialists and others with very radical moral theories who want to play down the revisionary consequences of those theories. In showing that his shocking-sounding theory could in fact accommodate important moral data which had appeared to present a difficulty for it, Epicurus has in fact expanded his notion of pleasure so much for it to be fit to be an agent's final end that it falls into convenient vagueness where the interests of others, and virtue, are concerned. A later Epicurean account of ethics presents this bland result nicely:

> [It is impossible for one to live pleasantly] without living intelligently and finely and justly, and also courageously and temperately and generously and making friends and being humane, and in general without having all the other virtues; for the greatest errors occur in the moral choices and avoidances, when some people perform each act while they believe in the opposite views and thereby are afflicted by evils.[32]

Epicurean ethics might seem in fact to be, apart from its misleadingly iconoclastic exterior, a theory which tries very hard to be intuitive. Pleasure, after all, is prominent in many people's notions of happiness, if they stress the suggestions of satisfaction and positive attitude. Epicurus avoids the counter-intuitive results of the Cyrenaics by giving us a conception of pleasure which could plausibly be thought to be complete, the point of all our activities: namely, *ataraxia*. He also claims to

---

[31] Athenaeus XII 546f (U 409) and VII 280a (U 67).

[32] Col. XIV of PHerc. 1251. This papyrus is generally known, after its first editor, as the *Ethica Comparetti*. The work was first assigned to Epicurus, but for arguments that the author is Philodemus, see M. Gigante (1983a). I follow the translation of V. Tsouna McKirahan, who is producing a new edition and translation of the papyrus, together with Giovanni Indelli. I have modified the translation only to produce consistency with the way I have translated some key terms in this book.

accommodate the facts that we intuitively expect our final end to involve developing the virtues, and caring for the interests of (some) others for their own sakes. Even if he is not successful in the latter attempt, we can see him trying to produce a hedonism which both fits the formal requirements people expect a serious theory to have, and is intuitively acceptable.

We might object that *ataraxia* is too negatively defined to be a plausible conception of *pleasure*; the ethical appeal of pleasure is that it is something that we positively want to go for, whereas mere freedom from trouble and frustration falls short of this.

Epicurus' answer to this is to be found in his view of nature and how we fall short of living naturally. In his view, most of us are living highly unnatural lives, since we are uncritical and mostly mistaken about our desires, and this in turn is so because we have uncritical and false beliefs about our needs. (We might in turn ask why this is so, but the further answer seems merely to be that we pick up wrong beliefs and attitudes from our society. And the question, how society got that way, is not the question seen as of primary importance; more urgent is the question, how then am I going to rid myself, by reflection, of these false and harmful beliefs?) By the time we have a correct view of what it is our needs really are, we will, Epicurus thinks, have revised our view as to the negative character of *ataraxia*. The reason most people expect to get a positive charge from their activity comes from their false beliefs and the unhealthy emotional attitudes that these tend to produce. By the time we are clear about our natural desires, Epicurus thinks, we will see that freedom from pain and trouble is in fact what we really want; the more exciting, positively attractive goals turned out to be ones which brought more pain and frustration in their wake. We may, of course, question this whole story about nature and natural desires, but without doing so we cannot really object that the final end is too negative and unexciting. To the extent that this is unintuitive, Epicurus has an account ready of how and why our intuitions on this topic are untrustworthy.

On one point, however, Epicurus' account of pleasure as our final end is surprising and distinctive.

> Epicurus, however, denies that duration of time adds anything to living happily, and says that no less pleasure is experienced in a short period of time than if it were everlasting. This is completely inconsistent. Although he places the final good in pleasure, he denies that pleasure becomes greater in a life lasting an infinite time than in one which is finite and even modest. . . . How can someone who thinks that life is rendered happy by pleasure be consistent with himself if he denies that pleasure is increased by duration? If not, then pain is not either. But if the longest pain is the most wretched, does not duration make pleasure more to be desired? . . . Remove Jupiter's everlastingness, and he is no happier than Epicurus; both enjoy the final good, that is to say, pleasure.[33]

This is more than the thesis that pleasure does not become any more pleasant or enjoyable with added time; it is the strong and counter-intuitive thesis that pleasure, the final end of a life, does not make a longer life any better, and thus more desirable, than a shorter life. If (*if*) Epicurus enjoys as much static pleasure as Jupiter,

---

[33] Cicero, *Fin* II 87–88.

then he is as happy as Jupiter, even though he will go out of existence sooner.[34] More to the point for us, if (*if*) you have achieved *ataraxia* at the age of eighteen, you have no reason to want to live till seventy rather than to die at eighteen. If you are already happy, then further time cannot give you anything you don't now already have, so you have no reason to prefer having further time to dying now.

> Infinite time contains equal pleasure with finite time, if one measures pleasure's limits by reasoning.[35]

> The flesh took the limits of pleasure to be infinite, and only infinite time would satisfy it. But the intellect, making a rational calculation of the final end and limit of the flesh , and dispelling the fears about eternity, brought about the complete [*pantelēs*] life, and there is no further need of infinite time. Still, it did not avoid pleasure, nor, when events brought about exit from life, did it leave as though missing any part of the best life.[36]

If we achieve the right sort of pleasure, we have a 'complete life'. How can this be compatible with our having less of it than we might have had?

This thesis is clearly linked to another central Epicurean thesis, namely that 'death is nothing to us'. Some of the death arguments make the point that death itself does not affect either the living or the dead, not being a bad event in the experience of either. But one prominent reason we fear death is that it deprives us of goods that we might otherwise have had; and so Epicurus has to establish that, when we die, we have not been deprived of anything we needed for happiness by dying. The thesis that a happy life is made no better by duration thus has a fundamental role in Epicureanism, since it considers our (mistaken) fear of death, to be the source of many of the false beliefs which make it so hard for us to achieve Epicurean happiness.[37]

Epicurus believes that once we fully appreciate the nature of *ataraxia*, the pleasure which is our final end, we will cease to make a certain mistake about life and duration. But what mistake is this, exactly? The relevant passages are not completely clear.

One suggestion is that we make the mistake of wanting immortality, a life that does not end.[38] But it is hard to think that the fear of death and what it deprives us of, is merely a fear of being mortal. Perhaps Epicurus is thinking of a certain irrational attitude; we sometimes say of reckless young people that 'they think they're immortal', meaning that although they know that they will age and die, and should avoid doing things now which will impair their future lives, they do not act on this knowledge but rush to satisfy irrational desires whose satisfaction hinges on

---

[34] It is worth pointing out that the Epicurean gods enjoy happiness, and that it has been claimed that Epicurus prefers the *makarios* family of words to the *eudaimōn* family of words in talking about happiness, because the former are traditionally more closely associated with talking of the gods' happiness. See Decleva Caizzi (1988), pp. 286–288.

[35] *KD* 19.

[36] *KD* 20.

[37] The death arguments have recently received much attention, especially from the point of view of deprivation of goods. The following is very selective: Furley (1986); Rosenbaum (1986), (1989a), (1989b), (1990); Luper-Foy (1986); Mitsis (1989); Striker (1989); Alberti (1990b).

[38] Striker suggests that this is all that the arguments can in fact meet.

ignoring this kind of fact. Fully appreciating the conditions of one's mortality, however, falls far short of the view that it is indifferent how much longer one lives.

More plausibly we make a mistake about duration; we think that, if a happy life is good, then more of it is in itself better than less. Epicurus can meet this point by showing us that the pleasure that is fit to be our final end is not the kind of thing that is improved by having more of it. Living a life free of frustration, trouble and disturbance is good, without being made better by going on longer. Some objections fall to this response. Cicero's objection above, for example, is that if more pleasure is not preferable to less, then less pain will not be preferable to more; but the latter is absurd, so the former is also. Patently this relies on talking about kinetic pleasure, the pleasure experienced as pain or lack is removed; of that it is plausible to say that it is like pain in this respect. But Epicurus is talking about static pleasure, and the point does not carry over.

What support can Epicurus get for his claim that *ataraxia* has this property? He can get some help from the death arguments, particularly the so-called symmetry argument.[39] According to this argument, we are upset when we think of what our death deprives us of in the future; but we are not upset when we think of what we were deprived of in the past before our birth. But this asymmetry is irrational; what could the relevant difference be between the past and the future? There is no rational basis for my getting upset at what my death will deprive me of, but not upset at what I was deprived of by being born at the time I was born.

This argument has called forth a great deal of sophisticated argument, but from the present point of view it completely misses the point.[40] When we think of death as depriving us of goods, what we have in mind is not sheer duration, but the thought of a life's being cut short before its proper time, or a death which is premature. For we operate with the idea, admittedly extremely vague, of a life's having a shape, progressing from youth to middle age and then to old age, and activities and interests that develop accordingly.[41] And, although we cannot say with any specificity just what need and need not go into a human life for it to have the proper shape, we certainly share the intuition that a normally endowed person who dies at eighteen, with hopes and projects unfulfilled, has had a premature death, whereas someone who dies at seventy-five, with a reasonable proportion of her projects fulfilled, has not. We think of death as depriving Mozart and Schubert of something that Wagner and Elgar were not deprived of. As Striker says, our lives are in this respect something like operas; opera plots vary widely, from the incoherent to the compellingly plotted, but whatever the opera is like, someone is deprived who expected to see all five acts and is told to leave after the first.

So, when Epicurus tells us that death brings no greater deprivation than we get from our non-existence before birth, he is in effect telling us that we are wrong to think of our lives this way, and to feel deprived if we have to die with projects unfulfilled and talents undeveloped. Since we manifestly have to take the death arguments seriously, we have to take seriously the idea that Epicurus is telling us that the eighteen-year-old who dies is not being deprived of anything that the seventy-

[39] This is stressed by Mitsis. The argument is at Lucretius III 972–977.
[40] As is clearly seen by Striker.
[41] See Slote (1983) for a development of this idea.

five-year-old has had. This holds, of course, only if the eighteen-year-old had achieved happiness, that is, *ataraxia*. Epicurus can perfectly well hold that an ordinary teenager who dies has been deprived to some extent, since he has been deprived of the chance to achieve happiness, which perhaps becomes easier after one's youth. And so the thesis does not clash as immediately and massively with our everyday attitudes as we might at first think. But even on reflection we surely find it a hard saying that, once you have progressed to shedding false beliefs, living naturally and achieving a state where you are not bothered by troubles and upsetting desires, there is *nothing* to choose between living like that for forty years and dying tomorrow.

Epicurus has taken great pains to preserve the idea that the happy life is complete; but he has radically shifted the application of completeness. If we are happy by achieving a condition of *ataraxia*, then our happiness resides not in what we actually do or produce, but in our condition of being untroubled about it. There is this much to ancient criticisms that for Epicurus our final end is too passive; it is located not in what we actually do, but in how we feel about what we do.

> The Epicurean philosophers do not accept [the final end's] being said to be in activity [*energoumenon*], because of supposing the final end to be passive [*pathētikon*], not active [*praktikon*]; for it is pleasure.[42]

As Rosenbaum, a sympathetic modern interpreter, puts it:

> [T]he Epicurean view of the significance of projects for human life lies in the way they may or may not engage the natural capacities of the human, not in their completion. Completeness thus lies in a certain time-independent quality of one's activities, not in whether the activities produce specific (future) results. If one's natural capacities are engaged by the projects one adopts, and one pursues those projects without desires which can interrupt engagement in those projects, then one has katastematic pleasure. No passage of time is required to bring about such engagement. It is not that the completion of projects in the future is unimportant, but rather that being unimpededly engaged in the activity of completing them is the only essential aspect of their contribution to one's well-being.[43]

So happiness is, on reflection, radically internalized. It depends on what one does—one cannot achieve Epicurean happiness by engaging in any old course of action—but happiness itself is not constituted by one's activities, but by what could be called one's attitude to or point of view on those activities. We should recall here that there were two levels of being an Epicurean: some lived in Garden communities like Epicurus, while others tried to lead a distinctively Epicurean life while engaged in standard personal and civic activities. This makes perfect sense if we stress the point that Epicurean happiness depends on attaining an inner attitude to one's activities, whatever they are. One is more likely to attain that attitude living in a supportive, non-competitive community; but some people are, by the conditions of their life, unable to make that commitment. Still, although their chances of attaining the right kind of pleasure are smaller, there is no reason in principle why they should be debarred from achieving it, or at least getting some way towards it. This is

---

[42] Arius' introduction to ethics, 46.17–20.
[43] Rosenbaum (1990) p. 37.

reminiscent of the two levels that emerged within Christianity: there are those who dedicate themselves wholly to the religious life, and live a special and, by comparison with others, highly restricted life, and also the bulk of ordinary Christians who try to attain a spiritual life while engaged in ordinary activities. Living the religious life is obviously a better course for those aiming to live a spiritual life; indeed, that is the reason for withdrawing from the world, and choosing it. But it is no guarantee. What matters is the condition that you succeed in bringing yourself into with regard to your activities, not your activities themselves.[44]

The relationship of happiness to one's activity in Epicureanism is thus quite subtle; as we shall see, there are extensive parallels with the Stoic view. What one seeks as one's final end is a condition of 'untroubledness', a state of freedom from misery and frustration. This can only be achieved by reflecting on one's actions and deliberations and realizing that one needs to change them if one has any chance of being happy. (For it is a datum for Epicurus that most people are unhappy, and live unnatural, corrupted lives.) And so one learns and internalizes the theories of Epicurus in order to direct one's desires in the right way, and learns how to monitor one's desires, and to fulfil them in ways that are not reliant on empty beliefs. One can only get the right kind of pleasure if one gets this right; so it is important to guide one's behaviour in the correct ways. But what one aims at is not the activity, still less the consequences of the activity, but the resulting condition of static pleasure, *ataraxia*. Epicurus' thesis that when once we have this, nothing further is gained by going on longer, gives the inner state definite priority over the external achievement—to the extent of denying the importance of our intuitive beliefs about the shape of a developing human life.[45]

This thesis stands in *prima facie* conflict with (at least) two other Epicurean ideas, which consequently have to be reinterpreted to fit. One is the idea that mental pleasures are superior to bodily pleasures, on the grounds that the latter concern only the present, while the former give equal weight to past and future, and thus involve the agent's whole life. This thesis seems to give weight to rational prudence and planning for one's whole life, as opposed to short-sighted indulgence in the pleasures of the moment. However, it is a somewhat reinterpreted notion of rational prudence, since it must be consistent with the thesis that there is nothing rationally to regret if all one's projects are cut off in the next five minutes. Epicurus could say that the thesis that death does not deprive us of goods does not make rational planning pointless; indeed, there is all the difference in the world between the person who, finding herself about to die, can face it with a mental attitude that has achieved untroubledness through considering her life as a whole, and the person who, face to face with death, is obsessed with the pleasure or pain of the recent moment.[46] Nevertheless, one might wonder whether, from the inside, the demand for rational prudence over one's whole life might not seem lessened in cogency by the thought

[44] On the early emergence of two 'grades' of Christians, see Lane Fox (1987).

[45] Forschner (1982), suggests the interesting idea that Epicurus' account of happiness involves a distanced and 'aesthetic' view of one's life. Cf. p. 171: Epicurus 'setzt vollendetes menschliches Glück in eine *ästhetische Lebensform*. Die autark gemachte Seele des Weisen vollendet ihr Glück in heiterer Gelöstheit von allem unbedingten Streben' and p. 188: for Epicurus happiness has the 'Struktur eines *zweckfreien Spiels*.' Unfortunately, Forschner does not develop the idea very far.

[46] One might compare the parable of the wise and foolish virgins.

that what matters is just the prudential attitude, not the application and results of the prudence, which is what intuitively seems to be important about it.

It is only in the light of this radical internalization of happiness that we can understand Epicurus' thesis that the wise person will be happy even when tortured on the rack, although he will, if so tortured, scream and groan.[47] Many have found this unjustified at best, paradoxical at worst. How can an ethical theory which tells us that our final end is pleasure, and which, moreover, has some pretensions to be empiricist, and to begin from and depend on common sense, possibly commit itself to so counter-intuitive a thesis? Not only is it odd for a hedonist to admit that one can be happy on the rack, it is even odder for a hedonist to admit that this can be accompanied by extreme pain, and by the normal reactions to pain.

But Epicurus' response to this is obvious by now. The right kind of hedonist does not have her mind on particular episodes of pain and pleasure, but on achieving the state that results from fulfilling only the right kind of desires. This will involve rational thought and planning over one's life as a whole, perhaps at the expense of certain intense episodes. Thus the thesis that the wise person can be happy on the rack is just a logical extension of the point that sometimes, in our search for *ataraxia*, we pass over some pleasures and accept some pains. The assumption being made, in talking about the wise person, is that he has ended up on the rack not through stupidity or lack of intelligence on his own part, but through bad luck, the incursions of the external world. We should remember that Greek citizens were not normally subject to torture; only slaves and foreigners were. So the assumption here is that either the wise person is a slave or a foreigner, or that, if he is a citizen, he has been victimized by a tyrannical and lawless government, probably by a personal tyrant (like some of the Hellenistic successor kings). In any case, the painful fate is taken to result from bad external luck which does not affect what the wise person has achieved for himself. The Epicurean can, even in these circumstances, retain happiness if happiness has been achieved: for that, as we have seen, depends not just on what is happening now, but on the attitude that the person has achieved to any of the happenings in his life—an attitude based on rational consideration of all parts of his life.

Thus, while it is noteworthy, it is not in any way illogical that the good Epicurean should be said to be happy even while screaming in pain on the rack. For he has what matters: the right internal attitude to what happens to him, and this is not removed by present pain—unless the pain were to result from something he had himself done which would detract from his untroubled state. If we find this illogical, it is because we are resisting the thought that happiness could become so detached from the effects of admitted disasters. But this problem is not a problem specifically for Epicurus; the Stoics also face a version of it. Most theories give us an answer to the question, what happiness is, which conflicts with some of our intuitions. Epicurus' thesis about happiness on the rack appears paradoxical only if taken out of context; it makes perfect sense given his stress on two points. First, happiness is a condition that involves our life as a whole, and does not come and go with particular intense episodes of pleasure or pain. But second, happiness is not to be identified with the course of our life as a whole, but with the inner attitude the agent has to

---

[47] Diogenes X 118 (U 598 and 601; see the latter for parallel passages).

that extended course, an attitude that is not dependent on the way that course goes on. Thus, being happy is consistent with the collapse or reversal of the outward course of one's life; and it is not curtailed when the course of one's life is curtailed.

Is this plausible? Here we would do well to look at what for the Epicureans was a star example, namely Epicurus' behaviour on his deathbed, when he claimed that his present extreme bodily pains were more than outweighed by the pleasures of recollected philosophical conversations.[48] Here we clearly see the idea that happiness is a matter of the attitude one has built up over one's life as a whole, and thus is not undermined by present pain. But, against the reverence felt by Epicureans for the Master's dying letter, we find the reaction of Plutarch, who sees here only false theatricality:

> Not one of us would believe Epicurus when he said that, while dying with the greatest pains and diseases he was cheered on his way by the memory of the pleasures he had enjoyed before. A person could sooner notice a reflection of a face in the troubled deep and waves than a smiling memory of pleasure in so great a convulsion and spasm of the body.[49]

Plutarch is harsh, but he has a point: memories of *pleasure* do not seem robust enough to do the work required here. The Epicurean response would presumably be that while our memories of pleasure might not do this, it would be different for a wise person like Epicurus. But at least Plutarch's objection underlines the unintuitive nature of Epicurus' conclusions.

The extent of the way in which Epicurus has redefined and relocated what matters is more obvious in cases where we have dramatic reversals, but can be seen also, less dramatically, in lives where things do not go wrong. For the thesis involves some rethinking of the activities that vary the condition of *ataraxia*. We have seen that it is wrong to think of this as a state of inertia; it can be varied by the activities that the agent performs -and we have seen that there is actually wide scope for variety here, since not only are there many potentially blameless ways of fulfilling natural desires, but different people find different kinds of activities suitable to development as an Epicurean. But the force of this concession is again somewhat weakened when we reflect that this variety has no value in itself. An Epicurean has no reason to value varied over monotonous activity: what matters is only the state of pleasure that results. To revert to the opera analogy, he has no reason to prefer a complex to a stereotyped plot, a poetic to a hack libretto. For what matters is internalized; it is not the activities but the agent's attitude to them. Epicurus has produced a bland rather than shocking hedonism by fitting pleasure into a eudaimonistic framework; the radical and interesting part of his theory lies in his internalizing of our final end, so that what we aim at, what we bend our lives towards and monitor our actions to achieve, is something which, once achieved, is altogether indifferent to the temporal shape of a human life.

---

[48] Diogenes X 22.

[49] Plutarch, *Non posse* 1099 d-e. Cf. Cicero, *TD* V 75, who compares the attempt to cope with actual overheating by calling up memories of bathing in cold water.

17

The Sceptics: Untroubledness Without Belief

We have seen that the ancient sceptics all take themselves to be different from the other schools in not recommending one favoured way of solving common problems and achieving a shared goal. Rather, they radically reject the basic assumption of all the other schools, namely that we can achieve anything by shared philosophical thinking and endeavour. For they all hold that continued genuine enquiry will face the thinker with situations where there is no option but to suspend belief; intellectual enquiry is thus, if properly done, self-abolishing, since the enquirer finds that all serious disputes are unsettleable, all debates endless, and the only honest outcome, detachment from the original questions.

Prima facie it is odd to combine this with a systematic presentation of scepticism as a philosophy like any other school philosophy—a definition, a criterion, a set of principles, and, most of all, an account of its final end. Among ancient sceptics, only the later Pyrrhonists, represented for us by Sextus, do this. Pyrrho himself wrote nothing, and in the accounts by his follower Timon, we find, apart from brief descriptions of sceptical strategy, nothing but a positive portrayal of Pyrrho as an attractive model, and highly negative portrayals of other, dogmatic philosophers, presenting them as ridiculous and pretentious. The general moral is clear: follow Pyrrho and you will avoid the paths of pompous idiocy, which is all other philosophers offer. What you will positively get is presented as calm and tranquillity,[1] but we have no positive indications as to how tranquillity is linked to sceptical enquiry, or as to why we should expect tranquillity to be what the sceptic ends up with. The Academic sceptics, who do stress enquiry and philosophical argument, do not claim that tranquillity will result from this: they do not, indeed, represent it as having any further point beyond itself. It is only in Sextus that we find that the later Pyrrhonists explicitly claimed both that sceptical enquiry will result in suspension of belief and that the sceptic is in fact doing what the other schools do, namely specifying our final end. For suspension of belief results in untroubledness (*ataraxia*), and this is in fact the only satisfactory final end for us to seek.

It might seem that there is a conflict here right at the start. For the sceptics tell us that if we enquire vigorously, we will reach suspension of judgement. But if we are, as sceptics, seeking a final end, happiness, then surely we are seeking suspension of judgement in order to be happy. But then how can we be enquiring in a genuine way? Surely we will be tempted not to enquire as vigorously as we might, if we are

---

[1] See Burnyeat (1980b).

aiming at being happy, but suspect that truly vigorous enquiry will leave us committed to a conclusion, rather than leading to suspension of belief.

This is not a problem for sophisticated sceptics, however. Sextus follows his claim that sceptics do have a final end by giving a narrative account of what happens to the sceptic. The sceptic begins just like anyone else, he says, seeking to escape troubles and frustrations by finding the answers to various questions. But when he enquires about them vigorously, he finds that there is as much to be said on the one side as on the other; hence he reaches equipollence, and so finds himself suspending judgement. And happiness, in the form of peace of mind, follows 'by chance', *tuchikōs*. It is like what happened to the painter Apelles, who tried and tried to produce in his painting the effect of a horse's foam, until he finally gave up and flung at the painting the sponge he used to wipe off his brushes; and thus produced, by chance, exactly the effect he had unsuccessfully been trying for.[2] So, even if sceptical enquiry makes you happy, you will not achieve happiness by trying for it directly, but only by going in for sceptical enquiry.

We might think the Apelles story is a discouraging one; success would appear to be a rare occurrence. But Sextus adds another analogy; peace of mind follows suspension of judgement the way a shadow follows a body. That is, it is a regular result, indeed one you cannot prevent. So the sceptic can perfectly well predict that sceptical enquiry and the resulting suspension of judgement will make her happy, and there is no real conflict. The only odd result is that the sceptic's aim is one that she cannot pursue directly; she has to pursue something else—sceptical enquiry—in order to get it. This result, however, may seem less odd if we reflect on the thinness of happiness in ancient theories as a specification of our final end. In telling us that we must philosophize sceptically in order to be happy, the sceptics are not giving us a roundabout route to a definite goal, but a definite strategy for achieving a vaguely specified end.

There is a problem, however, in Sextus' description of the sceptic's final end: not in having such a thing, but in having a developed philosophical view of what kind of thing it is. For *prima facie* there is a straight conflict between giving strategies to lead to suspension of belief on any topic (any topic, that is, on which there is serious dispute) and spelling out a set of philosophical beliefs about our final end, what it is and how scepticism is the best way of achieving it. Sextus, of course, is not to be caught in this easy trap. He points out that he is not committing himself to *belief* in any of what he puts forward about our final end; it is simply his appearances—the way things go on appearing to him even after he has been led to suspension of belief about it by recognizing the force of the matched difficulties on each side. That one is left with an appearance or set of appearances after reaching suspension of judgement and loss of belief shows that the appearances do not depend on rational sources. But realizing this is no basis for dismissing them; indeed, something so hard to get rid of by rational means is something it is advisable to take note of. So in presenting what he does about our final end, Sextus is merely pointing out what appears to him to be the case about something we shouldn't ignore; he does not have to have beliefs about it.

---

[2] *PH* I 26–29. See chapter 8, pp. 209–10, for a translation of this passage.

Nevertheless, we have already seen[3] that difficulties lurk in Sextus' claim that scepticism is a way of achieving our final end. We have looked at two aspects of this. A sceptic can appeal to nature to found the pursuit and practice of scepticism; but the nature he appeals to cannot serve as a selective and regulative ideal for life. Rather, whatever the sceptic ends up doing counts as conforming to nature, and the notion has become empty as far as ethics is concerned. Further, since Sextus cannot promote what he says about our final end as being something he believes, but only as the content of his own appearances, we have seen that there is a chronic problem as to the sceptic's relation to others. As far as concerns what is internal to the sceptic's appearances, he can care about others, and indeed we find Sextus ascribing to the sceptic a positive therapeutic aim, namely to help others escape the disease of holding beliefs. But the sceptic's untroubledness results from losing beliefs, and thus he is left without the beliefs needed to ground real concern for others; the only running concern that is plausibly left is the continuing irritation that the sceptic feels from the fact that others hold beliefs. Even larger difficulties, however, remain for the sceptic's recommendation of scepticism as a recipe for our achieving our final end when we consider it as a recipe for happiness.

Sextus argues at the beginning of the *Outlines* that the sceptic has a final end, as any school of philosophy would make the claim.

> Now a final end [*telos*] is that for the sake of which everything is done or considered, while it is not itself done or considered for the sake of anything else. Or: a final end is the final object of desire.[4]

That is, the sceptic accepts that the starting point of ethical reflection is that of one's life as a whole, and what one is aiming at in all one is doing. Clearly this is an assumption common to all the philosophical schools. But is the *sceptic* entitled to make it? Sextus can only put it forward as the content of his appearances, that is, as what he is left finding it inevitable to hold, even after suspending belief on the subject. So the assumption cannot itself depend on having a substantial belief. Nor can it depend on having suspended beliefs after only superficial argument, or after argument about only a small part of the subject. For in all these cases there would obviously be further argument which would remove the sceptic's ground for putting forward this assumption. (Sextus does not present himself, in his book, as a perfect sceptic; but clearly it would be unwise for him to put forward claims which could be undermined by obvious objections.)

This assumption, that the sceptic shares with the dogmatist an appearance about our having final ends (though the sceptic, of course, does not *believe* this), may seem like an unsafe assumption for the sceptic to make. What if, as a matter of fact, those who have been through the process of sceptical argument end up with no such appearance, taking anarchic lives and unorganized aims for granted? Sextus is assuming that, as a matter of fact and not of argument, most people do have and take for granted the notion of a final end as what unifies and makes sense of their lives. Otherwise he would hardly have this appearance himself as what organizes the content of his other appearances. So, if Sextus' procedure is to work, it must be true

---

[3] Chapters 8 and 11.
[4] *PH* 1 25.

that this notion of a final end is not dependent on philosophers' arguments, which can always be queried, but is part of what people accept and live by regardless of argument.

This seems an acceptable assumption; we have seen that in the ancient world people found it natural to reflect about their lives as wholes and to unify their concerns in terms of a final end, posing the basic ethical question in the form, what is the content of our final end?[5] So Sextus is able here, as elsewhere, to present himself as being on the side of *bios* or 'Life', against the philosophers' abstractions.[6] We might ask, however, how articulate the ordinary person's conception of their final end is supposed to be? Presumably not many unphilosophical Greeks spelled out the notion as Sextus does. Perhaps Sextus takes it for granted that most people can acquire some low-level philosophical articulation of the notion without leaning on particular theories, and so without importing beliefs that could be argued against.

In the initial passage Sextus does not mention happiness, but goes right ahead to the claim, 'Up to now we say the final end of the sceptic is untroubledness [*ataraxia*] in matters of opinion and having moderate feelings [*metriopatheia*] in matters forced on us.'[7] The claim is discussed further in the two versions of his section on ethics, *PH* III 235-238, and *M* XI 110-161. In the longer of these two passages it is abundantly clear that what is at stake is whether the sceptic has a better strategy for attaining happiness (*eudaimonia*) than the dogmatists. These passages are in the ethics section, but they are relevant to sceptical philosophizing as a whole. For, the claim is that the dogmatist has, and the sceptic lacks, beliefs about things being good and bad; and if you lack the belief that anything is good, you cannot have the belief that it is good to spend time on logic, say, or physics.[8] So belief, or the lack of it, about values affects one's life, and thus one's sceptical philosophizing, as a whole. And we find, made out in some detail, the claim that the sceptic will be happy, and the dogmatist correspondingly unhappy, because becoming a sceptic brings with it two things: untroubledness in matters where beliefs are relevant, and moderation in what one feels in matters where belief is not relevant. These are interesting and strong claims, and it is important to look at the way the sceptic tries to argue us to them, and the relation of the arguments to the result that is supposed to follow.

Sextus spells out the relevant connection for us at *M* XI 112-113: Unhappiness always comes from some trouble, *tarachē*. People feel troubled because they pursue or avoid things 'intensely', *suntonōs*. And the causes of intense pursuit and avoidance, in turn, are people's beliefs that various things are good or bad. The villains are thus beliefs that things are good and bad. Sextus' strategy is simple in form. He produces lots of arguments to get us to the point of suspending judgement about values, so that we no longer have beliefs that things are good and bad. If they

---

[5] The Cyrenaics, the only school seriously to query the importance of considering the agent's life as a whole, were notably unsuccessful and marginal in ethical debate.

[6] Cf. some other passages where Sextus claims to be the plain blunt man defending Life: *PH* II 246, where he dismisses the usefulness of knowing how fallacies come about; just before this (244-245), he approvingly mentions various philistine 'refutations' of philosophical problems, e.g., getting up and walking to 'refute' Zeno's paradoxes about motion. Cf. also *PH* III 2 (on religion), *M* VII 29-30 (the criterion of choice in everyday life) and *M* VIII 157-158 ('signs' in everyday life).

[7] *PH* I 25.

[8] So, although Sextus gives culpably little time to ethics, as compared with physics and logic, these passages are crucial for the sceptical enterprise as a whole, and not just for scepticism about ethics.

work, we find that losing these beliefs removes the intensity from our lives; thus we are no longer annoyed by troubles, and so are happy. There is a complication; this strategy will not save us from troubles that we cannot be avoided by not having beliefs—prominently, physical pain. However, even in these cases, says Sextus (147–160) the sceptic will be better off than the dogmatist, even though neither can completely avoid trouble. For the main reason that we are troubled by things like physical pain is that we believe them to be bad; so the sceptic, who merely suffers the pain, is better off than the dogmatist, who believes pain to be a bad thing. Thus the sceptic lives a life which is as free of troubles as anyone's life can be. This is a more pessimistic estimate of the chanches for happiness than we find in the positive ethical theories. According to the sceptic, nobody is actually happy, given that nobody can avoid the conditions of physical pain, hunger and so on. His claim, then, is a comparative one: the sceptic is *happier* than the dogmatist who accepts a positive ethical theory. We shall return to the status of this strategy after considering the arguments and their intended effect.[9]

Sextus' arguments about good and bad are to be found in three places: the Tenth Mode (*PH* I 145–163),[10] *PH* III 168–238, and *M* XI 1–167. The Tenth Mode follows the pattern of the other sceptical Modes or argument-schemata: it gives us a schema for setting up 'oppositions' that will lead to 'conflicting appearances'.

Sextus lists what he calls lifestyle (*agōgē*), customs (*ethē*), laws (*nomoi*), mythical beliefs (*muthikai pisteis*) and dogmatic conceptions (*dogmatikai hupolēpseis*). We use these factors to construct cases of 'oppositions': the same thing (object or course of action) appears to one set of people to have positive value and to another set to have negative value. Sextus uses examples which are familiar, indeed come to him from a long tradition, where, for example, a practice such as male homosexuality is, he claims, a custom in one place (Persia) but against the law in another (Rome). In all these cases we find that the practice is acceptable to one set of people because of one factor (their custom) but unacceptable to another, because of another factor (their law). Clearly, the practice can't in fact be both acceptable and unacceptable. But we have no grounds for preferring one factor to another; why should we be more impressed by Persian custom than by Roman law? Neither gives us, in itself, a rational ground for preferring one way of viewing the practice. Hence, thinks Sextus, we will find ourselves in a state of equipollence, and so will suspend judgement. We will, of course, continue to find the practice acceptable or unacceptable, depending on which of the factors has more weight with us, but we lose whatever belief we had on the subject. There are two ways in which these factors enter into our continuing to have 'appearances' of value or disvalue in these cases. If we are neither Persian nor Roman, we will understand why both sides feel the way they do, but cease to think that there is really any matter of dispute between them. But if we are ourselves Persian, or Roman, then we will have lost our belief that *our* practice has rational justification; though of course we will still regard it, strongly, in one or other way, because of the effect of the factors of custom or law.

The argument-pattern of the Tenth Mode is stronger than often supposed. We may find it weak because Sextus uses weak (often blatantly fictional) examples, and

---

[9] In what follows I draw on some material in Annas (1986) and (1993b).

[10] On this see Annas and Barnes (1985) ch. 13, where there are translations and discussion of this Mode in Sextus and also in its other appearances in Diogenes and Philo.

frequently uses examples where the conflict is merely superficial, and is easily seen to rely on deeper agreement. However, Sextus is not bound to his examples: he is offering us an argument-pattern which will be effective if we can find examples of it which work, in our case. And it does not require enormous efforts of imagination to come up with examples which might have force in dislodging beliefs about values.

A stronger objection is that even forceful examples are unlikely to get us to equipollence; usually, when faced by conflicting valuations, we come down on one or the other side. This is not fatal to Sextus' strategy, however; for he will merely press us for the grounds we give as to *why* we prefer one side to the other. He thinks that once we give due weight to the various factors on the basis of which people approve or disapprove of different practices, we will come to see that, if our preference is due *merely* to some such factor, we will become detached from that preference, seeing it as rationally ungrounded. And this is, of course, what it is to lose our belief in the value of the practice.

At this point, however, most people would make a move to look for a more theoretical justification for the practice in question; if commonsense discussion leads to an impasse, we move to ethical theory. So Sextus needs his more theoretical discussions in *PH* III and *M* XI. These arguments are designed to remove any reliance we might be tempted to place on the rational support given to various practices by the available theories. For, if all the support given by theories collapses, we revert to equipollence on the subject, and thus to suspension of judgement.

Sextus' performance here is, unfortunately, disappointing. In the sections of his book on logic and physics we find not only general argumentative strategies but a host of detailed refutations of particular theories (often preceded by extensive accounts of them). But Sextus was clearly something of a philistine about ethics, and he gives us appallingly little by way of exposition and demolition of particular ethical theories; we find large gaps where we expect detailed discussions of Stoic, Epicurean and Aristotelian theories of the final good, virtue and so on.[11] Thus even in Sextus' own terms, his arguments are woefully lacking. If I try to justify a practice by appeal to central Stoic or Aristotelian theses, Sextus has said nothing to show that this will not do. Instead, he relies on a few very general arguments purporting to show that ethics, as a discipline, is in bad shape. There is, he says, disagreement both about the basic concepts of ethics, such as good, bad and indifferent, and also about ethical judgements—what things and actions are good or bad. The disagreement is widespread, fundamental and chronic. Hence we cannot commit ourselves to beliefs about the truth of ethical claims, for in every area of ethics we find conflict and no hope of resolving it.[12] Sextus is not the only philosopher to make the condescending assumption that in ethics, as opposed to other areas of philosophy, nothing more is required than a single general argument, with no need to consider the detail of other theories. Nor is he the only one to assume that in ethics, as opposed to other areas of philosophy, disagreement is enough in itself to preclude the assumption of enough

---

[11] We get some discussion of particular theories, but only as a by-product of larger bits of argument (e.g., *PH* III 183–190, *M* XI 79–89; *PH* III 193–6, *M* XI 96–109). Sextus' criticism is also frequently clumsy, missing the point—for example, his over-lengthy and tedious demolition of the Stoic skill (*technē*) of life at *PH* III 239–279 and *M* XI 168–256, where a golden opportunity to discuss central ethical issues is frittered away in trivialities.

[12] *PH* III 179–182; *M* XI 68–78.

consensus to ground belief. Still, this is no excuse; both assumptions are clearly misguided. The mere fact of continued disagreement no more leads us to suspension of judgement on its own in ethics than it does in other areas of philosophy; massive amounts of detailed argument are needed, which Sextus shows himself unaware of the need for.[13]

Thus the argumentative part of Sextus' implementation of his strategy is very weak. However, let us assume that Sextus has enough arguments, and that they are respectable, and ask how, if you find them successful, this makes you happy.

Losing your beliefs that things and courses of action are good and bad is taken to make you lose the intensity with which you care about these things. Thus, they no longer bother you, and you are happy. What is meant here by 'intensity'? Sextus talks about some subsidiary sources of anxiety; if one thinks that money is a good thing, then one will have continual anxieties about keeping one's own, fending off others' attempts to take it, and so on. But what he mainly has in mind is the thought that simply thinking a thing good is in itself a source of intensity and anxiety. If I believe that money is a good thing, then it will *matter* to me that I get some, and so on. If I cease to believe that it is a good thing, then it can't matter to me any more. I might, of course, still want some; but I can't have the same intensity of attitude to it that I had before.

The mechanism that Sextus indicates sounds a plausible one. There is a real enough distinction between just wanting or going for something, on the one hand, and, on the other, thinking it good. And it is only if the thing actually has the value in question that one can find it *worth* pursuing; and, in turn, only if one finds it worth pursuing that one can *care* about whether or not one successfully pursues it. The problems for Sextus begin rather when we ask what the sceptic who has lost beliefs is left with. For, obviously, the sceptic is left with something; Sextus pours scorn on the idea that the sceptic is left inert, like a vegetable.[14] Rather, the sceptic is left with the appearances—with the way that things stubbornly go on appearing to one, even after all the arguments *pro* and *con* have produced equipollence and so suspension of belief. The sceptic will lose the belief that pursuing money, say, is good; but will be left with the fact that money still appears something to go for. (At least, she may be; what appearances she is left with will of course depend not on her intellectual state but upon the factors such as lifestyle and custom which have moulded her. Let us suppose, however, that in most cultures money will retain an attractive appearance even to the sceptic.) If Sextus is right, the sceptic left with this appearance will be happy, because she no longer has the nagging anxiety that follows believing that it is really worth having.

But, given that the sceptic will not be left motivationally inert like a vegetable when faced by this appearance, what will happen? As we have seen,[15] the sceptic relies on nature here; it is natural for us, when we lose our beliefs, not to become motivationally paralyzed, but rather to live by the appearances—to respond to the way things appear to us, and to act accordingly. Sextus indeed relies on this when saying that the sceptic will live a normal life, even being active in his profession, and

---

[13] This is strange, given the existence of works like Cicero's *De Finibus*, in which we find just this sort of argument.

[14] *M* XI 163.

[15] Chapter 5.

that when faced with difficult moral decisions he will respond adequately, in terms of his moral upbringing.[16] But—a problem that we have already explored—if living by the appearances is as motivationally adequate as this, it seems to come down to what most people mean by having beliefs, and scepticism seems to change nothing. If the sceptic lives normally, reacts to the same stimuli as other people, pursues his profession, earning money and, for example, writing books, then losing one's beliefs seems to make no difference in one's active life. The sceptic will, of course, be dismissive of philosophical arguments and claims, but his active life would seem to be the same as that of anyone else.

Neither outcome bodes well for Sextus' claim that the sceptic will be happier than the dogmatist. Manifestly, a life of inert vegetating, or of being pulled from under carts and back from precipices by unsceptical friends (as in the unfriendly biographical tradition about Pyrrho)[17] is not a good candidate for happiness. But neither is a life in which one dismisses the force of theoretical arguments, but does much the same as others. The other tradition about Pyrrho's life has him living the life of an honoured citizen and high priest[18] —a somewhat complacent view of the happy life.

What the sceptic needs, and will insist on having, is a middle way: losing one's beliefs about value will produce a difference in one's active life, a difference which will not only not land the agent in paralysis but will plausibly make her life happier than a life which has not lost these beliefs.[19] If such a way exists, it will depend on the sceptic's detachment from her beliefs. The sceptic who no longer has the belief that money is a good thing (nor, of course, that it is not a good thing) may still find money attractive, but can no longer feel commitment to this idea. She knows, if she thinks about it at all, that she finds it attractive only because of her upbringing, culture and so on, not on any rational grounds, and so cannot think of it as something to be seriously held, argued for, defended and so on. However, it is still to play a serious role in her life; she is to act on it, not just on particular occasions but in a systematic way, building other projects around it, and so on. Can these attitudes be combined? It is natural for us to think of the result of combining them as resulting in a kind of alienation from oneself— a sort of splitting of the self into the part which acts in accordance with the appearances, and a part which remains detached and uninvolved, somewhat like a spectator who is aware that all of this lacks backing.[20]

It could be countered to this that we do in fact combine these attitudes in parts of our lives; we have strong commitments for which we realize that there is no rational backing (to sports or other leisure activities, for example; one can be a passionate tennis player while realizing that one could perfectly well have gone in for riding instead). But these are typically optional activities, which engage only part of our energy and cover only part of our lives; it is quite another thing to suggest that one's whole life might be marked by this sort of detachable commitment. For this

---

[16] *PH* I 23–24; *M* XI 166.

[17] Diogenes IX 62, 63, 66; (cf. Aristocles, ap. Eusebius, *Praep Ev* XIV 18. 25–26).

[18] Diogenes IX 64–5.

[19] For a powerful defence of the view that Pyrrhonism can provide just such a middle way, see McPherran (1988) and (1990b).

[20] Cf. the comments by Burnyeat (1983).

would be to suggest that one could regard serious and central commitments, such as one's job or one's marriage, as though they were trivial matters like sports. And it is hard to see how one could do the latter without a division of one's life and efforts into the part which acts in a committed way and a part which stands back.

The price of the sceptic's detachment, together with continuing involvement in her practical life, would seem then to be a kind of division of the self, of a sort that seems unlikely, on most views, to conduce in itself to happiness. The sceptic could retort again that this is not the effect which detachment has to have; rather, instead of the agent dividing into an active self and a detached, spectator self, what happens is that the agent carries on as an agent, and any distinct sense of self tends to disappear: the agent's activities simply cease to be accompanied by unifying and critical reflection of the kind that we think accompanies having a sense of one's self.[21] It is hard for us to make ready sense of this idea. But, even if we understand adequately how real detachment does not prevent an active and practical life, we are still left with the point that this is a strange conception of happiness. Even if it is objected that it is not meant as a conception of happiness in general, but only of the sceptic's specific candidate for happiness, *ataraxia*, the result is still strange; for being detached from one's appearances, what one used to hold as beliefs, seems like overkill if all we are seeking is a state of not being troubled.

But, even supposing that the sceptic's arguments are cogent, and that being convinced by them would plausibly lead to being in a state of untroubledness (and mild troubledness in the case of what cannot be avoided), and that untroubledness is agreed to be the content of happiness, the question still remains, whether Sextus' diagnosis is correct—that is, given that nobody can be completely happy (because of pain, hunger, etc.), still, the sceptic will be happier than the dogmatist.

Here again Sextus does not give us specific arguments against the claims of the different theories, but rather a general argument. If anxiety attaches to believing things to be good and bad, then ethical theories can never rid us of anxiety. For all they do is to tell us to revise our priorities: to consider virtue, for example, good rather than money. And all that this exercise does is to redirect our concern. We will believe different things to be good, but, in still believing them good, we will have as much anxiety as ever. Ethical philosophers are thus as much use in helping you to achieve happiness as a doctor who rids you of one disease by giving you another one. Further, ethical theories may actually make things *worse* for you. For if you become convinced that virtue is *more* valuable than money, you will care about it more, and so become more anxious about having it; so the ethical philosopher in question has in effect cured you of a cold by giving you pneumonia.[22]

Much here seems to hang on the assumption (which we shall examine in due course) that it is believing things to be good and bad which gives rise to anxiety. However, this dependence does not nullify the argument here, since Sextus is comparing scepticism's procedure to those of ethical theories, and as we have seen, the major ancient ethical theories did start from the assumption that most people are unhappy and troubled, and that the cause of this is the valuations that they put on

---

[21] This is argued by McPherran, and also explored in Nussbaum, 'Skeptical Purgatives', a chapter in (forthcoming b).

[22] *M* XI 130–140.

things. Sextus is right that scepticism is the only really distinctive alternative here. All the major ethical theories do think that they can help people to live happier lives by getting them to think through and revise their priorities. The sceptic is the only one who takes this to be a systematic waste of time.

Sextus has been sharply criticized here[23] for missing the point of the rival ethical theories. For they do not just think that it is changing our priorities as such, valuing B rather than A, which will make us happy. They give reasons why the things most people go for—money, power—will not produce a satisfactory life. These things cannot give us a final end which is complete and self-sufficient, for a start. And the different theories argue that their own candidates do fulfil these conditions. So at the end of the day we have not just made a different selection among things all of the same kind, and with the same kind of effect. We have gone from inadequate to adequate candidates for being our final end, the ultimate thing we are going for in our lives as wholes.

Sextus actually notices one main way in which this could reasonably be held to reduce anxiety in particular. For in the shorter version[24] Sextus recognizes that dogmatic ethical theorists might claim that their goods cannot be lost. For the Stoics, for example, it is reasonable to be anxious if you think health or money a good; but when you realize that these are merely indifferents and that only virtue is good, your anxiety does not transfer to virtue. For to the extent that you are virtuous, this is your achievement and not something which is dependent on external factors; you cannot lose it in the way that you can lose your money. And all theories stress that, rightly conceived, your final end is up to you to achieve; it involves what you make of your life, and so is under your control in ways that money and power, for example, are not. Properly understood, then, ethical theories are not merely redirecting anxiety from one good to another, but directing us towards the kind of good that we should not be anxious about. Sextus replies to this merely that this view can be disputed—like all theses of dogmatic ethics, it is open to sceptical refutation. He conspicuously fails to refute it, however, so leaving the dogmatist with the advantage; for Sextus' argument now rests on an assumption which is challenged, and Sextus has not met the challenge.[25]

Actually, it is open to Sextus to meet this point. He could retort to the Stoic, for example, that he has pointed out a genuine difference between ends like money and ends like virtue. But he could query the claim that the latter free the agent from anxiety. A Stoic can pride herself on not being dependent on external things like money, since she thinks that only virtue is good. But her happiness is still dependent—not, now, on crude contingencies like the stock market, but on its

---

[23] By Striker (1990).

[24] *PH* 235–238, esp. 238. I think that Striker is being over-bold in seeing the *PH* version as a more cautious one, designed to meet obvious objections to the *M* version. For, while the chronology of Sextus' works is puzzling in many ways, Janáček's studies (1972) certainly suggest that *M* is the later work, and it is unsafe to base an interpretation on the supposition that the *PH* version must be later.

[25] Striker's own objection is different: she says that even the possibility of a viable alternative view here defeats Sextus, since it shows that there are alternative equally good ways to achieve *ataraxia*. Sextus, however, would probably not see things this way; what matters is not just whether there is an alternative view, but whether it is in fact viable. Hence it is an admission of weakness not to produce an actual refutation, but to rest, presumably, on the possibility of producing a refutation—for until one is actually produced, Sextus' own procedure so far is undermined.

being *true* that virtue is good while money is not. This will only be the case, of course, if Stoic ethical theory is the correct one, and other ones false. And it seems reasonable for someone who holds this, to worry about it; for there are, after all, many ways in which theories can go astray, and Stoic theory is complex and extensive, and open to question at very many points. So, even if anxiety is altered in its nature, and not just redirected, by a switch from money to virtue as a final end, there is still scope for the sceptic to argue that anxiety is still lurking—indeed, to argue that the new kind of anxiety might be worse than the initial kind.[26]

Is it a weakness in Sextus' account that he allows that the happy sceptic will still be bothered by things like pain and hunger? Certainly this leaves the sceptic making a far more modest claim than ethical theories that say that happiness lies completely in the agent's control—the Stoics, for example, who say that virtue is sufficient for happiness and that virtue is in the agent's control. However, such theories do not deny that pain, hunger, etc., happen to the agent, and that the agent has reason to mind them and to try to avoid them; they simply say that they do not detract from the agent's happiness. Sextus indeed seems to be actually borrowing from Epicurean arguments[27] when he claims that pain is bearable if spread over a long period, and, if it is unbearable, does not last long. He is quite entitled to do so, since all theories agree (how could they fail to do so?) that pain, hunger, etc., are negative things, to be avoided whenever possible by the agent, and differ only in whether or not they take them actually to detract from happiness. Sextus could indeed claim that his account is the most realistic, and most in accordance with our everyday notion of happiness. Indeed, that is why he claims that the sceptic is happier than the dogmatist, even if nobody can be completely happy, given the human condition.[28] So Sextus is consciously realistic here; and what he says ties in neatly with the rest of his account, since what makes pain, hunger, etc. more bearable for the sceptic is (allegedly) just what is distinctive of the sceptic's approach, namely the fact that the sceptic lacks beliefs.

We can thus see how Sextus would implement his strategy, and show that the sceptic is happier than the dogmatist; despite obvious weaknesses on Sextus' part, we can see how the strategy might be taken seriously. However, we must return at this point to the question of the status of the strategy itself. Sextus has proceeded on the assumptions that unhappiness always comes from being troubled, and that troubles come from holding beliefs about values. But how is he entitled to any of these assumptions? Isn't the sceptic after all depending on beliefs—and rather specific beliefs at that—in order to get us to be sceptical?

There is nothing wrong with the sceptic's depending on beliefs in his argument, if the beliefs in question are held by the opponent; it only becomes objectionable if the sceptic's argument depends on them, while the opponent rejects them. Sextus is

---

[26] Might not this point rebound on the sceptic's own head (as Terry Irwin has suggested to me)? For a sceptic might be troubled by worry that perhaps *epochē* is the wrong reaction to finding oneself in a state of equipollence. Perhaps sceptical reliance on nature could block this worry; *epochē* can't be a radically inappropriate reaction, or we would just not have it; we would react in other ways.

[27] *M* XI 150–155.

[28] Hence I think Striker (1990) unjustified in seeing it as a weakness in Sextus' claim, that Epicureans could do as well on this issue. For Sextus' account can claim to be more intuitive on the relation of the negative factors to happiness.

presumably assuming that all ancient ethical theories would accept these assumptions; so the only real question is, which theory—sceptical or dogmatist—succeeds in fulfilling these conditions? But this weakens Sextus' argument still further. For, first, not all theories would accept these assumptions, at least, not in the form in which Sextus puts them to work. We have seen that some theories challenge the idea that every belief about value brings *tarachē* or trouble, at any rate the same kind of trouble.[29] Second, the argument ought not to be directed just at supporters of various ethical theories, it ought to be directed as well to ordinary people. Sextus, after all, is the one who claims that he is the supporter of Life against the theorists. And it is far less clear that everyday intuitions in the ancient world were agreed on Sextus' assumptions. The idea that happiness is untroubledness, that *all* unhappiness is traceable to frustrations and troubles, has some plausibility—but so do various opposing views, which link happiness with activity and achievement. To defend his strategy, Sextus ought to put more work into defending the assumptions that he uses to set it up.

Further, Sextus is in the end reliant, as other philosophers are not, on the actual outcome when people are argued to suspension of judgement and find themselves living by the appearances. If the result of this were in fact massive rejection of the idea that happiness is untroubledness to the extent that we can achieve that, then Sextus has nothing to say; it appears differently to him, but since he is not putting forward any of his strategy as a matter of belief, but only of appearance, he can hardly engage in argument about it. If Sextus were to find himself so to speak outvoted on the issue of what most people's appearances about happiness are, we might suppose that this would not bother him; he would only be bothered, of course, if he thought that his appearances were preferable, and this thought betrays a commitment to belief about value, thus letting in *tarachē*. However, if Sextus were to be completely untroubled about having appearances about happiness and how to achieve it that differed from those of everyone else, this would cast some doubt on the therapeutic motivation that the sceptic has, to better the condition of those who are ill with the disease of having beliefs.

So, if we disagree with Sextus, either about what happiness involves or about the claim that scepticism is the best way to happiness, there seems to be a standoff. What we say seems to conflict; but there seems no way to resolve it. Sextus can only say that if we disagree, it is because we have dogmatic beliefs; if we became sceptical we would lose those beliefs and then, he predicts, we would have appearances like his. There is nothing to be done but to try and see. And if, when we do this, there still seems to be lack of agreement there is nothing to be done then either.

The situation might superficially seem to be like that between the ordinary person and the ethical theorist—the Stoic or Epicurean, say. The theorist makes claims about happiness which may well strike the ordinary person as counter-intuitive, even flatly false. The theorist has no direct response to this, except to say that if ordinary people reflect and follow up the theory honestly, then they will themselves come to the conclusion that they previously thought was counter-

---

[29] Epicurus would argue, for example, that correct beliefs bring *ataraxia*. Of course Sextus has a comeback; see pp. 360–61. But this could be further disputed; Sextus is at least not entitled to take the point for granted.

intuitive. However, there is a difference between the sceptic and other ethical philosophers. When Epicurus, say, tells us that our final end is *ataraxia*, he can appeal to some of our beliefs, and then develop arguments which, if successful, show us how we get from here to there, how we go from our intuitions to becoming Epicureans. But the sceptic cannot appeal to anything to show us that we are going in the right direction. He simply predicts what will happen. For any arguments that engaged with our beliefs and showed us that we ought, for example, to have certain beliefs about happiness could only be more of the dogmatism that he says that he is helping us to escape.

It is interesting that when he is telling us that the sceptic is happy, Sextus quotes from Timon's approving picture of Pyrrho: 'Happy is the person who lives on without being troubled and, as Timon used to say, set in quietness and calm: 'for calm spread everywhere' and 'him I noticed, in a windless calm'.[30] After centuries and centuries of argument there is still nothing better that the sceptic can do to persuade us that scepticism will lead to the happy life, than to give us an image that he hopes we will find attractive.

---

[30] Sextus, *M* XI 141. Timon was Pyrrho's disciple, who praised Pyrrho and wrote satirical verses against other philosophers.

18

Aristotle: An Unstable View

Aristotle in the *Rhetoric* tells us what most people take happiness, in outline, to be. In this work, where he is concerned with what actually convinces people, he gives us the *endoxa* or reputable views of most people, without subjecting them to philosophical criticism.[1] Thus we find

> Nearly everyone has a kind of target [*skopos*], both privately for each person and in common, in aiming at which they make their choices and avoidances, and this is, in brief, happiness and its parts. . . . Let happiness then be said to be doing well together with virtue [*eupraxia met'aretēs*], or self-sufficiency of life, or the most pleasant life together with security, or affluence in possessions and slaves together with the power to protect and make use of them. For virtually all agree that happiness is one or more of these things. If happiness is something like this, then its parts must necessarily be good birth, having many friends, having good friends, wealth, having good children, having many children, a good old age; further, the bodily virtues, such as health, beauty, strength, size, competitive power, and reputation, honour, good luck and virtue. For a person would be most self-sufficient, if he possessed the goods internal to him and external, since there are no others. Internal are those of the soul and in the body, and external are good birth, friends, money and honour. Further, we think that there should be powers, and luck; for this is how one's life would be most secure.[2]

We shall return to the point that Aristotle talks in this context of parts of happiness. It is also worth noting that here he divides goods into two kinds: internal and external to the person. Elsewhere he sometimes takes it that the interesting dividing-line is that between the goods of the soul on the one hand, and the goods of the body together with external goods on the other. Clearly the idea is that goods divide into those external to, and those internal to, the agent. Here, in reporting popular views, Aristotle takes the agent to be, commonsensically, soul and body. In the ethical works he sometimes tends to treat the agent as being the soul. This does not import dualism, or indeed any metaphysical view of the soul; Aristotle is simply distinguishing between what is up to the agent and what is not, since it is up to us to make choices, but not up to us to be tall or beautiful.[3]

---

[1] As is clearly brought out, in contrast with the ethical works, by Natali (1990c).

[2] *Rhet* I 5, 1360 b 4–29.

[3] As already stressed, the acceptance that some things are 'up to us' is indifferent as to which theory is accepted to explain how this can be the case.

Prior to philosophical reflection, then, we assume that happiness is one or more of the above. That is, there are different strands in the ordinary notion of happiness, and it is indeterminate enough to allow people to stress just one, or more than one, even though doing the latter will clearly lead to tensions. Some people think that happiness requires affluence, though they stress that one must feel confident about keeping it, thereby showing that they think of happiness not just as being prosperous *now*, but as leading a prosperous whole life. Some stress self-sufficiency and security, freedom from being troubled or frustrated in the everyday sense of running out of money or being let down by others. Some insist that the happy life be one that the agent experiences as satisfying and enjoyable. Some take happiness to be 'doing well together with virtue'. The notion of 'doing well', pre-philosophically, has implications of success, and not just of the performance of virtuous actions themselves. And virtue, as a 'part' of happiness, has an odd and inconspicuous place in this chapter; Aristotle discusses it in the *Rhetoric* as what we are praised for, which is hardly a satisfactory definition, but it is clear that we praise and value virtue for its own sake, not for its contribution to any of the agent's other aims, and indeed for its tendency to get the agent to benefit others. Nonetheless, it is clear that even prior to philosophical reflection there is a foothold for the idea that virtue might be required for a happy life.[4]

The notion of happiness current and acceptable in everyday life thus clearly shows two things. One is what I shall call *the intuitive requirement*: happiness must involve our enjoying the good things of life. It must be a pleasant life, in which we have access to what in our society counts as affluence. The other is what I shall call *the theoretical pull*: happiness must involve not just a satisfying state now, but self-sufficiency over one's whole life, and it must involve morality, which we praise and value for its own sake, and not because of its contribution to further ends. Thus already in the selection of reputable views which he puts forward Aristotle displays what is to be the biggest source of tension in his own views, and the locus of the continuing debate. On the one hand, we are drawn by the theoretical pull to two ideas: that happiness consists in having what we value only for its own sake, and that happiness consists in being self-sufficient and secure. This will lead to the idea that happiness consists in possession of what matters most, what is most valuable, and that this will be something in the agent's own control, something making her self-sufficient and so secure and independent of what is external to her. On the other hand, we are drawn by the intuitive requirement to demand that happiness involve what we normally take to be enjoyment of life's advantages, and to the extent that we do, we will make happiness dependent on external goods, and so on luck, on what is not under the agent's control.

In the *Nicomachean Ethics* Aristotle argues, as we have seen,[5] that reflection reveals to us that in all we do we are aiming at something we value in our lives as a whole, our final end. He goes on to say more about happiness.[6] There is consensus

---

[4] Cf. fragment B 2 (Düring) of the *Protrepticus*: happiness lies no more in external goods than in care of the soul. Aristotle is here addressing a non-philosophical audience. The *Protrepticus* must be used with care, however, since it is often unclear how much exact Aristotelian terminology has survived in what we have.

[5] Chapter 1.

[6] *NE* I 4–5, 7.

that our final end is happiness, but this is not substantive, since people disagree about what happiness is, most people thinking it is something obvious, like pleasure, wealth or honour, and indeed switching their views at different times, while philosophers give a different kind of account. The kind of view people hold tends to reflect the kind of life they lead; Aristotle distinguishes three kinds of life, that devoted to pleasure and gratification, that devoted to public life and seeking honour, and that devoted to philosophy.[7] Aristotle relies on the theoretical pull to reject pleasure and honour. Those who favour pleasure, he says, are slavish, since the life of pleasure is a life fit only for animals. Thus he feels justified in dismissing an account which pays absolutely no attention to the elements in popular understanding of happiness which stress concern for one's life as a whole and independence of external goods. (But this does not dismiss pleasure altogether; the intuitive requirement is still felt, and Aristotle will give pleasure a place in happiness.) The political life devoted to honour is too 'superficial'; it makes one dependent on the people providing the honouring, and honour seems not to be sought for its own sake, but for the sake of confirming that one *deserves* it, so that what matters to the agent cannot be the honour, but his being virtuous and so worthy of it. Clearly what is being pressed is the idea of completeness, and this is explicit in the following rejection of virtue itself as an end.

> But [virtue] also is too incomplete [to be a final end]. For it seems to be possible to be asleep while possessing virtue, or to be inactive all one's life, and also to suffer evils and the greatest misfortunes; and someone with a life like that no one would call happy, unless they were defending a thesis at all costs.[8]

Of the two objections here, the first is feeble, with force only against a popular notion of virtue which Aristotle does not share; on the kind of account he accepts, virtue is a disposition to action, and a perpetual sleeper or person in a coma just would not be virtuous. Aristotle mentions it here only because it shows that even by intuitive criteria, which are all we have so far, virtue is not complete, that is, it can't be what forms our final end; our final end is not just to be virtuous but to live a certain kind of life. However, the second objection, that being virtuous is compatible with great misfortunes, is one which Aristotle does take seriously. It violates the intuitive constraint; happiness must be experienced as satisfactory and enjoyable. This will turn out to be of crucial importance for Aristotle. Finally, Aristotle rejects the life devoted to money-making as obviously unsatisfactory; it is clear that we desire money for the sake of what we can do with it, so wealth cannot be our final end.

In Book I 7, Aristotle turns to establishing the formal conditions on our final end, which we have already seen. Our final end must be complete: chosen only for its own sake and never for the sake of anything further. Further, our final end is self-sufficient, and most choiceworthy; and this is what happiness is. Aristotle is establishing on his own account the theoretical bounds of happiness; any candidate

---

[7] I am standing aside from the dispute as to whether in Book I Aristotle is indicating that the best life is the life of theoretical contemplation and, if so, how this relates to the passage on the life of contemplation in Book X. (For my own view of this dispute, see chapter 9 n.1.) The issues I am dealing with do not depend on resolution of this problem. For extensive discussion of it see Kraut (1989).

[8] 1095 b 31–1096 a 2.

for happiness must meet these formal criteria. In the process he briefly rules out some candidates: honour, pleasure, understanding and every virtue are not complete in the theoretical sense of 'complete' that has been established, for while we choose them for their own sake (shown by the fact that we would choose them even if they had no further result), we also choose them for the sake of happiness. And Aristotle also introduces his own outline account of happiness. Humans, like other kinds of things, have an *ergon*, a characteristic activity; and what characterizes humans is living according to reason, the function of the soul that characterizes humans as opposed to animals and plants. What has an *ergon* has a corresponding *aretē*, excellence or way of doing it well. *Aretē* in humans is, of course, virtue. So

> the good for humans is activity of the soul in accordance with virtue (if there are more than one virtue, in accordance with the best and most complete)—in a complete life. For one swallow does not make a summer, nor does one day; similarly, a person is not made blessed [*makarios*] or happy [*eudaimōn*] in one day or a short time.[9]

So Aristotle rejects virtue as a candidate, but accepts as his own candidate a lifetime's virtuous activity. What is the crucial difference? Aristotle has added that the virtuous activity must be rational activity of a kind appropriate to human beings. But this might have been thought to be implicit in the original suggestion, and Aristotle's addition is in other ways infelicitous. Perhaps Aristotle thinks that it is crucially important that happiness is virtuous *activity*, not just the state of being virtuous. But, again, given his own account of virtue, it is hard to see how the agent could be properly called virtuous in the first place unless she were leading an active life of virtue—doing the right thing as a result of correct deliberations, and with feelings and emotions that had reached the appropriate degree of harmony with those deliberations.[10] Aristotle has in fact not yet distinguished his own suggestion meaningfully from the proponent of virtue; but this is because he has not yet filled out his own suggestion. In the following chapters Aristotle turns to widespread views about happiness to help fill out his suggestion. And his conclusion is, 'What then prevents us calling a person happy who is active in accordance with complete virtue and supplied adequately with the external goods, not just for any old length of time, but for his complete life?'[11] The active life of virtue needs external goods to make it complete, that is, a suitable candidate to be the happy life.[12] For the active life of virtue requires external goods if anything is actually to be achieved;[13] and in any case our life will be lacking and unsatisfactory if we lack certain external

---

[9] *NE* 1098 a 16–20. I ignore the complications raised by the parenthesis, which is taken by some to refer forward to the account of contemplation in Book X.

[10] Of course one might develop a virtuous disposition and then be struck down into a comatose state. But this does not seem to be what worries Aristotle; the intuitive objection, at least, is that one might be asleep or inactive 'throughout one's life' (1095 b 32–33).

[11] 1101 a 14–16.

[12] That this is Aristotle's procedure, so that the definition of happiness is not complete until *Nicomachean Ethics* I 10, is argued forcefully by J. Cooper (1985). However, I do not follow Cooper in his further claims that the *Nicomachean Ethics* is distinctively different from the *Eudemian Ethics* on this score, and that subsequent debate centred on the *Nicomachean Ethics* alone. For one of the passages most important for Aristotle's insistence that external goods are required, is in a common book (1153 b 14–25).

[13] 1098 b 30–1099 a 7, 1099 a 31–b 2.

goods.[14] Happiness, then, is an actively virtuous life which has available to and for it an adequate supply of external goods. This is the account of happiness which Aristotle sums up in the *Politics* when he says, 'If it was well said in the *Ethics* that the happy life is the life according to virtue which is unhindered [*ton kat'aretēn (bion) anempodiston*], and that virtue is a mean,'[15] then the best life must display a 'mean' or be middling in some way.

It is Aristotle's combination of virtue and external goods to produce the happy life which is the source of the instability of his position, and hence of the ensuing debate with the Stoics. But before examining this, we should examine more closely how he has been motivated to reach this position. It is obvious that he is trying to do justice to both the theoretical pull and the intuitive requirement in our common-sense views about happiness. But how does his definition do this?

Although a life of virtuous activity turns out in the end not to be complete, Aristotle clearly regards it as the most serious competitor, other than his own candidate. What is it about a life of virtuous activity that could make it reasonable to think that this is an agent's final end, the overall end she values and aims at in all her actions?

Two kinds of facts about virtue are relevant here. One is what could be called the outer kind of fact, and is familiar by now from the previous extensive discussion of different aspects of virtue. Aristotelian virtues are not simply dispositions to do the morally right thing. They are settled dispositions of character, and, as we have seen, have both an affective and an intellectual aspect. On the intellectual side, the person who has developed so as to be fully virtuous will have developed practical intelligence or *phronēsis*. He will not have to figure out what to do, or have to follow rules, as a beginner in virtue would; he will have developed and refined habits of good intellectual deliberation, and will have familiarized himself with the various kinds of reasons given for courses of action, and the types of justifications that can be offered. He will thus be ready for unfamiliar situations and for new kinds of intellectual challenges to his deliberations; like the expert, and unlike the beginner, he has familiarity with and intellectual mastery of what he is dealing with. The fully virtuous person, then, has no trouble in discerning what is the morally right thing to do; indeed, we have seen that sometimes Aristotle uses the language of perception to express the immediacy of this discernment in the person who does not suffer from competing intellectual forces.

On the affective side, we find even stronger results of the point that virtues are developed dispositions. To be fully virtuous is to have one's feelings and emotions trained and habituated in one way rather than another. As has been stressed, this is not a mindless process, but one that is interdependent with the development of the intellectual aspect. As one becomes more temperate, for example, one comes to appreciate in ever deeper ways, for many kinds of reasons, the undesirability of eating and drinking to excess. And, as a result of this, one comes to find stuffing oneself, and getting drunk, disgusting rather than attractive. And, because one finds it disgusting, one is rendered more sensitive to further reasons for its undesirability; one has no motive for ignoring or repressing relevant information, and so on. Recall

[14] 1099 b 2-7.
[15] 1295 a 35-8.

the important distinction between the fully virtuous person and the merely encratic. The latter can do the morally right thing, but in an important respect doing the right thing is not what matters most to all of him, since he has desires which do not go along with his deliberations. The fully virtuous person, on the other hand, is unified in motivation and deliberation. He does not have to summon up willpower to do what he sees to be the right thing, for he does not have to fight down countering desires.

The fully virtuous person thus finds himself with no motivation not to do the right thing. He will, of course, still appreciate that certain factors in the situation give other, not fully virtuous people reason to act otherwise; but these factors do not tempt him—if they did, he would merely be encratic, not yet fully virtuous. The dispositional and affective aspects of Aristotelian virtue in fact render the agent quite uncompromising; the more unified is the developed moral personality, the more extreme is the rejection of the rejected course of action.

Aristotle is indeed arguably more demanding than Kant in one respect: the virtuous person, by contrast with the merely encratic, actually *enjoys* acting virtuously. This condition might sound like an attempt to do justice to the intuitive requirement: the agent's final end must be something which is experienced as satisfying and pleasant. In fact Aristotle is far from our intuitions here, since intuitively it is odd to say that the exercise of a virtue like temperance or courage is itself pleasant. Aristotle himself draws attention to this in the case of courage.[16] The brave person may do what she knows makes it likely that she will be killed; and she will mind about this, and rightly so. Yet she takes pleasure in acting bravely—the appropriate pleasure, for it is not the brave action itself which is pleasant, but rather the action as done for the right reason. She has nothing to regret, and is not tempted to act otherwise. And Aristotle insists that acting virtuously, insofar as it does achieve its goal and is done for the right reason, is pleasant. Clearly this is not a pleasure which could tempt the coward, just as the brave person is not tempted by the pleasures of running away and avoiding danger. Similarly, the pleasure of acting temperately is available only to the temperate, not to the greedy and uncontrolled person; and the pleasures of pigging out do not tempt the temperate. What you find pleasant depends on what you value. Aristotle is relying on his own account of pleasure as unimpeded activity, or what perfects an activity, in rejecting the commonsense idea that pleasure is a single thing available to the virtuous, encratic and vicious alike. Rather, pleasures differ in kind, to the extent that those who do not share a common view of what is good do not share a common view of what is pleasant. Aristotle thus commits himself to a view of pleasure as something which depends on what you value in your activity.[17]

There is thus a sense in which virtue is the only aim of the virtuous person. She will go for health, money and so on in the normal course of things; but if she is fully virtuous, and virtue demands ignoring or losing these things, she will not only perform the virtuous action but she will be completely motivated to do it. She will note the losses, and may regret them for many reasons, but they do not so much as tempt her to reject the virtuous course. To be fully virtuous, from both the affective

---

[16] 1117 a 36–b 16.
[17] Cf. Annas (1980).

and the intellectual side, is to be someone who does what virtue requires just for that reason and not for any ulterior reason, without having to battle down counter-motivation. And to be this sort of person is to be a person who aims at the life of virtuous activity for its own sake.

So far this is just the outer kind of fact about virtue. That it is a motivationally unified disposition of this kind would not show that virtuous activity could be complete in the sense required for it to be a candidate for being happiness, unless there were also the inner fact about virtue, that it is sought for its own sake. If virtue were essentially a matter of aiming at something for the sake of a further thing, it could not itself be complete in the desired way.

Here a fact about virtue that has been hitherto not much stressed becomes important. The virtuous person, insofar as she is virtuous, has a characteristic aim. This is the *kalon*, a term which has been translated as 'fine', but which some translators render as 'noble', and which in some contexts is the ordinary Greek word for 'beautiful'. If we examine what it comes down to, for the virtuous person to have the fine as her characteristic aim, we shall see the sense in which virtue is sought only for its own sake by the virtuous person.

In his discussion of the virtues Aristotle frequently describes the virtuous person as aiming at the *kalon*. 'Actions in accordance with virtue are fine, and they are done for the sake of the fine.'[18] The brave person

> will be afraid of such things [as normal people find frightening], but will stand up to them as he ought and as reason demands, for the sake of the fine, for this is the aim [*telos*] of virtue. . . . Thus the person who stands up to and is afraid of the things he ought, for the sake of the right end, as he ought and when he ought, and feels confident in similar ways, is brave; for the brave person's actions and experiences are in accordance with things' worth, and as reason demands. The aim of every activity is to be appropriate to its state [of character]. To the brave person bravery is a fine thing; and so similarly will be its aim, since each thing is defined by its aim. So it is for the sake of the fine that the brave person stands up to, and does, what bravery requires.[19]

So it is aiming at the fine which characterizes the virtuous person,[20] as opposed to the person who does what she does because she has to do it,[21] or does it because she just wants to do it, or finds it useful to do it.[22] The fine is the internal aim of virtue.

Aristotle also insists, in his definition of virtue, that the virtuous person does virtuous actions for their own sakes, because they are virtuous actions and not because of some further reason.[23] Thus doing a virtuous action for the sake of the fine does not imply that the agent has an aim different from that of doing the action for its own sake. Rather, we can see that 'for the sake of the fine' is functioning rather like the Kantian notion of doing one's duty for the sake of doing one's duty; it characterizes what morality requires. This is Aristotle's way of bringing out what we would call the moral aspect of virtue. It is not enough to do, for example, the brave

[18] *NE* 1120 a 23–24.
[19] 1115 b 11–13, 17–24.
[20] Cf. also 1117 b 7–9, 1119 b 15–18, 1122 b 6–7, 1123 a 19–25.
[21] 1116 b 2–3.
[22] Cf. 1104 b 30–34, 1169 a 3–6.
[23] 1105 a 28–34. Cf. 1144 a 13–20, 1176 b 7–9.

action; one must do it from a developed disposition in which affective and intellectual aspects have progressed to a unified standpoint. But what marks the *virtuous* disposition is that the virtuous person now does the virtuous action just for its own sake; discerning that this is what virtue requires is enough to motivate her, and no counter-motivation is produced in her. This is what it is for her to act 'for the sake of the fine'.

Some have felt frustrated that Aristotle says so little, in the *Ethics*, about the fine. Because he leaves it unanalyzed some have concluded that Aristotle thinks that the virtuous person has something like perception of what he ought to do.[24] This would be something unarguable, not open to rational discussion. However, given Aristotle's stress on the development of the intellectual side of virtue, this can scarcely be the right account. It is more illuminating to compare Aristotle's own use of the *kalon* in the ethical works, with the account he gives in the *Rhetoric* of ordinary reputable, but unreflected views, of the *kalon*, and of virtue.

In the *Rhetoric*, Book I section 9, Aristotle introduces the popular view of what is *kalon* as being what is chosen for its own sake and is praised (or praiseworthy), or what is good and is pleasant because it is good. Neither of these characterizations, of course, is much use for understanding what the fine is. The one in terms of pleasantness is quietly dropped. The suggestion that the fine is what is chosen for its own sake, and so found intrinsically valuable, and also found to be praiseworthy, is not illuminating for the obvious reason that we would have to know what is praiseworthy about it for our understanding to be furthered. However, Aristotle is not here giving us philosophical analysis, but locating the concept in people's ethical views. Hence he infers that virtue must be fine, because people find it praiseworthy.[25] Further rundown of popular views reveals that actions are considered fine if done not for your own sake (*mē hautou heneka*), or done for the sake of others,[26] or are profitless, with no payoff.[27] Virtue also is characterized by benefitting others; the greater virtues are taken to be those that are most useful to others.[28] In the popular conception, then, both virtue and the *kalon* are associated with acting in ways which benefit others rather than yourself, or with acting in a way which brings no further benefit to yourself. In Aristotle's own ethical works, he ignores these points. Clearly, he thinks that they are only the more noticeable, and in a way superficial marks of virtuous action and acting for the sake of the *kalon*. For what characterizes virtue is a commitment to doing the virtuous action, regardless of whether it brings personal loss or gain to the agent—doing it for its own sake. Aristotle takes this to be the most basic and important fact about the *kalon*. To many people the most prominent fact about a virtuous person may well seem to be that they are prepared to act in others' interests, and against her own, in ways that non-virtuous people are not prepared to act. But this does not characterize virtue; on occasion the fine thing to do might be that which disadvantaged others and happened to coincide with one's

---

[24] This is well criticized in Irwin (1985b). I have learned much from this article, though I disagree with Irwin on the relation of the *Rhetoric*'s account of the *kalon* to that in the *Nicomachean Ethics*; see below.

[25] 1366 a 33–36.

[26] 1366 b 36–1367 a 6.

[27] 1367 a 20–23, 26–27.

[28] 1366 b 3–9.

own interests. What properly marks out virtue and the *kalon* is rather the point about the *kalon* which is stressed in the *Ethics*: to do an action for the sake of the fine is to do it for its own sake, that is, because it is a virtuous action.[29]

Surely, however, virtue is chosen for the sake of happiness? After all, it has been stressed that happiness is generally agreed to be what our final end in outline is; so it must be obvious that virtue, along with everything else, is sought for the sake of happiness, and is not sought for its own sake in the way a complete end has to be— that is, sought for its own sake and never sought also for the sake of something further. Aristotle says explicitly,

> We say that what is pursued for its own sake is more complete than what is pursued for something else, and that what is never chosen because of something else is more complete than things that are chosen both for themselves and because of something else; and that something is *simply* complete if it is chosen always for its own sake and never because of something else. Now happiness seems most to be something of this kind.[30] For we always choose it because of itself and never because of anything else, while we choose honour, pleasure, understanding and every virtue for its own sake indeed (we would choose each of them even if they were to have no result) but choose them also for the sake of happiness, supposing that because of them we shall be happy.[31]

Why is Aristotle so certain that, although virtue is chosen for its own sake, it is also chosen for the sake of happiness? He is sure that virtue is necessary for happiness. We find no explicit argument for this in the ethical works; later Aristotelian writers will pick up the idea that virtue is the right use of non-moral goods, so that they are useless to the person without it. But Aristotle takes it as intuitively obvious that, given that virtue is a developed disposition to do the morally right thing, only the virtuous person has the right values, and that having the right values must be involved in our having an overall aim in all we do. Aristotle is insistent, however, that virtue is not sufficient for happiness. In a passage cited above[32] he says that no one would call a virtuous person happy who was inactive through life, or suffering evils, unless they were defending a thesis at all costs. And in an even stronger passage he says that

> Everyone thinks that the happy life is pleasant, and weaves pleasure into happiness, and this is reasonable; for no activity is complete which is hindered, and happiness is complete. Hence the happy person has need of the goods of the body and external goods and luck, so as not to be impeded in these ways. Those

---

[29] Thus it is a mistake to see Aristotle as analyzing the fine in the *Rhetoric*, but leaving it unanalyzed in the *Nicomachean Ethics*. In the former work he does not analyze it at all, he merely collects popular views about it. In the latter, his considered view is that the fine can best be characterized in a different kind of way, as the distinctive aim of the virtuous person in acting virtuously.

[30] 'Most' is syntactically ambiguous, reflecting a common such ambiguity with *malista* in Greek.

[31] 1097 a 30–b 6. Part of this passage is discussed in Kraut (1976). Kraut defends an 'anti-Kantian' interpretation of Aristotle on virtue and happiness. I think that one can agree with Kraut's conclusions while not rejecting the idea that Aristotelian virtue has much in common with a Kantian notion of morality.

[32] P. 366

who assert that the person broken on the wheel and falling into great misfortunes is happy, if only he is good, are, willingly or unwillingly, talking nonsense.[33]

Aristotle finds the thesis that virtue suffices for happiness grossly counter-intuitive. Hence, even if we seek virtue for its own sake—which is, after all, the point of being virtuous—we also seek it for the sake of happiness, which includes not only virtue but also other kinds of thing—bodily and external goods, and luck or fortune.[34]

If we read Aristotle in isolation, we are apt to find this position unremarkable, for it may seem that, even given the ancient understandings of virtue and of happiness, it is indeed grossly counter-intuitive to think that virtue could suffice for happiness. Even given the complexity and depth of virtue in ancient theories, it still does not seem to suffice for any account of happiness that respects the intuitive requirement. How can the person suffering great misfortunes, or reduced to a wretched and ignominious criminal's death, be happy, however virtuous they are? The Stoics are going to respond that, nonetheless, virtue does suffice for happiness. They are prepared to accept the counter-intuitive consequence of saying this, for they claim that the results of the thesis are not counter-intuitive in their theory as a whole, even if they seem so in isolation. Aristotle, they think, runs into deep trouble by giving in here to the intuitive requirement. It is important, therefore, to look carefully at Aristotle's grounds for rejecting the sufficiency of virtue, to see whether he is wise to respect the intuitive requirement here.

First, however, we should look at the kind of luck which Aristotle holds that the happy person requires. He discusses luck at length in a moral context in a passage of the *Eudemian Ethics*.[35] As often, he starts out with a problem, resolving which leads to distinguishing more than one sense of the relevant term. We regard it as a fact, he begins, that 'it is not only intelligence that produces acting well in accordance with virtue; we also say that lucky people act well, implying that good luck produces good action, and the same results as knowledge does.'[36] That is, virtuous action can be the product not only of developed deliberation, but of luck. This is a very radical thesis for Aristotle to entertain; the suggestion is that we can actually be virtuous by luck. Given what we have seen about virtue, this would be very surprising; how could mere luck account for the development of our affective and intellectual dispositions

---

[33] 1153 b 14–25. This seems to have been a noted passage because of the reference to the wheel, which recurs in later discussions; Cicero has to explain the reference to a Roman audience (*TD* V, 24).

[34] We could seek virtue for its own sake and also for the sake of happiness, even if virtue were sufficient for happiness; for it could be that we come to specify our final end as virtue by seeking happiness and specifying it correctly. (This point has been put to me by Terry Irwin.) Aristotle, however, does not seem to regard this as a serious possibility; and this is surely due to his conviction that it is hopelessly counter-intuitive to think that virtue alone could be what correctly specified happiness as our final end.

[35] *EE* VIII, 2. The passage is extremely corrupt in the manuscript tradition, and this, as well as the rather abbreviated nature of the argument at times, has brought it about that the passage is not as well known as it deserves to be. I have been greatly helped in my understanding of the passage by Kenny (1988). I differ from Kenny in my analysis of the passage, but owe much to his article, which first enabled me to make sense of the chapter as a whole. I use the text reconstructed by Jackson (1912). Jackson makes extensive use of the mediaeval Latin tradition contained as part of the work *de Bona Fortuna*, consisting of this chapter and *Magna Moralia* Book II chapter 8. At several points Jackson accepts that the Greek and Latin traditions contain, not differing versions of the same clause, but different clauses from a fuller original. On this passage, see also the commentary by Woods (1982).

[36] 1246 b 36–1247 a 2. I read *kat'aretēn* with Jackson.

in the right way? It is true that on occasion one might by luck happen on what is in fact the right thing to do; but why should Aristotle be impressed by this? He takes it seriously because he also takes it to be a popular belief that not only are there lucky shots at action, there are *lucky people*, people who continuously succeed much better than they are entitled to do on the basis of their skill or knowledge alone. If people are indeed lucky and unlucky in this continuous and reliable kind of way, then their success suggests that being virtuous might itself actually be a matter of luck, at least partly. So Aristotle investigates what it is for someone to be a lucky person (*eutuchēs*).

It clearly cannot, he says, be a matter of a developed state; for that would involve practical intelligence, and in that case the lucky could give reasons for their success; but this is precisely what they cannot do, and what gives rise to the puzzlement. Nor can it be a matter of having a spirit (*daimōn*) or guardian angel guiding you from the outside; for why would the divine favour those who are not intelligent? So it must be a matter of nature; but this again will not do, since nature is the cause of what is so always or for the most part,[37] while luck is the opposite; it is just what can't be counted on to recur. Thus there seems to be *no* appropriate explanation for the existence of lucky people. Aristotle rejects the kind of solution that would cut the knot by claiming that there is no such thing as luck, or that there is, but that it is not a cause; as usual, he wants to account for as many of the well-based phenomena as he can. So he offers an account of the luck of the reliably lucky person, but then at once adds that this is only one kind of good luck, and distinguishes others.[38]

How is it that some people regularly succeed in ways that cannot be explained by their intelligence or knowledge?

> Are there not impulses [*hormai*] in the soul, some of which come from reasoning, and some from non-rational desire [*orexis*]? And the latter are prior, at least in nature. If the desire for the pleasant, brought about through appetite [*epithumia*], is natural, so also it will be natural for desire to go for the good in every case. If, then, some people have good natures (just as untrained musical people who have no understanding of singing nevertheless are naturally good at it) and are impelled without reason in nature's way, and feel desire [*epithumousi*] then and there, as they ought and for what they ought and when they ought—then these people will succeed, even if they happen to be foolish and irrational, just as the others will sing well, although unable to teach what they do. Therefore it will be by nature that lucky people are lucky.[39]

---

[37] 1246 a 31–33. We have seen the importance of this thought in an ethical context, in chapter 2, pp. 150ff.

[38] The account of the lucky person, in terms of underlying good desires, goes from 1247 b 18 ff.; Aristotle suggests that *eutuchia* has more than one form at 28 ff. (Literally, he suggests that it *pleonachōs legetai*, has more than one sense or application; but 'has many senses' would be misleading, since Aristotle is not cataloguing senses of terms but giving a philosophical analysis by making various distinctions.) Kenny finds that in what follows Aristotle distinguishes four kinds of luck, the first two of which are set aside as not properly being luck. I find a single distinction throughout the passage, between (i) the kind of 'natural' luck which comes down to having good non-rational desires and (ii) the kind of luck which consists in succeeding whatever the state of one's desires. On my reading Aristotle is enlarging on his original distinction at the end of the passage, not introducing a new one.

[39] 1247 b 18–28. I follow Jackson's text.

Obviously this is mere nature, not nature in the strong sense. As a solution to Aristotle's problem, it is rather elegant. Strictly, if the factor involved is nature, it cannot be luck, for the reason given. However, Aristotle has found an explanation, in terms of nature, for what on the level of human affairs is luck—for he has revealed that we consider a success lucky if the agent brought it about in a way owing nothing to his intelligence. Hence we have a kind of luck which is repeatable and reliable, just because it is due to nature, which explains regularities. This is *natural luck*; the appearance of paradox here is merely superficial, since something of this kind is what we needed if we were successfully to explain the notion of a lucky person.

Aristotle at once adds that this is not the only kind of luck. For, while we call people lucky who get what they were aiming at when their reasoning was at fault, we also call people lucky who succeeded in getting a good which they were not actually aiming at. This kind of luck of course cannot depend on having good non-rational desires. Hence, we have to admit that there are two kinds of good luck. The previous argument does not show that all good luck is merely something natural; rather it shows that when we refer to good luck we are sometimes referring to what we could call luck proper—achieving a success one had not aimed at—and sometimes to something else, which does have a natural, and thus reliable basis, namely the operation of non-rational desires which are part of the agent's (mere) nature.

Aristotle now refines somewhat the notion he has introduced of natural luck. Someone may object that the idea of a person being lucky cannot just come down to his having naturally good impulses (good instincts as we might say). For such a person just has the right desires at the right time for the right thing and so on—and surely it must be due to luck, and not just the person's nature, that this happened in this way? Aristotle objects that if having the right desires is a matter of luck, so will be having any desires, and indeed having any thoughts, and so luck will be responsible for everything. For when we ask why we have certain reasons and desires, we answer by citing other reasons and desires. But obviously this cannot go on for ever—a halt has to be called somewhere. There has to be what Aristotle calls here an *archē*, a first principle. And what can be the principle of movement in the soul other than God, which is the principle of movement in the world as a whole? This move is rather abrupt; Aristotle presumably is relying on the analogy of the world which as a whole needs a divine mover, as well as the intuitive point that what starts off thought and knowledge must be superior to them, and only the divine is that. And so, he concludes, lucky people operate by a principle which is in effect divine. In fact it is better for them not to deliberate, since they are like inspired people for whom reasoning is just an interference. One might think that this is a rather hasty conclusion. Why should we conclude that lucky people, who operate by good natural instinct, are more properly said to work by a divine principle than ordinary deliberators, whose thoughts have a divine starter also? Aristotle is clearly moved by the desire to classify these luckily instinctive people along with others who are ordinarily thought to operate by divine inspiration, like prophets and people who have significant dreams.[40]

At any rate, there is clearly a contrast between this and the other kind of luck, about which Aristotle says less: succeeding independently of or even contrary to one's aim. Both are cases of luck, because the event is explained without reference to the agent's plan or reasoning. What Aristotle says about natural or divine luck has some interesting ethical implications. He accepts, so it seems, that some people have a kind of impulse or instinct which is regular and reliable because natural, but also divine, because nothing in the natural world accounts for its operation. This is an instinct for nothing less than virtue: these people just naturally are brave, or temperate, although they cannot give an account of the virtue or explain their own actions. What Aristotle has in mind seems to be what he calls natural virtue in the *Nicomachean Ethics*.[41] He distinguishes it from full virtue on just these grounds, that the naturally virtuous person does the right thing and has the right feelings, but can give no account of this.

In a way Aristotle is not conceding much to luck. What is a matter of luck is merely whether we are naturally virtuous, and this falls far short of being fully virtuous. Further, while Aristotle envisages natural luck as giving some people a head start, an advantage over others in that they have the right temperament and do not have to struggle, this point is limited in two ways. One is that he does not envisage many people like this, so he does not see it as a serious problem. There is a norm; most people have to struggle, to some extent, to be brave, temperate and so on. The phenomenon of natural virtue interests Aristotle enough for him to investigate it, but he does not see it as a source of ethical problems. Second, Aristotle thinks only of some people having divinely produced good natural impulses which make them lucky; he never thinks of the divine as giving people *bad* luck, saddling them with especially difficult temperaments. God gives some people a push from behind, as it were, but does not trip others up. If I fail to become virtuous, Aristotle does not think that I can blame bad luck, my having a certain temperament and impulses; I have only myself to blame. However, if I succeed, it might be that I should thank God for my impulses as well as praising myself for what I have made of them. Thus, if we were to object to the unfairness implied by God's giving some people better temperaments than others, Aristotle could rightly reply that God does not handicap anyone, and that if he helps a few we have no reason to be envious; we can do it anyway for ourselves.

Nonetheless, by allowing that some have an advantage in having a nature (even mere nature) more fitted than others' natures for virtue, in having impulses which just naturally go right, Aristotle has committed himself to what we might call the thesis that there is such a thing as constitutive moral luck. If I ask myself why I did not become virtuous, I might well complain that my neighbour had a head start, since she had better natural impulses. Aristotle does not think that this difference makes any difference to questions of responsibility. I am just as responsible, blameworthy, etc., for not becoming virtuous as someone who did have a better natural temperament. But we might well ask why the natural difference, if it makes a

---

[40] On the difficult issue of the role of *nous* in this passage, see Wedin (1993).

[41] See chapter 4, pp. 143–44.

difference as far as becoming truly virtuous is concerned, should not make a difference to responsibility and blameworthiness. If I have been dealt a less good natural hand, temperamentally, it seems reasonable for me to complain at being held to the same standards of responsibility for my character as the more fortunate.

Thus, although Aristotle does not in fact appear to think that it is morally relevant what kind of starting temperament one has, we might well think that he has allowed for a fair degree of constitutive moral luck. While he does not see his naturally lucky people as a moral problem, we might. On this issue we can see the Stoics taking a distinctively different line. They see moral progress in terms of the development of the agent's reason, and thus, like Kant, they see morality as open to all regardless of their pre-moral temperament. Indeed, they typically see the divine as working through reason in humans, not through pre-rational impulses. They do not, however, go as far as Kant does in resting morality on a notion of reason which is sharply cut off from our empirical nature as such. But like him they reject even the amount of constitutive moral luck which Aristotle lets in.

Aristotle himself thinks of the virtuous person as in need of luck—presumably not the kind of natural luck just described, as it is hard to see how the virtuous person could be said to *need* that, but rather the other kind of luck, the sort that enables you to succeed in what you have not explicitly aimed at. But this kind of luck is, of course, sporadic and unreliable. More important are the other kinds of goods mentioned: bodily and external goods. Sometimes both together are lumped together as 'external goods', bodily goods being seen as external to what is under the agent's control.[42] Aristotle does not discuss what has been called 'situational luck', the luck of having been born in one particular milieu rather than another.[43] Presumably he does not think that accidents of situation are central to issues of moral development. What he does stress are external goods and their role in the life of the virtuous person, a role that makes them necessary for the virtuous person to be happy.

The *Rhetoric* treats external goods as 'parts' of happiness. In the *Eudemian Ethics*, however, Aristotle points out that frequently there are fruitless disputes about what happiness consists in, because some treat as parts of happiness what are really necessary conditions for it; hence we must scrutinize any account of happiness to see whether it is counting a necessary condition as a part.[44] It is hard to know how exactly to apply this advice to Aristotle's own account of happiness in the first book of the *Nicomachean Ethics*, which firmly embeds activity in accordance with virtue in an adequate supply of external goods. Are health, friends and the like included in happiness, or are they merely what needs to be present for happiness? This point has attracted a great deal of discussion,[45] but, while it is clearly important, it is perhaps not crucial, since in the debate which we are tracing what matters about Aristotle's

[42] As Cooper (1985) stresses.

[43] Kenny (1988) gives the example of not having been born in Nazi Germany and so been tempted to wrong-doing.

[44] 1214 b 14–27.

[45] For an extensive attack on 'inclusivism' (the parts view) see Kraut (1989). Kraut's main thesis is that for Aristotle our good consists in *theōria* ('contemplation') throughout the ethical works, but large parts of his discussion aim to establish that for Aristotle happiness consists solely in virtuous activity (not including the external goods), however that is to be further understood.

position is that he is committed to the view that external goods are necessary for happiness. This is the point on which the Stoics disagree. The point, whether external goods are parts of virtue, included in an account of it, or merely necessary conditions, does not determine this issue.

Aristotle in his account of external goods in *Nicomachean Ethics* I 8–10 distinguishes two ways in which they contribute to happiness. First, they are clearly instrumental to the production of virtuous activity.

> Nevertheless happiness evidently is in need of the external goods, as we said, since it is impossible, or not easy, to do fine actions if one lacks resources. For many actions are done by means of friends, wealth and political power, just as by means of tools.[46]

And they have a further role: they matter in themselves for happiness.

> Further, when deprived of some things people ruin their happiness—things such as good birth, good children, beauty. Someone is not exactly a happy kind of person if he is completely hideous or of low birth, solitary and childless, and perhaps even less if his children and friends are utterly evil, or are good but die. So, as we said, happiness seems to need this kind of prosperity too.[47]

In other passages Aristotle repeats this and similar language: external goods are necessary and useful for the exercise of virtue, and they also 'adorn' it.[48]

Aristotle represents his own view as doing justice both to the theoretical pull and to the intuitive requirement; his own view, that happiness requires exercise of virtue and external goods, explains why some identify happiness with virtue (following the theoretical pull) while others identify it with prosperity (following the intuitive requirement).[49] But exactly how can Aristotle satisfy both constraints, and have the best of both worlds? How are we to understand the metaphors of ruining and adornment? Aristotle's view is crucially vague and metaphorical (as happens elsewhere in his works where he has located a problem, but not yet worked out a completely satisfactory solution). His words lend themselves to two quite distinct interpretations, each of which, as we shall see, contains difficulties.

I shall call the first the 'internal-use view'. It has been vigorously defended by John Cooper.[50] On this view, there are not really two distinct roles for the external goods, only the first one, instrumentality for virtuous action. The external goods do not just in themselves have any intrinsic value, or add anything to the good life. The fully virtuous person has no reason to aim at getting them just for their own sake, for what they unaided can contribute to his life. Rather, their value is never independent of their contribution to the agent's virtuous activity. But this can happen in two ways, which is why Aristotle characterizes external goods in the above two ways. Sometimes they are necessary for the performance of virtuous activity at all. We

---

[46] 1099 a 31–b 2.
[47] 1099 b 2–7.
[48] Cf. 1099 b 25–28, 1100 b 22–30.
[49] 1099 b 7–8.
[50] In Cooper (1985). In Annas (1988–9) I call this view the 'proto-Stoic' view, by contrast with the 'Peripatetic' view. I now think it is more useful to characterize the interpretations in ways which do not point forward in a proleptic way to the Stoic and Peripatetic responses.

cannot be generous without money, for example. In particular, the social virtues that Aristotle describes, such as the virtues of spending money on public festivals, clearly presuppose quite a lot of external goods. However, sometimes they are necessary for the exercise of virtuous activity in 'preferred' or 'superior' circumstances.[51] That is, without them, one will still have the virtue, but its exercise will be in a limited and cramping sphere. One has reason to prefer a life in which one not only acts virtuously, but does so in circumstances that are favourable, in which the virtues can be developed in a wide and varied range of activities. On this view, the virtuous person will aim at, and so get, the external goods in the course of, and as a way of achieving, virtuous activities. But has he any motivation to seek these goods for their own sakes?

> Though he recognizes that external goods are very often objects of pursuit in the virtuous man's activities, and things therefore that he values for themselves, Aristotle has good reason for thinking that external goods are a *second* component of *eudaimonia*, alongside the virtuous activity, only because of the effect they have in enabling the virtuous person to live, and go on living, a fully virtuous life.[52]

One might wonder whether this account does justice to the ways in which Aristotle characterizes the external goods as adorning happiness, and their loss as ruining it, but clearly it would be unsafe to press Aristotle's vague language here. It is questionable, however, whether on this view the agent really can consider external goods to be a second component of happiness, alongside virtue.

On this view, when we have the external goods, they make no intrinsic contribution of their own to happiness. Thus, when we act virtuously, we are aiming at virtuous activity for its own sake; we do not have acquisition of the external goods as a further aim, over and above this. However, virtuous activity itself will typically take the form of action which is apparently aimed at acquiring external goods. Temperance, for example, is apparently directed towards acquiring and keeping one's health. How can we make sense of the virtuous person's activity if we have to take it that her end is just virtuous activity, and not health? Since virtuous activity does not take place in a void, we have to make sense of the way in which the virtuous person apparently aims at achieving external goods. On this interpretation, we have to combine this with the idea that the virtuous person is not actually concerned to get these for their own sakes at all; their only value lies in the contribution they can make to virtuous activity, or to virtuous activity in favourable situations. This is a deep difficulty. If only virtuous activity has intrinsic value for the virtuous person, and she is concerned with external goods merely as means to this, it looks as though the virtuous person's activity can never get started. If I act out of temperance, I seem to be aiming at health; but on this view, I am really aiming at health in order to have a decent field of activity for my exercise of temperance. But the exercise of temperance must aim at something beyond itself, or we would never have any independent access to the idea of what the temperate person does. Nor

---

[51] Cooper cites in this connection the Arius Didymus Peripatetic passage, where there is said to be a use of virtue which is *proēgoumenē*. Cooper rightly rejects Wachsmuth's emendation of these passages to *chorēgoumenē*.

[52] Cooper, pp. 195–96.

would we ever come to see what we intuitively assume to be the point of being temperate, rather than self-indulgent. This is not an insoluble problem; we shall see that the Stoics have a solution to it. But Aristotle gives us no indication of how he would meet the difficulty.

Problems are arguably even worse for *loss* of the external goods. On the internal-use view, the loss of external goods will affect one's happiness only because of the way it prevents one from exercising the virtues. External goods have no intrinsic value for one's happiness, so this is indeed the only way in which one could be adversely affected by their loss.

> Aristotle does not count the failure of the virtuous man to have good children who grow to maturity as disfiguring his happiness because it frustrates plans he conceived and acted on precisely *as* a virtuous man. The failure to have good children only affects his happiness insofar as it prevents the subsequent activities he might have engaged in together with them; it does not affect it by rendering his earlier actions aimed at producing and educating his children ineffective.[53]

Intuitively this is outrageous. We feel that sterility is in itself frustrating, if one wants children; and we especially feel that losing children is a terrible thing in itself, and not just because it deprives us of the chance to help our children on their careers and to look after grandchildren.[54] Indeed, this interpretation gets more outrageous the worse the effect of losing external goods. It would seem, for example, that the virtuous person broken on the wheel fails to be happy only because his prospects for future virtuous activity are dim. But surely being broken on the wheel must be intrinsically bad, if anything is.

Further, this interpretation can make no sense of our intuitive comparison of various losses. We normally do not compare external goods with a view only to their possible contribution to virtuous activity; we think that health is straightforwardly to be preferred to disease, for example. On this interpretation such comparisons are mistaken, and the virtuous person will not make them: he will ask only if health or disease will contribute more to his future virtuous activity. He will prefer the one with the greater yield in this respect, and if there is nothing to choose between them he will be indifferent. But on this view it seems that there would be nothing rationally to choose between being broken on the wheel or dying a painless death (or being in an irreversible coma). For all are on a par as far as concerns contributing to one's future virtuous activity. Aristotle, however, actually says[55] that it is worse, from the viewpoint of happiness, to have friends or children who die or turn out bad than never to have had friends or children at all. On the internal-use view we might expect the opposite, if anything; losing children or friends or coping with their misdeeds calls for greater exercise of virtue than never having any.[56]

Again, moves can be made which will avert these undesirable consequences; but Aristotle does not make them, and leaves us without indication of how he would deal with the problem. It is ironical, of course, that Aristotle runs into these counter-intuitive consequences as a result of respecting the intuitive requirement. The

[53] Cooper, p. 189.
[54] See Jost (forthcoming).
[55] 1099 b 2–7.
[56] In this last paragraph I am indebted to David Gill.

problems indicate that we should try another interpretation, which I shall call the 'external-use view', which has been defended by Terence Irwin and Martha Nussbaum.[57]

On this view, Aristotle straightforwardly allows that external goods have two roles in the happy life. They do enable us to exercise the virtues, and to do so in preferable circumstances. But this is not their only role. As is suggested by Aristotle's addition of a point that external goods 'adorn' happiness and 'ruin' it when lost, they also have intrinsic value of their own, so that a life of virtuous activity without an adequate supply of them ranks lower for achieving happiness than a life with such an adequate supply. While health enables us to exercise the virtue of temperance, it is also just a good thing to be healthy.

This seems a more natural and attractive interpretation; but problems lurk here too. Suppose that, on this view, I am living a life of virtuous activity and have access to adequate external goods; thus I am happy. We might first wonder how we are to establish a workable level for 'adequate' external goods. Does Aristotle mean that there is a minimum level that one must meet in order to qualify? But how do we set this? Aristotle says that when we say that happiness is self-sufficient

> we do not mean for someone by himself, living a cutoff life, but rather for parents, children and wife, and in general for friends and fellow-citizens, since humans are by nature social [*politikon*]. (But we must put a limit to this—if we extend it to parents and descendants and friends' friends it will go on *ad infinitum*; but we must investigate this another time.)[58]

But Aristotle never does; and we are left with the unhappy result that happiness on his view presupposes quite a high level of external goods, but no obvious means of setting any minimum level.

In any case, suppose that we can agree on some intuitively acceptable level of external goods for rendering someone happy. Having some of these things is needed to make me happy; so surely having more of them will make me happier? If, for example, good health is required to make me happy, surely excellent health will make me even happier? If I need wealth in order to exercise virtues such as generosity, surely more wealth will make me able to exercise even larger-scale virtues, such as paying for public festivals? The more external goods I have, the more I can expand the range and scope of my virtuous activity. This, however, runs into the claim that happiness is complete and self-sufficient. Something which meets these conditions precisely cannot be made better by the addition of any other good. It looks as though Aristotle is faced with an awkward choice. Either he has to say that external goods are required to make a person happy, but cannot make him happier by being increased. But this is deeply mysterious. Or, he has to say that happiness is not complete, since it can be increased by the addition of further goods. But this would be to go back on a fundamental point of his ethical structure. Again, Aristotle has avoided a counter-intuitive thesis at the cost of running into counter-intuitive results.

---

[57] Irwin (1985c); Nussbaum (1986a) chapters 11 and 12.
[58] 1097 b 8–14.

Various ways out of the problem suggest themselves. One ingenious one is offered by Irwin. Since the completeness of happiness is threatened if increase of external goods makes what you have a better good, the contribution of external goods is so understood that they do not give me a better good than I have when I am happy, but merely increase the extent to which I am happy, by increasing the scope and variety of my activities. Specifically,

> The goods that are components of happiness are determinable types of goods; these are exemplified in determinate types of goods and in determinate tokens of these types. . . . Aristotle probably believes that the complete good is composed of a sufficient number of tokens of some determinate types of each of the determinable types of good. . . . In saying that no good can be added Aristotle means that no determinable type of good can be added to happiness to make a better good than happiness.[59]

Thus more external goods are to be preferred to fewer, since they add further tokens of some determinate types of a determinable good, but they do not produce a better good than I already had, for they do not add any further determinable good. In the texts, however, Aristotle shows no explicit interest in anything which lines up with our distinction between determinables and determinates, and at this point we are focussing on the available resources internal to the Aristotelian position.

Another solution, nearer to the text, suggests itself: perhaps Aristotle thinks that there is a minimum level of external goods needed for happiness, but that increase of them produces something better, which we could call true happiness; and perhaps he marks this distinction by talking not only of the happy but of the 'blessed' person. We shall return to this when we have looked at the problem of losing external goods.

The problems are even worse where loss of external goods is concerned. On this interpretation, losing external goods is a genuine loss, and makes you less happy. But if so, there should surely come a point where losing enough external goods makes you not happy at all, or positively unhappy. However, Aristotle denies that the virtuous person could ever become unhappy.

> Many happenings come about in accordance with luck [*tuchē*], happenings differing in importance or unimportance. Small cases of good fortune [*eu-tuchēmata*], and similarly the opposite, clearly will not tip the balance of one's life, but if important things frequently turn out well they will make one's life more blessed [*makarios*]; for they themselves naturally add adornment to it, and one's use of them turns out fine and good. If they turn out the opposite way they cramp and ruin blessedness, for they import pains and impede many activities. Nevertheless, even in these cases what is fine shines through, when someone bears many great misfortunes uncomplainingly, not because of insensitivity, but because he is noble and great of soul. If activities are indeed what control one's life, as we said, no blessed person could become miserable; for he will never do hateful and low actions. We think that the truly good and sensible person bears all chances with dignity and always does the finest actions he can, given his circumstances, just as a good general uses the army he has in the best military way he can, and a shoemaker makes the finest shoe he can out of the hides given to

---

[59] Irwin (1985c), pp. 98–99.

him—and similarly for all other craftspeople. If this is so, the happy person could never become miserable—but he is not blessed either, if he meets with fortunes like Priam's.[60]

This is a puzzling passage. Aristotle wants to hold two theses that sort ill together. Loss of external goods matters to the virtuous person, because they are required for happiness. But loss of the external goods cannot, it appears, actually make the virtuous person unhappy. There are two obvious ways to make these theses coexist happily. One is to make explicit that happiness and unhappiness are not produced simply by possession or loss of external goods, and to introduce a different state, which is. This is the path taken by some later Hellenistic interpreters of Aristotle, including Arius Didymus.

The other is to read this passage as saying that there are two kinds or levels of happiness. Virtue suffices to make you happy, for however many external disasters you suffer you can never become unhappy, if you are virtuous. But the external goods are important also, for they take you to an improved state, better than happiness. It has often been suggested that Aristotle marks this point by using 'blessed' for the improved state. Antiochus' solution to the problem is essentially this, and he probably read this passage in this sense. However, it cannot be Aristotle's solution. For there is no more than a stylistic difference between 'happy' (*eudaimōn*) and 'blessed' (*makarios*); Aristotle is talking about a single thing, happiness, throughout this passage, not happiness and something else, 'true' happiness.[61] The passage in fact shows Aristotle struggling with the problem rather than finding a solution for it. On the one hand, he is clearly drawn to the idea that happiness really consists in virtuous activity; for he presents the opposite of happiness not as a state of abject suffering, but as a condition produced by doing bad, disgraceful actions. On the other hand, he seems to fight shy of fully accepting this idea, and he does not use the perfectly ordinary word for unhappiness, *kakodaimonia*. This is in spite of the fact that he does not hesitate to use the word in the *Poetics* in discussing the outcomes of plots.[62] For Aristotle also stresses heavily the importance of the external goods; nobody can be happy if they meet Priam's fate, even if they are virtuous. But although he wants to stress both, it is not clear how the claims of both are to be combined.

Thus both the internal-view and external-view interpretations of Aristotle's position on the place of the external goods in happiness lead to difficulties which Aristotle himself does not solve. He seems more inclined towards the external kind of view, and this is the one that his successors ascribed to him. But it is reasonable to conclude from what Aristotle says that he has not explicitly chosen between these interpretations; he feels entitled to use formulations appropriate to both, and tries to

---

[60] 1100 b 22–1101 a 8.

[61] See chapter 1, p. 44 and n. 62.

[62] The word occurs at *Poet* 1450 a 17. Kassel in his edition considers it dubious, but it is defended as 'genuine and important' by Halliwell (1987) and (1986). Aristotle more generally uses *eutuchia/dustuchia* in the *Poetics*, but that is because he is more often concentrating on success or failure rather than happiness itself. The word *kakodaimonia* occurs in B 46 of the *Protrepticus* (I. Düring, *Aristotle's Protrepticus*, Goteborg 1961, Acta Universitatis Gothoburgensis), but this may not be Aristotle's own wording. That *kakodaimonia* is a perfectly ordinary antithesis to *eudaimonia* can be seen from Sextus' discussion of ethics in M XI, for example.

meet as many constraints as he can. The theoretical pull is met by the insistence on the necessity of virtue, while the intuitive requirement is met by the insistence on the necessity of the external goods. But the result is problematic to a degree that Aristotle does not fully realize; once we start on the path of reflection about happiness, and bring in formal conditions such as completeness and self-sufficiency, we can no longer stop at a point which is intuitively satisfying. We have to face the difficult issues about use and loss of external goods which have been raised. Aristotle is reluctant to admit that pressing these issues forces us to make some counter-intuitive move somewhere.

As we found with the role in virtue of the emotions, common sense seems not to be consistent here. Our intuitions demand that happiness have something to do with experienced satisfaction; hence it is just absurd, to common sense, to call the virtuous person on the wheel happy. However, common sense is also ready to appreciate the importance of completeness and self-sufficiency; hence we pursue their implications. At some point we get a strain between the tendencies within common sense. If we are unwilling to count the virtuous person on the wheel as happy, because we find it absurd, we have to make external goods necessary for happiness. But then we find that we are forced to say other absurd-seeming things, such as that losing one's child affects one's happiness only to the extent that one has lost opportunities for virtuous parenting; or that, while getting more external goods makes you happier, losing them does not make you unhappy, without there being a point at which being happy can be distinguished from being still happier.

Philosophical reflection on the notion of happiness reveals that there is a distinct tension within it. Aristotle tries to overcome this tension and produce an account which will satisfy both tendencies within common sense, hence sometimes tends to the idea that virtue suffices for happiness, at least one kind of happiness, but at other times stresses the importance of the external goods to an extent incompatible with this, and so is ultimately unstable. Aristotle needs, but has not thought through, a satisfactory account of just how the external goods do figure in the happy life.[63]

We are enabled to be so critical, however, because the further stages in the debate, in sharpening the issues, build on Aristotle's achievement in posing the problem so vividly. When we find the Stoics saying that virtue is sufficient for happiness, this springs not from love of paradox, nor from the conviction that we often find in modern (especially consequentialist) theories, that common sense is primitive and must be mistaken, but rather from hard thought about the problems that are already inherent in the commonsense notion of happiness.

---

[63] This is supported by Ioppolo (1990).

19

Theophrastus and the Stoics:
Forcing the Issue

Aristotle wants to stress the importance of virtue for happiness, but also the importance of the external goods, and we cannot extract a single coherent view to be found in all the relevant passages, although he seems to be leaning more towards the view that gives the external goods independent value for happiness. Aristotle seems to have hoped that he was articulating the core of our everyday beliefs about happiness, but unfortunately our beliefs are more in tension than he seems to realize. After Aristotle we can see his successors pressing the tensions in his view and as a result being forced to come down more sharply on the role of the external goods. Aristotle's successor as head of his school, Theophrastus, goes one way, committing himself clearly to the necessity for external goods in the happy life. The Stoics go the other way, committing themselves to the thesis that virtue is sufficient for happiness, and doing so as part of a large-scale attempt to think through the relation of virtuous activity to the external goods which it characteristically obtains.

1. Theophrastus

Theophrastus wrote an *Ethics* and a work on Callisthenes, Aristotle's philosopher nephew who was put to death by Alexander the Great, but the ethical work which made most impact was a work *On Happiness*. We know little about its structure or contents, but we can see from later writers that in this work he was widely taken to have come down firmly for the view that external goods are necessary for happiness, and in particular that the virtuous person who suffers extensive loss of them loses his happiness. This point, about loss, is the one on which discussion fixes. Elsewhere we find a complaint that Theophrastus exaggerated the importance of wealth, but most references focus on the point that he said outright that happiness depends on external goods, and hence on fortune, so that virtue cannot guarantee happiness.[1]

It is precisely for this reason that Theophrastus attracted criticism from philosophers who held that to make happiness dependent on fortune in this way is incorrect: it fails to do any justice to the theoretical pull. Cicero complains that

---

[1] I refer to the fragments as in Fortenbaugh (1992) and (1984). Numbers (e.g., 495) refer to the former, L-numbers (e.g., L53) to the latter. The reference to wealth is 514 (= L76), Cicero, *Off* II.55–6 (Fortenbaugh [1984], pp. 246–8, thinks that Cicero may be mistaken here).

Theophrastus is the only Peripatetic to be consistent: they all think that bodily and external goods are genuinely good, as well as goods of the soul, but only Theophrastus thinks through the conclusion that loss of bodily and external goods is a genuine loss and can make the virtuous person lose his happiness.

> This is the point which Theophrastus was not able to sustain.[2] For when he had established that floggings, tortures, torments, overthrows of one's country, banishments and bereavements have great power to make life bad and miserable, he did not dare to speak in a lofty and ample style, since his thoughts were low and abject. But how well he spoke is not in question; certainly he was consistent; and I certainly do not enjoy criticizing the conclusions once one has granted the premises. However, this most elegant and learned of all philosophers is not greatly criticized when he says that there are three kinds of good, but he is attacked by all, first for that book that he wrote on the happy life, in which he offers many arguments to show why the person who is tortured and tormented cannot be happy. In it he is even thought to say that the happy life does not ascend on to the wheel (that is a kind of Greek torture). He doesn't say exactly this anywhere, but what he does say has the same force. Then, when I have conceded to someone that bodily pains are among evils, that shipwrecks of fortune are among evils, can I be angry with him when he says that not all good people are happy, since the things which he counts among evils can fall upon any good person? This same Theophrastus is attacked in all philosophers' books and lectures because in his *Callisthenes* he praised the saying, 'Fortune, not wisdom, rules life'. They say that nothing more feeble was said by any philosopher. That is indeed correct, but I don't see that anything could have been said more consistently. If there are so many goods in the body and outside the body which are in the power of chance and fortune, is it not reasonable that fortune, which is the mistress of things both external and relating to the body, should have more power than our judgement?[3]

The passage raises an important point of interpretation before the substantial one. What exactly was it that Theophrastus said? There are many other passages where Cicero says confidently that Theophrastus came right out and said that severe loss of external goods was incompatible with happiness.[4] Indeed, if he did not do this, it is hard to see why he should have attracted abuse; and he clearly did, so we are not just relying on Cicero's own personal opinion. However, it is noticeable that Cicero cannot actually lay his hand on a passage where Theophrastus can be quoted as saying the notorious thesis. Moreover, there are two passages, admittedly not such good sources, where Theophrastus is presented as stressing the importance of the agent's own virtue and judgement and as downplaying the importance of the goods of fortune.[5]

---

[2] The point made by Antiochus, that although virtue is not sufficient for the happiest life, it is sufficient for the happy life. For Antiochus see the next chapter.

[3] Cicero, *TD* V 24–5 (Fortenbaugh 493 [=L53]).

[4] Cf. Cicero, *Fin* V 77 (Fortenbaugh 495 [=L 55]); *Fin* V 85–6 (Fortenbaugh 496 [=L 56]); *Varro* 33, 35 (Fortenbaugh 497 [=L 57]; *Fin* V 12 (Fortenbaugh 498 [=L 58]); *TD* V 85 (Fortenbaugh 499 [=L 59]).

[5] John of Lydia, *On the Months* 4.7 (Fortenbaugh 490 [=L 50]) and Vitruvius, *On Architecture* 6, Introduction 2 (Fortenbaugh 491 [=L 51]). Fortenbaugh (1984, 215–217) is more doubtful about the first text, but points out that this side of Theophrastus' position has been generally neglected because so much of our information comes from Cicero, who emphasizes Theophrastus' stress on the importance of fortune.

Cicero's reference to philosophical books and lectures probably gives us the clue. Theophrastus' own position may very well have been subtle, and tried, like Aristotle's, to do justice to our thought that virtue must be important as well as our intuitions about the importance of external goods. But he clearly expressed himself in the work *On Happiness* in ways which led to his position being perceived in an over-simple way. Philosophical books and lectures have through the ages been filled with such over-simplifications. The work itself is lost, and in the present context the general perception of it is perhaps as important as its actual stance. For it is clear that the works of Aristotle, Theophrastus and the Stoics soon came to be seen in terms of the problem: Is virtue sufficient for happiness, or not? Aristotle's own works are hard to interpret on this point, as we have seen, and clearly Theophrastus' work was seen with relief as giving a clear answer on the Aristotelian side. If Theophrastus wanted to sit on the fence with Aristotle, he did not succeed. Henceforth the 'Peripatetic' view was seen in contrast to the Stoic one, as a position which allowed that loss of external goods did detract from happiness. Theophrastus was seen as holding that the virtuous person on the wheel loses his happiness; later Aristotelian kinds of theory made different moves. And Theophrastus was seen as diverging in this respect from the more circumspect Aristotle.[6]

Why, then, did Theophrastus move more clearly in the direction of allowing that loss of external goods did destroy happiness? Cicero represents him as forced to do so to avoid being inconsistent with another thesis he holds, namely that goods of the soul, goods of the body and external goods are all genuine goods. This thesis is certainly Aristotelian, although it is not a prominent part of Aristotle's ethics; he seems to regard it as a piece of common sense, to which his theory does justice.[7] The important point is clearly that virtue, which we achieve by means of the soul, that is, by our own agency and efforts, is a good, and so are beauty and wealth, which do not depend on our efforts in this way—and they are not importantly different kinds of good. Of course they are vastly different, but insofar as they are good, they can all be assessed on the same scale. Thus, if I have virtue and prosperity, and then lose the prosperity, I have retained a good but lost another. By Cicero's time this position was standardly set against the Stoic view, for which the value of virtue is not straightforwardly comparable with the value of other kinds of thing. But although Cicero's explicit context may be a later imposition, he is surely right in taking Theophrastus to be facing up, probably more explicitly than Aristotle, to the point that if the value of virtue is not different in kind from the value of other kinds of things, then the person with virtue and external goods simply has *more goods* than the person with virtue alone. And, since we recognize torture, banishment and so on as great evils, it becomes absurd to insist that virtue alone always is a great enough good to outweigh these evils in a person's life to the extent of rendering them

[6] Cf. Cicero, *Fin* V 12 (Fortenbaugh 498 [=L 58]), where the speaker claims that Aristotle and Theophrastus are in general agreement on ethics, and can safely be used together as sources, except for the one point on which they do disagree, namely the importance attached to fortune in Theophrastus' *On Happiness*.

[7] *Pol* VII 1 discusses happiness in what are presented as the popular and accessible terms of the three kinds of good. At *NE* I 8, 1098 b 12 ff, Aristotle presents his own more theoretical approach as doing justice to the common view that there are these three types of goods.

happy.[8] Cicero is probably right in seeing Theophrastus' move in this context, rather than in Aristotle's own context, of simply finding it grossly counter-intuitive to say that virtue suffices for happiness when the person is on the wheel.

We may be surprised by the violence of reaction to Theophrastus' position. He 'hamstrings virtue', he is guilty, we are repeatedly told, of a weak-kneed, contemptible response to pain and misfortune.[9] The fact that Aristotle is not abused in similar terms, when his own position can be interpreted along these lines, suggests that perhaps style has something to do with it: people are always readier to attack a simplified position than a more nuanced one which they are afraid they might be getting wrong. However, why would philosophers feel anger and contempt even at the simplified position?

Clearly Theophrastus was felt to be denying something central to happiness in making it depend on possession of external goods. But it is interesting to recall Aristotle's vehemence in denying that virtue suffices for happiness, regardless of other losses. Both sides here not only feel strongly, but think that the other side is *obviously* wrong. We could assume that general opinion had simply shifted: Aristotle counted on general agreement that virtue could not suffice for happiness, but Theophrastus, reaffirming this, found himself generally rejected. But so large a shift would be implausible, and once again we should recall Cicero's reference to philosophy books and lectures. The relation of virtue and happiness has now become a philosophical problem, much debated. A position that seemed mere common sense to Aristotle now seems contemptible in the philosophical schools. Common sense no longer offers any defence—indeed, it is seen as being itself contemptible if it supports the Theophrastean position. How could this come about? Presumably this is because the thesis can now be understood in terms of a large theory, within which it is compelling rather than silly—the Stoic theory. And contributors to the debate are now themselves rejected as unserious if they do not meet the Stoic theory on its own terms.

2. *The Stoics*

The thesis that virtue is sufficient for happiness, is a prominent element in Stoic ethics. We find the formulation that virtue is 'self-sufficient' (*autarkēs*) for happiness;[10] or the claim that virtue is both a 'productive' good, which brings about happiness, and a 'completing' good, which makes up happiness,[11] or more often an identity claim:

> One's aim, [the Stoics] say, is being happy, for the sake of which everything is
> done, while it is not done for the sake of anything further; and this consists in

---

[8] We shall see this Stoic argument in more detail, pp. 392–94.

[9] See the passages in n. 4.

[10] Diogenes VII 127–128. This is in the context of a puzzling 'argument' ascribed to Chrysippus: if *megalopsuchia* is sufficient for putting us above things, and is part of virtue, then virtue is self-sufficient for happiness. Presumably Diogenes has extracted this from a fuller context in which we could have made more sense of the train of thought.

[11] Arius 71.15-72.13; Diogenes VII 97. In this formulation the virtues are said to be 'parts' of happiness, which together constitute it.

living according to virtue, in living in agreement and further (it is the same thing) in living according to nature.[12]

We have examined, in chapter 6, how these claims about virtue and nature are to be taken together; we must now face the task of showing how the virtuous (and so natural) life could be taken to amount to, to be 'the same thing' as, the happy life. This was the Stoics' most famously counter-intuitive claim, though the larger theory that it forms part of is, as we shall see, not simply to be dismissed as counter-intuitive.

The quotation makes it clear that the Stoics explicitly accept that our final end must have the formal feature of being complete; and we might expect arguments to show that virtue is, in fact, complete and self-sufficient. What we find is rather different, though we shall see at the end that the Stoics have what amounts to an argument for this.

Such positive arguments as we find for the thesis are at first sight embarrassing. We frequently find the claim, for example, that virtue is what benefits us, since virtue is good and good is what benefits us. And since according to the Stoics *only* virtue is good, only virtue will benefit us.

> Goods, therefore, are the virtues—intelligence, justice, courage, temperance and the rest; evils are the opposites—folly, injustice and the like. Neither [goods nor evils] are things which neither benefit nor harm, e.g., life, health, pleasure, beauty, strength, wealth, good reputation, natural nobility; also their opposites—death, disease, annoyance, ugliness, weakness, poverty, obscurity, natural baseness and the like. . . . For these things are not goods, but indifferents preferred according to kind. For just as it is special to heat to heat, not to chill, so it is of good to benefit, not to harm. But wealth and health benefit no more than they harm; neither wealth nor health, therefore, is good. They further say that what can be used both well and badly is not a good; but wealth and health can be used both well and badly; wealth and health, therefore, are not good.[13]

If virtue is essentially beneficial, and if only virtue benefits by its own nature, whereas other kinds of seemingly good things such as wealth and health benefit only sometimes, and can bring harm, then virtue is the only thing which is guaranteed to benefit; thus it can plausibly be seen as the only thing which is really good. Thus we need it, rather than wealth or health, to be happy. The argument here is a descendant of an argument in Plato's *Euthydemus*,[14] and makes immediately better sense if we reflect that virtue is taken by the Stoics to be a *technē* or skill. The thought is: just having wealth and health may either help or harm you; but having the skill of rightly using and evaluating things like wealth and health can only benefit you, never harm you. Once virtue is thought of as a skill and other seeming goods like health as the things which the skill is exercised upon, it is clear that the objects of the skill need the skill if they are to be used properly and in a way which is bound to benefit the owner of the skill. Thus it is the skill, virtue, which you need to be happy, not the more intuitively obvious candidates such as wealth and health.

---

[12] Arius 77.16–19.

[13] Diogenes VII 102–103.

[14] *Euthyd* 278e–282e and 289e–292e. For discussion of this argument, and its relation to Stoic moral theory, see my (1993c).

There are several problems with this argument. First, although it makes an acceptable point, it falls far short of showing that virtue is *sufficient* for happiness. That we need virtue to make a proper use of other valued things shows that virtue is necessary for happiness if, as seems plausible, we need to make a right use of these things, rather than just having them, to be happy. But how is virtue alone sufficient for happiness? For this we need the special Stoic premise that only virtue is good at all, since the other valued things should be called not good but indifferent, having a value of a different kind. And in the Diogenes passage we do find the distinction of good and indifferent *before* the point about benefit. But this robs the argument of force for any but an already convinced Stoic.

Perhaps the Stoics are partly trying to meet this point when they elaborate different ways in which things can benefit, insisting that virtue benefits by its own nature, and hence cannot fail to benefit.[15] But this again quite fails to show that virtue is *all* we need for happiness. However reliable a source of benefit virtue is, we might still need further things, such as health and wealth. The argument thus does not produce the conclusion that the Stoics want, unless we already accept strong Stoic premises.[16]

Apart from the structure of the argument, however, we might well consider it doomed for another reason. Intuitively, we understand being benefitted as getting what is good for us, and we understand the latter in terms of our perceived wants. The Stoics, of course, do not mean this: virtue gives us what is good for us whether we realize it or not, and whether we want it or not, and health and wealth can harm us even if we deny that we are being harmed. The notion of benefit that the Stoics are using here is a completely objective one, and this is only to be expected, since they are characterizing a completely objective notion of good. But this limits the intuitive appeal of the claim, reducing it in fact almost to nothing. I may well accept that I am happy if I am getting what benefits me; but if I am then told that what benefits me does so whatever I think about it, the notion of happiness in play comes to seem highly unintuitive. The Stoics seem to be appealing to intuitions in a quite hopeless way, since it is crucial to their claim that the key terms are used in special ways in Stoic theory, and these are utterly unintuitive.

Nevertheless we find that the Stoics put some energy into this kind of claim, and we find extensive descriptions of good and of virtue which are clearly meant to be attractive, and to encourage us to see the happy life as requiring these alone.

> To virtue they apply many names. It is good, they say, because it leads us to the correct life; acceptable, because it is approved with no suspicion; of great value, because it has value which cannot be surpassed; excellent, because it is worth great concern; to be praised, because it would be reasonable to praise it; fine, because it is such as to call towards itself those who reach for it; expedient, because it brings with it what contributes to living well; useful, because it is beneficial in use; to be chosen, because from it comes what it would be reasonable to choose; necessary, because it benefits by its presence, while when it

---

[15] Diogenes VII 94; Arius 69.17–70.7; Sextus, *PH* III 171–72 and *M* XI 21–30.

[16] Perhaps this is not a failure; some Stoic arguments are clearly not intended to go from premises shared by the opponent to a conclusion which the opponent would not otherwise accept. Rather, they seem intended as encapsulations of Stoic doctrine, clarifying relations of dependence among already accepted theses. See Schofield (1983).

is not present one cannot be benefitted; profitable, because the benefits from it are greater than the efforts contributing towards them; self-sufficient, because it suffices for the person who has it; want-free, because it is rid of all lack; and adequate, because in its employment it is sufficient and extends to every use in life.[17]

And so on and so on. We also find the claim that people are in fact intuitively attracted by virtue and repelled by vice.[18]

But even if these appeals to our intuitions are successful, they cannot establish a thesis as strong as the thesis that virtue is sufficient for happiness. If this is all that the Stoics have to support that thesis, their position seems woefully dogmatic and undefended. We should remember two points here, however. One is that these appeals to intuitions were probably not intended to carry much weight on their own, but to make a supplementary contribution. The Stoics were aware that in isolation the thesis that virtue suffices for happiness sounds completely counter-intuitive. Aristotle, after all, regarded the thesis as one that nobody could seriously support. The Stoics maintain, however, that their theory does answer to our intuitions and is consistent with 'life'.[19] What they mean is not that all our initial intuitions support it, but that when we consider the theory in a variety of respects we will see that our intuitions overall cohere in a way that shows it not to be counter-intuitive as a whole. The second point is that Stoic ethical theory, while it does claim support from our intuitions, is revisionary. If the Stoics are right, then most of us have radically wrong priorities in practical matters, and we should revise and improve our practical beliefs in the light of Stoic theory. We should therefore expect that the consensus of our intuitions will show considerable changes and modifications from our initial responses, once we have absorbed the implications of the thesis that virtue is sufficient for happiness. That is, after all, what it is to revise your priorities: the result is that you judge differently from the way you did before. The Stoics hold both that coming to think in terms of Stoic moral theory will revise your priorities, and that when you have done so, you will nonetheless find that your revised position is in accord with the (revised and modified) consensus of your intuitions. We might doubt whether it is reasonable of them to hold both these things; but since they do, we cannot fault them for wishing to show that their position is in some respects in accordance with our intuitions about, for example, the attractive force of goodness and virtue.

Nonetheless, any support which the theory gets from our intuitions comes after we have been convinced by Stoic theory, not before; so they do not support the

---

[17] Arius 100.15–101.4. Cf. Arius 69.11–16; Diogenes VII 99–100.

[18] Cicero, *Fin* III 36–39. Cf. Cicero's *Stoic Paradoxes* 1 and 2: 'That virtue is the only good' and 'That virtue is sufficient for happiness'. Cicero tries to make them sound plausible and even compelling to a Roman audience, without much success: these theses are just not plausible on their own, only as parts of a larger theory. On the rhetorical strategy of the *Stoic Paradoxes*, see Englert (1990).

[19] See Plutarch, *Sto rep* 1041 e-f. Plutarch there claims that Chrysippus' statements elsewhere that Stoic ethics sets up an ideal which is not found in human life contradicts his claim in the third book of his *Protreptics* or conversion writings that 'his account of goods and evils is most in harmony with life and most closely latches on to the *prolēpseis* we are born to have'. (Chrysippus is not claiming that we are born with intuitions about good and bad already formed; the Stoic account of concept acquisition is completely empiricist. He means only that our nature as human beings gives us tendencies to acquire some concepts.)

theory in the sense of indicating why it, rather than, say, Aristotle's theory, is to be accepted. The Stoics' real defence here is attack. They hold that the Aristotelian (and later the Peripatetic) account of happiness, namely as virtuous activity together with an adequate supply of external goods, is fundamentally flawed; for it fails to recognize the difference of kind between the value of virtue and the value of other kinds of things. Once we recognize the nature of this difference, we shall see that thinking that external goods are also necessary constitutes making a fundamental mistake about what happiness is. The Stoics, in arguing that Aristotle's account of happiness is wrong, are in effect, though not in so many words, producing an argument that virtue alone is complete and self-sufficient, and thus competent to form our final end, without the addition of external goods. Since the Stoic arguments hinge so crucially on showing that virtue has a different kind of value from Aristotle's external goods, Cicero is exactly right in making his Stoic protagonist claim that 'unless it can be established that only what is moral [*honestum*] is good, it can in no way be proved that the happy life is achieved by means of virtue.'[20]

The core argument here is seen most clearly in Cicero's account of Stoic ethics in *de Finibus* III. The Stoic speaker, Cato, begins his account with a description of the process of 'familiarization' or *oikeiōsis*; we start from affinity to and concern for ourselves and for natural advantages, but as reason develops we come to discover that what matters to us as rational beings is something which is distinct in kind from these, namely the moral point of view. Just as we move from most valuing one friend to most valuing the person to whom he introduces us, we move from valuing natural advantages in a rational way to valuing our rationality itself, and appreciating the demands it makes on us. This is what it is properly to appreciate what virtue is.[21] This enables us to understand what good really is, and to see that it is different in kind from the natural advantages which we previously considered to be good.

> Just as honey, though very sweet, is felt to be sweet because of its own kind of taste, not by comparison with other things, so this good that we are considering is indeed what is most to be valued, but its value depends on the kind of thing it is, not its quantity.[22]

Virtue and other kinds of things are in a way incommensurable, but not in a way strong enough to prevent us from saying that it is more to be valued than they are.

With this important distinction in hand the Stoic turns to criticize the Aristotelian account of happiness.[23] The Peripatetics think that all of their three

---

[20] *Fin* III 11. I do not think that this is in conflict with *TD* V 18–19, where Cicero says that the Stoics write separate books on our final end and on what is morally good; they do not merely prove that only virtue is good from the sufficiency of virtue for happiness and vice versa. Cicero is here contrasting the method of mathematicians, who just assume what has been proved without discussing it, with that of philosophers, who proceed more discursively, and so sometimes prove A from B and sometimes B from A. This does not imply that we have nothing but trivial circular proof; only that it can sometimes be instructive to take as premise what was previously a conclusion. That the *Fin* statement expresses something important about the structure of Stoic ethics is confirmed by its prominence in the arguments of the *de Finibus*.

[21] *Fin* III 16–24. For a fuller discussion of this, see chapter 5.

[22] *Fin* III 34.

[23] *Fin* III 41 ff.

kinds of goods—external and bodily goods, and goods of the soul, particularly virtue, contribute to happiness. The Stoics disagree, saying that only virtue is good and contributes to happiness, although it is also natural, and rational, for humans to have a proper concern for natural advantages, such as wealth and health, which they call preferred indifferents. It can well seem that these two positions, although they initially look very different, really differ only verbally. The Stoics deny that anything but virtue is good; but they allow that what Aristotelians call bodily and external goods are reasonable objects to pursue. They go to great lengths, in fact, to show that their position on virtue does not commit them to the absurd thesis that we have no rational basis for choice between any aims other than virtue. They stress that proper pursuit of the preferred indifferents is a crucial part of the virtuous person's life; they are the 'material for virtue'. The Stoics thus might appear to be restoring with one hand what they took away with the other, and to differ only in their refusal to call things other than virtue good.

Cato, the Stoic spokesman in *de Finibus* III, strongly disagrees. The Stoic thesis about virtue, he claims, does make a real difference, especially to one's conception of happiness. In this he is surely right. He expounds two ways in which the difference shows up, and then explains this by the Stoic conception of virtue and its relation to other valuable things.

First, he says, the Stoics allow that the wise and virtuous person is happy even on the rack, whereas the Aristotelians cannot possibly allow this. This shows that the two schools do not just differ as to whether they call valued things other than virtue good or not; they differ on the kind of value that they think virtue has. For while both schools call it good, only the Stoics think that it has the kind of value which enables the person who has it to be happy whatever else happens. However, while the Stoics are right on this point, is it to their credit that they embrace the thesis which Aristotle could not take seriously? That will depend on their explanation of the value of virtue.

Second, he points out that on the Aristotelian position that we need goods of all three kinds to be happy, it will follow that the more goods a person has, the happier she will be.[24] Cicero's Stoic points out that the Stoics do not have to hold this. While the Aristotelians are committed to an additive view of happiness—the more goods you have, the happier you should be—the Stoics are not, and thus they avoid the objections awaiting that view.

Both these points are distinctive in the Stoic position, and both rely on their explanation of the value of virtue. It is clear by now that the Stoics have to meet two constraints. They have to avoid the additive position by claiming that in a sense virtue is not commensurable with other kinds of goods; its value is different in kind. But they must also show that it can in a way be compared, for it always takes precedence over other kinds of things.

> If being wise [here meaning being virtuous] is to be sought, and so is being healthy, both together is more to be sought than being wise alone. But it is not true that, if each has a value, then both together have more of it than being wise

---

[24] Unless we have a plausible independent argument for there being a point beyond which increase of external goods does not make the agent happier; but just this is what Aristotle, for one, notably fails to produce.

alone has. [*Neque tamen, si utrumque sit aestimatione dignum, pluris sit coniunctum quam sapere ipsum separatum.*] We judge health to be worthy of a kind of value, but we do not judge it a good; and we do not think there to be any value so great as to be preferred to virtue. This the Peripatetics do not hold, for they have to say that an action which is moral [*honesta*] and without pain is more to be sought than would be the same action without pain. . . . Compare the way the light of a lamp is obscured and overpowered by the light of the sun, and the way a drop of honey is lost in the extent of the Aegean sea; compare adding a penny to the riches of Croesus and taking one step on the journey from here to India—if the final good is what the Stoics say it is, it is necessary for all the value of bodily things to be obscured and overwhelmed, indeed to be destroyed, by the brilliance and the size of virtue.[25]

We have already seen briefly[26] that the Stoics are pointing to the difference between moral and other value. Virtue is not the same kind of thing as other things that we value. Adding other kinds of things to it as though they were on the same scale shows a lack of comprehension of what it is. Hence, although the Peripatetics call virtue good as the Stoics do, they fail to do justice to what virtue is in treating it simply as a good, which could have other goods added to it to produce a better good. The Stoics allow that it is rational to choose virtue and health rather than virtue and disease, but insist that this must not be construed as though one were adding more of the same kind of value. Virtue and other kinds of valued thing are thus incommensurable in this sense: they cannot be added (or, of course, subtracted) on a single scale of goodness.

If the Stoics are right, then, their account is recommended as an account of happiness by their arguments to show that they give a true account of virtue, unlike the Aristotelians. While Aristotle appears at first to give a more intuitively satisfactory account of happiness, his account must be rejected because, on reflection, it can be seen to give an unsatisfactory account of virtue and its relation to other valued things. And so, to reverse the argument, the Stoic theory, which gives a better account of this, must be accepted, despite its giving what seems at first like a less satisfactory account of happiness. We see, when we reflect on virtue, that we must reject the intuitions about happiness that Aristotle relied on.

The above is the nearest that the Stoics get to an argument to show that virtue is complete and self-sufficient, and therefore an acceptable candidate for giving the content of happiness. Clearly, given that they accept the formal conditions, they have to hold this; but they do so not directly but by arguing for a theory which gives virtue such a special and pre-eminent place by comparison to other valued things that none of them *can* be added to virtue to create a better good, and so to contribute to happiness.

An important issue presents itself here. The above line of thought was presented from the Stoic point of view; that is, it was accepted that Aristotle gave an inadequate account of the special kind of value that virtue is taken to have. But could it not be objected to the Stoics that they mistake what people think? Perhaps people do not in fact think that virtue is as special as all that; perhaps ordinary moral deliberations accept the additive view. If so, the Stoics will be disagreeing with

---

[25] *Fin* III 44–45.
[26] Chapter 2, section 7, pp. 122–24.

Aristotle not over the explanation which moral theory gives of the data, but over the question of what the data are. We shall return to this issue in the next section, where we look at the Peripatetic responses to the above Stoic moves.

The Stoics have more to say about the distinctive nature of happiness, but these characterizations are best approached by considering how the Stoics meet kinds of problems which their position obviously faces—problems as to the relation of virtue to the other kinds of valued thing.

The Stoics are not open to the kind of objection they find in the Aristotelian view—namely, that it is additive, so that increases in health, wealth and so on would seem automatically to lead to increases in happiness.[27] They allow, as we have seen, that virtue together with preferred indifferents is preferable to virtue alone. Indeed, any rational agent will prefer virtue together with health and wealth to virtue with sickness and poverty. They insist, though, that this is not to be construed as adding more of the same kind of value that we have when we have virtue alone. Thus they can hold both that it is preferable to live a virtuous life and also to be healthy, wealthy, and so on, and that health and wealth are not straightforwardly added on to virtue to produce a better good. In holding this they are faithful to the point that they take to be most crucial, namely that the value of virtue is different in kind from the value of other kinds of thing.

However, the Stoics seem in consequence to be landed with the unsatisfactory consequence that it is rational for us to aim at two different kinds of value which cannot be put on the same scale. It is rational for us to go for the natural advantages such as health and wealth, and also rational for us, as developed rational beings, to go for virtue; and these must be, it appears, quite distinct aims, since it is so crucial to the Stoic position that the values in question cannot be put on the same scale. But is it not a fault in a theory, especially one which lays so much weight on rationality, to have to say that we just go for two distinct goals, and, further, for two goals which are not commensurable in terms of one standard of value, so that there is no rational strategy for working out how much time, attention, etc., should be paid to each? A prominent argument against the Stoics in antiquity is just this, namely that they give us two separate goals, virtue and the natural advantages.[28] Further, by identifying virtue with happiness, they find themselves saying that the natural advantages are rational objects of pursuit, but irrelevant for happiness.[29] And by appealing so prominently to nature in their account of how we develop as moral beings, they are landed with the result that they appeal to nature to set up the natural advantages as objects of our pursuit, thereby giving us a plausible means of distinguishing between them as 'preferred' and 'dispreferred', but then turn around

---

[27] For a defence of the claim that they are open to a version of it, since they allow that 'the Total' (virtue plus indifferents) is more to be chosen than virtue alone, see Irwin (1986).

[28] This is the major argument of *Fin* IV, which tries to impale the Stoics on the dilemma: Either only virtue is good and other things are not good in not being rational objects of pursuit, but are truly 'indifferent', in which case we have no criterion for choosing rationally between health and sickness, etc. Or we do have rational grounds for choosing between them, in which case they are goods in all but name, and the Stoic position is only verbally, and perversely, different from Aristotle's.

[29] Cf. *Fin* IV 30–31.

and say that our final goal, virtue, is something quite distinct, and is unlike our previous goal in giving us no natural basis for choice of actions.[30]

These objections are akin to modern objections that are often raised against theories which are 'pluralist', which give us more than one end and deny that there is a single means of ranking the different ends that we have. The motivation which is common to ancient and modern objections is the thought that a moral theory ought to give us a single rational strategy for achieving all those of our aims which are relevant to the moral life. To give us two (or more) goals, and no single method of relating them, is to give up too soon; a moral theory ought to give us a single strategy for our whole life. Whatever its force against modern theories, it is clear that this objection is forceful against the Stoics, if it is successful. For, as we have seen at length,[31] ancient ethical theories begin from the agent's reflection on her life as a whole, and attempt to answer the demand for a clarification and unification of her aims. Although they all seek to revise her priorities to greater or lesser extent, none of them (with the exception, as often, of the Cyrenaics) concludes that she is wrong to aspire to have a single overarching aim which will make sense of her minor aims and enable her to discern the correct priorities between them. For it is a datum of ancient ethical thinking that we do, inchoately, have already such an overarching aim, namely happiness, and that the task of ethical theory is to lead us from a vague and partial understanding of this to a clearer and more definite conception, which will enable us to reorder and rethink our commitments and values. Thus if the Stoics are really giving us two aims and no common strategy, and are telling us to direct our life by two incommensurable values, they are falling short of what other ethical theories take to be necessary, namely giving us an aim which will make sense of and help to direct the agent's life overall.

In fact, however, the charge does not succeed. The objection as stated so far simply takes Stoic points about virtue and other valued things in isolation; it fails to take account of other aspects of the Stoic position. Chiefly important here is that for the Stoics virtue is a *skill*, a developed intellectual disposition of the agent.[32] Aiming at virtue is therefore to be construed for them as aiming at *being virtuous*, coming to have this skill. They underline this point by insisting that strictly what we aim at is not happiness but *being happy*, and that this is our overall *telos* or goal,[33] not our immediate *skopos* or target. In doing this the Stoics are merely sharpening the intuitive idea that our final good must be something that we do, not just a good object or state of affairs. Thus for the Stoics the relation of virtue to our other goals takes the form of asking what the relation is between virtue, the developed intellectual skill which the virtuous person possesses, and the other objects of our rational pursuit, which the virtuous person will go for, and which are the objects of virtue. Virtue is indeed sometimes said by the Stoics to be the 'skill of living' (*technē peri tou biou*)—that is, the skill of living one's life as a whole in a clear and intellectually well-based way.[34]

---

[30] Cf. *Fin* IV 47–48.

[31] Chapter 1.

[32] See chapter 2, section 4.

[33] Cf. Arius 77.16–27.

[34] See Sextus, *M* XI 168–256; unfortunately Sextus' own objections are all trivial and unrevealing of Stoic motivation.

It is presumably in order to stress this point that later heads of the Stoic school produce definitions of our final end which emphasize the fact that virtue is a developed disposition to deal rationally with its objects. They seem to have been building on ideas already present in Chrysippus, but altering the perspective.

> Chrysippus. . .expanded as follows: 'living in accordance with experience of what comes about by nature'. And Diogenes: 'being reasonable in the selection and counter-selection of the things according to nature'. And Archedemus: 'living making all one's due actions complete'. And Antipater: 'living selecting things according to nature and counter-selecting things contrary to nature invariably'. Often he also added: 'doing everything one can invariably and unalterably towards obtaining the things that are preferable according to nature'.[35]

Happiness, then, lies not in aiming at virtue *plus* external goods, as though they were the same kind of thing, but rather in aiming at external goods in a way which constitutes the exercise of virtue, that is, of a developed rational disposition to select among the indifferents, to give them their proper priorities and relations. For virtue is the skill of rightly selecting among and making use of the other valuable things. We seem to have avoided the charge that the Stoics are setting up two ends.

Or have we? We find in the ancient sources some powerful criticisms of this use of the idea of virtue as a skill. Virtue is for the Stoics the skill of making right use of other things such as health and wealth—its 'material'. It is also the only thing which is good, everything else, such as health and wealth, being merely indifferents, preferred if it is rational for us to go for them. Because it is the only thing which is good, it is sufficient for happiness. Various ancient arguments try to show that it is hopeless to try to combine these theses: if virtue has the special kind of value that the Stoics claim, then it cannot without absurdity be a skill. And if there is difficulty in construing it as a skill, then obviously the Stoic strategy of avoiding the claim of having two final ends cannot go through.

These objections have come down to us mainly in a long essay by Alexander of Aphrodisias and an unfortunately rather corrupt passage of Plutarch.[36] Alexander's main objections are the following: a skill needs equipment and objects to be exercised on, and furthermore needs them in good condition. A flute-player, for example, cannot exercise her skill if she has no flute; and, even if she has one, she cannot exercise the skill if the conditions are not good, for example if the flute is damaged and she has a heavy cold.[37] Analogously, if virtue is the skill of rightly using the indifferents, then we must set value on the existence and good state of these, as well as of the virtue which makes right use of them.

Is it true that we need good conditions for the exercise of a skill? If James Galway has a really bad cold and a really inferior flute, the result may not sound wonderful. It might even sound worse than a performance on a good flute, in good conditions, by a greatly inferior flautist. We do need, it seems, good conditions to get the good results that we expect from the skilled person. However, this need not be the right way of looking at it. It might be that even though the inferior player

---

[35] Arius 76.6–15.
[36] Alexander, *De An* II 159.16–168.20; Plutarch, *Comm not* 1071a–1072f.
[37] For the first objection, see 160.1–20; 160.21–31; 162.22–163.18; 163.18–32; 163.32–164.21; 165.26–29. For the second, see 160.31–161.3; 164.21–28; 166.21–35; 166.35–167.13.

produced a better-sounding result, nonetheless the better performance was produced by James Galway. Results need not be the basis for judging that there has been an exercise of skill.[38] But it looks different with the claim that there must be appropriate objects for a skill to work on for there to be such a thing as an exercise of skill. The flautist can perform even with a bad cold and a damaged instrument, but he needs at least a flute to perform at all. The analogue for virtue, of course, is something like the Aristotelian claim that you cannot be generous without owning some property to be generous with. And this does look like a decisive objection. Without a flute, James Galway can do *something*: whistle the tune, perhaps, or think of it in his head. But this is not an exercise in *flute-playing*. A sculptor deprived of materials or an architect deprived of a commission can think up and contemplate her creation; but this does not seem to be *sculpting* or *architecture*. We do not seem to have an exercise of skill at all in the absence of suitable equipment and objects for the skill to be exercised on to produce its results. Analogously, we do not seem to have an exercise of generosity in the case of someone with no money to be generous with.

The Stoics have to find a way of meeting this objection. For they are committed to the thesis that virtue has a value of its own which is different in kind from the value of anything that it might produce. And since the value that virtue has always overrides the other kinds, they are clearly committed to the Kantian thesis that virtue shines with its own light even when stepmotherly nature lets us down. This problem can be solved in one way by distinguishing two ways in which a virtuous action can be regarded. It can be described so as to include its outcome—'generous giving of money', say—and as so described it may be either a success or a failure. It will obviously be a failure if there is no money to be generous with. It may also, however, be described simply as an exercise of the agent's virtue—'actively being generous', say—and as so described it is not necessarily a failure just because it is a failure when described in terms of its outcome. It is open to the Stoics to say that failure to have money need not imply failure to exercise the virtue, even when the usual results are not forthcoming. However, this kind of resolution alone is not enough for the Stoics. For they have to hold that the successful exercise of virtue is itself an action, and one, moreover, which is itself an exercise of skill. For only so will they be able to defend their rejection of the objection that they set up two final ends and not one.

Is it not, however, paradoxical to hold that the exercise of a skill can take place in the absence of the right results? The Stoics here do need some help from their theory of action. In one passage[39] we hear of a dispute between Cleanthes and Chrysippus as to what walking is. In Stoic theory of action, every action involves what we would call a mental assent to a proposition, located (since the Stoics are materialists) in the 'governing part' of the soul in the heart. As a result, messages are sent out in the *pneuma* (very roughly, the physical way the soul works) and bodily movement takes place. Cleanthes, however, said that walking was *pneuma* sent to the feet by the governing part, while Chrysippus said it was the governing part itself. Details apart, the interesting point here is that both Stoics defined walking without

---

[38] See Striker (forthcoming). This would not seem to hold of all skills, for example, not of the productive ones; but it would be enough for the Stoics if there were some plausible cases where we did evaluate performance in terms of skill regardless of poor results in unfavourable circumstances.

[39] Seneca *Ep* 133.23.

reference to the movement of the feet; walking is rather identified with what we would call the mental event of assent, while Cleanthes seems to have wanted to include some causal result of this within the body (perhaps the trying to move the feet, as a result of the mental assent). So the Stoics held that an action which is usually described in terms of causal result can be described without essential reference to that result. We would normally say that I cannot walk without moving my feet. But the Stoics are willing to say that properly speaking I walk when I assent in my mind to the thought that normally leads to the movement of the feet.[40] Thus they are, quite apart from their ethical views, committed to the idea that an agent can correctly be said to have performed some action when he has made an inner (we would say mental) assent to some proposition. So it is not paradoxical for a virtuous agent to perform a virtuous action, even without the normal result.

But how can this be an exercise of *skill*? Many skills are so defined that we cannot sensibly talk about an exercise of the skill in the absence of the outcome. Whatever my mental performance, how can I be said to have cooked anything if there is nothing to eat, or to have cleaned the clothes if they are still dirty?[41] If we stick with this point as a basic feature of skills, we will probably conclude that the Stoics would have done better to abandon the idea that the virtuous person cheated of any actual outcome to his actions has nonetheless exercised a skill, and held instead the more Kantian position that what he has achieved is merely the antecedent of an action, a virtuous intention or act of will. But the Stoics were unwilling to make this move, probably because the thesis that virtue is a skill seemed to them the best way of avoiding the 'two ends' problem which their distinction of moral from non-moral value seemed to face them with.

The Stoics seem rather to have abandoned the intuitive conception of a skill, and with this to have accepted that in everyday terms their position here is counter-intuitive, since normally when we think of skills, we think of the outcome, so that it makes no sense to talk of an exercise of the skill in the absence of the objects and conditions that make that outcome possible. What the Stoics appealed to was what mattered to them most in the thesis that virtue is a skill, namely the intellectual structure of skill. What is important for them about a virtuous action is not the intuitive analogy with the practical aspect of skill, but rather the point that the virtuous agent, like the possessor of skill, has a unified and articulate grasp of the principles which unite and justify her decisions. As we have seen, the Stoics, who accept the unity of the virtues, develop this point quite extensively; the virtuous

---

[40] For more on the Stoic theory of action, see Annas (1992a), ch. 4. Here I cannot enter into the interesting theory of *lekta* (roughly corresponding to propositions), which is what the agent assents to. Our evidence is too scanty for detailed comparison to be possible, but the Stoic theory resembles modern theories that identify actions with tryings, which when they succeed are described in terms of their causal result, and when they do not succeed are merely tryings. I cannot here go into the question of what motivated the Stoics to this striking view, but it is plausible that it was, at least in part, the desire to identify one's action with what one is responsible for, together with the obvious thought that often one is not responsible for the causal result of one's action.

[41] This is not just a feature of the productive skills. Intellectual skills raise problems also; how can I be said to have exercised my mathematical ability if I have achieved no solutions?

person will accept a unified system of principles in terms of which she develops her virtuous dispositions and justifies her decisions and actions.[42]

The Stoics are thus in effect identifying the exercise of skill with the exercise of its intellectual basis. An agent counts as exercising the skill of virtue if he exercises the right thoughts, even in the case where those thoughts do not have the appropriate practical result. The agent is taken to be exercising a skill, and not merely having the right intentions to exercise a skill, because the Stoics are prepared to abandon some of the intuitive aspects of our conception both of action and of skill, and to redefine these in terms of the needs of their theory. As we have seen, the moral theory is held to answer to our intuitions overall, but in the process some of these need to be modified, and among these the internalizing of the notion of skill, to meet the demands on virtue, is certainly striking.

Given the results so far about the virtuous person in bad conditions nevertheless exercising a skill, we might expect the Stoics to make some explicit modifications to the conception of the skill which is virtue. Otherwise, it would be easy for opponents to press difficulties on them by foisting on them the everyday conception of skill, in which its exercise is dependent on available materials, and valued for its results. And we do find such explicit modification.

The standard account of how the Stoics did this, however, seems incorrect. It is worth briefly investigating why this is so, since the standard account rests on plausible views about success and failure in the exercise of skill, and seeing why the Stoics do not adopt it is itself illuminating as to their views of skill. This is the suggestion that the Stoics identified virtue with a particular kind of skill, a *stochastic* skill. These are characterized[43] as skills in which a failure, because of contingencies, to achieve the outcome is different from a failure in the exercise of the skill itself.[44] This has been seized on by modern scholars[45] as a point which might help the Stoics to save their theses about virtue. An exercise of virtue can tolerate certain kinds of failure, namely those that come from contingent failure of materials and circumstances, provided that there is no failure to act in accordance with the skill itself; this is allowed for by the conception of a stochastic skill.

Unfortunately, there is no good reason to think that the Stoics did make this use of the notion of a stochastic skill. The main basis for claiming so is the fact that, among the later heads of the Stoa who characterized the final end in terms of virtue's being a disposition to deal rationally with its objects,[46] Antipater added a second

---

[42] See chapter 2, sections 3 and 4, especially pp. 67–8, 96.

[43] By Alexander of Aphrodisias, *Quaest* II 1–28, also *In Top* 32.11–34.5. Alexander himself discusses stochastic skill because Aristotle does, especially at *Rhetoric* 1355 b 10 ff. and *Topics* 101 b 5 ff. Although Alexander rarely misses an Aristotelian idea with anti-Stoic potential, he does not himself relate it to the Stoics (with the possible exception of 34.3–4 of the *In Top* passage, where, in a corrupt passage, he seems to be opposing the Stoic final end to the Aristotelian one). Given that he has batteries of arguments against the Stoic claim that virtue is a skill, this lack of connection suggests that Alexander does not take the Stoics to have thought of virtue as a stochastic skill. However, von Arnim put the *Quaest* passage into his collection of Stoic 'fragments', and this has encouraged the idea that it must be relevant to the Stoics.

[44] Inwood (1986a) discusses another aspect, namely that in such skills there is no 'definite' way of exercising them; they are the kind of skills where excellence demands the ability to improvise as well as to follow rules. Here I shall merely discuss the point about admitting certain kinds of failure.

[45] Rieth (1934), Long (1967), Alpers-Gölz (1976), Striker (1986a) and (1991).

[46] See p. 397.

definition: 'doing everything one can invariably and unalterably towards obtaining the things that are preferable according to nature'. We are told that Antipater was cornered into verbal manoeuvrings by Carneades,[47] who set up a systematic framework for discussing ethical theories. First, he insisted that every skill has an object distinct from itself, going on to assume that the practical intelligence of the virtuous person is a skill. This skilled intelligence must be directed at pleasure, tranquillity or natural advantages, *or* at endeavouring to get one of these three, even if one does not succeed. The Stoic view he of course identifies with the view that our final end consists of the skilled endeavour to get natural advantages, even if one does not succeed.[48] Scholars have thought that Antipater was reacting to Carneades, and defending the Stoic view by claiming that virtue can be thought of as the kind of skill where failure to achieve the outcome does not imply failure to exercise the skill.

One can see why this is an attractive suggestion. The Stoics need to hold that virtue is a skill and that virtue is the sole good and sufficient for happiness; but they also have to accommodate the commonsense point that virtuous action does often fail to achieve anything, when stepmotherly nature, as Kant puts it, lets us down. On this view, virtue is defined as the kind of skill that can tolerate a certain kind of failure, namely failure of outcome. However, it does not seem to have been a suggestion that the Stoics in fact welcomed. Firstly, Antipater's definition does not look much like a definition of a kind of skill, and the wording is different from standard accounts of stochastic skills.[49] On the face of it, what is distinctive about Antipater's definition is that it characterizes virtue in terms of *trying* or attempting. This does not itself characterize a kind of skill, certainly not a stochastic skill, which is defined, not as a skill which consists in attempting to do something, but simply as a skill where certain sorts of failure do not count as failure in the skill, if one has done all that the skill requires.

Further, standard discussion of stochastic skill involve a distinction between the outcome aimed at, the *skopos*, and the *telos* or goal of performing in accordance with the skill. But the Stoics held to quite a different distinction of their own between these terms, and so it is unlikely that they would have taken over the terminology of stochastic skills as it stood.[50]

---

[47] Plutarch, *Comm not* 1072 f. Actually the comment comes at the end of a long series of objections to defining the *telos* in terms of rational selection or endeavouring to select natural advantages, and does not clearly pick out Antipater's second definition in particular. The passage confuses Diogenes' and Antipater's ideas, as well as being corrupt. Long (1967), p. 75 n. 43, points out that 'sources favourable to Stoicism' tell us virtually nothing about the alleged great controversy between Carneades and Antipater. Although there seems to have been some influence, it would be rash to inflate its importance, or to use Antipater's definition to illuminate Stoic moral theory generally.

[48] Cicero, *Fin* V 20–22.

[49] Antipater says that the agent should *pan to kath'hauton poiein*; Alexander's wording is *panta to par'autas* (i.e., the skills) *poiēsai*. Aristotle talks of what *endechetai*. Alpers-Gölz (1976), pp. 67–68, collects passages discussing stochastic skills; none is close to Antipater's wording.

[50] In the standard distinction, our *skopos* is *eudaimonia*, while our *telos* is *eudaimonein* (Arius 77.1–5, 16–27). See chapter 1, p. 34. The idea that Antipater took over the distinct use of these terms is often simply asserted, e.g., by Alpers-Gölz (1976), p. 70. A passage of Posidonius, quoted by Galen (*SVF* III 12), which is sometimes held to display the second use of *skopos*, in fact shows the opposite, since Posidonius is precisely not suggesting a special Stoic use of *skopos*, but rather referring to non-Stoic final ends.

It is fairly certain that Antipater used the image of an archer to illustrate his view of how we achieve our final end, happiness. The archer exercises his skill of archery in order to hit the target, but his real or proper aim is the exercise of his skill, not hitting the target.[51] It is often assumed that archery is here introduced as an example of a stochastic skill.[52] But there is no reason to do this, and since Antipater is not concerned with stochastic skills in any case, it makes much better sense to interpret the image as an illustration of the idea that we achieve happiness indirectly, by aiming at something else, namely the preferred indifferents. In this case, there is no reference in the archer example to the possibility of failure, and so nothing to connect it to the idea of a stochastic skill.[53] In any case, if archery were considered as a kind of stochastic skill, it would be an unfortunate example, since, while we might not count an individual exercise a failure even if the archer did not hit the target, archery as a skill can hardly be said to be the skill of shooting whether or not one hits the target. A good archer just is one who hits the target.

Finally, the archer example in this context has prompted suggestions that sports provide examples of stochastic skills which are suitable as an analogy for virtue. Virtue is supposed to be analogous to the disposition to 'play up! and play the game!'[54] However, archery in the ancient world is a military skill, not sport. And further, sports are fundamentally unsuitable as a model of virtue, for a number of reasons.[55] If this were the implication of the archer example, it would be a bad one.

Attractive as the idea of a stochastic skill might seem at first to be, in order to accommodate the intuitive kind of failure that Stoic virtue as a skill has to encounter in the world, it did not recommend itself to them. We can also see two principled objections that they would have to accepting it. First, the virtuous person must actually succeed in achieving happiness, so virtue could not be thought of by a Stoic as entirely stochastic.[56] And second, the problem with the archer image is a general one: a stochastic skill can accommodate cases where the agent fails to achieve her aim because of contingent bad luck or lack of the appropriate means or instruments, but the skill as such has essential reference to the outcome whose success demands these contingencies. To take a standard example: a doctor may fail to cure without failing in his skill, but medicine is practiced for the sake of curing, not for the sake of doctoring.

There is a possible way for the Stoics to retain the position about failure embodied in the notion of a stochastic skill, while avoiding the above difficulties.[57]

[51] Cicero, *Fin* III 22; Plutarch, *Comm not* 1071 b-c.

[52] As by Alpers-Gölz (1976), p. 80.

[53] Cf N. White (1990), n. 36, who makes this point about the archer image.

[54] According to Long (1967), n. 56, this was first suggested by F. Sandbach. It is discussed in detail by Striker (1986a) and (1991).

[55] Sports are based on the idea of (often violent) competition. Ancient writers, who were less coy than we are about the nature of violent competition, are never tempted to take them as analogues for virtue, a major concern of which is to *overcome* competitive and violent impulses. Modern scholars, who use sanitized examples of comparatively non-violent sports, and focus on the modern concern of rules in sports, often miss this.

[56] Cf. Inwood (1986a) p. 551.

[57] This has been suggested to me by Terence Irwin and also by Brad Inwood. In the discussion of this issue I have been greatly helped by comments from an audience at Cornell, where I read a paper discussing this issue, and in particular from comments by Phillip Mitsis.

They could say that a virtuous action is the exercise of skill in the ordinary sense, and to that extent a success, while it is *also* an exercise of stochastic skill, in a way tolerating failure of outcome. Thus virtuous action would be an exercise of skill in two ways, one of them accounting for its success in terms of intellectually grasping principles, the other allowing for failure of outcome because of contingencies. However, there is no basis in the texts for this solution. We should conclude that the Stoics took the analogy of virtue with skill to suggest success, not failure, and that this was because they stressed the intellectual requirements and structure of skill, being prepared to jettison the intuitive side of the analogy when it came to failures of outcome.

It remains true that Antipater's definition stands out as somewhat unorthodox, and it is interesting to reflect why. Antipater seems to have been forced by Carneades into characterizing virtue in terms of trying in a certain kind of endeavour, regardless of success. We have seen why he might well have been forced this way; it is very plausible to think that the virtuous person who has failed to achieve her intended outcome has nevertheless successfully produced an intention of some kind, and that what matters is thus whether one tries, rather than whether one succeeds. But this is not a position which a Stoic can comfortably take, for it creates problems for the central thesis that virtue is a skill. As Plutarch points out in talking about Antipater, there is something absurd about a skill which is supposed to be valued for itself, and yet which appears to consist entirely in trying to get something else.[58] So while we can sympathize with Antipater, we have to recognize that what the Stoics have to do is to reject, at the cost of counter-intuitiveness, any connection of skill with failure, and insist that virtue is a skill the exercise of which is always successful, described as an exercise of virtue, even though it may be a failure if described in terms of its outcome.

The Stoics do, though, modify the straightforward claim that virtue is a skill, as we can see from a long passage in Cicero's *De Finibus* III.[59]

> [24]. . .And we (Stoics) do not consider intelligence [the practical intelligence of the virtuous person] to be like medicine or navigation,[60] but rather to acting, which I just mentioned, and dancing, in that its end, that is, the achievement of the skill,[61] is included in the skill itself, and is not to be sought outside it. However, there is another difference between intelligence and these skills, because in them, what is rightly done does not yet contain all the parts of which the skill consists, whereas when we talk about right actions or rightly done actions (if this will do), which the Stoics call *katorthōmata*, they do contain 'all the numbers of virtue'. For only intelligence is completely self-concerned, which does not happen with the other skills. [25] It is inept, then, to compare the end of medicine and navigation with the end of intelligence.[62] For intelligence embraces

[58] These are not objections which arise for a stochastic skill.

[59] Paragraphs [24] and [25], and also paragraph [32], which seems displaced where it is. Several scholars have thought that it belongs after [25]; Wright (1991) prints it there.

[60] Standard examples of stochastic skills in Alexander.

[61] There are three occurrences of *effectio*, all in Cicero's philosophical writings. At *Varro* 6 it is clearly a technical term meaning 'efficient cause'. Reid notes there that at the other two occurrences (here, and *Fin* III 45) 'it has the more natural sense of *praxis*, accomplishment'. At III 45 Cicero remarks that he uses *recta effectio* to translate *katorthōsis*, since *rectum factum* translates *katorthōma*.

[62] I agree with Madvig that this sentence is ineptly placed, and belongs neither with what immediately precedes nor with what immediately follows.

greatness of soul and justice and the judgement that all that can happen to a human being is beneath it, which again does not happen with the other skills. Indeed, no one can even have these virtues which I have just mentioned unless he has realized that there is nothing which is not indifferent and unimportant besides what is moral and immoral. [32] In the other skills, when something is said to be skilfully done, it is to be taken to be something which is in some way subsequent, and a result, which the Stoics call *epigennēmatikon*. But in the case in which we say that something is done intelligently, it is said to be done with complete correctness right from the start. For whatever is initiated by the wise person must forthwith be complete in all its parts, since in this is located what we say is to be sought. As it is wrong to betray one's country, to be violent to one's parents, to rob temples—actions defined by their effects—so being afraid, being depressed, being in a state of lust [examples of emotions] are wrong even without effects. Indeed, just as these are wrong not subsequently and in their effects, but forthwith and right from the start, so actions initiated by virtue are to be judged right beginning from their first inception and not in their completion.

Three points of importance about virtue emerge. First, ordinary skills are local; you can be a good navigator but a terrible person in other respects. Virtue, on the other hand, is a global skill in the agent's life. As we have seen,[63] by this is meant not just that virtue is required in all areas of the agent's life, but rather that each exercise of virtue involves not only an appreciation of the requirements of the particular situation, but also a global appreciation of the principles which the agent lives by in her life as a whole. Given the unity of the virtues, each virtuous decision, however parochial the content, reflects the agent's overall virtuous state and the values in his life as a whole.

Second, intelligence *in se tota conversa est*, which I have rendered as 'is completely self-concerned'. The point is, of course, not that intelligence is self-absorbed or self-indulgent, but rather than it is self-reflexive in a way that skills like medicine and pottery-making are not. By this is meant nothing more dramatic than that the virtuous person's thoughts will crucially involve reflection on the nature of virtue itself, whereas potters and weavers need not, indeed probably should not, reflect on the nature of their skill in exercising it. Presumably, virtue is *completely* self-concerned in that every exercise of virtue involves reflection (not, of course, conscious reflection) on what virtue requires. This point is put forward as a reason for the first; what is the connection? Presumably the thought is something like the following: it is because virtuous reasoning involves reflection on the nature of virtue that it requires a global grasp of one's principles in one's life as a whole.[64]

It is the third point which distinguishes most sharply between virtue and other skills. Both in [24] and in [32] it is claimed that virtue achieves its end in a way distinguishing it from most other skills. Because of its characteristic features, an exercise of virtue is successful, achieves its end, as soon as it is initiated and regardless of whether it achieves its intended outcome.[65] In this respect it clearly

---

[63] Chapter 2, sections 3 and 4.

[64] Cf. *Fin* III 50, where virtue is distinguished from other skills by the fact that it requires a great deal of reflection (*commentatio*) and practice (*exercitatio*), as well as stability over one's life as a whole.

[65] A minor puzzle here is that the same seems to be true of some ordinary skills in [24], namely dancing and acting. But presumably these contrast with virtue in not being global and requiring reflection

contrasts with most intuitive examples of skills. It would obviously be absurd to say that an exercise of skilled car repair is successful from its inception, regardless of whether the car actually gets fixed or not. But this just underlines the point that virtue is different. What is successful from its inception in a virtuous action is the exercise of intelligence, the making of the right decision in the light of reflection on the agent's principles and the particularities of the case at hand. We would of course identify this successful element with an intention or act of will, but we have seen that the Stoics have good reason to retain the thesis that the virtuous agent succeeds in exercising the skill which constitutes her virtue.

Thus the Stoics have a coherent and viable conception of virtue as a skill which is indifferent to results; to do so they have to frankly leave behind much of the analogy with ordinary skills and rest with the aspect of skill which has already been drawn out: there is an intellectual difference between the skilled and the unskilled, and this makes a real difference even in cases where the circumstances are unfavourable, where normal activity is not possible, or where the exercise of skill fails to lead to the expected result. In the Stoic development of this idea one thing which notably comes to the fore is the extent to which this results in an internalization of virtue.

It has always been noted that Stoic moral theory makes virtue, and hence happiness, internal to the agent. The virtuous agent has within himself all that matters, regardless of external outcome. Frequently, however, this is misunderstood; it is thought that for the Stoics virtue must be internal since it must be under the agent's control; happiness cannot depend on what is outside the agent's control. Nowhere, however, do we find this as an assumption in Stoic moral theory.[66] Rather, the internalization of virtue emerges as a result of argument, of serious attempts to work out the consequences of theses which require considerable mutual modification. Hence, the idea that virtue is internal to the agent is not one that can be characterized by the simple thought that it is something which is up to the agent. We can, however, grasp it through a number of striking theses about virtue—made more striking, of course, by the point that for the Stoics virtue amounts to happiness.

First is the thesis that virtue is not a matter of degree; this has the notorious consequence that strictly speaking it is impossible to progress by degrees in becoming virtuous. The Stoics of course recognize that there is such a thing as moral progress (*prokopē*), but insist that this is not a gradual process which when complete consists in being virtuous, on the Aristotelian pattern. Such a picture would risk softening the all-important distinction between the value of virtue and the value of other things. Rather, learning to be virtuous requires the development of one's ability to choose and make use of indifferents until one does so in a rational way, and this develops to the point when one grasps something distinctively new, namely the difference between the values of the things one has chosen between, and the value of virtue which is marked off decisively from all of these. Thus for the Stoics the process of habituation in virtuous habits of action and patterns of response is merely a prelude to the all-important move to grasping the value of virtue—the

---

on their own nature. On acting as a skill in Stoic moral philosophy, see Ioppolo (1980), pp. 188–193, 197–202.

[66] See the conclusion to this part, p. 430.

moral point of view. This move is, according to the Stoics, instantaneous, and goes unperceived;[67] something easily ridiculed by opponents, but underlining an important point. Whether you are virtuous, for the Stoics, depends on whether you do in fact grasp what matters: the distinctive value of virtue. Whether you do, is not a matter of degree, and so there is no process of coming to grasp it, which you might be aware of.

The Stoics employed several analogues to make this point. Puppies on the verge of opening their eyes are just as blind as newborn puppies; someone just beneath the surface of the water is just as unable to breathe as someone on the bottom.[68] The analogues make the point that, while there is progress by degrees towards being able to become virtuous, becoming virtuous is not itself a matter of degree, but a transformation from one state to another. Unfortunately, hostile critics interpreted the idea perversely, claiming, wrongly, that the Stoics are denying the existence of moral progress, or implying that trying to progress is a waste of time.[69]

Virtue, and thus happiness, once achieved, is not subject to quantitative measurement. This leads to two consequences, both striking and frequently misunderstood. One is that happiness is not increased by duration. 'Chrysippus says that the happiness of an instant is not different from the happiness of Zeus, [and] that the happiness of Zeus is in no way more to be chosen or finer or more dignified than the happiness of wise people.'[70] This thesis is equally startling when posed in terms of virtue; opponents were equally shocked by the idea that 'Zeus does not exceed Dion in virtue'.[71] The point is clear, however; while we ordinarily give a sense to locutions implying that some people are more or less happy (or virtuous) than others, a proper conception of virtue and happiness shows us that they make no real sense. For virtue, properly conceived, is the skill of rightly selecting among indifferents—that is, it is a disposition to get things right both intellectually and in one's reactions. And this is not the kind of thing that there can be more or less of. The Stoics claim that virtue belongs to the kind of thing whose goodness is a matter of fitting or being right, and that the goodness of this kind of thing is not increased by duration. The goodness of a shoe consists in its fitting the foot; the goodness of a childbirth consists in things happening in the right way at the right time. It makes no sense to say that the childbirth would be better if it lasted longer, or that the shoe would fit better if there were more shoes like it. Similarly, virtue is valuable because it is a disposition to get things right; it makes no sense to want *more* of this.[72] Hence, a longer rather than shorter life is of no value to the person who has achieved virtue (though it is still, of course, of value to you and me who are still trying). We are reminded of Epicurus here: duration can add something, perhaps variation, but happiness is not the kind of thing that can be increased.

Since there cannot be more or less virtue, the Stoics are also compelled to revise our ordinary beliefs to the effect that acting in difficult circumstances, say, requires more virtue than doing an easy action. They hold the thesis that all virtuous actions

---

[67] Plutarch, *Comm not* 1062 b-d.
[68] *Fin* III 48; cf. IV 64–65; Plutarch, *Comm not* 1063 a-b.
[69] See the excellent article by Decleva Caizzi and Serena Funghi (1988).
[70] Arius 98.20–99.2.
[71] Plutarch, *Comm not* 1076 a.
[72] Cicero, *Fin* III 46–48.

are 'equal' ; for they all express virtue, which is a matter of getting things right, and not a matter of degree. This is an easy thesis to deride, and Plutarch duly claims that the Stoics are, unwillingly, committed to finding courageous endurance of surgery no more praiseworthy than courageous endurance of an insect bite, and so on.[73] For both are examples of courage, and the Stoics refuse to give any sense to one being more courageous, or demanding more courage, than the other. Again, however, the Stoics are not committed to absurdities here,[74] as long as we remember to distinguish the inner from the outer aspect of virtuous action. Insofar as a virtuous action is an exercise of virtue, the disposition to get things right, to do the right thing for the right reason, all virtuous actions, whether easy or difficult, display it equally, just because there cannot be more or less of it. This does not mean, of course, that the other features of the action, those making it easy or difficult, are irrelevant. The Stoics can perfectly well allow that they are relevant to what we care about in our actual practices of praise and blame, and thus that a Stoic will not diverge greatly from others in what he says by way of praise of reactions to severe pain and to insect bites. As Cicero puts it, 'One context in which one goes wrong [*in quo peccatur*] is more or less important, even though the actual going wrong is a single thing, whichever way you turn it.'[75] But he insists that there is something in every virtuous action which is the same, something which is simply an exercise of virtue in that it is a choice of the right action for the right kind of reason, whatever else is true of the action and the kind of indifferents involved in it.

> Virtue is a single thing, virtue in agreement with reason and continual consistency; nothing can be added to it to make it more of virtue, and nothing removed in a way that leaves it with the name of virtue. Indeed, if what is done well is what is done correctly, and there is nothing *more correct* than correct, certainly nothing can be found that is *better than* good. . . . And since the virtues are equal, correct actions when they proceed from the virtues must be equal.[76]

Here the Stoics come close to Kant's notion of the good will, and to his conception of virtue as strength of will.

The same can plainly be said of the even more notorious thesis that all actions which fail to be virtuous actions[77] are equally failures; in their case the actual Stoic view is easier to see.

> They say that all failures are equal, though not similar. For they are all in their nature produced as from the single fountainhead of vice, and the judgement in all failures is the same. However, depending on the external cause, since there is

[73] Plutarch, *Sto rep* 1038 e–1039 d. The example comes from Chrysippus, as does the unpleasantly sexist example of resisting the sexual attractions of an old woman, as opposed to resisting those of an attractive young one. On this passage, see, for an improved text, Algra (1990).

[74] See the sensible comments of Irwin (1990).

[75] *PS* 3, para. 20.

[76] *PS* 3, para. 22. Note that this 'paradox' on its own is not nearly as hopelessly out of tune with our intuitions as the other five which Cicero enlarges on. Wright (1991), p. 202, calls it 'the hardest to accept', but while it is initially unintuitive, it requires only a simple and fairly obvious distinction to defend it.

[77] The word is *hamartēmata*, which means a failure or mistake; the traditional rendering, 'all sins are equal' is highly misleading.

diversity in the means which are the objects of the completed judgements,[78] failures become different according to their quality.[79]

Cicero puts the point more intuitively:

'It is a small thing,' you say. But the fault is great; for failures [*peccata*, translating *hamartēmata*] are not to be measured by their consequences [*rerum eventu*] but by the vices of the agent.[80]

Just as virtue is getting it right, so vice is going wrong; but no more than getting it right can this be something that itself comes in degrees, even though there are degrees of goodness and badness in its consequences.

How could [failures] appear more trivial, since whenever one goes wrong one goes wrong through an upset of reason and order, while, once reason and order have been upset, nothing can be added to make it appear that one could go *more* wrong?[81]

So what matters, for the Stoics, is not what we achieve in what we do, but rather the attitude we have managed to develop to what we do. This inner achievement is not the kind of thing that can be measured; once it is achieved, nothing further is gained by staying in it longer. This is, of course, reminiscent of Epicurus, and to a certain extent the two theories are similar: both end up defending their candidate for happiness by extensively internalizing it. But there are equally significant differences. Epicurus' ideal of happiness, a quality of one's life which is experienced, allegedly, as extremely pleasant, is passive in two ways. It is negatively conceived, as untroubledness, absence of frustration and nuisance; and it is passive in that it happens to the agent who successfully adjusts her desires, but is not identified with anything she does. Although the Stoics agree that happiness is an inner state which, once achieved, cannot be increased, rather than in any condition of one's external circumstances, they identify happiness with something positive and active. It is the active exercise of virtue, involving everything we have seen by way of a developed disposition to do the right thing for the right reason, with all that that entails. We have seen that, because they sharply distinguish the value of virtue from that of other things, the Stoics are led to divorce the active exercise of virtue from its actual results, and to identify it with what I have called the inner aspect of virtuous action. But virtue is still taken to be something that the agent actively exercises, not a state that she passively is in.

This point emerges sharply in the Stoic attitude to suicide. They were widely ridiculed by their opponents for their view that, faced by illness, poverty and pain, it is rational to end it all. How can this be the case, however, when these things have merely selective value, while only virtue is good? Surely it should be loss of virtue alone which justified ending one's life? The Stoic response is perfectly clear: virtue is not just a state which the virtuous person has, but a disposition which is exercised, and life is not worth living if one is deprived of the chance of exercising one's virtue.

---

[78] Accepting Heeren's conjecture *mesōn* (genitive plural) for *meson*. The Greek is awkward and possibly the corruption goes deeper.

[79] Arius 106.21–26.

[80] *PS* 3, para. 20

[81] *PS* 3, para. 26.

Of course not every loss of a preferred indifferent will reduce one to that state. But it is realistic to allow that some conditions of deprivation are such that one has no chance of virtuous action. As we have seen, virtuous action can succeed even when the intended outcome fails, so these conditions will have to be extreme, so extreme as to threaten the agent's intellectual and affective state. When this happens, and there is 'not even the hope' of virtuous action, it is rational for the agent to commit suicide.[82] Happiness, then, is not just a state in which the agent is passively virtuous, but a state in which he exercises virtue, acts virtuously.

However, the Stoics add further characterizations of happiness, which stress the point that it is in fact a desirable state that one would reasonably want to be in. They characterize it as a condition of consistency, both internal (agreement with oneself) and external (agreement with nature).[83] The first point is easy to understand: the virtuous, and so happy person, will not be troubled by internal conflict. Since the virtuous person gets it right, she will not be troubled by regrets about having done the wrong thing. (She may, of course, regret undesirable consequences of a virtuous action, but that is a different thing.) And since the virtues are unified, an action in accordance with one virtue will not lead to regret or other kinds of conflict with actions done in accordance with another virtue.[84] (Again, this may leave room for some kinds of regret, but not regret for having done the wrong thing.) Agreement with nature comes in, in two ways. As humans who are part of the physical world, have bodies and so on, we cannot help but agree with nature in what we do. As rational beings we can reflect on our nature, and, when we realize that we are not just physical, etc., but also rational beings, we can choose either to agree with our rationality, and to think and act rationally, or to go against it and to think and act irrationally. If it is thinking rationally which leads us to grasp the distinctive viewpoint of virtue, we can see why the virtuous person will be the person in agreement with herself and with nature; the virtuous person is fully rational, and so her reflections do not lead her to go against the demands of her rationality.

Further, although the Stoics do not agree with Epicurus that untroubledness or tranquillity (*ataraxia*) amounts to happiness, they do hold that happiness will include tranquillity. From Zeno on they characterized happiness as 'a smooth flow of life' (*eurhoia biou*). And it is clear that their conception of the virtuous life would imply that it is undisturbed by internal conflict, given that the virtuous person lives in accordance with his rationality; he does not confuse moral with non-moral value, and so, much though he may be affected by damaging results of a virtuous action, say, he will not waver in his adherence to the virtuous attitude and what it demands. And he is not affected by emotions, which might disturb his attachment to the demands of rationality. But we have seen that the virtuous person is not affectless;

---

[82] Clement, *Strom* IV 6 (SVF III 765).

[83] Arius 75.11–76.6 tells us that Zeno called our aim living in agreement, and that Cleanthes added 'with nature'. However, Diogenes 87–88 tells us that the longer formula went back to Zeno. Clearly they were not felt to be very different, as indeed they are not, if agreement is thought of primarily as agreement in beliefs, and if our nature is that of a rational being, who will naturally be concerned about agreement in beliefs. See Inwood (1985) for an interesting discussion of the way this notion of agreement connects with Stoic philosophy of mind, in which all our mental acts, not just the ones that we call beliefs, involve assent to propositional content, and thus involve some kind of belief.

[84] See chapter 2, section 3.

his tranquillity does not exclude his having feelings, as long as these do not interfere with thinking and acting rationally.

In some authors we find the role of tranquillity in Stoic theory somewhat expanded; it figures as an attraction of the Stoic conception of happiness, a positive feature of Stoicism which makes us feel secure. Not only do we have what matters for happiness, according to these authors, but we feel secure about it, and this is an attraction of the Stoic position.[85] However, we do not find tranquillity figuring in this way in the early accounts of Stoic theory, and it seems illegitimate to let the notions of security and tranquillity play any major role in the theory. If we are tempted to seek virtue because it will make us tranquil and secure, we are missing the point about virtue that is most important; it is virtue itself that matters, not its results.

These claims about tranquillity and inner agreement bring Stoic happiness somewhat nearer to the intuitive conception. But no great weight can be laid on them, and probably none was meant to be. The weight of the Stoic case for the view that virtue suffices for happiness can never rest on our views about happiness. The Stoics have to assume that our intuitions about happiness are capable of quite extensive revision, and that this will happen once we are sure of the fundamental point about virtue and its kind of value. It is the peculiar nature of virtue which we have to understand if we are to understand Stoic happiness.

The Stoic insistence that the value of virtue and that of other kinds of things are not straightforwardly commensurable may seem one of most immediately accessible parts of their theory, for it is bound to seem to us like an insistence on the difference between moral and non-moral value. What is likely to seem most frustratingly alien is to find this insistence in a theory of the ancient pattern, which begins from reflections about one's final end and promises to produce a clear and decisive conception of happiness. Our first reaction may well be that the Stoics would have done better to eschew concern with happiness, and produce a theory of a more Kantian type, which exalted the importance of virtue but allowed that this could be at the expense of the agent's happiness. But this would be mistaken. We have seen that the Stoic insistence on the distinctive value of virtue plays a central role in their arguments about virtue and happiness. Indeed they establish their own account of virtue by way of criticising the Aristotelian theory for allowing that other valuable things besides virtue might be goods, and required for happiness.

The Stoics claim that their moral theory, as a whole, answers to life, and to our intuitions. But they are also aware that their claims about virtue appear, at least at first sight, paradoxical. There is no deep problem here, if we take it that, once the arguments about virtue and happiness have brought home the nature and importance of virtue, the agent revises her priorities accordingly, and revises her intuitions about happiness in line with this. After all, we knew that we had to revise our priorities; the only question is, how much. The Stoics are not afraid to begin by demanding a large step on the part of the agent, for they take it that, once the distinctive nature of the

---

[85] Cicero stresses tranquillity in the fifth book of the *TD*; this may be a personal slant on Stoic theory, however. Seneca is firm that the joy and pleasure that arise from virtue are not to be identified with virtue, the final good itself (*Vit Beat* 15.1–3). Marcus and Epictetus sometimes write as though what matters most about the Stoic final end is the tranquillity it produces; but if they seriously mean this, they are sliding into heterodoxy. See Irwin (1986) and Striker (1990).

value of virtue is recognized, the other adjustments will follow without too much trouble. Certainly they seem to have been well-advised in making this move; for they bring about a climate of thought in which, while an Aristotelian kind of theory is still seen as a possible option, Theophrastus is widely berated for defending the intuition that virtue is not sufficient for happiness. The Stoic arguments are sufficiently powerful that this is now seen, not as rock-solid common sense, as Aristotle saw it, but as highly vulnerable. Aristotelian theories henceforward need counter-arguments to defend themselves. The Stoics may not have convinced everyone, but they succeeded in shifting the terms of the debate.

20

Aristotelian Responses

Once the Stoic position had been put forward, would-be defenders of an Aristotelian position about happiness now required a more theoretically adequate defence. The Stoic view struck many, then as now, as outrageous, and they felt that something must be wrong with a position that makes virtue sufficient for happiness; but of course it is one thing to think this, and quite another to be able to defend it by producing cogent arguments and a defensible alternative. Theophrastus' reiteration of common sense merely cast doubt on common sense, as we have seen, in the face of the Stoic arguments. But the Stoic position produced fruitful reaction and rethinking of an Aristotelian kind. I shall consider three versions of this: (a) further developments in Aristotle's own philosophical school, the Lyceum; (b) the account of Aristotelian ethics that we find in Arius Didymus, a product of later Hellenistic thought in which Aristotelian ideas are presented in ways which owe a great deal to Stoic thinking; and (c) the theory of Antiochus, who produced a synthesis of Platonic, Stoic and Aristotelian thought, which he claimed to be the original tradition shared by all three schools. Antiochus' ethical theory tries to be a synthesis of Stoic and Aristotelian ideas; in so doing it respects our initial intuitions more than the Stoics do, but also aims to defend Aristotelian ideas against Stoic objections.

The Aristotelian response is, as we can see, fragmented. This is because, on the one hand, Aristotle's own school did not survive in the Hellenistic period as a powerful institution, particularly in ethics; on the other hand, the Stoic position is one which is bound to call forth powerful reactions, and it clearly seemed to many people that some form of Aristotelian theory about happiness must be the right one, even if they were not agreed on the moves to be made to defend it against the Stoic alternative. It is clear from Cicero's ethical writings, for example, that he is convinced that the most important ethical question is whether Stoics or Aristotelians are right about happiness. For ethics begins from reflections about our final end and how we should conceive of it. And the Stoic and Aristotelian views seem to Cicero to be the most serious contenders, and the ones most worth a reflective person's serious consideration.

1. *Aristotle's School*

Aristotle's own school, the Lyceum, petered out rapidly as far as ethics was concerned. It had in any case a troubled history in the Hellenistic period, because of damage and disruption during periods of war.[1] And the head of the school after Theophrastus, Strato, turned the school to a narrow concern with science. Some later heads of the school did write on ethical topics, but what we know of them gives us no reason to argue with Cicero's verdict that philosophically they were lightweights.[2] An interesting thread that can be traced through this rather unrewarding period of the school is a concern with a more hedonic view of happiness than we find in Aristotle. We find formulations which associate happiness and our final end with pleasure and tranquillity, freedom from pain and trouble.[3] However, they are merely formulations, with no supporting arguments. And the more they suggest the idea of tranquillity and freedom from pain, the less they sound like anything Aristotelian, as Cicero forcibly and correctly points out.[4] It is possible, of course, that these later writers were developing Aristotle's thoughts on pleasure, and Aristotle's suggestion that pleasure, so construed, might indeed be our final end.[5] But if so, there is little sign that they did so satisfactorily, or in a way that did justice to Aristotle's main discussions of happiness.

The only one of Aristotle's successors who defended an Aristotelian conception of our final end is the otherwise not very distinguished Critolaus. Cicero picks him out as the only explicit defender of the Aristotelian tradition.[6] He characterized our final end as 'the fulfilment of all the goods', where 'all the goods' explicitly meant, 'all three kinds of goods', that is, external and bodily goods as well as goods of the soul.[7] This may well seem a not very interesting suggestion. It explicitly claims that all three kinds of goods are needed for happiness, as against the Stoic view that only virtue, the good of the soul, is required. But we have no arguments, and it is not

---

[1] Lynch (1972).

[2] *Fin* V 13.

[3] Strato produced an account of the *telos* in terms of 'completing' potentiality and so actualizing it (Wehrli fr. 134); this becomes less mysterious if allied to Aristotle's conception of pleasure as unimpeded activity. Lycon characterized our final end as 'true joy of the soul' (Wehrli fr. 20). Hieronymus held that our end is freedom from pain (*vacuitas doloris, aochlēsia*; Wehrli frs. 8–18). Diodorus' view is represented as *to aochlētōs kai kalōs zēn* (Wehrli frr. 3–6), morality and freedom from trouble being combined in a way that we know little about; Cicero, our main source, sees it as an unsatisfactory combination.

[4] *Fin* V 14. Cicero claims that Hieronymus and Diodorus are not Peripatetics, at least in ethics. He contrasts them sharply with Critolaus and with Antiochus, who both, though in utterly different ways, defended an Aristotelian position.

[5] *NE* 1153 b 7–9.

[6] *Fin* V 14. The sentence is: *Critolaus imitari voluit antiquos; et quidem est gravitate proximus et redundat oratio; ac tamen is quidem in patriis institutis manet*: 'Critolaus wished to imitate the former [Peripatetics], and indeed is nearest to them in weightiness, and his style is copious; and he indeed remains within his inherited tradition'. Editors have generally inserted a *ne* before *is quidem*, feeling that the final clause draws a sharp contrast, given the *ac tamen*, which is lost unless Cicero is denying that Critolaus succeeded in imitating the ancients. (For a defence of this insertion, see especially Madvig *ad loc.*) The thought is then: 'but even he did not remain within his inherited tradition'. It is not necessary, however, to make Cicero write off every single later Peripatetic, as the insertion would do; he is clearly pointing out that Critolaus forms an exception to the dismal rule, and we should not destroy this point by a needless insertion.

[7] Arius 46.10–13: *to ek pantōn tōn agathōn sumpeplēroumenon (touto de en to ek tōn triōn genōn).*

clear what motivated Critolaus' choice of the idea of fulfilment to characterize the production of happiness.[8]

What is interesting about this formulation is that in one of our sources, Arius, it is ascribed to Critolaus, and severely criticized, on noteworthy grounds.[9] Only the goods of the soul are appropriate, says the critic (whether Arius or someone earlier), because it is activities of the soul alone that can make up happiness. Critolaus should have said 'activation' (*energoumenon*), rather than 'fulfilment' (*sumplēroumenon*), to stress the point that virtue is a *making use* of the other goods.[10] Critolaus' view, in other words, makes happiness too passive; it makes it sound as though we just need to have all three kinds of goods, and these will then make up happiness. The critic associates Critolaus with Epicurus in underestimating the need to consider happiness as *activity*, as a matter of what we *do*, rather than states of affairs which come about in our lives. Further, the criticism is taken to be a specifically Aristotelian one. In Arius' account of Aristotelian ethics, Critolaus' account is again rejected, in the interests of establishing as the proper account of happiness the Aristotelian one, that it is activity according to virtue.[11] A properly Aristotelian account of happiness, it is assumed, must make it essentially a matter of activity, and Critolaus' account fails to do this.

In another of our sources, however, Diogenes Laertius, Critolaus' definition is ascribed to Aristotle himself. Further, it is listed alongside another definition, that of 'making use of virtue', which contains just the element which Critolaus was criticized for lacking, that of doing something or acting.[12] Diogenes' account of Aristotle's philosophy is based on the kind of Hellenistic account of which we have an example in Arius;[13] but clearly we have a striking disagreement here. Critolaus' formulation 'updates' Aristotle by explicitly referring to three kinds of goods, and thus taking a stand against the Stoics. One interpretation of Aristotle's ethics, however, regards it as obviously in tune with Aristotle's stress on happiness as an active life according to virtue, and thus as also being in tune with another reformulation in terms of *making use*. Another interpretation, however, regards it as equally obvious that Critolaus' formulation is a mistake, just because it suggests that happiness is not essentially something active.

As for a solution to the problem of the relationship of virtue and the external goods in happiness, we know that Critolaus was the source of a striking image which is prominent in Antiochus' account, so presumably his solution was on Antiochus' lines; but we lack any independent account of Critolaus' reasoning.[14]

---

[8] The idea appears at *Fin* III 41 and 43, in a contrast of Stoics and Peripatetics; perhaps it was a common term in Hellenistic debates.

[9] Not necessarily Stoic, as Wehrli claims in his commentary (the passage is his fr. 19).

[10] Arius 46.13–20. See chapter 1, pp. 36–7.

[11] Arius 126.12–127.2. See p. 415.

[12] Diogenes V 30. The first definition is *chrēsis aretēs*. The critic in Arius says that Critolaus ought to have emphasized (but didn't) *to chrēstikon tēs aretēs*. Diogenes' version differs from Arius' only in having *sumplērōma* instead of *sumplēroumenon*.

[13] See Moraux (1986); cf. especially pp. 289–90 on the account of ethics: 'On ne peut guère concevoir que l'exposé de Diogène ait vu le jour à une époque ou on lisait attentivement et commentait dans le detail un traité comme l'*Éthique à Nicomaque*. . . . Tout nous engage plutôt à y voir une sorte de catalogue des positions que la doxographie tenait pour caractéristique de l'aristotélisme'.

[14] Cicero, *TD* V 50–51.

The somewhat depressing conclusion that it seems reasonable to draw from this is the following. As far as Aristotle's own school went, only Critolaus made a serious attempt to recast an Aristotelian position about happiness; and whatever it was that he said to motivate his view, it was not enough to prevent its being taken in radically different ways. No progress seems to have been made, in Aristotle's own school, in recasting Aristotle's ethical position in up to date and defensible ways.

2. *Arius Didymus' Account of Aristotelian Ethics*

Arius' account of Aristotle's ethics diverges from Aristotle's own, as we have seen,[15] in that it does not start by developing the notions of final end and happiness as Aristotle does in the *Nicomachean Ethics*; rather it begins from a long account of *oikeiōsis*, recast to produce Aristotelian rather than Stoic conclusions. This culminates in an account of happiness which distinguishes the Aristotelian position sharply from the Stoic one in two ways.

First, as we have already seen,[16] Arius insists that all three kinds of goods are required for happiness—bodily and external, as well as virtue, the good of the soul, which according to the Stoics is all that is required.[17] However, this position is open to more than one kind of interpretation, and Arius distinguishes his from Critolaus' kind. External and bodily goods, he insists, are not actually parts of happiness; they are necessary prerequisites, but are not the right kind of thing to make up happiness.

> Those who think that [bodily and external goods] fulfil [*sumplēroun*] happiness do not know that happiness is life, and life is the fulfilment of [*sumpeplērōtai*] action. No bodily or external good is in itself an action, or in general an activity.[18]

Arius is concerned not to let one important feature of Aristotelian ethics—recognizing other kinds of valued things besides virtue as good, and thus as desirable in the happy life—conflict with another, the characterization of happiness as activity. The result is a useful distinction: bodily and external goods are not part of the active life which constitutes happiness, although they are, *contra* the Stoics, required for it. Later the point is made that bodily and external goods are like tools and materials for virtue, as a skill or *technē*, to make use of.[19]

Second, happiness is characterized consistently as requiring both virtue and external goods. The point is made in terms of actions or circumstances which are 'preferred' (*proēgoumena*). This is a non-Aristotelian term, which by Arius' time has become established as the term to express the idea that virtue must be exercised in a

---

[15] Chapter 12, section 3.

[16] Chapter 12, section 3, pp. 284–85.

[17] The long *oikeiōsis* passage has provided an argument against the Stoics for insisting on this: namely, that an adequate account of our natural development will show that a rational attitude to our life requires prizing all three kinds of goods, rather than leading to an attachment to virtue which is different in kind from our other attachments, and which leads us to downgrade the value we attach to them.

[18] Arius 126.22–127.2. See chapter 1, pp. 36–37.

[19] 129.19–130.12.

life which is adequately equipped with bodily and external goods, for the person's
life to be happy.[20]

Several definitions of happiness are given in the course of the Arius passage.
Before the discussion of happiness and virtue proper, we find two statements to the
effect that happiness is virtuous activity 'in' or consisting 'of' actions which are both
fine (and thus characteristic of virtue) and 'preferred'.[21] These formulations are
explained when we are given three different definitions of happiness, regarded as
equivalent:

> Happiness is 'a preferred making use of complete virtue in a complete life', or 'the
> activity of a complete life in accordance with virtue', or 'unimpeded making use
> of virtue among things in accordance with nature [*ta kata phusin*, i.e., natural
> advantages]'.[22]

The second formulation is close to one in the *Eudemian Ethics*,[23] but the other two
recast Aristotle's ideas in later terms. There is no doubt, however, that the point of
them is to sustain and clarify Aristotle's point that virtue does not suffice for
happiness; bodily and external goods are also required. In fact we find the bald
claims that 'not every fine action is such as to produce happiness', and that virtue is
sufficient for a life which is fine, but not for one which is happy.[24]

Arius not only accepts, but explicitly develops, the 'external-use' interpretation
of Aristotle. Bodily and external goods enable us to develop and exercise the virtues,
but they also have intrinsic value of their own, and have sufficiently important value
that a certain level of them is necessary for the person to be happy. They do not
themselves form part of happiness, but they are necessary conditions for it.

Arius gives us no help with the problem of setting a workable minimum level of
external goods. He simply assumes that there is a level which is 'preferred', but does
not discuss what that level is. Nor does he discuss the problem that, if addition of
external goods makes a virtuous person happy, adding more goods should, it seems,
make her even happier. He assumes, that is, that there is an intuitively acceptable
'floor' of bodily and external goods for happiness, and likewise an intuitively
acceptable 'ceiling': after a certain point these goods will not make you any happier.
He is perhaps more entitled to hold this than Aristotle is, since he has taken over the
Stoic idea that virtue is a skill or *technē*, and also the idea that it consists in a way of
making use of other things. If bodily and external goods are thought of as necessary
material for exercising a skill, it might well seem patent that beyond a certain level,
more will not necessarily mean better; what matters is the use that is made of the
materials, and more than a certain amount cannot readily be put to use.

Arius does, however, meet head on the problem that puzzled Aristotle, about
the effect of losing external goods.[25] His answer is straightforward: external goods

---

[20] Wachsmuth consistently emends *proēgoumena* and variations to the corresponding form of
chorēgoumena, a term used by Aristotle. But this is needless; see Moraux (1973), p. 353, n. 117, and J.
Cooper (1985).

[21] 126.18–20, 129.19–20.

[22] 130.18–21.

[23] *EE* 1219 a 38–39. See Moraux (1973), p. 355.

[24] 131.12–13, 145.3–10.

[25] See chapter 18, pp. 380–381, 382–83.

are necessary conditions for happiness, so if and when you lose them, you do lose happiness, although you retain your virtue.

> The activity of virtue is 'preferred' because it is utterly necessary for it to exist among things that are by nature goods, since among evils the good person would make fine use of virtue, but will not be blessed [*makarios*]; among torments he would display nobility, but will not be happy [*ou mēn g'eudaimonesēi*].[26]

Arius in the Introduction denied that there was any real difference between using *eudaimōn* and using *makarios*,[27] and the solution is clearly not to distinguish two levels or kinds of happiness. Rather, Arius follows up the other trend in Aristotle's discussion, of distinguishing the state of the virtuous person who loses external goods from unhappiness. Unlike Aristotle, he freely uses the ordinary word for unhappiness, *kakodaimonia*.

> The person who has lost happiness is not unhappy [*kakodaimōn*], like the person who never had it at all, but can be in the middle. For both the wise person and the unwise sometimes live what is called the middle life, a life that is neither happy nor unhappy. . . . Happiness exists in beings which can live a rational life, but not always even for these, but only when they can live a preferred life. Just as happiness is called a making use of virtue, so is unhappiness a making use of vice; but it is not the case that just as vice is sufficient for unhappiness, so is virtue for happiness.[28]

This is one way of solving Aristotle's problem; Arius shares it with whoever is the source for Diogenes Laertius' Life of Aristotle,[29] and it is, as we shall see, distinctively different from the solution produced by Antiochus.[30] It retains the commonsense point that virtue does not suffice for happiness, allowing us to retain our intuition that, for example, Priam (assuming him to be virtuous) was happy, but ceased to be so during and after the Trojan War. The position is clearer than Aristotle's, however, in committing itself to the thesis that happiness and unhappiness are not exclusive opposites. The person who is virtuous but loses external goods reaches only a state 'in the middle'.

This is at first sight a solution that grants a great deal of weight to the intuition that virtue cannot suffice for happiness, because of the intuitive demand that happiness require some measure of success in worldly terms: health, money and so on. But it is not a wholly intuitive solution, as we can see if we reflect on the notion of unhappiness required. Unhappiness is no longer, as we might expect, a state of being miserable because of abject poverty, pain and so on. Rather, being vicious is sufficient for being unhappy, even if one has all one wants by way of bodily and

---

[26] 132.8–12.

[27] 48.6–11.

[28] 133.7–11, 19, 134.1. Moraux (1973), pp. 357–58, is right in seeing this passage as an example of later Aristotelians defending their position against the Stoics, but surely wrong to see the significance of the 'middle' state in its denial of a Stoic thesis; it provides an answer to an Aristotelian problem.

[29] See Diogenes V 30: 'Virtue is not sufficient for happiness; there is also need of bodily and external goods, since the wise person will be unhappy, if in troubles and poverty and the like. But vice is sufficient for unhappiness, even if external and bodily goods are present as much as you like'.

[30] In my view this is one of the main reasons for not treating the Arius passage and Antiochus in *Fin* V as variations on or derivative from a single common source.

external goods.[31] Thus we get the rather startlingly Platonic position that a paradigm of worldly success and fame is really unhappy, if she is wicked and immoral.

Aristotle, and any Aristotelian view, is committed to revising our intuitive notion of happiness, since they insist that happiness, as that recommends itself to the reflective, is not to be identified with mere worldly success, but requires virtue. This rules out from the start the position that one could be happy merely by having health, money, etc. Thus it might seem natural to deny that one becomes unhappy merely by losing these things. But there are, of course, a number of options about unhappiness. One could bite the bullet and say that the virtuous person does become unhappy when she loses health and money. Or one could say that happiness and unhappiness are symmetrical: just as the former requires virtue and also external goods, so the latter requires the absence of both: both vice and lack of health and money. This leaves room for a 'middle' state: the person who has lost health and money but remains virtuous. Nothing here requires the strong thesis that vice alone produces unhappiness, which renders happiness and unhappiness asymmetrical.

Further, the strong thesis is not only unnecessarily strong, it is so counter-intuitive that it undermines the motivation for holding that virtue is only a necessary, not a sufficient condition of happiness. What is the point of holding, as Arius so insistently does, that virtue in rags is not happy, if we have to hold that the wicked person in luxury, apparently flourishing and unrepentant, is really unhappy? Why is vice so much more powerful in its effects than virtue?

Thus Arius has chosen to defend a less counter-intuitive view of the relation of virtue and happiness than the Stoic one, but has done so by appeal to a position which is counter-intuitive in other directions. We can see the motivation for denying that the virtuous person who loses health and money becomes unhappy: that suggests an identification of the states of being happy and unhappy with mere possession of worldly goods. Happiness requires virtue; so we would expect that unhappiness would require vice. Both revise our intuitions, but equally so, and we are now able to recognize a middle state which makes the Aristotelian theory consistent. (The Stoics, of course, would deny the existence of any such middle state, but not on any clearly independent grounds.)[32] The position, however, seems to be weakened rather than strengthened by redefining unhappiness considerably more than happiness was redefined. In defending a plausibly Aristotelian account of happiness, Arius has produced a distinctly unAristotelian account of the relation of happiness to unhappiness.

---

[31] The latter point is clearer in Diogenes V 30 than in Arius.

[32] They hold that there is no middle ground between virtue and vice, and hence have to hold that there is none between happiness and unhappiness; but Aristotelians precisely deny that virtue is sufficient for unhappiness, at least. Later in the Arius passage the 'middle life' is described in Stoic terms (144.21–145.10). It is the state of the person who has not yet achieved virtue (and thus performs only *kathēkonta*) and is not yet virtuous; Aristotelians claim that it is also the state of the person who has achieved virtue but has lost the external goods. This is a little awkward; it would have been better to use different terms for these two states.

3. *Antiochus*

Antiochus, as we have seen,[33] produced an ethical theory which synthesized Stoic and Aristotelian ideas, and which, he claimed, represented the true Academic tradition, shared by Academics, Peripatetics and Stoics (though the Stoics perversely altered the terminology). On some issues Stoic and Aristotelian ideas are reasonably easy to harmonize; and Antiochus also applied Stoic approaches, for example giving a long account of *oikeiōsis* as the basis of ethics, to produce Aristotelian conclusions. However, on this issue, of the relation of virtue and external goods in happiness, the Stoics and Aristotelians are, and realize themselves to be, far apart. How could any theory *synthesize* them on this score?

At the outset of the presentation of Antiochus' ethics in Cicero's *de Finibus* V, the speaker insists that the Peripatetics present a unified view—with the exception of Theophrastus' book *On Happiness*, which admits the importance of factors not under our control. Piso, Antiochus' spokesman, dismisses with sneers the position which he understands as claiming that happiness is substantially dependent on factors outside our control.[34] And the position eventually defended is surprising. Our final end is to achieve all or the greatest natural advantages;[35] Antiochus holds that this is common ground to Stoics and Peripatetics. His long developmental account of how we develop naturally takes us from primitive self-concern which we have as children, to the rational concern that we will have as adults for goods of the soul, rather than bodily and external goods. And once we understand the nature of virtue we will grasp that its value far exceeds that of other kinds of goods, so much so that we require nothing further to be happy. Antiochus presents this as the consensus of the only philosophical schools that he takes seriously: 'And so the whole of that philosophy of the past grasped that the happy life is located in virtue alone.'[36] Antiochus has to hold this if he can claim to be using, rather than discarding, Stoic views on virtue and happiness. And he has particular reason to insist on the Stoic position on this point. It would be awkward to claim that he was producing the common core of a tradition if he had to reject the main thesis of one of its theories.

But he faces an obvious problem. He does reject the Stoics' insistence on the distinctiveness of virtue and the way its value cannot be straightforwardly compared with the values of other things- the move that necessitates calling virtue alone good, and inventing a great deal of artificial terminology. Without *this*, what could motivate the claim that virtue suffices for happiness?

Antiochus' position is especially problematic here, because he is a prime defender of the idea that there are three kinds of goods: external, bodily and goods of the soul: a position which renders impossible the Stoic kind of defence of the special value of virtue, and thus of its sufficiency for happiness. Antiochus' way of presenting natural development as a smooth and uninterrupted progression from primitive self-love to grasp of morality relies heavily on the idea that we progress from one kind of good to another, preferable kind, with no awkward leap from one

---

[33] Chapters 6 and 12.

[34] See above, chapter 19, for doubts as to whether Theophrastus' position was in fact all that different from the Aristotelian one.

[35] *Varro* 22, from a short summary of Antiochus' ethics.

[36] *Varro* 22.

kind of value to another, as the Stoics make out. But the more strongly you hold this, as Cicero and other critics point out, the harder it is to defend the idea that virtue suffices for happiness. If pain, poverty and disgrace are evils, then how can the virtuous person on the wheel be happy?[37]

Antiochus' solution is an ingenious distinction between happiness and complete happiness. Or, more accurately, he avoids talking of happiness at all, preferring to talk about the happy life (*vita beata*) or living happily (*beate vivere*), and holding that this does not amount to the completely happy life. Thus, while the happy life is located in virtue alone, 'yet the completely happy life [(*vita*) *beatissima*] is not so located, unless goods of the body are added, as well as the other things already mentioned, which are suitable for use by virtue.'[38] Given the premises Antiochus holds, this is what he has to say,[39] but he can only do so by dropping what for the Stoics is the main prop of the thesis that virtue suffices for happiness—namely the impossibility of comparing the value of virtue with the value of other kinds of things, and with it the impossibility of making virtue a greater good than it is by adding other kinds of things to it. Antiochus combines the Stoic thesis that virtue suffices for happiness with the commonsense point that some people can be happier than others, and that bodily and external goods make you happier than you would be without them. 'Those things which we call goods of the body do indeed make up [*complent*] the completely happy life, but in such a way that the happy life can exist without them.'[40] This is an ingenious solution. On the one hand it maintains the basic Stoic thesis, but refuses to reject the intuitive point that happiness does come in degrees.[41] On the other, it uses this solution to present a view which can be called both Stoic and Aristotelian. Antiochus almost certainly read the puzzling passage at *Nicomachean Ethics* 1100 b 22–1101 a 8[42] as distinguishing between two levels of happiness, and tailored his own view accordingly. For in that passage Aristotle talks not only of the happy person (*eudaimōn*) but also of the blessed person (*makarios*), and says that, since virtue shines through misfortune, 'the happy person could never become miserable—but he is not blessed either, if he meets with fortunes like Priam's'. The distinction between *eudaimōn* and *makarios* is merely stylistic, but Antiochus may have thought that Aristotle's use here indicated, if only implicitly, a distinction between a kind or level of happiness achieved by virtue, and a further kind, requiring also other, worldly advantages. Antiochus realized that he could use such a distinction, along with the intuitive point that happiness comes in degrees, to defend a view of happiness which emphasized the power of virtue to ensure happiness, with the Stoics and against Theophrastus, but also allowed that external

---

[37] See *Fin* V 84.

[38] *Varro* 22.

[39] As Cato, the Stoic spokesman, points out at *Fin* III 43.

[40] *Fin* V 71.

[41] There is a slight problem translating *beata*/*beatissima*. The latter is the ordinary superlative of the adjective, and so it might seem that the right translation must be 'happy/happiest'. But in English superlatives commonly have a suggestion of ranking: we assume there to be alternatives among which a winner has been ranked happiest. In Latin (and Greek) superlatives can commonly be used merely to indicate a very high degree of the quality; and I have accordingly translated *beatissima* as 'completely happy', to indicate that happiness can be a matter of degree, and there can be a very high or even maximal degree of it, but without suggestion of ranking among alternatives.

[42] See chapter 18, pp. 382–83.

goods can make the happy person even happier, with common sense and with the Peripatetic doctrine that virtue and other things are all good, have the same kind of value.[43]

This solution is not only ingenious, it is patently different from the kind of solution we have seen in Arius; and it is equally clear that the differences spring from Antiochus' desire to produce a theory which can be said to be Stoic as well as Aristotelian. It preserves the thought that virtue is sufficient for happiness, but refuses to abandon common sense; other things, like health, are good and their opposites bad. Aristotle is interpreted as holding, implicitly, what this theory brings out, a two-kind or two-level view of happiness. It is certainly a gallant try.

Is it, however, also a gallant failure? We find obvious objections to it in Cicero, who makes it clear that they were already standard. The theory takes pride in doing two things together: in making morality the most important thing in a happy life, and in refusing to flout our intuitions. Antiochus thinks that the Stoics are right in insisting that there is something special about virtue, that it is not *just* like other goods, but of its nature more important than they are, and that it is part of normal rational development to come to grasp this. But he also thinks that they are wrong to cut the value of virtue off so sharply from that of other kinds of things, and to say counter-intuitive things, such as that only virtue is good. But are these two aims compatible? Can a theory which pushes Aristotle so far in a Stoic direction really claim to be compatible with our intuitions? And, if it is in fact compatible with our intuitions, is it really pushing Aristotle over to the Stoics, or trying but failing to do so?

Cicero presents himself as a critic of the theory,[44] and makes some forceful points. He begins by claiming that it is inconsistent to hold (with the Peripatetics) that virtue is a good, not different in kind from other goods, and also (with the Stoics) that virtue suffices for happiness. Piso, the defender of Antiochus, answers this problem by means of Antiochus' famous distinction: virtue suffices for the happy life (*vita beata*) but not for the completely happy life (*vita beatissima*). Cicero objects to this making happiness a matter of degree. It implies absurdities, he claims, such as that someone can be happy but not happy enough, or too happy. These objections are less trivial than they may sound, for they should force Antiochus to define more clearly the sense in which happiness does come in degrees. But, whether fairly or not, Piso ignores this and retorts that it is even more absurd to deny that happiness does come in degrees: that commits you to saying that a virtuous person with every worldly success and comfort is no happier than a virtuous person in pain and disgrace.[45] This is, of course, what the Stoics do say, and it is, in isolation, extremely counter-intuitive. Cicero points out that Antiochus does not have as great

---

[43] Augustine, *Civ. Dei*. XIX 3, reports at length 'Varro on the authority of Antiochus', which would seem to be a reference to the second edition of the *Academica*; it adds one feature which is not in the part of *Varro* which we possess, namely that to achieve happiness we need virtue and the other goods of mind and body without which we would not have virtue. But life is happier if we have these other goods in their own right, and completely happy if we have them all. The last claim seems completely wrong, however; at *Fin* V 68 an account of Antiochean ethics contains the point that no one could ever achieve their final good if all those things which we find desirable were part of one's final good.

[44] In *Fin* V 77 ff.; also in *TD* V 50 ff.

[45] Cicero uses the Roman *exempla* of Quintus Metellus and Regulus, which gives us a striking example, but has to make it conditional—'*if* these people were virtuous.'

an advantage here as he might hope. From the point of view of what is intuitive, Antiochus has just taken over what is hardest to defend in the Stoic system: the claim that virtue suffices for happiness. And from the theoretical point of view the position is unsatisfactory. Someone might accept the Stoic thesis on theoretical grounds, unworried by its being counter-intuitive; but she would find this inconsistent with accepting that other things have the same kind of value as virtue, and can be added to it to make a better good than virtue alone. Cicero gives Antiochus a dilemma: either health, wealth, and so on are goods or they are not; but if they are, this is inconsistent with his Stoic thesis (virtue suffices for happiness) and if they aren't, this is inconsistent with his Peripatetic thesis (virtue is not incommensurable with other kinds of good).[46]

Piso's reply[47] appeals to intuition: *of course* health, wealth and so on are goods, and lack of them evil; and everyone thinks so, whatever they say. *But*, he adds, loss of them does not remove happiness, for virtue is so great a good that it will always on its own outweigh loss of other goods. Virtue can make us happy even among poverty, pain and so on; to deny this is like denying that a crop is good if there are a few weeds in it, or a business profitable overall if it sustains a few losses. 'Won't you judge of the whole [of life] from its greatest part? And is there any doubt that virtue so occupies the greatest part of human affairs that it obliterates[48] the other parts?'[49] Inconsistency is avoided by insisting that the effect of allowing that loss of external goods detracts from happiness is not as bad as feared. It *is* worse to be in pain than not, to be poor rather than rich, and so on. However, it is not *that* bad; not bad enough to make you unhappy if you are virtuous.

> Thus I will venture to call the other natural things 'goods'; I will not cheat them of their old name rather than think up a new one;[50] but I will place the great bulk of virtue in the other scale of the balance. That scale will weigh down both earth and sea, believe me.[51]

The weakness of this suggestion is obvious; it relies on the claim that we value virtue so highly that it is guaranteed to make us happy even among poverty, pain and so on. And, while Antiochus tries to defend this at length in his developmental account of how we come to recognize the claims of virtue, it remains unconvincing.[52] He is not, of course, claiming that we do in fact all value virtue as highly as this, but rather that people who develop naturally, and reach the natural culmination of their rational faculties, would do so. But even this claim is dubious; it certainly is not established by the kind of appeal that Antiochus makes to the results of our development.

---

[46] *Fin* V 86.

[47] *Fin* V 90–95.

[48] *Obruat.* Since Antiochus is talking of the power of virtue as against external evils, not external goods, this, unusually, comes near the thought that morality *overrides* other counter-considerations.

[49] *Fin* V 91.

[50] The text is corrupt here (see Madvig *ad loc*), but this does not affect the sense of what follows.

[51] *Fin* V 91–92. The image of the balance comes from Critolaus (*TD* V 51). It is sad that we cannot reconstruct Critolaus' own position on this issue; presumably he did not feel the same need that Antiochus did to synthesize Aristotle's ideas with Stoic ones, but it is hard to see what else could motivate such a position.

[52] See chapter 6, pp. 185–86.

Antiochus could indeed be said to get the worst of both worlds. He tries to produce an intuitive position, but parts of it remain stubbornly counter-intuitive, in spite of special pleading. And he does not produce a theoretically satisfactory position either; there is an ineliminable tension between the Stoic and Peripatetic elements in his account. We can see the depth of the problem if we reflect back to the most important formal constraint on the notion of happiness. Happiness must be complete; it must in some way include all the agent's valued goals. The Stoics can claim that virtue is sufficient for happiness only by insisting that goals other than virtue are not relevant for happiness, because they cannot meaningfully be brought into comparison with virtue. Antiochus rejects this move, and yet is left saying that the happy life requires virtue alone. Is the happy life then complete? But this is flatly inconsistent with recognizing that bodily and external goods matter to us, and are goods, objects of rational striving.

At this point Antiochus can make two moves, both bad ones. He can allow that the happy life (*vita beata*) is *not* complete; what *is* complete is the completely happy life (*vita beatissima*). But this utterly trivializes the thesis that virtue suffices for the happy life; this becomes no longer an interesting (and Stoic) claim about our final end, but an uninteresting (and unStoic) claim about what helps to make up our final end. Or he could insist that the happy life *is* complete. But then, what is added that is worthwhile by the external goods, in order to produce the completely happy life? How can it be better than something that is already complete? Further, if the external goods are of such little importance for the happy life that it can be achieved without them, why do they matter for the completely happy life?[53]

Cicero is correct here; the position that 'all virtuous people are always happy, but it is possible for one to be happier than another' is a problematic one, which needs to be defended 'again and again',[54] and does not withstand being thought through. Antiochus' solution is much weaker than the one we find in Arius; and it is no more intuitive, hard though Antiochus tries to do justice to as many intuitions as possible.

There is more than one Aristotelian response to the challenge of the Stoic position about virtue and happiness. Antiochus' is the most familiar, and may have been the most famous. Certainly he openly tries to be more intuitive than the Stoics, in an Aristotelian spirit, and he builds on what he takes to be an implicit distinction in Aristotle between two kinds of happiness, one secured by virtuous activity and one not. But his theory is not theoretically satisfactory nor, in the end, particularly intuitive. We find a more interesting and viable answer in Arius, one which seems to have been shared in Hellenistic accounts of Aristotle's ethics. But it, too, is not as a whole an intuitive position.

The debate between Peripatetics and Stoics on the nature of happiness, and the importance in it of virtue, seems in fact to have produced a result which is interesting in itself, quite apart from one's views about the respective merits of the answers. Aristotle begins by giving an account of happiness which includes both virtue and bodily and external goods. In so doing, he is trying, in standard

---

[53] For the last point, see Cicero, *TD* V 51.
[54] *Fin* V 95.

Aristotelian fashion, to do justice to our intuitions, to produce an account which will answer directly to some of them, modify others, and produce an account of why some others again are unjustified, or wrong. But with an issue like the relative importance for happiness of virtue and external goods this project turns out to be more elusive and difficult than Aristotle thinks. For it seems as though our common views themselves, the basis of the whole project, are deeply divided. Unreflectively, we associate happiness with success and with actual possession of affluence, worldly goods and success. But the account of happiness which an ethical theory has to produce must satisfy people who have reflected on virtue and what its significance is in our lives. And to those who do this, it seems clear that worldly success is not the point at all, that what matters is being virtuous, being a moral person as we nowadays say, and that if this is what matters, one has all one needs for happiness even if one loses all the worldly goods. This second set of thoughts may not be found in the majority of people, who do not reflect on their lives and final ends. But they are found in the people who need a proper answer to the question, what their final end consists in, namely the thoughtful people who have chosen to reflect on their goals, and in particular on virtue and its significance in their lives.

Thus, from the philosopher's point of view, the intuitions that must be satisfied are mixed, and pull in different directions. In the *Rhetoric*, where Aristotle is talking about everyday unreflected views about happiness, we can see that things like money and security are paramount. People find it important to be virtuous, but certainly not something to centre one's life around. In the *Ethics* we see the result of reflection: thoughtful people appreciate that what matters is being virtuous, rather than having various things like money and security. But how much more does it matter? Can being virtuous achieve happiness at the cost of pain and poverty? Aristotle is unwilling to allow this; he thinks of the original intuitions as still having considerable weight. It is just absurd, he thinks, to say that the virtuous person is happy on the rack. When we find the Stoics accepting this, and Theophrastus reviled for repeating Aristotle's rejection, it is clear that the debate has shifted. The intuitions of the *Rhetoric* no longer have any weight on their own. We have to choose between competing theories.

Can either side be said to win the debate? The Stoic position is clearly consistent, and each individually counter-intuitive thesis is well motivated and defended. On theoretical grounds it is clearly preferable to Aristotle's position, and certainly to Antiochus'. But it is possible, as we see from Arius, to produce a more consistent version of Aristotle's theory, which arguably retains the original motivation. And by the time we have these alternatives before us, how do we rationally make a choice? By this time none of the theories answer directly to the original intuitions; all of them make moves which have to be defended both by theory and by intuition. For here we clearly see, for the second and more important time,[55] the limits of ethical theory, at least of theory that aims to stand in a realistic relation to people's ethical views. Sometimes reflection serves to organize and unify our thoughts about an issue. But sometimes it reveals deep sources of division, and the more thorough the reflection, the more intractable the division appears. In the

---

[55] The first time was the division of our intuitions about emotion and its place in moral action; see chapter 2, section 2.

case of happiness, we find that *no* theory is satisfactory. Even one which is consistent, and well defended, finds a rival with equal advantage. We are led to reflect on the nature of our lives, and our search for happiness; but reflection delivers no one satisfactory answer. We shall see more about the implications of this in the next chapter.

21

Happiness and the Demands of Virtue

In this part we have looked at several extremely different account of happiness—pleasure conceived of as untroubledness, virtue alone or together with external goods. While these accounts differ, they emerge from a similar pattern of thought, which is the attempt to do justice to two sources of intellectual pressure.

On the one hand, what we need an account of is *happiness*, a life that can reasonably be said to be enjoyable or at least preferable. For ethical reflection takes its starting point from reflections on one's life as a whole, and begins by realizing that one has a final end, and seeking to make this more precise; and we cannot proceed to do this any other way than by asking what happiness consists in, since happiness is the only thing on which there is consensus that it is our final end: we all go for it, and we do not go for it for the sake of something further. On the other hand, happiness so far is a thin and unspecific notion, and so subject to considerable revision as the philosophical account progresses. A philosophical account of happiness has to be revisionary, for two reasons. One is that the drive to ethical reflection is a revisionary drive to begin with; it is dissatisfaction with one's life and with the conventional forces that have shaped it that leads to the reflection that seeks clearer and better answers through philosophy. The other is that ethical reflection leads us to see that virtue and the interests of others must play a role in my final end. Thus while we seek happiness, it is a happiness which must make accommodation to the intrinsic value of virtue, and to the interests of others, and the account of it will accordingly be revisionary of our ordinary views about happiness.

The Cyrenaics are the only school who deny the first point, that our final end is happiness; for they deny the fundamental point, that our final end must be what we seek in our life as a whole, and thus they seek to maximize episodes of pleasure, rather than looking for an aim that a person has in his life as a whole. The Sceptics accept this point—not as a premise that they believe in, of course, but as an appearance, a view of things that we are inevitably left with when argument *pro* and *con* has left us with no reasoned belief. Sextus indeed assumes not only that we are bound to organize our ethical thoughts around the conception of a final end but that, without accepting any theoretical beliefs, we will articulate it to some extent and will accept that the only thing that we really aim at is absence of pain and frustration. However, the Sceptics reject the second point—the need to revise our initial notion of happiness in order to accommodate the importance of virtue and the interests of others. Sextus shows no interest in giving virtue, or the interests of others, any role in our final end. He does not think that this makes the sceptic immoral and selfish; he assumes that he will have proper moral intuitions and will care for others, indeed have a 'philanthropic' desire to cure them of the miseries of their beliefs. But he makes no effort to give morality and other-concern a theoretically grounded place in our lives. And, as we have seen, the sceptic in fact has problems here; the assumption that we will care for these things, ungrounded by beliefs, is dubious, or even tends to conflict with other parts of the sceptical position. But it is clear why Sextus refuses to revise the sceptic's notion of happiness to include virtue and other-concern; it is because, as a sceptic, he rejects the very notion of reflection that leads to giving them this role. All the other theories urge us to revise our priorities; but for Sextus this is useless, or even harmful, since ethical reflection is dogmatic, assuming that things are good or bad, and for the Sceptic what matters is to get rid of beliefs, not to exchange some beliefs for others. It is because he rejects the very idea of ethical reflection that the Sceptic refuses to revise the content of the notion of happiness which, he alleges, we find ourselves stuck with.

It is obvious, however, that these are special cases. The Cyrenaics are unique among ancient ethical schools in rejecting any final end over the agent's life as a whole. And the Sceptics are unique in rejecting ethical reflection as useless for happiness. Those who do not share these special restrictions all work out their ethical theories within a common pattern: we seek happiness, but reflection reveals that happiness is very different from what we thought it was.

Happiness must be complete and self-sufficient, for our final end must be complete and self-sufficient; nobody except the Cyrenaics rejects that. Even Sextus takes it to be part of the notion of a final end which we can't help but have, that it has these properties. The felt pressure of these formal constraints on ancient theories is very strong. Epicurus' theory that happiness is pleasure, for example, appears most peculiar unless we see it as an attempt to cast pleasure as our end within such a eudaimonist framework. Epicurus insists that the pleasure we seek is not the kind of pleasure we grasp from pleasant felt experiences, but a negatively defined state of not being troubled; he insists that we require the virtues, and true friendship, to achieve it; and he emphasizes that we should restrict our desires, and lower our expectations, so as to avoid disappointments. None of this makes sense within the framework of classical hedonism; it makes sense only, as I have stressed, if we see Epicurus as putting forward a candidate for happiness which has to be shown to fit the formal requirements of being complete and self-sufficient. It is because pleasure must be complete that virtue must be shown to be intelligibly a way of achieving it; because it must be shown to be self-sufficient that it must make us invulnerable to disappointed desires; and so on. Given these constraints, we can see why the ideal hedonist is happy while screaming and groaning on the rack, a thesis that Bentham would certainly have regarded as lunatic.

Nor can we fully understand the debate between Stoics and Aristotelians about happiness, unless we bear in mind the importance of these formal features. Aristotle explicitly says that happiness must be complete and self-sufficient, and this lies behind his conviction that virtuous activity cannot itself amount to happiness, but must be supplemented by external goods. We have seen that the Stoic rejection of this thesis rests on their thesis that virtue has a value which is different in kind from that of other things, so that they cannot be added to it to make it a better good than it was before. Thus, the improvement in our lives that accrues when, as well as being virtuous, we are healthy and wealthy, is not to be construed as making virtue complete by adding other goods; virtue was complete to begin with, since the other kinds of things which we aim at and desire to have as well as virtue cannot be added to it in the way that goods can be added to an incomplete good to make it complete. The further debate of Stoics and Aristotelians on this score and the discomforts of Antiochus' theory spring from the importance of completeness.

Given the common character of the points already stressed, the different theories nonetheless come up with highly divergent accounts of happiness; and it might seem that little or nothing could be said that was generally true about them. But this is not so; and two unifying points in particular emerge from the theories that we have looked at. One is the idea that happiness, properly understood, is up to us; the other is the dominance of virtue.

We see clearly in Epicurus and the Stoics that happiness, though they construe it very differently, is taken to be up to us or in our power—not of course in the sense that I can here and now decide to be virtuous, but in the sense that virtue turns out to be an internal state, one which, once I achieve it, depends only on me and not on the success of my efforts in the outer world. This is a striking result, and worth investigation, but it should be stressed that it is a *result* of the two theories' development. Sometimes it is claimed, or implied, that ancient ethical theories, at least the Hellenistic ones, demand from the outset that happiness be shown to be something which is in the agent's power- that is, that it is a formal condition on happiness, at least for Epicurus and the Stoics, that happiness must be something which is up to me. This is a mistake, however. We have seen that the formal conditions which do do a great deal of work in various theories emerge naturally from intuitive reasoning; but it is hard to see how we could motivate an initial demand that happiness be up to me. Before any philosophical reflection has taken place, to say that happiness is up to me is simply to say something very silly. Obviously happiness, at the intuitive level, is *not* up to me; it involves success in ways which depend heavily on other people, and the world generally. And the demand, ahead of any actual theorizing, that happiness must turn out to be something which is not in this way dependent, is just wishful thinking. If this demand were in fact to be a formal demand prior to giving happiness content, it would be arbitrary in the extreme. But it is not in fact such a prior demand. If it were, the actual theories would develop in ways rather different from the ways in which we have seen that they do develop. The position that happiness lies in something internal to the agent and thus does not depend on actual success or achievement, is one which emerges as a result of the developments of theory, not as a demand which shapes the development itself.[1]

---

[1] It has been put to me (by Terry Irwin) that the picture looks somewhat different if one takes into account the uncompromising attitudes of Socrates, which were held as an ideal by many of the Hellenistic schools (particularly the Stoics and Sceptics). For it is the thrust of many passages in Plato's Socratic dialogues that, appearances notwithstanding, happiness is up to the agent. I am far from denying that such Socratic ideas were influential, but I would hesitate to give them a role in the actual philosophical arguments and theories of the schools. They seem to belong rather at the level of rhetorical presentation of the theory in terms of an ideal philosophical type (a theme excellently discussed in Decleva Caizzi's 1988 book). They are prominent in the Cynics, who deliberately do not even have a worked-out

The Sceptics are the furthest from thinking that happiness is something which is up to the agent, for according to them our conception of our final end is freedom from trouble, and there are some troubles which nobody can escape, namely physical pain and the like. They urge that the person who successfully loses all his beliefs will in fact be better off than the person who has not, since a great deal of the negative aspect of pain, for example, lies in the agent's belief that pain is a bad thing, and so the person who lacks this belief will be better off than the person who has it. But this does not, of course, remove the pain; it only makes it (allegedly) easier to bear. For the Sceptics, happiness is never going to depend just on the agent, since, being human, we all care about pain and the like, which we are exposed to. And the Sceptic quietism on this score seems to be due to their refusal to engage in ethical reflection and theory. If we start from what we must take for granted, and refuse to engage in belief or reasoning about it, we will never develop theoretical grounds for holding that happiness is up to us. The Sceptics are in fact a useful test case for showing that this thesis could never have been an initial demand of ancient ethical theory. The Sceptic, with her final end of untroubledness, is the person, if anyone is, to want to have a final end which brings with it independence of the world. But the Sceptic's end is actually *less* up to the agent to achieve than the Stoic or Epicurean end is, and this is because the Sceptic refuses to go in for ethical theorizing.

Epicurus, as we have seen, holds the thesis that pleasure is not increased, only varied, by duration; and theses which are mutually dependent with this one are central in his thought, notably that death is not an evil, not even though it appears to deprive us of future goods. This thesis would be completely unaccountable in a classical hedonist; it would make no sense at all to Bentham, for example. Why does Epicurus hold it? Under pressure from the formal conditions, he specifies the pleasure which is our final end as *ataraxia*, freedom from trouble. So conceived, it is clearly not to be identified with pleasant feelings, but is a state of tranquillity which, once achieved, is displayed in all one's actions. But a state of such a kind is not the kind of thing one can have more or less of, or aggregate amounts of. Hence, once one has achieved it, there is no reason to go on wanting more of it; hence no reason to feel deprived if one dies sooner rather than later. As we have seen, this will only work if one is prepared to discount the natural shape of one's life, for we intuitively feel that the person who dies at eighteen (even supposing him to have achieved a state of untroubledness) is deprived of something which would have improved his life, whereas according to Epicurus he is not. Here we find that Epicurus is led by the effect of the formal constraints on his concept of pleasure, if it is to serve as a candidate for our final end, to locate our final end in a state which is indifferent to the normal contours of a human life. Pleasure is our final end; but for it to be complete and self-sufficient it must be the kind of pleasure which is *ataraxia*; but this turns out not to be the kind of end which can be increased over a lifetime, since it is not the kind of thing which can be aggregated at all.

The Stoic final end, virtue, also turns out to be indifferent to the characteristic temporal shape of a human life. It differs from Epicurus' end in that the latter is passive, a state that one gets into by altering one's attitudes but which, once

---

philosophical theory. From the fact that a theory takes Socrates as a 'type' suitable for presenting itself, we cannot infer that Socratic ideas serve as premises in that theory.

achieved, is defined by what does *not* go on: one is not frustrated, troubled and so on.[2] The Stoics, however, stress that virtue is a skill, a way of putting other factors in one's life to use. Thus their theory has more continuity with the initial intuitions that happiness is a matter of activity, of living one's life, not a state of affairs that just happens to you.[3] However, because of the sharp line they draw between the value of virtue and the value of other kinds of things, it turns out that the worth of a virtuous action resides solely in its inner aspect, as an exercise of a virtuous disposition, and not at all in the outer aspect, the actual result achieved in terms of indifferents. Hence for them also virtue becomes something internal to the agent, for in various circumstances the actual exercise of virtue may make no mark at all in the external world. A virtuous action may be completely frustrated; or courage may be shown in a very trivial action, and so on. It is odd to think of the virtuous person as having, in these cases, successfully exercised his skill. Virtue seems in these cases to have lost the features which made ordinary skills a good analogue for virtue in the first place. And in the modern world we are inclined to identify the inner aspect of Stoic virtue not with an activity but with the antecedent of activity, some kind of intention or willing. Whether counter-intuitive or not, however, Stoic virtue is firmly internalized to the agent.

It is not, however, internalized in response to a prior demand that happiness be something which does not depend on external contingencies. We can underline this point by looking back at the Aristotelian-Stoic debate over happiness. The Stoics hold a position which implies that happiness is in the agent's power, since virtue is, and virtue constitutes happiness. The Aristotelians hold that happiness also requires external goods, and thus is not in the agent's power, but also depends on the contingencies of fortune which distribute bodily and external goods. We have seen that different Aristotelian responses differ in the emphasis they put on this point, with Theophrastus being seen at one end, and Antiochus at the other. But this debate does not start from the assumption that happiness must be in the agent's power. Rather, it is a debate about the nature of virtue and its relation to other valued things. Can virtue fulfil the formal conditions for being happiness all on its own? Intuitively we think that health, wealth, etc., make a virtuous life better; but, as we have seen, it does not just follow that virtue is not complete, for that depends on the view one takes as to the relation of virtue to other valued things. Debates as to whether happiness is or is not up to us are a result of this debate; they are not what starts it off. Indeed, as I have emphasized, until the philosophical debate gets going it is dubious what sense there is to saying that happiness is up to us; the philosophical debate starts from everyday views about happiness, and, at the level of those views, the thesis is just silly.

The other unifying thought is what I shall call the dominance of virtue. Only the Sceptics are uninterested in establishing a place for virtue as part of or needed for

---

[2] Of course nobody is exempt from physical pains, so it might look as though Epicureans here are in the same position as the Sceptics; but they are not, given Epicurus' strategies to produce an attitude which will diminish the importance to the agent of the physical pains when they happen. The Sceptics actually take over some of these strategies (see above, chapter 17, p. 361), but with less force, since for them they are not embedded in an overall theory, but merely put forward (implausibly) as recommendations which all will agree on.

[3] See chapter 1, pp. 36–37.

happiness; and this is because they reject any role for ethical reflection and theory in achieving happiness. Epicurus, as we have seen, has to claim that virtue is required to achieve happiness, implausible as that claim is when happiness is conceived as pleasure, and unsuccessful as Epicurus' own attempts turn out to be. In all the other theories we can see that an acceptable account of happiness has to give virtue a dominant role. Indeed, the Aristotelian-Stoic debate takes the form of asking, Is virtue sufficient for happiness, or necessary but not sufficient?

In twentieth century moral philosophy it is often regarded as problematic whether virtue is even necessary for happiness, and these ancient discussions may seem alien; frequently they are not taken really seriously. Much of the reason for this, however, lies in misunderstandings which I hope have been removed by now. In modern theories happiness is often treated as a definite goal, independently specifiable as a state of pleasure or satisfaction; and this can lead to regarding the ancients as engaged in the high-minded but quixotic and hopeless task of showing us that virtue leads to *that*. Or the ancients may be presented with more credible views by endowing them with a different task: that of showing that certain dispositions to excel in various useful ways lead to happiness. But it is clear by now that both these approaches are mistaken. Another source of misunderstanding is that in modern moral philosophy the notion of virtue employed is often impoverished and radically unintellectual; but again it should be clear by now how different this is from the ancient notion.

Ancient debates about virtue and happiness are recognizably debates about the place of morality in happiness; and, giving due weight to the greater flexibility and revisability of the ancient notion of happiness, we could perhaps best restate them as debates about the place of morality in the good life, or the life one would choose to live. Intuitive views give *some* role to morality, but not a dominant one. Aristotle revises the commonsense notion of happiness in insisting that virtue is necessary for happiness: health, wealth and the goods of popular esteem cannot make a person's life satisfactory. Our lives will only achieve a final end which is complete and self-sufficient—the aim that we all inchoately go for, and try to make precise through philosophy—if our aims and actions are subordinated to, and given their roles and priorities by, a life of virtuous activity: a life, that is, lived in a moral way, from a disposition to do the morally right thing for the right reason, and with one's feelings endorsing this. Nonetheless, happiness requires external goods as well: morality is required to give a life shape in a way that will render its final end complete and self-sufficient, but it seems absurd to talk of happiness when someone meets great misfortunes and is virtuous, but dying on the wheel.

When the Stoics challenge this, and argue that virtue is sufficient for happiness, they are left with the conclusion that the virtuous person slowly dying on the wheel is happy. We can regard them here as simply accepting an intuitive absurdity for the sake of a theory. In some parts of twentieth-century ethics this is regarded as a kind of advantage: a sign of the bold theorist untrammelled by old-fashioned intuitions. But we have seen that in ancient ethics the picture is more complex. For once we have two developed theories going, the answer as to which of them is right on this issue is no longer regarded as settled by intuition; we also have to look at the issue of which side's arguments against the other are the stronger. Hence the complex debate which gets more and more sophisticated in isolating key principles and their roles in the arguments.

However, intuitions cannot be left out of the picture altogether. On the one hand Aristotle appeals to the absurdity of saying that the virtuous person on the rack is happy, and later Antiochus to the absurdity of saying that the prosperous and successful virtuous person is no happier than the virtuous person on the rack. But on the other side, the Stoics' arguments to show that adding prosperity to virtue does not add more of what was there already depend on accepting a point which they cannot prove, but must rely on, namely that virtue cannot be assessed against other kinds of things, but has a different kind of value. Kant does not argue that moral reasons are different in kind from other kinds of reason; he asks how best we are to account for this. Similarly the Stoics do not ask whether virtue is different in kind from other things, and produces demands which cannot be weighed up against other demands but must sweep them away; rather they produce a theory which accounts for this, and criticize the Aristotelians for putting virtue on the same scale as health and wealth. At many points the Stoics take for granted something which their theory accounts for, and which other theories do not: the distinctiveness of virtue. The process of *oikeiōsis* results in moral development when the agent realizes the distinctive nature of virtue and the reasons stemming from virtue; virtue is said to be good and all other valued things indifferent because of what is distinctive in kind about it; virtue suffices for happiness, though this may initially shock, because other kinds of valued things are not the kinds of things that could make virtue any better. In all this it is amply clear by now that what is being got at is the distinctive nature of morality, and that the Stoics are claiming that only their theory does justice to this. It is too simple, therefore, to see the Stoics as simply producing a more counter-intuitive theory of happiness than Aristotle does. They claim that only their theory does justice to our intuitions about the nature of morality. And it is easy to see how they would be able to claim that these are deeper and more important intuitions than the ones about happiness that Aristotle appeals to. For we have repeatedly seen how indefinite are ancient views of happiness, and the Stoics may reasonably have thought that they should give way before a theory which properly articulates our views about virtue.

This raises again an issue which was briefly touched on above.[4] Are the Stoics right in thinking that this is what is demanded by intuitions about virtue? Could not Aristotelians retort that the Stoic theory is, indeed, counter-intuitive, since intuitively we do treat virtue, health and wealth as all being goods, all capable of being assessed on the same scale? These may seem useless questions, since of course we cannot do an opinion poll on ancient views about virtue and find out empirically which theory answers best to most people's views. But this response would be a mistake, for as we have seen no ancient theory thinks that the views of most people, just as they stand, form a suitable criterion for testing ethical theories. Rather, a good theory is not the one which makes most common opinions turn out to be true, but the one which answers to the most important ones, and can show why others have to be rejected or modified. Thus, an ancient Stoic, faced by an opinion poll which showed that most people found Aristotle's theory more convincing, would

---

[4] Chapter 19, pp. 394–95.

simply reply that that was because most people gave too much uncritical weight to their intuitions about happiness, and that when they reflected on virtue they would come to see that only the Stoic theory answered to their considered intuitions about virtue.

The real problem is rather that even on the level of reflection it is not clear whether the Stoics or Aristotelians are right. We can see this just from the indecisive result of centuries of discussion. Cicero in his philosophical works uses the Stoic theory to demolish the Aristotelian one and vice versa—not out of irresponsibility, but because he genuinely sees the difficulties on each side. Even to someone familiar with all the arguments and the different demands which the different theories make on our intuitions, it can seem unclear where the truth lies. I have already said that this resembles our modern situation in ethical theory: there are a number of established theories, all of which have familiar arguments against one another, and also claim support from our intuitions.[5] While the ancient debate about virtue and our final end does not answer exactly to any modern debate, we can easily see the analogue. We all agree that morality matters, and that it should play a part in our lives. But how big a part? Is morality so important that it should override other considerations? Is a moral life one that is lived with a disposition always to let morality override these other considerations? Kant thinks that on reflection we will agree that this is what we think. But to many it has seemed that our reflected views do not support a position as strong as this. How are we to find the truth? By developing theories, but also by appealing to the results of our reflection—and we are likely to find this as indecisive as the ancients did.

Cicero is particularly interesting to us here, because in him we can see an educated and intelligent person, who is aware of the arguments on either side and of the considerations which either side considers to be convincing, and who finds it genuinely difficult to commit himself to either position. Technically, Cicero writes always as an Academic Sceptic—that is, as someone who is presenting what seems to him at the time to be the most plausible and convincing position, but who is not committed to its truth. He seems to find a personal kind of satisfaction in the Stoic account of happiness that he fails to find in the Aristotelian alternatives.[6] In the last book of the *Tusculan Disputations* and the last book of the *De Officiis* he defends Stoic views on the final end with energy and passion. Yet he is always aware that this is what seems to him convincing at the moment, that he has defended opposing views in the past, and may do so again in the future. 'He may not have made up his mind to his dying day concerning the sufficiency of virtue to happiness and the importance of external goods'.[7] Cicero is always aware that, however personally committed he may be at any given time to a theory, it is still a *theory*, with arguments for and against. Each side is convincing in its appeal to intuitions, but both sides appeal to intuitions, and they seem to have equal force. For our unreflective views here seem to be divided against themselves, and the result of reflection is to make

---

[5] Some theories, like consequentialism, make a great virtue of rejecting ordinary intuitions in the name of theory. But theory has to be supported somewhere (at least ethical theory, which has to be lived by); and consequentialist arguments in fact appeal all the time to our reflected intuitions for support.

[6] Cf. *TD* IV 53, where he says that, however accustomed he is to attacking them, as Carneades used to, still, 'I fear that they may be the only philosophers'.

[7] Glucker (1988), p. 69.

the difference sharper, rather than to resolve it without further question. And so the state of being convinced by a theory, and by the intuitions it appeals to, can never be the end of the story—at least, not to a reflective person, who will sooner or later rehearse the counter-arguments.[8]

A passage of Cicero[9] expresses very well the predicament of the thoughtful and seriously reflective person in the ancient world, faced by the dialectical development of various theories about happiness. On the one hand, nothing could be more important than to settle in determinate terms the question of what our final good, happiness, actually is. For this is the central question of ethics, not a trivial detail. To the thoughtful person, theories that make happiness a form of pleasure have some obvious advantages, but these turn out on inspection to be superficial; the only theories worthy of serious consideration are those that give virtue a dominant role. But this takes us right into the debate between the Stoics and the Aristotelians: how dominant is virtue? It should be important in one's life. But can it be important enough to sweep aside other kinds of valued aim so completely that we can be said to be happy if we are virtuous, regardless of pains and disasters? Isn't it more reasonable to hold that, while virtue matters, it is not the only thing that matters for happiness; we need some level of bodily and external goods as well?

> Zeno thinks that the happy life is located in virtue alone. What does Antiochus think? 'Well, happy,' he says, 'but not completely happy'. The former is a god, holding that virtue lacks nothing; the latter a mere mortal, thinking that there are many things other than virtue which are in part dear to humans, in part even necessary. And yet I fear that Zeno ascribes to virtue more than nature permits, especially since Theophrastus argues the opposing case at length and eloquently. But still, I am afraid that *he* [Antiochus] is scarcely consistent when he says that there are certain evils of the body and of fortune, and yet holds that a person who is among all of these will still be happy, provided that he is virtuous.[10] I am dragged in different directions—at one time one view seems more convincing to me, at other times the other. Still, unless one or other of them is the case, I firmly believe that virtue is defeated. But—just on this issue they disagree.

We can feel sympathy for this position. For it is abundantly clear by now that the ancient debate about the place of virtue in happiness is not some conceptually alien debate that we can barely understand, but closely akin to a debate about the place of morality in our lives. We too can agree that morality must have an important place in our lives, and that theories which deny this, or have difficulty in accommodating it, are to that extent discredited. But this leaves us with the problem: How important should morality be? We see a grossly immoral person flourishing, and a moral person in circumstances reduced by injustice or bad luck. We too are torn: we can see the

---

[8] It is often assumed that Cicero comes down in the end for the Stoic view, because of the vigour with which he presents it in writings produced at the very end of his life. But the passion involved internally, in presenting a position, is always matched by awareness that this is only one possible position. See the end of Annas (1989a) and Glucker (1988), who points out that Cicero's situation at this time made the question of virtue and happiness salient and pressing for him, and that just this fact stood in the way of his accepting any one solution to it.

[9] *Luc* 132–141. The passage translated comes from 134.

[10] '*He*' cannot refer to Theophrastus, as we might expect, since his view was clearly that the virtuous person in misfortune is *un*happy.

point of claiming that the latter has everything that really matters, and that she has not lost anything worth having as long as she has not compromised her integrity. But we can also see the point, all too clearly, of the claim that the first person has things that matter too, and that it sounds odd to say that the second person is better off.

Cicero tells us that Carneades, the great Academic sceptic, frequently used to argue that 'whatever be the opinion of the philosophers with their disagreements about final ends, still virtue has adequate security for a happy life.'[11] This sounds as though it could defensibly be claimed that the intuitions about virtue to which the Stoics make appeal had to be recognized even by those who rejected Stoic arguments; and this would indicate that Stoic arguments had an advantage here. But we are also told that Carneades did not commit himself to this thesis, but used it only to argue against the Stoics.[12] So there is no bedrock here that can be used to decide between theories. Once we have started reflecting, we cannot go back. But reflection on the fundamental question of ethics—the determinate nature of our final end—leaves us with decisions still to make, arguments to decide between.

Sometimes it is thought to be a peculiarly modern predicament that we live in an age when no one type of ethical theory commands general allegiance, and, while some are clearly better than others, none has an overwhelming superiority. We can see from Cicero that there is nothing new about this predicament. It is clear that morality is important to us, but what we urgently need to know is, just how important. But on this, it appears, reflection can never be decisive.

---

[11] *TD* V 83.

[12] Why *against* the Stoics? Presumably he was attacking their arguments here, rather than their conclusions.

V

Conclusion

22

Morality, Ancient and Modern

In this part I will try to draw together some of the themes that have emerged from the lengthy explorations of the previous four parts. Before doing so it is, I think, a good idea to reiterate two points made initially in the introduction. One is that the form of ancient ethical theory, as I discern that, has emerged from the comparative discussions of different ancient theories. I have tried to lead the reader along with me in the process of seeing this happen, rather than laying out the entire abstract structure beforehand and then going through the ancient material for confirmation, checking off similarities and differences as noted. Some readers will undoubtedly have felt dissatisfaction; they will have felt that I have not ascended quickly or firmly enough to the universal, and have spent longer than they desired on the detail of the theories, rather than devoting time to sharpening and making precise the extracted principles which define ancient ethics. Some will even feel that I have presented the material for a study of the form of ancient ethical theory, rather than that study itself.

In fact I would not feel that the book had been a failure even if that was all that it had achieved. For study of ancient ethical thinking has long been confined to the minute study of particular theories, particularly Aristotle's; it surely cannot be a bad idea to supplement and enrich this with study of issues that appear pressing, or indeed appear for the first time, when different theories are put together with a view to discerning their common structure. And I would further repeat the point that we are not yet at a stage where we should feel confident in proceeding very far with formalizing the principles of ancient ethics and subjecting them to rigorous discussion in the abstract. Before we do this we should check them against the detail of different theories and establish whether they do indeed emerge in the way that I have claimed that they do, or whether the picture I have presented should be corrected in minor or major ways. Nevertheless, we can draw some conclusions, definite if not rigorously formalizable, and that is what I have tried to do in this part, as well as in the opening and concluding remarks to each of the previous parts.

The second preliminary point which bears repeating is that in discussing ancient theories alongside, and in terms of, modern moral theories, the aim has not been to give the ancient theories a factitious glamour by showing them to be of interest to moderns. The aim has been the opposite: instead of imposing modern concerns on ancient theories, I have tried to remove modern preconceptions as to what they are theories of. And this is best done by facing, rather than by trying to ignore, our own viewpoints and assumptions about the relevant matters. If we embark directly on a historical study of ancient ethics without first reflecting on our own expectations from ethics, we shall simply carry our own concerns with us without noticing; instead of a purely historical account we shall produce an account coloured by our own unquestioned perspective. Making our own concerns and expectations explicit is our only hope of minimizing, if not removing entirely, our own preconceptions, and of recovering what is most distinctive about ancient ethics. Of course we cannot step outside our own ethical framework to write about the Epicureans and Stoics; this is why writing about ancient ethics is methodologically much harder than writing about ancient medicine or physics. However, getting clear about what we are doing, reflecting on our own ethical theories and concepts, affords at least the hope of coming to see ancient theories in a way which is comparatively free of the distortions produced by not noticing our own perspective.

1. *The Shape of Ancient Ethical Theory*

Throughout this book we have seen that the entry point for ancient ethical reflection is very different from the one we have been taught to find standard. It is the point of view of a reflective person who realizes that all her various aims and values do hang together in a pattern in her life, and that her life is given a definite direction by whatever it is that she takes to be her overarching value or view of what matters. Ancient ethics begins from this viewpoint. Only the Cyrenaics tell us to discard it; all other theories tell us that the task of reflection is to clarify, rather than to reject, our final end, and to revise and organize our aims and priorities. The theories differ in the amount of reordering that they require, and thus in the distance they demand that the agent travel from the intuitions that she has as a result of education in her particular society. Aristotle is in this respect notably less demanding than either Epicurus or the Stoics.

In thinking about her final end, which is assumed to be happiness, the agent is told to reflect on what is natural and, in the light of this, to criticize and modify what is merely conventional in her ethical beliefs, acquired by upbringing in society. Perhaps the single most widespread misconception about ancient ethics is that this appeal to nature consists of an appeal to a conception of human nature which is both determinate and established by reasoning which is not itself ethical. This misconception lies behind a number of drearily familiar criticisms of ancient ethics, on the ground that it presupposes such a thing as 'the single best way of life for a human being', which we moderns reject. We moderns do have good reasons for rejecting any such conception; but so did the ancients. In fact, as we have seen, nature enters into ancient ethics in two ways. In one way it sets the limits that any theory must respect; to be livable, a theory must be in accord with human nature in the sense that it must be a theory that can be lived by a human being, with the characteristic needs, basic desires and so on that human beings have. So understood, however, the appeal is relatively uncontroversial. Nature also enters in another, stronger role (and here theories differ as to how coherently this is connected with the first). Nature provides us with an ideal, in terms of which we can identify and perhaps discard the merely conventional element in our moral beliefs and practices. So, for the Epicureans, it is only when we understand what constitutes a natural desire that we can reform many of our actual desires, which depend for their strength on our accepting merely conventional goals as being of importance in our lives. And only when we do this, of course, will we achieve freedom from the unhappiness which comes from having goals imposed on us which do not accord with our nature. Nature in this sense provides a substantial ideal. But it is not a pre-ethical ideal; for each theory it is part of the theory. The Epicurean concept of nature as an ideal differs widely from that of the Stoic. For there can be no such thing as a substantial ideal of the natural which is not dependent on holding certain ethical theses to be true. A Stoic's idea of the natural life differs from that of an Epicurean in just the way, and for just the reasons, that Hobbes' theory of a state of nature differs from Aristotle's; they disagree about what is natural for humans because they disagree about what matters ethically for humans.

The ancient appeal to nature could hardly be further away from modern 'naturalism' in ethics. The latter is the attempt to found ethics on something safely non-ethical, and enshrines the presupposition that there is something a bit insecure about ethics, which needs to be founded on something different and more robust. Ancient ethical theories do not have to answer to any such preconceptions, because ancient philosophy as a whole does not contain any such bias against the ethical, as an area which is peculiarly frail and in need of external support. Nature comes into ancient ethical theories as a notion which can help to illuminate and clarify the other elements in the theories. We suspect, for example, that in the ethical beliefs that we have, there is much that rests merely on conventions that we accept, and has no proper ethical backing; asking what is natural about the way we live helps us to work out what this is. But the notion of nature is not the kind of notion that could, just by itself, give rise to ethical theses.

Ethical reflection proceeds to revise and reorder the agent's priorities; in the process the proper place has to be found for virtue. I have argued frequently through the book that this task is not fundamentally different from modern attempts to determine the proper place in an agent's life for morality. Virtue is not a neutral kind of excellence (still less, an excellence in achieving some non-morally specified way of life). It is a complex disposition to do the morally right thing for the right reason in a consistent and reliable way, in which one's emotions and feelings have so developed as to go along with one's decisions. The question, exactly what place virtue should have in one's life, is the fundamental question of ancient ethics. Further, there is the question of one's relations to others. While in a sense this is already covered by virtue, the issue of one's relations to others, and the scope and demands of other-concern, are sufficiently complex to warrant separate treatment. Third, virtue and other-concern have to be given their proper place and status in a life whose priorities will undoubtedly have been considerably modified and revised from one's pre-reflective, conventional opinions; but this life is still taken to be aimed at some version of happiness, the overall goal that all agree on.

Thus we have three elements: virtue, other-concern and happiness. Ancient ethical theories differ most obviously in the way they distribute their emphasis between these elements. Epicurus pays attention to our normal, ongoing conception of happiness and to its standard implications of desirableness and satisfaction. As a result, his theory has some difficulty with accommodating the other two elements. The Stoics place most weight on virtue, and make the strongest demands on other-concern; as a result theirs is the hardest account of happiness for common sense to accept. All theories see it as their task to work with these elements to produce an overall theory which will revise the agent's priorities in the best way. They differ as to how to do this; but, with the single striking exception of the Cyrenaics, the exception which proves the rule, they do not disagree on what they take the basic task of ethical theory to be. In the different parts of this book I have made clear what great divergencies there are between theories where each of the elements is concerned. Aristotle and the Stoics, for example, differ strongly as to the scope of other-concern, and the subsequent hybrid theories assimilate the weaker to the stronger theory. But these differences also make clear how much the different theories share by way of assumed framework. Aristotle's account of happiness, for example, is more intuitive than that of the Stoics; and this is not an isolated point of comparison, but can clearly be seen to be linked to the point that he makes weaker demands than they do on the scope of other-concern, and allows conventional goods an essential role in happiness, where they insist on virtue alone. Stoic criticisms of Aristotle on the role of virtue are linked directly to criticisms of his account of happiness.

2. *The Tasks of Ethical Theory*

It is obvious by now both that ancient ethical theories are indeed theories, and that they are quite different from many modern ethical theories. We have seen from many different angles that ancient theories are not hierarchical and complete. There is no favoured set of primitive terms or theses, from which other less basic terms or theses are derived. By contrast, many modern ethical theories have as their ideal the model of derivation, from a set of favoured primitive terms or theses, of all applications of these primitives to areas which the theory is supposed to cover. Often this is because the intellectual model which is seen as appropriate for ethics is that of a scientific theory.[1] In the ancient world science was undeveloped; scientific theories were not notable for either rigour of structure or for predictive success. Ethical theorists had no reason to see them as being paradigmatic for the form a theory should take. This is not to say that they had no model available of a theory in which specific results were derived from a set of favoured primitives; they were, in the form of mathematics, the theory which Plato found compelling as a model for knowledge in general. But from Aristotle onwards philosophers are never tempted to construe ethical theories on the mathematical model; it seemed a completely unsuitable model for practical knowledge. Rather, we have seen the compelling force of the model of a practical skill or craft, *technē*, in ethics. Virtue is seen, in theories which are explicit about its intellectual structure, as having the intellectual structure of a skill. The Stoics think of it as actually being a kind of skill, and this point plays an important part in the way they relate virtue to the other kind of valued things which make up a satisfactory life. For virtue as a skill provides a way of relating virtue intellectually to the other things that we value; it is our intellectually reflective way of obtaining them. Morality is not, as often in modern theories, essentially opposed to other

---

[1] Or rather what is in philosophy textbooks the orthodox model of a scientific theory.

kinds of value, but represented as the appropriate way of selecting things with non-moral value. And taking virtue to be a skill also emphasizes the importance of the moral agent's need for reflection, to reach a unified and organized intellectual basis which will explain and justify her particular decisions and actions. A truly moral agent is not just the person who discerns what is the right thing to do, but the person who does this on the basis of a reflectively achieved ability to justify in terms of rules and principles under which the decisions and actions can be brought.

Ancient ethical theories, then, have a structure, but it is not the structure of a theory in which the less basic is derived from the basic. This general point has several implications for what are and are not seen as the tasks of ethical theory. With ancient theories there is no expectation that the theory can be formalized in such a way that particular answers to ethical questions can be derived from general principles. Indeed, ethical theories are not seen *primarily* as mechanisms for answering ethical questions at all; they arise from the reflection provoked in an intelligent person about the shape and course of his life, not from the presumption that the intelligent agent will find lots of ethical questions facing him and will require a theory to answer them for him.[2] Hence, although the agent who has absorbed an ethical theory will thereby be provided with means to solve the problems that confront him, there is no expectation that ethical theory will provide a decision procedure for solving hard cases which would lack a solution without it. In part this reflects the fact that the context of ancient theories is not one in which ethical conflict is seen as basic and pressing, so pressing in fact as to provide the primary job of ethical theory. This is not because there was no ethical conflict in the ancient world; it would be naive to assume that the ancients lived in a world in which consensus was the norm. Rather, it is because in the ancient world ethical theory was not seen primarily as something generated by the need for a problem-solving mechanism. Ethical theory arises from the need, for each person, to reflect on his final end, and of the place and role of virtue in his current conception of happiness. This is a task to which the solution of ethical conflict is secondary. We do in fact have lists of textbook problem cases from the Stoics, together with their answers to them. And it is not hard to find passage like that in which Cicero comments on the importance of rules and principles in moral philosophy, because of the need to determine one's duty in all areas of life. But the theory is not driven, or structured, by this demand; the energy, and the basic arguments, are devoted to producing a convincing account of our final end. If modern ethical theories pay more insistent attention to solving difficult problems, this is not because we disagree more than the ancients did, but because we have acquired a different view of the task of ethical theory. It is hard not to suspect that this picture of ethical theory as introduced by puzzlement over hard cases, and as primarily focussed towards resolving these cases, is not heavily influenced by science. It certainly does not seem to have become widespread until an age which was influenced by modern science. It is difficult to

---

[2] Cf. the opening of Brandt (1959), 'What is ethical theory about? Someone might propose as an answer: "Everyone knows what an ethical problem is: ethical theory must be about the solutions to such problems".'

believe that we had to wait till the modern age for people to start disagreeing about ethical matters.[3]

Ancient ethical theories, however, are supposed to have impact, greater or lesser, on the agent's ethical beliefs. Theories begin from intuitions, but in the light of philosophical reflection and argument those intuitions have to be refined and modified. The Stoic theory indeed demands that we make some rather large alterations in our intuitions, although they still think that overall the theory recommends itself to our reflected views.[4] Ancient theories are not tools to help us make decisions, but they give us ways in which through reflection and argument we come to understand the basis for our moral views, and to refine and modify them.

Thus if we try to compare the structure of ancient ethical theories with that of modern theories, we find that we have to make distinctions. The ancient theories are unlike modern moral theories which have, or aspire to, a structure like that of scientific theories; they are not hierarchical and complete. However, it would be a mistake to conclude that they therefore reject the very idea of systematic theory and structure, as some modern forms of virtue ethics do.[5] In some modern discussions the turn from deontology and consequentialism to virtue has been accompanied by a rejection of the very idea of moral *theory* at all. Concentration on character and virtue has often gone with the rejection of any aspiration to systematize ethical thinking into a single structure. One ground put forward for this is that moral theory is useless; it cannot do anything for us which our own deliberations do not already do, or do better.[6] Another ground is that our ethical beliefs are deeply marked by conflict, and that the project of unifying them ignores the constant potential for conflict between the different sources of our ethical positions.[7] Ancient theories are not so despondent on either ground. They are based on the assumption that ethical beliefs can in fact be unified, without ignoring forces of deep significance for ethics, and that they can be refined and improved; the person who has reflected and reordered his priorities in the light of theory is in a better state than the person who has simply stuck with his original beliefs.

Thus ancient ethical theories are strikingly different in structure from modern theories which retain a commitment to being hierarchical and complete; they thus differ from most versions of consequentialism and Kantianism. They are, however, comparable to modern theories which reject this commitment, and which base themselves on a method such as reflective equilibrium, and thus aim to unify, order and modify our intuitions, rather than establishing first principles from which applications can be rigorously derived. They are theories in a weaker understanding

---

[3] It has been recognized that modern ethical theories lay immense weight on the supposed fact of massive ethical conflict. Cf. Baier (1989). Baier, however, takes Mill to be the first moral philosopher who writes against a background of assumed conflict. It is arguable that moral philosophy was affected by this assumption much earlier. See the writings of J. B. Schneewind, especially (1990b) who locates it as part of the turn in moral philosophy first evident in writers of the age of Grotius.

[4] The Stoics also, as we have seen, hold that Stoic philosophy as a whole holds together, and that within this the ethical theory can be best understood in the light of their conception of cosmic nature. For the purposes of this book I have left this stage aside. In any case one can well query how cosmic nature can in fact illuminate the distinctive theses of Stoic ethics, except in the most general way.

[5] Clarke (1987); Clarke and Simpson (1989); Louden (1990).

[6] Noble (1989).

[7] Hampshire (1989).

of theory, one which rejects any assimilation to the kind of theory appropriate in science.

However, there remains a striking difference even from modern theories of this kind. A standard complaint against methods that rely on starting from and eventually answering to intuitions is that they hold only for the community whose intuitions are in question, and must thus fall short of making claims that hold of every agent. 'Reflective equilibrium can. . . apply only to judgements that might be expressed in a single moral practice. For that reason it does not generate norms that are universal in the sense of binding everyone.'[8] As long as we appeal to intuitions, it is thought, and have a theory which answers to them rather than generating principles which are used to derive answers independently of them, the theory will lose claims to universality and thus to objectivity. It will merely be a theory that rationalizes what some people happen to think. Any such theory is open to the charges of relativism and of moral conservatism. And indeed, since it is clear that ancient theories do aim to answer to our intuitions,[9] ancient ethical theories have been held guilty of both these charges, particularly the second.[10]

Ancient theories, however, are conspicuous for their appeal to human rationality and to the results of thinking in a rational way. This is particularly clear in the Stoics, who argue that the moral point of view is grasped by the agent whose reason has developed in the appropriate way. Thus, although we have to start from the specific intuitions on moral matters which are current in society, the theory is not committed to endorsing these, or to producing results which will best harmonize them. All the theories in question argue for positions which greatly revise some of our intuitions, and do so as a result of argument of a rational kind, and appeals to rational thinking and argument. The closest analogue here is the method of Rawls in *A Theory of Justice*,[11] which starts from our intuitions and employs reflective equilibrium to unify and modify them, but which nevertheless makes claims to universality and objectivity, because the method employs the rational point of view, and makes use of what is established by reasoning from that point of view. It is quite wrong, then, to hold that ancient theories hold positions which are explicitly limited to one particular community, and thus fall into relativism. Ancient theories always start from the intuitions of ancient Greek societies. Where else could they start? But they hold that these intuitions can be unified and revised, not just in the light of each other, but in the light of reasoning and argument which reflects the rational point of view. And thus their positions are meant to be objective. We can, of course, query whether this method is always followed as rigorously as it should be. Aristotle notoriously fails to grasp that his society's consensus on slavery is not in fact underpinned by rational reflection. It is, of course, easier for us than for Aristotle to see this. When we are looking at a theory developed in a historical context very different from our own, it is often clear to us where rational reflection has been confused with conventional social views. Further, and more deeply, we can raise the

---

[8] Clarke and Simpson, Introduction to (1989), p. 11.

[9] At least it is clear that Aristotle's does, and this has been the theory that has received most attention, and is often regarded as paradigmatic of ancient ethics.

[10] For a powerful defence of virtue ethics against relativism, see Nussbaum (1988b).

[11] I ignore in this context the methodological complications raised by Rawls' later works.

question whether this is a strong enough method actually to achieve what moral theory requires— though plausible alternatives are hard to find.[12]

The answer to the charge of moral conservatism is clearly similar. It is often assumed that ancient theories serve as rationalizations of the current moral views held in ancient society; but this ignores the large part played in these theories by appeal to rational reflection, and thus ignores the counter-intuitive nature of many of the conclusions that the theories draw. Again, this point is clearest in the Stoics, who make the strongest appeal to rationality, and draw conclusions greatly at variance with conventional opinion; it is as open for a slave or a woman to become virtuous as for a prosperous citizen, for example, given their views of virtue and what it is to acquire it. It remains true that the more 'applied' parts of the theory, even Stoic theory, contain a great deal that is merely conventional. We find Panaetius and Epictetus, for example, reading off moral duties from conventional social roles, without laying much stress on the rational reflections which would greatly modify the force of these roles.[13] But this seems to be a point which holds of all moral theories. The more 'applied' element of any theory will run the risk of absorbing or rationalizing merely conventional opinions; this is as true of applied consequential-ism as of applied Stoicism, with the difference, of course, that historical perspective makes the point much clearer with the latter.

There is a very persistent assumption in modern ethical discussion that ancient ethical theories are morally conservative.[14] This assumption has no good basis. It seems to be due to many factors: failure to see the extent to which ancient theories appeal to rational reflection; over-concentration on areas where ancient theories do make the mistake of rationalizing conventional opinions; over-emphasis on the importance to ancient Greeks of their social context and practices, especially those of the city-state. Over-emphasis on Aristotle's comparatively conservative theory, and neglect of the more radical theories of the Epicureans and Stoics, may also have played a role. In general the importance and extent of rational reflection in ancient ethics has been greatly under-estimated, and so has the importance to the reflective individual of rationally testing and modifying, rather than just taking over, the ethical beliefs that were conventional in his society.

3. *Structural Contrasts*

Some of the striking features of ancient ethics which have emerged from the discussion in this book may become more salient by contrast with prominent modern theories. (The contrasts are not meant to do more than this.)

---

[12] Even Sidgwick, whose *Methods of Ethics* is the origin of much modern moral theorizing of the kind which despises intuitions and derives applications directly from principles, has no way of reaching his own allegedly self-evident first principles than from reflection on our moral intuitions.

[13] See the end of chapter 2, section 4, pp. 107–8.

[14] This is partly due, of course, to over-emphasis on Aristotle, whose theory is less counter-intuitive and more respectful of consensus than the theories of the Stoics and Epicureans.

Consequentialism

Modern forms of consequentialism are defined by their adherence to the principle that the right thing to do is the action which will produce the best consequences. This principle has turned out to be the part of traditional utilitarianism which has had the most enduring philosophical appeal, so that now it is this concept of maximizing rationality, rather than the nature of its final end, which characterizes utilitarianism. Few modern forms of consequentialism adhere to the classical kind of hedonism defended by Bentham and by Mill.[15] But the idea that the correct method of reasoning in ethics is that of maximizing remains strong. Often it is simply taken for granted, but sometimes defended on the grounds that maximizing is an obviously rational thing to do.[16]

The only ancient ethical thinkers to espouse maximizing are the Cyrenaics. And, as we have seen from more than one angle, their commitment to maximizing went with a rejection of the whole eudaimonistic framework. What they sought to maximize were episodes of pleasure; and this led them to reject the significance of happiness, or the agent's overall end. Hence the chronic difficulty that the school faced in finding a place in their theory for virtue and other-concern, at least a place that would satisfy reflective common sense. Some members of the school turned to accommodating common sense at the expense of theoretical rigour, others stuck to a position of rejecting common sense. All of them found the school's position difficult to defend, and not merely because they were hedonists, but because they chose to aim at a kind of pleasure which could be maximized. Epicurus' very different form of hedonism avoids the problems plaguing the Cyrenaics, because he chooses to set up pleasure as an end within a eudaimonist framework, and so to see pleasure as an aim which is complete and self-sufficient, and which orders the agent's priorities over the whole of her life. In so choosing, Epicurus rejects maximizing as the appropriate form for ethical reasoning. Even his cruder pronouncements are not to be construed on the model of maximizing.

There is only one passage in the whole of ancient ethical literature in which we find both a recommendation of maximizing as a form of ethical reasoning, and the assumption of eudaimonism, namely that one's concern be with one's final good, and with one's life as a whole. This is Plato's *Protagoras*, a work which is technically outside the scope of this book, but should be mentioned in this context anyway. In it we find Socrates putting forward, as a kind of skill to make life more secure, the ability to calculate amounts of pleasure so as to produce the best result overall, without the distortions of perspective that make us prefer the present moment to the future, or the nearer to the further pleasure. The *Protagoras* is indeed comparable to the classical utilitarianism of Bentham and Mill (in the above respects, though not in others which will shortly be pointed out). However, the *Protagoras* is puzzling in many ways. It is far from clear that Socrates is presented as putting forward the theory in its own right, rather than *ad hominem*. Even if Plato does mean to put

---

[15] This trend is seen very strikingly in Griffin (1986), who explicitly says that utilitarians need not begin from a determinate conception of the end which they seek to maximize, but need start only from a vague notion of 'welfare' and achieve greater precision as the theory proceeds.

[16] See Scheffler (1985), who gives no argument for the point that a form of reasoning which is common or prestigious in other areas should be a suitable form of reasoning in ethics.

forward the theory as Socrates' own, it is risky to identify Socrates' point of view here with Plato's own.[17] And even if we were justified in doing so, this would only be a temporary position of Plato's; it is inconsistent with his views on pleasure in other dialogues, notably the *Gorgias*.[18] What is most notable, in fact, about the *Protagoras*, is its total lack of influence. Subsequent ethical theories continue to be eudaimonist in form, but abandon the idea of maximizing reasoning, as even the hedonist Epicurus does. The only maximizers are the Cyrenaics, who seek to maximize episodes of pleasure, and thus abandon the eudaimonistic framework of the *Protagoras*.

Another notable difference between ancient and modern theories which propose that our final end is pleasure, in some form, is that for the ancient theories the pleasure in question is always the agent's pleasure. This indeed is why even Epicurus, who has a very expanded notion of pleasure, has difficulty in accommodating virtue and other-concern in his theory. Modern forms of consequentialism, by contrast, take the pleasure aimed at to be the pleasure of all pleasure-experiencing beings. This difference has of course been noticed, but a further point has less often been stressed. This is that modern forms of consequentialism often take a form which is given its classic formulation by Sidgwick, who argues that it is the constraints of rationality which force us into pursuing, not our own pleasure, but pleasure regardless of whose it is. Considerations that are compelling to rational people force us to be impartial as to whose, or where, is the pleasure which we seek to maximize. There is nothing corresponding to this in Epicurus, or any ancient hedonist. There is, however, something strikingly analogous in the Stoics, namely their position that we are led by our nature as rational beings to be 'familiarized' equally to all rational beings, even 'the furthest Mysian'. Thus we find hedonism in Epicurus. And in the Stoics we find strong demands made of rationality, which is taken to compel us to a position impartial between ourselves and others; but this goes with a *rejection* of hedonism. Thus modern consequentialism has no ancient structural analogue; different elements of it turn up in different theories, but in ancient terms it is itself a monstrous hybrid.

Kantianism

It is familiar that there are deep analogies and some deep differences between the Stoics and Kant, differences which in the present context will be deployed to strengthen our understanding of the former. They are strikingly alike in that they both hold that it is the uncorrupted development of reason which leads the agent to grasp the moral point of view. The Stoics fall far short of Kant in giving formal criteria for identifying the moral point of view. There is nothing in the ancient texts which corresponds even remotely to Kant's formula of universal law, or to an

---

[17] This is very disputed among scholars. It seems to me that the *Protagoras* is merely an obvious case of a dialogue where Socrates is presented as arguing *ad hominem*, and that it is very incautious to identify Socrates' position with that of Plato, as often in the dialogues. For two scholars who agree that the *Protagoras* presents Plato's own view, though not his settled view, see Irwin (1976) chapter 4, and Nussbaum (1986a) chapter 4. These discussions refer to the considerable recent secondary literature on the dialogue.

[18] This is another much discussed question. For a recent addition to the discussion, see Kahn (1988).

interest in universalizability as a necessary or sufficient condition of a reason's being a moral reason.[19] The Stoics rely rather on the agent's coming to grasp the distinctive nature of the kind of value that virtue has. We might expect to find here some analogue to Kant's formula of treating humanity, whether in one's own person or that of another, as an end in itself. For Kant obviously does not mean that humanity is the kind of end that we seek in action; an end is not just something we go for, but something that we are motivated to seek because of the kind of value that we take it to have, and the point of Kant's formulation is that there is a kind of value exhibited by people, just by virtue of their rational humanity, which is different in kind from the value that other things have. The Stoics indeed mark a distinction of kind between the value of virtue and the value of other kinds of things. And in both cases we are justified in speaking of a distinction between moral and other value. But the Stoics never locate moral value in rational humanity just as such.[20] The contrast for them is between rational humanity in its achieved or perfected form—the virtuous—and rational humanity in any other state; they devote some energy to drawing extreme contrasts between the ideally virtuous and everybody else, who is by contrast worthless and bad. And hence, although the Stoics are more 'democratic' than Aristotle in that for them virtue comes from the development of reason alone, and they lay far less weight than he does on habituation in specific social contexts, they do not achieve the extreme 'democracy' of Kant's account, in which it is rational humanity just as such which is the locus of moral value.

The most striking dissimilarity is of course that the Stoics see the development of reason which leads to adopting the moral point of view as a natural part of the development of human nature. Kant by contrast sees it as something which could never spring from the development of empirical nature alone, and hence as requiring a noumenal self, a conception of one's agency as independent of all the empirical factors in one's context and makeup. Relatedly, the Stoics see the development of virtue as part of one's development of a clarified and corrected conception of happiness. Kant by contrast sees morality as standing in the sharpest possible contrast with happiness, indeed sometimes only to be achieved by sacrificing happiness. So for the Stoics there is no essential opposition between the pursuit of virtue and the pursuit of other goods. Indeed, virtue is the skill which one exercises in selecting these other goods, whereas for Kant there is something deeply suspicious in the idea of morality being shown in one's pursuit of what one desires. Famously, he thinks that we can get our clearest idea of what it is to do one's duty for the right reason, that is, just because it is our duty, in cases where all our interests and pursuits of other goods pull *against* doing what morality requires. One thing that this illustrates is the flexible and indeterminate nature of the ancient notion of happiness, compared to the limited and narrow concept that Kant employs. But more deeply this is a difference about the role of nature. The Stoics see morality and the development in humans of a moral point of view as being something natural, namely, what is natural for rational beings. However much they stress the distinctiveness of virtue and the kind of value that it has, it is not for them something which is so alien

---

[19] It could well be argued that they have the materials for this idea, in the concept of *oikeiōsis*; but the connection is not drawn.

[20] The nearest we get is in the Stoic-influenced, but Aristotelian, theory put forward by Arius. See chapter 12, pp. 283–84.

to all our other concerns that it is not part of the natural world at all. Whereas for Kant that is exactly what it is; the sources of virtue and of other kinds of values are, for him, so distinct that he cannot conceive of them even falling under a single scheme of explanation. The Stoics preserve what Kant sees as vital—the difference in kind between moral and other value—but without his violent dualism between the world of nature and the world of morality.

Like Kant, the Stoics stress rules and principles more than Aristotle's theory does; and they also stress, with him and against Aristotle, the inner aspect of virtue, the value of what may make no impact in the outer world. But these aspects of their theory come naturally from the way that they press the distinctive nature of moral value within a eudaimonistic theory. They do not give rules and principles the basic kind of status that they have for Kant. And the inward aspect of virtue is for them the result of their conception of virtue as a skill whose value does not depend on its results; it is not linked, as it is in Kant, with a distinction of two fundamentally different aspects of the whole self, the noumenal and the phenomenal.

Modern Virtue Ethics

Modern versions of virtue ethics are as yet fairly undeveloped, and the differences from ancient ethical theories are as striking as the similarities. Modern virtue ethics displays a number of connected tendencies, including the tendency to reject a significant role for ethical theory; to reject or be wary of the notion of the impartial viewpoint in ethics; to make low demands on rationality in ethics and to stress the role of habit and practice; to employ a non-intellectual and habitual concept of virtue; and to rehabilitate traditional forms of moral conservatism, in opposition to revisionary moral theories like consequentialism.[21] By contrast, ancient ethics is an ethics of virtue, but stands in opposition on all these points. Ethical theory is regarded as crucial; it is only reflection, argument and theory that can lead us to fruitful ethical practice and the needed revision of our priorities. Impartiality does not figure in Aristotle, but once introduced by the Stoics is thereafter seen as required by ethical theory in the Stoic and Aristotelian traditions. Habituation and practice are accorded a significant role, but not at the expense of deliberation and choice; in particular, virtue is not a non-intellectual notion, or tied closely to habituation in actual practices. It is complex and highly intellectual and, since it includes the notion of having a disposition to do the ethically right thing, requires whatever amount of ethical reflection and theorizing is required to have a proper grasp of what the right thing to do is. Hence, ancient ethical theory never (with the problematic exception of the Sceptics) serves to canonize tradition. It always has the role of questioning tradition from the rational point of view. Hence it is not morally conservative but the opposite; it always queries tradition and convention in the name of an ethical ideal.[22]

[21] No one work displays *all* these tendencies, of course. See, apart from the collections of work on virtue ethics already referred to in the notes for this chapter and for the introduction, Schnädelbach (1986).

[22] Aristotle's theory is the most morally conservative, but even he revises common opinions a great deal just in insisting on the primacy of virtue for happiness. Further, even the more revisionary Stoic

The most important lesson which modern virtue ethics can learn from ancient ethical theories, in fact, is that virtue ethics, given a proper conception of virtue, has no tendency towards moral conservatism. Rather, it expresses a tendency to question and to reflect on conventional morality. For a proper conception of morality will give due emphasis to its intellectual and reflective side. To people in the ancient world, ethical reflection has to start from the intuitions that they have. But these intuitions will tend to support the view, for example, that success in worldly matters is an essential component of happiness, and that it is utterly absurd that the virtuous person on the wheel could be happy. But, as we have seen, this position is not as uncontroversial as common sense would have us think. Once the Stoics challenge it, and reflective people come to study the considerations for and against, it becomes a matter for theory to pronounce on, whether the virtuous person on the rack, rather than the prosperous and successful citizen, is happy. The unreflective person relying merely on the initial intuitions is not the arbiter of the question. Ancient ethical theories are not morally conservative in either of two respects. They have no tendency to preserve or rationalize the majority of the current moral intuitions. And despite the stress they lay on habituation as necessary to produce full virtue, they do not set up as an ideal the life of effortlessly habituated activity, the life in which one does not need to reflect on one's moral views and work them out. Rather, their ideal is one of the examined life, the life which has been through considerable reflection and argument on the subject of one's final good, and which has committed itself to search for a determinate form of that good in the light of a possibly very demanding theory. If we think of ancient ethics as characterized by the life of the person who feels at home in his society's ethical views, in contrast to anomic moderns faced by a plurality of types of theory, we are thinking of a type of life which may or may not have existed (probably it never did except in modern fantasy and projection).[23] We are not thinking of a life informed by ancient ethical theory.

One of the few modern thinkers to have got this point right is Michael Oakeshott. Contrasting the moral life as *a habit of affection and behaviour* on the one hand, with the moral life as *the reflective application of a moral criterion*, he correctly notes that ancient ethics is an example of the latter, in the particular form of *the self-conscious pursuit of moral ideals*.

> [The Greco-Roman age was] an age of intense moral self-consciousness, an age of moral reformers who, unavoidably, preached a morality of the pursuits of ideals and taught a variety of dogmatic moral ideologies. The intellectual energy of the time was directed toward the determination of an ideal, and the moral energy toward the translation of that ideal into practice. Moral self-consciousness itself became a virtue; genuine morality was identified with 'the practice of philosophy'. And it was thought that for the achievement of a good life it was necessary

---

theory was susceptible to more morally conservative interpretation, as we have seen. There does not seem to be anything essentially morally conservative about the *structure* of either theory.

[23] Alasdair MacIntyre, in his influential books (1981) and (1988), goes too far in his presentation of ancient ethical life as one where deeply unsettling reflection did not arise, and the virtues were essentially constituted by certain shared practices.

that a man should submit to an artificial moral training, a moral gymnastic, *askesis*; learning and discipline must be added to 'nature'.[24]

Ancient Christianity and its effects were similar, he adds, so that

> The fact. . . .remains that the moral inheritance of western Europe, both from the classical culture of the ancient world and from Christianity, was not the gift of a morality of habitual behaviour, but of a moral ideology.[25]

We have seen the ultimately indecisive nature of the major serious debate in ancient ethics, that between Stoic and Aristotelian theories about the relation of virtue and happiness. We have thus seen that once started, reflection and argument acquire a life of their own, and may point up a division in the original moral views, a division which, instead of being healed by reflection, is more and more exacerbated as reflection proceeds. And this in turn indicates that thoughtful agents in the ancient world may well have found themselves in a similar position to that of some moderns: ethical reflection has destroyed one's initial certainties, while seeming to make it impossible to attain any certainty on the theoretical level. Cicero, arguing passionately now for the Stoic and now for the Aristotelian view, has many modern analogues. But the ancient problem remains in a way more superficial than the modern one. For the modern problem is one of facing diverse theories which spring from diverse sources, rather than different answers to the same problem. In the modern world we do not face different answers about our final end; we face theories which disagree as to the very subject matter: virtue, obligation, good consequences. We can see why Cicero, despite his genuine inability to decide, should be motivated to continue the search for the right answer. In the modern world we can be less sure that we are even looking for the right kind of answer.

4. *Ancient Ethics and Modern Morality*

Is ancient ethics then modern morality? Yes; and also, Perhaps. Yes, in any intuitive understanding of morality. I hope to have established that the ancient theories are not theories of some alien mode of thought, but theories of morality, in the same sense that Kant's and Mill's theories are. Perhaps, in that our intuitive notion of morality might be thought to be unsatisfactorily vague; and there are certainly definitions of morality in a narrower and more technical sense which make it harder to identify the object of the ancient theories with morality. If Bernard Williams is right, for example, in the suggestion that the modern concept of morality is essentially one of obligation,[26] then, since ancient theories are wide of that mark, they will not count as theories of morality in that sense. Thus a satisfactory answer to the question about ancient ethics and modern morality must await the same kind of reflection at this end, about the concept of modern morality and the various

---

[24] Oakeshott (1989).

[25] Ibid., p. 201. Oakeshott, incidentally, finds this to be a bad thing: the 'form [of European morals] has, from the beginning, been dominated by the pursuit of moral ideals. In so far as this is an unhappy form of morality, prone to obsession and at war with itself, it is a misfortune to be deplored' (p. 202).

[26] Williams (1985), chapter 10.

kinds of moral theory available, that I have tried to begin at the other end, for the ancient theories. In the meantime, however, I hope to have established that ancient theories are theories of morality, rather than theories of something else, something which is of no serious moral interest to us.

Any serious comparisons must bear in mind the two major points of dissimilarity which I pointed to in the Introduction. Modern moral theories often conceive themselves to have different tasks from the ancient ones; and modern moral concerns are influenced by a number of sources. We cannot just wish away any concern with good consequences, or other twentieth-century issues. Our entry point for ethical reflection is different, and so is the shape of our reflection itself.

Nonetheless, there are some ways in which a study of ancient ethics may improve our understanding of what we are doing with our own ethical theories. I give two examples; more would be reasonably easy to develop.

Although in recent years more serious ethical attention has been paid to the notion of happiness,[27] we still find problems in finding a role for happiness in ethical theory. We also still tend to find, in studying ancient ethical theories, the same difficulty, springing from the point that our concept of happiness is more determinate, than the ancient one. Our concept of happiness is certainly not limited to feelings of pleasure or euphoria; we can sensibly talk of a happy life. Moreover, we can think of a happy life as a life which contains the resources which would reasonably make a person feel happy; so for some of our uses of 'happy' it does not follow that if you think you are happy, then you are.[28] Still, the notion of happiness is more bound to the notions of felt pleasure and experienced satisfaction than the ancient concept is. And thus the modern concept is more *rigid*. Not only is it paradoxical, for us, to hold that the virtuous person on the wheel is happy, the paradox persists until we interpret happiness in a more indeterminate and flexible way than we are used to. The Stoic thesis remains paradoxical for us, given our rigid concept of happiness. This is, of course, the reason I have insisted throughout the book that in ancient theories happiness is to be taken as an unspecific concept, capable of far more by way of revision than our notion of happiness is.

One response to this situation, familiar by now in work on ancient ethics, is to use a different term to translate the Greek *eudaimonia*, such as 'human flourishing' or the like.[29] But this risks missing the affinity between the starting points in both cases. For both ancients and moderns, the starting point for considering happiness is a conventionally successful life which the agent finds satisfactory. We find it hard to expand this concept to the extent that a moral, but outwardly disastrous life still counts as happy. The ancients clearly did not feel the difficulty as intensely. Perhaps this is a signal to us that, at the very least, we are missing something, Perhaps our rigid concept is less useful, just because it makes it difficult for us to express the idea that the criteria for success in a life should take in morality as well as other ends, or that what matters in a life is to revise our priorities so that morality has the proper weight in its relation to other ends. We have no concept which readily covers both the unreflective notion of success in life from which we start, and the revised notion

---

[27] Cf. Telfer (1980).
[28] See Kraut (1979).
[29] This suggestion has been given currency by Cooper (1975).

of success in life with which we end if and when we have appropriately revised our priorities, and given morality its appropriate place in our life. The fact that we lack such a concept doubtless owes something to our tendency to see the pursuit of morality as being always likely to be in tension or conflict with the pursuit of other ends. Thus we tend to see the process of making morality more important in your life as one which will tend to lead to loss of happiness, rather than as an achievement of happiness properly conceived. This goes, of course, with our tendency to respect in our moral theories, in ways that the ancient philosophers did not, our everyday tendency to oppose morality to self-interest, and to regard moral and prudential reasoning as though they were different kinds of reasoning.

It is unlikely, of course, that we can now make happiness into a more flexible and amenable concept, and more likely that we need to put to use something like the notion of a satisfactory life. It is fairly clear, however, that if we stick to our rigid notion of happiness, we shall completely fail to understand the ancient theories. And if we put some effort into sympathetically understanding them, we are likely to appreciate the shortcomings of the rigid concept. This may at least make us reflect on the ways in which in our ethical theorizing we may canonize automatically the unreflective tendency to oppose morality to happiness, and if we do this we may take these ways less for granted.

In modern moral philosophy we often find ourselves working with another assumption: that commonsense morality includes elements of only two kinds, or rather of two kinds that can be developed theoretically: deontological and consequentialist. Sidgwick, in *The Methods of Ethics*, made this assumption explicit, and since then many writers on ethics have taken it absolutely for granted. Sidgwick sees commonsense morality as being explicitly deontological but implicitly consequentialist.[30] That is, we explicitly recognize the force of moral rules, but can be led by argument to see that underlying these rules we see the achievement of good consequences as a justifying element, indeed the only element strong enough to produce a unified justification of our moral beliefs.[31] Hence the deontological element provides the static or rigid element in commonsense morality, while the implicit consequentialism, if made explicit, provides the element which, when laid out, can lead to change and flexibility. This view of commonsense morality has been very widespread in the twentieth century. It has been especially popular with consequentialists, who see themselves as proponents of the moveable element in commonsense morality, and who have seen nothing standing in their way but mindless adherence to rules.[32]

---

[30] Sidgwick refers to utilitarianism rather than consequentialism, but in this respect his position depends entirely on the consequentialist element, and not at all on his favoured conception of the final end (which Sidgwick takes to be pleasure).

[31] Sidgwick's argument here ingeniously appeals to the point that consequentialism can explain not only why we have the moral rules we have (a point as old as Hume) but also our practice of allowing certain exceptions to these rules, and can also explain why we have the exceptions that we have. Sidgwick never pauses to justify his crucial assumption that all these phenomena both need and have one single justification. (Insofar as he has any grounds, they lie in his unargued premise that ethical method is like scientific method.)

[32] This belief about the components of commonsense morality is especially obvious in consequentialists like Scheffler (1982) and Kagan (1990).

But such a view of what commonsense morality contains is a deformed one, and can only be maintained by not paying attention to what commonsense morality actually is. For one thing that is abundantly clear is that at the level of actual moral belief and practice people have never ceased to have concern for virtue and character as well as for rules, obligations and the production of good consequences. For most of the twentieth century there has been no room in conventional moral philosophy for considerations of character and virtue, so they have gone undiscussed in moral philosophy, and those who have noticed them have been at a loss as to how to categorize them theoretically. But they have not gone away. It is a great puzzle, why Sidgwick's analysis, which demotes the virtue aspects of commonsense morality to a sub-theoretical level, has been so successful. (And Sidgwick at least struggles with the problem of what to do with our concern with virtue, character and disposition, whereas his successors have dismissed these matters as though solved.)[33] One main reason why twentieth-century mainstream moral philosophy has been, until the last decade or so, so barren, and why it has failed to engage with other practical concerns, is that it has totally failed to engage with those aspects of commonsense moral thinking which involve virtue and character, and thus has systematically omitted a whole aspect of moral thinking; unsurprisingly, the result has often been inadequate or wrong.

All serious discussion of moral thinking would benefit from recognizing, and giving due attention to, the element in our moral thinking which is concerned with virtue and character. But after decades of neglect this is a difficult task to carry out. Reflection on ancient ethical theory may make it easier for us to do this; for we need to study theories which make these notions primary in order to recover a proper understanding of them, an understanding which will prevent us from making mistakes such as identifying virtue with a consistent mindless adherence to certain practices, or thinking that eudaimonistic theories are egoistic. Here, as elsewhere in this book, the relation of ancient and modern is complex. To recover a decent understanding of elements in our own moral thinking, we should study the ancient theories. But we will only do this well rather than badly, and with respect for the historical study that this requires, if we become aware of, rather than ignoring, our own ways of moral thinking and the place of virtue in them. The primary aim of this book has been to further the historical study of ancient ethical theories. But it is not an accident, I think, that this study may be of direct help in further articulating, and trying to understand, our own moral point of view.

---

[33] For Sidgwick's treatment of virtue notions, see Schneewind (1977), especially ch. 8, ch. 9 iii and ch.11 i.

Cast of Characters

The following gives biographical information which is intended to help non-specialist readers; hence the entries are selective, mentioning only information useful for this book (for example, only Aristotle's ethical works are listed). More information on many of these people can be found in *The Oxford Classical Dictionary* and *Die Kleine Pauly*. All authors listed below wrote in Greek except those marked (L) for Latin. Cross-references to people with entries are indicated by capital letters.

ACADEMY. Philosophical school founded by PLATO, named after the Academy gymnasium. For some generations after Plato's death the 'Old Academy' taught metaphysics and ethics. However, the name 'Academic' came to be attached to members of the school after ARCESILAUS turned it to scepticism (the sceptical Academy is sometimes called the 'New Academy'). It continued to teach and practice sceptical argument, producing no positive doctrines, until it petered out after PHILO.

AENESIDEMUS of Cnossus. Philosopher who in the first century B.C. broke away from the ACADEMY, which he regarded as having got too close to dogmatism, and founded a more radical sceptical movement which harked back to PYRRHO. He is the source of many arguments in SEXTUS, notably the Ten Modes (of which the Tenth, concerning value, is discussed in this book).

ALEXANDER of Aphrodisias. Late second-century or early third-century A.D. PERIPATET-IC philosopher, best known for his commentaries on works of Aristotle. He also wrote various essays and collections of notes, usually defending an Aristotelian position against later criticisms, particularly by the Stoics. Some of these are of interest for ethics.

ANDRONICUS of Rhodes. First century B.C. Editor of ARISTOTLE's works, probably in the second half of the century. Andronicus' edition seems to have been based on rediscovered original texts of Aristotle's own research and lecture notes; in any case, it became standard, and is the basis for subsequent text and arrangement of Aristotle's works, while the 'published', more popular works were gradually lost.

ANNICERIS of Cyrene. Third century B.C. The founder of a distinctive type of CYRENAIC philosophy, making more concessions than the original to ordinary beliefs.

ANONYMOUS COMMENTATOR ON PLATO'S THEAETETUS. Probably from the first century B.C. We have only the beginning of the commentary (on papyrus). The Commentator opposes the sceptical interpretation of Plato, which was supported by passages in the *Theaetetus* such as the 'midwife' passage, where Socrates disclaims the holding of positive views and represents himself as merely testing the views of others. He also includes interesting material (of doubtful relevance to the *Theaetetus*) on Stoic *oikeiōsis* and Pyrrhonist sceptics.

ANTIOCHUS of Ascalon, c. 130/120–68 B.C. Member of the late ACADEMY under PHILO, with whom he had an acrimonious debate over epistemology. Some time after the end of the Academy he founded his own school (which did not long outlast him). He put forward a frankly dogmatic system of philosophy, breaking away from the sceptical tradition. In ethics he put forward an interesting synthesis of Stoic and Aristotelian ideas, which he presented as the 'original tradition' of the Old Academy, displaying the essential convergence of the Platonic, Aristotelian and Stoic ethical theories. Antiochus' theory, however, is far more Peripatetic than Stoic in content. Along with ARIUS DIDYMUS' account of Peripatetic ethics, it is our major source for the interaction of Stoic and Aristotelian arguments in ethics.

ANTIPATER of Tarsus. Second century B.C. head of the STOA, successor to DIOGENES of Babylon. He appears to have been basically orthodox in approach and views, but in two respects introduced ethical matters of interest: his debate with Antipater over the ethically permitted attitude to institutions like sale, and his second definition of the final end, which tries to allow that virtue can be a skill and yet be compatible with failure in certain respects.

ARCESILAUS of Pitane, c. 315–240 B.C. On becoming head of the ACADEMY, he turned it to thorough scepticism, possibly supporting this by appeal to the *Theaetetus* (see ANONYMOUS COMMENTATOR). His practice was to argue only against the views of others, putting forward no positive doctrines himself. The result he claimed to be suspension of judgement, a feature absent from Socratic practice and suggesting influence by PYRRHO.

ARCHEDEMUS of Tarsus. Second century B.C. Stoic, probably a pupil of Diogenes; notable only for his characterization of our final end.

ARISTIPPUS of Cyrene. Fourth century pupil of Socrates, who adopted a version of hedonism in Socratic spirit; he served as the figurehead for the CYRENAICS, although he probably did not formulate or teach philosophical doctrines.

ARISTIPPUS the YOUNGER. Son of ARISTIPPUS' daughter Arētē. Probably the first to formulate and teach CYRENAICISM as a philosophical position.

ARISTOCLES of Messene. Second century A.D. Peripatetic philosopher. He wrote a history of philosophy, of which we have long extracts quoted by Eusebius.

ARISTON of Chios. Pupil of ZENO; he had a large but short-lived influence. In many ways his position differed from that of other early Stoics like CLEANTHES, the official head of the school. Later, because of the prestige of the works of CHRYSIPPUS, Ariston's position came to be regarded as 'deviant' from the orthodox Stoic line. In ethics his main divergence from this line was his position on rules in ethics.

ARISTOTLE of Stageira. 383–322 B.C. Founder of the PERIPATETIC school; pupil of PLATO and teacher of THEOPHRASTUS. His works relevant to moral theory are his two *Ethics, Rhetoric* and *Politics*. The *Magna Moralia* is a work of Aristotelian ethics, generally regarded as a product of the early Peripatetic school, but showing no great independence from Aristotle's thought; it may be lecture notes. The *Nicomachean* and *Eudemian* versions of the *Ethics* share three books; otherwise they differ in several ways. It is uncertain which is the earlier, but the *Nicomachean* version has the more influential tradition and the better text.

ARIUS DIDYMUS. First century B.C. Court philosopher to the Emperor Augustus; wrote a consolation to Livia on the death of her son Drusus. He seems to have had Stoicizing tendencies, but while we know little of his own ideas, he is an important source because of his histories of philosophy. In ethics he is the author of three important passages preserved in the collection of excerpts by John Stobaeus: an introduction to ethics, an account of Stoic ethics and an account of Peripatetic ethics. These have been abbreviated, probably more than once, but are still among our most important sources for ancient ethics. The Stoic passage is one of our three major sources for early Stoic moral theory. The Peripatetic passage is a valuable account of Aristotelian theory at a time when Stoic theory was setting the theoretical agenda, and shows many signs of engagement with Stoic ideas. Along with ANTIOCHUS it forms our best source for Aristotelian reactions to Stoic moral theory.

CARNEADES of Cyrene, 214–129/8. After ARCESILAUS, the most famous head of the New or sceptical ACADEMY. He put forward no positive positions of his own, but argued against the views of others, and also worked out, and argued against, the argumentative structure of sets of theories. In ethics, he is responsible for such a structure, 'Carneades' division', in CICERO'S *De Finibus* V. Carneades' arguments also are thought with much plausibility to lie behind many of the arguments of the *De Finibus* in general, and are mentioned in some other sources such as Plutarch.

CHRYSIPPUS of Soli, c. 280–207 B.C. Third head of the STOA. A voluminous writer, he was responsible for formulating the most influential form of Stoic doctrine in a number of areas, and was regarded as a 'second founder' of the Stoa.

CICERO (L) 106–43 B.C. Roman politician, well educated in philosophy, who at the end of his life wrote a series of philosophical works in Latin systematically discussing the major topics of Greek philosophy. The most important of these for ancient moral philosophy is *On Final Ends* (*De Finibus*), which presents and criticises Epicureanism, Stoicism and Antiochus' ethics. Also of interest are the *Tusculan Disputations* and *On Duties* (*De Officiis*). Cicero writes as a sceptical Academic, always arguing both sides of a question without committing himself to either as the rationally preferable alternative. Because of this he is a most valuable source for the argumentative structure of ancient ethics. Cicero's works on political philosophy, the *Republic* and *Laws*, which hark back to Plato in their format, were written at an earlier period of this life, and we possess only fragments of them.

CLEANTHES of Assos, 331–232 B.C. Pupil of ZENO, succeeding him as head of the STOA. As with ARISTON, his ideas were later overshadowed by the influence of CHRYSIPPUS. Cleanthes is the most religious Stoic, best known for his theistic 'Hymn to Zeus'. He was interested in the Presocratic Heraclitus, finding analogies between his ideas about the cosmos and those of the Stoics.

CRITOLAUS of Phaselis. Early second century B.C. head of the PERIPATETIC school. We have from him only a few fragments on ethical topics; his work seems to show more academic rigour than his immediate predecessors.

CYNICS. Philosophical movement deriving from Antisthenes of Athens (c.445–360 B.C.), a follower of SOCRATES, and Diogenes of Sinope (c. 400–325 B.C.). The Cynics were never an established school, since they programmatically despised academic learning and theory, and were more like street preachers, relying on personal example and forceful message. They stressed the importance of 'returning to nature', but because of their lack of interest in ethical theory they did not mean anything very precise by this, other than protest at many social conventions; stories about them often represent them as flouting taboos, particularly about sex. 'Cynic' comes from the Greek for dog, the dog being a symbol of lack of shame.

CYRENAICS. Philosophical school founded by ARISTIPPUS, though probably established as a philosophical school by his grandson ARISTIPPUS the YOUNGER. Its main positions were hedonism in ethics, and an extremely empiricist epistemology. In ethics, the school fragmented in different intellectual directions under HEGESIAS, ANNICERIS and THEO-DORUS, and petered out, probably unable to compete with EPICURUS' version of hedonism.

DIOGENES of Babylon, c. 240–152. Head of the STOA. Had a variety of interests, particularly in the theory of language and poetic theory. In ethics, his debate with ANTIPATER over the moral status of institutions like sale is of great interest.

DIOGENES LAERTIUS. Probably third century A.D., but date very uncertain. Author of a 10-book *Lives of the Philosophers*, containing much chatty and unintelligent gossip, but also much important information about the ideas of several philosophers.

DIOGENES of Oenoanda. Second century A.D. wealthy Epicurean citizen of Oenoanda in Asia Minor, who had a massive stone inscription carved for the benefit of his fellow-citizens, displaying some classic Epicurean texts and some passages of his own. Fragments of the inscription were first discovered in 1884; in recent years more have been found.

EPICTETUS of Hierapolis, c. 50–130 A.D. Stoic philosopher and former slave. He taught orally; his pupil Arrian wrote down his teachings in four books and a handbook. His major focus is always on practical ethics, and he is less interested in argument than in practical conversion and improvement.

EPICURUS of Athens, 341–270 B.C. Founder of the Epicurean school. Taught at first in Asia Minor, then in a 'Garden' at Athens. He wrote voluminously on many topics, including ethics, but all we have is a short letter and collections of sayings, together with a few fragments; hence the structure of his ethical theory is necessarily speculative. He defends a form of hedonism, which was much attacked in antiquity, often on the basis of misunderstandings; sources are often hostile and have to be used with care.

GALEN of Pergamum, 129–late second century A.D. Doctor and self-styled philosopher who wrote copiously on many subjects, and is often useful as a source for the Stoics, though because of his hostility to them he has to be used with caution.

HECATON of Rhodes. Late second century- first century B.C. Stoic philosopher, pupil of PANAETIUS. He wrote mainly on ethics. We have some passages in CICERO which derive from his treatment of 'applied ethics' and problem cases, but we know little about his general views.

HEGESIAS of Cyrene. Third century B.C. Leader of one of the distinctive developments within the CYRENAIC school.

HERMARCHUS of Mytilene. Younger contemporary of Epicurus; his pupil and associate, he succeeded him as head of the Epicurean school. His teachings were influential with later Epicureans, along with those of Epicurus himself and two other associates, Metrodorus and Polyaenus. A long passage in Porphyry deriving from him is important for the Epicurean theory of justice.

HIEROCLES. Second century A.D. Stoic philosopher. We know his *Elements of Ethics* from (a) a papyrus discovered a hundred years ago giving the beginning of the work and (b) extracts from later parts of the work (or similar works) preserved in the collection of extracts by John Stobaeus. Hierocles does not aim to be original, and his work is probably an elementary textbook. It shows an academic rather than sermonizing attitude to ethics, and is a useful source for Stoic ethical theory.

LUCRETIUS (L), c. 94–55 B.C. Roman Epicurean, author of a philosophical poem *On the Nature of Things*, in six books, in Latin hexameters. Unfortunately the poem concentrates on atomism and has little helpful on the content or structure of Epicurean ethics; nonetheless it is useful on some points.

MARCUS AURELIUS, 121–180 A.D.; Roman emperor 161–180 A.D. Author of twelve books of private 'meditations'. These are Stoic in content, but are not meant as philosophical teachings, and are sometimes misleading if taken as orthodox Stoicism.

PANAETIUS of Rhodes, c. 185–109 B.C. Stoic philosopher, succeeding Antipater as head of the Stoa; friend of aristocratic Romans of the circle of Scipio Aemilianus. He was more eclectic in interests than earlier Stoics, more prepared to find value in other philosophical traditions and more concerned to make Stoicism accessible to a non-academic audience, but his ethical views are not radically different from those of earlier Stoics.

PERIPATETICS. Philosophical school founded by ARISTOTLE. After THEOPHRASTUS, Aristotle's pupil, who emulated him by writing on a wide variety of topics, the school turned strongly to scientific research, especially under Strato of Lampsacus. Strato's successors returned to ethics (see CRITOLAUS), but we know almost nothing of the content of their writings. The account of Peripatetic ethics in ARIUS DIDYMUS is of uncertain origin and we do not know its relation to what was taught in Aristotle's own school. The school itself petered out in the first century B.C., but was replaced by a scholarly study of Aristotle's own philosophy.

PHILO of Larissa, c. 160–80 B.C. Last head of the ACADEMY, at a time when its scepticism was becoming less radical. He engaged in an epistemological debate with ANTIOCHUS. We have from him a long fragment presenting the task of ethical philosophy as a therapeutic one; since Academic sceptics argued *ad hominem* from opponents' premises, not their own, this presumably records a current assumption rather than an original view of Philo's own.

PHILODEMUS of Gadara, c. 110–40/35 B.C. Epicurean philosopher; friend of prominent contemporary Romans. Although he was not head of the school, his works are an important source for us, since large numbers of his books have been recovered, mostly in charred fragments, from a villa at Herculaneum destroyed in the eruption of Vesuvius. Philodemus writes in clotted academic prose, and this, as well as the fragmentary state of the papyri, makes the texts difficult to read and often inaccessible to the non-specialist. Few are available in English. This is unfortunate, as Philodemus is an important source for Epicurean views on a number of topics, as well as for contemporary debates.

PLATO of Athens, c. 429–347 B.C. Plato's immediate successors in the ACADEMY taught ethics which do not seem to have been directly related to what we read in the dialogues. After ARCESILAUS the Academy criticized the ethics of others, notably the Stoics, without putting forward any of their own. Plato's dialogues were available but not particularly influential, except that the *Theaetetus* influenced the sceptical Academy, and some isolated arguments may have had effect: for example, the argument at *Euthydemus* 278–282 and 288–292 probably influenced Stoic arguments about virtue and skill. However, in the period of explicit ancient ethical theory covered by this book, Plato was not a player. Platonic ethics were to have a comeback later, particularly in relation to Christianity.

PLUTARCH of Chaironeia, c. 50–120 A.D. Bellelettrist and essay-writer, author of parallel lives of great Greeks and Romans, and also of a large number of philosophical and religious essays, written from the standpoint of Middle Platonism, a philosophical movement reviving, in opposition to the sceptical ACADEMY, the idea that Plato's dialogues contain positive doctrines which can be systematized. Plutarch is an extensive source for Epicureanism and Stoicism, although he is relentlessly hostile to both, and makes his criticisms in a mechanical and often unfair way.

PYRRHO of Elis, c. 360–270 B.C. The first person in Greek philosophy to develop a sceptical position. Like Socrates, he wrote nothing (although his follower TIMON wrote some philosophical works and attacks on contemporary philosophers) and became a figurehead for later sceptical philosophers, particularly AENESIDEMUS, who broke away from the sceptical Academy to found 'Pyrrhonism' as a more radical form of scepticism.

SENECA (L), c. 4 B.C.–65 A.D. Stoic philosopher, tutor to the Emperor Nero, by whom he was eventually forced to commit suicide. Author of several philosophical essays and letters, in which various aspects of Stoic philosophy are presented. Seneca writes for a cultivated literary audience, not for academics, so his presentation of Stoic moral theory is not systematic, and he does not much discuss argument or structure. He is most interested in the practical difference which being a Stoic can make in a person's life.

SEXTUS EMPIRICUS. Date uncertain, but probably second century A.D. Doctor, and author of several works of sceptical philosophy. Others have been lost. Apart from attacks on specialized disciplines, Sextus' major works are a three-book *Outlines of Pyrrhonism* and a seven-book *Against the Professors*, answering to the last two-thirds of the shorter work. Ethical philosophy is treated in the third book of the *Outlines* and the eleventh of the longer work; also relevant is the first part of the *Outlines*, where sceptical methodology is discussed.

SOCRATES of Athens, 469–399. Philosopher, who wrote nothing himself. Several philosophers, including Plato, wrote dialogues in which he appears defending a variety of intellectual positions. In the Hellenistic period, he served as a figurehead for many philosophical schools (the sceptical Academy, the Stoics, the Cynics) and was widely regarded as a type of the ideal philosopher (the Epicureans alone were hostile to him). But, because so many different schools claimed to represent the real Socrates, the general edifying ideal of philosophy which he represented became abstracted from attachment to any particular set of doctrines.

STOA. Philosophical school founded by ZENO, and given its major intellectual foundation by CHRYSIPPUS. Named for the Stoa Poikilē or Painted Porch, where Zeno taught, the Stoa became one of the two major new philosophical schools after Aristotle (the other being Epicureanism).

THEODORUS of Cyrene. Third century B.C. Leader of one of the divergent tendencies among the CYRENAICS.

THEOPHRASTUS of Eresus, c. 370–288/5. ARISTOTLE'S pupil and successor. He continued Aristotle's tradition of widely based research. In ethics he wrote works which were perceived as sharpening Aristotle's position on the external goods, and were standardly cited in the Stoic-Peripatetic debate on the nature of happiness; but we know little of the details of what he said.

TIMON of Phlius, c. 320–230. Follower of PYRRHO; unlike him Timon produced written works. These were in a variety of prose and verse genres; many were satirical, pouring scorn on past and present dogmatic philosophers. Some of his *Python*, a prose dialogue featuring Pyrrho, has come down to us through ARISTOCLES.

XENOPHON of Athens, c. 428/7–354 B.C. Pupil of Socrates; wrote Socratic dialogues and reminiscences, which were influential in the Hellenistic period, promoting a picture of Socrates rather different from Plato's, though equally making him an ideal type of the philosopher.

ZENO of Citium, 335–263 B.C. The founder of the STOA. His writings, along with those of other early Stoics like CLEANTHES and ARISTON, were largely superseded by the works of CHRYSIPPUS, who restated Stoic positions in a stronger and more intellectually defensible form. In a few cases we have evidence for the divergent positions of early Stoics, for example, Ariston's position on the place of rules in ethics.

Primary Sources

There is no customary system of abbreviations which is accessible both to specialists and to non-specialists. On the one hand, 'Plutarch, *Comm. not* 1071f' is not perspicuous to philosophers not familiar with ancient texts. On the other hand, writing out in English the titles of every ancient work that is referred to would have made the notes too lengthy and clumsy. I have therefore used, in the footnotes, forms of abbreviation familiar to specialists, and add here a list of explanations of these for the non-specialist.

Alexander

de An II	Alexander of Aphrodisias, Book II of the Commentary on Aristotle's *de Anima* (*On the Soul*) containing a number of essays by Alexander on Aristotelian topics.
Fat	*De Fato* (*On Fate*)
Eth Pr	*Ethical Problems*
Quaest	*Quaestiones* (Questions for Discussion)
In Top	Commentary on Aristotle's *Topics*

Aristotle

EE	*Eudemian Ethics*
NE	*Nicomachean Ethics*
MM	*Magna Moralia* (*The Large Ethics*)
Pol	*Politics*
Top	*Topics*
Cat	*Categories*
Phys	*Physics*
Met	*Metaphysics*
Pr An	*Prior Analytics*
Post An	*Posterior Analytics*
Rhet	*Rhetoric*
Poet	*Poetics*
MA	*De Motu Animalium* (*The Movement of Animals*)
De An	*De Anima* (*On the Soul*)
Hist An	*Historia Animalium* (*Animal Researches*)
PA	*De Partibus Animalium* (*The Parts of Animals*)
Prot	*Protrepticus* (*Exhortation to Philosophy*)
Arius	Arius Didymus, in Stobaeus, *Eclogae* (*Selections*) Book II. There is an Introduction to Ethics, an account of Stoic ethics, and an account of Aristotelian ethics.

465

Augustine

Civ. Dei.   *De Civitate Dei* (*The City of God*)

Cicero

Fin   *De Finibus* (*On Final Ends*)

Off   *De Officiis* (*On Duties*)

TD   *Tusculanae Disputationes* (*Discussions at Tusculum*)

Rep   *De Republica* (*The State*)

Leg   *De Legibus* (*The Laws*)

Am   *De Amicitia* (*On Friendship*)

ND   *De Natura Deorum* (*The Nature of the Gods*)

PS   *Paradoxa Stoicorum* (*Paradoxes of the Stoics*)

Luc   *Lucullus*, the first version of the *Academica* (*Academic discussions*), a work on scepticism.

Varro   *Varro*, the second version of the *Academica*

Att   *ad Atticum Epistulae* (*Letters to Atticus*)

Diogenes   Diogenes Laertius, *Lives of the Philosophers* in ten books

Diogenes of Oenoanda   Fragments of an Epicurean stone inscription set up at Oenoanda. 'Fragments' edited by C. Chilton, 'New fragments' edited by M. Ferguson Smith.

Eusebius

Praep Ev   *Praeparatio Evangelica* (*Preparation for the Gospel*)

Epictetus

Disc   *Discourses*

Epicurus

KD   *Kuriai Doxai* (*Principal Doctrines*)

VS   *Vaticanae Sententiae* (*Vatican Sayings*)

Ep Men   *Epistula ad Menoeceum* (*Letter to Menoeceus*)

Ep Her   *Epistula ad Herodotum* (*Letter to Herodotus*)

Ep Pyth   *Epistula ad Pythoclem* (*Letter to Pythocles*)

[34] [32]   References to texts in G. Arrighetti, *Epicuro, Opere*, the standard edition of the texts and fragments from papyrus.

U   H. Usener Ed. *Epicurea*, the standard edition of testimonies about Epicurus and fragments in other authors.

Galen

PHP   *Placita Hippocratis et Platonis* (*The Doctrines of Hippocrates and Plato*)

Hierocles   *Elements of Ethics*

Lucretius   *De Rerum Natura* (*On the Nature of Things*)

Marcus   Marcus Aurelius, *Meditations*

Marcianus   *Institutes*

Philodemus

Anger	*On Anger*
Vices	*On Vices*
Grat	*On Gratitude*
Rhet	*Rhetoric*
Sto	*Against the Stoics*

Plato

Protag	*Protagoras*
Hipp Maj	*Hippias Major*
Repub	*Republic*
Euthyd	*Euthydemus*
Stat	*Statesman*
Theaet	*Theaetetus*
Laws	*Laws*

Plutarch

Virt mor	*De virtute morali* (*On moral virtue*)
Comm not	*De Communibus Notitiis* (*On Common Notions*)
Non posse	*Non posse suaviter vivi secundum Epicurum* (*That Epicurus actually makes a pleasant life impossible*)
Sto rep	*De Stoicorum repugnantiis* (*On Stoic self-contradictions*)
Ad Col	*Adversus Colotem* (*Against [the Epicurean] Colotes*)
De tranq an	*De Tranquillitate animae* (*On tranquillity of mind*)

Porphyry

Abst	*De Abstinentia* (*On Abstinence from Meat*)

Pseudo-Plato

Minos	*Minos*
SVF	H. von Arnim, *Stoicorum Veterum Fragmenta* (*Fragments of the Early Stoics*)

Seneca

Ira	*De Ira* (*On Anger*)
Ot	*De Otio* (*On Leisure*)
Vit Beat	*De Vita Beata* (*On the Happy Life*)
Ep	*Epistulae* (*Letters*)

Sextus

PH   Sextus Empiricus, *Pyrrhōneioi Hupotupōseis* (*Outlines of Pyrrhonism*)

M   *Adversus Mathematicos* (*Against the Professors*)

Simplicius

in Phys   *Commentary on Aristotle's Physics*

Stobaeus

Ecl   *Eclogae* (*Selections*)

Flor   *Florilegium* (*Treasury*)

Secondary Sources

Adkins, A.W.H. (1991) 'The Connexion between Aristotle's *Ethics* and *Politics*', in D. Keyt and F.D. Miller (Eds.) *A Companion to Aristotle's Politics,* 75–93. Oxford and Cambridge, MA.

Alberti, A. (1990a) '*Philia* e identità personale in Aristotele', in A. Alberti (Ed.) *Studi Sull'etica di Aristotele,* 203–302, Naples (*Elenchos* Collana XIX).

———. (1990b) 'Paura della morte e identità personale nell'Epicureismo', in A. Alberti (Ed.) *Logica, Mente e Persona,* 151–206. Firenze (Accademia Toscana di Scienze e Lettre 'La Colombaria', Studi CX).

———. (Ed.) (1990c) *Studi sull'etica di Aristotele,* Naples (*Elenchos* Collana XIX).

———. (Ed.) (1990d) *Logica, Mente e Persona,* Firenze (Accademia Toscana di Scienze e Lettere 'La Colombaria', Studi CX).

Algra, K. (1990) 'Chrysippus on Virtuous Abstention from Ugly Old Women (Plutarch, *SR* 1038e–1039a)', *Classical Quarterly* 40: 450–58.

Allan, D. J. (1953) 'Aristotle's Account of the Origin of Moral Principles', *Proceedings of the XIth International Congress of Philosophy, Brussels.* Amsterdam, 120–27.

———. (1955) 'The Practical Syllogism', *Autour d'Aristote: Recueil offert a Mgr. Mansion,* Louvain, 325–40.

Alpers-Gölz, R. (1976) *Der Begriff SKOPOS in der Stoa und seine Vorgeschichte,* Spudasmata VII, Hildesheim and New York.

Annas, J. (1977) 'Plato and Aristotle on Friendship and Altruism', *Mind* 86: 532–54.

———. (1980) 'Aristotle on Pleasure and Goodness', in A. O. Rorty (Ed.) *Essays on Aristotle's Ethics,* 285–99. Berkeley, Los Angeles, and London.

———. (1986) 'Doing without Objective Values: Ancient and Modern Strategies', in M. Schofield and G. Striker (Eds.) *The Norms of Nature,* 3–29, Cambridge.

———. (1987) 'Epicurus on Pleasure and Happiness', *Philosophical Topics* 15.2: 5–21.

———. (1988a) 'Naturalism in Greek Ethics: Aristotle and After', in *Proceedings of the Boston Area Colloquium in Ancient Philosophy* 4: 149–71.

———. (1988b) 'The Heirs of Socrates', *Phronesis* 33: 100–112.

———. (1988c) 'Self-Love in Plato and Aristotle', *The Southern Journal of Philosophy* 27, Supplement (Proceedings of the Spindel Conference 1988): 1–18.

———. (1988–9) 'Aristotle on Virtue and Happiness', *University of Dayton Review* 19: 7–22.

———. (1989a) 'Cicero on Stoic Moral Philosophy and Private Property', in M. Griffin and J. Barnes (Eds.) *Philosophia Togata,* 151–73, Oxford.

———. (1989b) 'Epicurean Emotions', *Greek, Roman and Byzantine Studies* 30.2: 145–64.

———. (1990a) 'The Hellenistic Version of Aristotle's Ethics', *The Monist* 73.1: 80–96.

———. (1990b) 'Stoic Epistemology', in S. Everson (Ed.) *Epistemology* (Companions to Ancient Thought 1), 184–203, Cambridge.

———. (1992a) *Hellenistic Philosophy of Mind,* Berkeley, Los Angeles, and London.

———. (1992b) 'Plato the Sceptic', in J. Klagge and N. Smith (Eds.) *Methods of Interpreting Plato and his Dialogues,* 43–72, Oxford (Oxford Studies in Ancient Philosophy, Supplementary Volume).

———. (1992c) 'Ancient Ethics and Modern Morality', *Philosophical Perspectives* no. 6, 119–36. J.E. Tomberlin (Ed.) Atascadero, California.

———. (1992d) 'Women and the Quality of Life: Two Norms or One?', in M. Nussbaum and A. Sen (Eds.) *The Quality of Life,* 279–96, Oxford.

_____. (1992e) 'The Good Life and the Good Lives of Others', in E. Paul, F.D. Miller, and J. Paul (Eds.) *The Good Life and the Human Good,* 133–48, Cambridge.

_____. (1993a) 'Virtue as a Skill', in the Proceedings of the 1991 Conference on Contemporary Attitudes to Ancient Thought at the University of Nevada, Reno.

_____. (1993b) 'Scepticism, Old and New', in M. Frede and G. Striker (Eds.) Festschrift for Gunther Patzig.

_____. (1993c) 'Virtue as the Use of Other Goods', in the Proceedings of *Socratic Studies,* a conference in honour of Gregory Vlastos, held at the University of California at Berkeley.

_____. (1993d) 'Reply to Fernanda Decleva Caizzi and Christopher Gill', in *Images and Ideologies, Proceedings of a Conference on Hellenistic Thought,* Berkeley, Los Angeles, and London.

_____. (1994) 'Aristotelian Political Theory in the Hellenistic Period', in the *Proceedings of the Sixth Symposium Hellenisticum,* Cambridge and Paris.

Annas, J., and J. Barnes. (1985) *The Modes of Scepticism,* Cambridge.

Anton, J.P., and A. Preus, Eds. (1983) *Essays in Ancient Greek Philosophy* vol. 2, Albany, NY.

_____. Eds. (1990) *Essays in Ancient Greek Philosophy* vol. 4, Albany, NY.

von Arnim, H. (1906) *Hierokles, Ethische Elementarlehre,* Berlin (Berliner Klassikortexte IV).

_____. (1924) *Die drei aristotelischen Ethiken,* Akademie der Wissenschaften in Wien, philososophisch-historisch Klasse, Sitzungsbericht 202.2, Vienna and Leipzig.

_____. (1926) *Arius Didymus' Abriss der peripatetischen Ethik,* Akadamie der Wissenschaften in Wien, philosophisch-historisch Klasse, Sitzungsbericht 204.3, Vienna and Leipzig.

Asmis, E. (1990) 'Seneca's *On the Happy Life* and Stoic Individualism', in M. Nussbaum (Ed.) *The Poetics of Therapy,* 219–56. *Apeiron* 23.4.

Atkins, E.M. (1990) '"Domina et Regina Virtutum": Justice and *Societas* in the *De Officiis',* *Phronesis* 35: 258–89.

Atkins, E.M., and M. Griffin. (1991) *Cicero, On Duties,* translation and notes, Cambridge.

Baier, A. (1989) 'Doing without Moral Theory?' in S.G. Clarke and E. Simpson (Eds.) *Anti-Theory in Ethics and Moral Conservatism,* 29–48, Albany, NY.

Baier, K. (1988) 'Radical Virtue Ethics', in P. French and others (Eds.) *Midwest Studies in Philosophy,* vol. 13: *Ethical Theory: Character and Virtue,* 126–35, Notre Dame.

Barker, E. (1906) *The Political Thought of Plato and Aristotle,* London.

Barnes, J. (1979) *The Presocratic Philosophers,* London.

_____. (1980) 'La méthodologie d'Aristote', *Revue Internationale de Philosophie* 133–34: 490–511.

_____. (1982) 'The Beliefs of a Pyrrhonist', *Proceedings of the Cambridge Philological Society* 208: 1–29.

_____. (1987) 'New Light on Antiphon', *Polis* 7 no. 1: 2–5.

_____. (1989) 'Antiochus of Ascalon', in M. Griffin and J. Barnes (Eds.) *Philosophia Togata,* 51–96, Oxford.

_____. (1990) 'Scepticism and Naturalism', in *Annales Universitatis Scientiarum Budapestinensis de Rolando Eotvos Nominatae,* Sectio Philosophica et Sociologica, 22–23: 5–19.

_____. (1991) 'Partial Wholes', in E. Paul and others (Eds.) *Ethics, Politics and Human Nature,* 1–23, Oxford.

Baron, M. (1984) 'On the Alleged Repugnance of Acting from Duty', *The Journal of Philosophy* 81: 179–219.

_____. (1985) 'Varieties of Ethics of Virtue', *American Philosophical Quarterly* 22: 47–53.

_____. (1987) 'Kantian Ethics and Supererogation', *The Journal of Philosophy* 84: 237–62.

Benson, J. (1990) 'Making Friends: Aristotle's Doctrine of the Friend as Another Self', in A. Loizou and H. Lesser (Eds.) *Polis and Politics: Essays on Greek Moral and Political Philosophy*, 50–68, Aldershot.

Bentham, J. (1834) *Deontology*, ed. J. Bowring, London and Edinburgh.

Bett, R. (1988) 'Is Modern Moral Scepticism Essentially Local?', *Analysis* 48: 102–7.

———. (1989) 'Carneades' *pithanon*: A Reappraisal of Its Role and Status', *Oxford Studies in Ancient Philosophy* 7: 59–94.

———. (1990) 'Carneades on the Difference between Assent and Approval', *The Monist* 73.1: 3–20.

Blickman, D. (1989) 'Lucretius, Epicurus and Prehistory', *Harvard Studies in Classical Philology* 92: 157–91.

Bollack, J. (1975) *La pensée de plaisir*, Paris.

Bradley, F. (1876) *Ethical Studies*, 2nd ed., Oxford.

Brandt, R. (1959) *Ethical Theory*, Englewood Cliffs, NJ.

Brink, C.O. (1956) '*Oikeiōsis* and *oikeiotēs*: Theophrastus and Zeno on Nature in Moral Theory', *Phronesis* 1: 123–45.

Brumbaugh, R. (1976) 'Plato's Relation to the Arts and Crafts', in W. Werkmeister (Ed.) *Facets of Plato's Philosophy*, 40–52, Assen and Amsterdam.

Brunschwig, J. (1986) 'The Cradle Argument in Epicureanism and Stoicism', in M. Schofield and G. Striker (Eds.) *The Norms of Nature*, 113–44, Cambridge.

———. (1991) 'On a Book-Title by Chrysippus: "On the Fact That the Ancients Admitted Dialectic along with Demonstrations",' *Oxford Studies in Ancient Philosophy* Supplementary Volume, 81–96.

Brunschwig, J., and M. Nussbaum. (forthcoming) *Passions & Perceptions, Proceedings of the Fifth Symposium Hellenisticum*, Cambridge and Paris.

Brunt, P. (1975) 'Stoicism and the Principate', *Papers of the British School at Rome* 43 (n.s. 30): 7–35.

Burnyeat, M. (1971) 'Virtues in Action', in G. Vlastos (Ed.) *The Philosophy of Socrates*, 209–34. New York, 1971.

———. (1980a) 'Aristotle on Learning to Be Good', in A.O. Rorty (Ed.) *Essays on Aristotle's Ethics*, 69–92, Berkeley, Los Angeles, and London.

———. (1980b) 'Tranquillity without a Stop: Timon Fragment 68', *Classical Quarterly* 72 (n.s. 30): 86–93.

———. (1983) 'Can the Skeptic Live His Skepticism?', in M. Burnyeat (Ed.) *The Skeptical Tradition*, 129–41, Berkeley, Los Angeles, and London.

Burnyeat, M. Ed. (1983) *The Skeptical Tradition*, Berkeley, Los Angeles, and London.

Cambiano, G. (1983) *La filosofia in Grecia e a Roma*, Roma and Bari.

———. (1988) *Il ritorno degli antichi*. Roma and Bari.

Charles, D. (1984) *Aristotle's Philosophy of Action*, London.

———. (1988) 'Perfectionism in Aristotle's Political Theory: Reply to Martha Nussbaum', *Oxford Studies in Ancient Philosophy* Supplementary Volume (*Proceedings of the Oberlin Ancient Philosophy Colloquium*), 185–206.

Charlton, W. (1990) 'Aristotle's Identification of Moral Philosophy with Ethics', in A. Loizou and H. Lesser (Eds.) *Polis and Politics: Essays on Greek Moral and Political Philosophy*, 35–49, Aldershot.

Clarke, S.G. (1987) 'Anti-Theory in Ethics', *American Philosophical Quarterly* 24: 237–41.

Clarke, S.G., and E. Simpson, Eds. (1989) *Anti-Theory in Ethics and Moral Conservatism*, Albany, NY.

Classen, C.J. (1958) 'Aristippos', *Hermes* 86: 182–92.

———. (1985) 'Bibliographie zur Sophistik', *Elenchos* 6: 75–140.

Clay, D. (1983) *Lucretius and Epicurus*, Ithaca and London.

Clowney, D. (1990) 'Virtues, Rules and the Foundations of Ethics', *Philosophia* 20: 49–68.

Cole, E.B. (1988-9) '*Autarkeia* in Aristotle', *University of Dayton Review* 19: 35–42.

Cooper, J. (1973) 'The *Magna Moralia* and Aristotle's Moral Philosophy', *American Journal of Philology* 94: 327–49.

_____. (1975) *Reason and Human Good in Aristotle,* Cambridge, MA.

_____. (1980) 'Aristotle on Friendship', in A.O. Rorty (Ed.) *Essays on Aristotle's Ethics,* 301–40, Berkeley, Los Angeles, and London.

_____. (1982) 'Aristotle on Natural Teleology', in M. Nussbaum and M. Schofield (Eds.) *Language and Logos: Essays in Honour of G.E.L. Owen,* 197–222, Cambridge.

_____. (1985) 'Aristotle and the Goods of Fortune', *Philosophical Review* 94: 173–97.

Cooper, N. (1989) 'Aristotle's Crowning Virtue', *Apeiron* 22: 191–206.

Copp, D., and D. Zimmerman, Eds. (1984) *Morality, Reason and Truth,* Totowa, NJ.

Couissin, P. (1929a) 'Le stoicisme de la nouvelle Academie', *Revue d'Histoire de la Philosophie* 3: 241–76, translated and reprinted in M. Burnyeat (Ed.) *The Skeptical Tradition,* 31–63, Berkeley, Los Angeles, and London, 1983.

_____. (1929b) 'L'origine et l'évolution de l'*epochē*', *Revue des Études Grecques* 42: 373–97.

Craik, E.M., Ed. (1990) '*Owls to Athens*': *Essays on Classical Subjects Presented to Sir Kenneth Dover,* Oxford.

Creed, J. (1989) 'Aristotle's Middle Constitution', *Polis* 8: 2–27.

Curzer, H. (1990) 'A Great Philosopher's Not So Great Account of Great Virtue: Aristotle's Treatment of "Greatness of Soul"', *Canadian Journal of Philosophy* 20.4: 517–38.

_____. (1991) 'Aristotle's Much Maligned *Megalopsuchos*', *Australasian Journal of Philosophy* 69.2: 131–51.

Dahl, N.O. (1984) *Practical Reason, Aristotle and Weakness of the Will,* Minneapolis.

Dancy, J., J.M.E. Moravcsik, and C.C.W. Taylor, Eds. (1988) *Human Agency: Language, Duty and Value. Philosophical Essays in Honor of J.O. Urmson.* Stanford.

Decleva Caizzi, F. (1981) *Pirrone: Testimonianze, (Elenchos Collana V)* Naples.

_____. (1985) 'Ricerche su Antifonte: A proposito di POxy. 1364 fr. 1', *Studi di filosofia Preplatonica,* Napoli, 191–208.

_____. (1986a) 'Il nuovo papiro di Antifonte: POxy LII 3647', in F. Adorno, and others (Eds.) *Protagora, Antifonte, Posidonio, Aristotele: saggi su frammenti inediti e nuove testimonianze da papiri,* Firenze.

_____. (1986b) 'Hysteron Proteron: la nature et la loi selon Antiphon et Platon', *Revue de Métaphysique et de Morale* 91: 291–310.

_____. (1988) *Felicità e Immagine del Filosofo nel Pensiero Antico,* Cooperativa Universitaria Studi e Lavoro, Università degli Studi di Milano, Facoltà di Lettere e Filosofia.

Decleva Caizzi, F., and M. Serena Funghi. (1988) 'Un testo sul concetto stoico di progresso morale', *Aristoxenica, Menandrea, Fragmenta Philosophica. Studi e Testi per il Corpus dei Papiri filosofici greci e latini* 3, 85–125, Firenze.

Dent, N.J.H. (1975) 'Virtues and Actions', *Philosophical Quarterly* 25: 318–35.

_____. (1984) *The Moral Psychology of the Virtues,* Cambridge.

Denyer, N. (1983) 'The Origins of Justice', SUZETESIS, *Studi Offerti a Marcello Gigante,* Naples, 133–52.

Diels, H. (1958) *Doxographi Graeci,* reprinted, Berlin.

Diels, H., and W. Schubart Eds. (1905) *Anonymer Kommentar zu Platons Theaetet* (Berliner Klassikertexte II), Berlin.

Dillon, J. (1977) *The Middle Platonists,* London.

_____. (1983) '*Metriopatheia* and *Apatheia*: Some Reflections on a Controversy in Later Greek Ethics', in J.P. Anton and A. Preus (Eds.) *Essays in Ancient Greek Philosophy,* vol. 2, Albany, NY.

Dillon, J., and A.A. Long, Eds. (1988) *The Question of "Eclecticism": Studies in Later Greek Philosophy,* 508–518. Berkeley, Los Angeles, and London.

Dirlmeier, F. (1937) *Die Oikeiosis-Lehre Theophrasts, Philologus* Supplement 30.1, 1–100 Leipzig.

Dorandi, T. (1982) 'Filodemo, *Gli Stoici* (PHerc 155 E 339)', *Cronache Ercolanesi* 12: 91–133.

Döring, K. (1988) *Der Sokratesschuler Aristipp und die Kyrenaiker,* Mainz.

Dover, K.J. (1974) *Greek Popular Morality in the Time of Plato and Aristotle,* Oxford.

Dudley, D.R. (1967) *A History of Cynicism,* reprinted, Hildesheim.

Engberg-Pedersen, T. (1981) 'For Goodness' Sake: More on *Nicomachean Ethics* I vii 5', *Archiv für Geschichte der Philosophie* 63: 17–40.

——. (1986) 'Discovering the Good: *oikeiōsis* and *kathēkonta* in Stoic Ethics', in M. Schofield and G. Striker (Eds.) *The Norms of Nature,* 145–83, Cambridge.

——. (1990) *The Stoic Theory of Oikeiōsis,* Aarhus.

Englert, W. (1990) 'Bringing to the Light: Cicero's *Paradoxa Stoicorum*', in M. Nussbaum (Ed.) *The Poetics of Therapy,* 117–42, *Apeiron* 23.4.

Erskine, A. (1990) *The Hellenistic Stoa,* Ithaca and London.

Everson, S. (1988) 'Aristotle on the Foundations of the State', *Political Studies* 36: 89–101.

——. Ed. (1990) *Epistemology* (Companions to Ancient Thought 1), Cambridge.

Farrar, C. (1988) *The Origins of Democratic Thinking,* Cambridge.

Feinberg, J., Ed. (1969) *Moral Concepts,* Oxford.

Finley, M. (1970) 'Aristotle and Economic Analysis', *Past and Present* 47: 3–25.

——. Ed. (1981) *The Legacy of Greece,* Oxford.

Flanagan, O., and A.O. Rorty, Eds. (1990) *Identity, Character and Morality, Essays in Moral Psychology,* Cambridge, MA and London.

Foot, P. (1978) *Virtues and Vices,* Oxford.

Forschner, M. (1981) *Die stoische Ethik,* Stuttgart.

——. (1982) 'Epikurs Theorie des Glücks', *Zeitschrift für philosophische Forschung* 36: 169–88.

——. (1986) 'Das Gute und die Güter, Zur Aktualität der stoischen Ethik', *Aspects de la philosophie hellénistique,* Entretiens Hardt 32 (Geneva): 325–60.

Fortenbaugh, W.W. (1975a) *Aristotle on Emotion,* London.

——. (1975b) 'Aristotle's Analysis of Friendship: Function and Analogy, Resemblance and Focal Meaning', *Phronesis* 20: 51–62.

——. (1984) *Quellen zur Ethik Theophrasts,* Amsterdam.

——. (1992) *The Fragments of Theophrastus.*

Fortenbaugh, W.W. Ed. (1983) *On Stoic and Peripatetic Ethics: The Work of Arius Didymus,* Rutgers University Studies in Classical Humanities 1, New Brunswick.

Fowler, D. (1984) 'Sceptics and Epicureans', *Oxford Studies in Ancient Philosophy* 2: 237–67.

Frankena, W. (1973) *Ethics,* 2nd ed., Englewood Cliffs, NJ.

Frede, M. (1986) 'The Stoic Doctrine of the Affections of the Soul', in M. Schofield and G. Striker (Eds.) *The Norms of Nature,* 93–110, Cambridge.

——. (1987a) 'The Skeptic's Beliefs', in M. Frede, (1987c), 179–200.

——. (1987b) 'The Skeptic's Two Kinds of Assent and the Question of the Possibility of Knowledge', in M. Frede, (1987c) 201–22.

——. (1987c) *Essays in Ancient Philosophy,* Minneapolis.

——. (forthcoming) 'Doxographie, historiographie philosophique et historiographie historique de la philosophie'.

French, P., Th. Uehling, and H. Wettstein, Eds. (1978) *Midwest Studies in Philosophy,* vol. 3: *Studies in Ethical Theory,* Morris, MN.

French, P., Th. Uehling, and H. Wettstein, Eds. (1988) *Midwest Studies in Philosophy,* vol. 13: *Ethical Theory: Character and Virtue,* Notre Dame.

Furley, D. (1981) 'Antiphon's Case Against Justice', in G. Kerferd (Ed.) *The Sophists and Their Legacy,* 81–91. *Hermes* Einzelschriften 44, Wiesbaden.

_____. (1983) 'Comments on Dr. Sharples' Paper: A Note on Arius and *Magna Moralia* I 1–2', in W.W. Fortenbaugh (Ed.) *On Stoic and Peripatetic Ethics: The Work of Arius Didymus*, 160–64, Rutgers University Studies in Classical Humanities 1. New Brunswick.

_____. (1986) 'Nothing to Us?', in M. Schofield and G. Striker (Eds.) *The Norms of Nature*, 75–91, Cambridge.

Furley, D., and R. Allen, Eds. (1975) *Studies in Presocratic Philosophy*, vol. 2, London.

Giannantoni, G. (1958) *I cirenaici*, Firenze.

_____. (1990) *Socratis et Socraticorum Reliquiae*, 2nd ed., Naples (*Elenchos* Collana XVIII).

Giannantoni, G., Ed. (1981) *Lo scetticismo antico, Atti del convegno organizzato dal Centro di Studio del Pensiero Antico del C.N.R.*, Naples.

_____. Ed. (1986) *Diogene Laerzio storico del pensiero antico*, Naples.

Gigante, M. (1981) *Scetticismo e Epicureismo*, Naples (*Elenchos* Collana IV).

_____. (1983a) 'Filodemo quale autore dell'*Etica Comparetti*', in M. Gigante, *Ricerche Filodemee*, 245–76, Naples.

_____. (1983b) *Ricerche Filodemee*, Naples.

Gill, C. (1988) 'Personhood and Personality: The Four-*personae* Theory in Cicero, *De Officiis* Book I', *Oxford Studies in Ancient Philosophy* 6: 169–200.

_____. (1990a) 'The Human Being as Ethical Norm', in C. Gill (Ed.) *The Person and the Human Mind*, 137–61, Oxford.

_____. Ed. (1990b) *The Person and the Human Mind*, Oxford.

_____. (forthcoming) 'Panaetius on the Virtue of Being Yourself', in *Images and Ideologies, Proceedings of a Conference on Hellenistic Thought*, Berkeley, Los Angeles, and London.

Gill, D. (forthcoming) 'Epicurus on Justice'.

Gill, M., and J. Lennox, Eds. (1993) *Self-Motion from Aristotle to Newton*, Princeton.

Giusta, M. (1964–7) *I dossographi di etica*, Torino.

Glidden, D. (1975) 'Protagorean Relativism and the Cyrenaics', in N. Rescher (Ed.) *Studies in Epistemology*, 113–40, Oxford.

_____. (1983) 'Epicurean Semantics', *SUZETESIS*, Naples, 185–226.

_____. (1985) 'Epicurean *Prolēpseis*', *Oxford Studies in Ancient Philosophy* 3: 175–217.

Glucker, J. (1978) *Antiochus and the Late Academy, Hypomnemata* 56, Göttingen.

_____. (1988) 'Cicero's philosophical affiliations', in J. Dillon and A.A. Long (Eds.) *The Question of "Eclecticism": Studies in Later Greek Philosophy*, 34–69, Berkeley, Los Angeles, and London.

Görgemanns, H. (1983) '*Oikeiōsis* in Arius Didymus', in W.W. Fortenbaugh (Ed.) *On Stoic and Peripatetic Ethics: The Work of Arius Didymus*, 165–89, Rutgers University Studies in Classical Humanities 1, New Brunswick.

Gosling, J. (1987) 'The Stoics and *akrasia*', *Apeiron* 20.2: 179–202.

Gosling, J., and C.C.W. Taylor (1982) *The Greeks on Pleasure*, Oxford.

Griffin, J. (1986) *Well-Being: Its Meaning, Measurement and Moral Importance*, Oxford.

Griffin, M. and Barnes, J. (Eds.) (1989) *Philosophia Togata: Essays on Philosophy and Roman Society*, Oxford.

Griswold, C., Ed. (1988) *Platonic Writings, Platonic Readings*, New York.

Hahm, D.E. (1990) 'The Ethical Doxography of Arius Didymus', *Aufstieg und Niedergang der Römischen Welt*, Teil II (Principat) Band 36.4, Berlin and New York, 2935–3055 and 3234–3243.

Halliwell, S. (1986) *Aristotle's Poetics*, Chapel Hill, NC.

_____. (1987) *The Poetics of Aristotle*, translation and commentary, Chapel Hill, NC.

Hampshire, S. (1989) 'Morality and Conflict', in S.G. Clarke and E. Simpson (Eds.) *Anti-Theory in Ethics and Moral Conservatism*, 135–64, Albany, NY.

Hankinson, R.J., Ed. (1988) *Method, Medicine and Metaphysics, Apeiron* 31.2.

Hardie, W.F.R. (1978) '"Magnanimity" in Aristotle's Ethics', *Phronesis* 78: 63–79.

Herman, B. (1981) 'On the Value of Acting from the Motive of Duty', *Philosophical Review* 90: 359–82.

_____. (1983) 'Integrity and Impartiality', *The Monist* 66: 233–50.

Heyd, D. (1982) *Supererogation*, Cambridge.

Homiak, M. (1981) 'Virtue and Self-Love in Aristotle's Ethics', *Canadian Journal of Philosophy* 11: 633–51.

Hossenfelder, M. (1985) *Stoa, Epikureismus und Skepsis*, Munchen.

_____. (1986) 'Epicurus, hedonist malgré lui', in M. Schofield and G. Striker (Eds.) *The Norms of Nature*, 245–63, Cambridge.

Huby, P. (1983) 'Peripatetic Definitions of Happiness', in W.W. Fortenbaugh (Ed.) *On Stoic and Peripatetic Ethics: The Work of Arius Didymus*, 121–34, Rutgers University Studies in Classical Humanities 1, New Brunswick.

Hudson, S. (1986) *Human Character and Morality*, Boston and London.

Hunt, H. (1954a) 'The Ethical System of Antiochus', in H. Hunt, *The Humanism of Cicero*, 89–97, Melbourne.

_____. (1954b) 'The Stoic and Antiochean Definitions of the Good', in H. Hunt, *The Humanism of Cicero*, 116–21, Melbourne.

_____. (1954c) *The Humanism of Cicero*, Melbourne.

Hursthouse, R. (1980–1) 'A False Doctrine of the Mean', *Proceedings of the Aristotelian Society* 81: 57–72.

_____. (1988) 'Moral Habituation', *Oxford Studies in Ancient Philosophy* 6: 201–20.

_____. (1991) 'Virtue Theory and Abortion', *Philosophy and Public Affairs* 20: 223–46.

Hutchinson, D. (1986) *The Virtues of Aristotle*, London and New York.

_____. (1988) 'Doctrines of the Mean and the Debate Concerning Skills in Fourth-century Medicine, Rhetoric and Ethics', in R.J. Hankinson (Ed.) *Method, Medicine and Metaphysics*, 17–52, Apeiron 21.2.

Inwood, B. (1983) 'Comments on Professor Görgemanns' Paper, "The Two Forms of Oikeiōsis in Arius and the Stoa"', in W.W. Fortenbaugh (Ed.) *On Stoic and Peripatetic Ethics: The Work of Arius Didymus*, 190–201, Rutgers University Studies in Classical Humanities 1, New Brunswick.

_____. (1984) 'Hierocles: Theory and Argument in the Second Century A.D.', *Oxford Studies in Ancient Philosophy* 2: 151–83.

_____. (1985) *Ethics and Human Action in Early Stoicism*, Oxford.

_____. (1986a) 'Goal and Target in Stoicism', *Journal of Philosophy* 83: 547–56.

_____. (1986b) 'Comments on Striker', *Proceedings of the Boston Area Colloquium in Ancient Philosophy* 2: 95–101.

Inwood, B. and Gerson, L. (1988) *Hellenistic Philosophy*, Indianapolis.

Ioppolo, A.-M. (1980) *Aristone di Chio e lo stoicismo antico*, Naples (*Elenchos* Collana I).

_____. (1986) *Opinione e Scienza: il dibattito tra Stoici e Accademici nel III e II secolo a. C.*, Naples (*Elenchos* Collana XII).

_____. (1990) 'Virtue and Happiness in the First Book of the *Nicomachean Ethics*', in A. Alberti (Ed.) *Studi sull'etica di Aristotele*, 119–48, Naples (*Elenchos* Collana XIX).

Irwin, T. (1976) *Plato's Moral Theory*, Oxford.

_____. (1985a) *Aristotle's Nicomachean Ethics*, translation and notes, Indianapolis.

_____. (1985b) 'Aristotle's Conception of Morality', *Proceedings of the Boston Area Colloquium in Ancient Philosophy* 1: 115–43.

_____. (1985c) 'Permanent Happiness: Aristotle and Solon', *Oxford Studies in Ancient Philosophy* 3: 89–124.

_____. (1986) 'Stoic and Aristotelian conceptions of happiness', in M. Schofield and G. Striker (Eds.) *The Norms of Nature*, 205–44, Cambridge.

_____. (1988a) 'Disunity in the Aristotelian Virtues', *Oxford Studies in Ancient Philosophy* Supplementary Volume, *Proceedings of the Oberlin Ancient Philosophy Colloquium*, 61–78, 87–90.

_____. (1988b) *Aristotle's First Principles*, Oxford.

_____. (1990) 'Virtue, Praise and Success: Stoic Responses to Aristotle', *The Monist* 73.1: 59–96.

_____. (1991) 'Aristotle's Defense of Private Property', in D. Keyt and F.D. Miller (Eds.) *A Companion to Aristotle's Politics*, 200–225, Oxford and Cambridge, MA.

Jackson, H. (1912) '*Eudemian Ethics* Theta i and ii', *Journal of Philology* 32: 170–221.

Jaggar, A. (1983) *Feminist Theory and Human Nature*, Totowa, NJ.

Janácek, K. (1972) *Sextus Empiricus' Sceptical Methods*, Prague.

Jost, L. (forthcoming) 'Moral Luck and External Goods in the *Eudemian Ethics*.'

Kagan, S. (1984) 'Does Consequentialism Demand Too Much? Recent Work on the Limits of Obligation', *Philosophy and Public Affairs* 13: 239–54.

_____. (1990) *The Limits of Morality*, Oxford.

Kahn, C. (1981a) 'Did Plato Write Socratic Dialogues?' *Classical Quarterly* 31: 305–20.

_____. (1981b) 'The Origins of Social Contract Theory', in G. Kerferd (Ed.) *The Sophists and Their Legacy*, 92–108, *Hermes* Einzelschriften 44, Wiesbaden.

_____. (1981c) 'Aristotle and Altruism', *Mind* 99: 20–40.

_____. (1983) 'Arius as a Doxographer', in W.W. Fortenbaugh (Ed.) *On Stoic and Peripatetic Philosophy: The Work of Arius Didymus*, 3–13, Rutgers University Studies in Classical Humanities 1, New Brunswick.

_____. (1985) 'Democritus and the Origins of Moral Psychology', *American Journal of Philology* 106: 1–31.

_____. (1988) 'On the Relative Date of the *Gorgias* and the *Protagoras*', *Oxford Studies in Ancient Philosophy* 6: 69–103.

Kenny, A. (1969) 'Happiness', in J. Feinberg (Ed.) *Moral Concepts*, 43–52, Oxford.

_____. (1978) *The Aristotelian Ethics*, Oxford.

_____. (1988) 'Aristotle on Moral Luck', in J. Dancy and others (Eds.) *Human Agency: Language, Duty and Value, Philosophical Essays in Honor of J.O. Urmson*, 105–19, Stanford.

_____. (1991) 'The *Nicomachean* Conception of Happiness', *Oxford Studies in Ancient Philosophy* Supplementary Volume, 67–80.

Kerferd, G. (1972) 'The Search for Personal Identity in Stoic Thought', *Bulletin of the John Rylands Library of Manchester* 55: 177–96.

_____. (1981) *The Sophists and Their Legacy*, *Hermes* Einzelschrift 44, Wiesbaden.

Keyt, D. (1991a) 'Three Basic Theorems in Aristotle's *Politics*', D. Keyt and F.D. Miller (Eds.) *A Companion to Aristotle's Politics*, 118–41, Oxford and Cambridge, MA.

_____. (1991b) 'Aristotle's Theory of Distributive Justice', in D. Keyt and F.D. Miller (Eds.) *A Companion to Aristotle's Politics*, 238–78, Oxford and Cambridge, MA.

Keyt, D., and F.D. Miller, Eds. (1991) *A Companion to Aristotle's Politics*, Oxford and Cambridge, MA.

Kidd, I. (1978) 'Moral Actions and Rules in Stoic Ethics', in J. Rist (Ed.) *The Stoics*, 247–58, Berkeley, Los Angeles, and London.

Kirwan, C. (1967) 'Logic and the Good in Aristotle', *Philosophical Quarterly* 17: 97–114.

Klagge, J., and N. Smith. (1992) *Methods of Interpreting Plato and his Dialogues*, Oxford Studies in Ancient Philosophy, Supplementary Volume.

Kosman, L.A. (1980) 'Being Properly Affected: Virtues and Feelings in Aristotle's Ethics', in A.O. Rorty (Ed.) *Essays on Aristotle's Ethics*, 103–16, Berkeley, Los Angeles, and London.

Kraut, R. (1976) 'Aristotle on Choosing Virtue for Itself', *Archiv für Geschichte der Philosophie* 58: 223–39.

_____. (1979) 'Two Conceptions of Happiness', *Philosophical Review* 88: 167–97.

_____. (1988) 'Comments on "Disunity in the Aristotelian Virtues"', *Oxford Studies in Ancient Philosophy* Supplementary Volume, *Proceedings of the Oberlin Ancient Philosophy Colloquium,* 79–86.

_____. (1989) *Aristotle on the Human Good,* Princeton.

Kruschwitz, R., and R. Roberts, Eds. (1987) *The Virtues,* New York.

Kuhlmann, W., Ed. (1986) *Moralität und Sittlichkeit,* Frankfurt am Main.

Kullman, W. (1991) 'Man as a Political Animal in Aristotle', in D. Keyt and F.D. Miller (Eds.) *A Companion to Aristotle's Politics,* 94–117, Oxford and Cambridge, MA.

Laks, A. (1988) 'Reply to Annas', *Proceedings of the Boston Area Colloquium in Ancient Aristotle* 4: 172–85.

_____. (1993) 'Anniceris et les plaisirs psychiques: quelques préalables doxographiques', in J. Brunschwig and M. Nussbaum (Eds.) *Passions & Perceptions, Proceedings of the Fifth Symposium Hellenisticum,* 18–50, Cambridge and Paris.

Lane Fox, R. (1987) *Pagans and Christians,* New York.

Larmore, C. (1990) 'The Right and the Good', in *Philosophia* 20: 15–32.

Lear, J. (1988) *Aristotle: The Desire to Understand,* Cambridge.

Lesses, G. (1989) 'Virtue and the Goods of Fortune in Stoic Moral Theory', *Oxford Studies in Ancient Philosophy* 7: 95–127.

_____. (forthcoming) 'Austere Friends: the Stoics on Friendship'.

Lloyd, G.E.R. (1968) 'The Role of Medical and Biological Analogies in Aristotle's Ethics', *Phronesis* 13: 68–83.

Loizou, A., and H. Lesser, Eds. (1990) *Polis and Politics: Essays on Greek Moral and Political Philosophy,* Aldershot.

Long, A.A. (1967) 'Carneades and the Stoic Telos', *Phronesis* 12: 59–90.

_____. (1970–1) 'The Logical Basis of Stoic Ethics', *Proceedings of the Aristotelian Society* 92: 85–104.

_____. (1971) '*Aisthēsis, prolēpsis* and Linguistic Theory in Epicurus', *Bulletin of the Institute of Classical Studies* 18: 114–33.

_____. (1986) 'Pleasure and Social Utility—the Virtues of Being Epicurean', in *Aspects de la Philosophie Hellénistique,* Entretiens Hardt 32 (Geneva) 283–324.

_____. (1988a) 'Socrates in Hellenistic Philosophy', *Classical Quarterly* 38: 150–71.

_____. (1988b) 'Stoic Eudaimonism', *Proceedings of the Boston Area Colloquium in Ancient Philosophy* 4: 77–101.

_____. (1992) 'Cyrenaic Hedonism', *The Cambridge History of Hellenistic Philosophy.*

_____. (1992) 'Cyrenaics', L. Becker (Ed.) *Encyclopaedia of Ethics,* New York and London, Vol I. 236–238.

Long, A.A., Ed. (1971) *Problems in Stoicism,* London.

Long, A.A., and D. Sedley. (1987) *The Hellenistic Philosophers,* Cambridge.

Louden, R. (1984) 'On Some Vices of Virtue Ethics', *American Philosophical Quarterly* 21: 227–36.

_____. (1990) 'Virtue Ethics and Anti-theory', *Philosophia* 20: 93–114.

Luper-Foy, S. (1976) 'Annihilation', *The Philosophical Quarterly* 37: 233–52.

Lynch, J. (1972) *Aristotle's School,* Berkeley, Los Angeles, and London.

MacDowell, J. (1980) 'The Role of *Eudaimonia* in Aristotle's Ethics', in A.O. Rorty (Ed.) *Essays on Aristotle's Ethics,* 359–76, Berkeley, Los Angeles, and London.

MacIntyre, A. (1981) *After Virtue,* London.

_____. (1988) *Whose Justice? Which Rationality?,* London.

_____. (1990) *Three Rival Versions of Moral Enquiry,* Notre Dame.

Mackie, J. (1978) 'Can There Be a Right-based Moral Theory?', in P. French and others (Eds.) *Midwest Studies in Philosophy,* vol. 3: *Studies in Ethical Theory,* 350–59, Morris, MN.

McKirahan, V. Tsouna. (1992) 'The Cyrenaic Theory of Knowledge'. *Oxford Studies in Ancient Philosophy* 10: 161–92.

Maconi, H. (1988) '*Nova Non Philosophandi Philosophia*', *Oxford Studies in Ancient Philosophy* 6: 231–53.

McPherran, M. (1988) '*Ataraxia* and *Eudaimonia* in Ancient Pyrrhonism: Is the Sceptic Really Happy?', *Proceedings of the Boston Area Colloquium in Ancient Philosophy* 5: 135–71.

———. (1990a) 'Kahn on the Pre-middle Platonic Dialogues', *Oxford Studies in Ancient Philosophy* 8: 211–36.

———. (1990b) 'Pyrrhonism and the Arguments Against Value', *Philosophical Studies* 60: 127–42.

Madvig, J.W. (1965) *M.T. Ciceronis de Finibus Bonorum et Malorum libri quinque*, Copenhagen 1876, reprinted Hildesheim.

Magnaldi, G. (1991) *L'oikeiōsis peripatetica in Ario Didimo e nel 'De finibus' di Cicerone'*, Firenze.

Mannebach, E. (1961) *Aristippi et Cyrenaicorum Fragmenta*, Leiden/Köln.

Meikle, S. (1991) 'Aristotle and Exchange Value', in D. Keyt and F.D. Miller (Eds.) *A Companion to Aristotle's Politics*, 156–81, Oxford and Cambridge, MA.

Melden, A.E., Ed. (1958) *Essays in Moral Philosophy*, Seattle.

Merlan, P. (1960) '*Hēdonē* in Epicurus and Aristotle', *Studies in Epicurus and Aristotle* I, Klassisch-philologische Studien 22, Wiesbaden.

Mette, H.J. (1986–7) 'Philon von Larisa und Antiochos von Askalon', *Lustrum* 28–29: 9–63.

Mill, J.S. (1874) 'Nature' in *Three Essays on Religion*, London.

Miller, F. D. (1989) 'Aristotle's Political Naturalism', in T. Penner and R. Kraut (Eds.) *Nature, Knowledge and Virtue, Essays in Memory of Joan Kung*, 195–218, Apeiron 22.4.

———. (1990) 'Aristotle on Property Rights', in J. Anton and A. Preus (Eds.) *Essays in Ancient Greek Philosophy*, vol. 4, 227–48, Albany, NY.

———. (forthcoming) *Nature, Justice and Rights in Aristotle's Politics*.

Mitsis, P. (1986) 'Moral Rules and the Aims of Stoic Ethics', *The Journal of Philosophy* 83: 556–58.

———. (1988) *Epicurus' Ethical Theory*, Ithaca.

———. (1989) 'Epicurus on Death and the Duration of Life', *Proceedings of the Boston Area Colloquium on Ancient Philosophy* 4: 295–314.

———. (1993) 'Seneca on Reason, Rules and Moral Development', in J. Brunschwig and M. Nussbaum (Eds.) *Passions & Perceptions. Proceedings of the Fifth Symposium Hellenisticum*. Cambridge and Paris, 285–312.

———. (forthcoming) 'Natural Law and Natural Right in Post-Aristotelian Philosophy: the Stoics and their critics', in W. Haase (Ed.) *Aufsteig und Niedergang der Römischen Welt* II, 36.7.

Moore, G.E. (1903) *Principia Ethica*, Cambridge.

Moraux, P. (1973) *Der Aristotelismus bei den Griechen* vol. 1, Berlin and New York.

———. (1986) 'Diogène Laërce et le Peripatos', *Diogene Laerzio storico del pensiero antico, Elenchos* (1986)1-2: 245–94.

Moraux, P., and D. Harlfinger, Eds. (1970) *Untersuchungen zur Eudemischen Ethik*, Berlin.

Mulgan, R. (1977) *Aristotle's Political Theory*, Oxford.

———. (1979) 'Lycophron and Social Contract Ideas', *Journal of the History of Ideas* 40: 121–28.

———. (1991) 'Aristotle's Analysis of Oligarchy and Democracy', in D. Keyt and F.D. Miller (Eds.) *A Companion to Aristotle's Politics*, 307–22, Oxford and Cambridge, MA.

Nagel, T. (1980) 'The Limits of Objectivity', in S. McMurrin, (Ed.) *The Tanner Lectures on Human Values* vol. 1: 77–139.

_____. (1986) Review of B. Williams, *Ethics and the Limits of Philosophy* (1985), *The Journal of Philosophy* 83: 351–60.

Natali, C. (1979–80) 'La struttura unitaria del libro I della *Politica* di Aristotele', *Polis* 3.1: 2–18.

_____. (1989) *La sagezza di Aristotele*, Naples, *Elenchos* Collana XVI.

_____. (1990a) 'Fino a che punto rispettare le opinioni in etica: Aristotele e gli *endoxa*', *Ermeneutica e filosofia pratica*, Atti del Convegno internazionale di Catania, ed, De Domenico, N., Di Stefano, A.E., Puglisi, 191–201.

_____. (1990b) 'Le chrématistique chez Aristote', in G. Patzig (Ed.) *Aristoteles: Politik*, 296–324, Akten des XI Syposium Aristotelicum, Göttingen.

_____. (1990c) 'Due modi di trattare le opinioni notevole. La nozione di felicità in Aristotele, *Retorica* I 5', *Methexis* 3: 51–63.

Nill, M. (1985) *Morality and Self-Interest in Protagoras, Antiphon and Democritus*, Leiden.

Noble, C.N. (1989) 'Normative Ethical Theories', in S.G. Clarke and E. Simpson (Eds.) *Anti-Theory in Ethics and Moral Conservatism*, 49–64, Albany, NY.

Nock, A.D. (1933) *Conversion*, Oxford.

Nussbaum, M. (1978) *Aristotle's De Motu Animalium*, Princeton.

_____. (1985) 'The Discernment of Perception: An Aristotelian Conception of Private and Public Rationality', *Proceedings of the Boston Area Colloquium in Ancient Philosophy* 1: 151–201.

_____. (1986a) *The Fragility of Goodness*, Cambridge.

_____. (1986b) 'Therapeutic Arguments: Epicurus and Aristotle', in M. Schofield and G. Striker (Eds.) *The Norms of Nature*, 31–74, Cambridge.

_____. (1987) 'The Stoics on the Extirpation of the Passions', *Apeiron* 20.2: 129–78.

_____. (1988a) 'Nature, Function and Capability: Aristotle on Political Distribution', *Oxford Studies in Ancient Philosophy* Supplementary Volume (*Proceedings of the Oberlin Colloquium in Ancient Philosophy*), 145–84 and 207–16.

_____. (1988b) 'Non-Relative Virtues: an Aristotelian Approach', in P. French and others (Eds.) *Midwest Studies in Philosophy*, vol. 13: *Ethical Theory: Character and Virtue*, 32–53, Notre Dame.

_____. (1989) 'Beyond Obsession and Disgust: Lucretius' Genealogy of Love', *Apeiron* 22: 1–60.

_____. (forthcoming a) 'Aristotle on Human Nature and the Foundations of Ethics', Festschrift for Bernard Williams.

_____. (forthcoming b) *The Therapy of Desire*.

_____. Ed. (1990) *The Poetics of Therapy, Apeiron* 23.4.

Nussbaum, M., and A. Sen (Eds.) (1992) *The Quality of Life*, Oxford.

Nussbaum, M., and M. Schofield (Eds.) (1982) *Language and Logos: Essays in Honour of G.E.L. Owen*, Cambridge.

Oakeshott, M. (1989) 'The Tower of Babel', in S.G. Clarke and E. Simpson (Eds.) *Anti-Theory in Ethics and Moral Conservatism*, 185–204, Albany, NY.

O'Connor, D. (1988) 'Aristotelian Justice as a Personal Virtue', in P. French and others (Eds.) *Midwest Studies in Philosophy*, vol. 13: *Ethical Theory: Character and Virtue*, 417–27, Notre Dame.

_____. (1989) 'The Invulnerable Pleasure of Epicurean Friendship', *Greek, Roman and Byzantine Studies* 30: 165–86.

O'Neil, E. (1977) *Teles, the Cynic teacher*, Missoula, MT.

Parfit, D. (1984) *Reasons and Persons*, Oxford.

Patzig, G. (1968) *Aristotle's Theory of the Syllogism*, Dordrecht.

_____. Ed. (1990) *Aristoteles: Politik*, Akten des XI Syposium Aristotelicum, Göttingen.

Paul, E., F.D. Miller, and J. Paul, Eds. (1991) *Ethics, Politics and Human Nature*, Oxford.

———. Eds. (1992) *The Good Life,* Cambridge.

Pembroke, S. (1971) '*Oikeiōsis*', in A.A. Long (Ed.) *Problems in Stoicism,* 114–49, London.

Pence, G. (1984) 'Recent Work on Virtues', *American Philosophical Quarterly* 21: 281–96.

Penner, T., and R. Kraut, Eds. (1989) *Nature, Knowledge and Virtue, Essays in Memory of Joan Kung, Apeiron* 22.4.

Pohlenz, M. (1940) *Grundfragen der stoischen Philosophie,* Göttingen.

Price, A. (1989) *Love and Friendship in Plato and Aristotle,* Oxford.

Prior, W.J. (1991) *Virtue and Knowledge: An Introduction to Ancient Greek Ethics,* London and New York.

Railton, P. (1988) 'How Thinking about Character and Utilitarianism Might Lead to Rethinking the Character of Utilitarianism', in P. French and others (Eds.) *Midwest Studies in Philosophy,* vol. 13: *Ethical Theory: Character and Virtue,* 398–416, Notre Dame.

Rawls, J. (1971) *A Theory of Justice,* Cambridge, MA.

Rees, D.A. (1970) '"Magnanimity" in the *Eudemian* and *Nicomachean* Ethics', in P. Moraux and D. Harlfinger (Eds.) *Untersuchungen zur Eudemischen Ethik,* 231–43, Berlin.

Rescher, N., Ed. (1975) *Studies in Epistemology,* Oxford.

Rieth, O. (1934) 'Über das Telos der Stoiker', *Hermes* 69: 13–45.

Rist, J. Ed. (1972) *Epicurus,* Cambridge.

———. Ed. (1974) 'Pleasure: 360–300 BC', *Phoenix* 28: 167–79.

———. Ed. (1978) *The Stoics,* Berkeley, Los Angeles, and London.

———. Ed. (1982) 'Are you a Stoic? The Case of Marcus Aurelius', in B.F. Meyer and E.P. Sanders (Eds.) *Jewish and Christian Self-Definition,* 23–45, 190–92, Philadelphia.

Roberts, R.C. (1984) 'Will Power and the Virtues', *Philosophical Review* 93: 227–48.

Rorty, A.O., Ed. (1976) *The Identities of Persons,* Berkeley, Los Angeles, and London.

———. Ed. (1980) *Essays on Aristotle's Ethics,* Berkeley, Los Angeles, and London.

Rosenbaum, S. (1986) 'How to Be Dead and Not Care: A Defense of Epicurus', *American Philosophical Quarterly* 23: 217–25.

———. (1989a) 'Epicurus and Annihilation', *The Philosophical Quarterly* 37: 81–90.

———. (1989b) 'The Symmetry Argument: Lucretius Against the Fear of Death', *Philosophy and Phenomenological Research* 50: 353–74.

———. (1990) 'Epicurus on Pleasure and the Complete Life', *The Monist* 73.1: 21–41.

Rutherford, R. (1989) *The Meditations of Marcus Aurelius: A Study,* Oxford.

Sandbach, F. (1985) *Aristotle and the Stoics,* Cambridge Philological Society, Supplementary vol. 10, Cambridge.

Saunders, T. (1977–78) 'Antiphon the Sophist on Natural Laws', *Proceedings of the Aristotelian Society* 99: 26–35.

Scheffler, S. (1982) *The Rejection of Consequentialism,* Oxford.

———. (1985) 'Agent-Centred Restrictions, Rationality and the Virtues', *Mind* 94: 409–19.

———. (1987) 'Morality Through Thick and Thin', a Critical Notice of B. Williams, *Ethics and the Limits of Philosophy* (1985), *Philosophical Review* 96: 411–34.

Schnädelbach, H. (1986) 'Was ist Neo-aristotelismus?' in W. Kuhlmann (Ed.) *Moralität und Sittlichkeit,* 38–63. Frankfurt am Main, 1986.

Schneewind, J. (1977) *Sidgwick's Ethics and Victorian Moral Philosophy,* Oxford.

———. (1990a) *Moral Philosophy from Montaigne to Kant,* 2 vols., Cambridge.

———. (1990b) 'The Misfortunes of Virtue', *Ethics* 101: 42–63.

———. (1991) 'Natural Law, Skepticism and Methods of Ethics', *Journal of the History of Ideas* 52: 289–308.

———. (1993) 'Modern Moral Philosophy: From Beginning to End?' in P. Cross (Ed.) *Philosophical Imagination and Cultural Memory,* Durham, N.C.

———. (forthcoming) 'Classical Republicanism and the Ethics of Virtue'.

Schofield, M. (1983) 'The Syllogisms of Zeno of Citium', *Phronesis* 28: 31–58.

———. (1984) 'Ariston of Chios and the Unity of Virtue', *Ancient Philosophy* 4: 83–96.

———. (1990) 'Ideology and Philosophy in Aristotle's Theory of Slavery', in G. Patzig (Ed.) *Aristoteles: Politik,* 1–27, Akten des XI Syposium Aristotelicum, Göttingen.

———. (1991) *The Stoic Idea of the City,* Cambridge.

Schofield, M., and others, Eds. (1980) *Doubt and Dogmatism,* Oxford.

Schofield, M., and G. Striker, Eds. (1986) *The Norms of Nature,* Cambridge.

Sedley, D. (1991) 'Is Aristotle's Teleology Anthropomorphic?' *Phronesis* 36: 179–96.

Sharples, R.W. (1983a) *Alexander of Aphrodisias on Fate,* translation with notes, London.

———. (1983b) 'The Peripatetic Classification of Goods', in W.W. Fortenbaugh (Ed.) *On Stoic and Peripatetic Ethics: The Work of Arius Didymus,* 139–59, Rutgers University Studies in Classical Humanities 1, New Brunswick.

———. (1990) *Alexander of Aphrodisias, Ethical Problems,* Ithaca.

Sherman, N. (1988) 'Common Sense and Uncommon Virtue', in P. French and others (Eds.) *Midwest Studies in Philosophy,* vol. 13: *Ethical Theory: Character and Virtue,* 97–114, Notre Dame.

Sidgwick, H. (1907) *The Methods of Ethics,* 7th ed., London.

———. (1931) *Outlines of the History of Ethics,* 6th ed., London.

Singer, M. (1958) 'Moral Rules and Principles', in A.E. Melden (Ed.) *Essays in Moral Philosophy,* 160–96, Seattle.

Slote, M. (1983) *Goods and Virtues,* Oxford.

———. (1988) 'Utilitarian Virtue', in P. French and others (Eds.) *Midwest Studies in Philosophy,* vol. 13: *Ethical Theory: Character and Virtue,* 384–97, Notre Dame.

———. (1989) *Beyond Optimizing,* Cambridge, MA.

Smith, N. (1991) 'Aristotle's Theory of Natural Slavery', in D. Keyt and F.D. Miller (Eds.) *A Companion to Aristotle's Politics,* 142–55, Oxford and Cambridge, MA.

Solomon, D. (1988) 'Internal Objections to Virtue Ethics', in P. French and others (Eds.) *Midwest Studies in Philosophy,* vol. 13: *Ethical Theory: Character and Virtue,* 428–41, Notre Dame.

Sorabji, R. (1980) 'Aristotle on the Role of Intellect in Virtue', in A.O. Rorty (Ed.) *Essays on Aristotle's Ethics,* 201–19, Berkeley, Los Angeles, and London.

Soreth, M. (1968) 'Die zweite Telosformel des Antipater von Tarsos', *Archiv für Geschichte der Philosophie* 50: 48–72.

de Sousa, R. (1984) 'Arguments from Nature', in D. Copp and D. Zimmerman (Eds.) *Morality, Reason and Truth,* 169–90, Totowa, NJ.

Sparshott, F. (1978) 'Zeno on Art: Anatomy of a Definition', in J. Rist (Ed.) *The Stoics,* 273–90, Berkeley, Los Angeles, and London.

Stopper, M. (1983) '*Schizzi Pirroniani*', *Phronesis* 28: 265–97.

Striker, G. (1980) 'Sceptical Strategies', in M. Schofield and others (Eds.) *Doubt and Dogmatism,* 54–83, Oxford.

———. (1981a) 'Über den Unterschied zwischen den Pyrrhonern und den Akademikern', *Phronesis* 26: 153–71.

———. (1981b) 'Epikur', in O. Höffe Ed., *Klassiker der Philosophie* I, 108–14, Munchen.

———. (1983) 'The Role of *Oikeiōsis* in Stoic Ethics', *Oxford Studies in Ancient Philosophy* 1: 145–67.

———. (1986a) 'Antipater, or the Art of Living', in M. Schofield and G. Striker (Eds.) *The Norms of Nature,* 185–204, Cambridge.

———. (1986b) 'The Origins of the Concept of Natural Law', *Proceedings of the Boston Area Colloquium in Ancient Philosophy* 2: 79–94.

———. (1988) 'Greek Ethics and Moral Theory', *Tanner Lectures on Human Value* 9: 182–202.

———. (1989) 'Comments on Mitsis', *Proceedings of the Boston Area Colloquium in Ancient Philosophy* 4: 315–20.

———. (1990) '*Ataraxia*: Happiness as Tranquillity', *The Monist* 73.1: 97–99.

———. (1991) 'Following Nature: A Study in Stoic Ethics', *Oxford Studies in Ancient Philosophy* 9: 1–73.

———. (forthcoming) 'Plato's Socrates and the Stoics', in P. Vander Waerdt (Ed.) *The Socratic Movement*, Ithaca, NY.

Tarrant, H. (1983) 'The Date of Anonymous *In Theaetetum*', *Classical Quarterly* 33: 161–87.

Taylor, C.C.W. (1967) 'Pleasure, Knowledge and Sensation in Democritus', *Phronesis* 12: 6–27.

———. (1990) 'Popular Morality and Unpopular Philosophy', in E.M. Craik (Ed.) *'Owls to Athens': Essays on Classical Subjects Presented to Sir Kenneth Dover*, 233–43, Oxford.

Taylor, R. (1988) 'Ancient Wisdom and Modern Folly', in P. French and others (Eds). *Midwest Studies in Philosophy*, vol. 13: *Ethical Theory: Character and Virtue*, 54–63, Notre Dame.

Telfer, E. (1980) *Happiness*, London.

Trianosky, G. (1986) 'Supererogation, wrongdoing and vice: on the autonomy of the ethics of virtue', *Journal of Philosophy* 83: 26–40.

Tsekourakis, D. (1974) *Studies in the Terminology of Early Stoic Ethics*, *Hermes* Einzelschrift 32, Wiesbaden.

Urmson, J. (1958) 'Saints and Heroes', in A.E. Melden (Ed.) *Essays in Moral Philosophy*, 198–216, Seattle.

———. (1973) 'Aristotle's Doctrine of the Mean', *American Philosophical Quarterly* 10: 223–30.

Vander Waerdt, P.A. (1987) 'The Justice of the Epicurean Wise Man', *Classical Quarterly* 37: 402–22.

———. (1988) 'Hermarchus and the Epicurean Genealogy of Morals', *Transactions of the American Philological Association* 118: 87–106.

———. (1991) 'Politics and Philosophy in Stoicism', *Oxford Studies in Ancient Philosophy* 9: 185–211.

———. (forthcoming a) *The Theory of Natural Law in Antiquity*, Ithaca.

———. (forthcoming b) 'Philosophical Influence on Roman Jurisprudence? The Case of Stoicism and Natural Law', in W. Haase, (Ed.) *Aufstieg und Niedergang der Römischen Welt* II, 36.7.

Vegetti, M. (1989) *L'etica degli antichi*, Roma and Bari.

Vlastos, G. (1945–6) 'Ethics and Physics in Democritus', *Philosophical Review* 54: 578–92 and 55: 53–64, reprinted in D. Furley and R. Allen (Eds.) *Studies in Presocratic Philosophy*, vol. 2, 381–408, London, 1975.

———. (1981a) 'The Individual as Object of Love in Plato', in G. Vlastos, *Platonic Studies*, 3–42, Princeton.

———. (1981b) *Platonic Studies*, Princeton.

Vlastos, G., Ed. (1971) *The Philosophy of Socrates*, New York.

Walker, A.D.M. (1979) 'Aristotle's Account of Friendship in the *Nicomachean Ethics*', *Phronesis* 24: 180–96.

Wallace, J. (1978) *Virtues and Vices*, Ithaca.

———. (1988) 'Ethics and the Craft Analogy', in P. French and others (Eds.) *Midwest Studies in Philosophy*, vol. 13: *Ethical Theory: Character and Virtue*, 222–32, Notre Dame.

Waterlow, S. (1982) *Nature, Change and Agency in Aristotle's Physics*, Oxford.

Watson, G. (1971) 'Natural Law and Stoicism', in A.A. Long (Ed.) *Problems in Stoicism*, 216–38, London.

Wedin, M. (1993) 'Aristotle on the Mind's Self-Motion', in M. Gill and J. Lennox (Eds.) *Self-Motion from Aristotle to Newton*, Princeton.

Wehrli, F. (1944–59) *Die Schule des Aristoteles*, Basel.

———. (1950) *Straton von Lampsakos*, Basel.

———. (1952) *Lykon und Ariston von Ceos*, Basel.

———. (1959) *Hieronymos, Kritolaos, Rückblick*, Basel.

Werkmeister, W., Ed. (1976) *Facets of Plato's Philosophy*, Assen and Amsterdam.

White, N. (1978a) 'The Basis of Stoic Ethics', *Harvard Studies in Classical Philology* 83: 143–78.

———. (1978b) 'Two Notes on Stoic Terminology', *American Journal of Philology* 50: 111–19.

———. (1985a) 'Nature and Regularity in Stoic Ethics', *Oxford Studies in Ancient Philosophy* 3: 289–305.

———. (1985b) 'The Role of Physics in Stoic Ethics', *The Southern Journal of Philosophy* 23, Supplement (Proceedings of the Spindel 1984 Conference): 57–74.

———. (1990) 'Stoic Values', in *The Monist* 73.1: 42–58.

———. (forthcoming a) 'Modern Morality in Ancient Stoic Ethics'.

———. (forthcoming b) 'The Imperative, the Attractive and the Repulsive: Sidgwick and Modern Views of Ancient Ethics'.

White, S. (1990) 'Is Aristotelean Happiness a Good Life or the Best Life?', *Oxford Studies in Ancient Philosophy* 8: 103–44.

———. (1992) *Sovereign Virtue*, Stanford.

———. (forthcoming) 'Peristoica: *oikeiōsis* and the Restructuring of Aristotelian Ethics'.

Whitlock Blundell, M. (1990) 'Parental Nature and Stoic *Oikeiōsis*', *Ancient Philosophy* 10: 221–42.

Wiggins, D. (1980) 'Deliberation and Practical Reason', in A.O. Rorty (Ed.) *Essays on Aristotle's Ethics*, 221–40, Berkeley, Los Angeles, and London.

Williams, B. (1962) 'Aristotle on the Good', *Philosophical Quarterly* 12: 289–96.

———. (1976) 'Persons, Character and Morality' in A.O. Rorty (Ed.) *The Identities of Persons*, 197–216, Berkeley, Los Angeles, and London.

———. (1980) 'Justice as a Virtue', in A.O. Rorty (Ed.) *Essays on Aristotle's Ethics*, 189–99, Berkeley, Los Angeles, and London.

———. (1981a) 'Philosophy', in M. Finley (Ed.) *The Legacy of Greece*, 202–55, Oxford.

———. (1981b) 'Utilitarianism and Moral Self-Indulgence', in B. Williams, *Moral Luck*, 40–53, Cambridge.

———. (1981c) 'Internal and External Reasons', in B. Williams, *Moral Luck*, 101–13, Cambridge.

———. (1981d) *Moral Luck*, Cambridge.

———. (1985) *Ethics and the Limits of Philosophy*, London.

Woodruff, P. (forthcoming) *Plato and Protagoras*.

Woods, M. (1982) *Aristotle's Eudemian Ethics* Books I, II and VIII, Oxford.

———. (1986) 'Intuition and Perception in Aristotle's Ethics', *Oxford Studies in Ancient Philosophy* 4, Festschrift for John Ackrill, 145–66.

Wright, M.R. (1992) *Cicero: On Stoic Good and Evil: De Finibus* III and *Paradoxa Stoicorum*, edited with introduction, translation and commentary, Warminster.

Young, C. M. (1988a) 'Aristotle on Justice', in *Aristotle's Ethics*, Proceedings of the Spindel Conference 1988, *The Southern Journal of Philosophy* 27, Supplement: 233–49.

———. (1988b) 'Aristotle on Temperance', *The Philosophical Review* 97: 521–42.

———. (forthcoming) 'Aristotle's Doctrine of the Mean'.

Zeller, E. (1961) *Die Philosophie der Griechen in ihrer geschichtlichen Entwicklung*, reprinted, Hildesheim.

Index Locorum

Alexander of Aphrodisias

Commentary on Aristotle's *Topics* (*In Top*)
32.11–34.5 400 n.43
34.3–4 400 n.43

De Anima Commentary Book II (*de An* II)
150–153 39 n.42, 277 n.95
150.20–21 35 n.22
151.3–18 277 n.95
153.29–156.27 76 n.94
154.1 76 n.94
154.16 76 n.94
154.30–32 123 n.252
155.24–28 131 n.267
155.38–156.27 76 n.94
156.29–159.14 145 n.16
159.16–168.20 397 n.36
159.34 169 n.36
160.1–20 397 n.37
160.21–31 397 n.37
160.31–161.3 397 n.37
162.22–163.18 397 n.37
162.34 35 n.22
163.18–32 397 n.37
163.32–164.21 397 n.37
164.21–28 397 n.37
165.26–29 397 n.37
166.21–35 397 n.37
166.35–167.13 397 n.37

De Fato (*Fat*)
XXVII 197.25–198.26 147 n.28

Ethical Problems (*Eth Pr*)
22 76 n.94

Quaestiones (*Quaest*)
II 1–28 400 n.43

Anonymous Commentator on the Theaetetus

col. 5.14–6.26 271 n.80
col. 7.20–25 280 n.106
col. 11.12–40 80 n.109

Aristotle

Categories (*Cat*)
8 b 26–9 a 13 50 n.7
8 b 27–35 50 n.7

De Anima (*De An*)
434 a 16–21 93 n.151

De Motu Animalium (*MA*)
701 a 11–15 92 n.149
701 a 16–17 93 n.150
701 a 17–22 92 n.145

De Partibus Animalium (*PA*)
641 b 24–26 152 n.45
696 b 2 ff. 139 n.13

Eudemian Ethics (*EE*)
I 1 33
1214 b 3–5 33 n.17
1214 b 6–14 32 n.16
1214 b 14–27 377 n.44
1215 a 9–12 44 n.61
1220 a 39-b 2 281 n.111
1220 b 18–21 51
1221 b 27–31 281 n.112
1219 a 38–39 416 n.23
1229 a 20–30 144 n.12
III 5 116 n.223
1234 a 24–34 144 n.12
VII 6 255 n.28
1242 a 19–28 314 n.99
VII 12 255 n.28
1246 a 31–33 374 n.37
1246 a 31-b 1 152 n.46
1246 b 36–1247 a 2 373 n.36
1247 b 18 ff. 374 n.38
1247 b 18–28 374 n.39
1247 b 28 ff. 374 n.38
VIII 2 373 n.35

Historia Animalium (*Hist An*)
588 a 31–33 281 n.111
588 a 33 183 n.12

Magna Moralia (*MM*)
1184 a 15–24 35 n.23
1184 a 25–30 36 n.26
1184 a 26–27 45 n.65
1185 b 3–13 281 n.112
1186 a 1 281 n.111
1194 b 37–39 152 n.46
1196 b 15–17 281 n.112
1200 a 5–11 78 n.98
1200 a 34–24 36 n.29
1205 b 6–7 145 n.18

Arius Didymus

Augustine

De Civitate Dei (Civ Dei)

Cicero

ad Atticum Epistulae (Att)

De Amicitia (Am)

De Finibus (Fin)

General Index